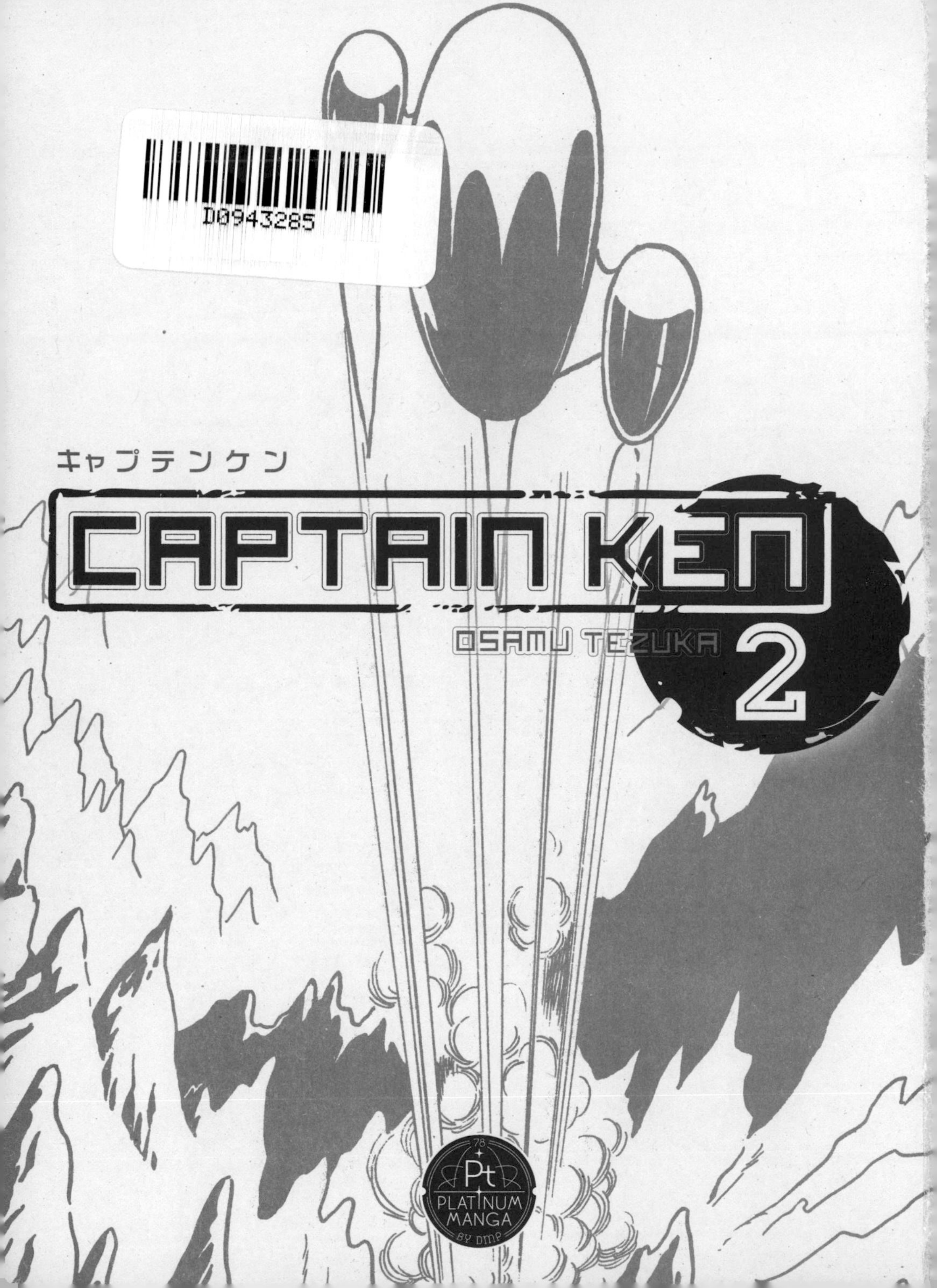
キャプテンケン
CAPTAIN KEN
OSAMU TEZUKA
2
Pt
PLATINUM MANGA
BY DMP

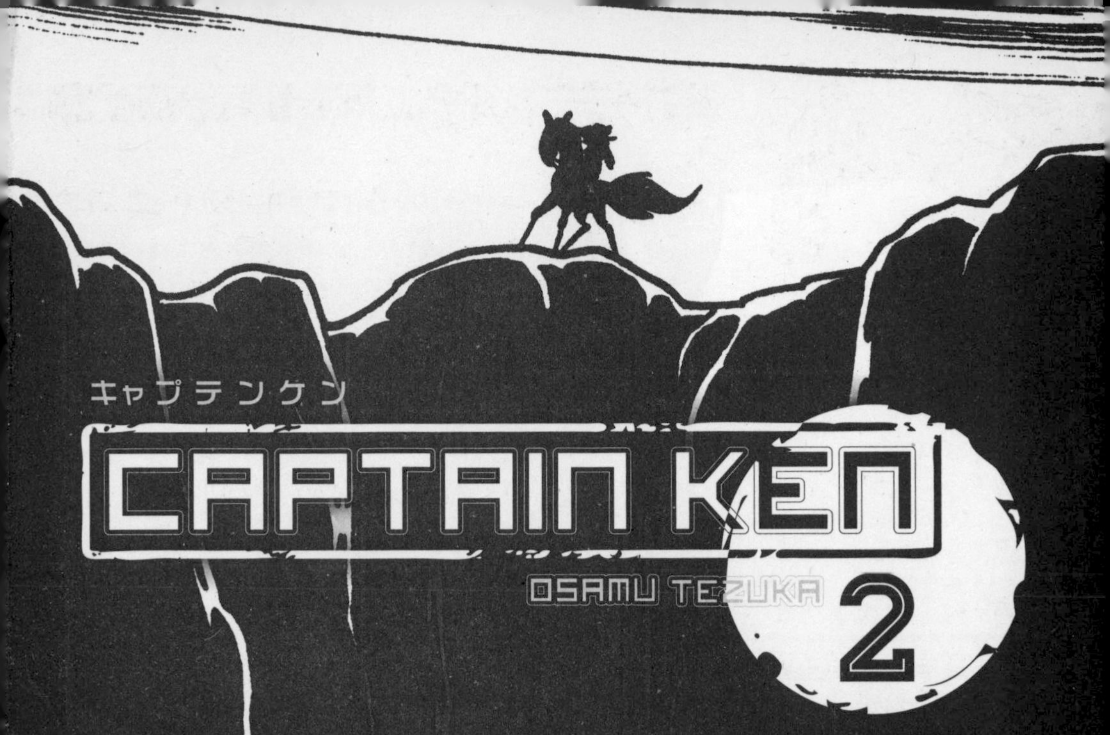
キャプテンケン
CAPTAIN KEN
OSAMU TEZUKA
2

CONTENTS

TRANSLATION	KYLE VANDERSTEEN	JAPAN RELATIONS	YOSHIO OGURA
EDITING	RACHELLE DONATOS LIPP	LICENSING, SALES & DISTRIBUTION	YOKO TANIGAKI
LETTERING	RAYMOND RAMIREZ	EDITOR IN CHIEF	FRED LUI
GRAPHIC DESIGN	JORDAN GARCIA	PUBLISHER	HIKARU SASAHARA

ENGLISH EDITION PUBLISHED BY
DIGITAL MANGA PUBLISHING
A DIVISION OF DIGITAL MANGA, INC.
1487 W 178TH STREET, SUITE 300
GARDENA, CA 90248
WWW.DMPBOOKS.COM
FIRST EDITION: MAY 2015
ISBN-10: 1-56970-339-6
ISBN-13: 978-1-56970-339-7
1 3 5 7 9 10 8 6 4 2
PRINTED IN CANADA

funded with KICKSTARTER
kickstarter.com/profile/digitalmanga
www.emanga.com
www.akadot.com
Become our fan on Facebook
Digital Manga Inc.
Follow us on Twitter
@DigitalManga

SPECIAL THANKS

Greg Baker, Digital Companion Producer

Special thanks to TezukaInEnglish.com
for your passionate and gracious
support for this project.

Aaron Wong
Ada Palmer
Barbie Wilson
Christina Liu
Connie C.
Daniel Taylor

David Rodríguez "DARO"
Dom Stevens
Edward W Sizemore
Jason S. Yadao
Jena Jenkins
Joe "Zeroagent" Aguilar
Kazakthule

Linnea Harper
Mary Danielson
Maura Werner
Sean Kemp
Tobias Wirth
Wesley Holtkamp

A. L. Miller
Aaron B.
Abdul Hadi Sid Ahmed
Abhilash Sarhadi
Adisakdi Tantimedh
Alan Sparrow
Alan Zabaro
Albert Cua
Alex Bullett
Alex Hoffman
Alex Martin
Alvin Yap Kean Hoo
Amy Watson
Ana N.
Andrew Cassady
Andrew Krawic
Andrew Morgan
Andrew Partridge
Anna Frohling
Annaliese Christman
Anonymous
Arety Jameson
Ash Brown
AstroBBoy (Brian)
Aubrey Chambers
Bahar Vaghari Moghaddam
Basil Berchekas III
Ben Applegate
Benjamin Jacobson
Blue Delliquanti
Bob Pelletier
Bobby Thickett
Braet Bjorn

Brandon Eaker
Brandon Lee Archer
Braver Cruz Montero
Brendan Hubbs
Brian S. Lang
Brian Sebby
Brian Sikkenga
Bryan Elliott
Caitlin Peterson
Calvin Atom Markle
Captain Kris
Carl Sterner
Chad Beaver
Charles Crapo
Charles Strobl
Chris Colvin
Chris Kirby
Chris Marsh
Chris Opinsky
Chris Walker
Christine Ng
Christopher Ball
Christopher Brenner
Christopher Burrows
Christopher Lew
Christopher M. Cox
Christopher Roman
Christopher Wilson
Christy Lewis
CJ Thom
Colleen Salisbury
Corinna Cornett
Craig Crosier

Crobdan
Curt Darragh
Cynthia Ann Foberg
D. Raines
Dallas Middaugh
Dan & Val Bailey
Dana
Daniel and Lael Blackburn
Daniel Dames
Daniel Grant
Daniel Hottinger
Daniel Lin
Daniella Orihuela-Gruber
Danielle Lavoie
Daryl Jenkins
David Merrill
David Northover
David Price-Hughes
David Tai
David Verigin
Dawn Oshima
Deb Aoki
Derek Tagg
Diana Mallery
Dirk
Doctor Swerve
Doug Wilder
Dr Jon Barker
drjiin
Duckling Delarosa
Dustin Cooper
Dylan M.
E. Whitehurst

Eddy Yue
Edward Delaney
Eleanor Walker
Elijah
Elisabeth Dufresne
Ellen Yu
Emily Bov
Eoin Marron
Eric Seyler
Eric Swanson
Erik Nelson
Evan Ritchie
Fabio Martins
Fabrice Armisen
Federica Lampugnani
Felicia Bhagwandin
Felipe Oliveros
FILIPPO CAMPANIOLO
finchiekins
François Blavoet
François Picot
Gabe Roginic
Garrett O'Boyle
Gene Verley
Gerardo Aguirre
Gianluca Gentili
Gina Curtice
Gina Fusco
Grant Alexander
Gray Hendricks
Gregory Prout
Guilherme e Renata

Gustav Jonsson
Guy Barnes
Guy Thomas
Gwyneth Holder
Heather Breckel
Heather Keys Matthews
Henrik Lindhe
Hoai Thanh Nguyen
Ian Stephen
Ian Wolf
Ihsaan
Ivan Doronin
J. Ryan Pas
Jack Donoghue
Jacob Welch
Jákup Fuglø
James Austin
James Weber
Janelle and Bob Billings
Japheth Campbell
Jason Glick
Jason Raquinio
Jay V. Schindler
Jean Harrison
Jeff Chan
Jeff Troutman
Jeffrey Kahn
Jenna Crawford
Jennifer Torkkola
Jeremy Dowdle
Jess Brand
Jimmie Maggard Jr
Jimmy A. Guerrero
JJ Harrison
Joan Rodas Cusidó
Joe Keatinge
Joel Schlosberg
Johan F
John Deemer
John J. Aylward
John Oppliger
Jon VanDuzee
Jonathan Betanoff
Jonathan Carter
Jose P Zagal
Jose Șagastume
Joseph Cortese
Joseph Parello
Joshua Chaplin
Joshua James Grigg
Joshua Kenney
Joshua Munro
Joshua Steadman
Julia S-J
Julian Vu
Justin R. Turbyfill
Justin Ryan
Karl W. Reinsch
Kasper Bornauw Vanderlocht
Kate Montgomery
Katherine S
Katy Norman
Keith Bowden
Kelly Breswick
Kelly Hoolihan
Kelvin the Lion
Kevin D. Bond
Kevin Derendorf
Kevin Freeman
Kin Chung Ken Ho
Kirk J. Westbeld
Kory Cerjak
Kosaka
Kotatsu
Kristin Bomba
Kunal Desai
Kwame Akosah
Ky
Laura Pinson
Liam Tate
Lillia Stevens
@LisaKraus
Lisa M. Geller
Lisette Sandoval
Liz Hencke
Lori
Lucille M. Hatfield
Luke Foster
Luke Osterritter
M. Raven Metzner
M.R. Turnage
Mahlon Landis
Marc Edwards
Marcus Woodman
Margaret Kunz
Marius Dagestad
Mark Cox
Mark Daly
Mark Pengryn
Mary Canada
Matt Parker
Matt Zitron
Matthew Geoffino
Matthew Latino
Maurizio "Kirio" Iorio
Melissa Gelfs
Michael Barbour
Michael Camacho
Michael Ferri
Michael K David II
Michael Whipp
Miguel Rana
Mike Meltzer
Mike Valentine Prower
Mohammed Kalkattawi
Monique Pihl
Murasaki Kitty
Nguyễn Văn Hà [Hanz]
Nicholas "The History Follower" Anderson
Nicholas Bray
Nicholas Chow
Nicholas S Del Guercio
Noel Arnold
NOM
oliver oakley
Owen Sayers
Pamela B.
Patrick King
Patrick McClafferty
Patrick Mohlmann
Patrick Mulderig
Paul C. Walcher
Paul M. H.
Penny
Peter A. Rose
Peter Fong
Peter Strömberg
Phil Binkowski
Philip
Philippe Lupien
Phillip O'Connor
Pierre Martinez
PJ
Pual Northcott
R. Snow
R. Todd Crockett
Rachael LeNoir
Rachel Susan
Rachelle Morissette
Randall Ramsey
Randy Cobb
Raymond Herrera
Rebecca Woolford
Reid Johnson
Rhel n DecVand
Ricardo Javier Peña García
Richard H.
Rick Grubel
Robert Kamphaus II
Robert Musser
Romane Milliard
Ronald & Dejah Whited
Rose Moran
Russell Martens
Ryan C. Baker
Ryan Schlegel
Ryan Visteen
S & M Cavanaugh
Sam Murdock
Scaut
Scott Bono
Scott Forgue
Scott Hastings Mitchell
Scott Rubin
Scott Underwood
Sean Brady
Sean Gaffney
Seth Isenberg
Seth Karp
SgLee
Sherri French
Shervyn
Sherwin Abesamis
Siddharth Gupta
Sleazy Dan Lester
Stephen G Matthews
Stephen J White
Stephen Rooney
Steve Hudson
Steve Rubin
Steven Wu
Susan Bermudez
Tabby Ramsey
Tariq Khonji
Teagan Nash
Tegan and Isabelle McCarty
Tenzing Thabkhe
TheLurkingTerror
Thomas Flintham
Thomas Fuchs
Thomas J. Wood
Thomas Jones-Low
Thomas Maluck
Thomas W. Harvey
Thorsten Gruber
Tiffany Beckley
Tom Pandich
Tyler Goulet
Van G. Wong
Vincenzo Averello
Will Hensley
Wilma Jandoc Win
Yamaneko
Zabuni
Zachary Rosenberg
Zack Rosenberg
Zack Walter
Zoë Grey Decena

THANK YOU ALL SO MUCH FOR YOUR SUPPORT!

CAPTAIN KEN

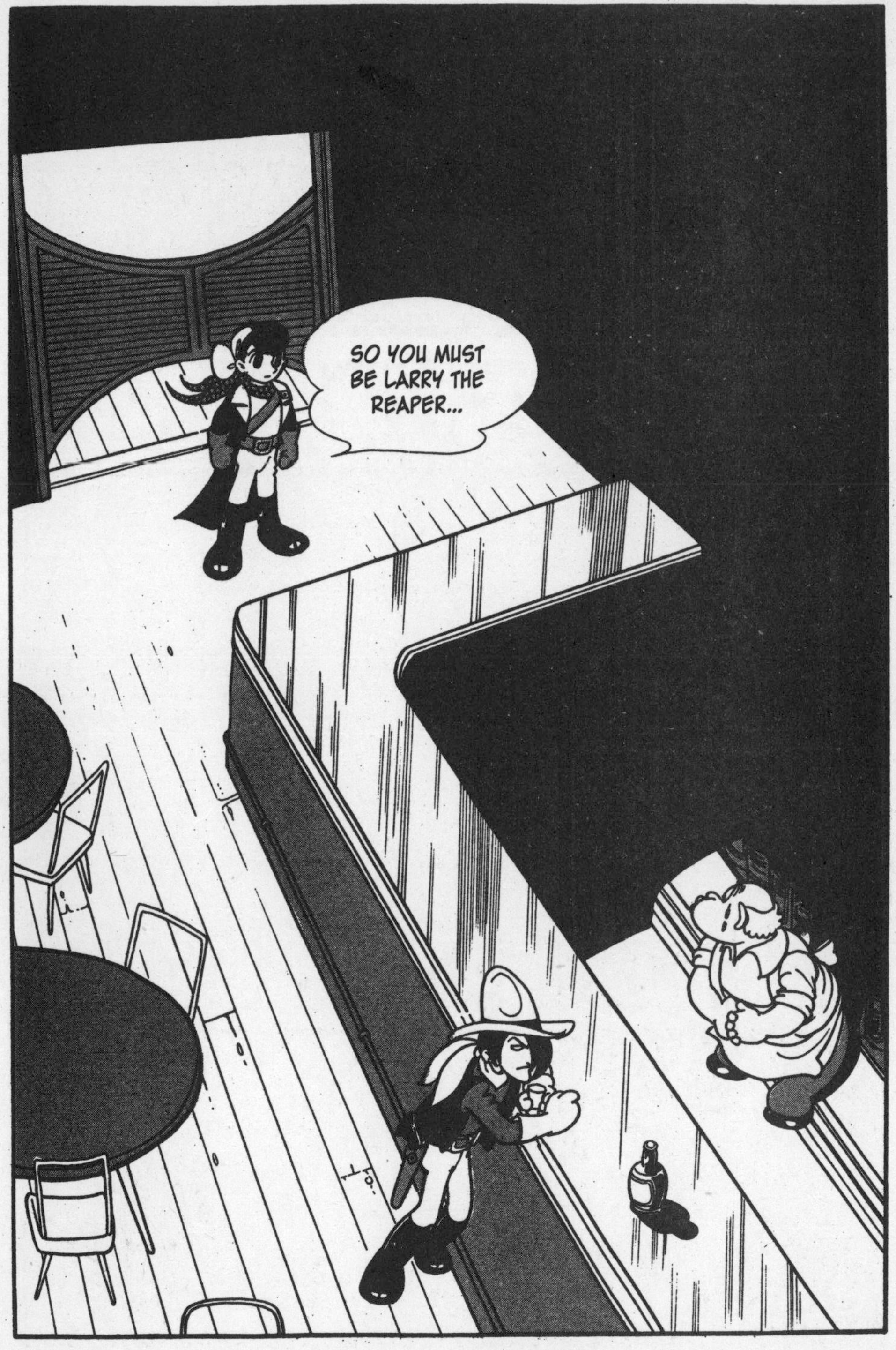
SO YOU MUST BE LARRY THE REAPER...

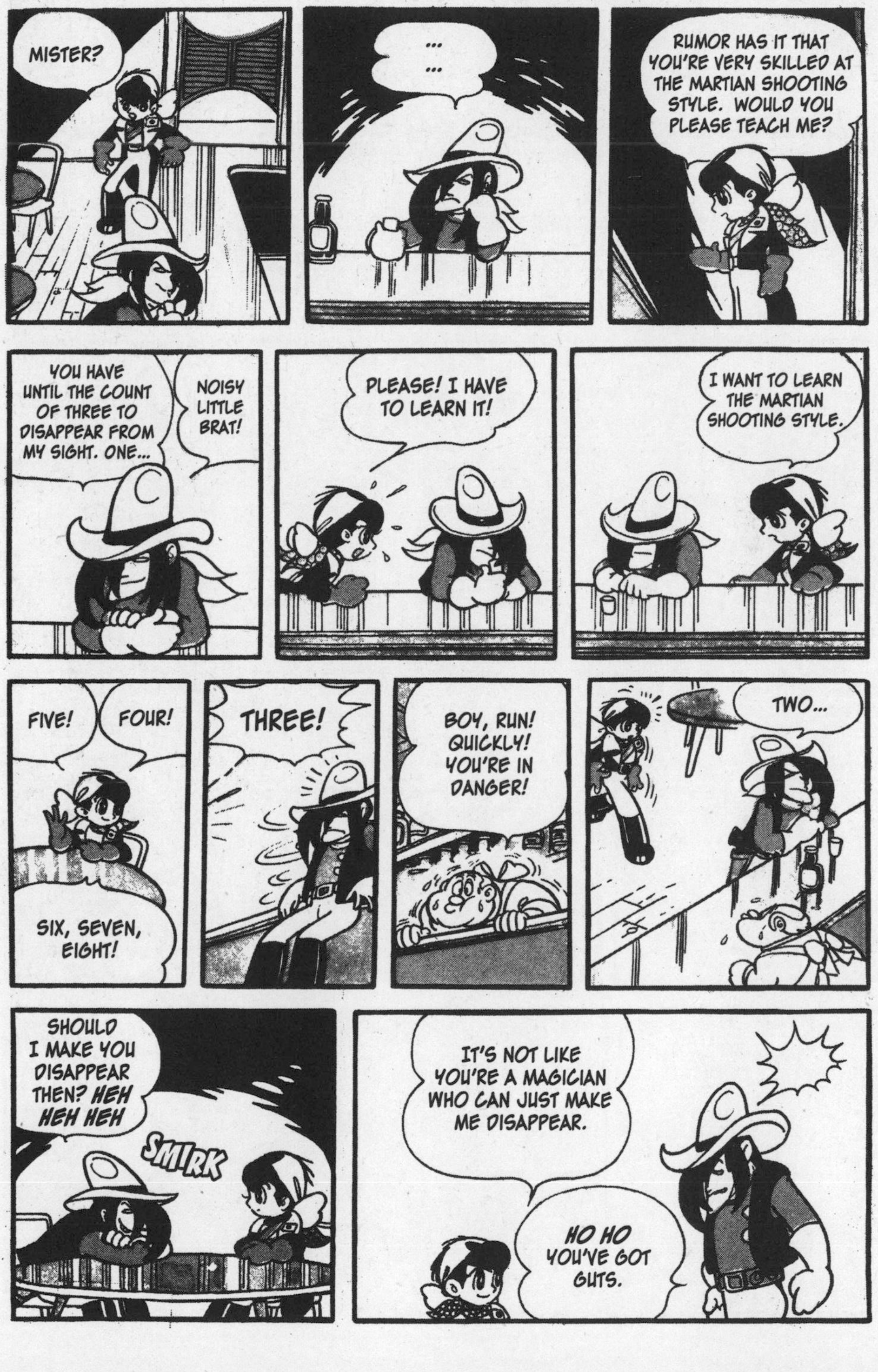
RUMOR HAS IT THAT YOU'RE VERY SKILLED AT THE MARTIAN SHOOTING STYLE. WOULD YOU PLEASE TEACH ME?
...
...
MISTER?
I WANT TO LEARN THE MARTIAN SHOOTING STYLE.
PLEASE! I HAVE TO LEARN IT!
NOISY LITTLE BRAT!
YOU HAVE UNTIL THE COUNT OF THREE TO DISAPPEAR FROM MY SIGHT. ONE...
TWO...
BOY, RUN! QUICKLY! YOU'RE IN DANGER!
THREE!
FOUR!
FIVE!
SIX, SEVEN, EIGHT!
IT'S NOT LIKE YOU'RE A MAGICIAN WHO CAN JUST MAKE ME DISAPPEAR.
HO HO YOU'VE GOT GUTS.
SHOULD I MAKE YOU DISAPPEAR THEN? HEH HEH HEH
SMIRK

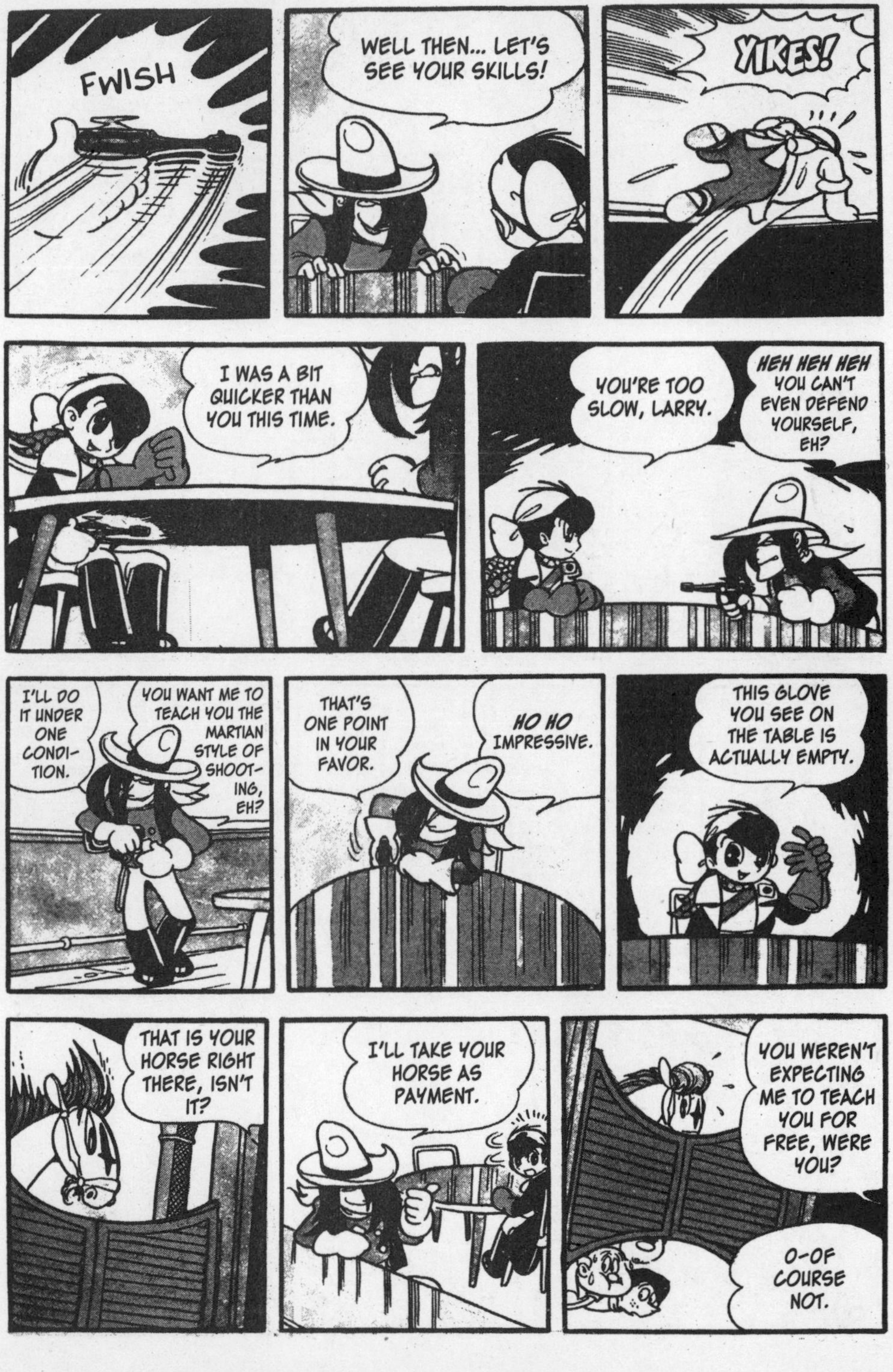
YIKES!
WELL THEN... LET'S SEE YOUR SKILLS!
FWISH
HEH HEH HEH YOU CAN'T EVEN DEFEND YOURSELF, EH?
YOU'RE TOO SLOW, LARRY.
I WAS A BIT QUICKER THAN YOU THIS TIME.
THIS GLOVE YOU SEE ON THE TABLE IS ACTUALLY EMPTY.
HO HO IMPRESSIVE.
THAT'S ONE POINT IN YOUR FAVOR.
YOU WANT ME TO TEACH YOU THE MARTIAN STYLE OF SHOOTING, EH?
I'LL DO IT UNDER ONE CONDITION.
YOU WEREN'T EXPECTING ME TO TEACH YOU FOR FREE, WERE YOU?
O-OF COURSE NOT.
I'LL TAKE YOUR HORSE AS PAYMENT.
THAT IS YOUR HORSE RIGHT THERE, ISN'T IT?

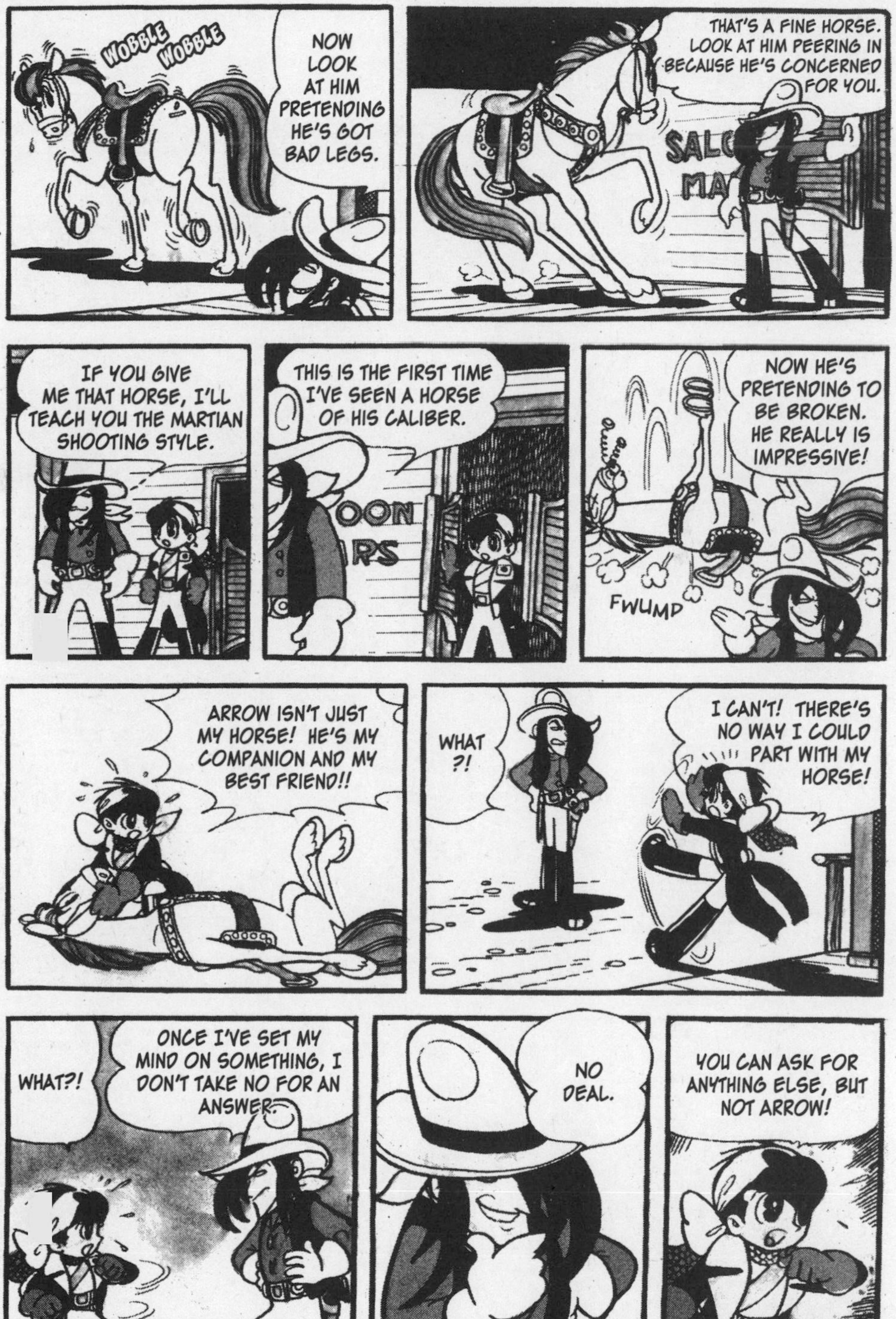
THAT'S A FINE HORSE. LOOK AT HIM PEERING IN BECAUSE HE'S CONCERNED FOR YOU.
NOW LOOK AT HIM PRETENDING HE'S GOT BAD LEGS.
WOBBLE WOBBLE
NOW HE'S PRETENDING TO BE BROKEN. HE REALLY IS IMPRESSIVE!
FWUMP
THIS IS THE FIRST TIME I'VE SEEN A HORSE OF HIS CALIBER.
IF YOU GIVE ME THAT HORSE, I'LL TEACH YOU THE MARTIAN SHOOTING STYLE.
I CAN'T! THERE'S NO WAY I COULD PART WITH MY HORSE!
WHAT ?!
ARROW ISN'T JUST MY HORSE! HE'S MY COMPANION AND MY BEST FRIEND!!
YOU CAN ASK FOR ANYTHING ELSE, BUT NOT ARROW!
NO DEAL.
ONCE I'VE SET MY MIND ON SOMETHING, I DON'T TAKE NO FOR AN ANSWER.
WHAT?!

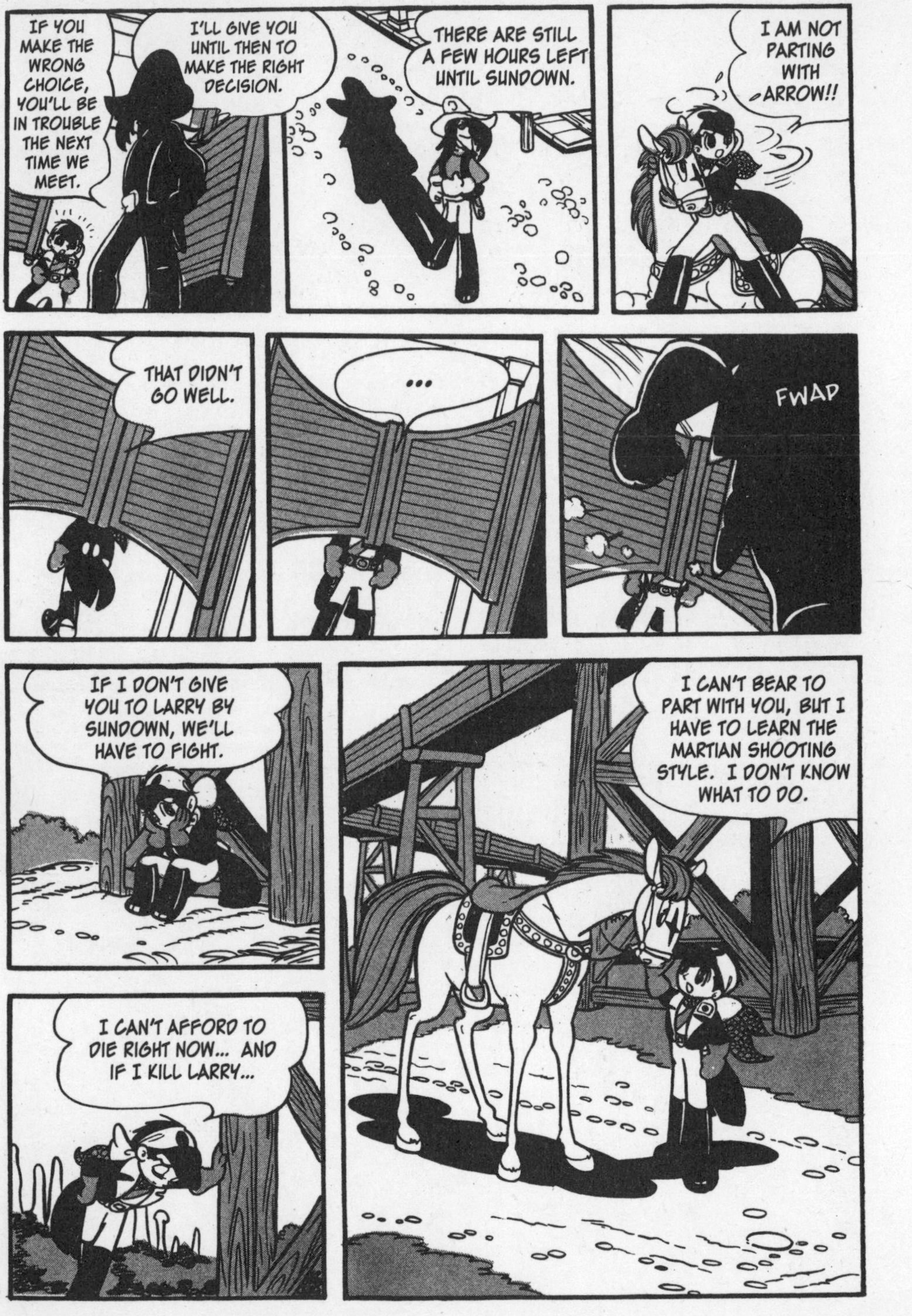
I AM NOT PARTING WITH ARROW!!
THERE ARE STILL A FEW HOURS LEFT UNTIL SUNDOWN.
I'LL GIVE YOU UNTIL THEN TO MAKE THE RIGHT DECISION.
IF YOU MAKE THE WRONG CHOICE, YOU'LL BE IN TROUBLE THE NEXT TIME WE MEET.
FWAP
...
THAT DIDN'T GO WELL.
I CAN'T BEAR TO PART WITH YOU, BUT I HAVE TO LEARN THE MARTIAN SHOOTING STYLE. I DON'T KNOW WHAT TO DO.
IF I DON'T GIVE YOU TO LARRY BY SUNDOWN, WE'LL HAVE TO FIGHT.
I CAN'T AFFORD TO DIE RIGHT NOW... AND IF I KILL LARRY...

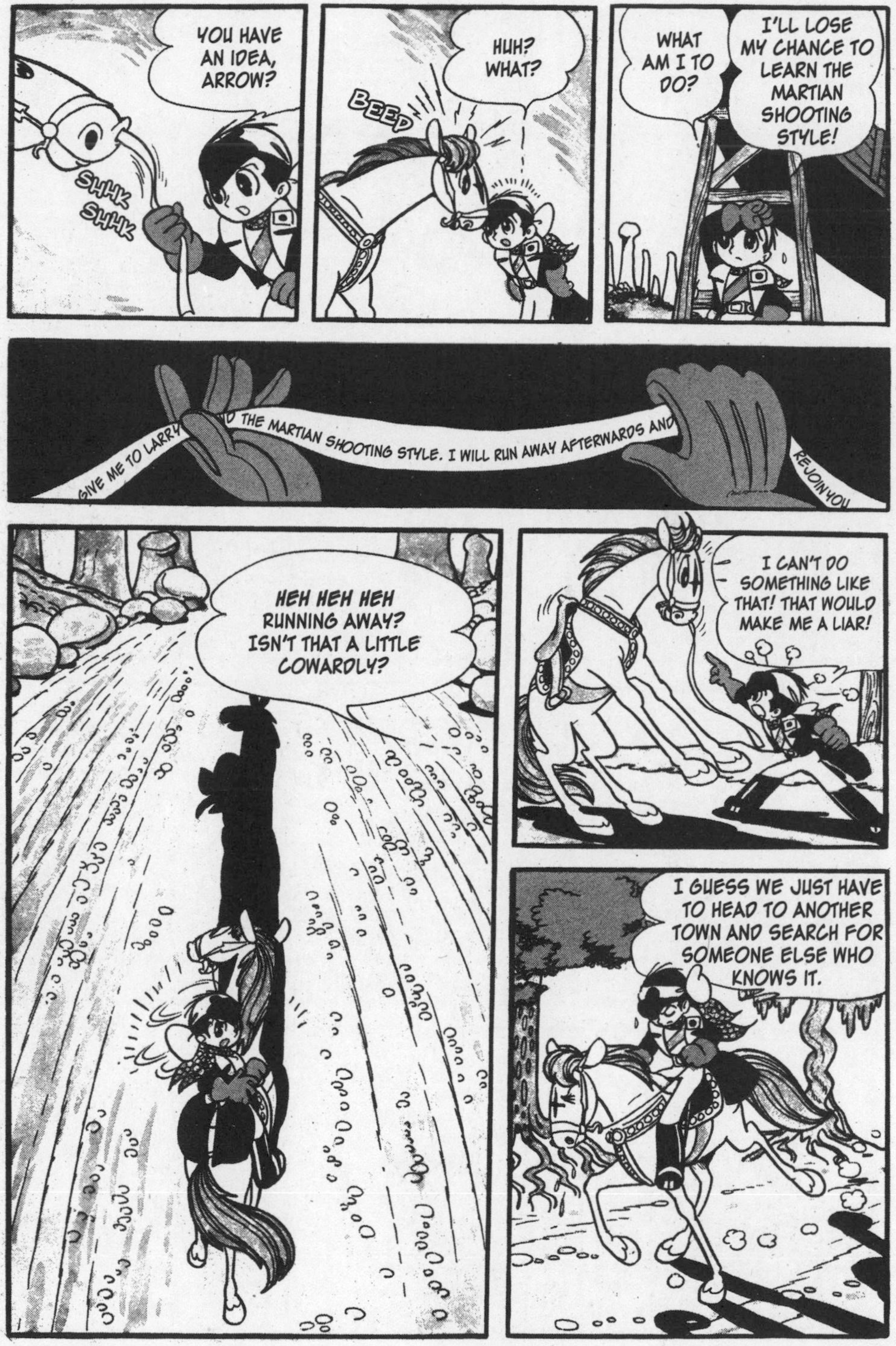
I'LL LOSE MY CHANCE TO LEARN THE MARTIAN SHOOTING STYLE!
WHAT AM I TO DO?
BEEP
HUH? WHAT?
YOU HAVE AN IDEA, ARROW?
SHHK SHHK
GIVE ME TO LARRY
D THE MARTIAN SHOOTING STYLE. I WILL RUN AWAY AFTERWARDS AND
REJOINYOU
I CAN'T DO SOMETHING LIKE THAT! THAT WOULD MAKE ME A LIAR!
I GUESS WE JUST HAVE TO HEAD TO ANOTHER TOWN AND SEARCH FOR SOMEONE ELSE WHO KNOWS IT.
HEH HEH HEH RUNNING AWAY? ISN'T THAT A LITTLE COWARDLY?

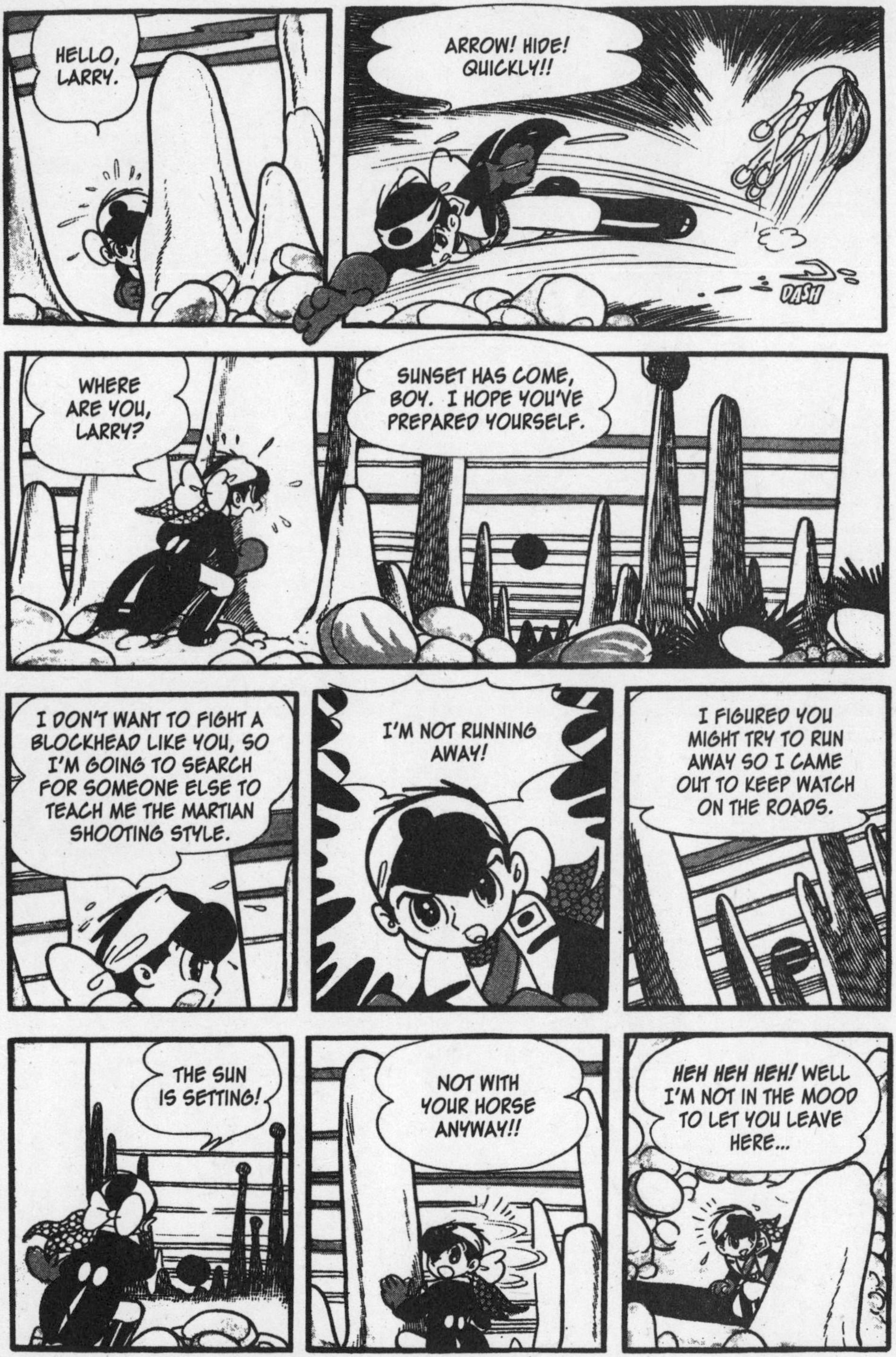
ARROW! HIDE! QUICKLY!!
DASH
HELLO, LARRY.
SUNSET HAS COME, BOY. I HOPE YOU'VE PREPARED YOURSELF.
WHERE ARE YOU, LARRY?
I FIGURED YOU MIGHT TRY TO RUN AWAY SO I CAME OUT TO KEEP WATCH ON THE ROADS.
I'M NOT RUNNING AWAY!
I DON'T WANT TO FIGHT A BLOCKHEAD LIKE YOU, SO I'M GOING TO SEARCH FOR SOMEONE ELSE TO TEACH ME THE MARTIAN SHOOTING STYLE.
HEH HEH HEH! WELL I'M NOT IN THE MOOD TO LET YOU LEAVE HERE...
NOT WITH YOUR HORSE ANYWAY!!
THE SUN IS SETTING!

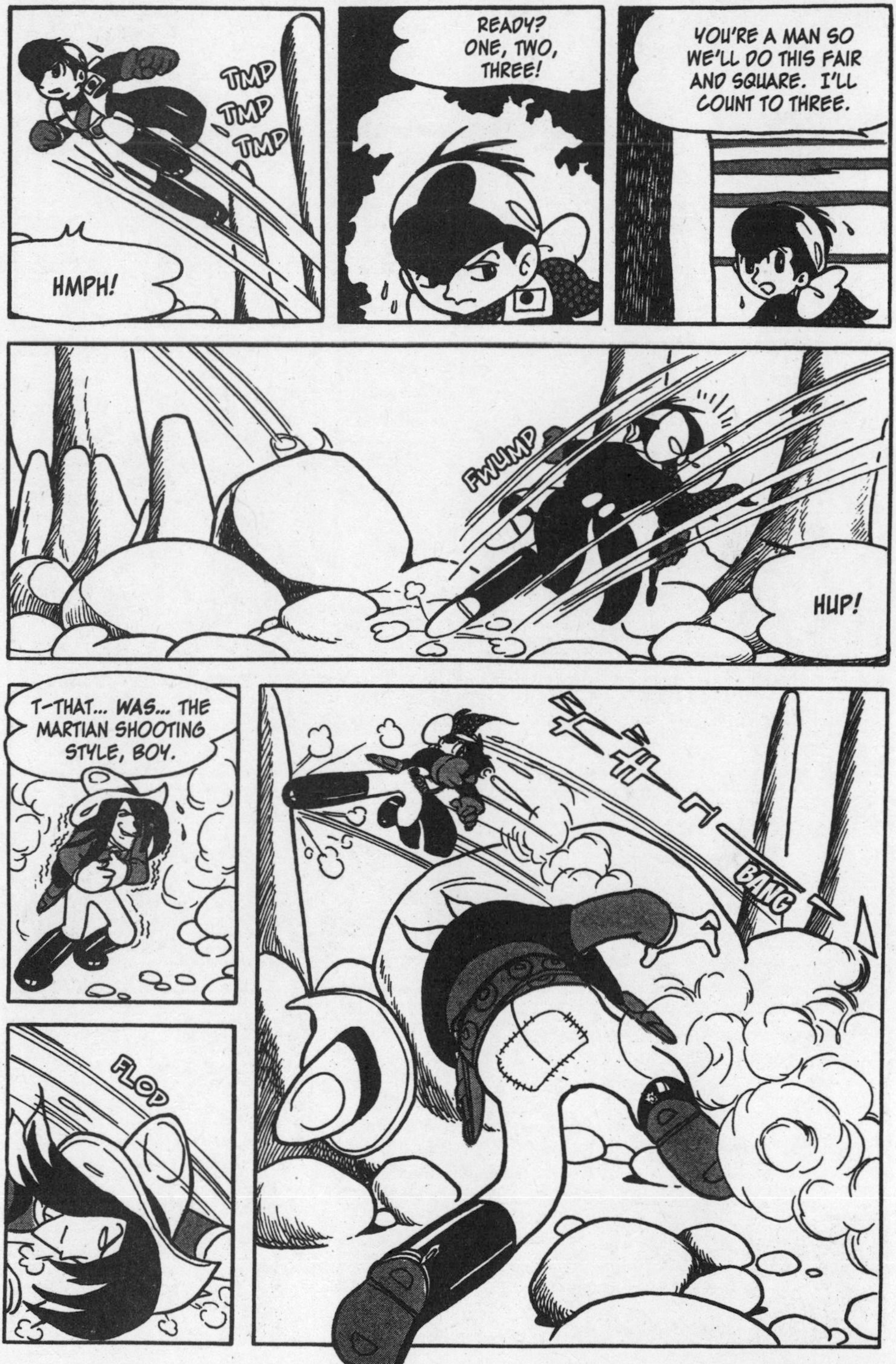
YOU'RE A MAN SO WE'LL DO THIS FAIR AND SQUARE. I'LL COUNT TO THREE.
READY? ONE, TWO, THREE!
TMP
TMP
TMP
HMPH!
FWUMP
HUP!
BANG
T-THAT... WAS... THE MARTIAN SHOOTING STYLE, BOY.
FLOP

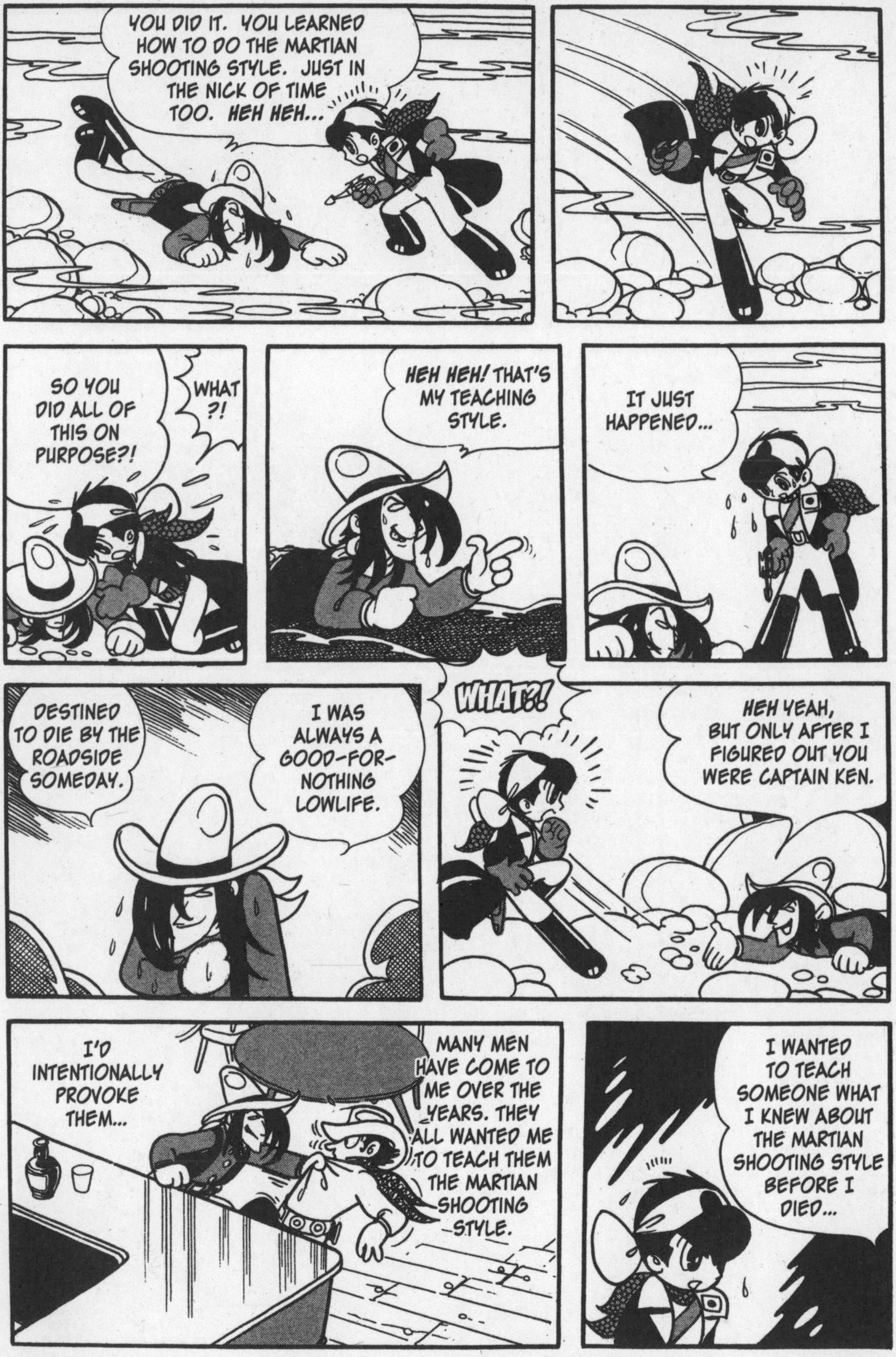
YOU DID IT. YOU LEARNED HOW TO DO THE MARTIAN SHOOTING STYLE. JUST IN THE NICK OF TIME TOO. HEH HEH...
IT JUST HAPPENED...
HEH HEH! THAT'S MY TEACHING STYLE.
WHAT ?!
SO YOU DID ALL OF THIS ON PURPOSE?!
HEH YEAH, BUT ONLY AFTER I FIGURED OUT YOU WERE CAPTAIN KEN.
WHAT?!
I WAS ALWAYS A GOOD-FOR-NOTHING LOWLIFE.
DESTINED TO DIE BY THE ROADSIDE SOMEDAY.
I WANTED TO TEACH SOMEONE WHAT I KNEW ABOUT THE MARTIAN SHOOTING STYLE BEFORE I DIED...
MANY MEN HAVE COME TO ME OVER THE YEARS. THEY ALL WANTED ME TO TEACH THEM THE MARTIAN SHOOTING STYLE.
I'D INTENTIONALLY PROVOKE THEM...

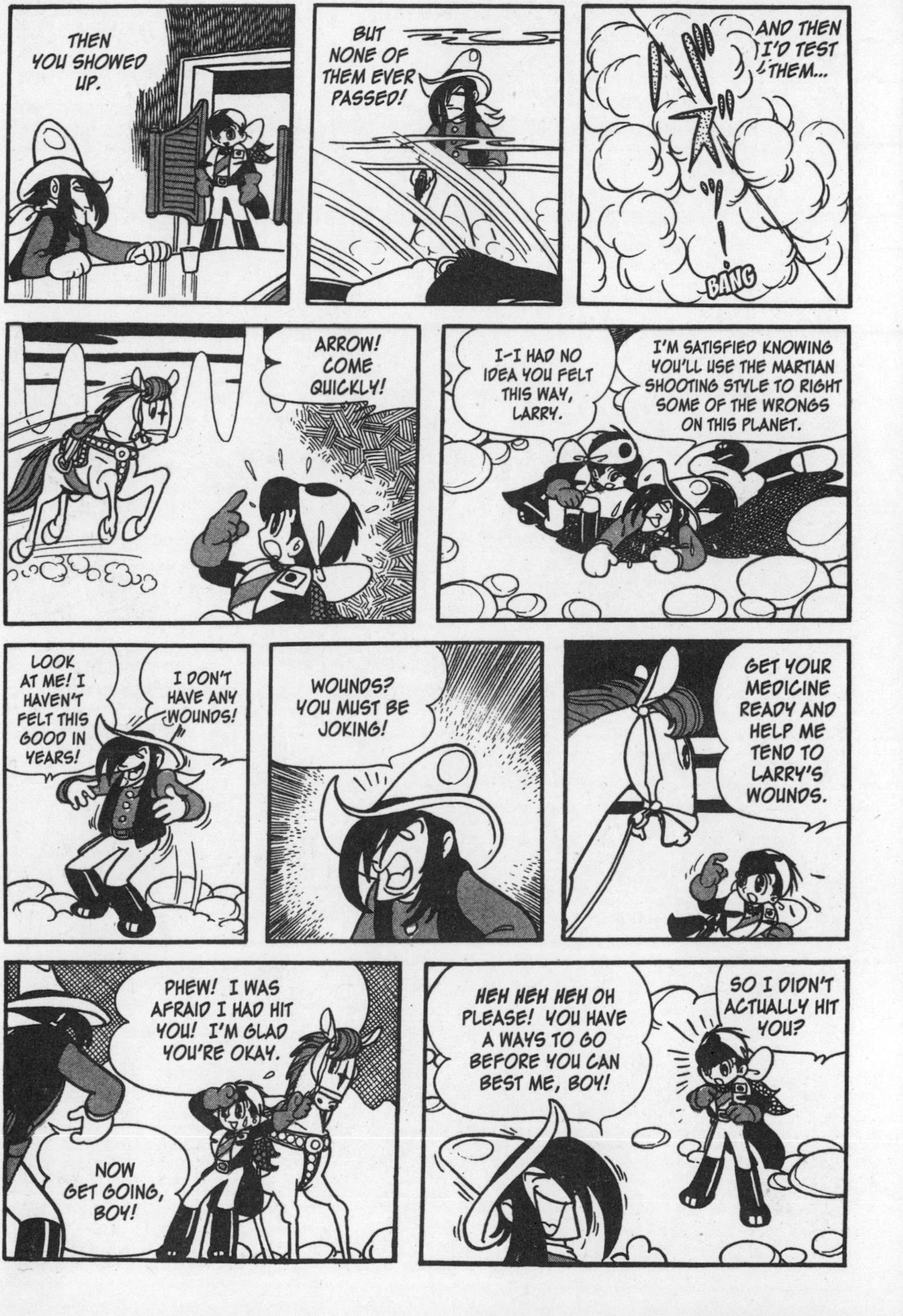
AND THEN I'D TEST THEM...
BANG
BUT NONE OF THEM EVER PASSED!
THEN YOU SHOWED UP.
I'M SATISFIED KNOWING YOU'LL USE THE MARTIAN SHOOTING STYLE TO RIGHT SOME OF THE WRONGS ON THIS PLANET.
I-I HAD NO IDEA YOU FELT THIS WAY, LARRY.
ARROW! COME QUICKLY!
GET YOUR MEDICINE READY AND HELP ME TEND TO LARRY'S WOUNDS.
WOUNDS? YOU MUST BE JOKING!
I DON'T HAVE ANY WOUNDS!
LOOK AT ME! I HAVEN'T FELT THIS GOOD IN YEARS!
SO I DIDN'T ACTUALLY HIT YOU?
HEH HEH HEH OH PLEASE! YOU HAVE A WAYS TO GO BEFORE YOU CAN BEST ME, BOY!
PHEW! I WAS AFRAID I HAD HIT YOU! I'M GLAD YOU'RE OKAY.
NOW GET GOING, BOY!

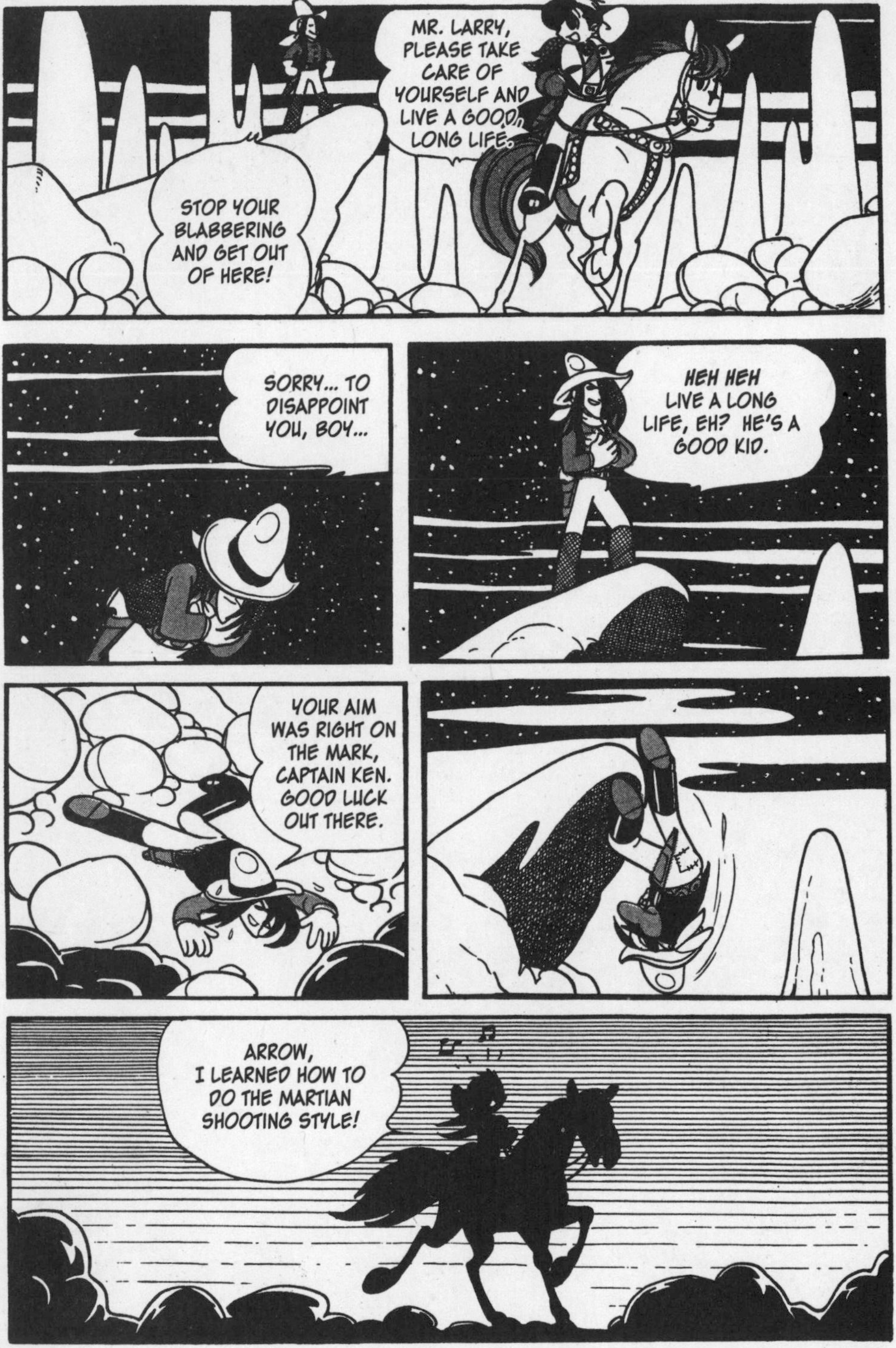
MR. LARRY, PLEASE TAKE CARE OF YOURSELF AND LIVE A GOOD, LONG LIFE.
STOP YOUR BLABBERING AND GET OUT OF HERE!
HEH HEH LIVE A LONG LIFE, EH? HE'S A GOOD KID.
SORRY... TO DISAPPOINT YOU, BOY...
YOUR AIM WAS RIGHT ON THE MARK, CAPTAIN KEN. GOOD LUCK OUT THERE.
ARROW, I LEARNED HOW TO DO THE MARTIAN SHOOTING STYLE!

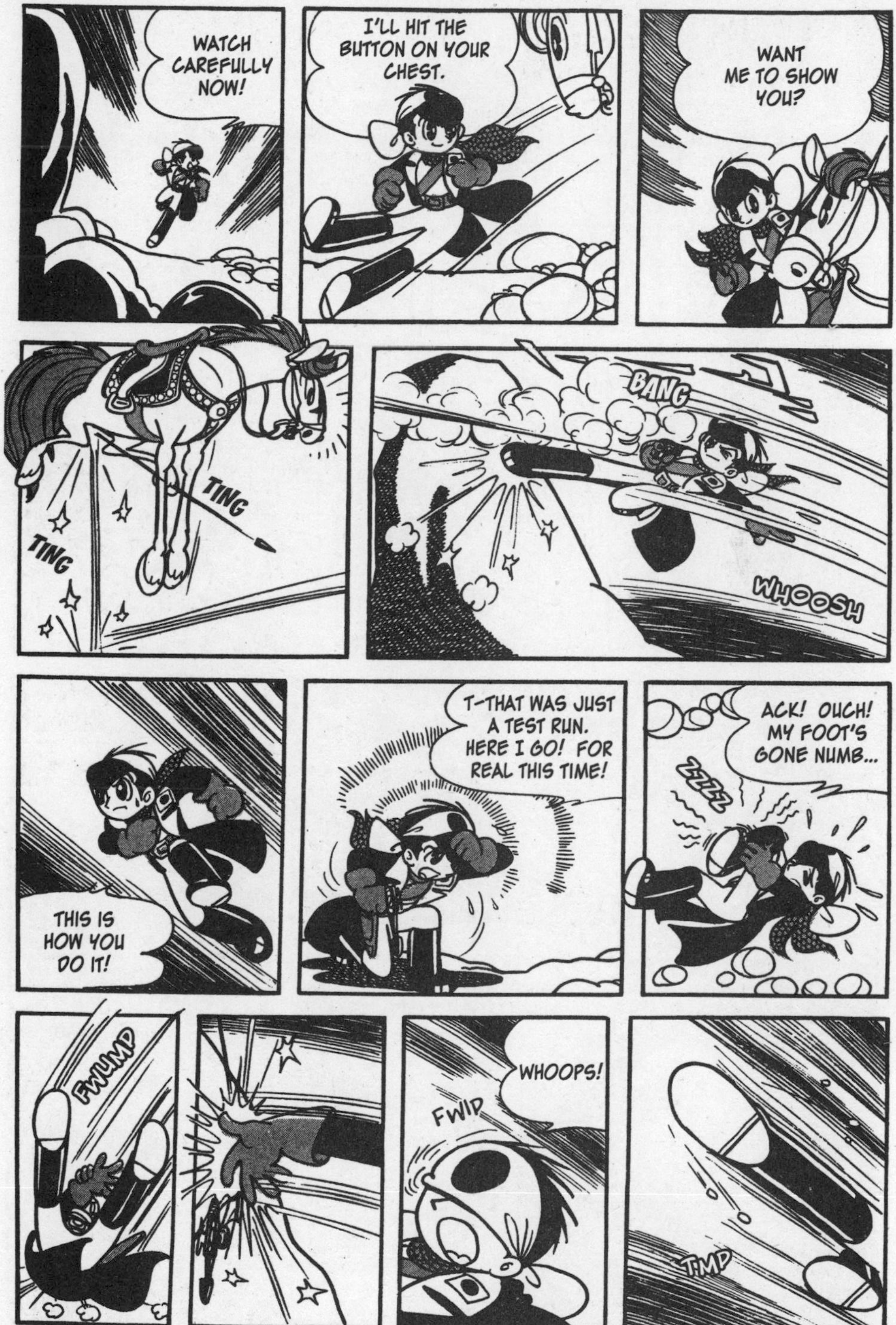
WANT ME TO SHOW YOU?
I'LL HIT THE BUTTON ON YOUR CHEST.
WATCH CAREFULLY NOW!
BANG
WHOOSH
TING
TING
ACK! OUCH! MY FOOT'S GONE NUMB...
ZZZZ
T-THAT WAS JUST A TEST RUN. HERE I GO! FOR REAL THIS TIME!
THIS IS HOW YOU DO IT!
TMP
WHOOPS!
FWIP
FWUMP

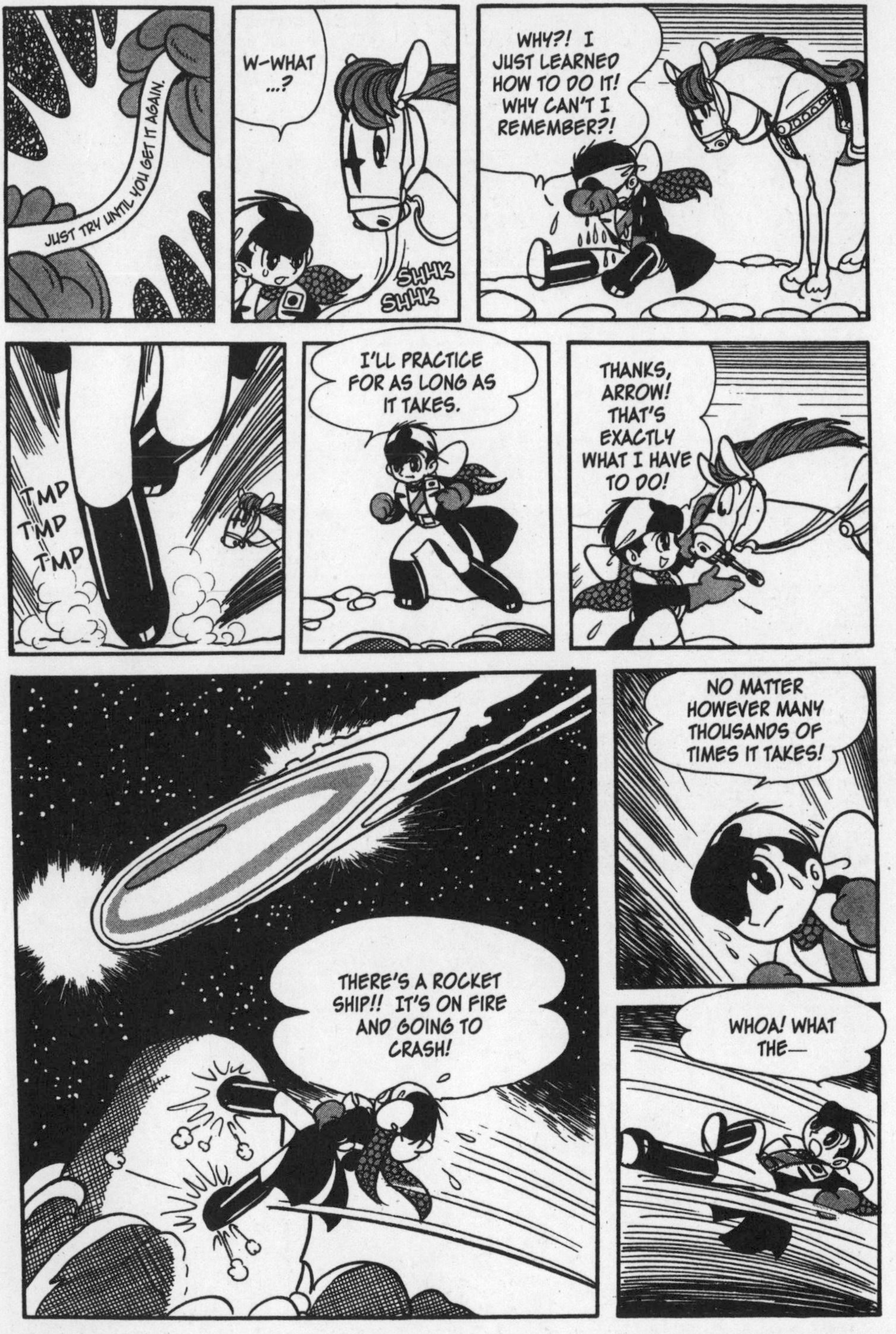
WHY?! I JUST LEARNED HOW TO DO IT! WHY CAN'T I REMEMBER?!
W-WHAT ...?
SHHK SHHK
JUST TRY UNTIL YOU GET IT AGAIN.
THANKS, ARROW! THAT'S EXACTLY WHAT I HAVE TO DO!
I'LL PRACTICE FOR AS LONG AS IT TAKES.
TMP TMP TMP
NO MATTER HOWEVER MANY THOUSANDS OF TIMES IT TAKES!
WHOA! WHAT THE—
THERE'S A ROCKET SHIP!! IT'S ON FIRE AND GOING TO CRASH!

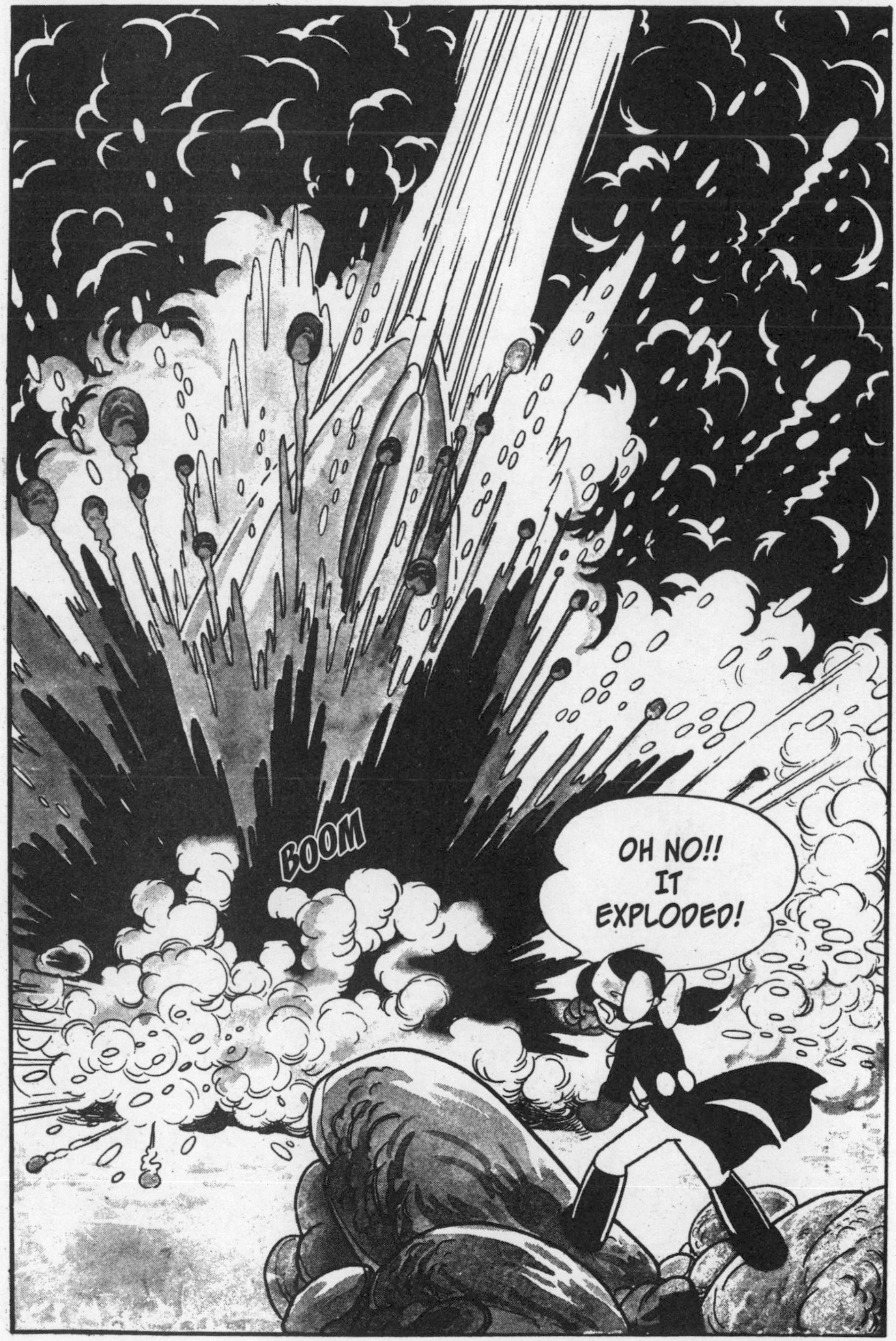
BOOM
OH NO!! IT EXPLODED!

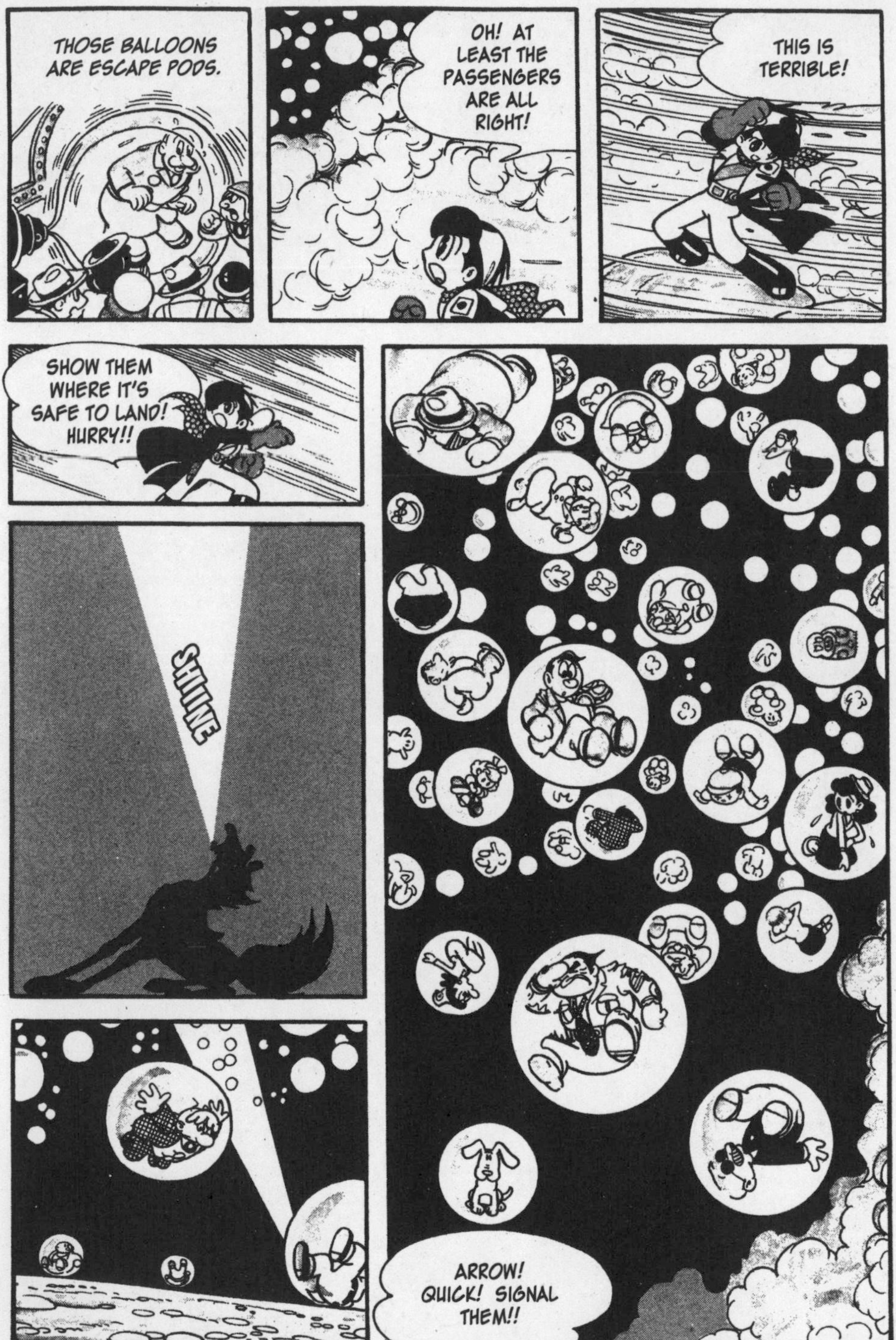
THIS IS TERRIBLE!
OH! AT LEAST THE PASSENGERS ARE ALL RIGHT!
THOSE BALLOONS ARE ESCAPE PODS.
ARROW! QUICK! SIGNAL THEM!!
SHOW THEM WHERE IT'S SAFE TO LAND! HURRY!!
SHINE

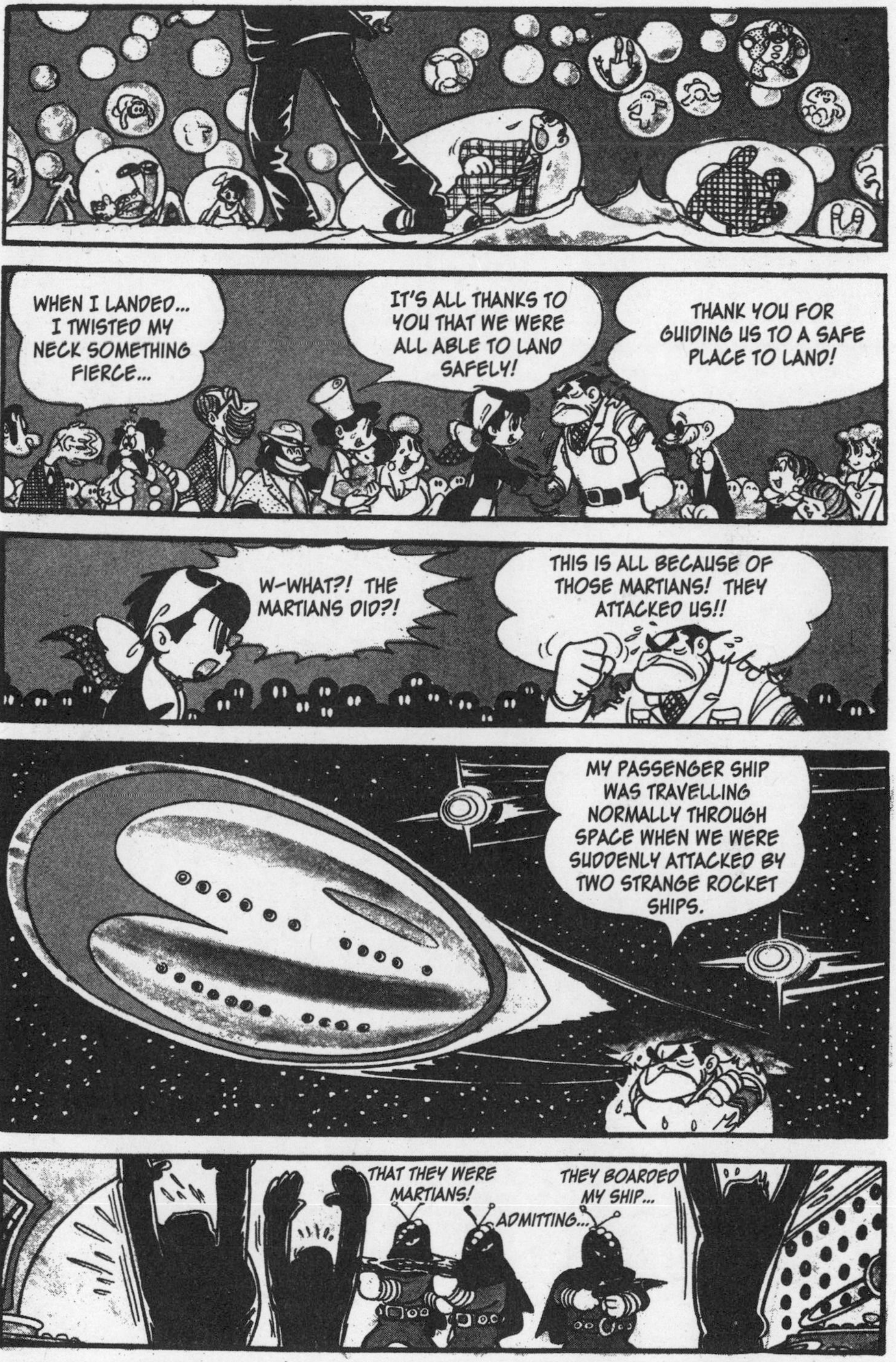
THANK YOU FOR GUIDING US TO A SAFE PLACE TO LAND!
IT'S ALL THANKS TO YOU THAT WE WERE ALL ABLE TO LAND SAFELY!
WHEN I LANDED... I TWISTED MY NECK SOMETHING FIERCE...
THIS IS ALL BECAUSE OF THOSE MARTIANS! THEY ATTACKED US!!
W-WHAT?! THE MARTIANS DID?!
MY PASSENGER SHIP WAS TRAVELLING NORMALLY THROUGH SPACE WHEN WE WERE SUDDENLY ATTACKED BY TWO STRANGE ROCKET SHIPS.
THEY BOARDED MY SHIP...
ADMITTING...
THAT THEY WERE MARTIANS!

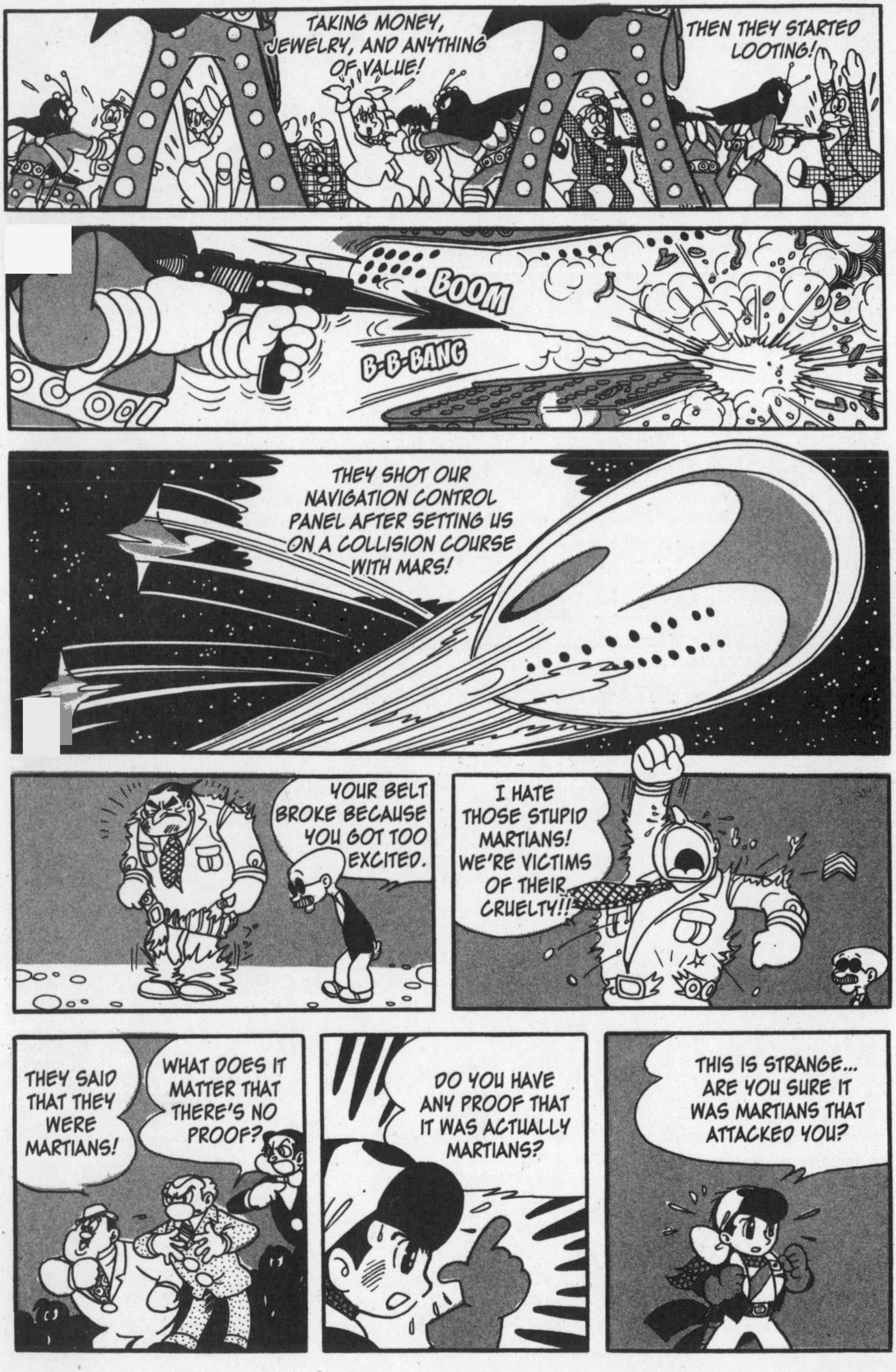
THEN THEY STARTED LOOTING!
TAKING MONEY, JEWELRY, AND ANYTHING OF VALUE!
BOOM
B-B-BANG
THEY SHOT OUR NAVIGATION CONTROL PANEL AFTER SETTING US ON A COLLISION COURSE WITH MARS!
I HATE THOSE STUPID MARTIANS! WE'RE VICTIMS OF THEIR CRUELTY!!
YOUR BELT BROKE BECAUSE YOU GOT TOO EXCITED.
THIS IS STRANGE... ARE YOU SURE IT WAS MARTIANS THAT ATTACKED YOU?
DO YOU HAVE ANY PROOF THAT IT WAS ACTUALLY MARTIANS?
WHAT DOES IT MATTER THAT THERE'S NO PROOF?
THEY SAID THAT THEY WERE MARTIANS!

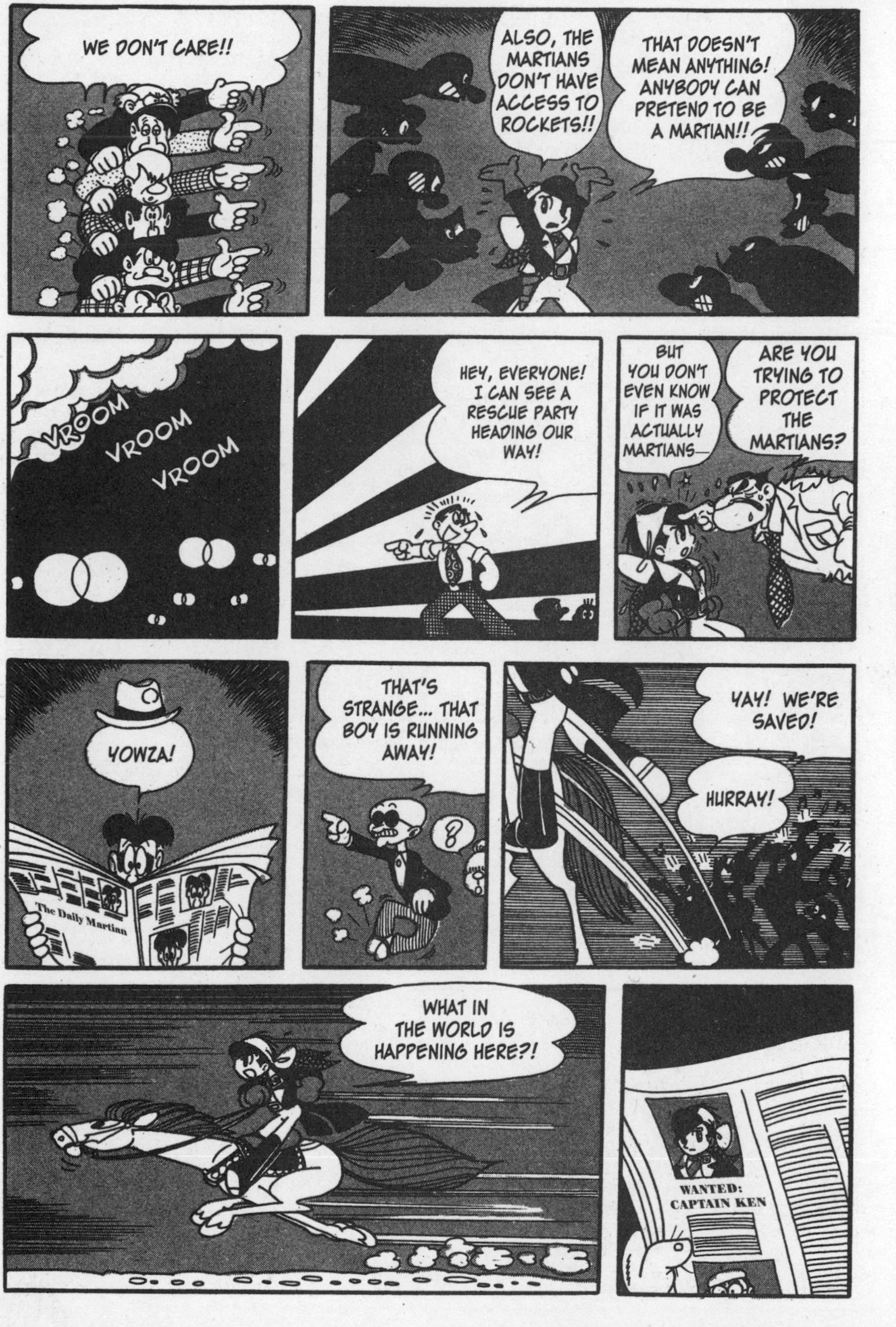
THAT DOESN'T MEAN ANYTHING! ANYBODY CAN PRETEND TO BE A MARTIAN!!
ALSO, THE MARTIANS DON'T HAVE ACCESS TO ROCKETS!!
WE DON'T CARE!!
ARE YOU TRYING TO PROTECT THE MARTIANS?
BUT YOU DON'T EVEN KNOW IF IT WAS ACTUALLY MARTIANS—
HEY, EVERYONE! I CAN SEE A RESCUE PARTY HEADING OUR WAY!
VROOM
VROOM
VROOM
YAY! WE'RE SAVED!
HURRAY!
THAT'S STRANGE... THAT BOY IS RUNNING AWAY!
?
YOWZA!
The Daily Martian
WANTED: CAPTAIN KEN
WHAT IN THE WORLD IS HAPPENING HERE?!

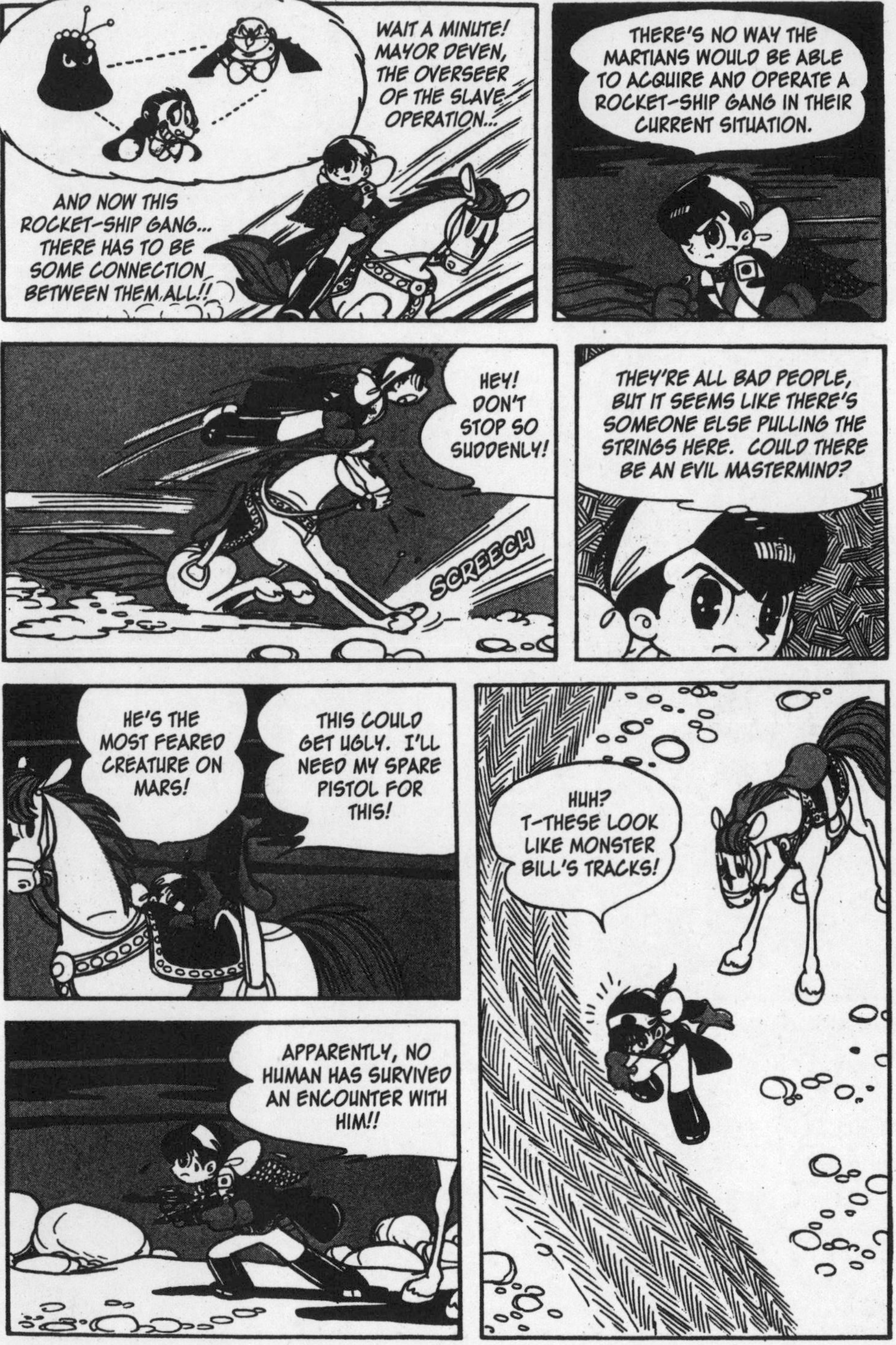
THERE'S NO WAY THE MARTIANS WOULD BE ABLE TO ACQUIRE AND OPERATE A ROCKET-SHIP GANG IN THEIR CURRENT SITUATION.
WAIT A MINUTE! MAYOR DEVEN, THE OVERSEER OF THE SLAVE OPERATION...
AND NOW THIS ROCKET-SHIP GANG... THERE HAS TO BE SOME CONNECTION BETWEEN THEM ALL!!
THEY'RE ALL BAD PEOPLE, BUT IT SEEMS LIKE THERE'S SOMEONE ELSE PULLING THE STRINGS HERE. COULD THERE BE AN EVIL MASTERMIND?
HEY! DON'T STOP SO SUDDENLY!
SCREECH
HUH? T-THESE LOOK LIKE MONSTER BILL'S TRACKS!
THIS COULD GET UGLY. I'LL NEED MY SPARE PISTOL FOR THIS!
HE'S THE MOST FEARED CREATURE ON MARS!
APPARENTLY, NO HUMAN HAS SURVIVED AN ENCOUNTER WITH HIM!!

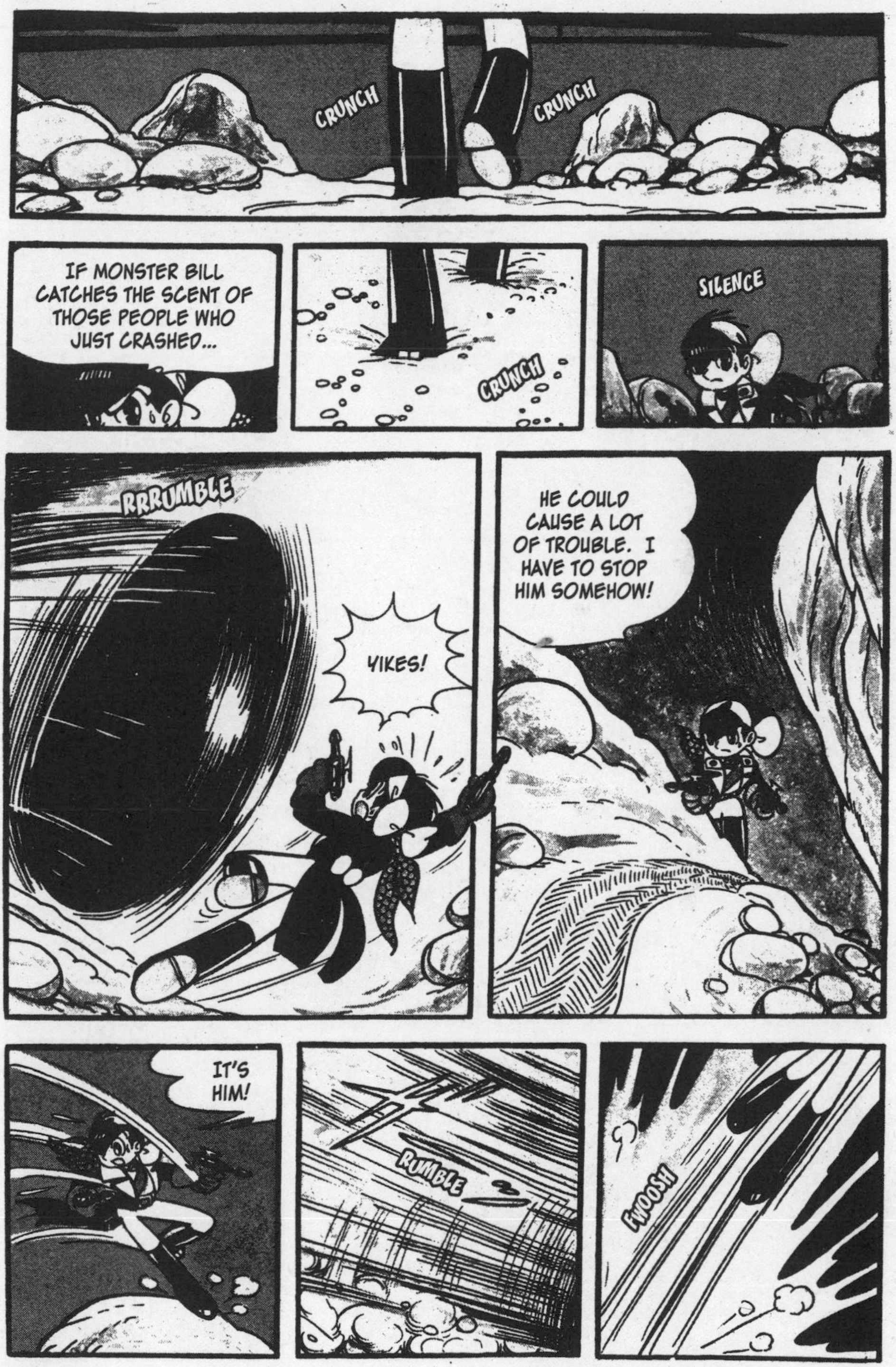
CRUNCH
CRUNCH
SILENCE
CRUNCH
IF MONSTER BILL CATCHES THE SCENT OF THOSE PEOPLE WHO JUST CRASHED...
HE COULD CAUSE A LOT OF TROUBLE. I HAVE TO STOP HIM SOMEHOW!
RRRUMBLE
YIKES!
FWOOSH
RUMBLE
IT'S HIM!

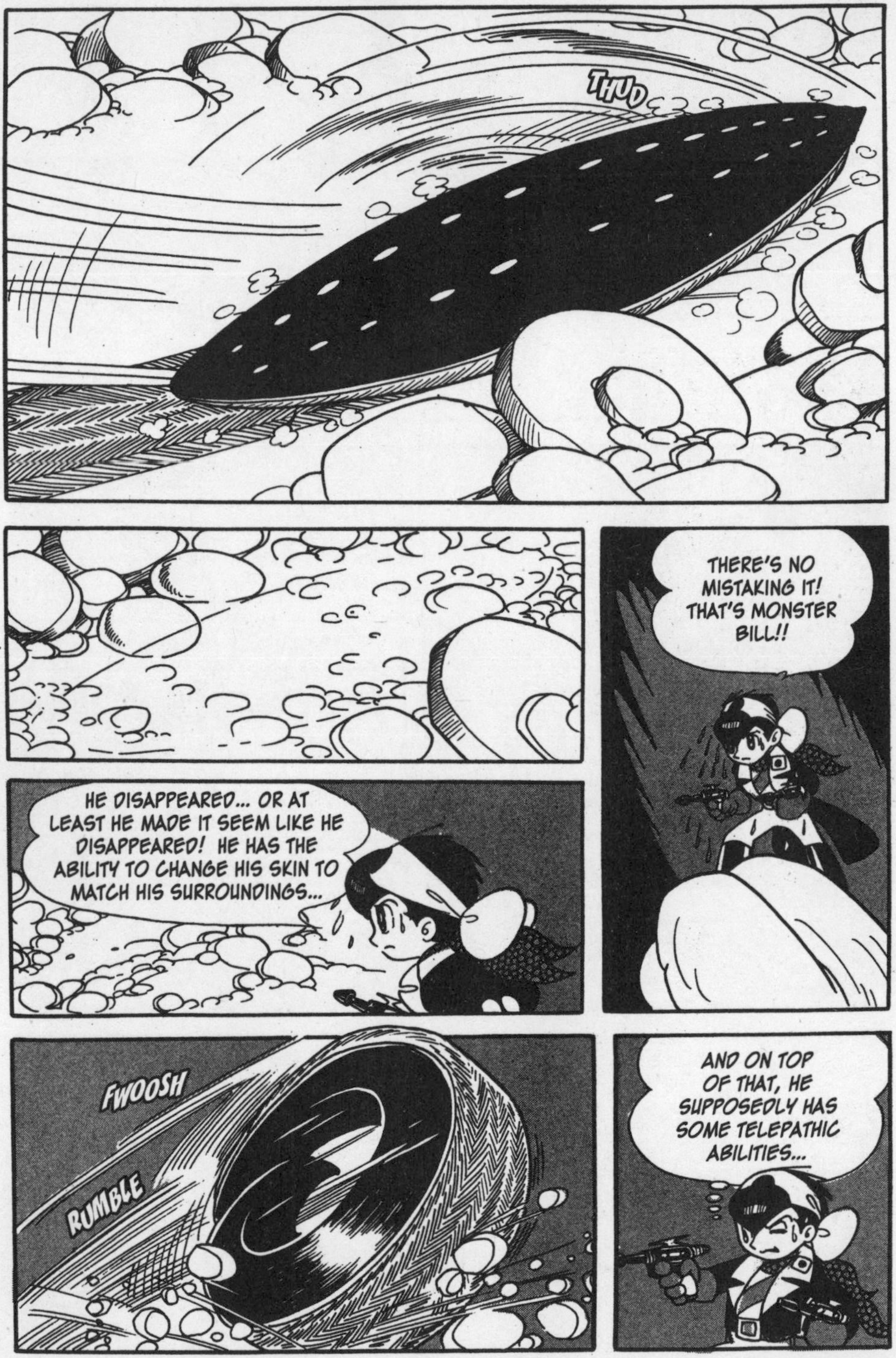
THUD
THERE'S NO MISTAKING IT! THAT'S MONSTER BILL!!
HE DISAPPEARED... OR AT LEAST HE MADE IT SEEM LIKE HE DISAPPEARED! HE HAS THE ABILITY TO CHANGE HIS SKIN TO MATCH HIS SURROUNDINGS...
AND ON TOP OF THAT, HE SUPPOSEDLY HAS SOME TELEPATHIC ABILITIES...
FWOOSH
RUMBLE

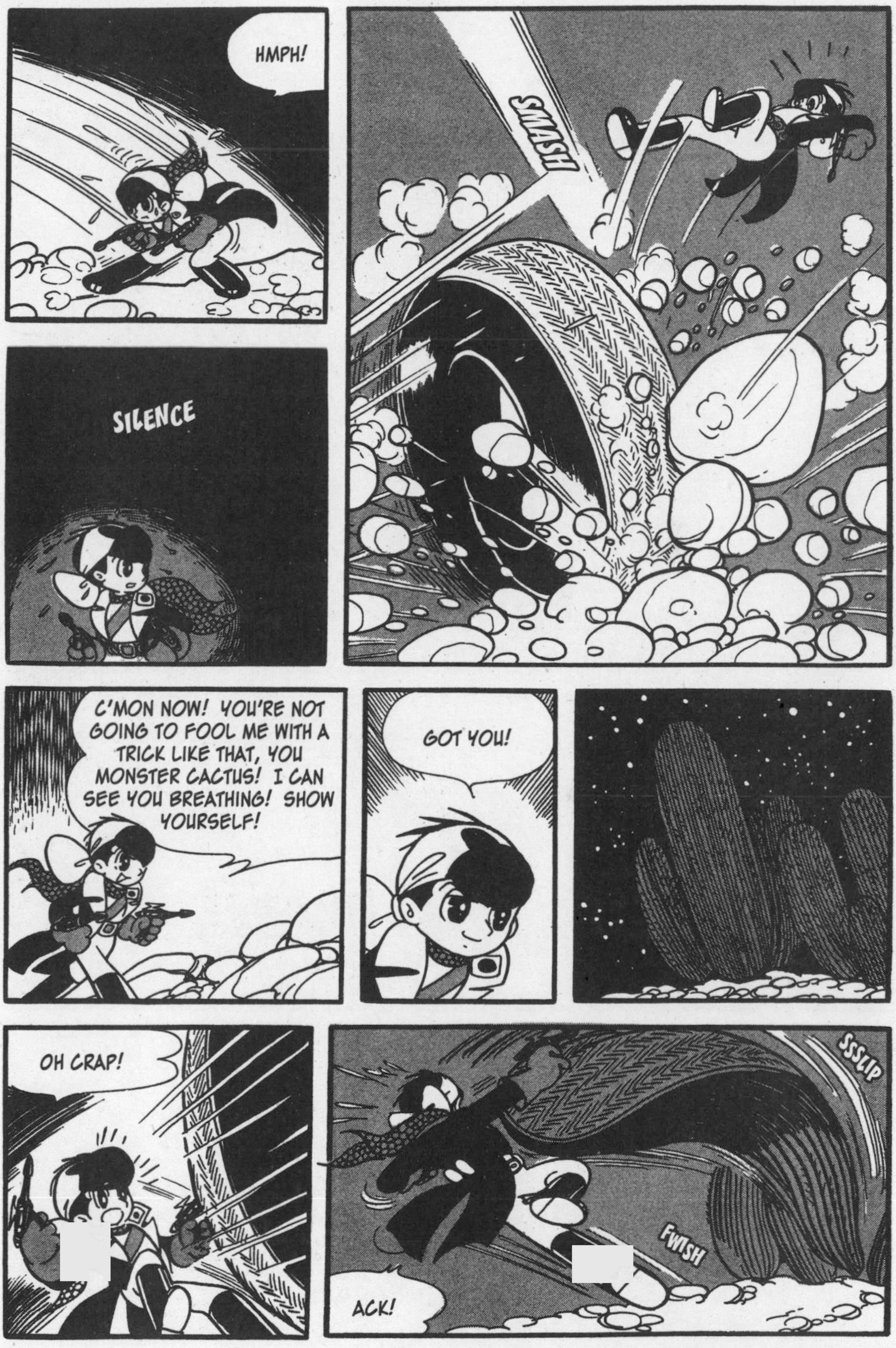
SMASH
HMPH!
SILENCE
GOT YOU!
C'MON NOW! YOU'RE NOT GOING TO FOOL ME WITH A TRICK LIKE THAT, YOU MONSTER CACTUS! I CAN SEE YOU BREATHING! SHOW YOURSELF!
SSSLIP
FWISH
ACK!
OH CRAP!

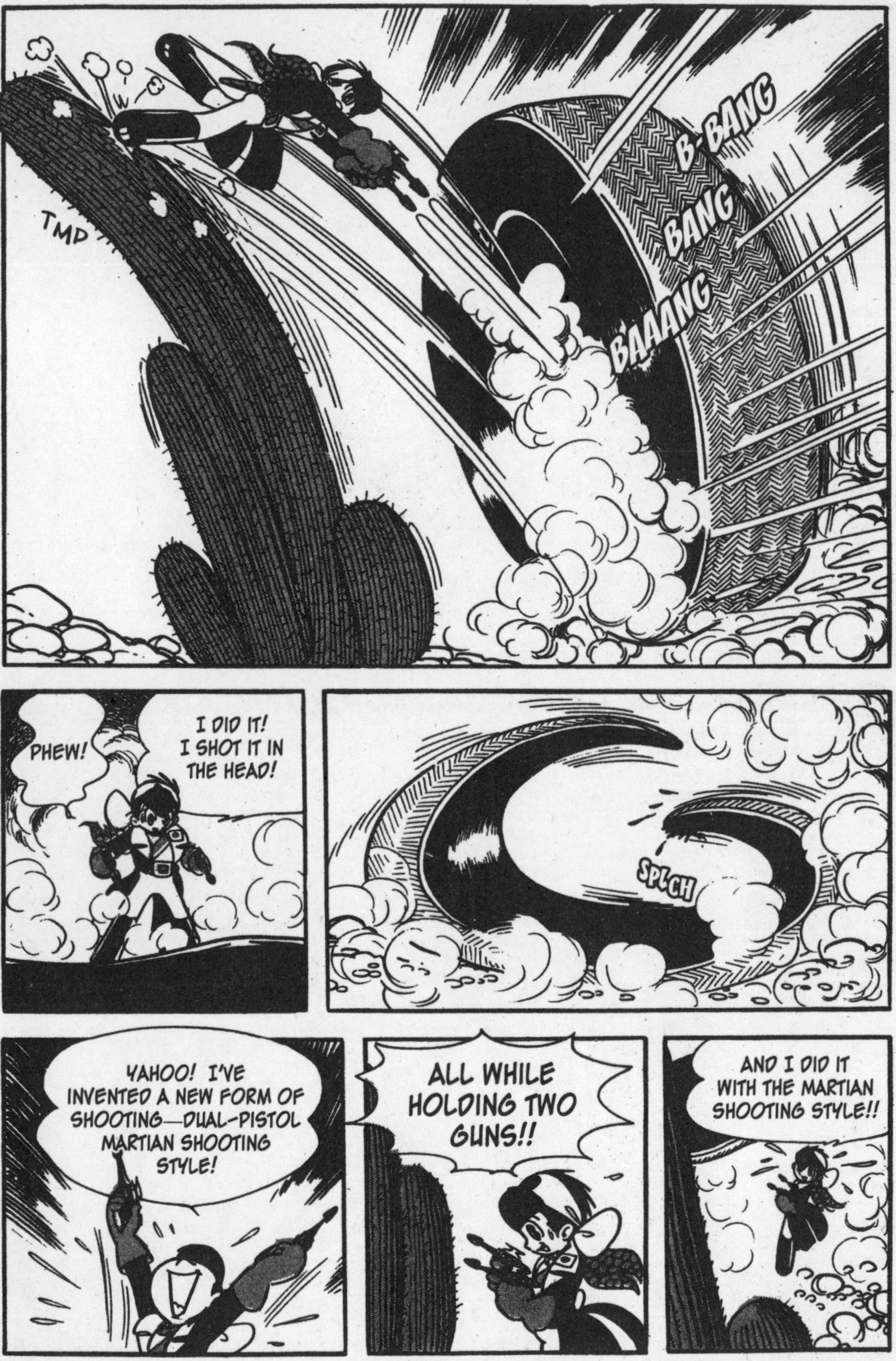
B-BANG
BANG
BAAANG
TMP
SPLCH
I DID IT! I SHOT IT IN THE HEAD!
PHEW!
AND I DID IT WITH THE MARTIAN SHOOTING STYLE!!
ALL WHILE HOLDING TWO GUNS!!
YAHOO! I'VE INVENTED A NEW FORM OF SHOOTING—DUAL-PISTOL MARTIAN SHOOTING STYLE!

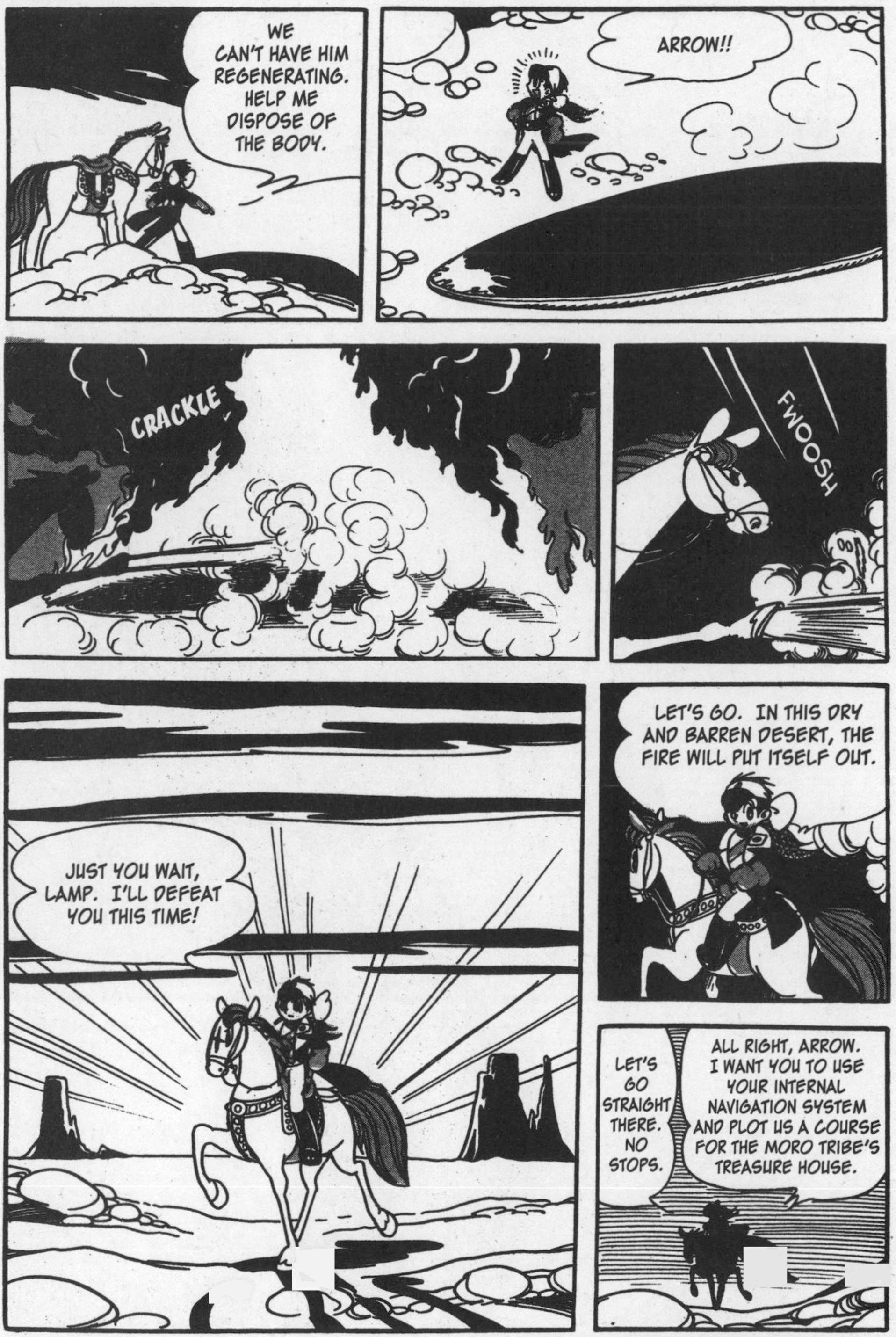
ARROW!!
WE CAN'T HAVE HIM REGENERATING. HELP ME DISPOSE OF THE BODY.
FWOOSH
CRACKLE
LET'S GO. IN THIS DRY AND BARREN DESERT, THE FIRE WILL PUT ITSELF OUT.
ALL RIGHT, ARROW. I WANT YOU TO USE YOUR INTERNAL NAVIGATION SYSTEM AND PLOT US A COURSE FOR THE MORO TRIBE'S TREASURE HOUSE.
LET'S GO STRAIGHT THERE. NO STOPS.
JUST YOU WAIT, LAMP. I'LL DEFEAT YOU THIS TIME!

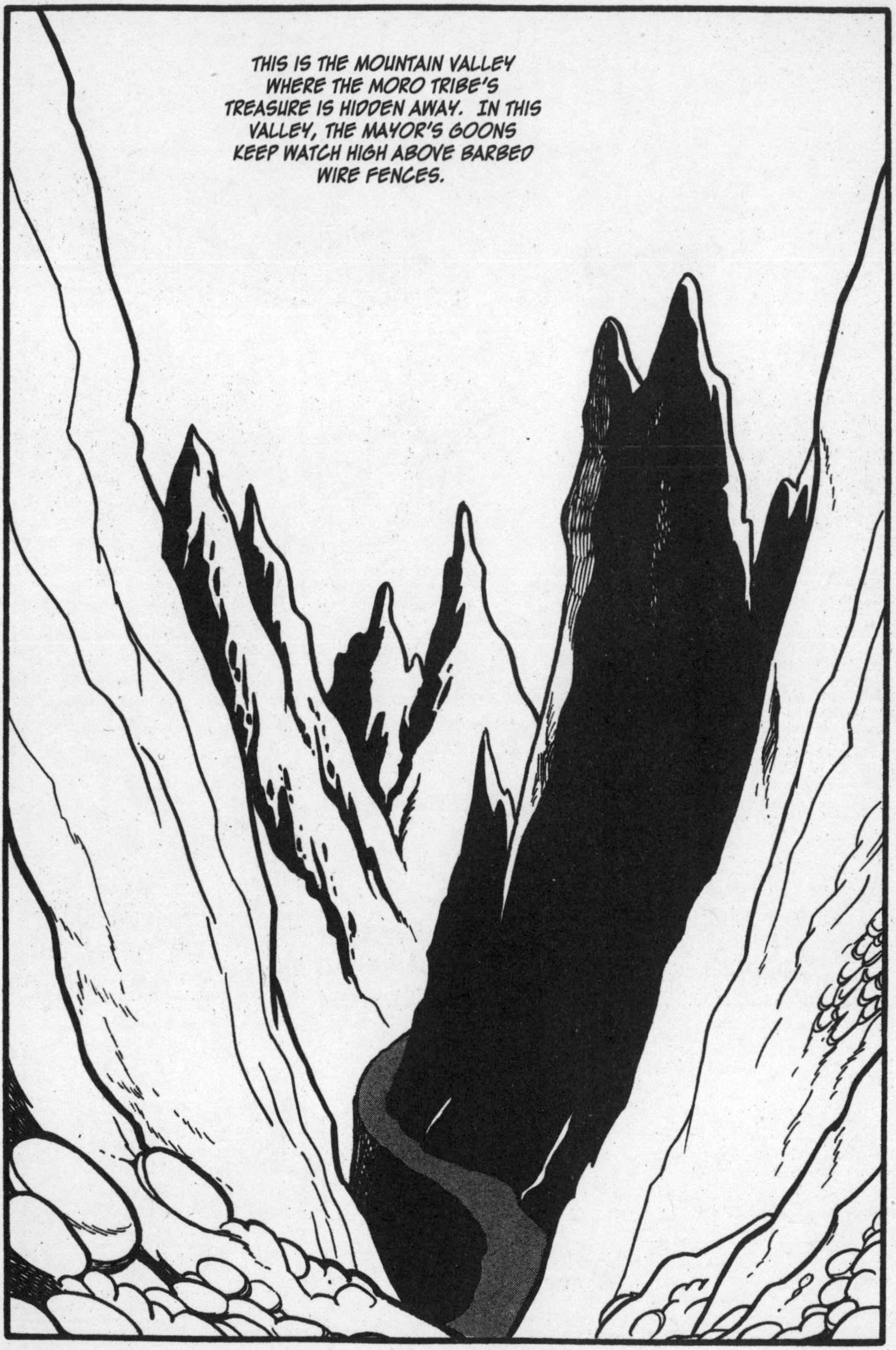
THIS IS THE MOUNTAIN VALLEY WHERE THE MORO TRIBE'S TREASURE IS HIDDEN AWAY. IN THIS VALLEY, THE MAYOR'S GOONS KEEP WATCH HIGH ABOVE BARBED WIRE FENCES.

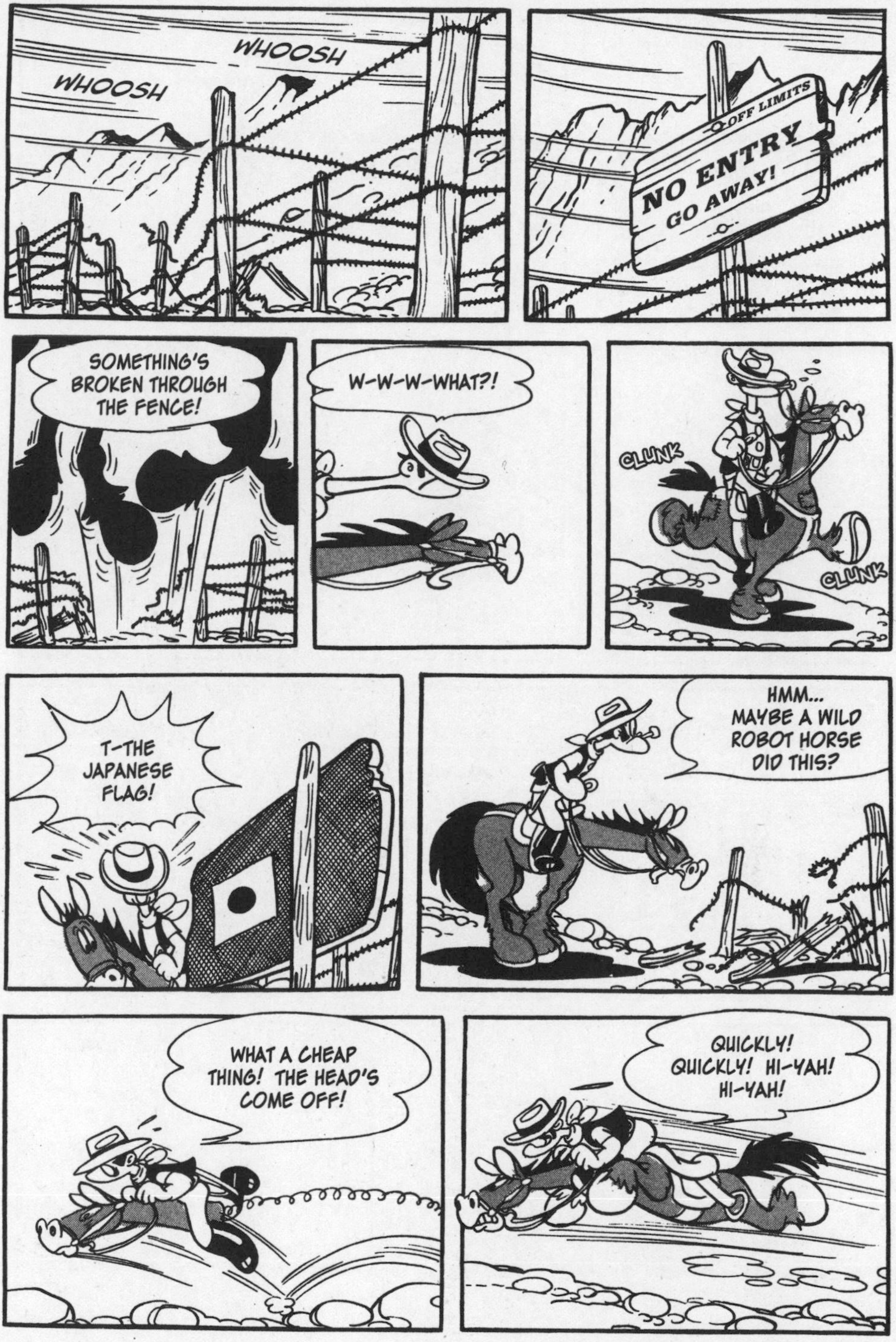
OFF LIMITS
NO ENTRY
GO AWAY!
WHOOSH
WHOOSH
CLUNK
CLUNK
W-W-W-WHAT?!
SOMETHING'S BROKEN THROUGH THE FENCE!
HMM... MAYBE A WILD ROBOT HORSE DID THIS?
T-THE JAPANESE FLAG!
QUICKLY! QUICKLY! HI-YAH! HI-YAH!
WHAT A CHEAP THING! THE HEAD'S COME OFF!

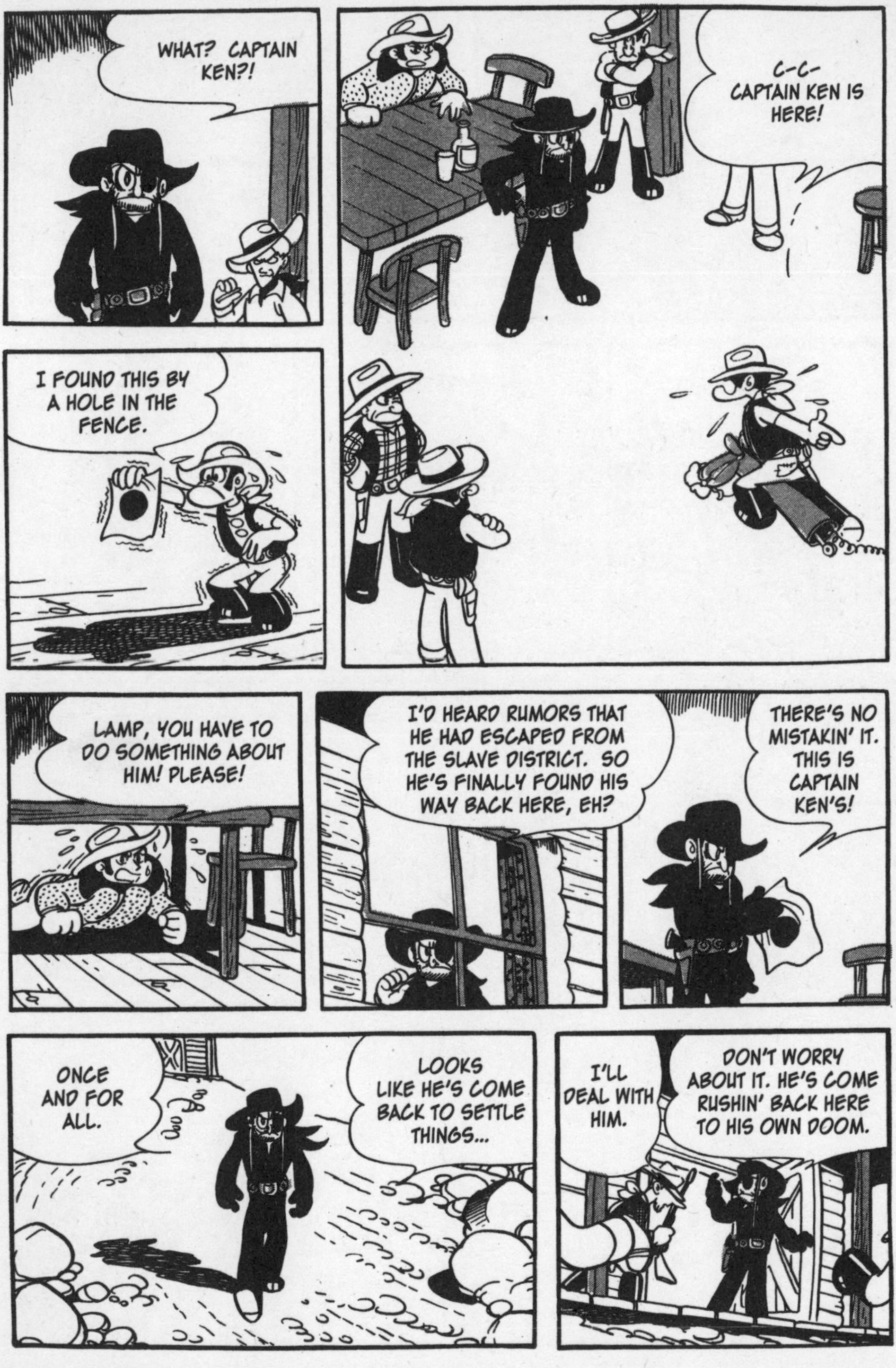
C-C-
CAPTAIN KEN IS HERE!
WHAT? CAPTAIN KEN?!
I FOUND THIS BY A HOLE IN THE FENCE.
THERE'S NO MISTAKIN' IT. THIS IS CAPTAIN KEN'S!
I'D HEARD RUMORS THAT HE HAD ESCAPED FROM THE SLAVE DISTRICT. SO HE'S FINALLY FOUND HIS WAY BACK HERE, EH?
LAMP, YOU HAVE TO DO SOMETHING ABOUT HIM! PLEASE!
DON'T WORRY ABOUT IT. HE'S COME RUSHIN' BACK HERE TO HIS OWN DOOM.
I'LL DEAL WITH HIM.
LOOKS LIKE HE'S COME BACK TO SETTLE THINGS...
ONCE AND FOR ALL.

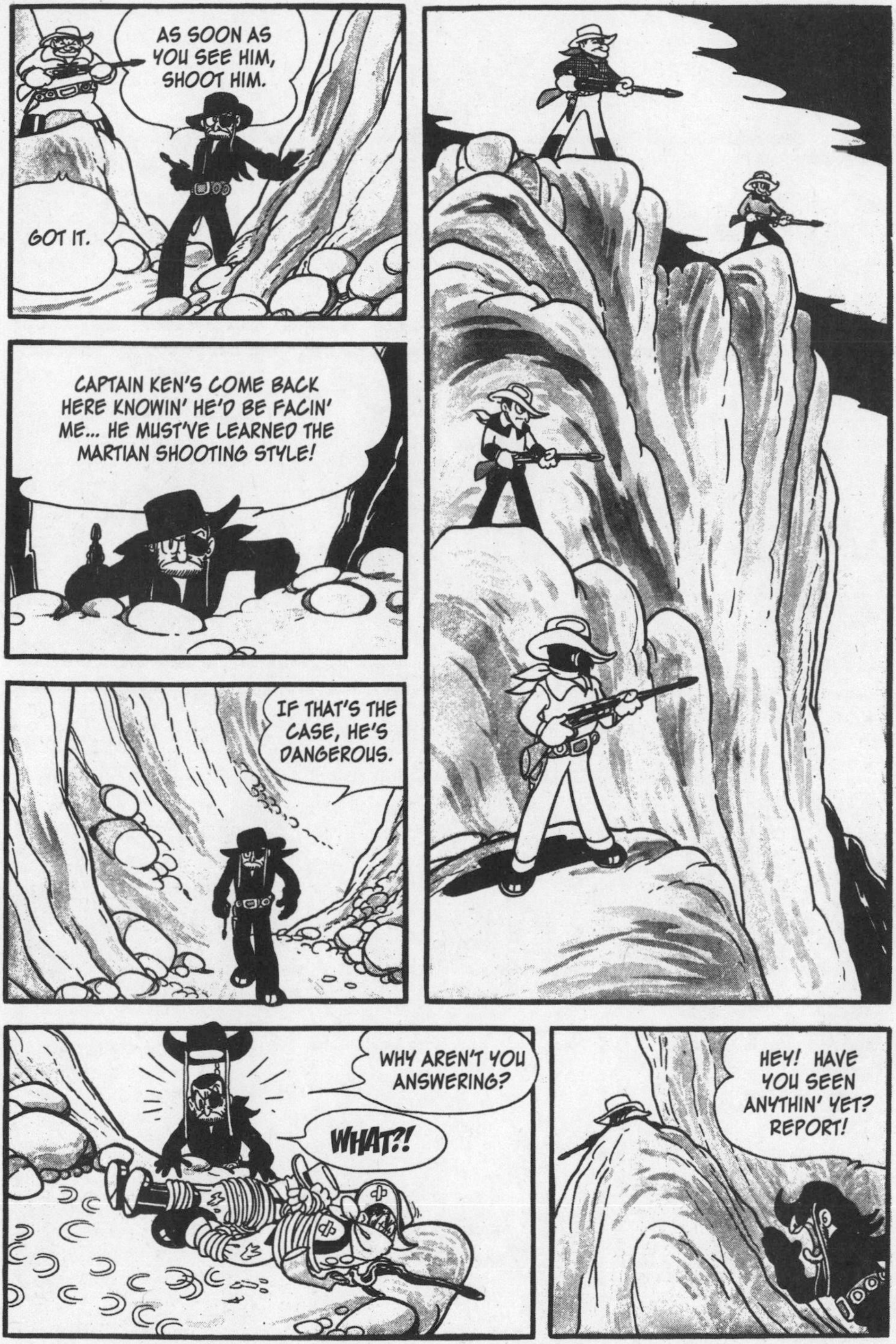
AS SOON AS YOU SEE HIM, SHOOT HIM.
GOT IT.
CAPTAIN KEN'S COME BACK HERE KNOWIN' HE'D BE FACIN' ME... HE MUST'VE LEARNED THE MARTIAN SHOOTING STYLE!
IF THAT'S THE CASE, HE'S DANGEROUS.
HEY! HAVE YOU SEEN ANYTHIN' YET? REPORT!
WHY AREN'T YOU ANSWERING?
WHAT?!

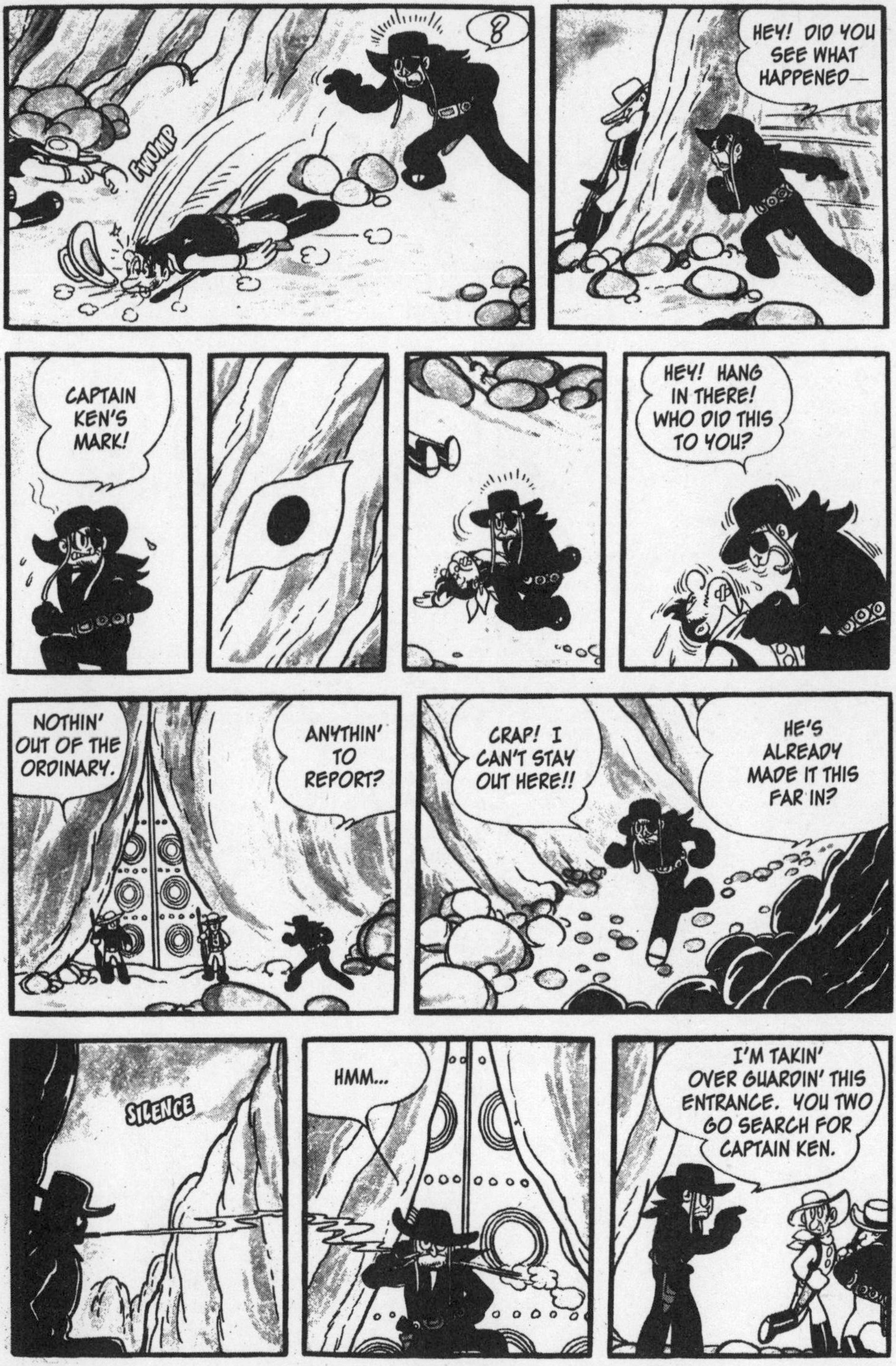
HEY! DID YOU SEE WHAT HAPPENED—
?
FWUMP
HEY! HANG IN THERE! WHO DID THIS TO YOU?
CAPTAIN KEN'S MARK!
HE'S ALREADY MADE IT THIS FAR IN?
CRAP! I CAN'T STAY OUT HERE!!
ANYTHIN' TO REPORT?
NOTHIN' OUT OF THE ORDINARY.
I'M TAKIN' OVER GUARDIN' THIS ENTRANCE. YOU TWO GO SEARCH FOR CAPTAIN KEN.
HMM...
SILENCE

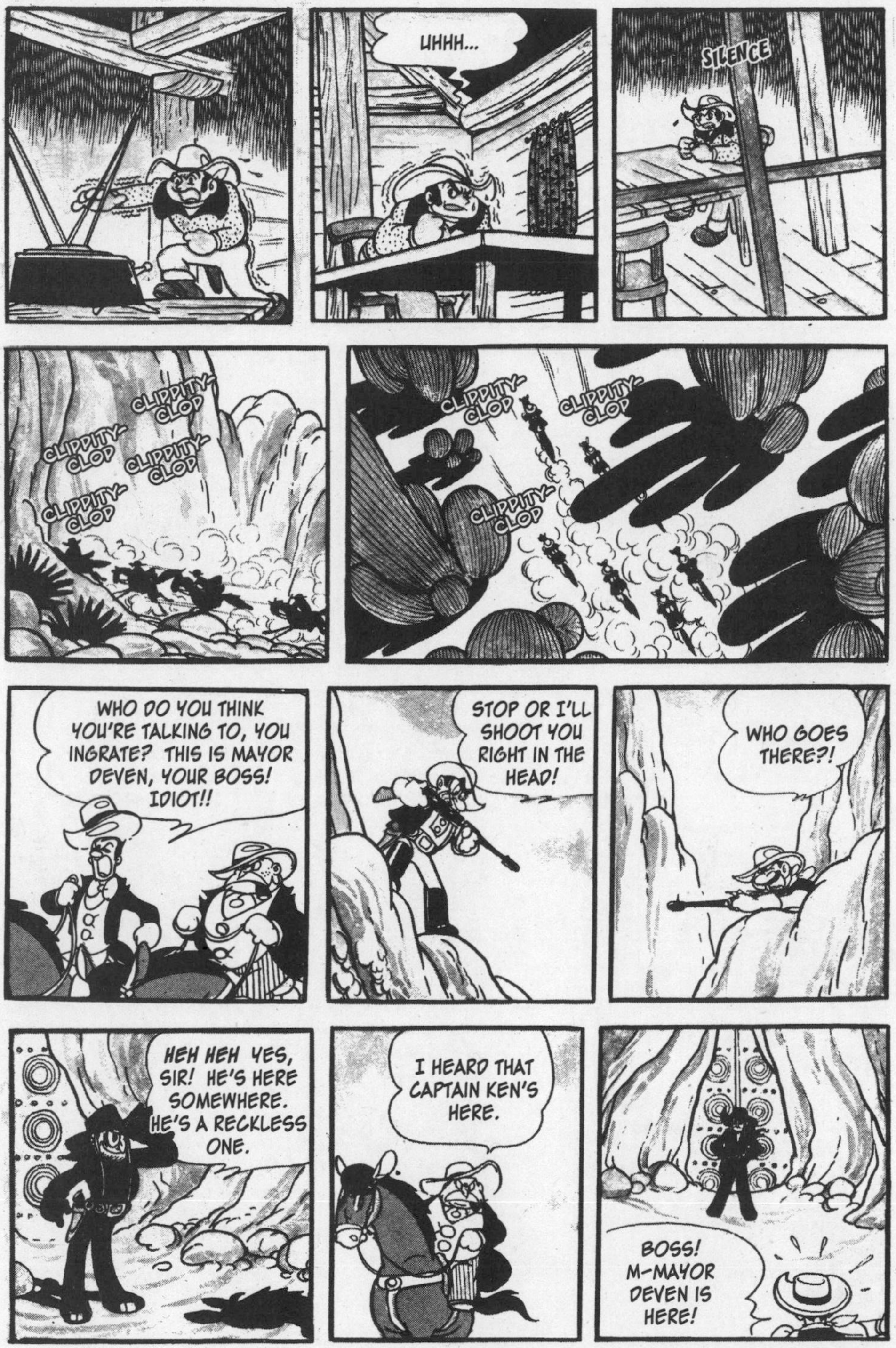
SILENCE
UHHH...
CLIPPITY-CLOP
CLIPPITY-CLOP
CLIPPITY-CLOP
CLIPPITY-CLOP
CLIPPITY-CLOP
CLIPPITY-CLOP
CLIPPITY-CLOP
WHO GOES THERE?!
STOP OR I'LL SHOOT YOU RIGHT IN THE HEAD!
WHO DO YOU THINK YOU'RE TALKING TO, YOU INGRATE? THIS IS MAYOR DEVEN, YOUR BOSS! IDIOT!!
BOSS! M-MAYOR DEVEN IS HERE!
I HEARD THAT CAPTAIN KEN'S HERE.
HEH HEH YES, SIR! HE'S HERE SOMEWHERE. HE'S A RECKLESS ONE.

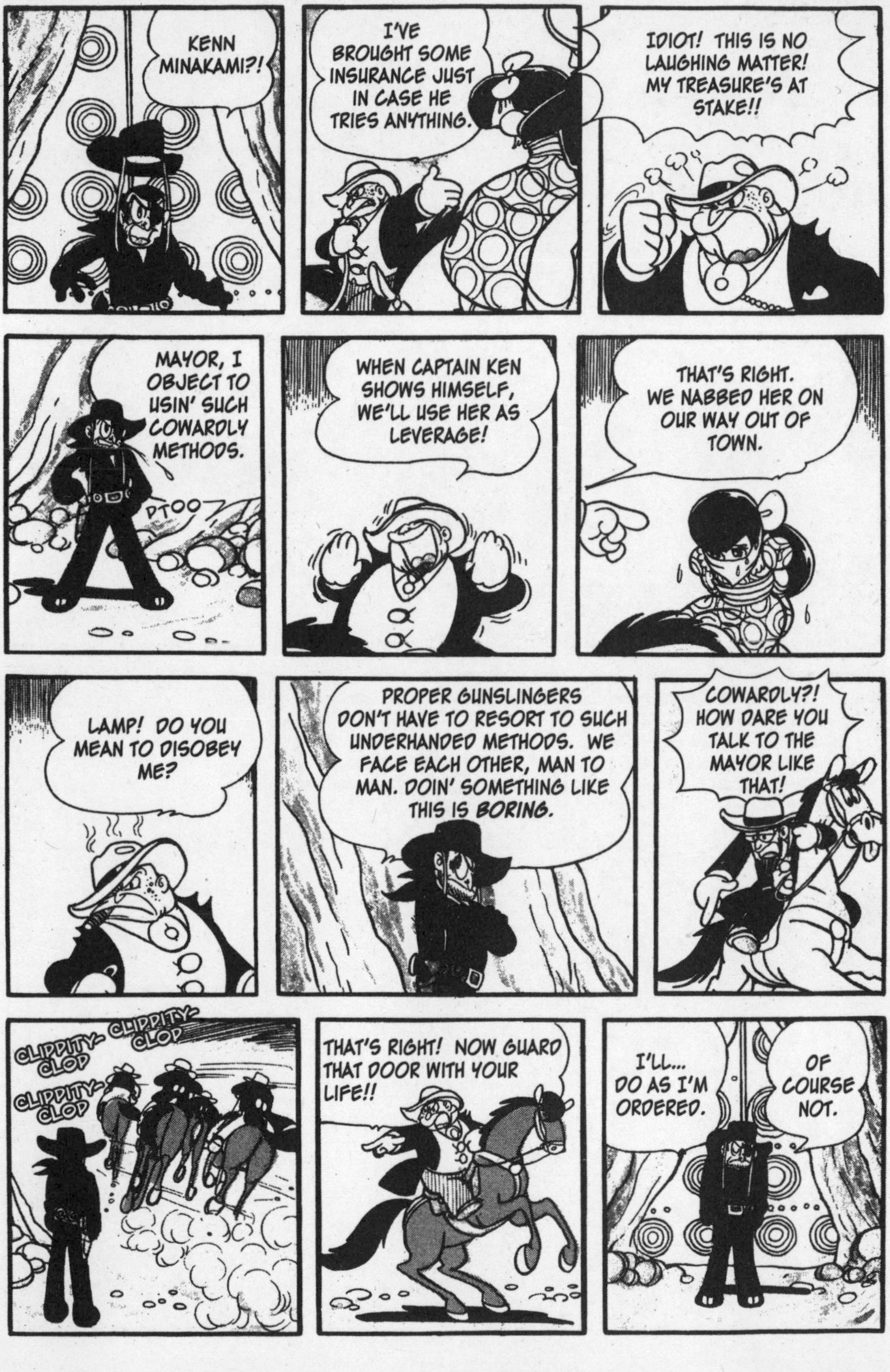
IDIOT! THIS IS NO LAUGHING MATTER! MY TREASURE'S AT STAKE!!
I'VE BROUGHT SOME INSURANCE JUST IN CASE HE TRIES ANYTHING.
KENN MINAKAMI?!
THAT'S RIGHT. WE NABBED HER ON OUR WAY OUT OF TOWN.
WHEN CAPTAIN KEN SHOWS HIMSELF, WE'LL USE HER AS LEVERAGE!
MAYOR, I OBJECT TO USIN' SUCH COWARDLY METHODS.
PTOO
COWARDLY?! HOW DARE YOU TALK TO THE MAYOR LIKE THAT!
PROPER GUNSLINGERS DON'T HAVE TO RESORT TO SUCH UNDERHANDED METHODS. WE FACE EACH OTHER, MAN TO MAN. DOIN' SOMETHING LIKE THIS IS *BORING*.
LAMP! DO YOU MEAN TO DISOBEY ME?
OF COURSE NOT.
I'LL... DO AS I'M ORDERED.
THAT'S RIGHT! NOW GUARD THAT DOOR WITH YOUR LIFE!!
CLIPPITY-CLOP
CLIPPITY-CLOP
CLIPPITY-CLOP

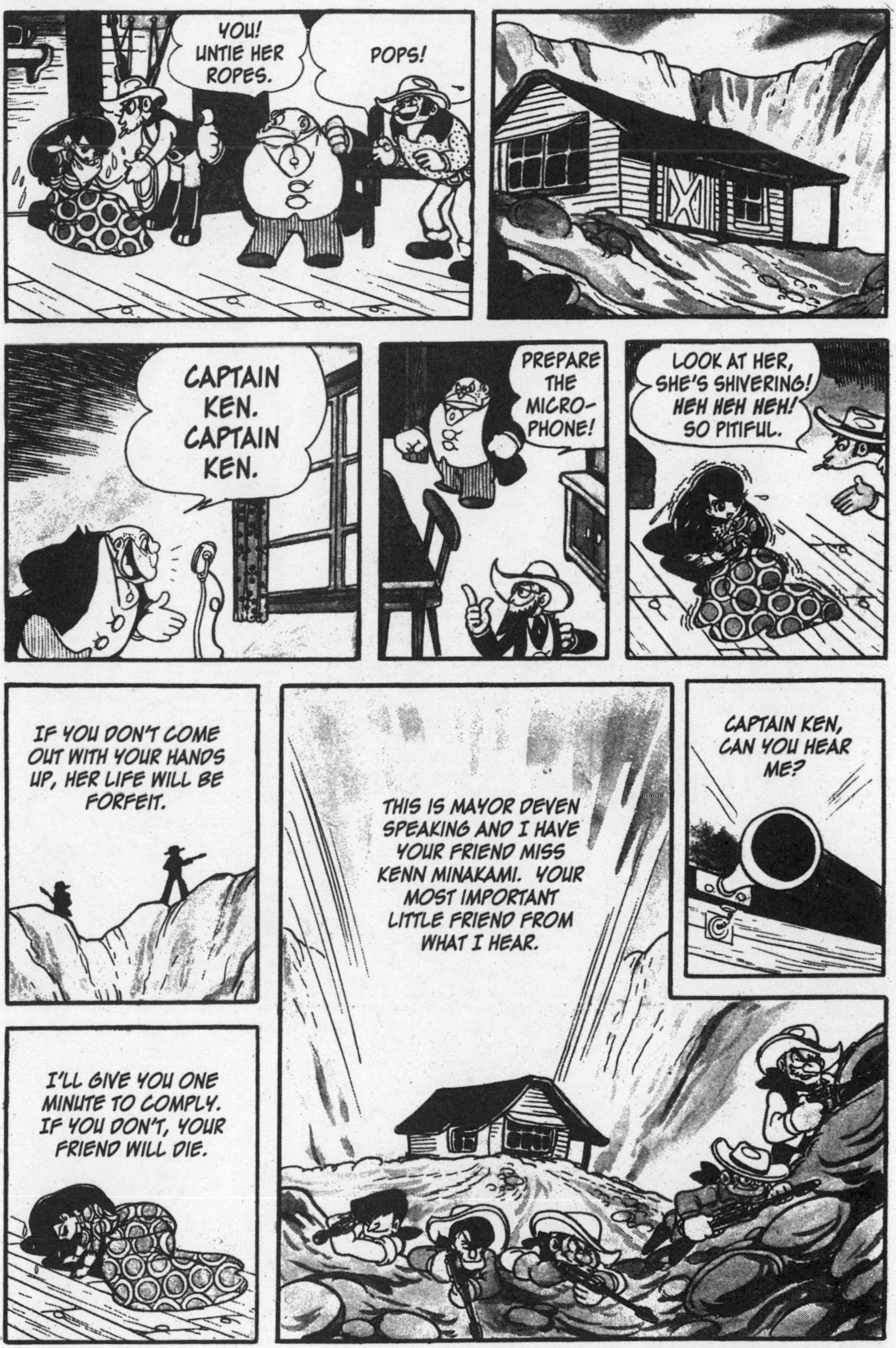
POPS!
YOU! UNTIE HER ROPES.
LOOK AT HER, SHE'S SHIVERING! HEH HEH HEH! SO PITIFUL.
PREPARE THE MICRO-PHONE!
CAPTAIN KEN. CAPTAIN KEN.
CAPTAIN KEN, CAN YOU HEAR ME?
THIS IS MAYOR DEVEN SPEAKING AND I HAVE YOUR FRIEND MISS KENN MINAKAMI. YOUR MOST IMPORTANT LITTLE FRIEND FROM WHAT I HEAR.
IF YOU DON'T COME OUT WITH YOUR HANDS UP, HER LIFE WILL BE FORFEIT.
I'LL GIVE YOU ONE MINUTE TO COMPLY. IF YOU DON'T, YOUR FRIEND WILL DIE.

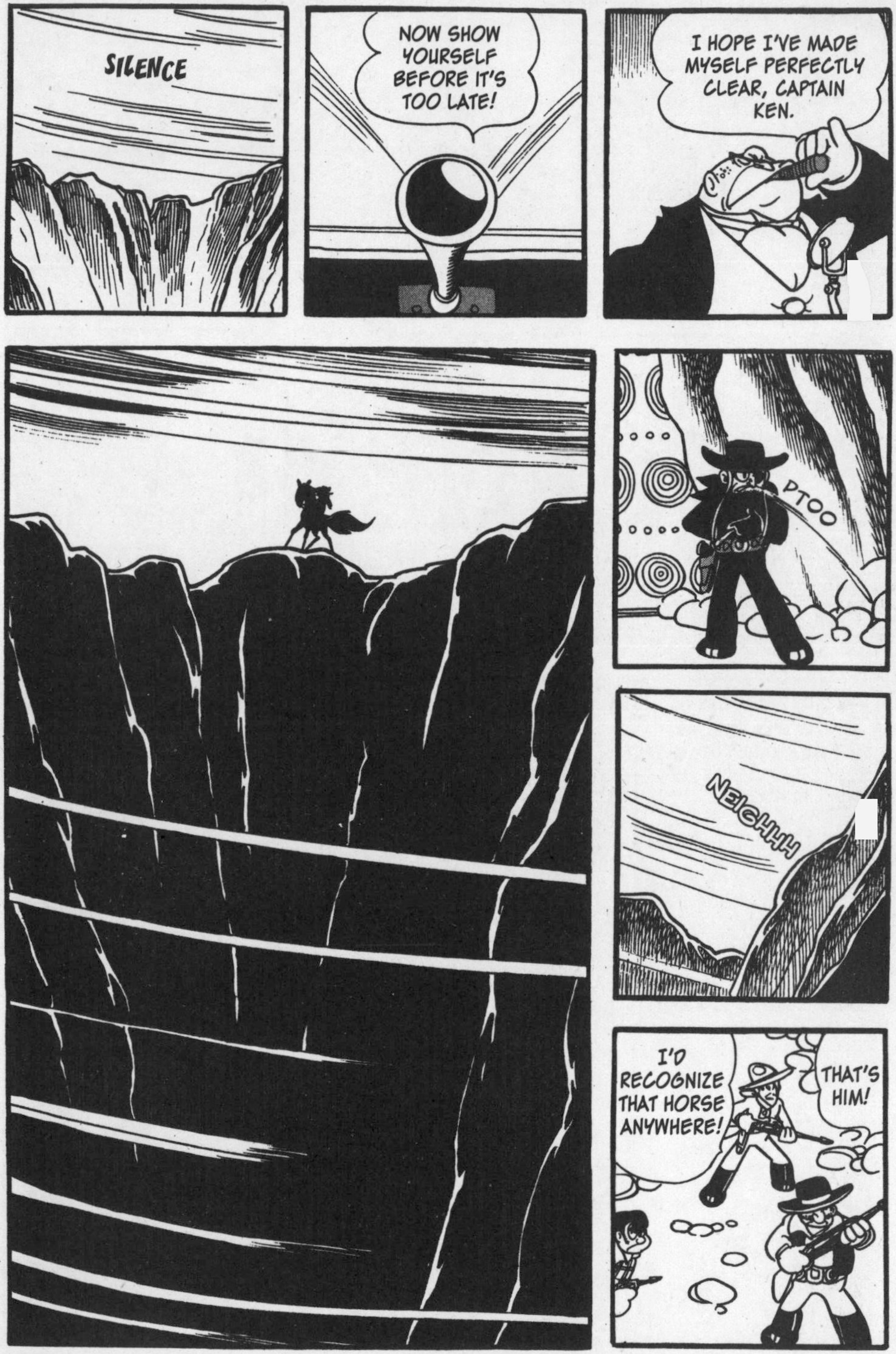
I HOPE I'VE MADE MYSELF PERFECTLY CLEAR, CAPTAIN KEN.
NOW SHOW YOURSELF BEFORE IT'S TOO LATE!
SILENCE
PTOO
NEIGHHH
THAT'S HIM!
I'D RECOGNIZE THAT HORSE ANYWHERE!

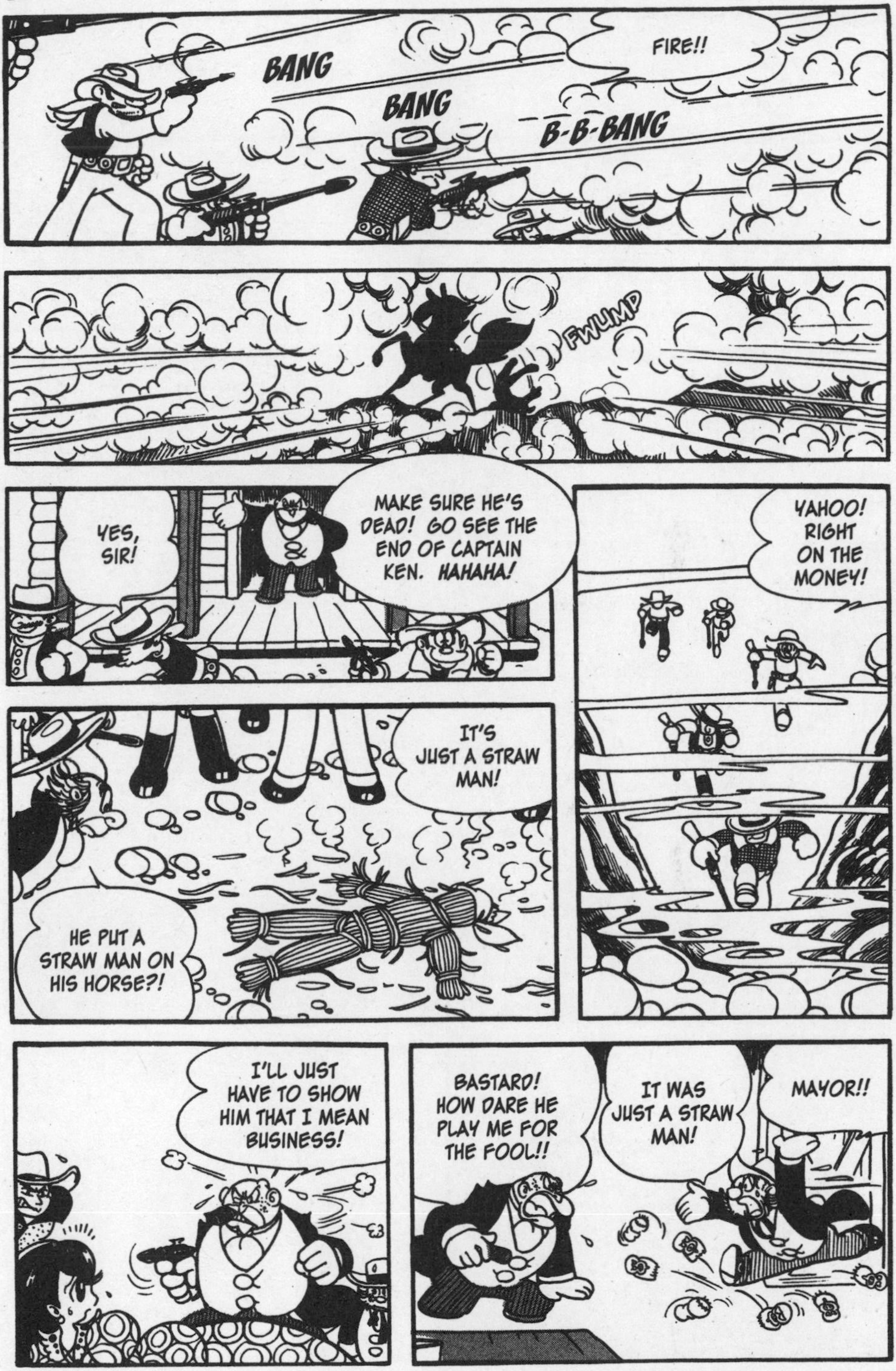
FIRE!!
BANG
BANG
B-B-BANG
FWUMP
YAHOO! RIGHT ON THE MONEY!
MAKE SURE HE'S DEAD! GO SEE THE END OF CAPTAIN KEN. HAHAHA!
YES, SIR!
IT'S JUST A STRAW MAN!
HE PUT A STRAW MAN ON HIS HORSE?!
MAYOR!!
IT WAS JUST A STRAW MAN!
BASTARD! HOW DARE HE PLAY ME FOR THE FOOL!!
I'LL JUST HAVE TO SHOW HIM THAT I MEAN BUSINESS!

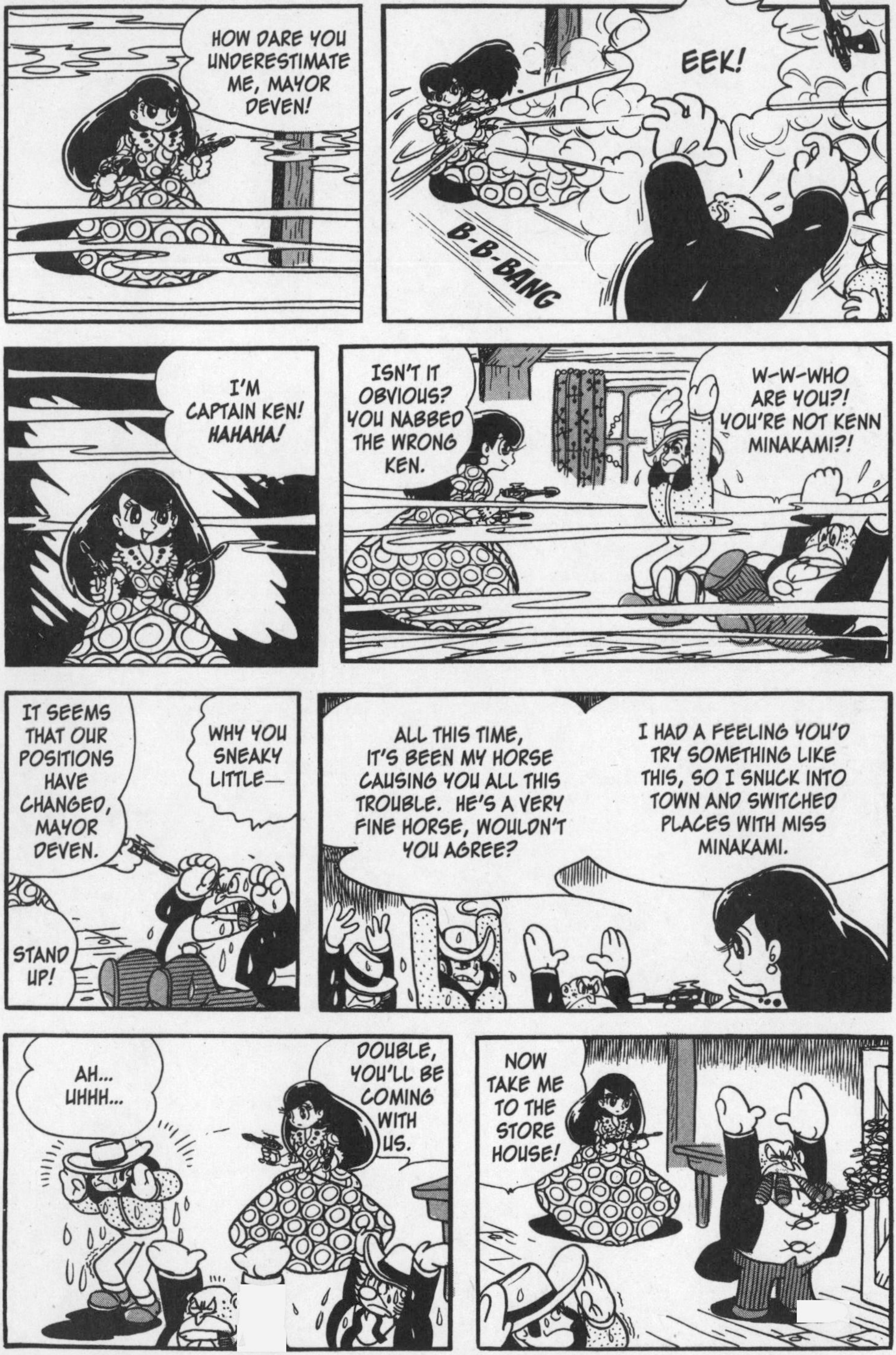
EEK!
B-B-BANG
HOW DARE YOU UNDERESTIMATE ME, MAYOR DEVEN!
W-W-WHO ARE YOU?! YOU'RE NOT KENN MINAKAMI?!
ISN'T IT OBVIOUS? YOU NABBED THE WRONG KEN.
I'M CAPTAIN KEN! HAHAHA!
I HAD A FEELING YOU'D TRY SOMETHING LIKE THIS, SO I SNUCK INTO TOWN AND SWITCHED PLACES WITH MISS MINAKAMI.
ALL THIS TIME, IT'S BEEN MY HORSE CAUSING YOU ALL THIS TROUBLE. HE'S A VERY FINE HORSE, WOULDN'T YOU AGREE?
WHY YOU SNEAKY LITTLE—
IT SEEMS THAT OUR POSITIONS HAVE CHANGED, MAYOR DEVEN.
STAND UP!
NOW TAKE ME TO THE STORE HOUSE!
DOUBLE, YOU'LL BE COMING WITH US.
AH... UHHH...

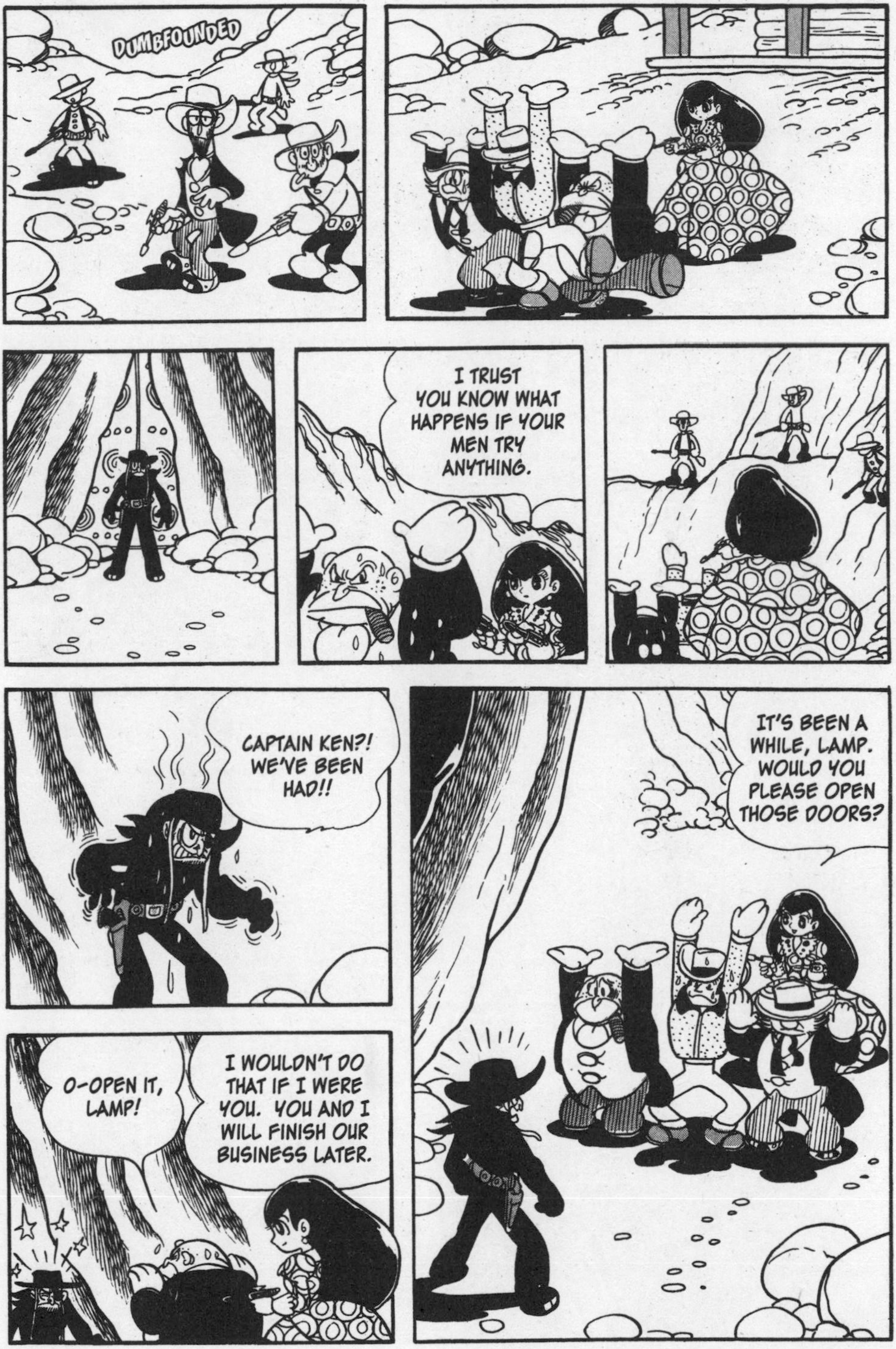
DUMBFOUNDED
I TRUST YOU KNOW WHAT HAPPENS IF YOUR MEN TRY ANYTHING.
IT'S BEEN A WHILE, LAMP. WOULD YOU PLEASE OPEN THOSE DOORS?
CAPTAIN KEN?! WE'VE BEEN HAD!!
I WOULDN'T DO THAT IF I WERE YOU. YOU AND I WILL FINISH OUR BUSINESS LATER.
O-OPEN IT, LAMP!

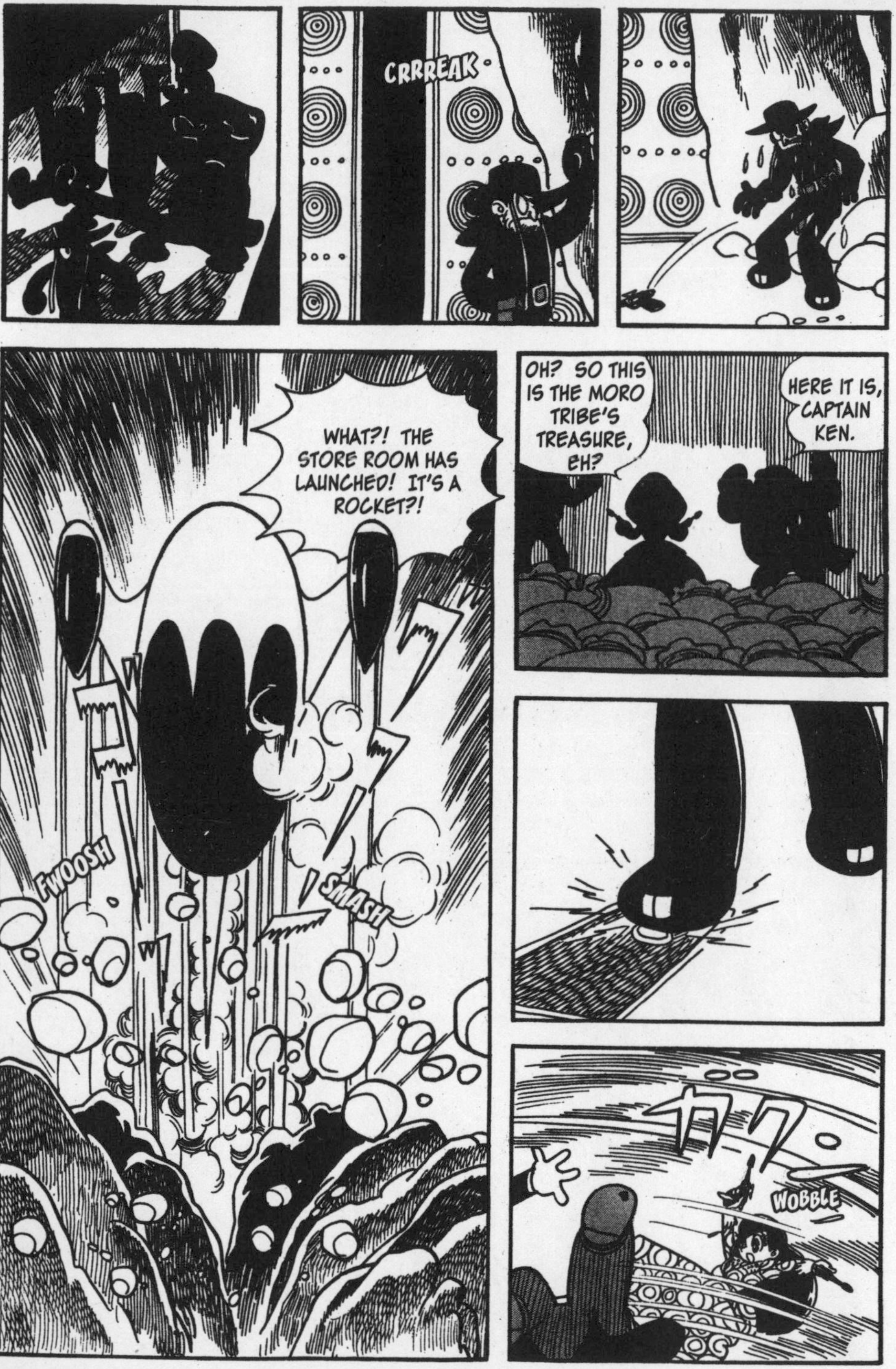
CRRREAK
HERE IT IS, CAPTAIN KEN.
OH? SO THIS IS THE MORO TRIBE'S TREASURE, EH?
カク
WOBBLE
WHAT?! THE STORE ROOM HAS LAUNCHED! IT'S A ROCKET?!
FWOOSH
SMASH

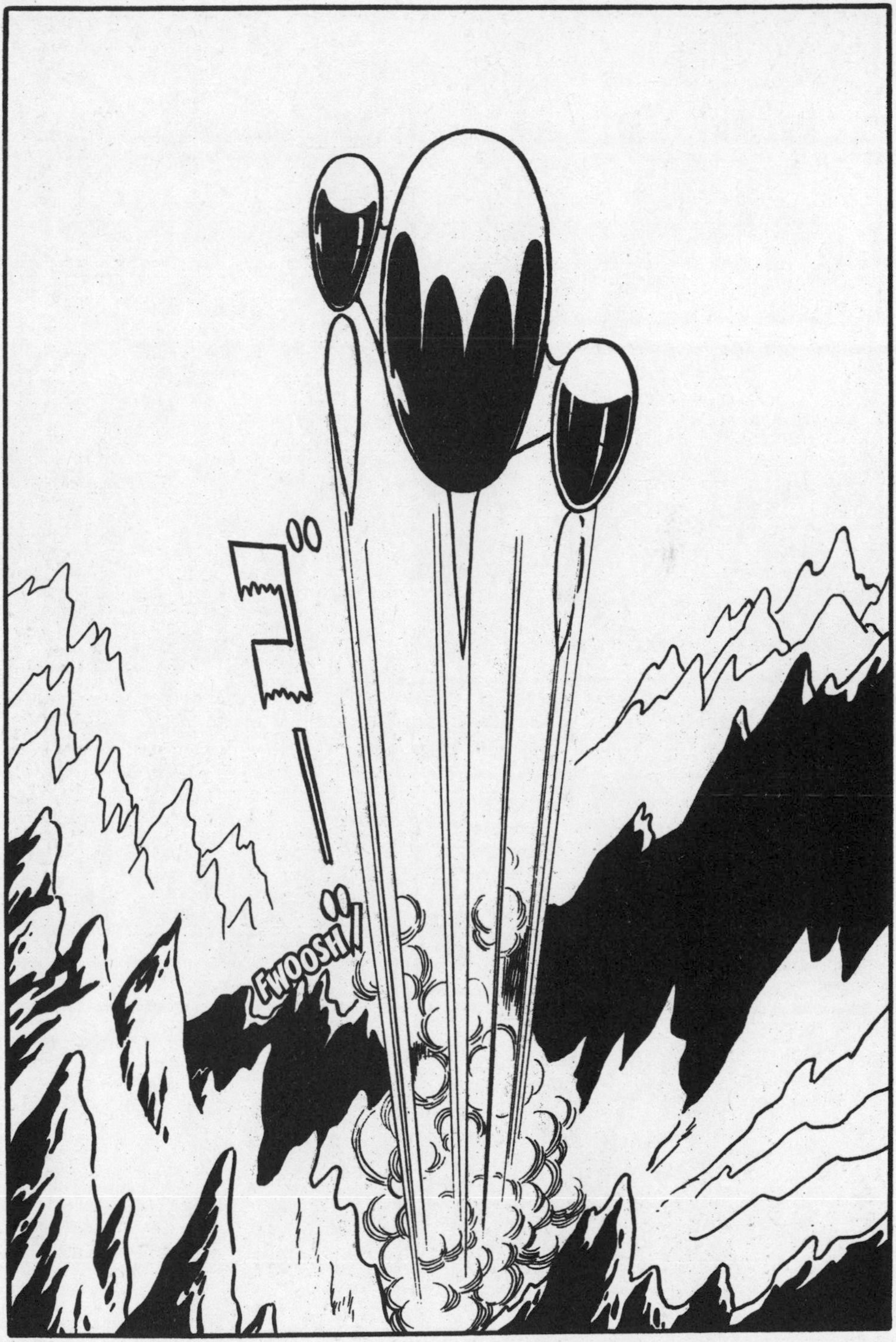
FWOOSH

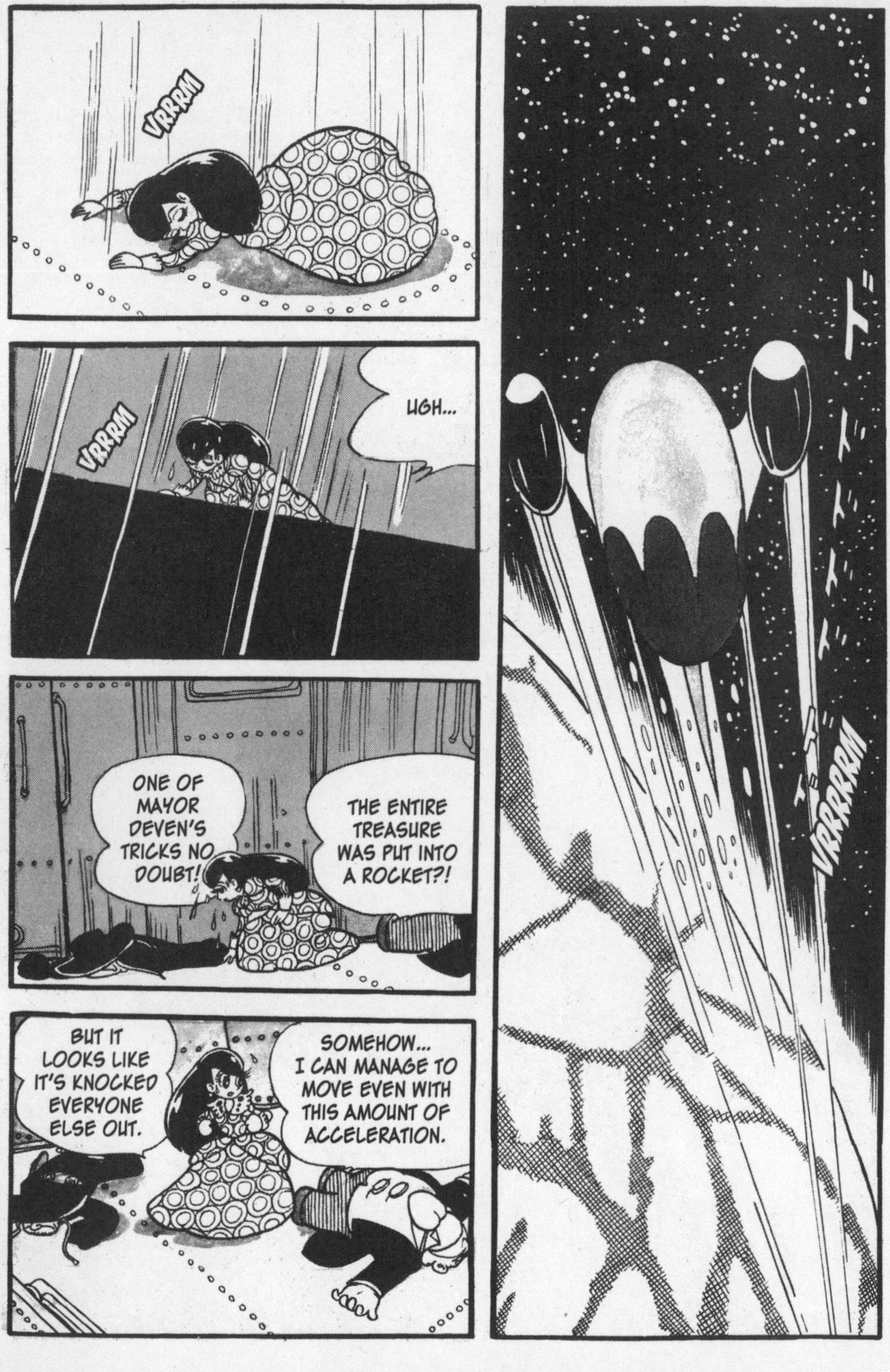
VRRRRRM
VRRRM
VRRRM
UGH...
THE ENTIRE TREASURE WAS PUT INTO A ROCKET?!
ONE OF MAYOR DEVEN'S TRICKS NO DOUBT!
SOMEHOW... I CAN MANAGE TO MOVE EVEN WITH THIS AMOUNT OF ACCELERATION.
BUT IT LOOKS LIKE IT'S KNOCKED EVERYONE ELSE OUT.

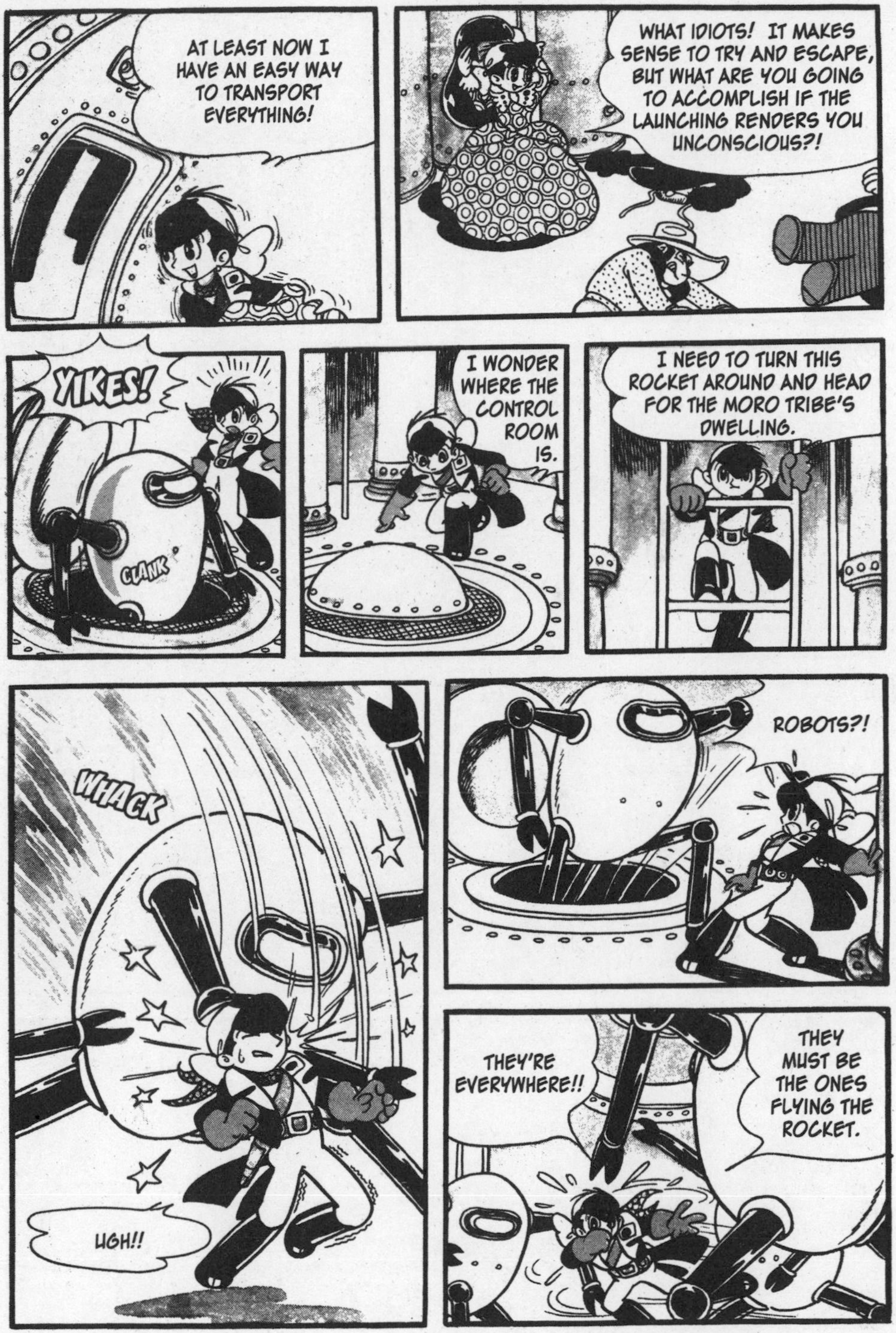
WHAT IDIOTS! IT MAKES SENSE TO TRY AND ESCAPE, BUT WHAT ARE YOU GOING TO ACCOMPLISH IF THE LAUNCHING RENDERS YOU UNCONSCIOUS?!
AT LEAST NOW I HAVE AN EASY WAY TO TRANSPORT EVERYTHING!
I NEED TO TURN THIS ROCKET AROUND AND HEAD FOR THE MORO TRIBE'S DWELLING.
I WONDER WHERE THE CONTROL ROOM IS.
YIKES!
CLANK
ROBOTS?!
THEY MUST BE THE ONES FLYING THE ROCKET.
THEY'RE EVERYWHERE!!
WHACK
UGH!!

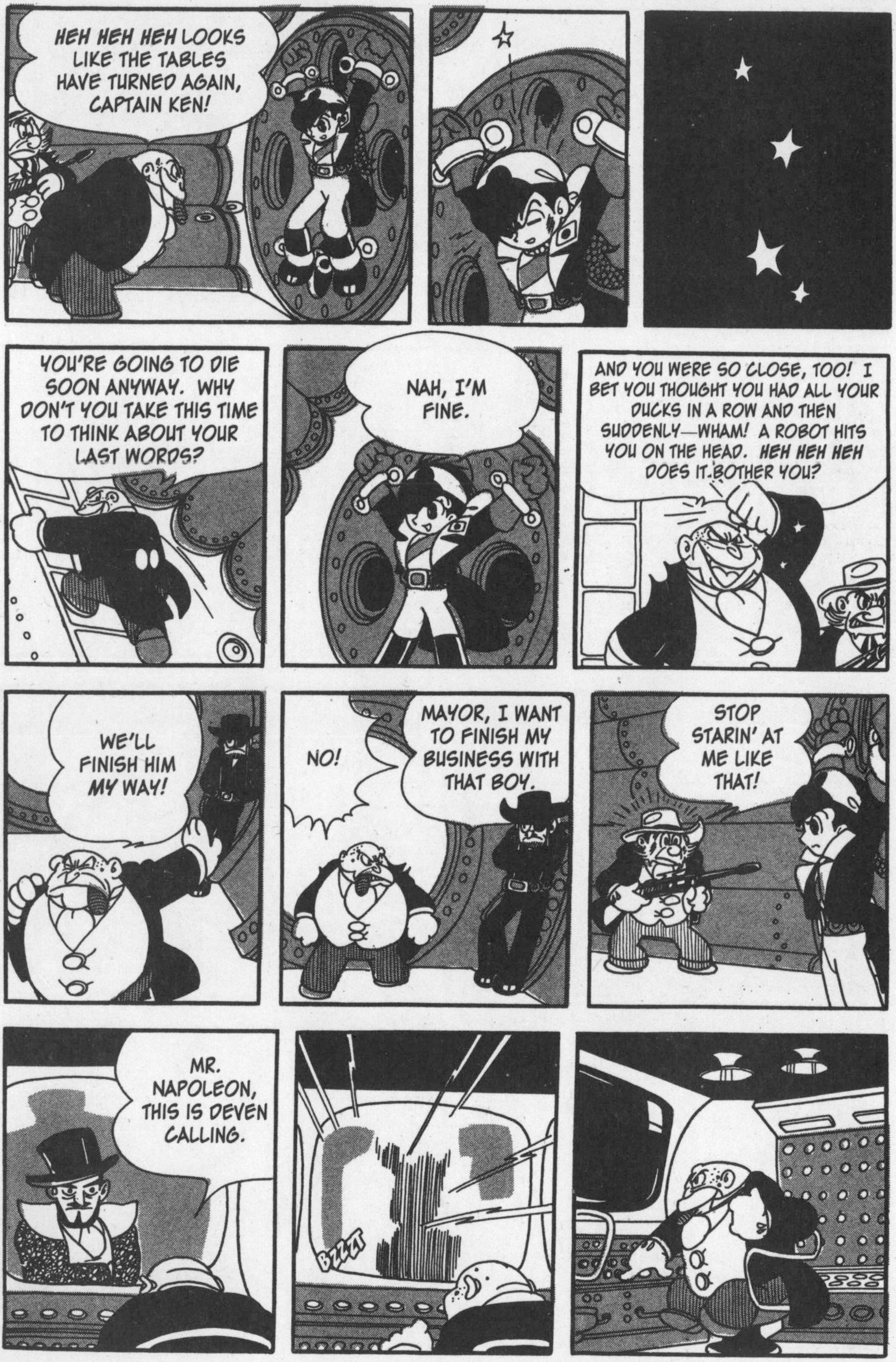
HEH HEH HEH LOOKS LIKE THE TABLES HAVE TURNED AGAIN, CAPTAIN KEN!
AND YOU WERE SO CLOSE, TOO! I BET YOU THOUGHT YOU HAD ALL YOUR DUCKS IN A ROW AND THEN SUDDENLY—WHAM! A ROBOT HITS YOU ON THE HEAD. HEH HEH HEH DOES IT BOTHER YOU?
NAH, I'M FINE.
YOU'RE GOING TO DIE SOON ANYWAY. WHY DON'T YOU TAKE THIS TIME TO THINK ABOUT YOUR LAST WORDS?
STOP STARIN' AT ME LIKE THAT!
MAYOR, I WANT TO FINISH MY BUSINESS WITH THAT BOY.
NO!
WE'LL FINISH HIM MY WAY!
BZZZT
MR. NAPOLEON, THIS IS DEVEN CALLING.

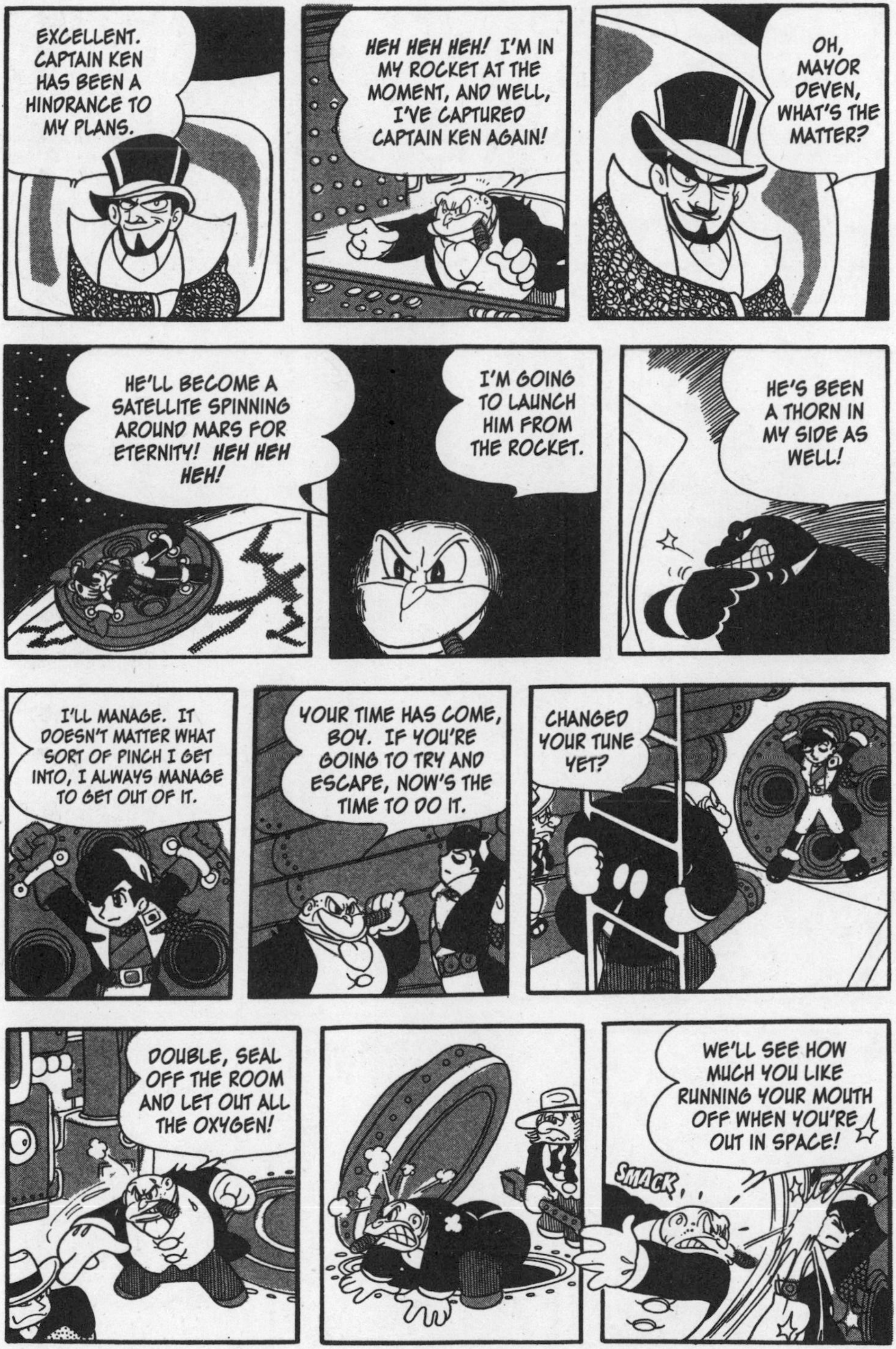
OH, MAYOR DEVEN, WHAT'S THE MATTER?
HEH HEH HEH! I'M IN MY ROCKET AT THE MOMENT, AND WELL, I'VE CAPTURED CAPTAIN KEN AGAIN!
EXCELLENT. CAPTAIN KEN HAS BEEN A HINDRANCE TO MY PLANS.
HE'S BEEN A THORN IN MY SIDE AS WELL!
I'M GOING TO LAUNCH HIM FROM THE ROCKET.
HE'LL BECOME A SATELLITE SPINNING AROUND MARS FOR ETERNITY! HEH HEH HEH!
CHANGED YOUR TUNE YET?
YOUR TIME HAS COME, BOY. IF YOU'RE GOING TO TRY AND ESCAPE, NOW'S THE TIME TO DO IT.
I'LL MANAGE. IT DOESN'T MATTER WHAT SORT OF PINCH I GET INTO, I ALWAYS MANAGE TO GET OUT OF IT.
WE'LL SEE HOW MUCH YOU LIKE RUNNING YOUR MOUTH OFF WHEN YOU'RE OUT IN SPACE!
SMACK
DOUBLE, SEAL OFF THE ROOM AND LET OUT ALL THE OXYGEN!

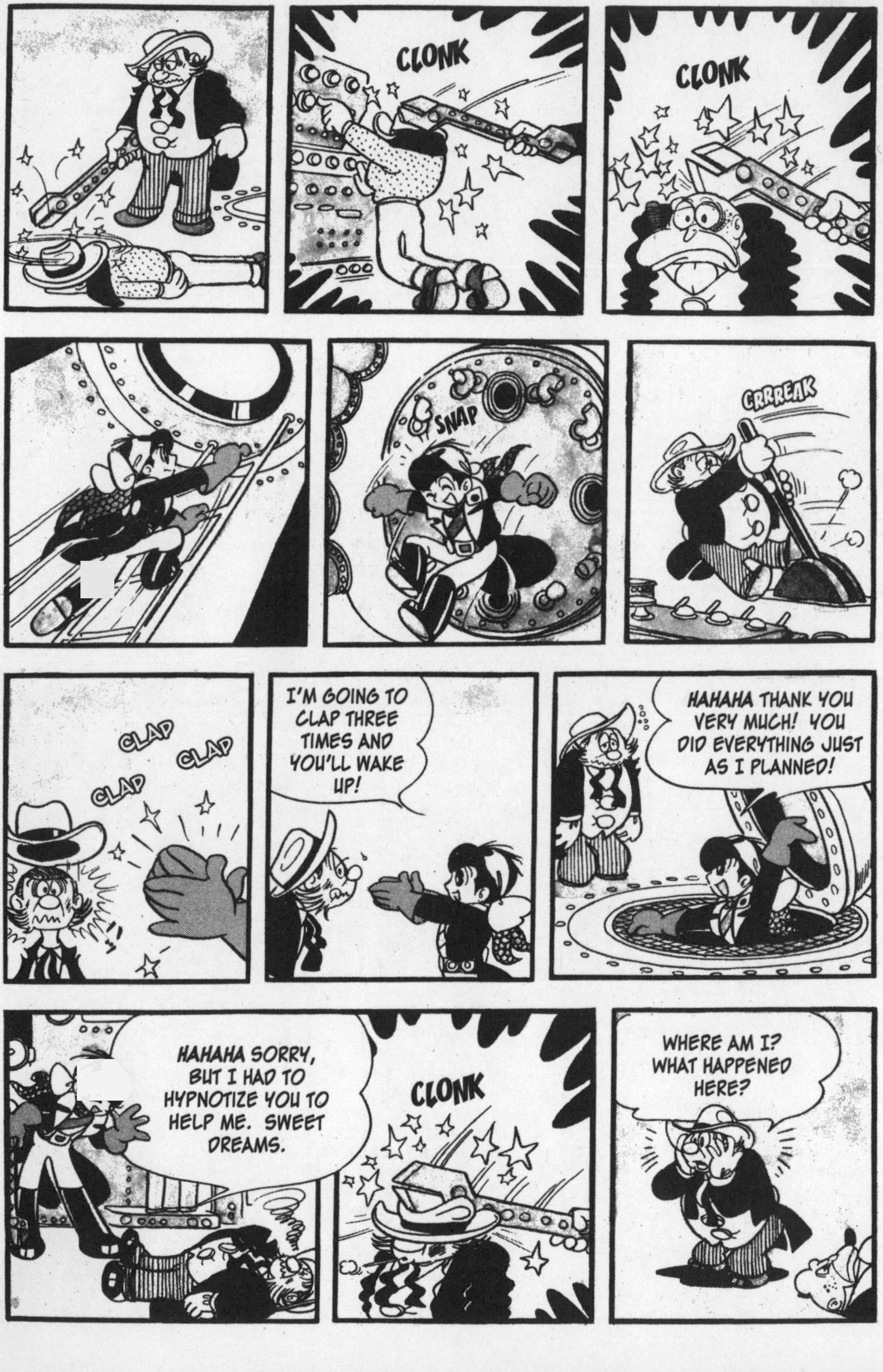
CLONK
CLONK
CRRREAK
SNAP
HAHAHA THANK YOU VERY MUCH! YOU DID EVERYTHING JUST AS I PLANNED!
I'M GOING TO CLAP THREE TIMES AND YOU'LL WAKE UP!
CLAP
CLAP
CLAP
WHERE AM I? WHAT HAPPENED HERE?
CLONK
HAHAHA SORRY, BUT I HAD TO HYPNOTIZE YOU TO HELP ME. SWEET DREAMS.

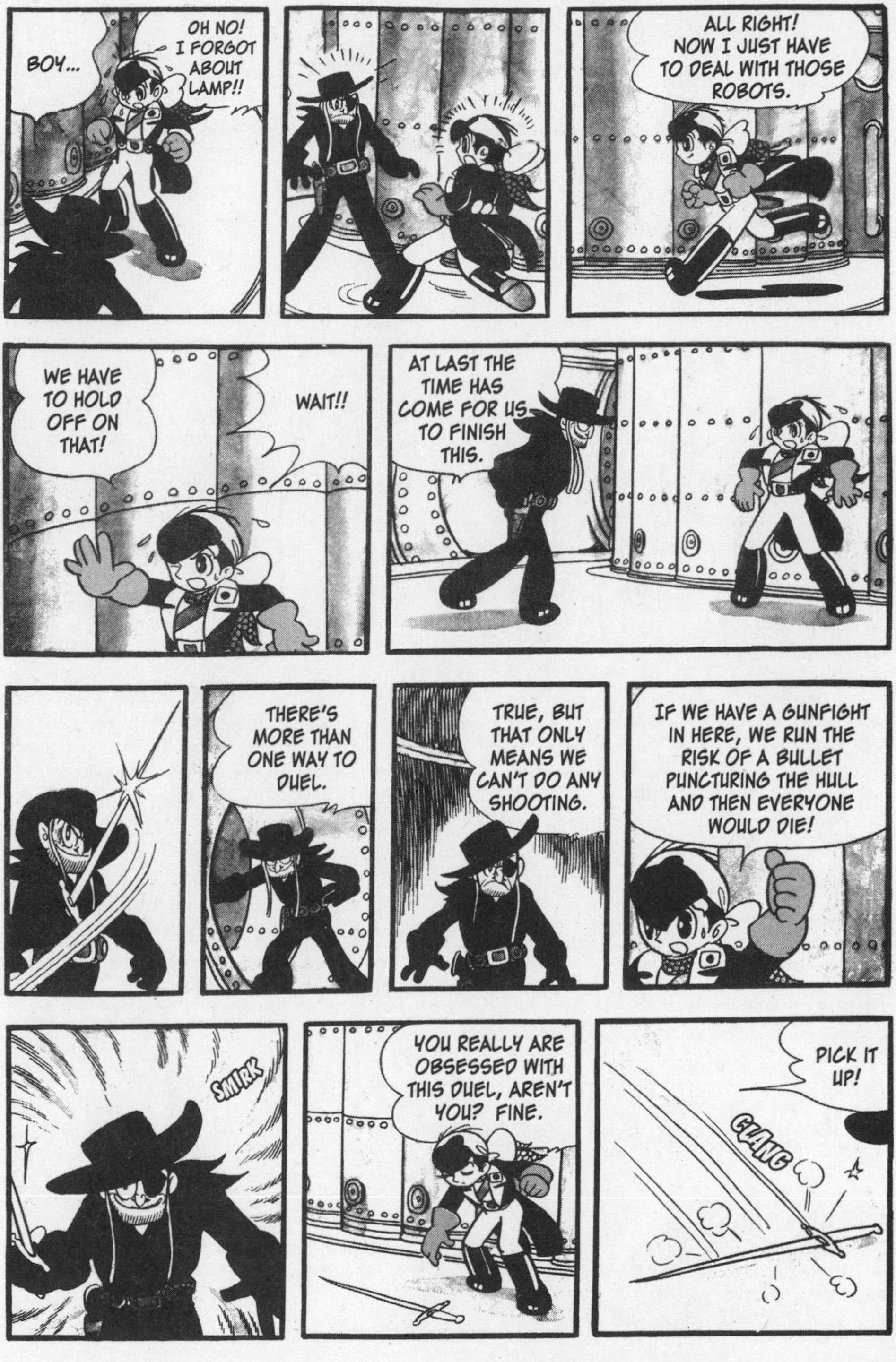
ALL RIGHT! NOW I JUST HAVE TO DEAL WITH THOSE ROBOTS.
OH NO! I FORGOT ABOUT LAMP!!
BOY...
AT LAST THE TIME HAS COME FOR US TO FINISH THIS.
WAIT!!
WE HAVE TO HOLD OFF ON THAT!
IF WE HAVE A GUNFIGHT IN HERE, WE RUN THE RISK OF A BULLET PUNCTURING THE HULL AND THEN EVERYONE WOULD DIE!
TRUE, BUT THAT ONLY MEANS WE CAN'T DO ANY SHOOTING.
THERE'S MORE THAN ONE WAY TO DUEL.
PICK IT UP!
CLANG
YOU REALLY ARE OBSESSED WITH THIS DUEL, AREN'T YOU? FINE.
SMIRK

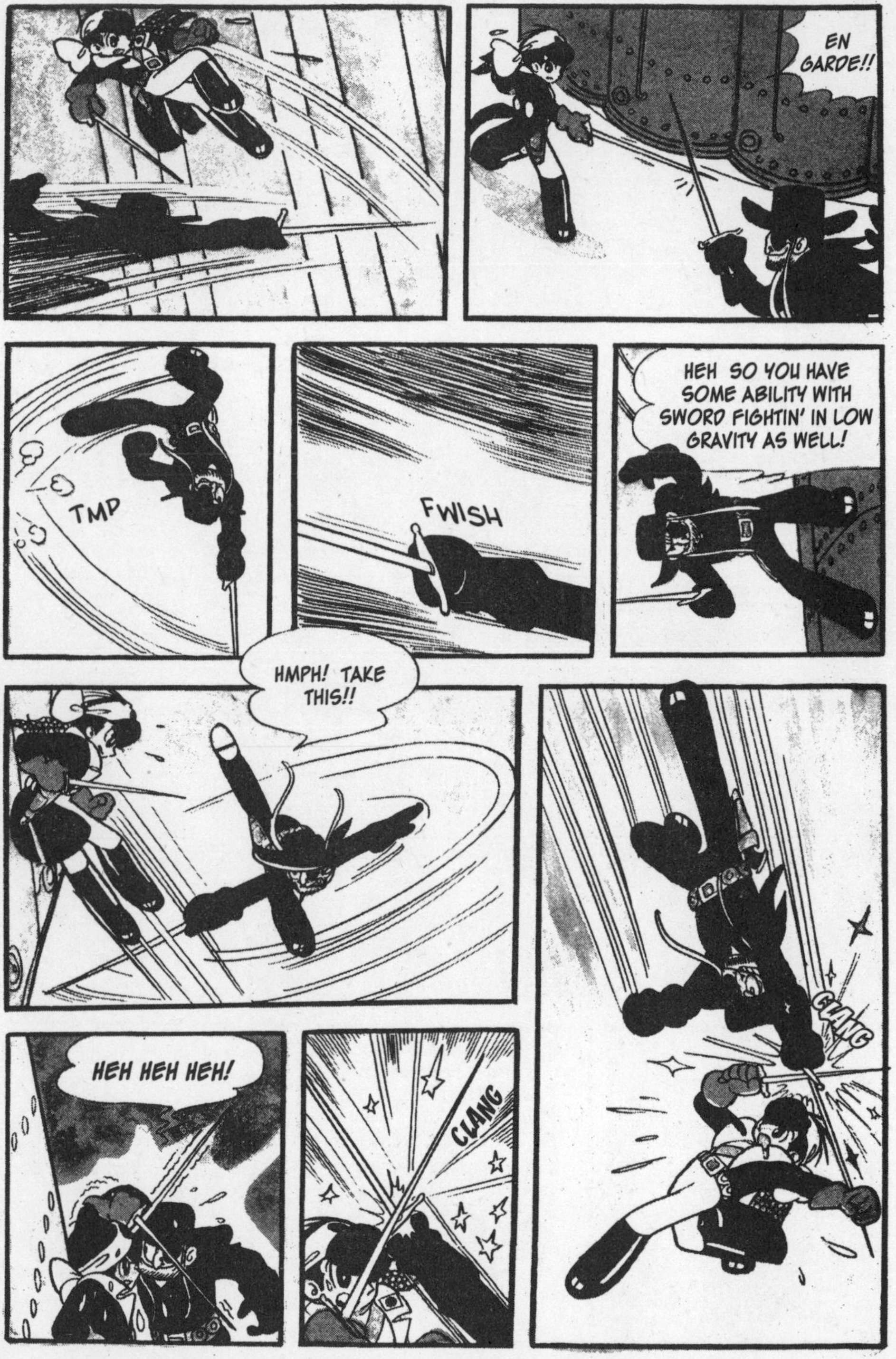
EN GARDE!!
HEH SO YOU HAVE SOME ABILITY WITH SWORD FIGHTIN' IN LOW GRAVITY AS WELL!
FWISH
TMP
CLANG
HMPH! TAKE THIS!!
CLANG
HEH HEH HEH!

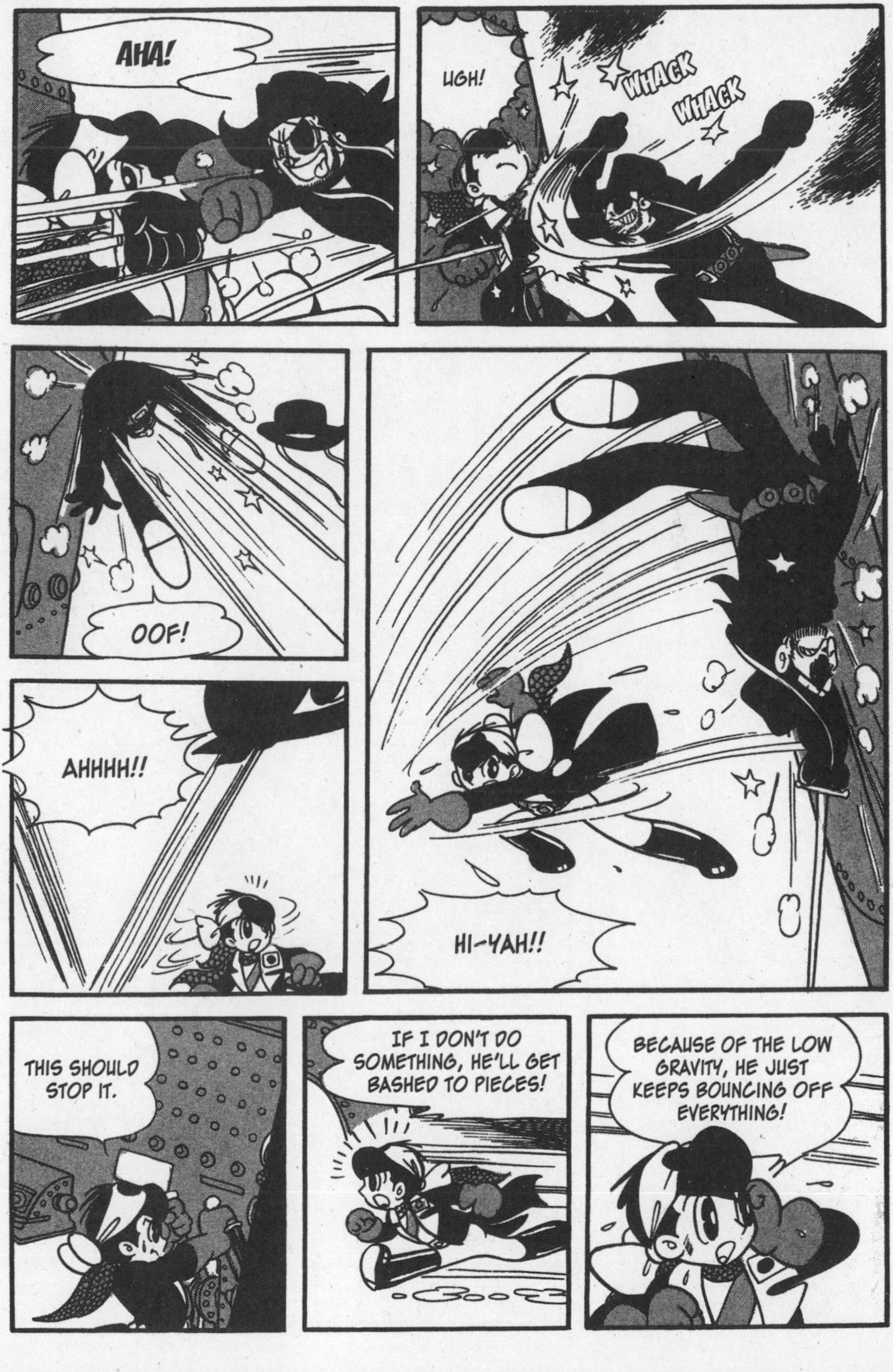
UGH!
WHACK
WHACK
AHA!
HI-YAH!!
OOF!
AHHHH!!
BECAUSE OF THE LOW GRAVITY, HE JUST KEEPS BOUNCING OFF EVERYTHING!
IF I DON'T DO SOMETHING, HE'LL GET BASHED TO PIECES!
THIS SHOULD STOP IT.

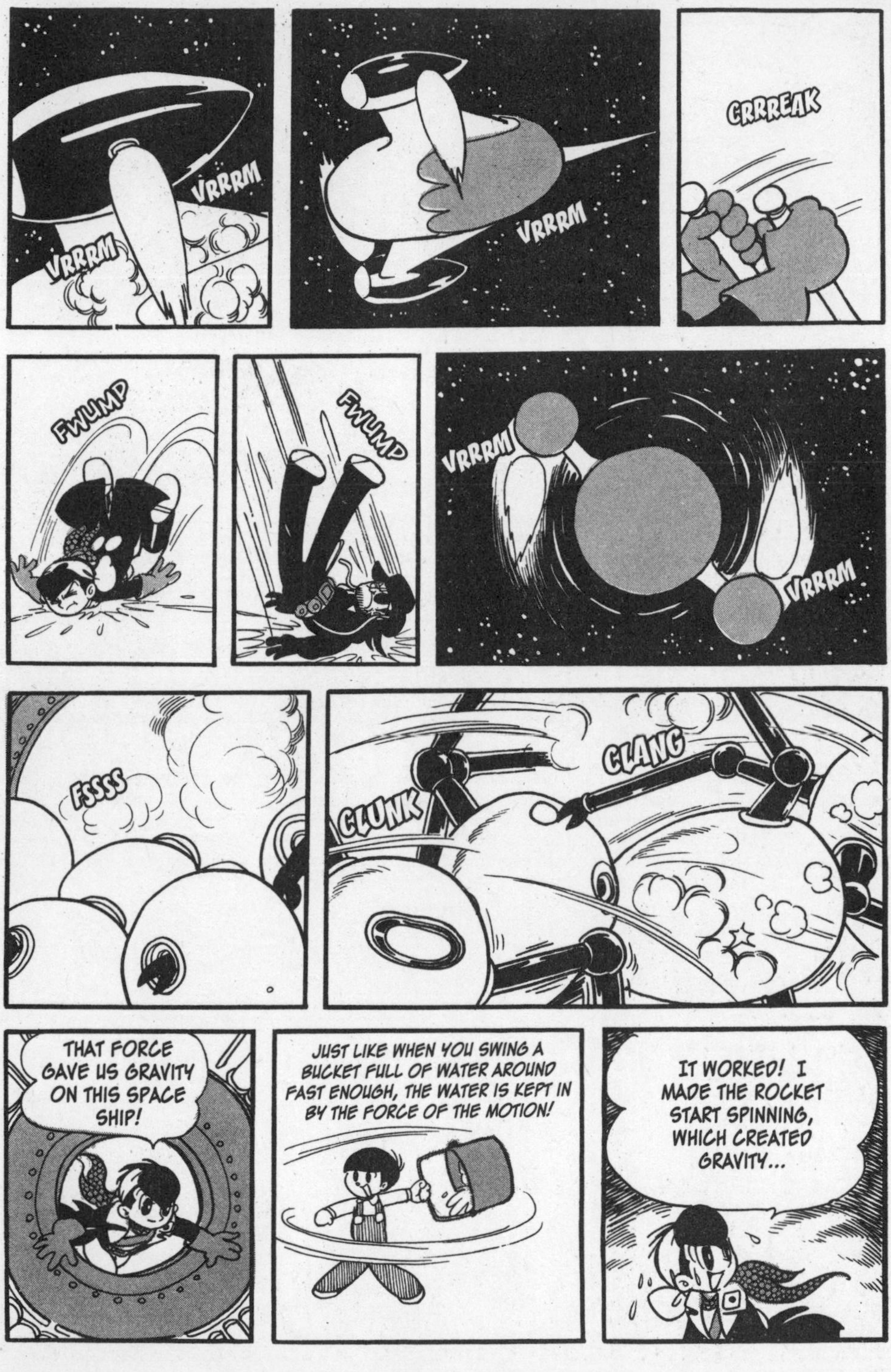
CRRREAK
VRRRM
VRRRM
VRRRM
VRRRM
VRRRM
FWUMP
FWUMP
CLANG
CLUNK
FSSSS
IT WORKED! I MADE THE ROCKET START SPINNING, WHICH CREATED GRAVITY...
JUST LIKE WHEN YOU SWING A BUCKET FULL OF WATER AROUND FAST ENOUGH, THE WATER IS KEPT IN BY THE FORCE OF THE MOTION!
THAT FORCE GAVE US GRAVITY ON THIS SPACE SHIP!

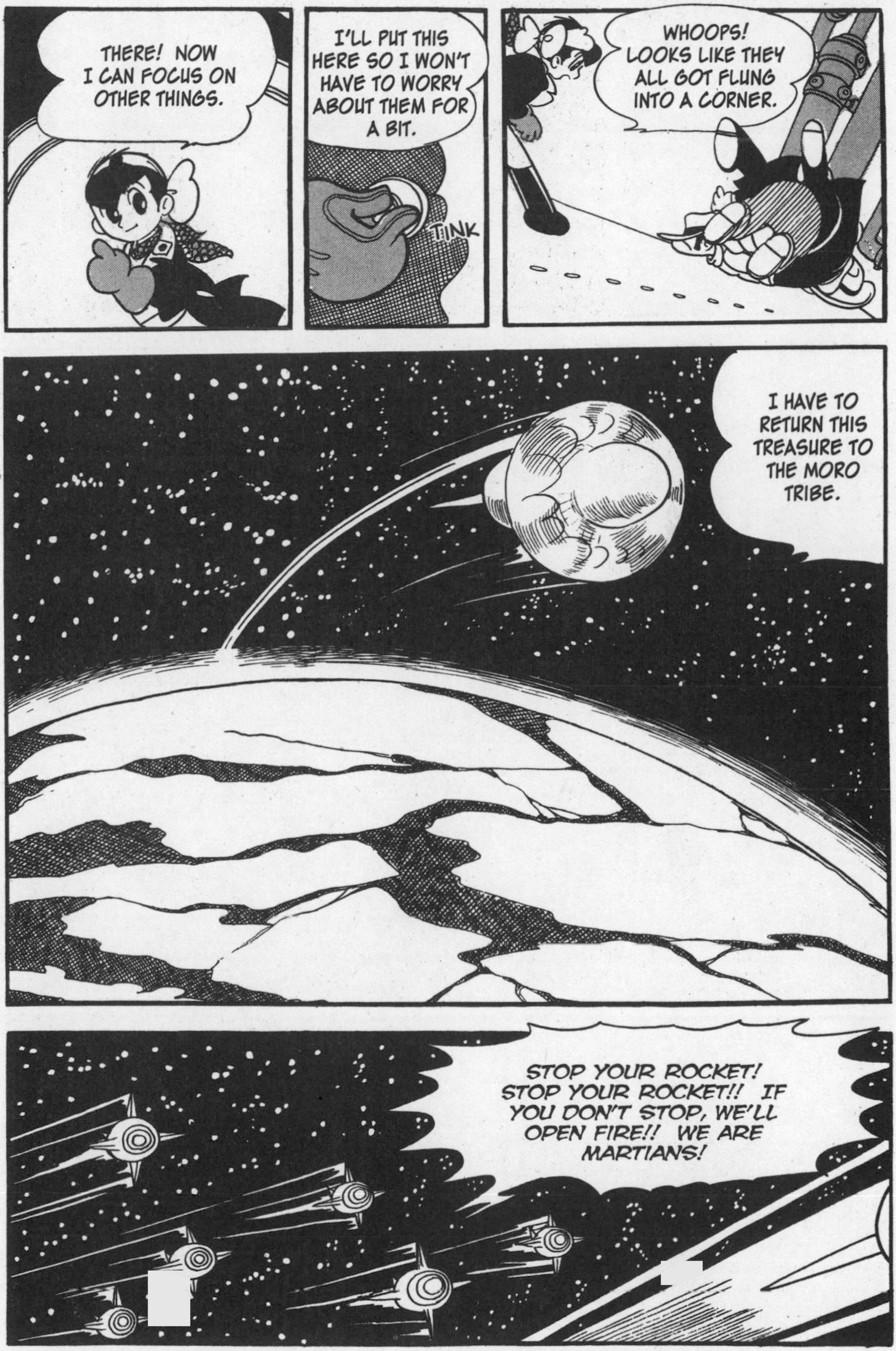
WHOOPS! LOOKS LIKE THEY ALL GOT FLUNG INTO A CORNER.
I'LL PUT THIS HERE SO I WON'T HAVE TO WORRY ABOUT THEM FOR A BIT.
TINK
THERE! NOW I CAN FOCUS ON OTHER THINGS.
I HAVE TO RETURN THIS TREASURE TO THE MORO TRIBE.
STOP YOUR ROCKET! STOP YOUR ROCKET!! IF YOU DON'T STOP, WE'LL OPEN FIRE!! WE ARE MARTIANS!

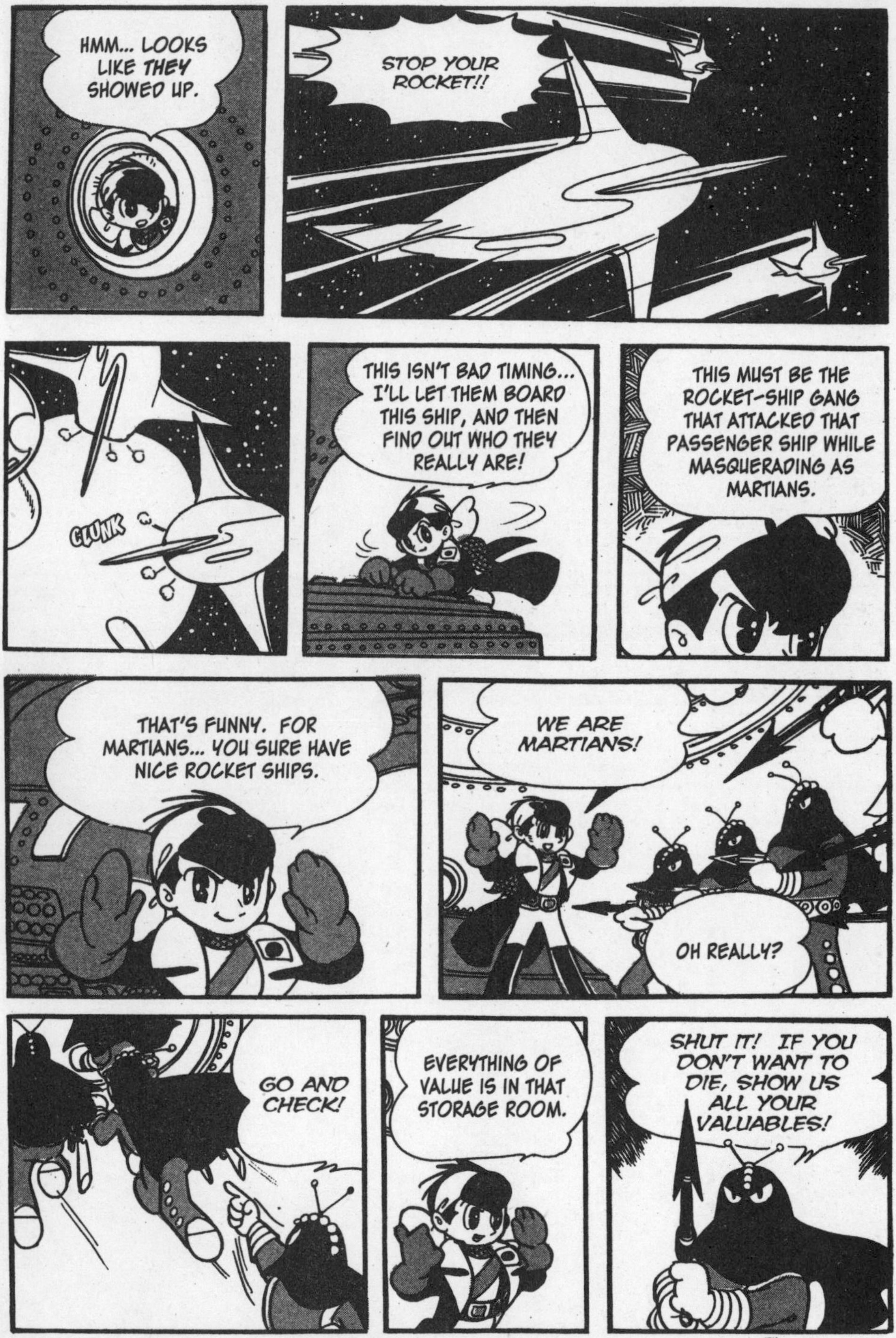
STOP YOUR ROCKET!!
HMM... LOOKS LIKE THEY SHOWED UP.
THIS MUST BE THE ROCKET-SHIP GANG THAT ATTACKED THAT PASSENGER SHIP WHILE MASQUERADING AS MARTIANS.
THIS ISN'T BAD TIMING... I'LL LET THEM BOARD THIS SHIP, AND THEN FIND OUT WHO THEY REALLY ARE!
CLUNK
WE ARE MARTIANS!
OH REALLY?
THAT'S FUNNY. FOR MARTIANS... YOU SURE HAVE NICE ROCKET SHIPS.
SHUT IT! IF YOU DON'T WANT TO DIE, SHOW US ALL YOUR VALUABLES!
EVERYTHING OF VALUE IS IN THAT STORAGE ROOM.
GO AND CHECK!

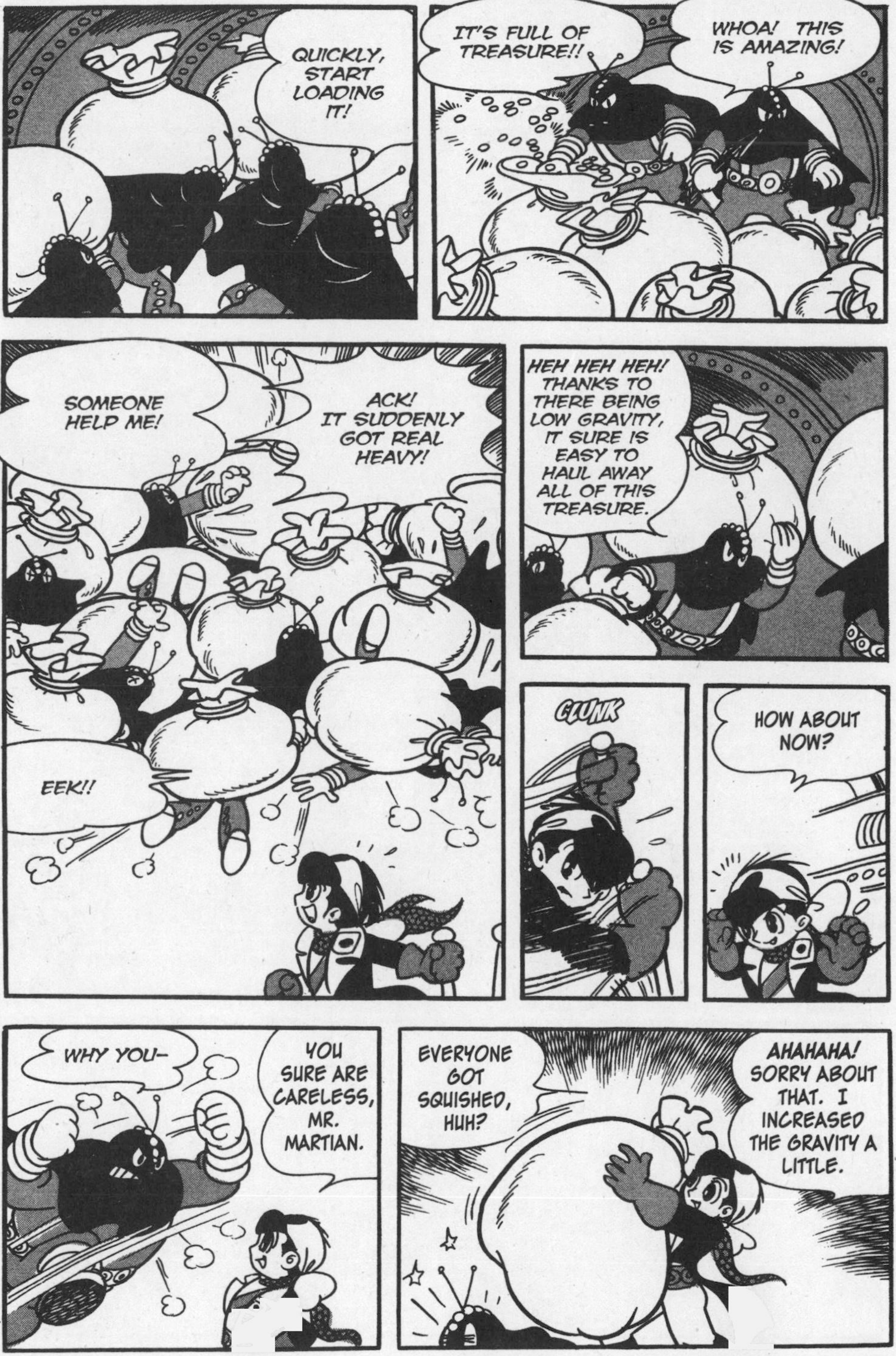
WHOA! THIS IS AMAZING!
IT'S FULL OF TREASURE!!
QUICKLY, START LOADING IT!
HEH HEH HEH! THANKS TO THERE BEING LOW GRAVITY, IT SURE IS EASY TO HAUL AWAY ALL OF THIS TREASURE.
HOW ABOUT NOW?
CLUNK
ACK! IT SUDDENLY GOT REAL HEAVY!
SOMEONE HELP ME!
EEK!!
AHAHAHA! SORRY ABOUT THAT. I INCREASED THE GRAVITY A LITTLE.
EVERYONE GOT SQUISHED, HUH?
YOU SURE ARE CARELESS, MR. MARTIAN.
WHY YOU-

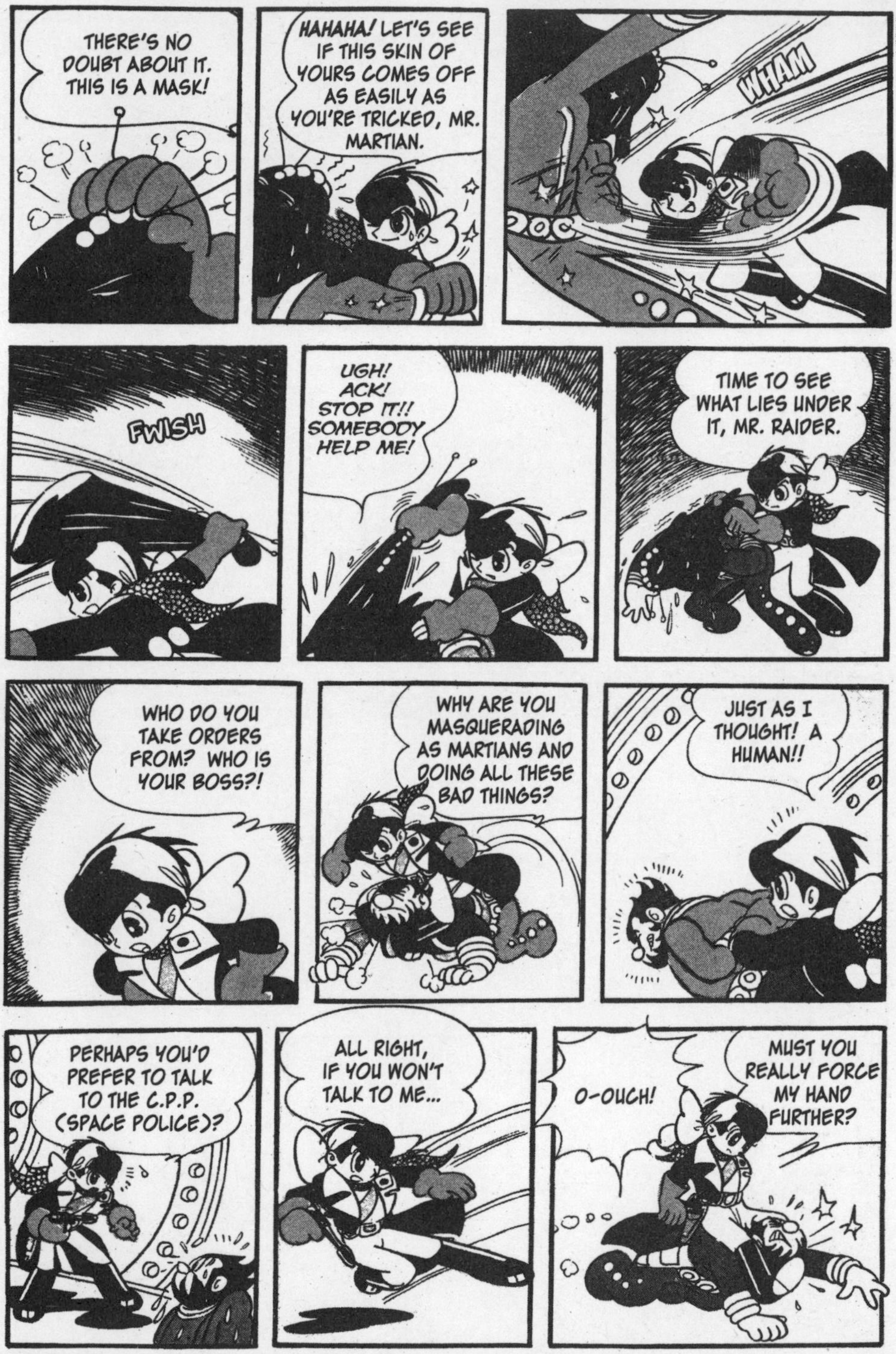
WHAM
HAHAHA! LET'S SEE IF THIS SKIN OF YOURS COMES OFF AS EASILY AS YOU'RE TRICKED, MR. MARTIAN.
THERE'S NO DOUBT ABOUT IT. THIS IS A MASK!
TIME TO SEE WHAT LIES UNDER IT, MR. RAIDER.
UGH! ACK! STOP IT!! SOMEBODY HELP ME!
FWISH
JUST AS I THOUGHT! A HUMAN!!
WHY ARE YOU MASQUERADING AS MARTIANS AND DOING ALL THESE BAD THINGS?
WHO DO YOU TAKE ORDERS FROM? WHO IS YOUR BOSS?!
MUST YOU REALLY FORCE MY HAND FURTHER?
O-OUCH!
ALL RIGHT, IF YOU WON'T TALK TO ME...
PERHAPS YOU'D PREFER TO TALK TO THE C.P.P. (SPACE POLICE)?

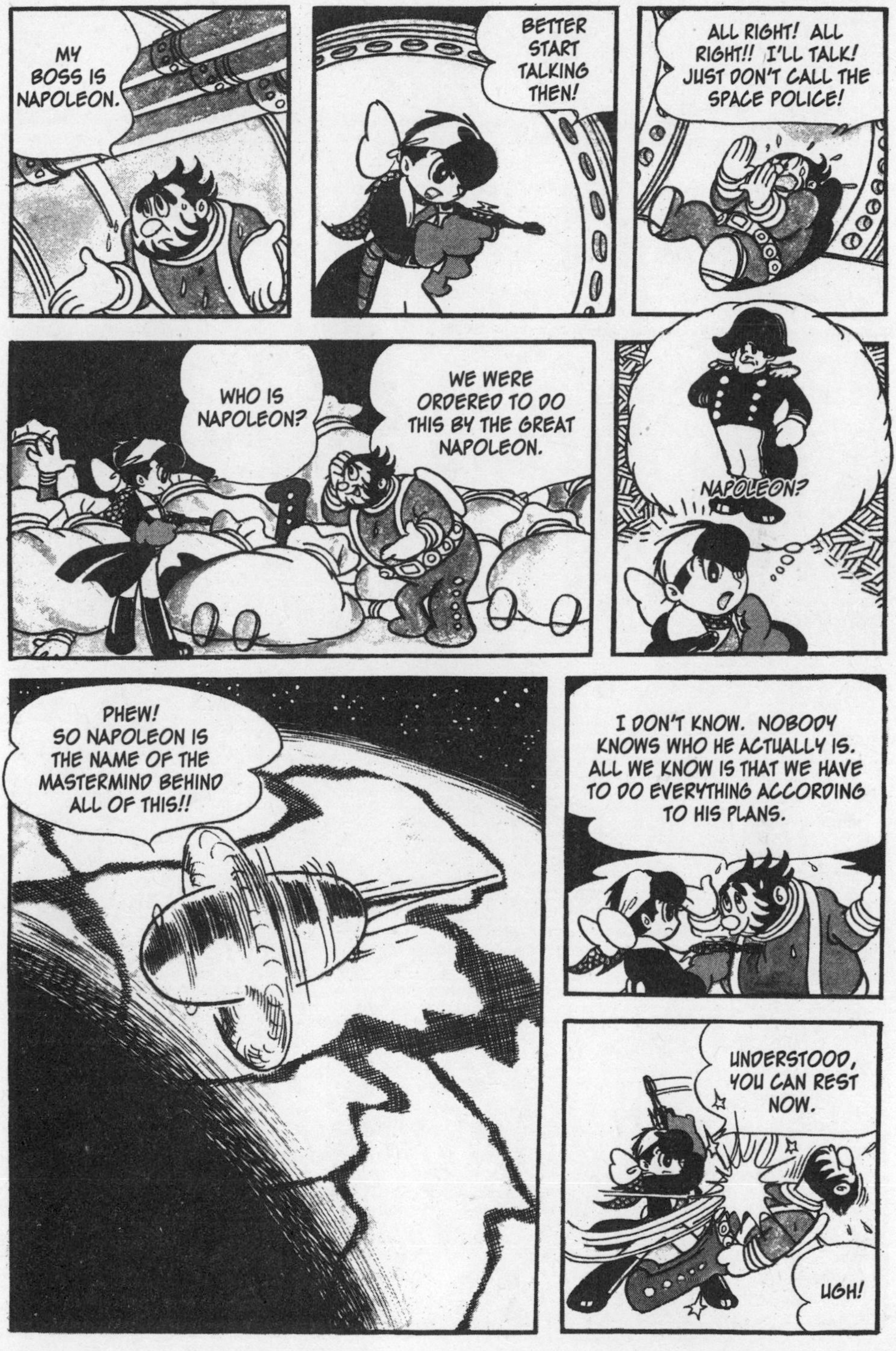
ALL RIGHT! ALL RIGHT!! I'LL TALK! JUST DON'T CALL THE SPACE POLICE!
BETTER START TALKING THEN!
MY BOSS IS NAPOLEON.
NAPOLEON?
WE WERE ORDERED TO DO THIS BY THE GREAT NAPOLEON.
WHO IS NAPOLEON?
I DON'T KNOW. NOBODY KNOWS WHO HE ACTUALLY IS. ALL WE KNOW IS THAT WE HAVE TO DO EVERYTHING ACCORDING TO HIS PLANS.
UNDERSTOOD, YOU CAN REST NOW.
UGH!
PHEW! SO NAPOLEON IS THE NAME OF THE MASTERMIND BEHIND ALL OF THIS!!

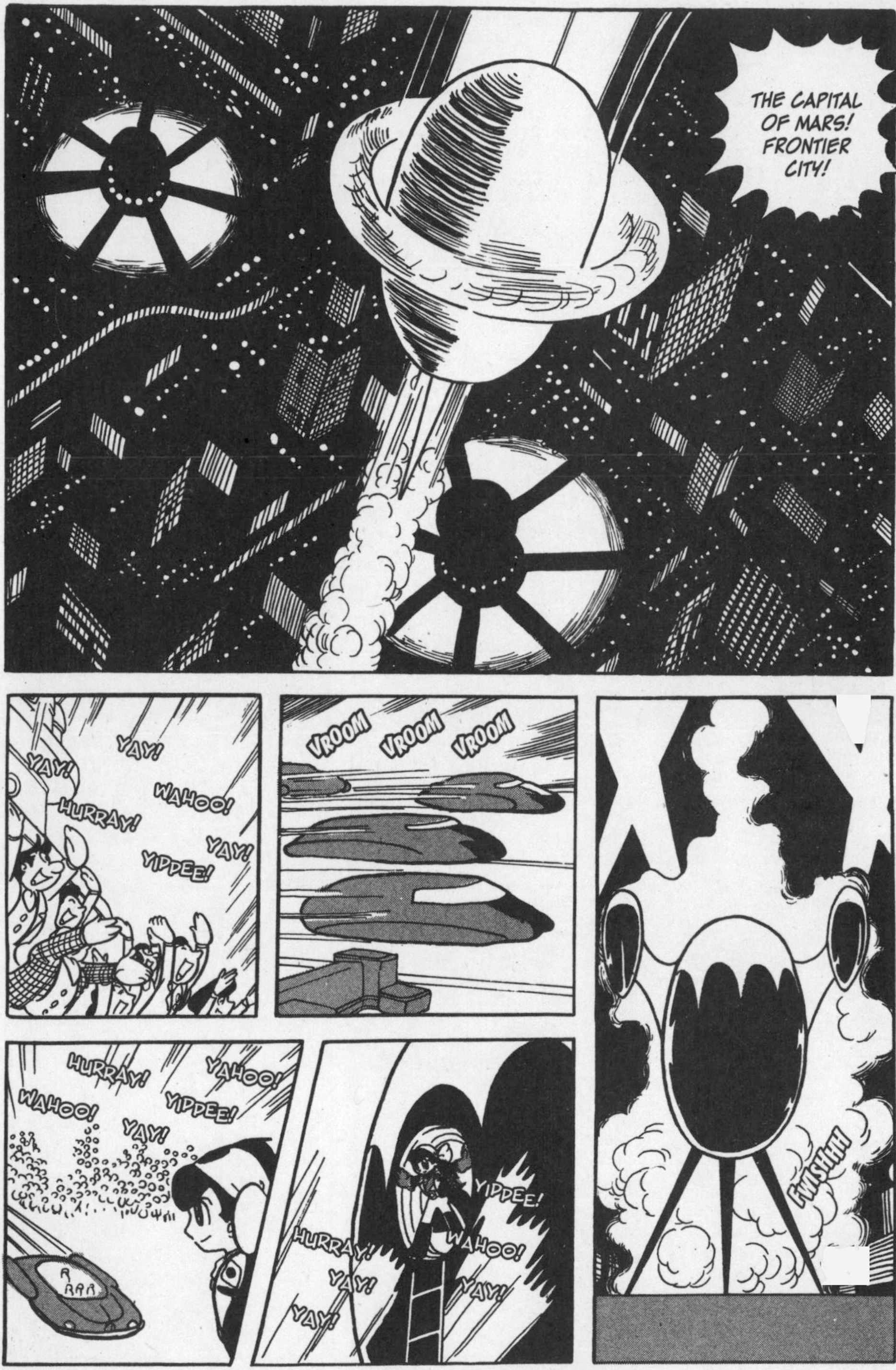
THE CAPITAL OF MARS! FRONTIER CITY!
FWISHHH
VROOM
VROOM
VROOM
YAY!
YAY!
WAHOO!
HURRAY!
YAY!
YIPPDEE!
YIPPDEE!
WAHOO!
HURRAY!
YAY!
YAY!
YAY!
YAHOO!
HURRAY!
YIPPDEE!
WAHOO!
YAY!

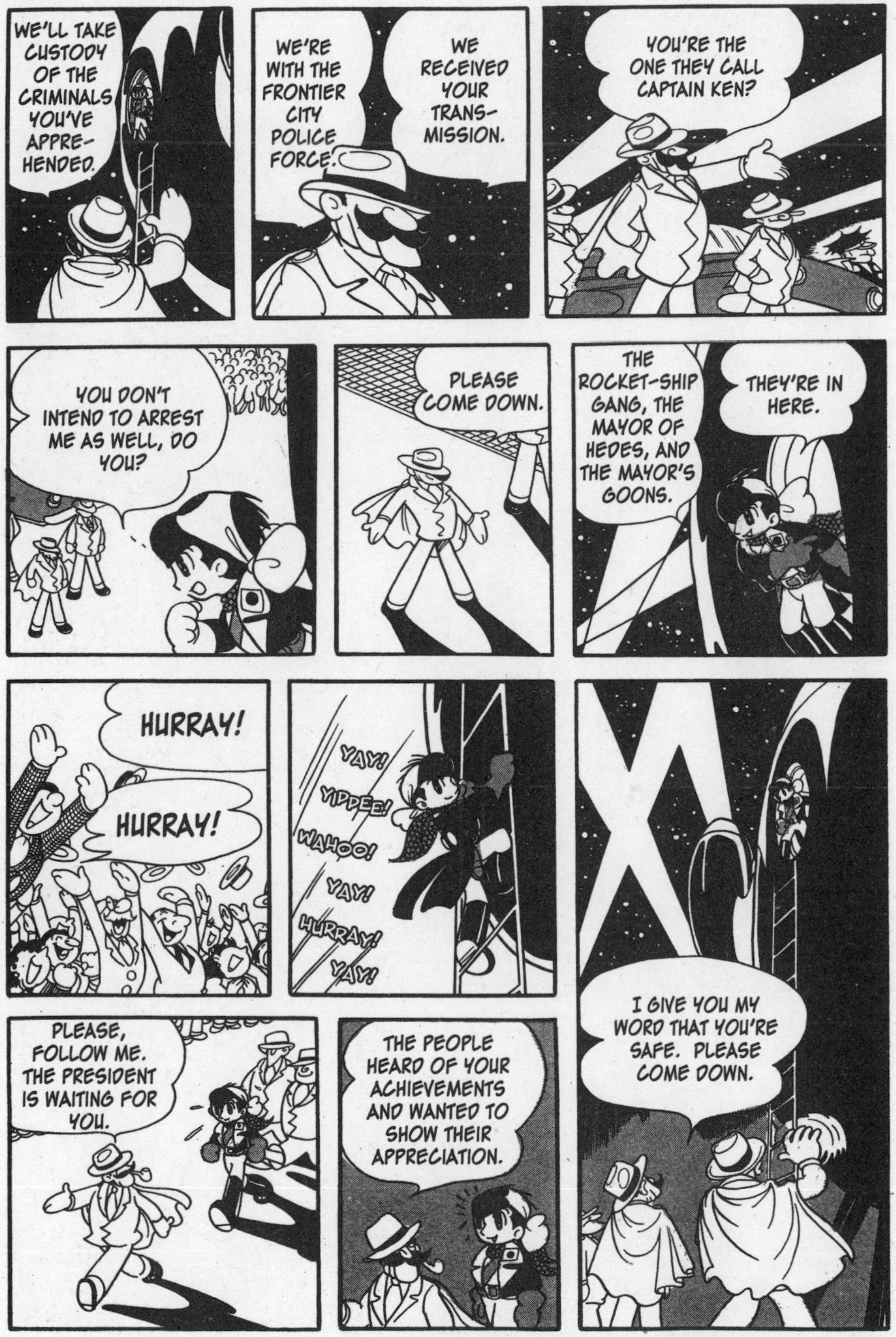
YOU'RE THE ONE THEY CALL CAPTAIN KEN?
WE RECEIVED YOUR TRANS-MISSION.
WE'RE WITH THE FRONTIER CITY POLICE FORCE.
WE'LL TAKE CUSTODY OF THE CRIMINALS YOU'VE APPRE-HENDED.
THEY'RE IN HERE.
THE ROCKET-SHIP GANG, THE MAYOR OF HEDES, AND THE MAYOR'S GOONS.
PLEASE COME DOWN.
YOU DON'T INTEND TO ARREST ME AS WELL, DO YOU?
I GIVE YOU MY WORD THAT YOU'RE SAFE. PLEASE COME DOWN.
YAY!
YIPPEE!
WAHOO!
YAY!
HURRAY!
YAY!
HURRAY!
HURRAY!
THE PEOPLE HEARD OF YOUR ACHIEVEMENTS AND WANTED TO SHOW THEIR APPRECIATION.
PLEASE, FOLLOW ME. THE PRESIDENT IS WAITING FOR YOU.

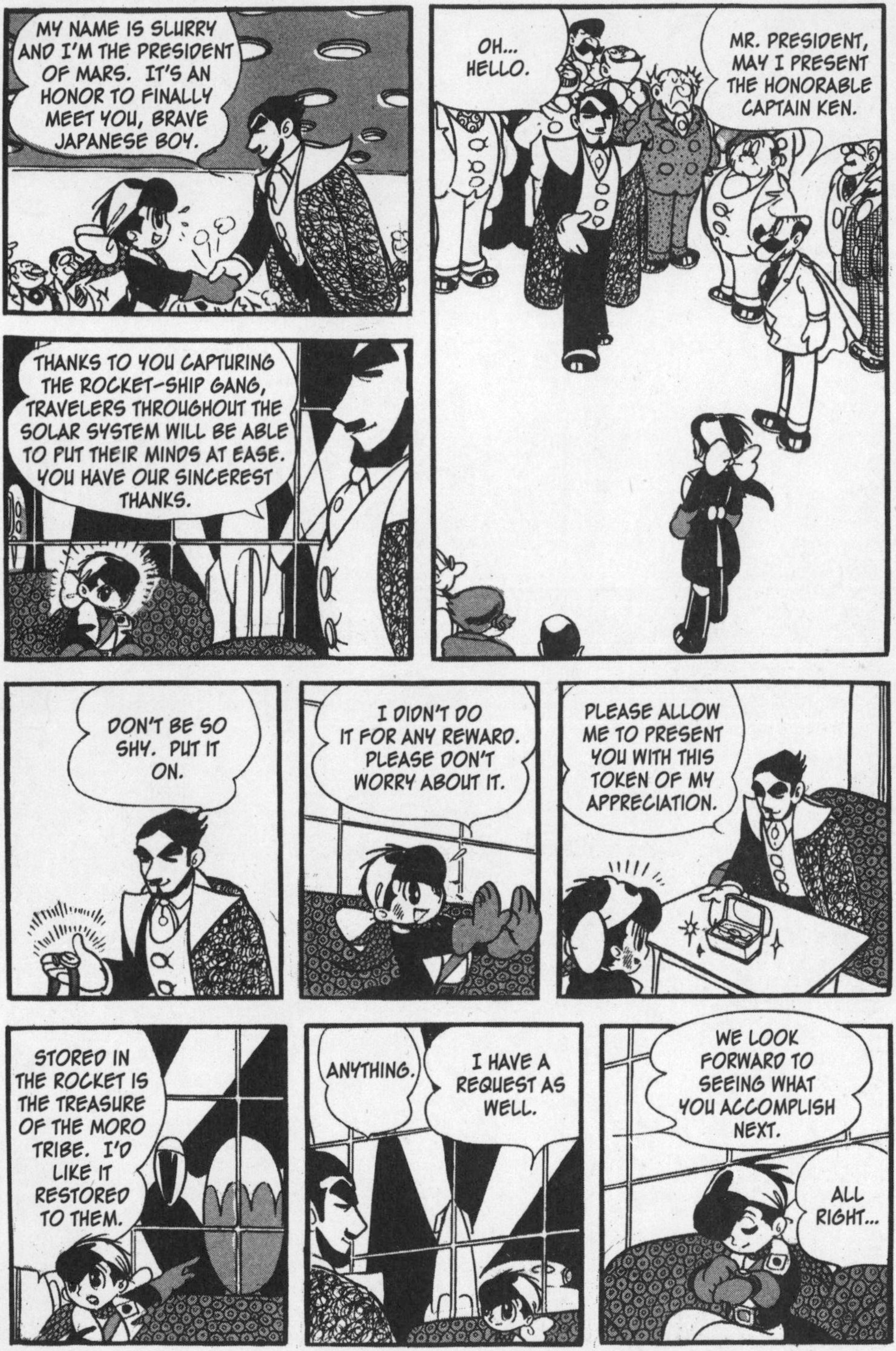
MR. PRESIDENT, MAY I PRESENT THE HONORABLE CAPTAIN KEN.
OH... HELLO.
MY NAME IS SLURRY AND I'M THE PRESIDENT OF MARS. IT'S AN HONOR TO FINALLY MEET YOU, BRAVE JAPANESE BOY.
THANKS TO YOU CAPTURING THE ROCKET-SHIP GANG, TRAVELERS THROUGHOUT THE SOLAR SYSTEM WILL BE ABLE TO PUT THEIR MINDS AT EASE. YOU HAVE OUR SINCEREST THANKS.
PLEASE ALLOW ME TO PRESENT YOU WITH THIS TOKEN OF MY APPRECIATION.
I DIDN'T DO IT FOR ANY REWARD. PLEASE DON'T WORRY ABOUT IT.
DON'T BE SO SHY. PUT IT ON.
WE LOOK FORWARD TO SEEING WHAT YOU ACCOMPLISH NEXT.
ALL RIGHT...
I HAVE A REQUEST AS WELL.
ANYTHING.
STORED IN THE ROCKET IS THE TREASURE OF THE MORO TRIBE. I'D LIKE IT RESTORED TO THEM.

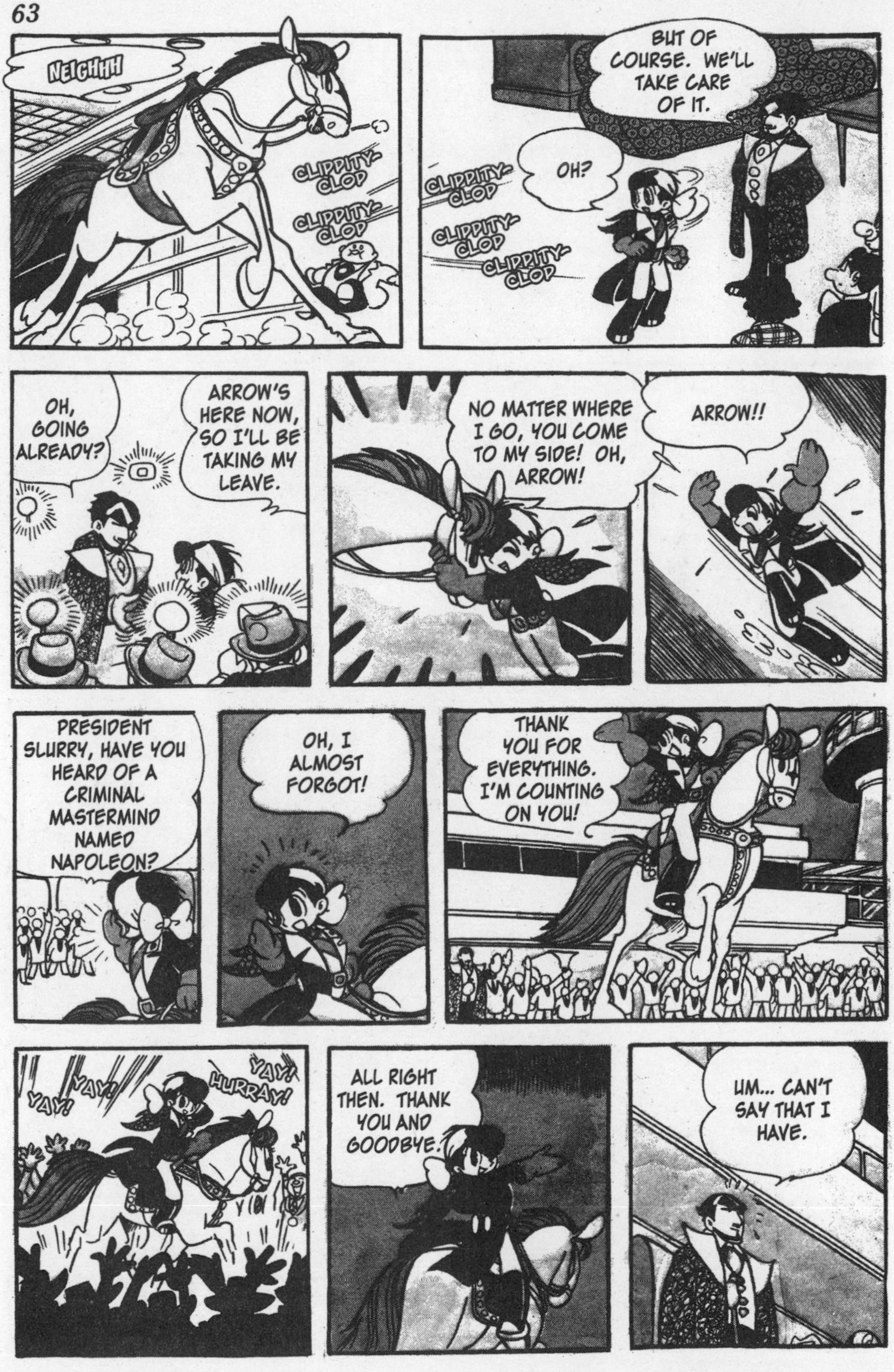
BUT OF COURSE. WE'LL TAKE CARE OF IT.
OH?
CLIPPITY-CLOP
CLIPPITY-CLOP
CLIPPITY-CLOP
NEIGHHH
CLIPPITY-CLOP
CLIPPITY-CLOP
ARROW!!
NO MATTER WHERE I GO, YOU COME TO MY SIDE! OH, ARROW!
ARROW'S HERE NOW, SO I'LL BE TAKING MY LEAVE.
OH, GOING ALREADY?
THANK YOU FOR EVERYTHING. I'M COUNTING ON YOU!
OH, I ALMOST FORGOT!
PRESIDENT SLURRY, HAVE YOU HEARD OF A CRIMINAL MASTERMIND NAMED NAPOLEON?
UM... CAN'T SAY THAT I HAVE.
ALL RIGHT THEN. THANK YOU AND GOODBYE.
YAY! HURRAY!
YAY!
YAY!

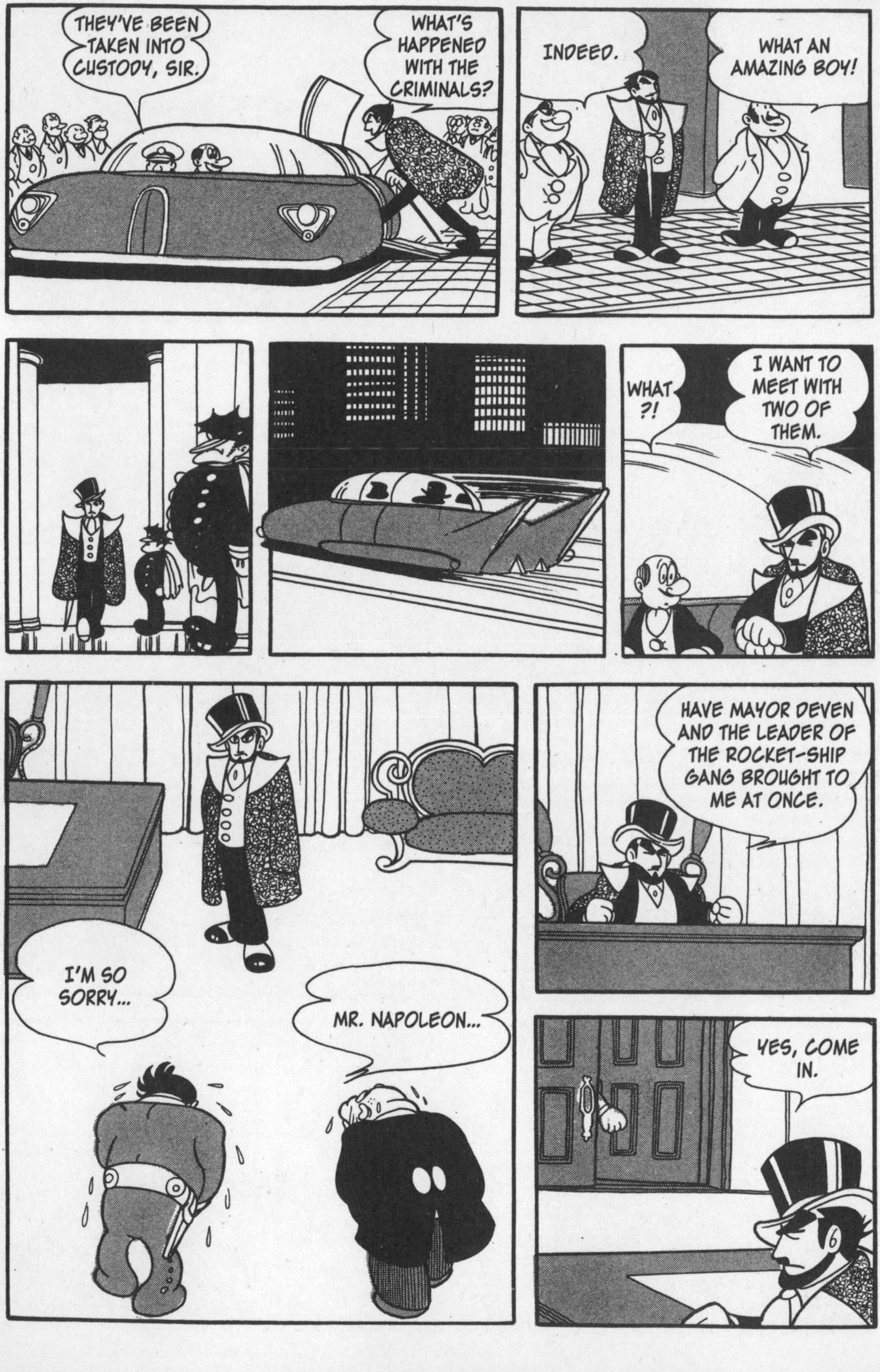
WHAT AN AMAZING BOY!
INDEED.
WHAT'S HAPPENED WITH THE CRIMINALS?
THEY'VE BEEN TAKEN INTO CUSTODY, SIR.
I WANT TO MEET WITH TWO OF THEM.
WHAT ?!
HAVE MAYOR DEVEN AND THE LEADER OF THE ROCKET-SHIP GANG BROUGHT TO ME AT ONCE.
YES, COME IN.
I'M SO SORRY...
MR. NAPOLEON...

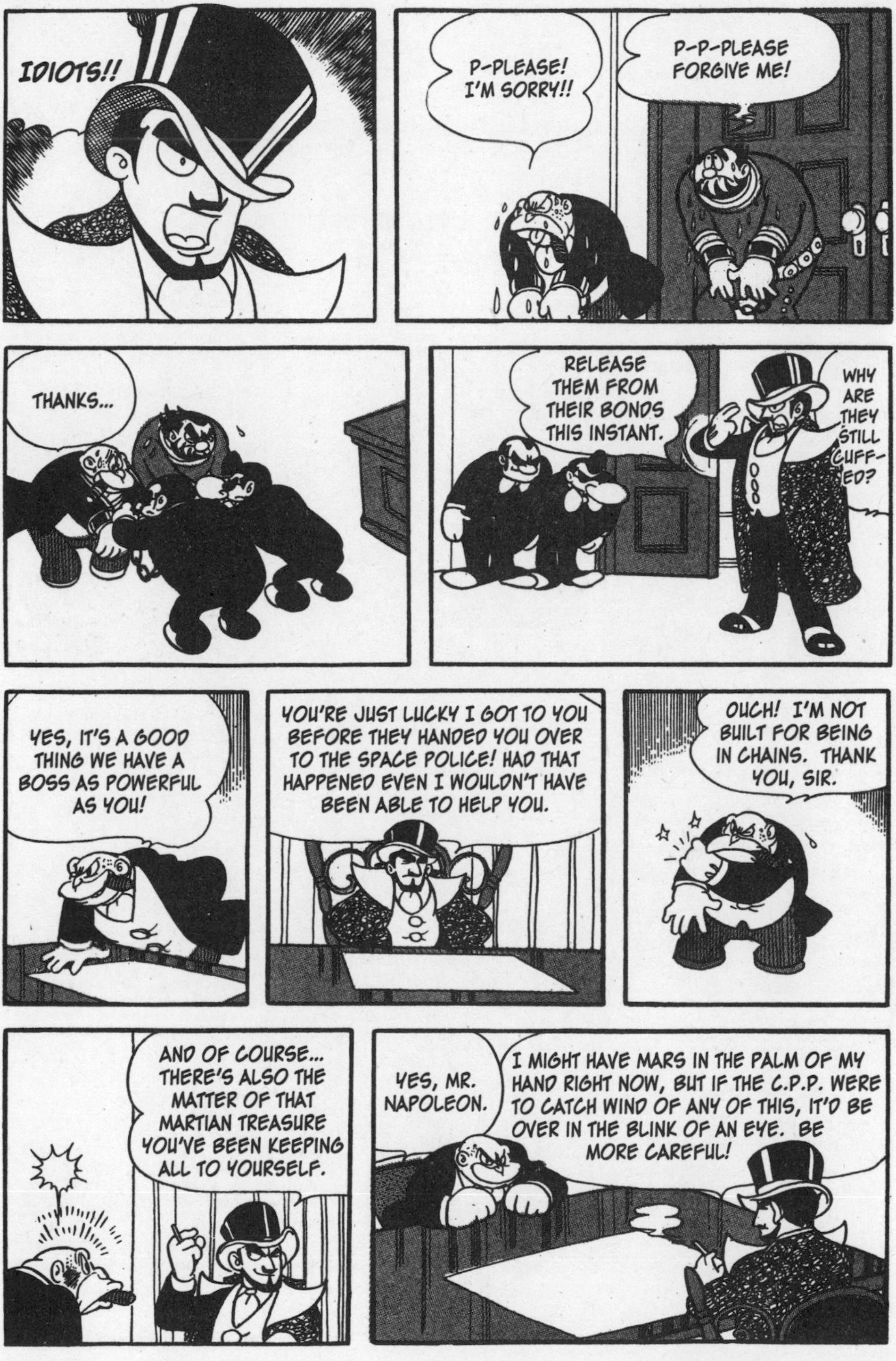
P-P-PLEASE FORGIVE ME!
P-PLEASE! I'M SORRY!!
IDIOTS!!
WHY ARE THEY STILL CUFFED?
RELEASE THEM FROM THEIR BONDS THIS INSTANT.
THANKS...
OUCH! I'M NOT BUILT FOR BEING IN CHAINS. THANK YOU, SIR.
YOU'RE JUST LUCKY I GOT TO YOU BEFORE THEY HANDED YOU OVER TO THE SPACE POLICE! HAD THAT HAPPENED EVEN I WOULDN'T HAVE BEEN ABLE TO HELP YOU.
YES, IT'S A GOOD THING WE HAVE A BOSS AS POWERFUL AS YOU!
I MIGHT HAVE MARS IN THE PALM OF MY HAND RIGHT NOW, BUT IF THE C.P.P. WERE TO CATCH WIND OF ANY OF THIS, IT'D BE OVER IN THE BLINK OF AN EYE. BE MORE CAREFUL!
YES, MR. NAPOLEON.
AND OF COURSE... THERE'S ALSO THE MATTER OF THAT MARTIAN TREASURE YOU'VE BEEN KEEPING ALL TO YOURSELF.

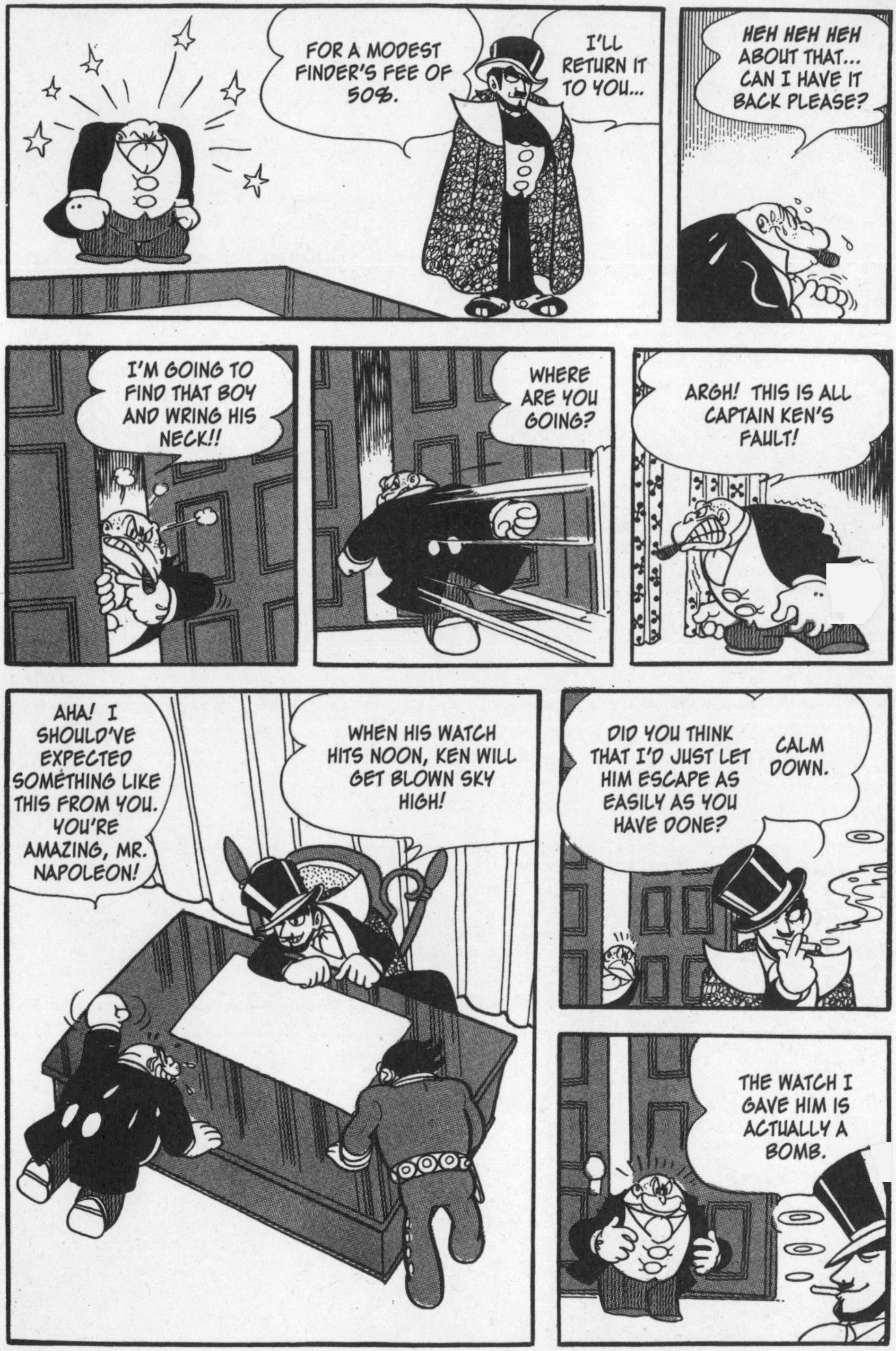
HEH HEH HEH ABOUT THAT... CAN I HAVE IT BACK PLEASE?
I'LL RETURN IT TO YOU...
FOR A MODEST FINDER'S FEE OF 50%.
ARGH! THIS IS ALL CAPTAIN KEN'S FAULT!
WHERE ARE YOU GOING?
I'M GOING TO FIND THAT BOY AND WRING HIS NECK!!
CALM DOWN.
DID YOU THINK THAT I'D JUST LET HIM ESCAPE AS EASILY AS YOU HAVE DONE?
THE WATCH I GAVE HIM IS ACTUALLY A BOMB.
WHEN HIS WATCH HITS NOON, KEN WILL GET BLOWN SKY HIGH!
AHA! I SHOULD'VE EXPECTED SOMETHING LIKE THIS FROM YOU. YOU'RE AMAZING, MR. NAPOLEON!

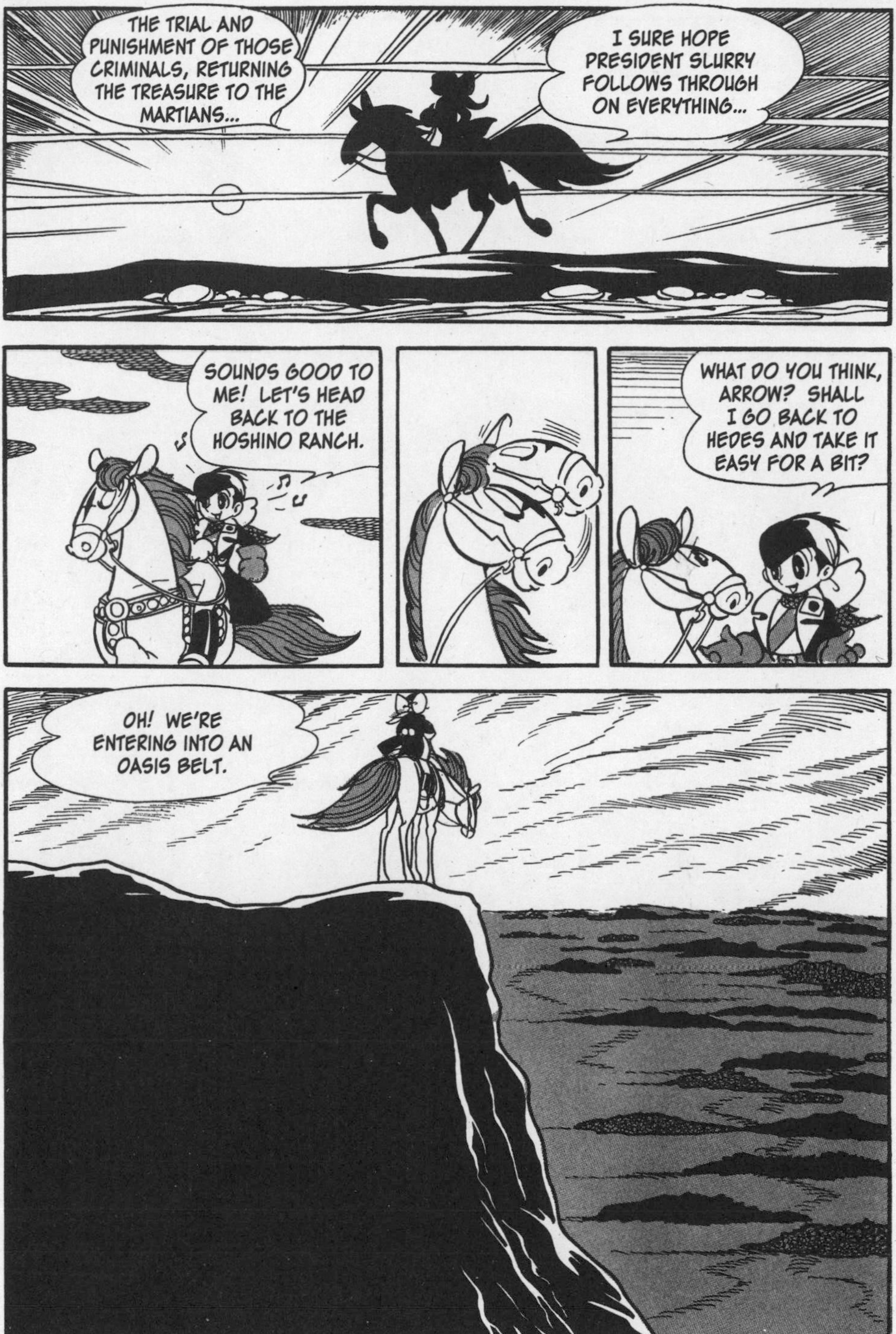
I SURE HOPE PRESIDENT SLURRY FOLLOWS THROUGH ON EVERYTHING...
THE TRIAL AND PUNISHMENT OF THOSE CRIMINALS, RETURNING THE TREASURE TO THE MARTIANS...
WHAT DO YOU THINK, ARROW? SHALL I GO BACK TO HEDES AND TAKE IT EASY FOR A BIT?
SOUNDS GOOD TO ME! LET'S HEAD BACK TO THE HOSHINO RANCH.
OH! WE'RE ENTERING INTO AN OASIS BELT.

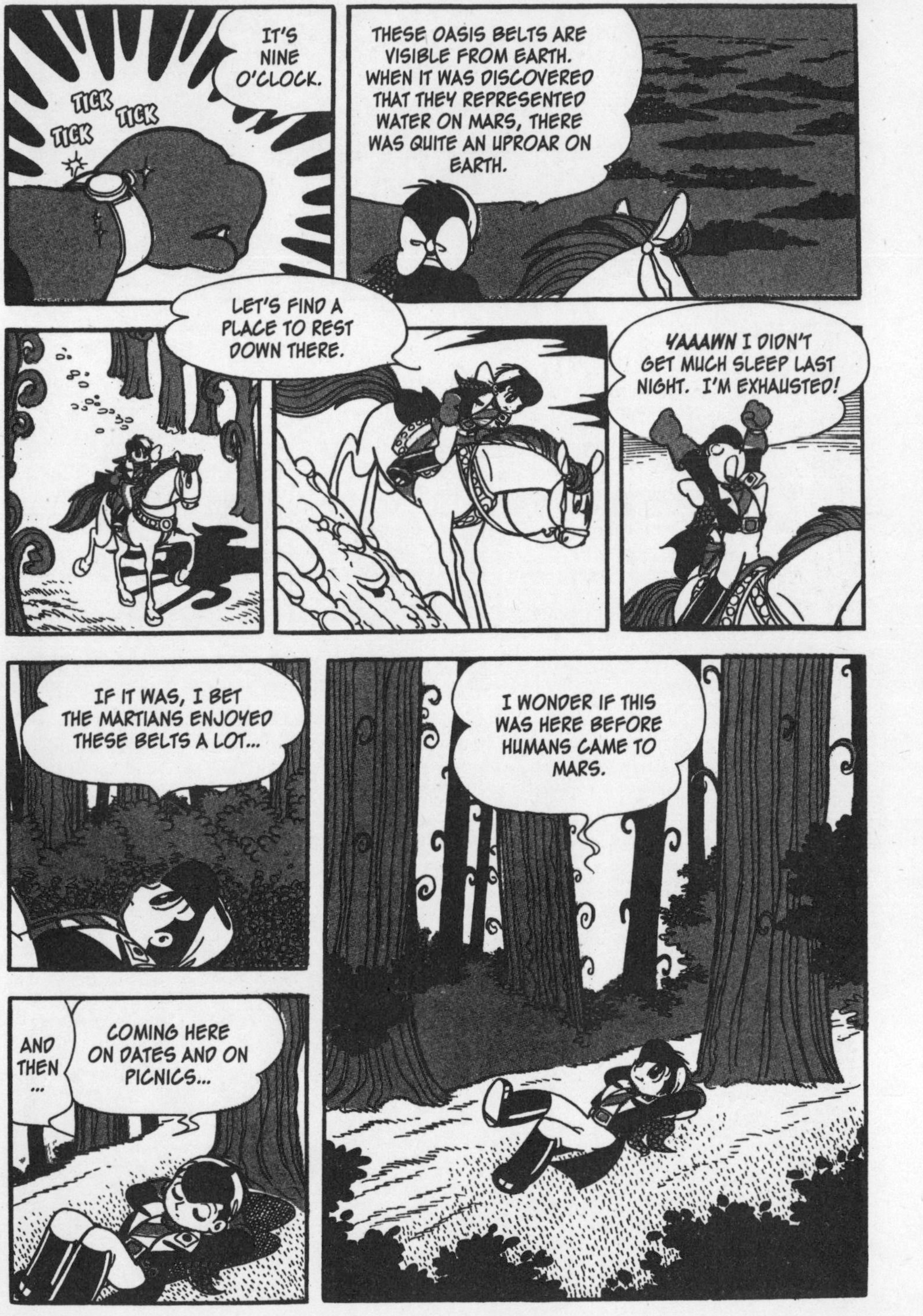
THESE OASIS BELTS ARE VISIBLE FROM EARTH. WHEN IT WAS DISCOVERED THAT THEY REPRESENTED WATER ON MARS, THERE WAS QUITE AN UPROAR ON EARTH.
IT'S NINE O'CLOCK.
TICK TICK
TICK
YAAAWN I DIDN'T GET MUCH SLEEP LAST NIGHT. I'M EXHAUSTED!
LET'S FIND A PLACE TO REST DOWN THERE.
I WONDER IF THIS WAS HERE BEFORE HUMANS CAME TO MARS.
IF IT WAS, I BET THE MARTIANS ENJOYED THESE BELTS A LOT...
COMING HERE ON DATES AND ON PICNICS...
AND THEN ...

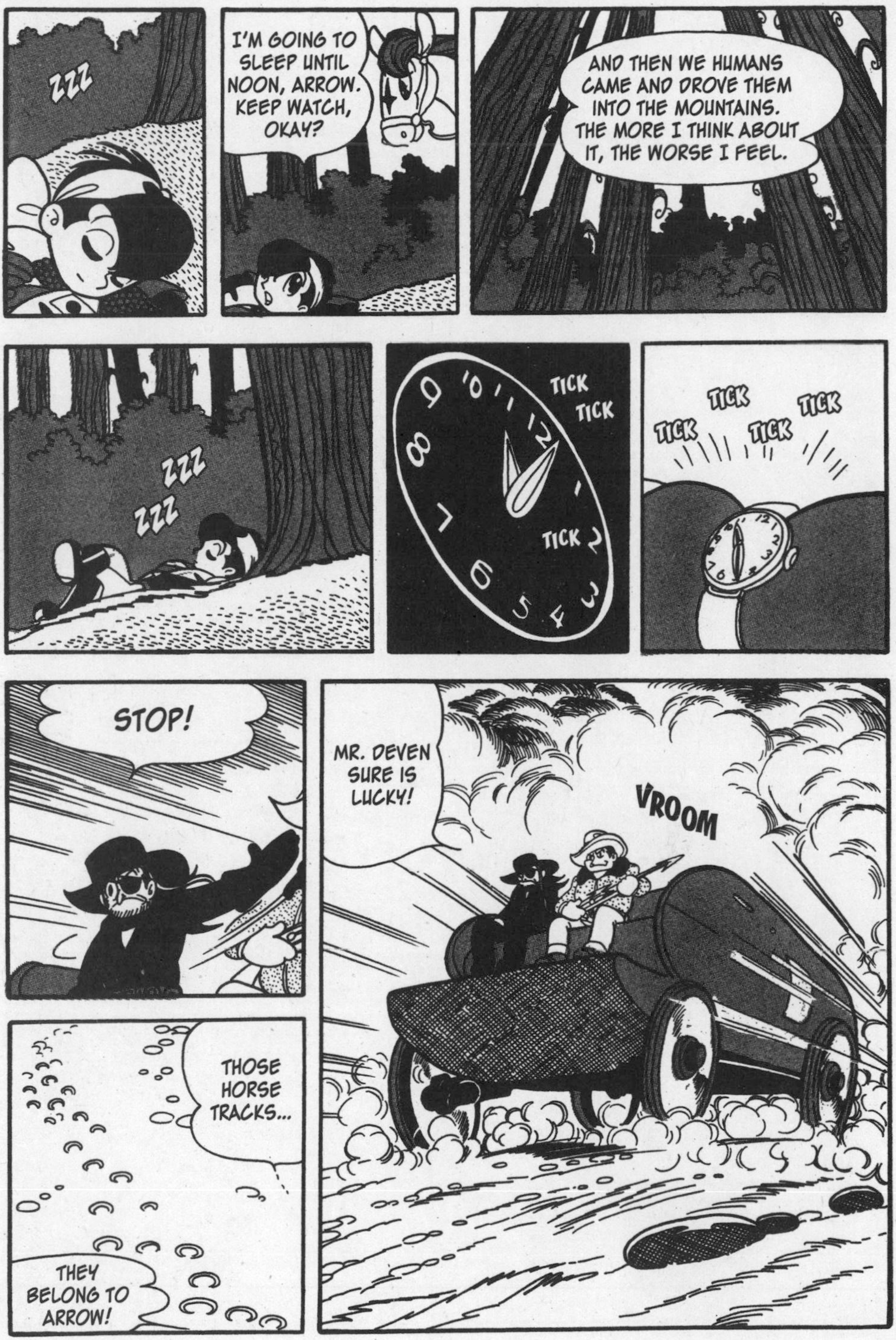
AND THEN WE HUMANS CAME AND DROVE THEM INTO THE MOUNTAINS. THE MORE I THINK ABOUT IT, THE WORSE I FEEL.
I'M GOING TO SLEEP UNTIL NOON, ARROW. KEEP WATCH, OKAY?
ZZZ
TICK
TICK
TICK
TICK
TICK
TICK
TICK
ZZZ
ZZZ
MR. DEVEN SURE IS LUCKY!
VROOM
STOP!
THOSE HORSE TRACKS...
THEY BELONG TO ARROW!

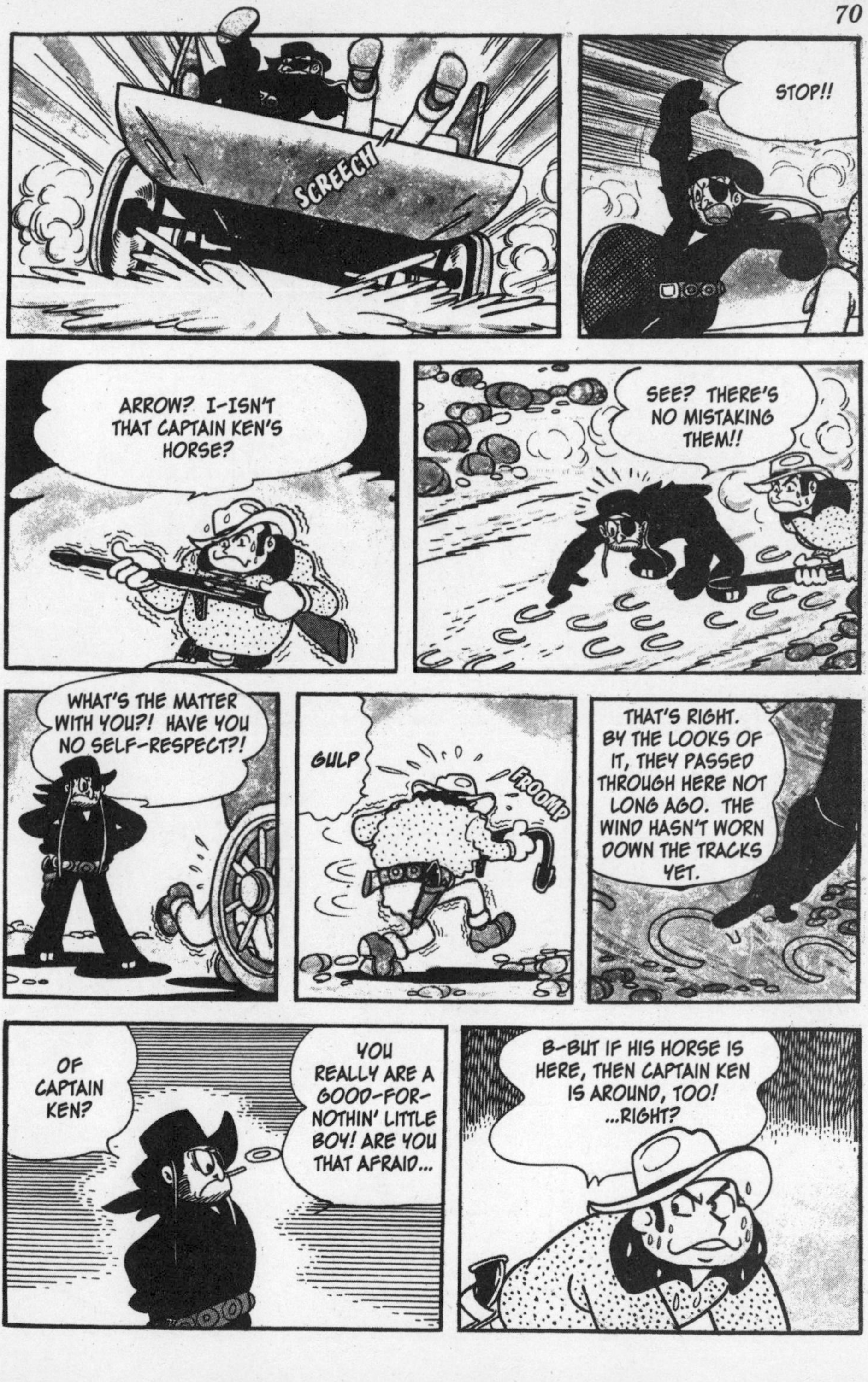
STOP!!
SCREECH
SEE? THERE'S NO MISTAKING THEM!!
ARROW? I-ISN'T THAT CAPTAIN KEN'S HORSE?
THAT'S RIGHT. BY THE LOOKS OF IT, THEY PASSED THROUGH HERE NOT LONG AGO. THE WIND HASN'T WORN DOWN THE TRACKS YET.
FROOMP
GULP
WHAT'S THE MATTER WITH YOU?! HAVE YOU NO SELF-RESPECT?!
B-BUT IF HIS HORSE IS HERE, THEN CAPTAIN KEN IS AROUND, TOO! ...RIGHT?
YOU REALLY ARE A GOOD-FOR-NOTHIN' LITTLE BOY! ARE YOU THAT AFRAID...
OF CAPTAIN KEN?

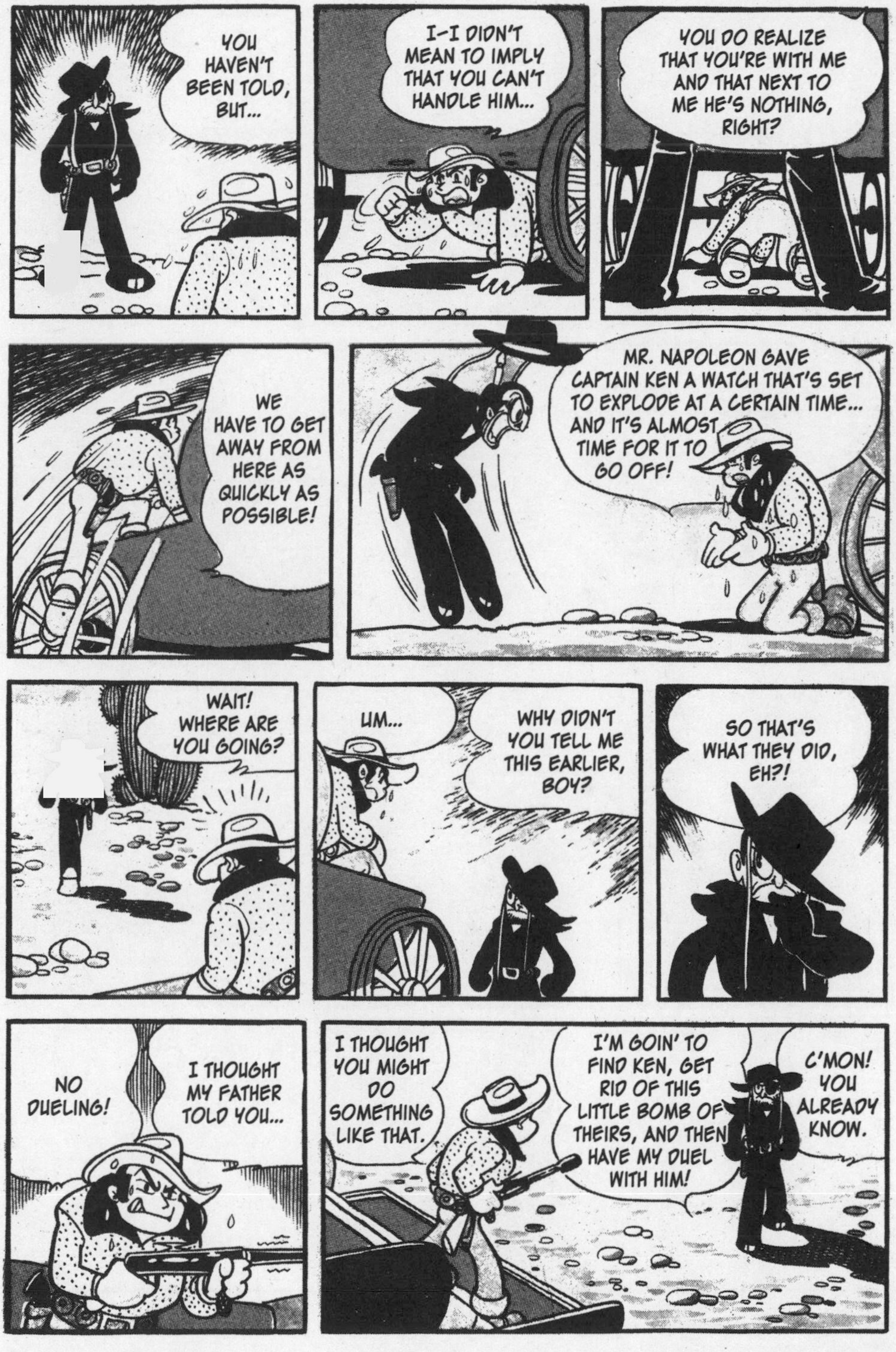
YOU DO REALIZE THAT YOU'RE WITH ME AND THAT NEXT TO ME HE'S NOTHING, RIGHT?
I-I DIDN'T MEAN TO IMPLY THAT YOU CAN'T HANDLE HIM...
YOU HAVEN'T BEEN TOLD, BUT...
MR. NAPOLEON GAVE CAPTAIN KEN A WATCH THAT'S SET TO EXPLODE AT A CERTAIN TIME... AND IT'S ALMOST TIME FOR IT TO GO OFF!
WE HAVE TO GET AWAY FROM HERE AS QUICKLY AS POSSIBLE!
SO THAT'S WHAT THEY DID, EH?!
WHY DIDN'T YOU TELL ME THIS EARLIER, BOY?
UM...
WAIT! WHERE ARE YOU GOING?
C'MON! YOU ALREADY KNOW.
I'M GOIN' TO FIND KEN, GET RID OF THIS LITTLE BOMB OF THEIRS, AND THEN HAVE MY DUEL WITH HIM!
I THOUGHT YOU MIGHT DO SOMETHING LIKE THAT.
I THOUGHT MY FATHER TOLD YOU...
NO DUELING!

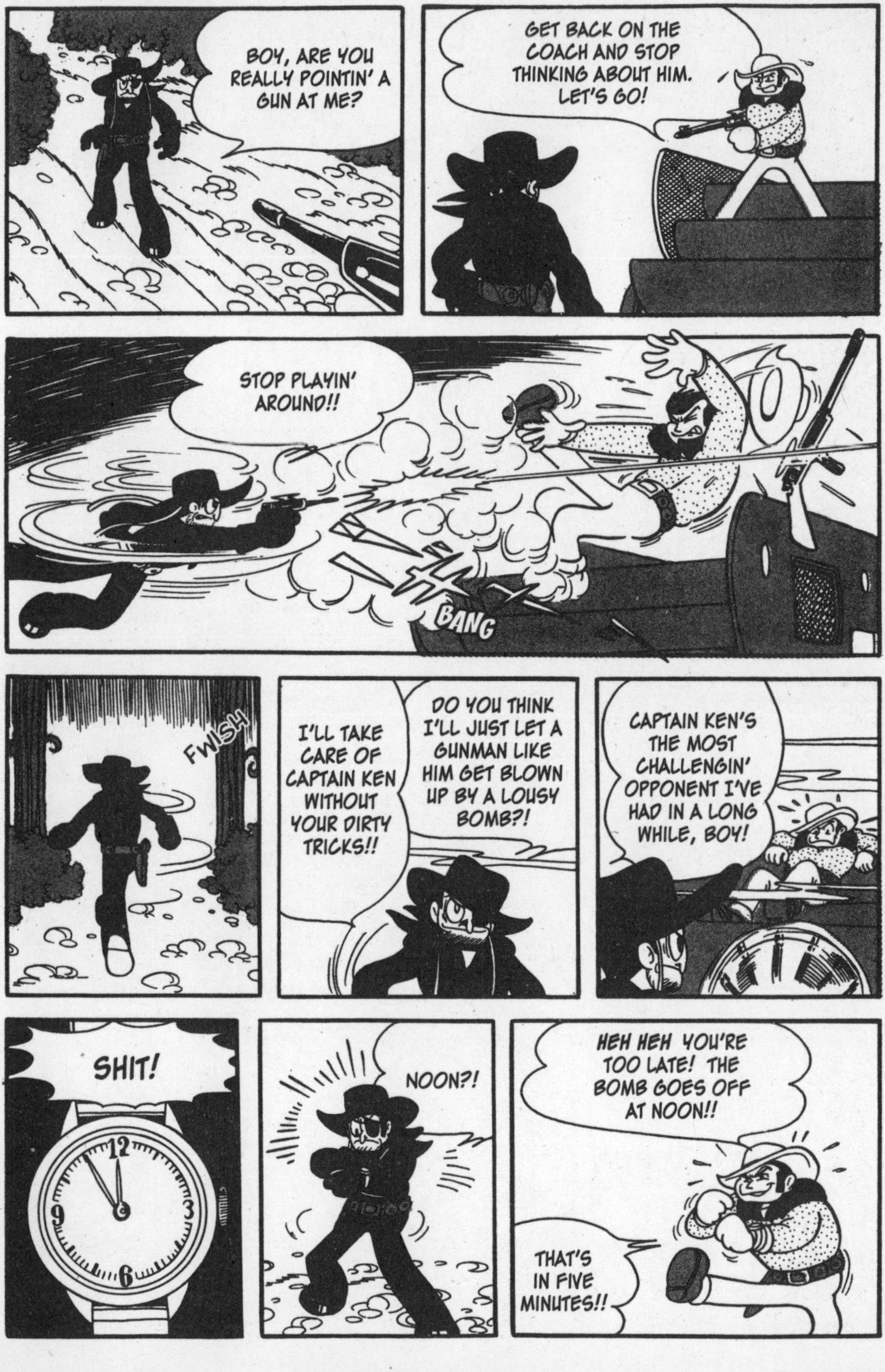
GET BACK ON THE COACH AND STOP THINKING ABOUT HIM. LET'S GO!
BOY, ARE YOU REALLY POINTIN' A GUN AT ME?
STOP PLAYIN' AROUND!!
BANG
CAPTAIN KEN'S THE MOST CHALLENGIN' OPPONENT I'VE HAD IN A LONG WHILE, BOY!
DO YOU THINK I'LL JUST LET A GUNMAN LIKE HIM GET BLOWN UP BY A LOUSY BOMB?!
I'LL TAKE CARE OF CAPTAIN KEN WITHOUT YOUR DIRTY TRICKS!!
FWISH
HEH HEH YOU'RE TOO LATE! THE BOMB GOES OFF AT NOON!!
THAT'S IN FIVE MINUTES!!
NOON?!
SHIT!

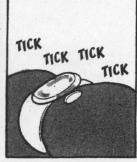

TICK
TICK TICK
TICK

ZZZ

SILENCE

SNAP

SILENCE

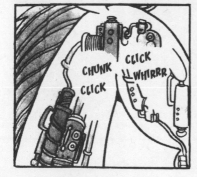

CHUNK
CLICK
CLICK
WHIRRR

HUMAN
MALE...

FOOT-
STEPS...

THE
SMELL
OF
GUN-
POWDER...

GUN-
MAN...

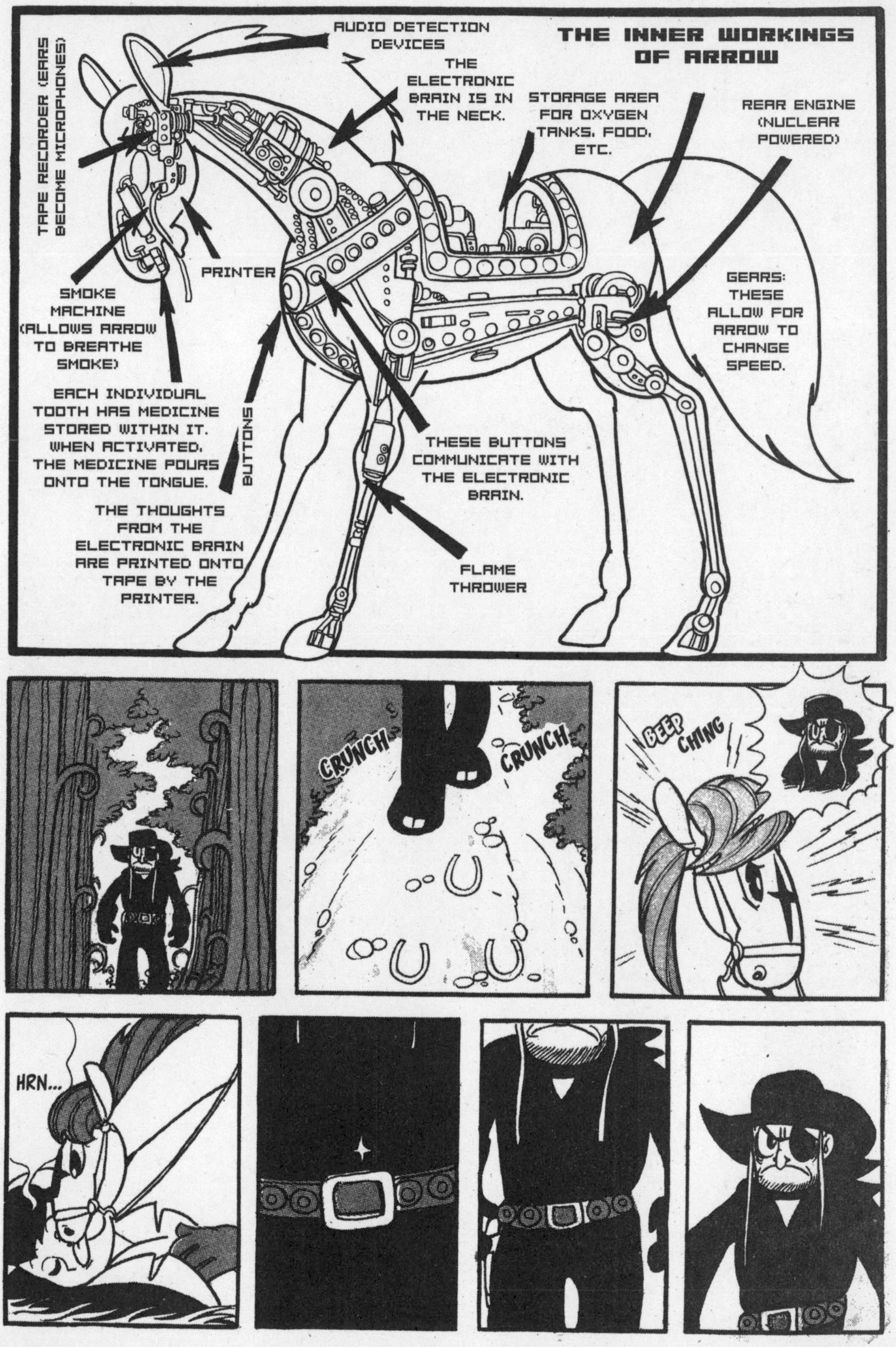
THE INNER WORKINGS OF ARROW
REAR ENGINE (NUCLEAR POWERED)
STORAGE AREA FOR OXYGEN TANKS, FOOD, ETC.
THE ELECTRONIC BRAIN IS IN THE NECK.
AUDIO DETECTION DEVICES
TAPE RECORDER (EARS BECOME MICROPHONES)
GEARS: THESE ALLOW FOR ARROW TO CHANGE SPEED.
PRINTER
SMOKE MACHINE (ALLOWS ARROW TO BREATHE SMOKE)
THESE BUTTONS COMMUNICATE WITH THE ELECTRONIC BRAIN.
BUTTONS
EACH INDIVIDUAL TOOTH HAS MEDICINE STORED WITHIN IT. WHEN ACTIVATED, THE MEDICINE POURS ONTO THE TONGUE.
FLAME THROWER
THE THOUGHTS FROM THE ELECTRONIC BRAIN ARE PRINTED ONTO TAPE BY THE PRINTER.
BEEP
CHING
CRUNCH
CRUNCH
HRN...

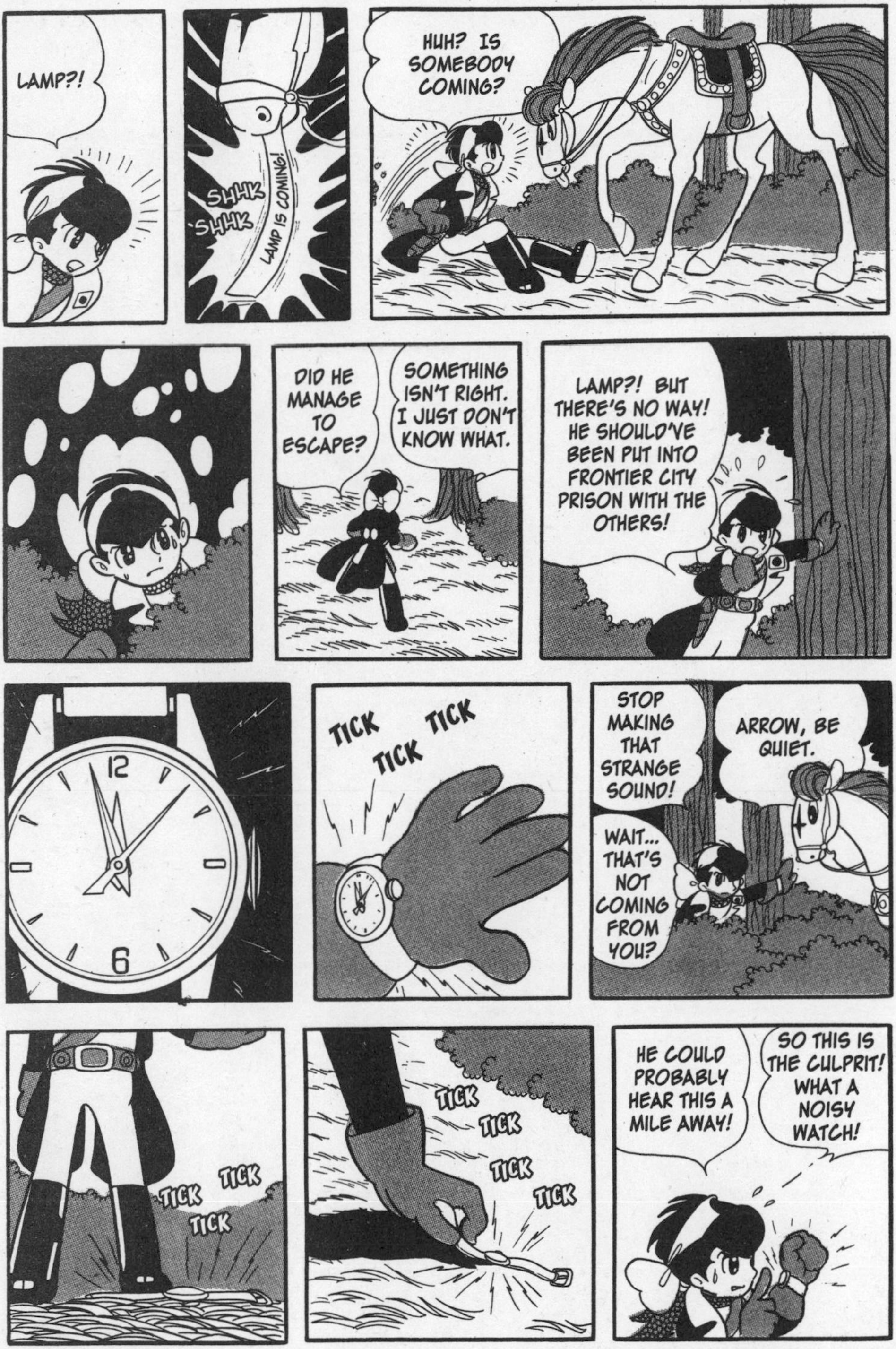
HUH? IS SOMEBODY COMING?
SHHK
SHHK
LAMP IS COMING!
LAMP?!
LAMP?! BUT THERE'S NO WAY! HE SHOULD'VE BEEN PUT INTO FRONTIER CITY PRISON WITH THE OTHERS!
SOMETHING ISN'T RIGHT. I JUST DON'T KNOW WHAT.
DID HE MANAGE TO ESCAPE?
ARROW, BE QUIET.
STOP MAKING THAT STRANGE SOUND!
WAIT... THAT'S NOT COMING FROM YOU?
TICK
TICK
TICK
12
6
SO THIS IS THE CULPRIT! WHAT A NOISY WATCH!
HE COULD PROBABLY HEAR THIS A MILE AWAY!
TICK
TICK
TICK
TICK
TICK
TICK
TICK

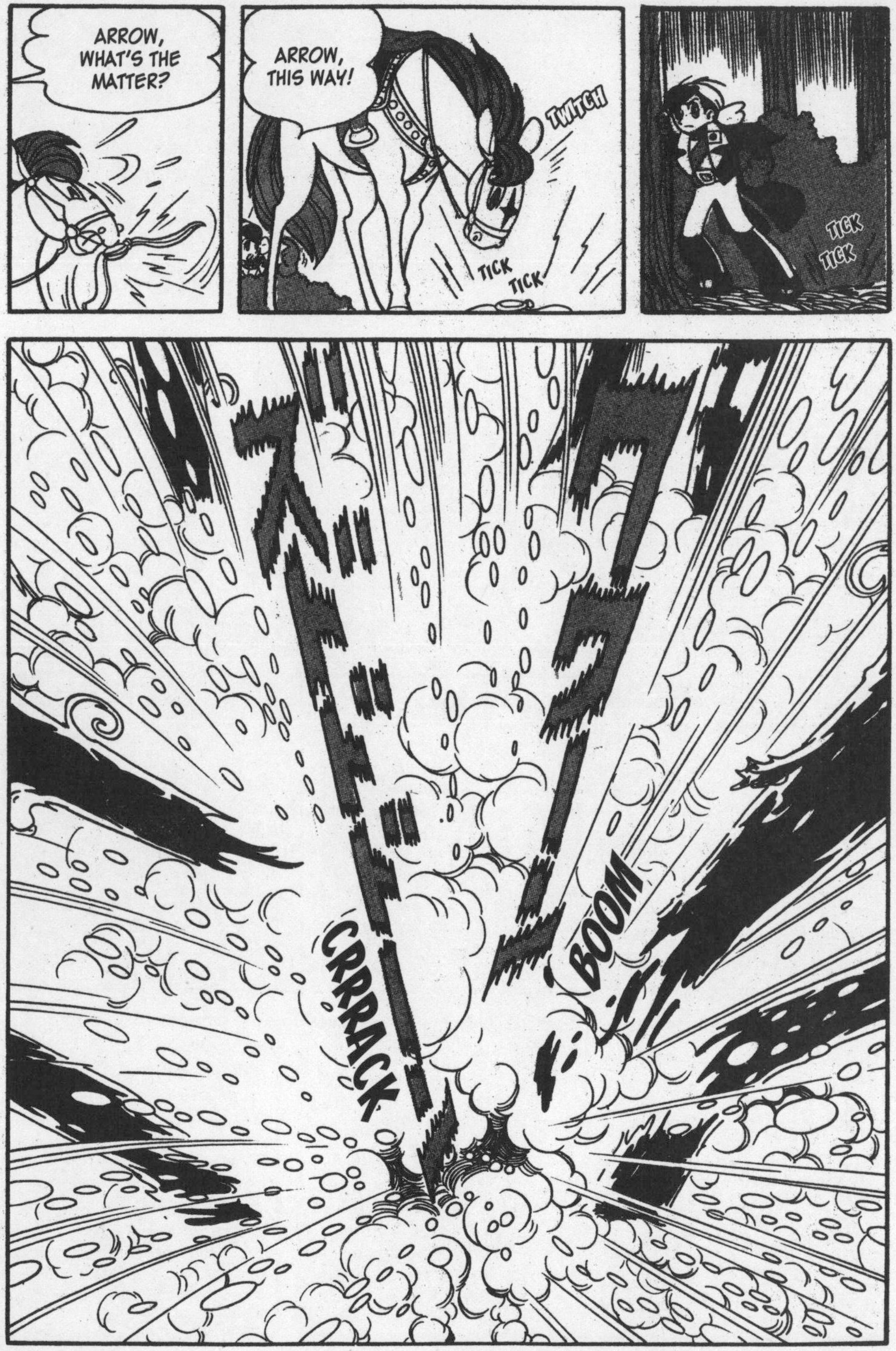
TICK
TICK
ARROW, THIS WAY!
TWITCH
TICK
TICK
ARROW, WHAT'S THE MATTER?
BOOM
CRRRACK

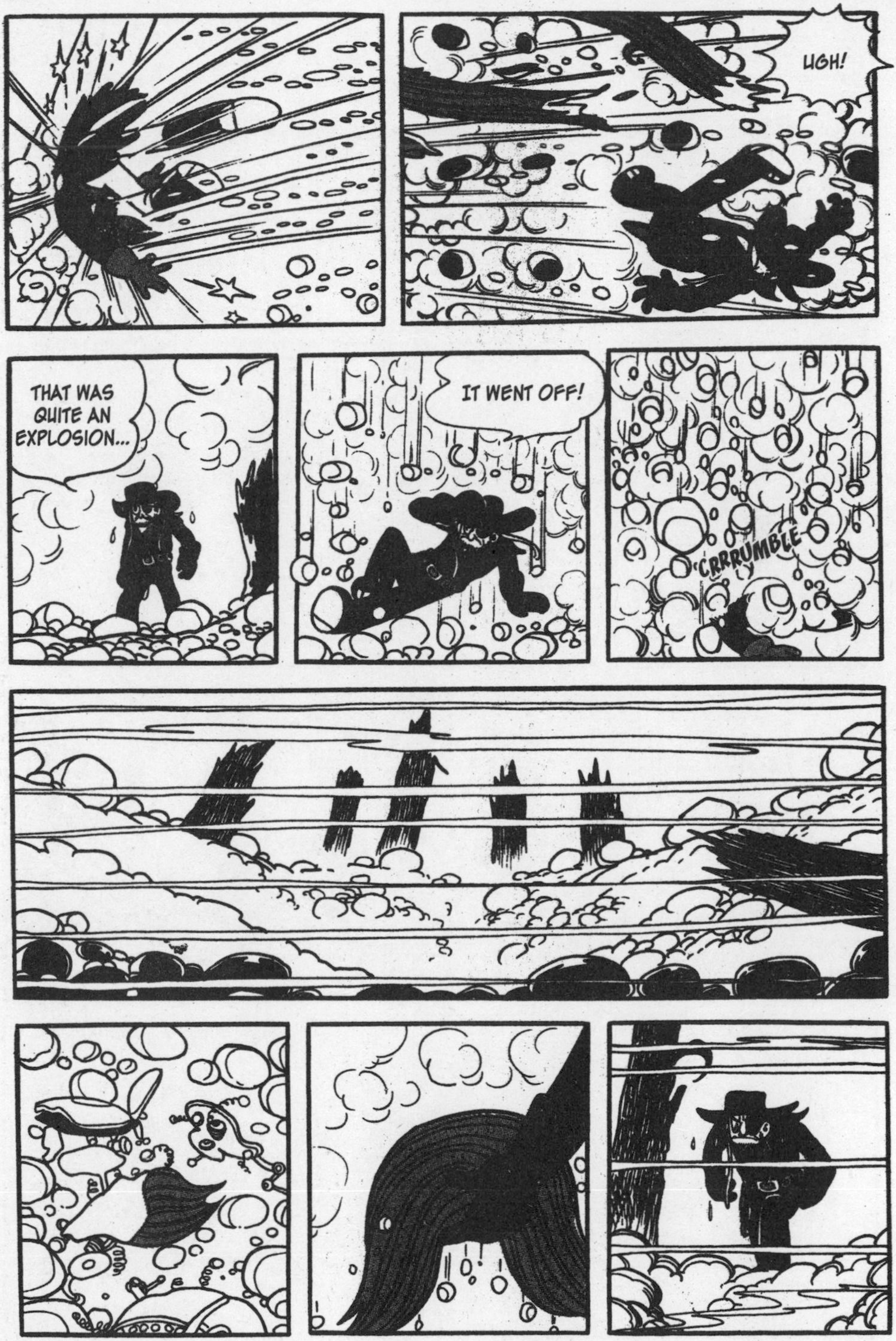
UGH!
CRRRUMBLE
IT WENT OFF!
THAT WAS QUITE AN EXPLOSION...

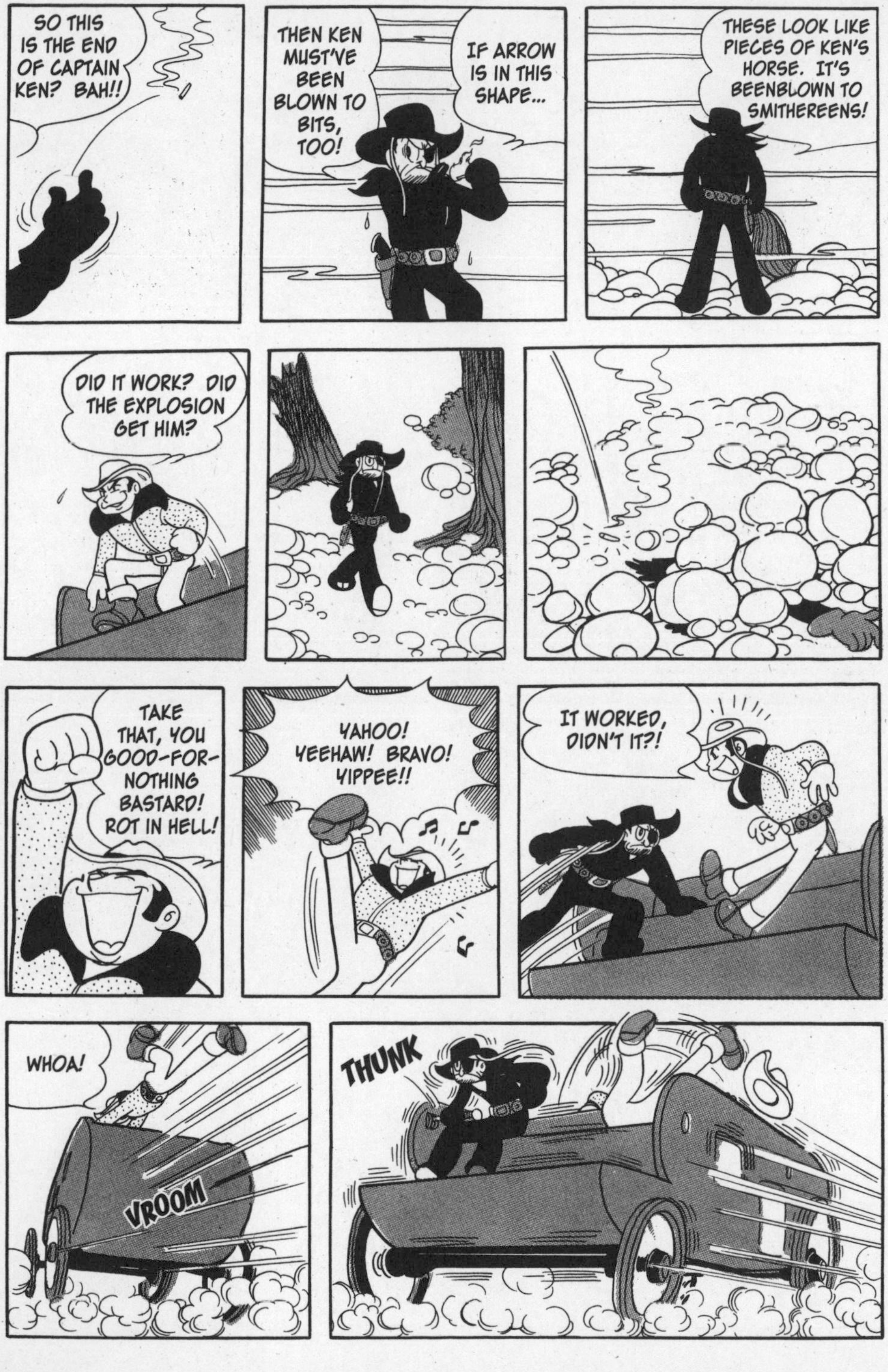
THESE LOOK LIKE PIECES OF KEN'S HORSE. IT'S BEENBLOWN TO SMITHEREENS!
IF ARROW IS IN THIS SHAPE...
THEN KEN MUST'VE BEEN BLOWN TO BITS, TOO!
SO THIS IS THE END OF CAPTAIN KEN? BAH!!
DID IT WORK? DID THE EXPLOSION GET HIM?
IT WORKED, DIDN'T IT?!
YAHOO! YEEHAW! BRAVO! YIPPEE!!
TAKE THAT, YOU GOOD-FOR-NOTHING BASTARD! ROT IN HELL!
THUNK
WHOA!
VROOM

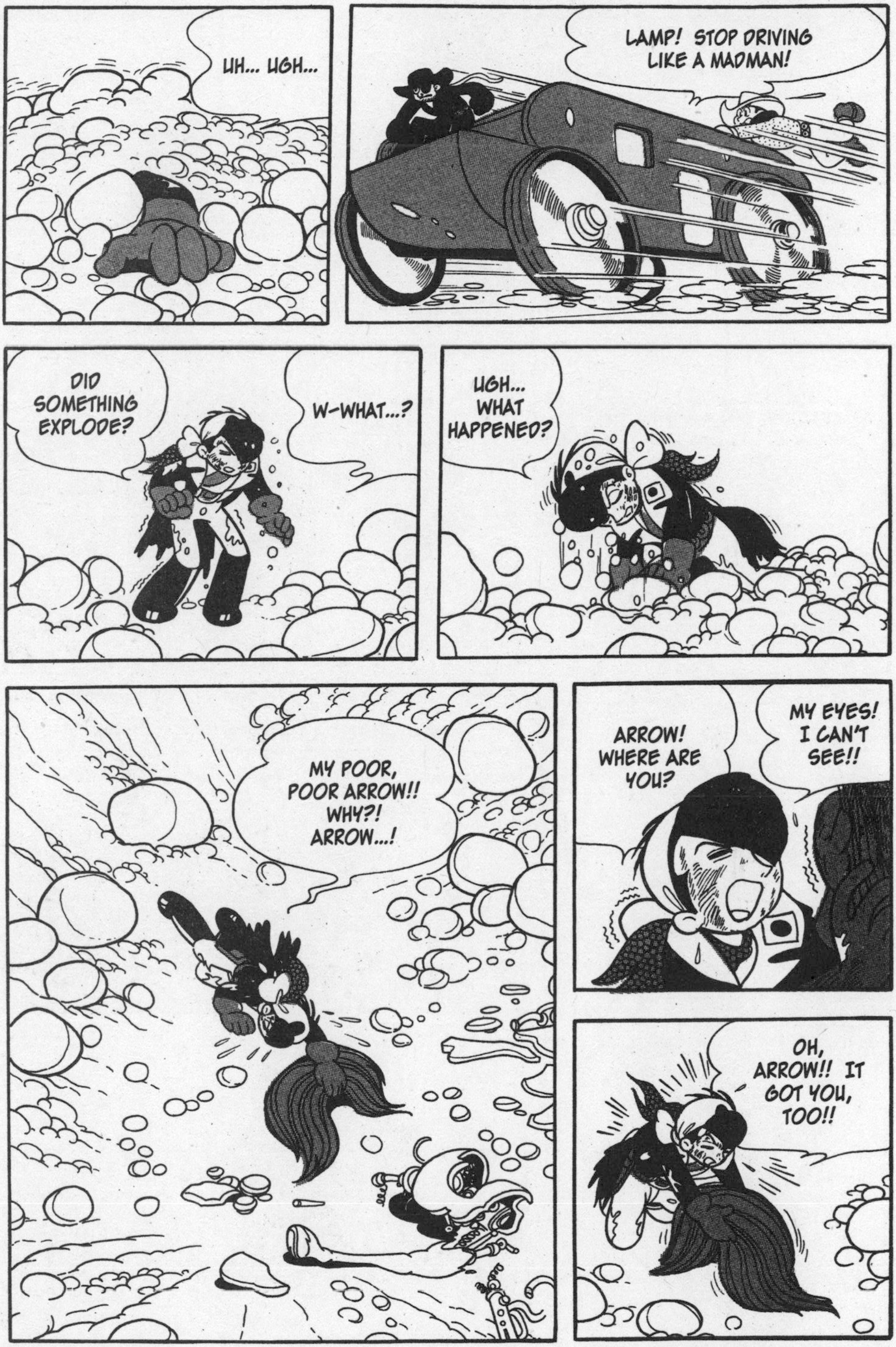
LAMP! STOP DRIVING LIKE A MADMAN!
UH... UGH...
UGH... WHAT HAPPENED?
W-WHAT...?
DID SOMETHING EXPLODE?
MY EYES! I CAN'T SEE!!
ARROW! WHERE ARE YOU?
OH, ARROW!! IT GOT YOU, TOO!!
MY POOR, POOR ARROW!! WHY?! ARROW...!

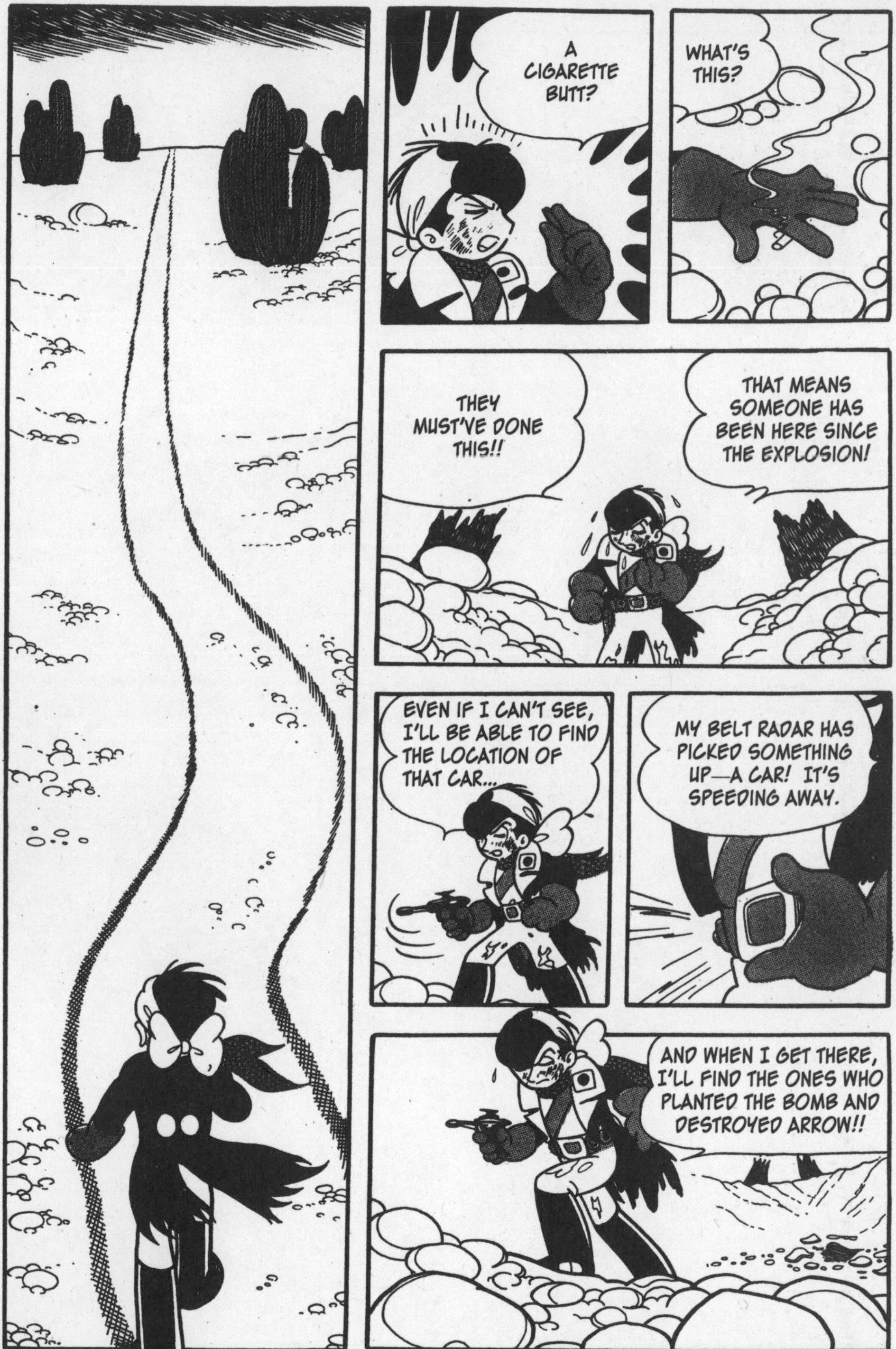
WHAT'S THIS?
A CIGARETTE BUTT?
THAT MEANS SOMEONE HAS BEEN HERE SINCE THE EXPLOSION!
THEY MUST'VE DONE THIS!!
MY BELT RADAR HAS PICKED SOMETHING UP—A CAR! IT'S SPEEDING AWAY.
EVEN IF I CAN'T SEE, I'LL BE ABLE TO FIND THE LOCATION OF THAT CAR...
AND WHEN I GET THERE, I'LL FIND THE ONES WHO PLANTED THE BOMB AND DESTROYED ARROW!!

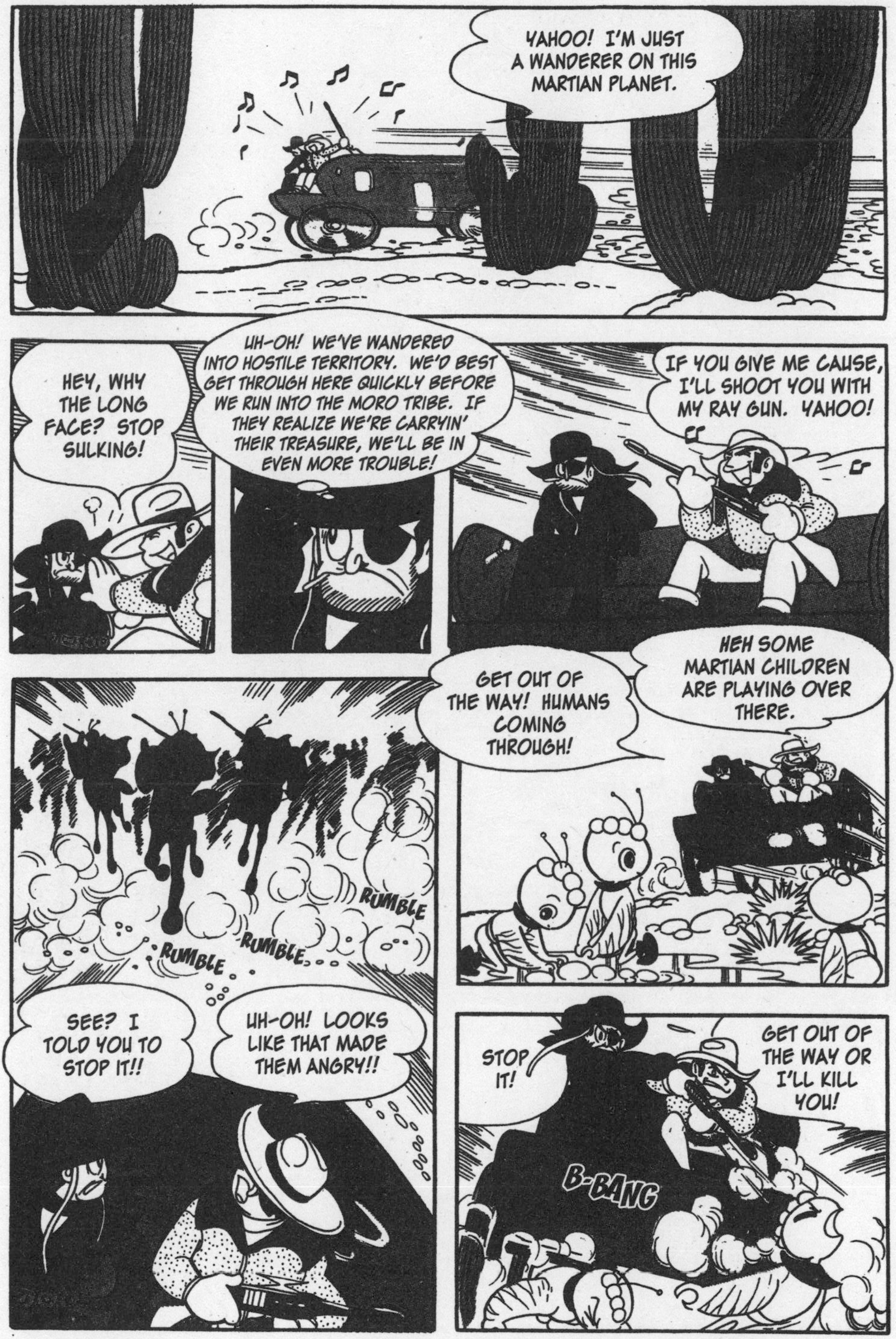
YAHOO! I'M JUST A WANDERER ON THIS MARTIAN PLANET.
IF YOU GIVE ME CAUSE, I'LL SHOOT YOU WITH MY RAY GUN. YAHOO!
UH-OH! WE'VE WANDERED INTO HOSTILE TERRITORY. WE'D BEST GET THROUGH HERE QUICKLY BEFORE WE RUN INTO THE MORO TRIBE. IF THEY REALIZE WE'RE CARRYIN' THEIR TREASURE, WE'LL BE IN EVEN MORE TROUBLE!
HEY, WHY THE LONG FACE? STOP SULKING!
HEH SOME MARTIAN CHILDREN ARE PLAYING OVER THERE.
GET OUT OF THE WAY! HUMANS COMING THROUGH!
GET OUT OF THE WAY OR I'LL KILL YOU!
STOP IT!
B-BANG
RUMBLE
RUMBLE...
RUMBLE
UH-OH! LOOKS LIKE THAT MADE THEM ANGRY!!
SEE? I TOLD YOU TO STOP IT!!

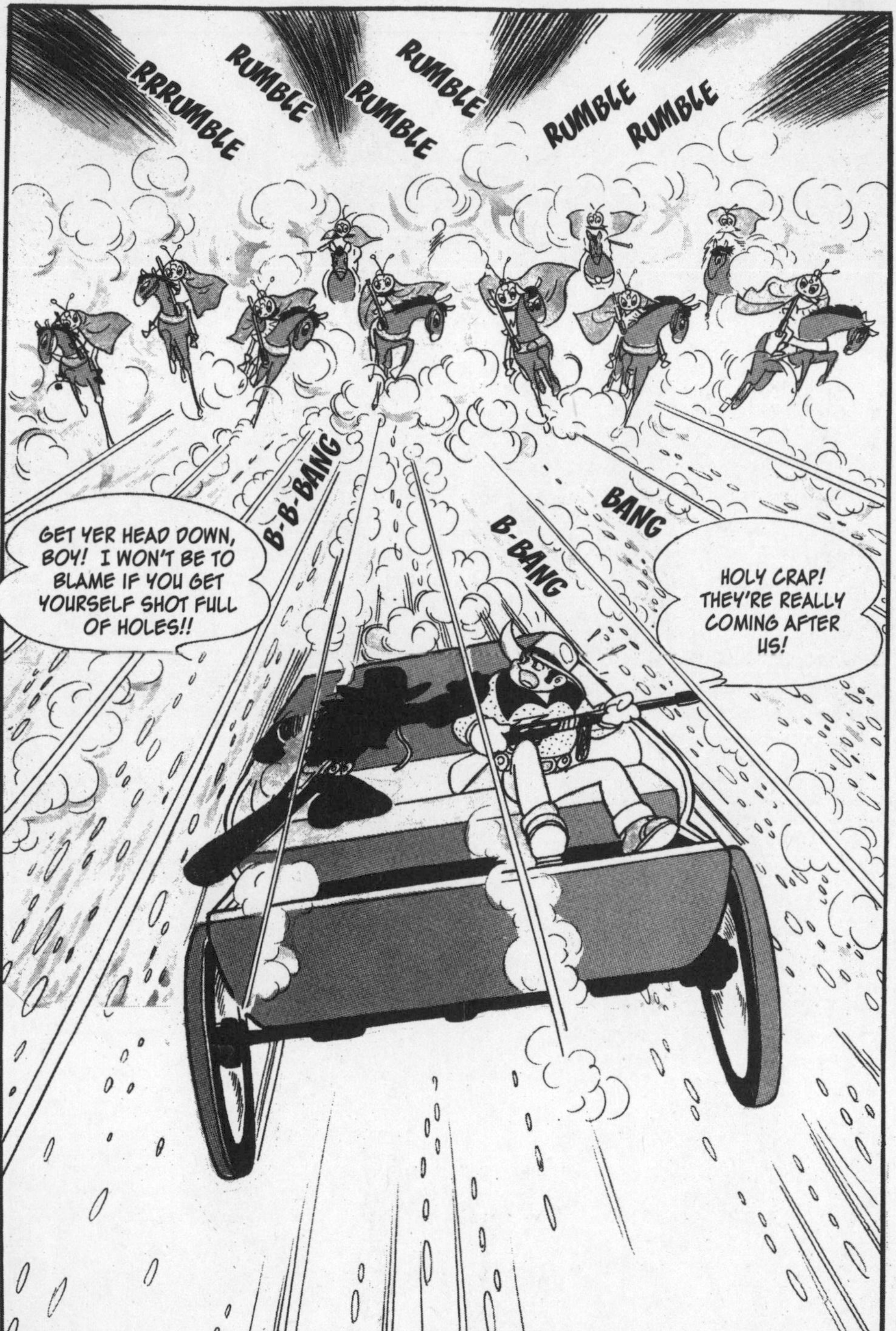
RUMBLE
RUMBLE
RUMBLE
RUMBLE
RUMBLE
RRRUMBLE
BANG
HOLY CRAP! THEY'RE REALLY COMING AFTER US!
B-BANG
B-B-BANG
GET YER HEAD DOWN, BOY! I WON'T BE TO BLAME IF YOU GET YOURSELF SHOT FULL OF HOLES!!

TAKE THIS!

BANG

DEWWW

B-B-B-BANG

BANG

RRRUMBLE

BANG

WHOA! I'M TIRED! SOMEBODY... SWITCH PLACES... WITH ME...

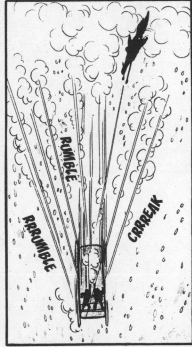

RUMBLE

RRRUMBLE

CRRREAK

CRACK

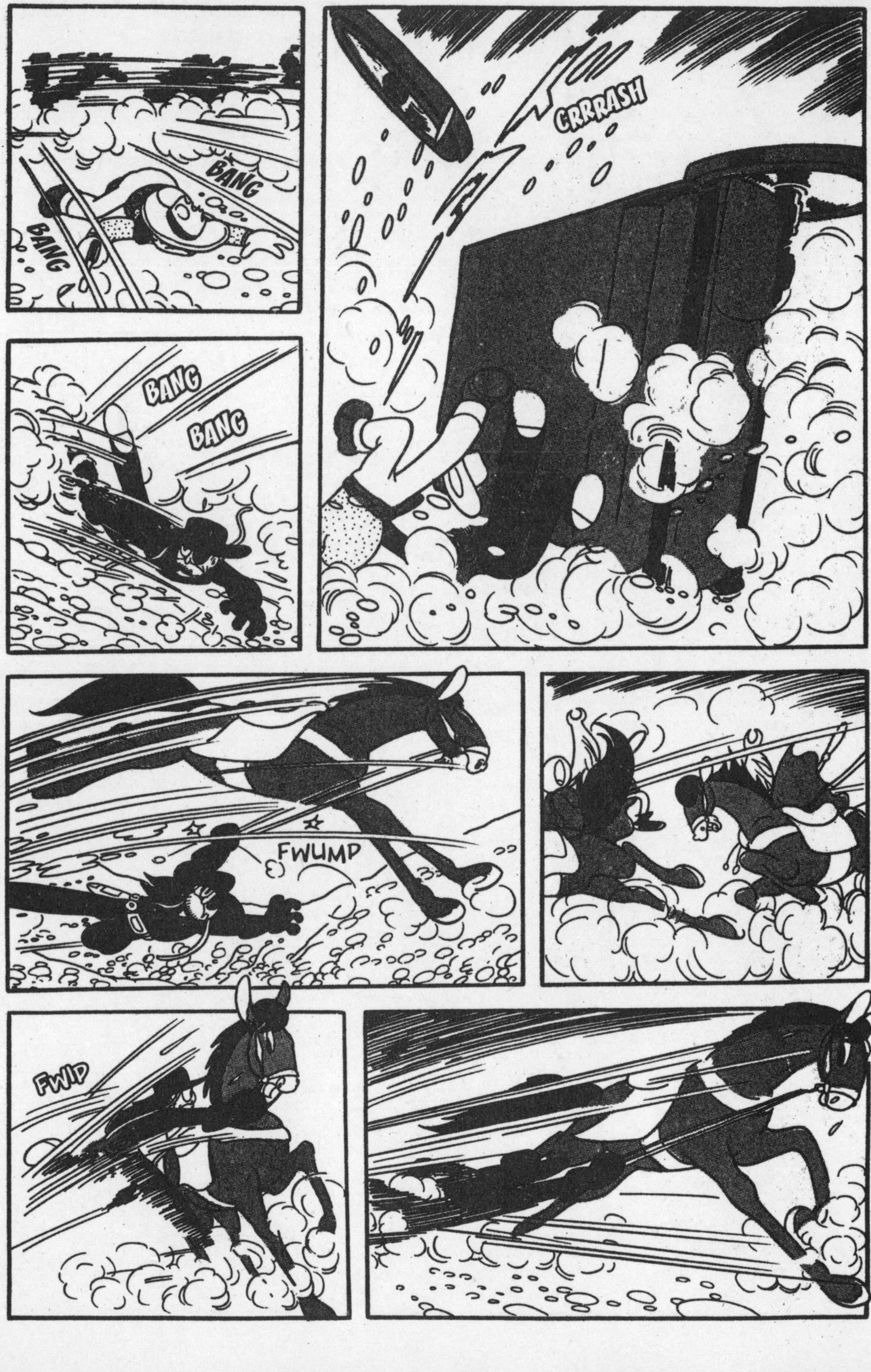
CRRRASH
BANG
BANG
BANG
BANG
FWUMP
FWIP

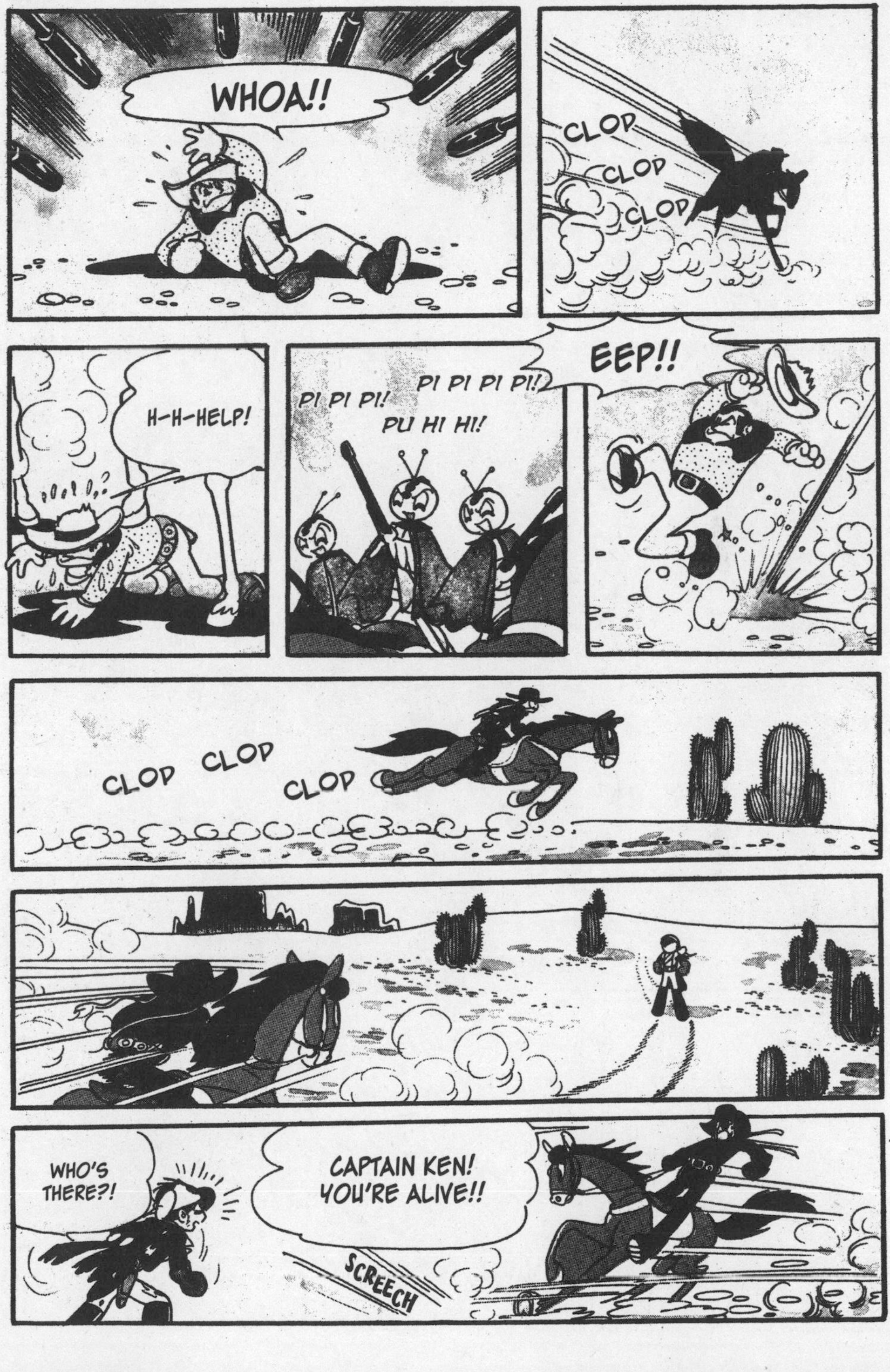
CLOP
CLOP
CLOP
WHOA!!
EEP!!
PI PI PI PI!
PI PI PI!
PU HI HI!
H-H-HELP!
CLOP
CLOP
CLOP
CAPTAIN KEN! YOU'RE ALIVE!!
SCREECH
WHO'S THERE?!

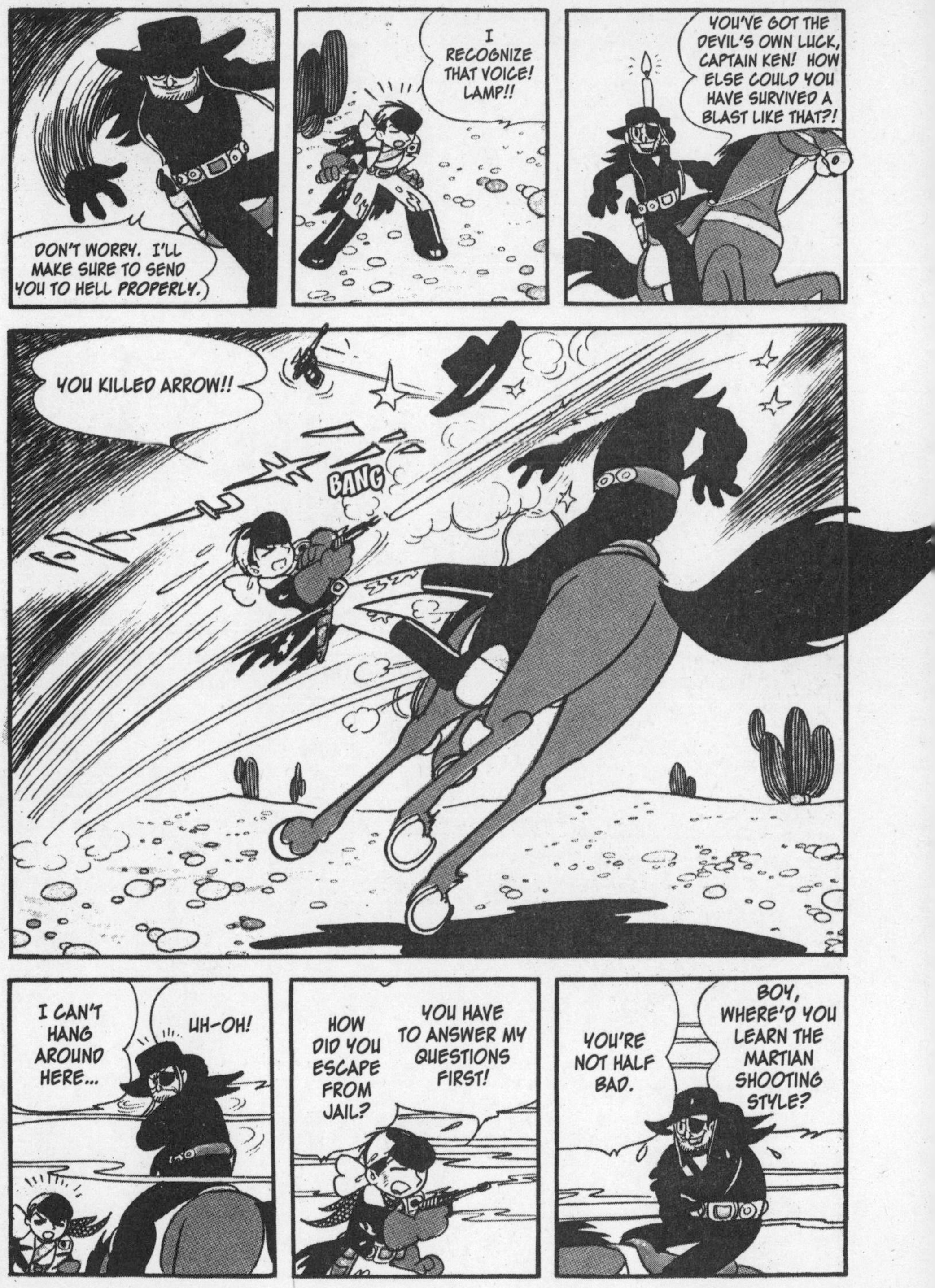
YOU'VE GOT THE DEVIL'S OWN LUCK, CAPTAIN KEN! HOW ELSE COULD YOU HAVE SURVIVED A BLAST LIKE THAT?!
I RECOGNIZE THAT VOICE! LAMP!!
DON'T WORRY. I'LL MAKE SURE TO SEND YOU TO HELL *PROPERLY*.
YOU KILLED ARROW!!
BANG
BOY, WHERE'D YOU LEARN THE MARTIAN SHOOTING STYLE?
YOU'RE NOT HALF BAD.
YOU HAVE TO ANSWER MY QUESTIONS FIRST!
HOW DID YOU ESCAPE FROM JAIL?
UH-OH!
I CAN'T HANG AROUND HERE...

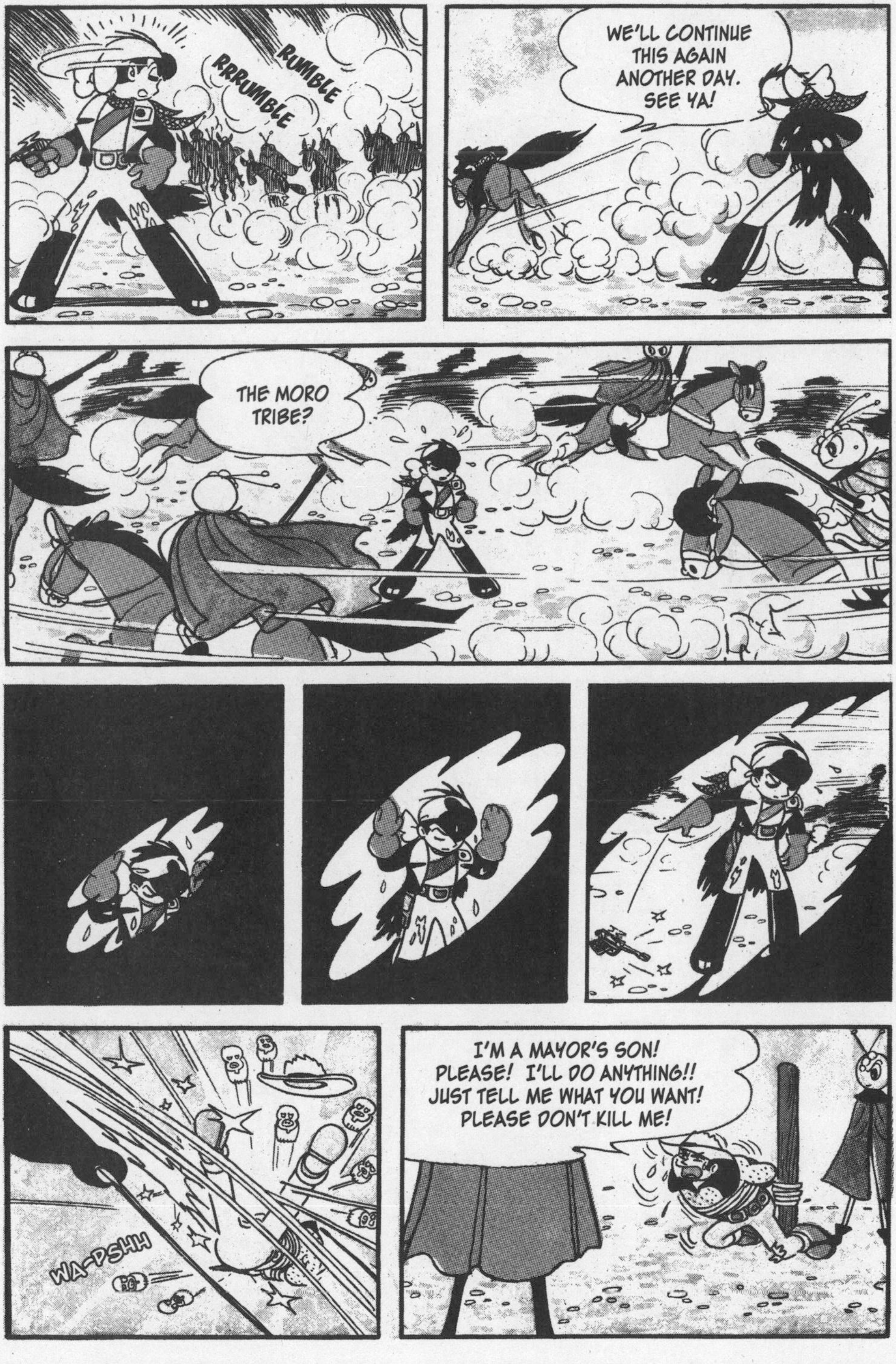
WE'LL CONTINUE THIS AGAIN ANOTHER DAY. SEE YA!
RUMBLE
RRRUMBLE
THE MORO TRIBE?
I'M A MAYOR'S SON! PLEASE! I'LL DO ANYTHING!! JUST TELL ME WHAT YOU WANT! PLEASE DON'T KILL ME!
WA-PSHH

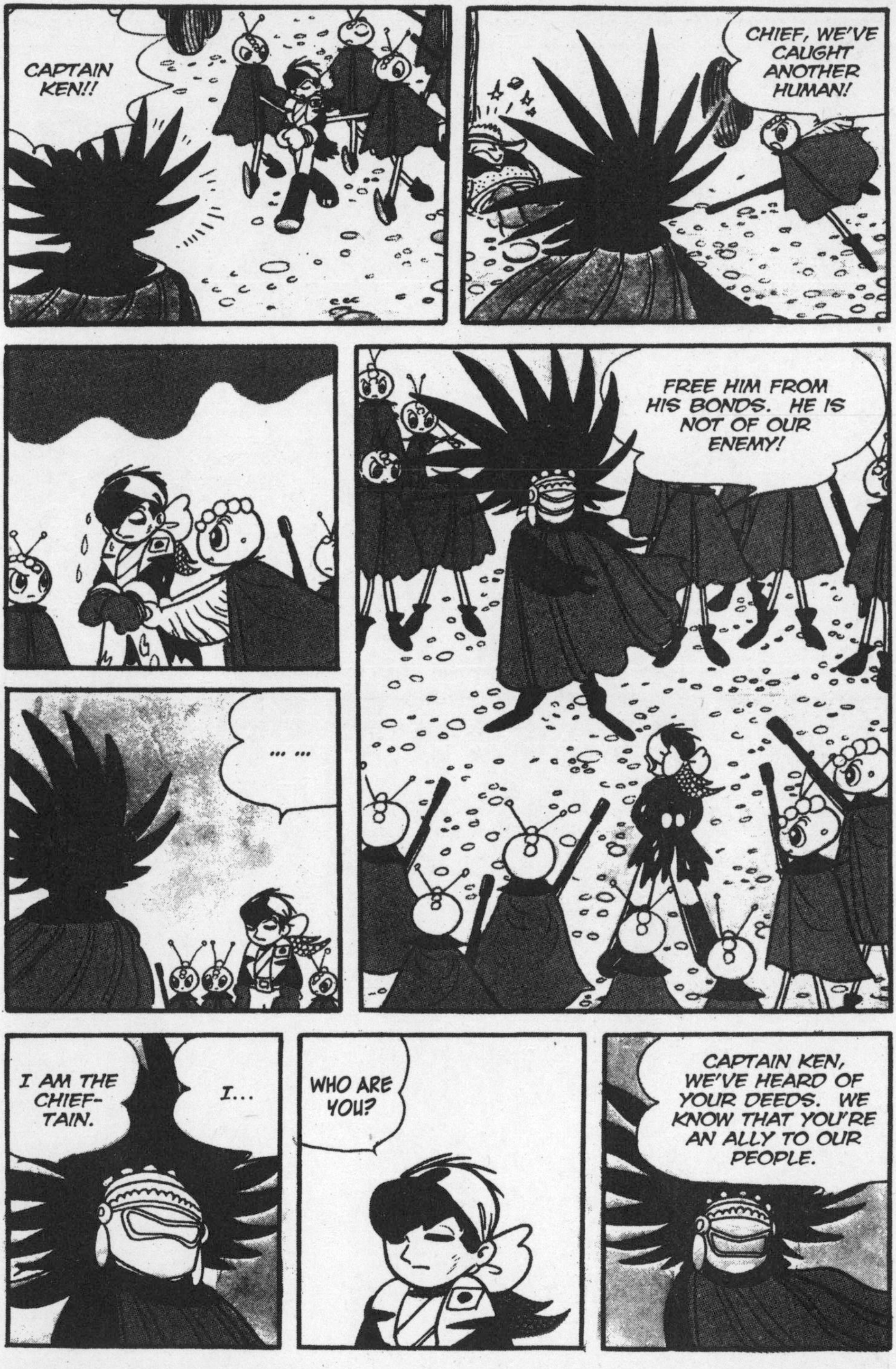
CHIEF, WE'VE CAUGHT ANOTHER HUMAN!
CAPTAIN KEN!!
FREE HIM FROM HIS BONDS. HE IS NOT OF OUR ENEMY!
... ...
CAPTAIN KEN, WE'VE HEARD OF YOUR DEEDS. WE KNOW THAT YOU'RE AN ALLY TO OUR PEOPLE.
WHO ARE YOU?
I...
I AM THE CHIEF-TAIN.

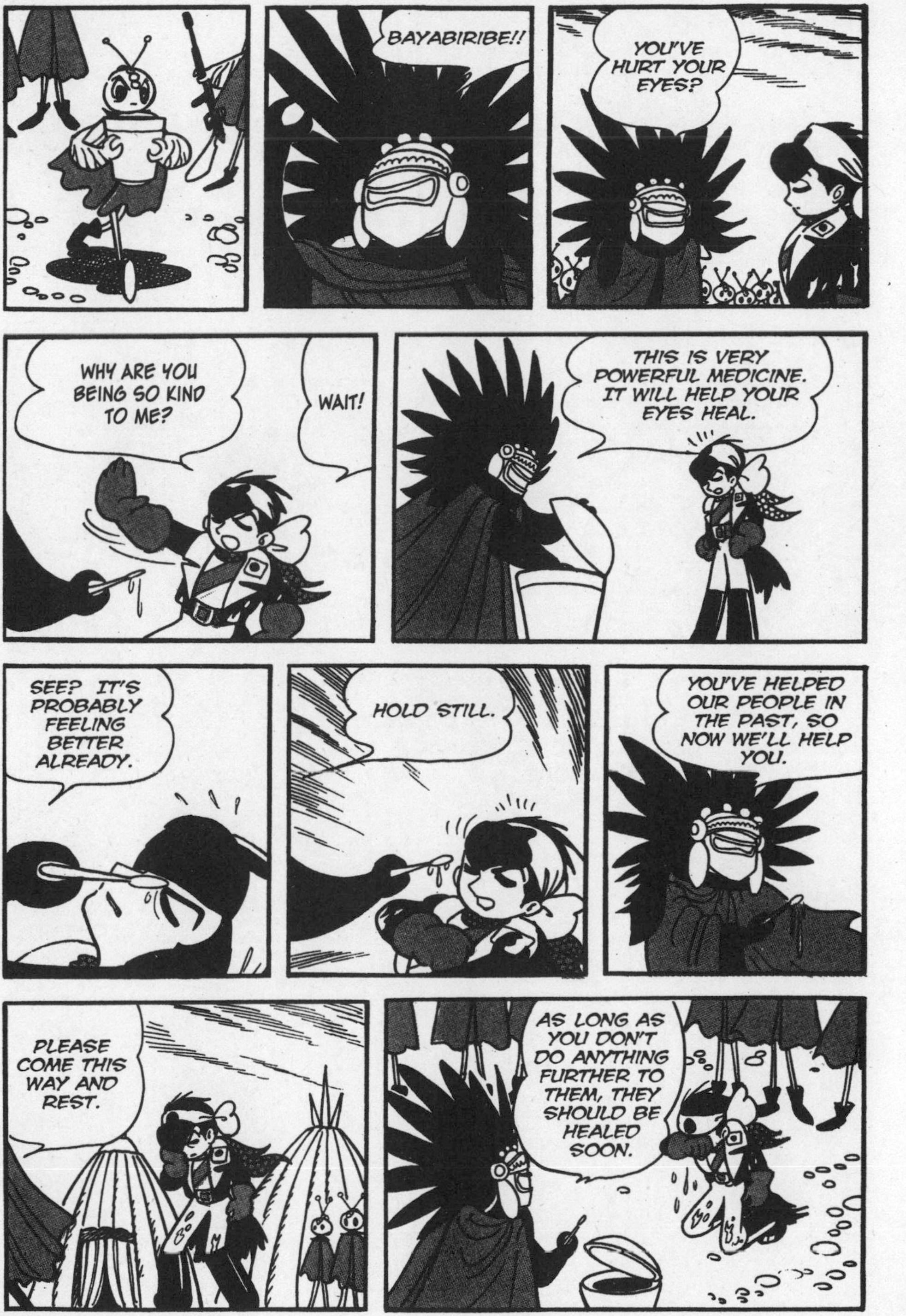
YOU'VE HURT YOUR EYES?
BAYABIRIBE!!
THIS IS VERY POWERFUL MEDICINE. IT WILL HELP YOUR EYES HEAL.
WAIT!
WHY ARE YOU BEING SO KIND TO ME?
YOU'VE HELPED OUR PEOPLE IN THE PAST, SO NOW WE'LL HELP YOU.
HOLD STILL.
SEE? IT'S PROBABLY FEELING BETTER ALREADY.
AS LONG AS YOU DON'T DO ANYTHING FURTHER TO THEM, THEY SHOULD BE HEALED SOON.
PLEASE COME THIS WAY AND REST.

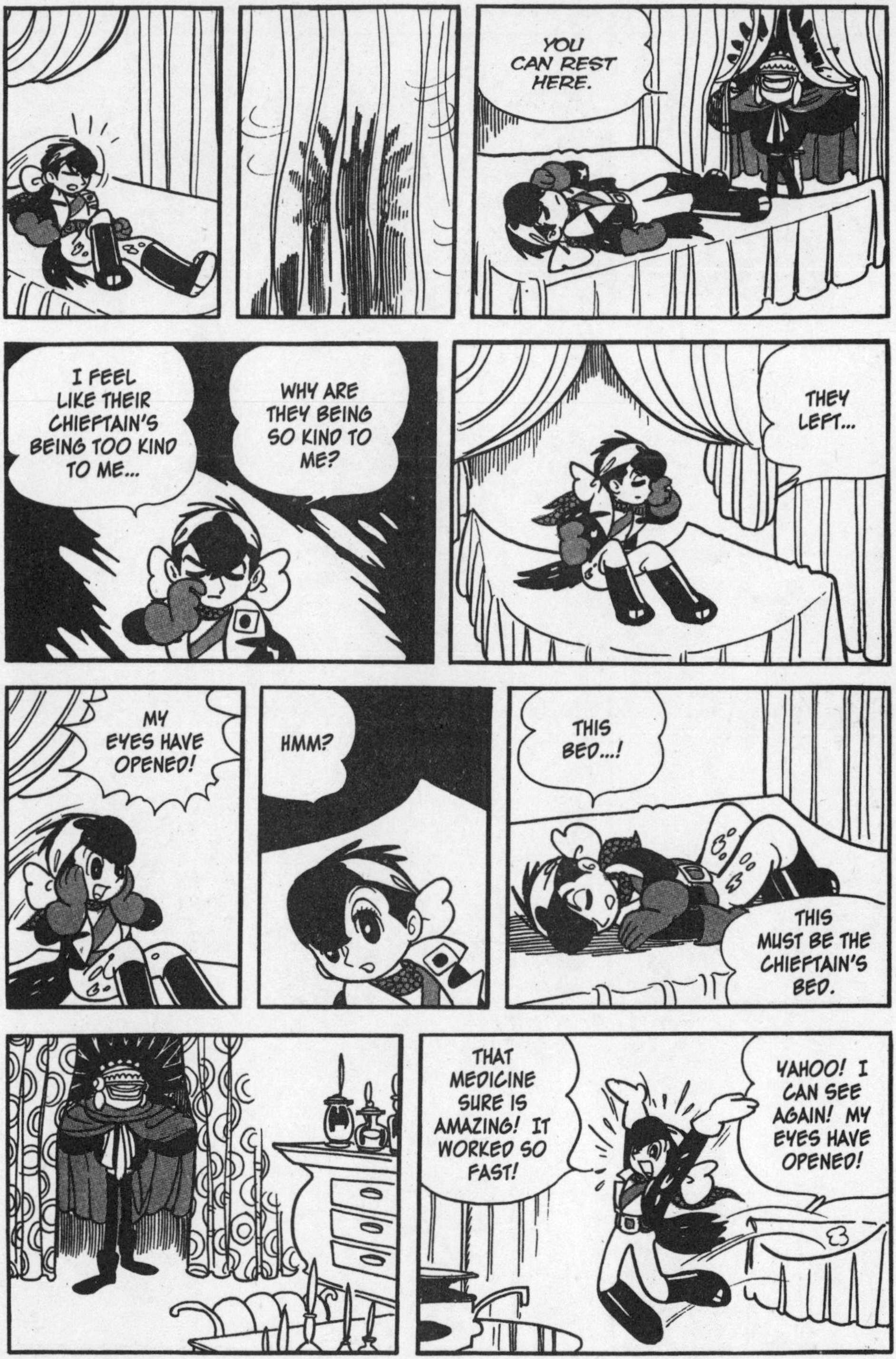
YOU CAN REST HERE.
THEY LEFT...
WHY ARE THEY BEING SO KIND TO ME?
I FEEL LIKE THEIR CHIEFTAIN'S BEING TOO KIND TO ME...
THIS BED...!
THIS MUST BE THE CHIEFTAIN'S BED.
HMM?
MY EYES HAVE OPENED!
YAHOO! I CAN SEE AGAIN! MY EYES HAVE OPENED!
THAT MEDICINE SURE IS AMAZING! IT WORKED SO FAST!

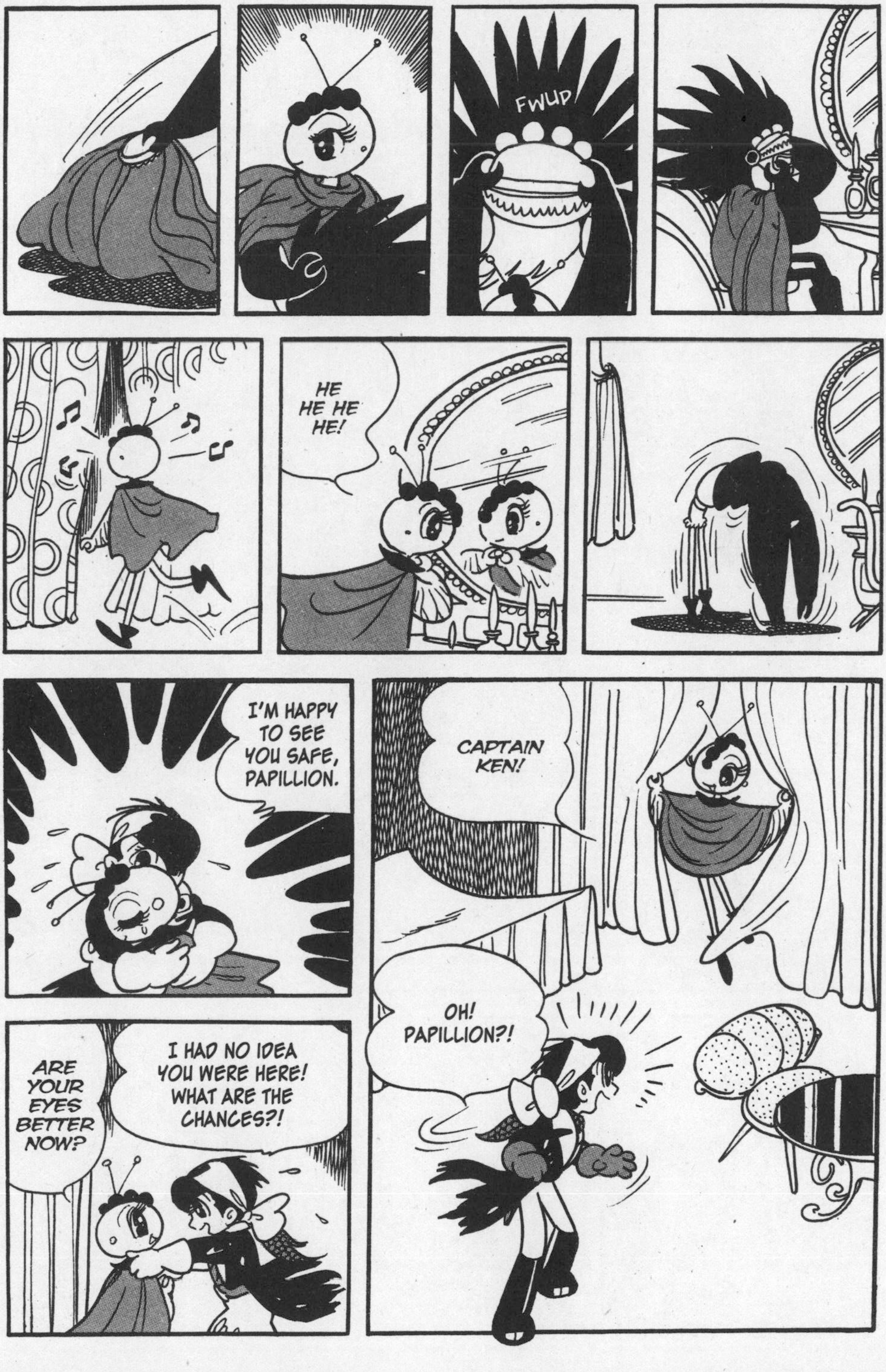
FWUP
HE HE HE HE!
CAPTAIN KEN!
OH! PAPILLION?!
I'M HAPPY TO SEE YOU SAFE, PAPILLION.
I HAD NO IDEA YOU WERE HERE! WHAT ARE THE CHANCES?!
ARE YOUR EYES BETTER NOW?

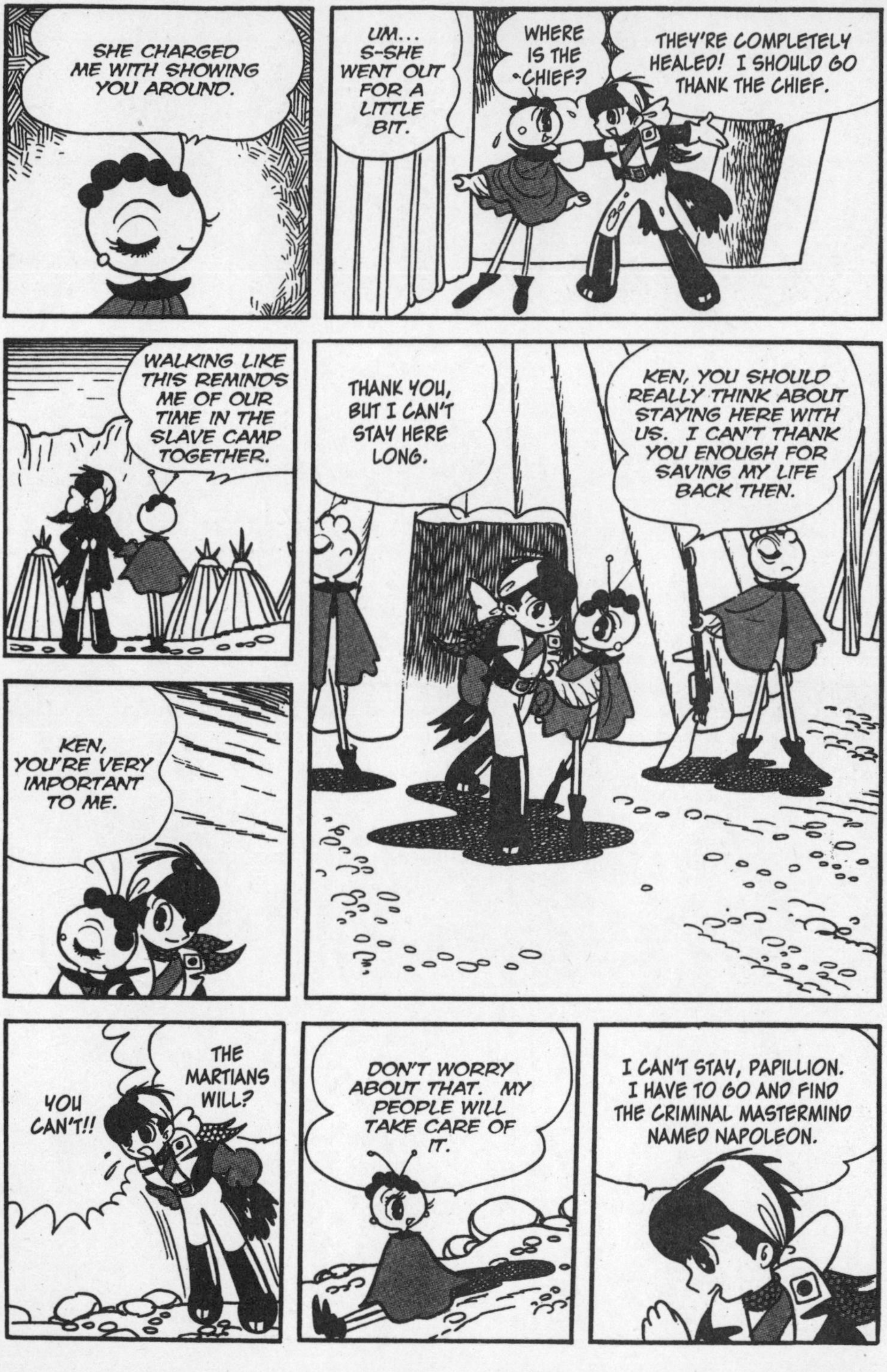
THEY'RE COMPLETELY HEALED! I SHOULD GO THANK THE CHIEF.
WHERE IS THE CHIEF?
UM... S-SHE WENT OUT FOR A LITTLE BIT.
SHE CHARGED ME WITH SHOWING YOU AROUND.
KEN, YOU SHOULD REALLY THINK ABOUT STAYING HERE WITH US. I CAN'T THANK YOU ENOUGH FOR SAVING MY LIFE BACK THEN.
THANK YOU, BUT I CAN'T STAY HERE LONG.
WALKING LIKE THIS REMINDS ME OF OUR TIME IN THE SLAVE CAMP TOGETHER.
KEN, YOU'RE VERY IMPORTANT TO ME.
I CAN'T STAY, PAPILLION. I HAVE TO GO AND FIND THE CRIMINAL MASTERMIND NAMED NAPOLEON.
DON'T WORRY ABOUT THAT. MY PEOPLE WILL TAKE CARE OF IT.
THE MARTIANS WILL?
YOU CAN'T!!

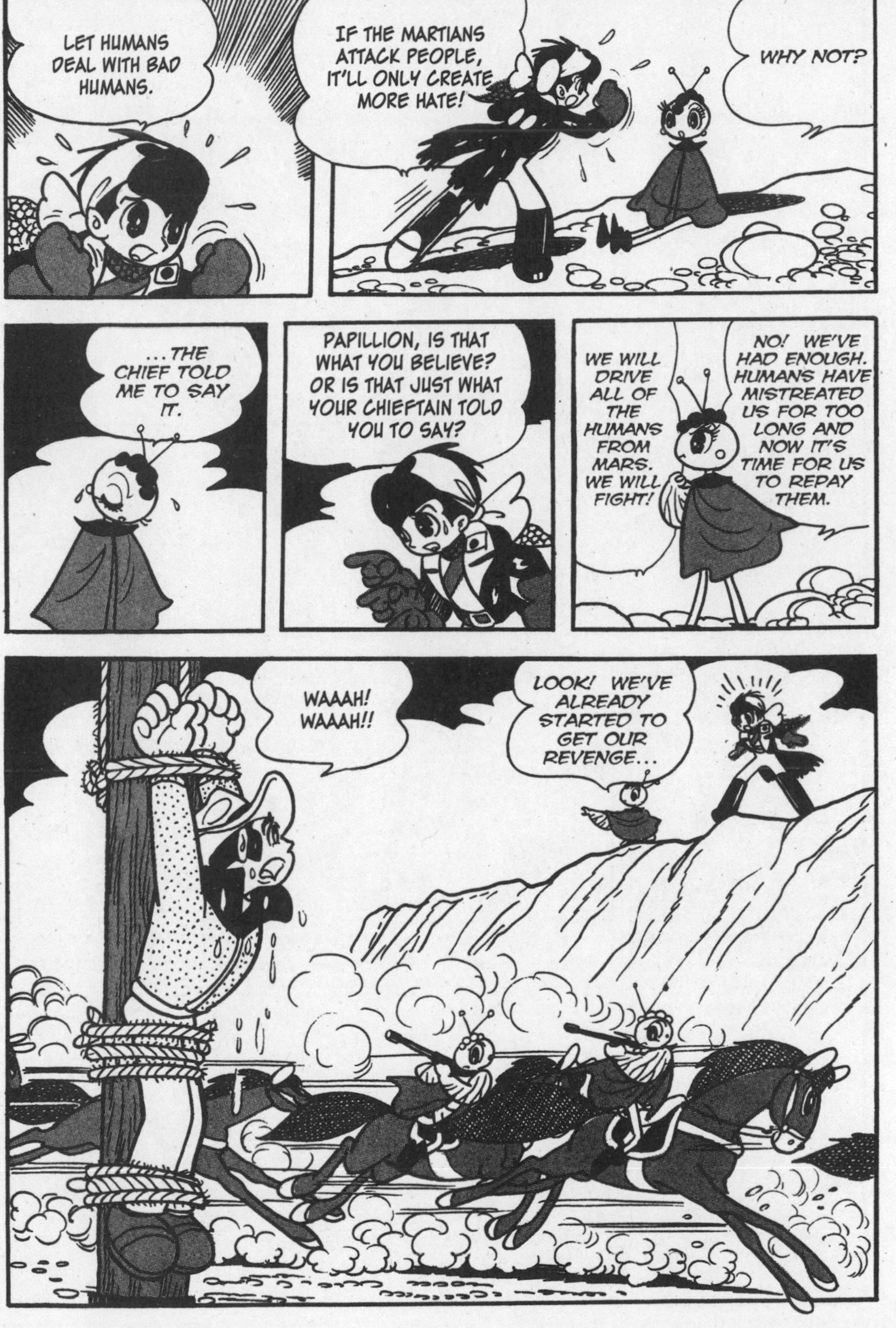
WHY NOT?
IF THE MARTIANS ATTACK PEOPLE, IT'LL ONLY CREATE MORE HATE!
LET HUMANS DEAL WITH BAD HUMANS.
NO! WE'VE HAD ENOUGH. HUMANS HAVE MISTREATED US FOR TOO LONG AND NOW IT'S TIME FOR US TO REPAY THEM.
WE WILL DRIVE ALL OF THE HUMANS FROM MARS. WE WILL FIGHT!
PAPILLION, IS THAT WHAT YOU BELIEVE? OR IS THAT JUST WHAT YOUR CHIEFTAIN TOLD YOU TO SAY?
...THE CHIEF TOLD ME TO SAY IT.
LOOK! WE'VE ALREADY STARTED TO GET OUR REVENGE...
WAAAH! WAAAH!!

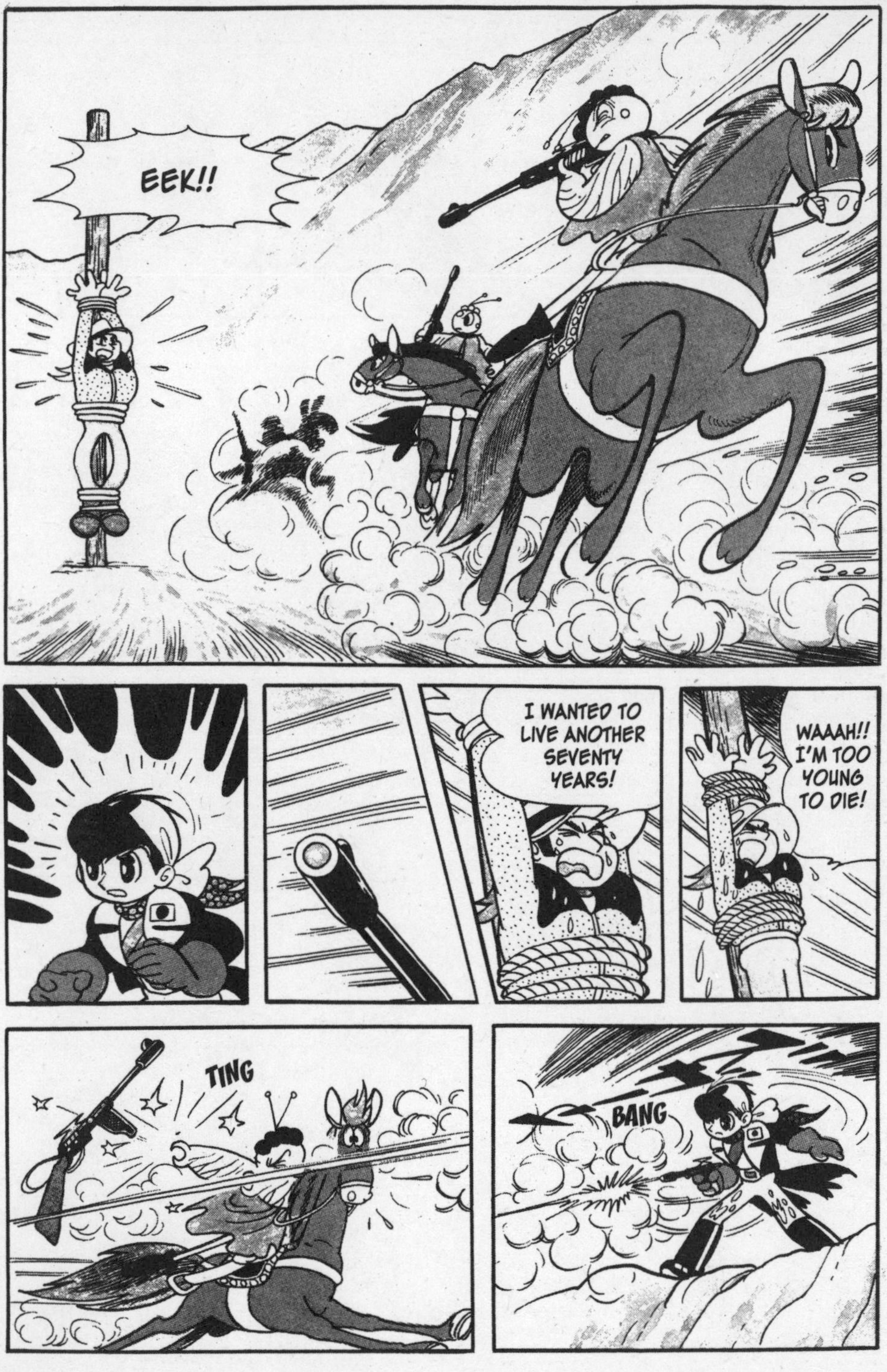
EEK!!
WAAAH!! I'M TOO YOUNG TO DIE!
I WANTED TO LIVE ANOTHER SEVENTY YEARS!
BANG
TING

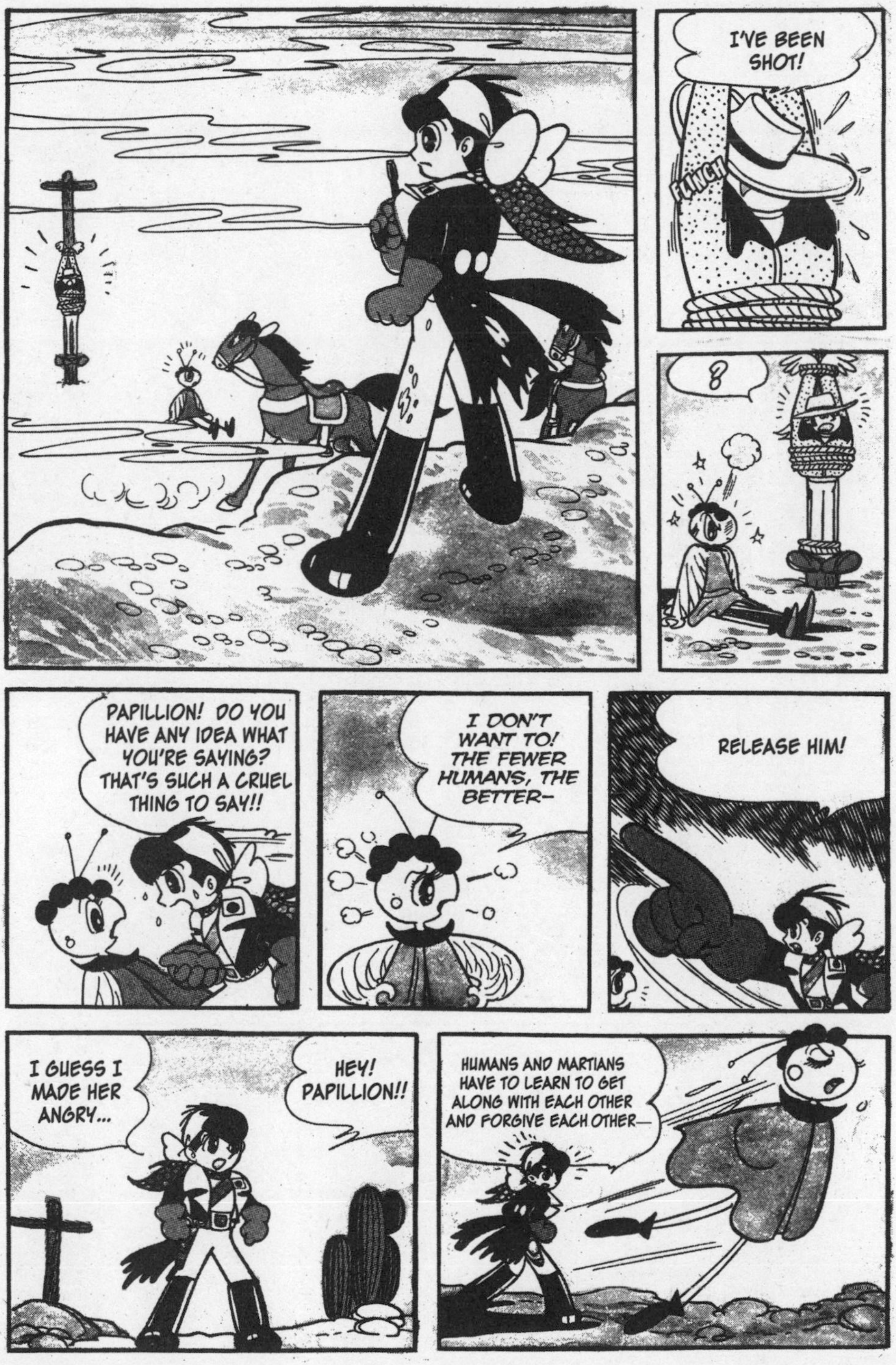
I'VE BEEN SHOT!
FLINCH
?
RELEASE HIM!
I DON'T WANT TO! THE FEWER HUMANS, THE BETTER—
PAPILLION! DO YOU HAVE ANY IDEA WHAT YOU'RE SAYING? THAT'S SUCH A CRUEL THING TO SAY!!
HUMANS AND MARTIANS HAVE TO LEARN TO GET ALONG WITH EACH OTHER AND FORGIVE EACH OTHER—
HEY! PAPILLION!!
I GUESS I MADE HER ANGRY...

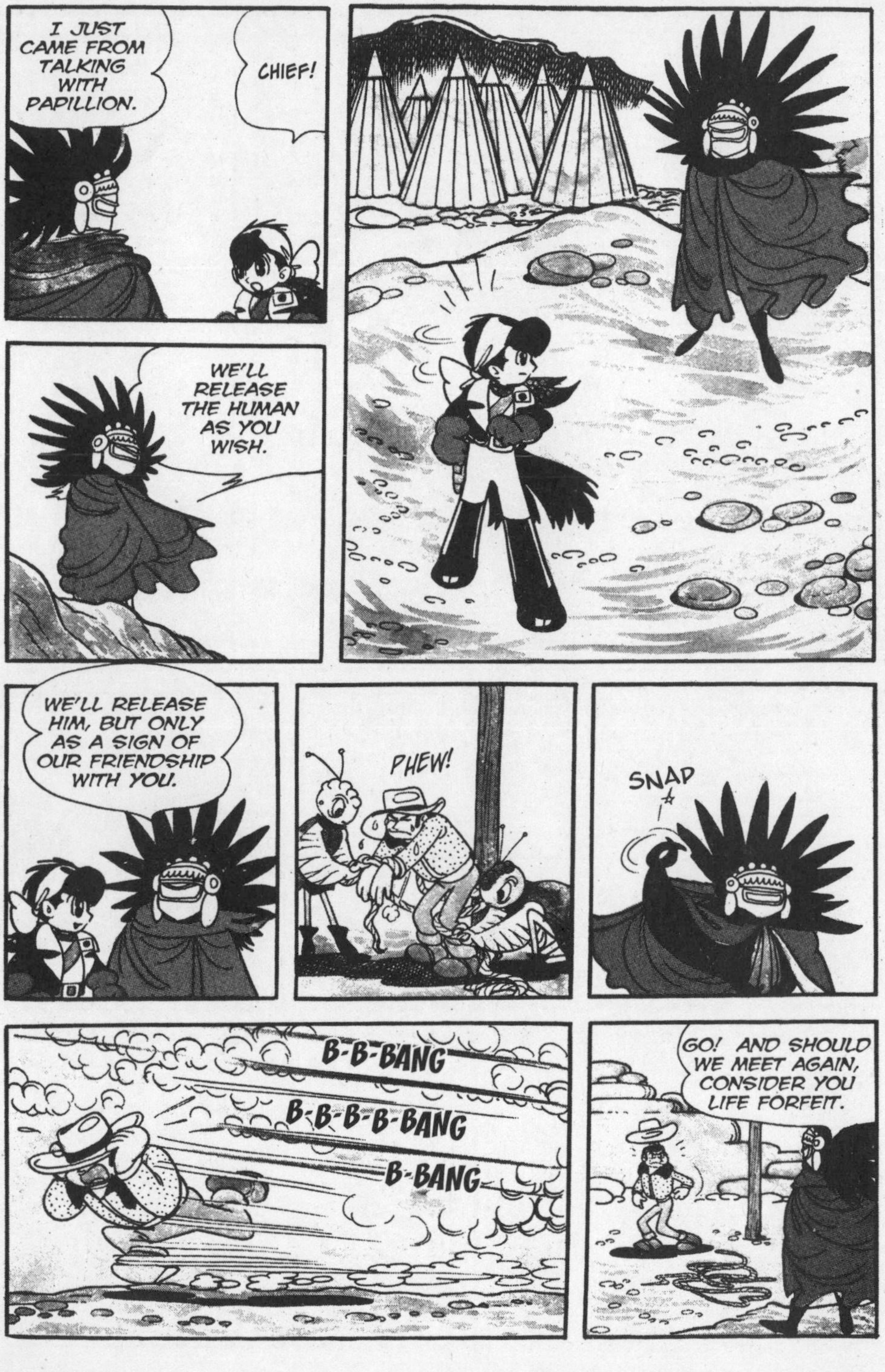
CHIEF!
I JUST CAME FROM TALKING WITH PAPILLION.
WE'LL RELEASE THE HUMAN AS YOU WISH.
SNAP
PHEW!
WE'LL RELEASE HIM, BUT ONLY AS A SIGN OF OUR FRIENDSHIP WITH YOU.
GO! AND SHOULD WE MEET AGAIN, CONSIDER YOU LIFE FORFEIT.
B-B-BANG
B-B-B-B-BANG
B-BANG

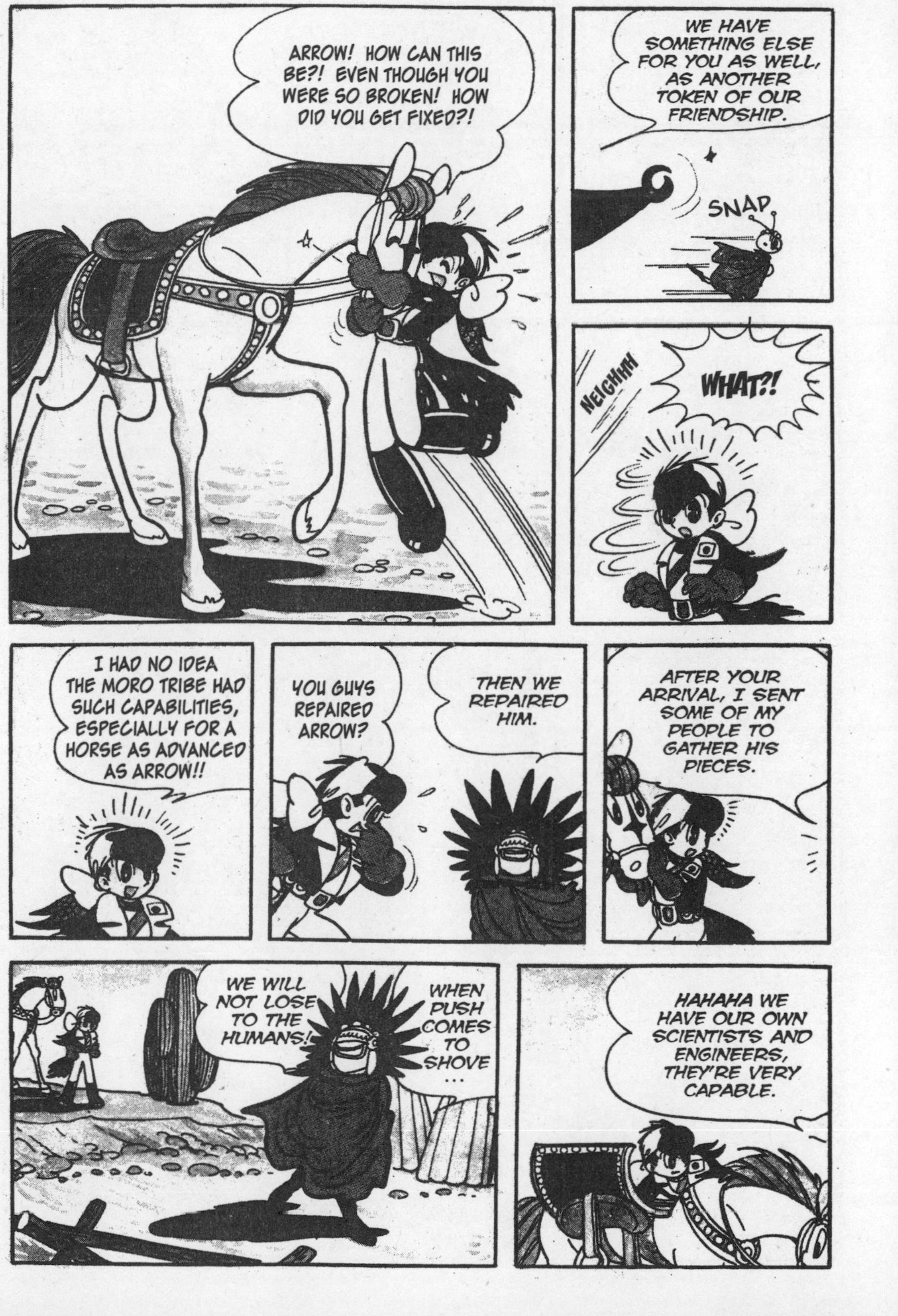
WE HAVE SOMETHING ELSE FOR YOU AS WELL, AS ANOTHER TOKEN OF OUR FRIENDSHIP.
SNAP
NEIGHHH
WHAT?!
ARROW! HOW CAN THIS BE?! EVEN THOUGH YOU WERE SO BROKEN! HOW DID YOU GET FIXED?!
AFTER YOUR ARRIVAL, I SENT SOME OF MY PEOPLE TO GATHER HIS PIECES.
THEN WE REPAIRED HIM.
YOU GUYS REPAIRED ARROW?
I HAD NO IDEA THE MORO TRIBE HAD SUCH CAPABILITIES, ESPECIALLY FOR A HORSE AS ADVANCED AS ARROW!!
HAHAHA WE HAVE OUR OWN SCIENTISTS AND ENGINEERS, THEY'RE VERY CAPABLE.
WHEN PUSH COMES TO SHOVE ...
WE WILL NOT LOSE TO THE HUMANS!

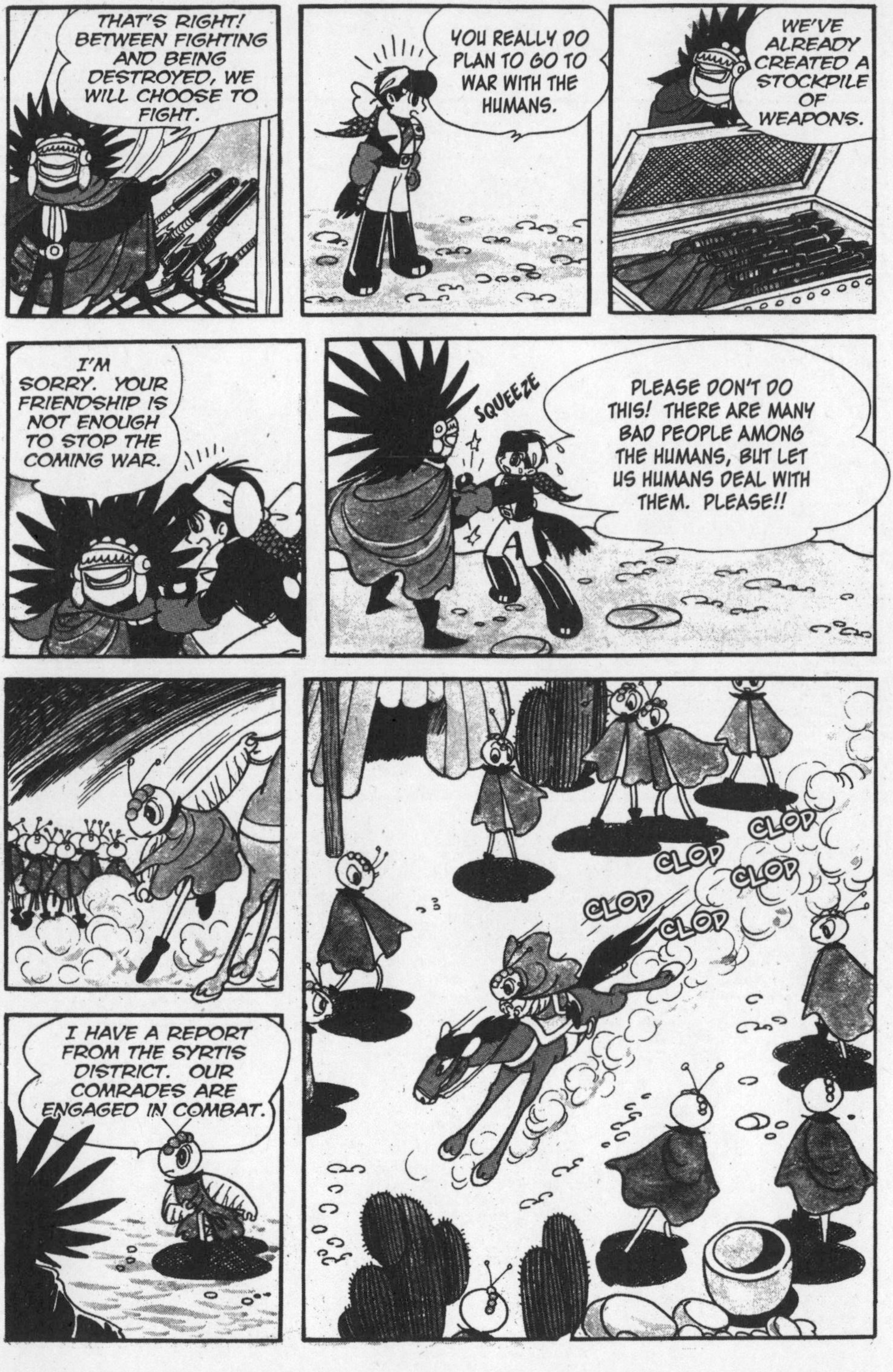
WE'VE ALREADY CREATED A STOCKPILE OF WEAPONS.
YOU REALLY DO PLAN TO GO TO WAR WITH THE HUMANS.
THAT'S RIGHT! BETWEEN FIGHTING AND BEING DESTROYED, WE WILL CHOOSE TO FIGHT.
SQUEEZE
PLEASE DON'T DO THIS! THERE ARE MANY BAD PEOPLE AMONG THE HUMANS, BUT LET US HUMANS DEAL WITH THEM. PLEASE!!
I'M SORRY. YOUR FRIENDSHIP IS NOT ENOUGH TO STOP THE COMING WAR.
CLOP
CLOP
CLOP
CLOP
CLOP
I HAVE A REPORT FROM THE SYRTIS DISTRICT. OUR COMRADES ARE ENGAGED IN COMBAT.

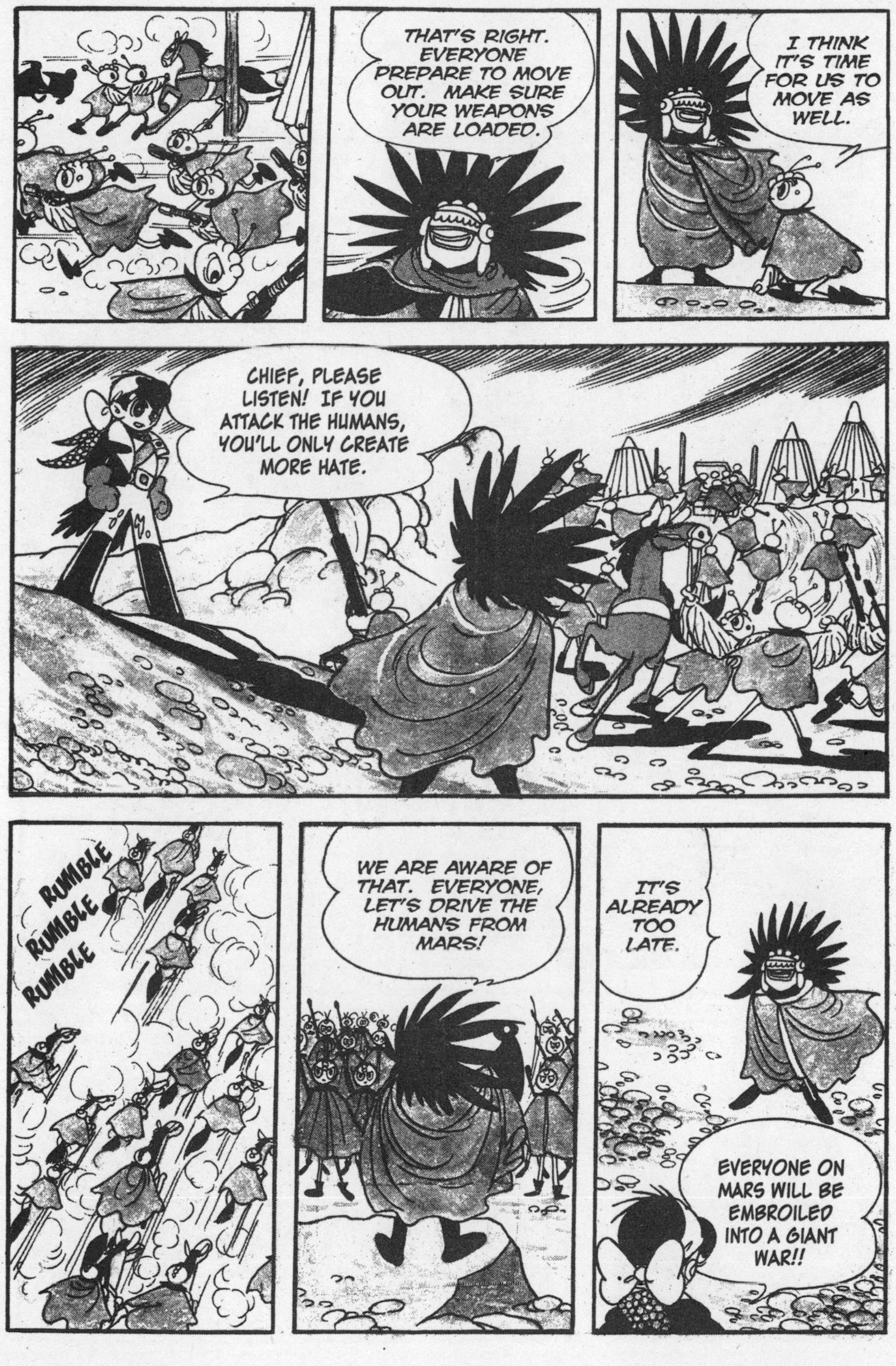
THAT'S RIGHT. EVERYONE PREPARE TO MOVE OUT. MAKE SURE YOUR WEAPONS ARE LOADED.
I THINK IT'S TIME FOR US TO MOVE AS WELL.
CHIEF, PLEASE LISTEN! IF YOU ATTACK THE HUMANS, YOU'LL ONLY CREATE MORE HATE.
RUMBLE
RUMBLE
RUMBLE
WE ARE AWARE OF THAT. EVERYONE, LET'S DRIVE THE HUMANS FROM MARS!
IT'S ALREADY TOO LATE.
EVERYONE ON MARS WILL BE EMBROILED INTO A GIANT WAR!!

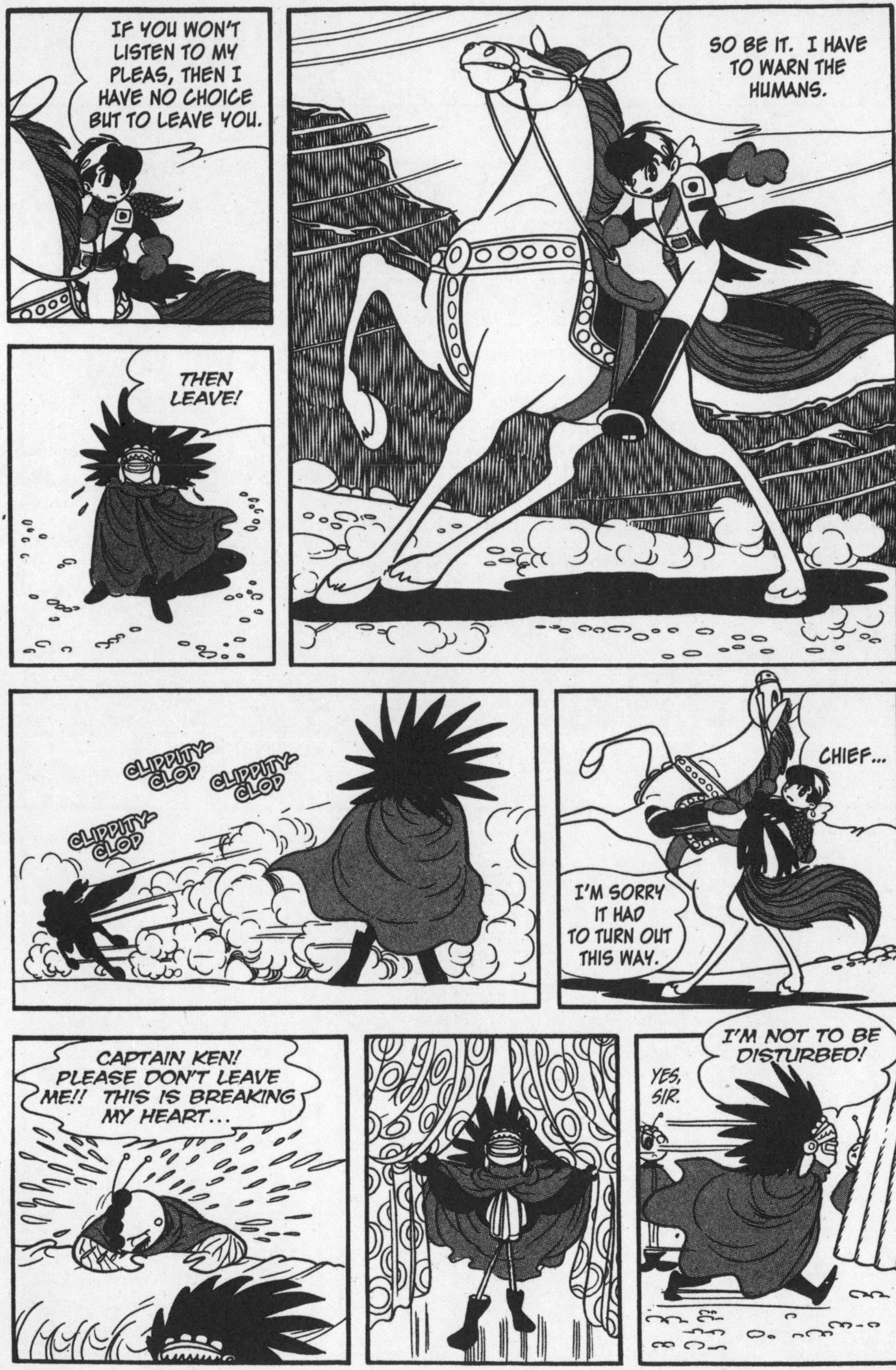
SO BE IT. I HAVE TO WARN THE HUMANS.
IF YOU WON'T LISTEN TO MY PLEAS, THEN I HAVE NO CHOICE BUT TO LEAVE YOU.
THEN LEAVE!
CHIEF...
I'M SORRY IT HAD TO TURN OUT THIS WAY.
CLIPPITY-CLOP
CLIPPITY-CLOP
CLIPPITY-CLOP
I'M NOT TO BE DISTURBED!
YES, SIR.
CAPTAIN KEN! PLEASE DON'T LEAVE ME!! THIS IS BREAKING MY HEART...

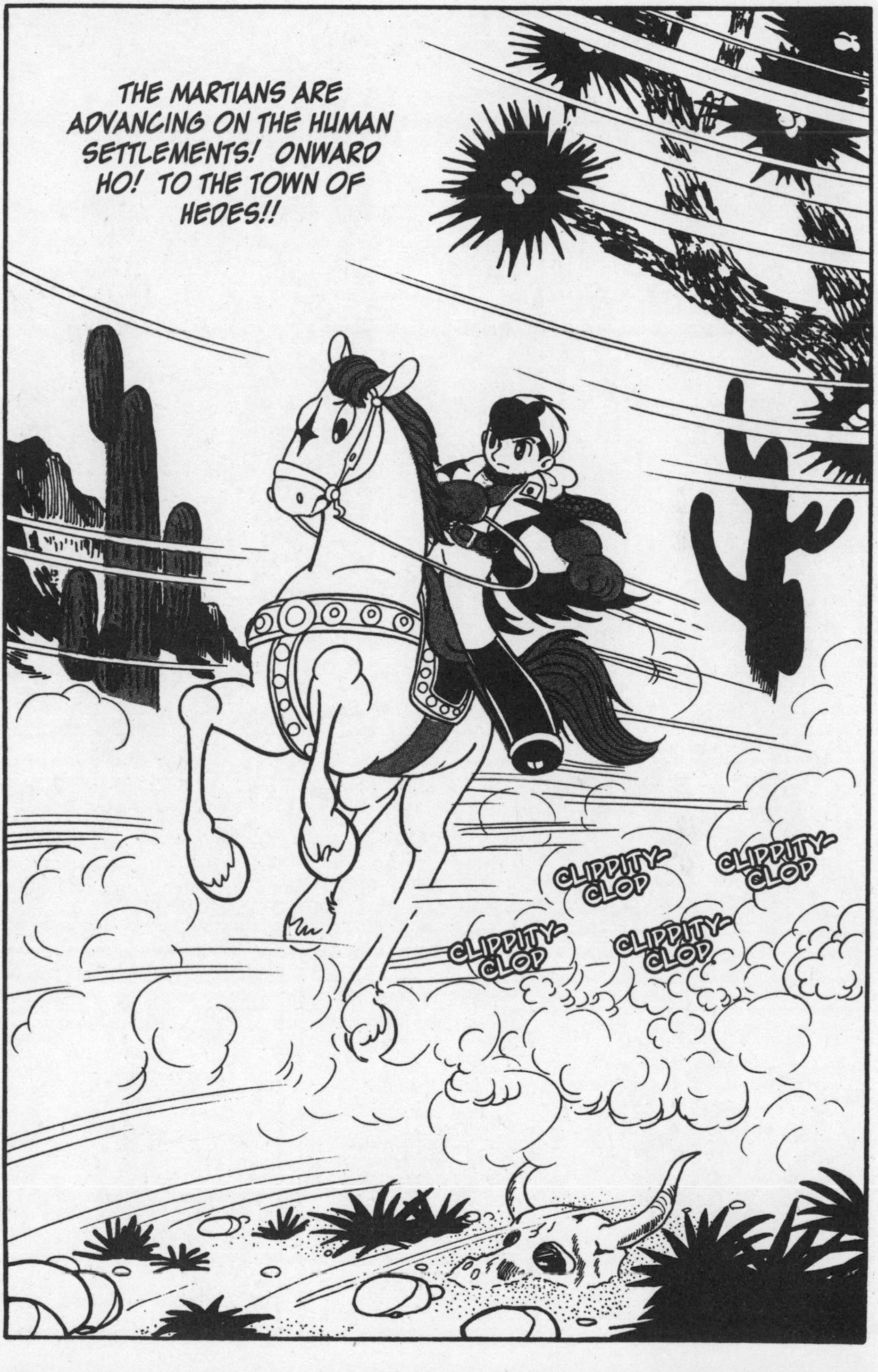
THE MARTIANS ARE ADVANCING ON THE HUMAN SETTLEMENTS! ONWARD HO! TO THE TOWN OF HEDES!!
CLIPPITY-CLOP
CLIPPITY-CLOP
CLIPPITY-CLOP
CLIPPITY-CLOP

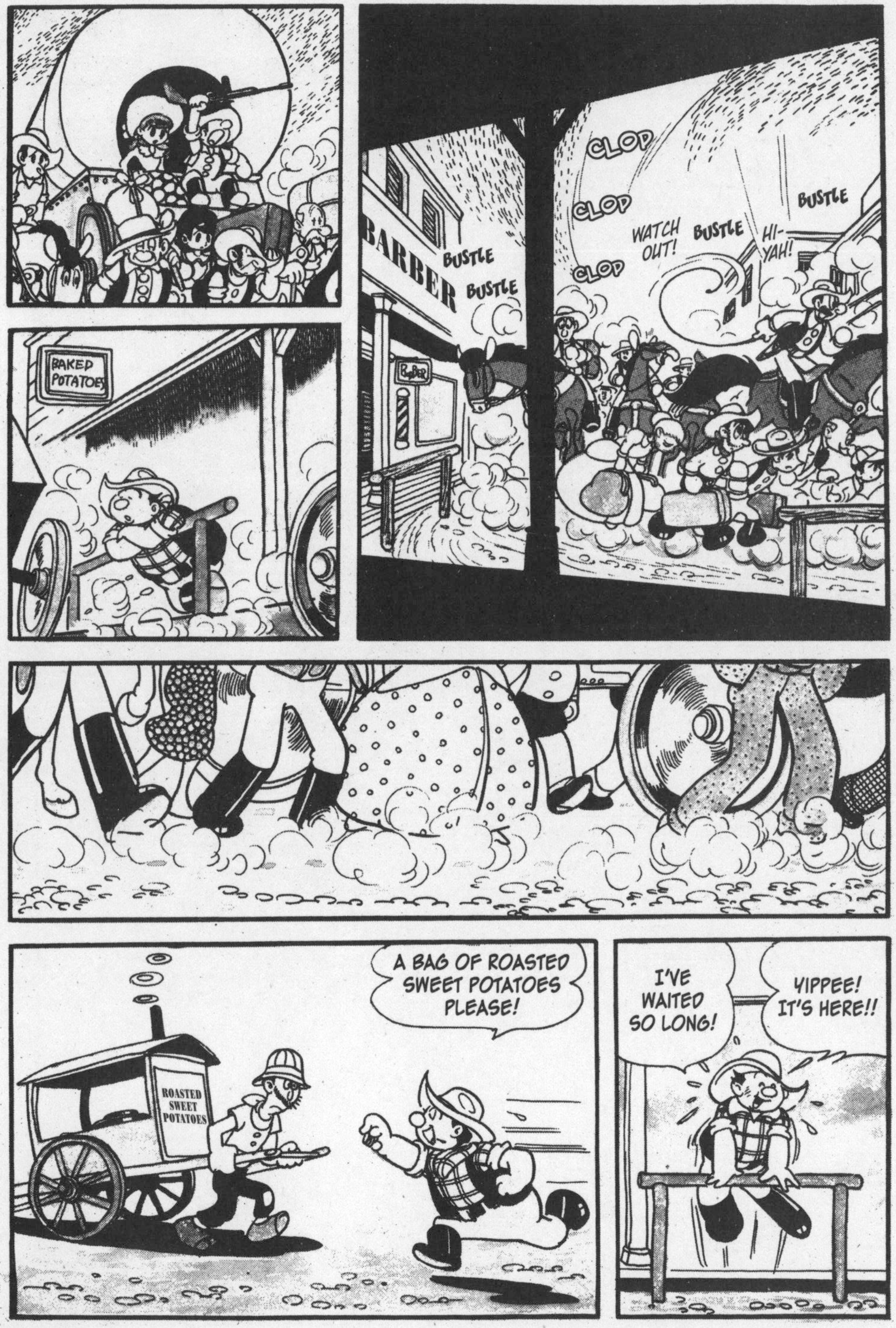
BUSTLE
HI-YAH!
BUSTLE
WATCH OUT!
CLOP
CLOP
CLOP
BARBER
BUSTLE
BUSTLE
BARBER
BAKED POTATOES
YIPPEE! IT'S HERE!!
I'VE WAITED SO LONG!
A BAG OF ROASTED SWEET POTATOES PLEASE!
ROASTED SWEET POTATOES

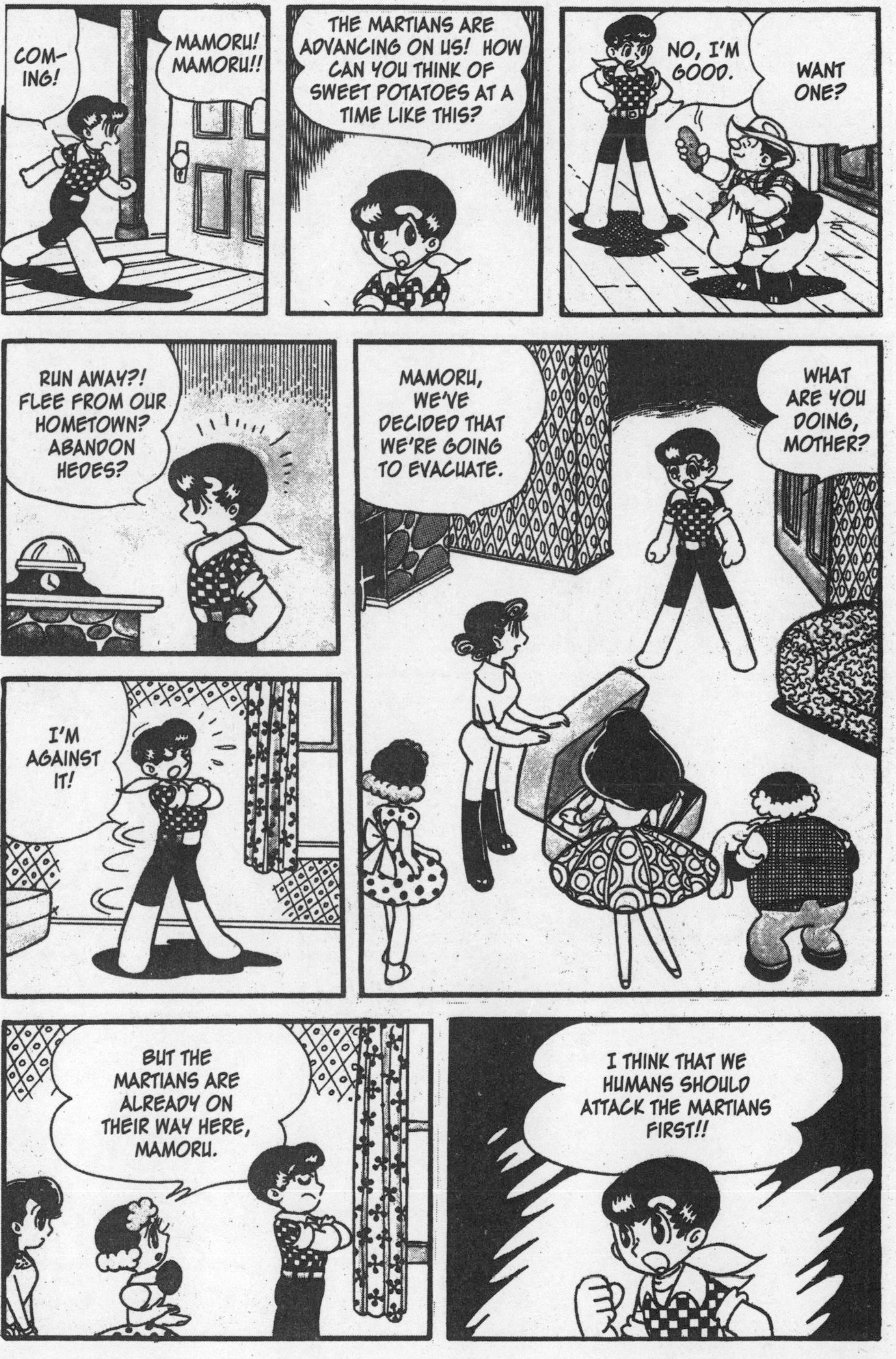
WANT ONE?
NO, I'M GOOD.
THE MARTIANS ARE ADVANCING ON US! HOW CAN YOU THINK OF SWEET POTATOES AT A TIME LIKE THIS?
MAMORU! MAMORU!!
COM-ING!
WHAT ARE YOU DOING, MOTHER?
MAMORU, WE'VE DECIDED THAT WE'RE GOING TO EVACUATE.
RUN AWAY?! FLEE FROM OUR HOMETOWN? ABANDON HEDES?
I'M AGAINST IT!
I THINK THAT WE HUMANS SHOULD ATTACK THE MARTIANS FIRST!!
BUT THE MARTIANS ARE ALREADY ON THEIR WAY HERE, MAMORU.

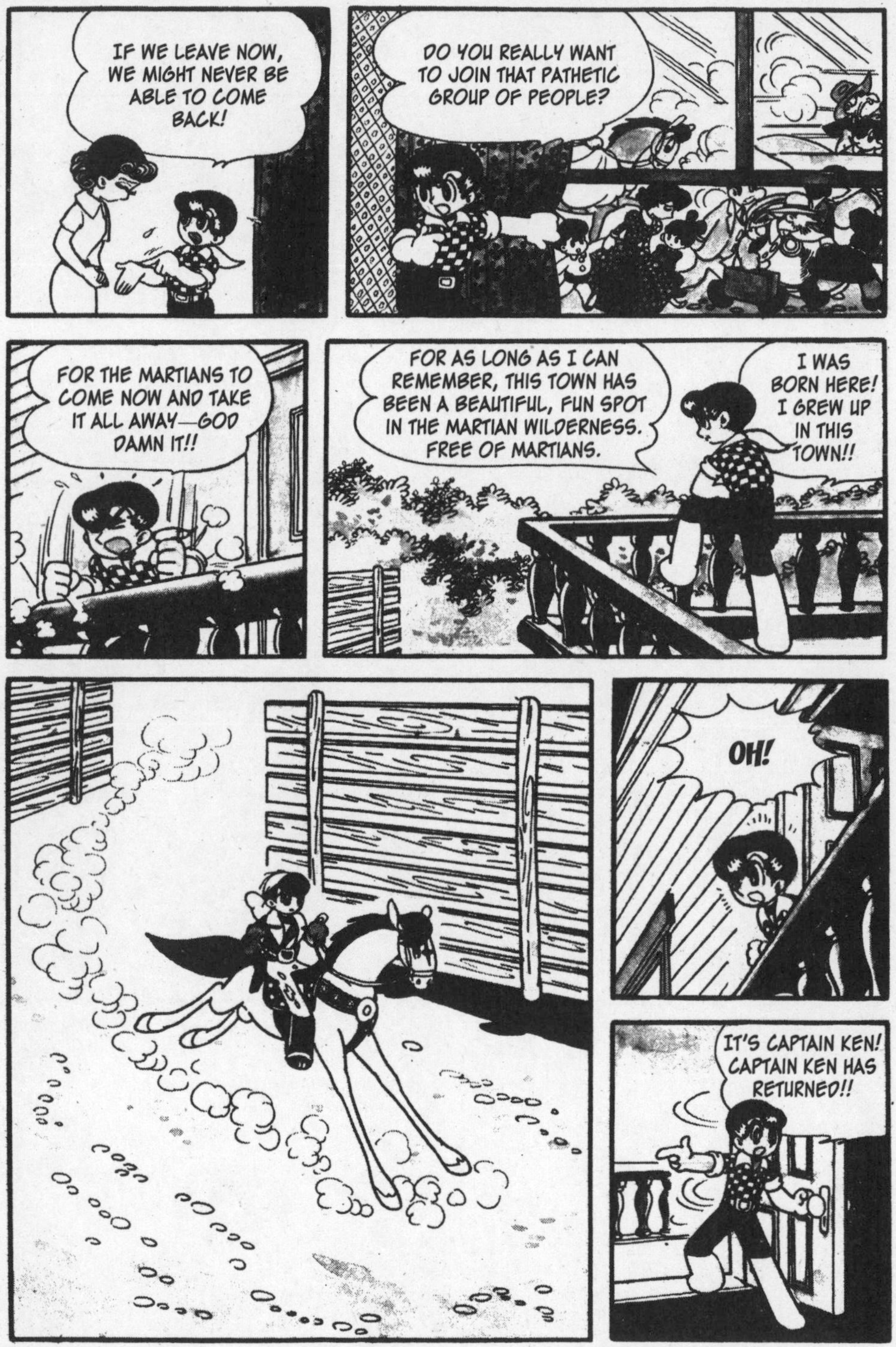
DO YOU REALLY WANT TO JOIN THAT PATHETIC GROUP OF PEOPLE?
IF WE LEAVE NOW, WE MIGHT NEVER BE ABLE TO COME BACK!
I WAS BORN HERE! I GREW UP IN THIS TOWN!!
FOR AS LONG AS I CAN REMEMBER, THIS TOWN HAS BEEN A BEAUTIFUL, FUN SPOT IN THE MARTIAN WILDERNESS. FREE OF MARTIANS.
FOR THE MARTIANS TO COME NOW AND TAKE IT ALL AWAY—GOD DAMN IT!!
OH!
IT'S CAPTAIN KEN! CAPTAIN KEN HAS RETURNED!!

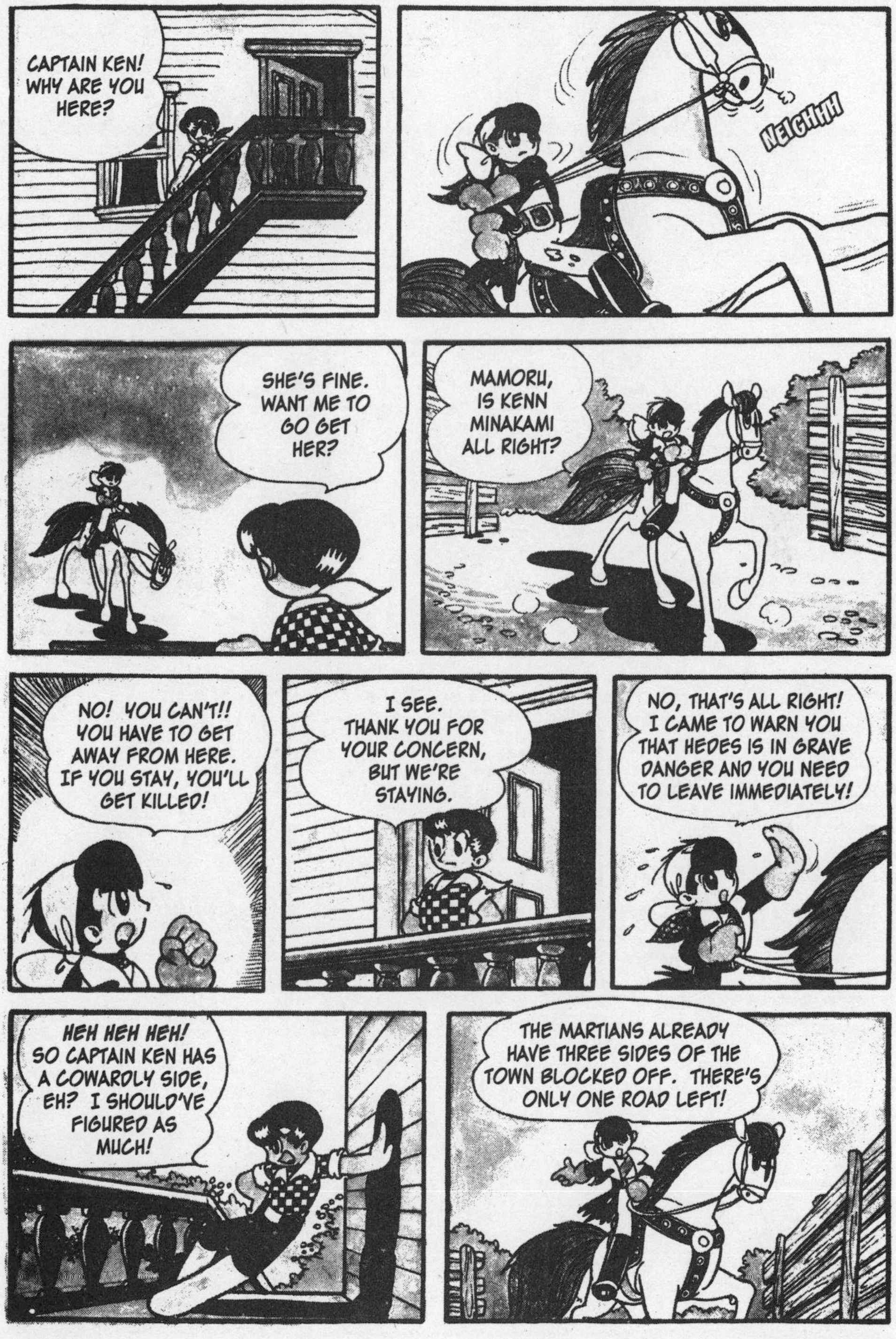
NEIGHHH
CAPTAIN KEN! WHY ARE YOU HERE?
MAMORU, IS KENN MINAKAMI ALL RIGHT?
SHE'S FINE. WANT ME TO GO GET HER?
NO, THAT'S ALL RIGHT! I CAME TO WARN YOU THAT HEDES IS IN GRAVE DANGER AND YOU NEED TO LEAVE IMMEDIATELY!
I SEE. THANK YOU FOR YOUR CONCERN, BUT WE'RE STAYING.
NO! YOU CAN'T!! YOU HAVE TO GET AWAY FROM HERE. IF YOU STAY, YOU'LL GET KILLED!
THE MARTIANS ALREADY HAVE THREE SIDES OF THE TOWN BLOCKED OFF. THERE'S ONLY ONE ROAD LEFT!
HEH HEH HEH! SO CAPTAIN KEN HAS A COWARDLY SIDE, EH? I SHOULD'VE FIGURED AS MUCH!

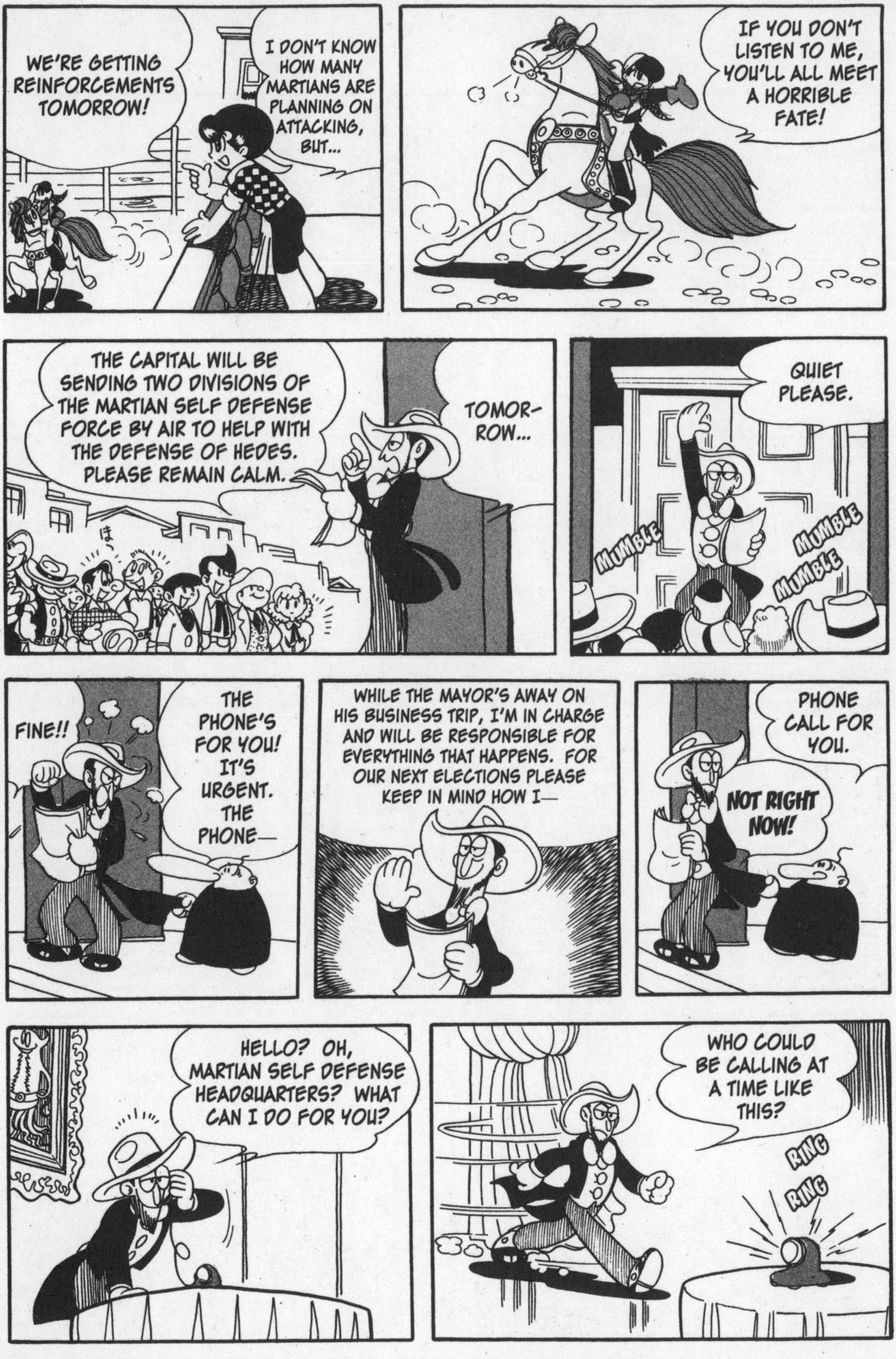
IF YOU DON'T LISTEN TO ME, YOU'LL ALL MEET A HORRIBLE FATE!
I DON'T KNOW HOW MANY MARTIANS ARE PLANNING ON ATTACKING, BUT...
WE'RE GETTING REINFORCEMENTS TOMORROW!
QUIET PLEASE.
MUMBLE
MUMBLE
MUMBLE
TOMOR-ROW...
THE CAPITAL WILL BE SENDING TWO DIVISIONS OF THE MARTIAN SELF DEFENSE FORCE BY AIR TO HELP WITH THE DEFENSE OF HEDES. PLEASE REMAIN CALM.
はっ
PHONE CALL FOR YOU.
NOT RIGHT NOW!
WHILE THE MAYOR'S AWAY ON HIS BUSINESS TRIP, I'M IN CHARGE AND WILL BE RESPONSIBLE FOR EVERYTHING THAT HAPPENS. FOR OUR NEXT ELECTIONS PLEASE KEEP IN MIND HOW I—
THE PHONE'S FOR YOU! IT'S URGENT. THE PHONE—
FINE!!
WHO COULD BE CALLING AT A TIME LIKE THIS?
RING
RING
HELLO? OH, MARTIAN SELF DEFENSE HEADQUARTERS? WHAT CAN I DO FOR YOU?

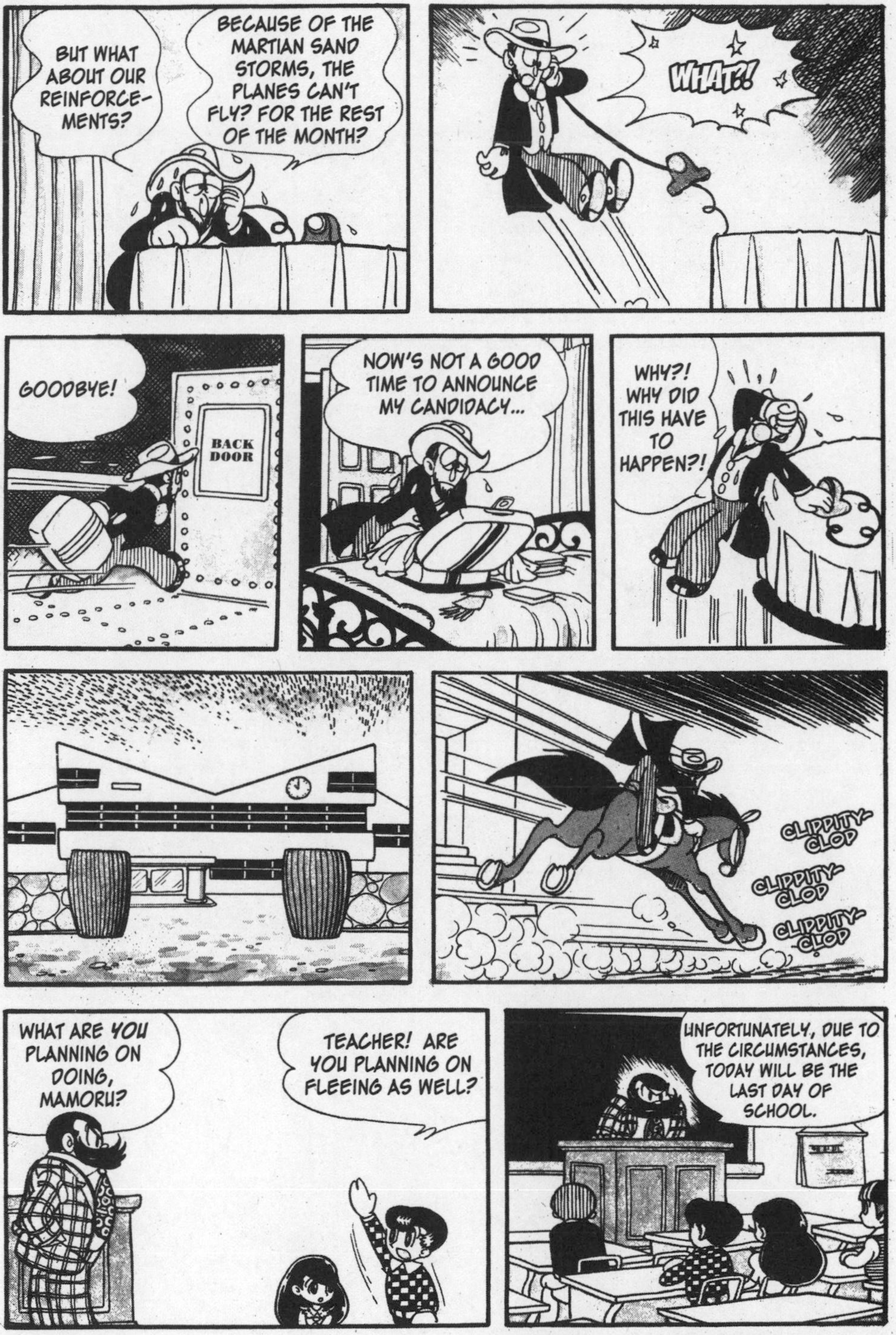
WHAT?!
BECAUSE OF THE MARTIAN SAND STORMS, THE PLANES CAN'T FLY? FOR THE REST OF THE MONTH?
BUT WHAT ABOUT OUR REINFORCE-MENTS?
WHY?! WHY DID THIS HAVE TO HAPPEN?!
NOW'S NOT A GOOD TIME TO ANNOUNCE MY CANDIDACY...
GOODBYE!
BACK DOOR
CLIPPITY-CLOP
CLIPPITY-CLOP
CLIPPITY-CLOP
UNFORTUNATELY, DUE TO THE CIRCUMSTANCES, TODAY WILL BE THE LAST DAY OF SCHOOL.
TEACHER! ARE YOU PLANNING ON FLEEING AS WELL?
WHAT ARE YOU PLANNING ON DOING, MAMORU?

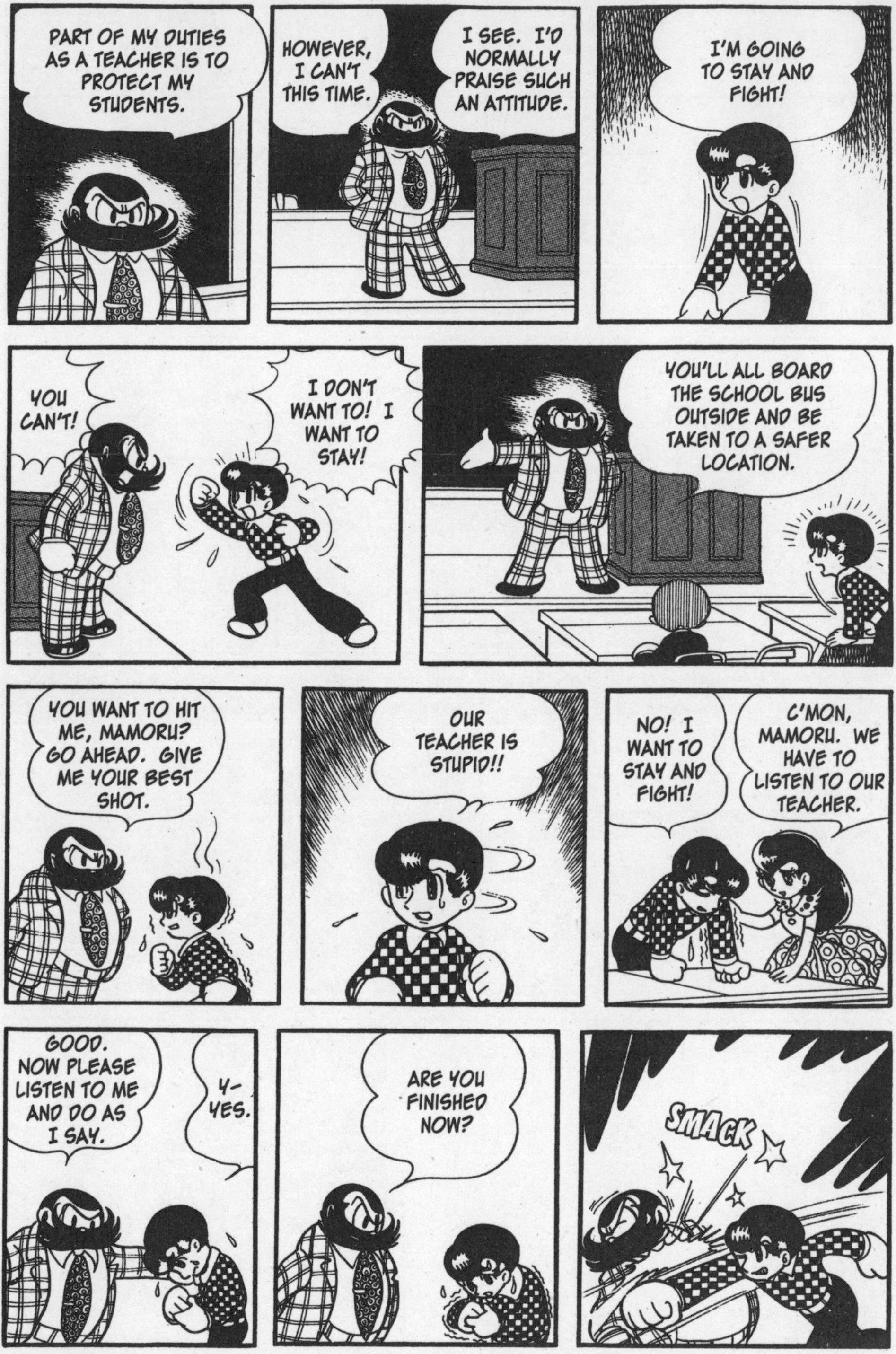
I'M GOING TO STAY AND FIGHT!
I SEE. I'D NORMALLY PRAISE SUCH AN ATTITUDE.
HOWEVER, I CAN'T THIS TIME.
PART OF MY DUTIES AS A TEACHER IS TO PROTECT MY STUDENTS.
YOU'LL ALL BOARD THE SCHOOL BUS OUTSIDE AND BE TAKEN TO A SAFER LOCATION.
I DON'T WANT TO! I WANT TO STAY!
YOU CAN'T!
C'MON, MAMORU. WE HAVE TO LISTEN TO OUR TEACHER.
NO! I WANT TO STAY AND FIGHT!
OUR TEACHER IS STUPID!!
YOU WANT TO HIT ME, MAMORU? GO AHEAD. GIVE ME YOUR BEST SHOT.
SMACK
ARE YOU FINISHED NOW?
Y-YES.
GOOD. NOW PLEASE LISTEN TO ME AND DO AS I SAY.

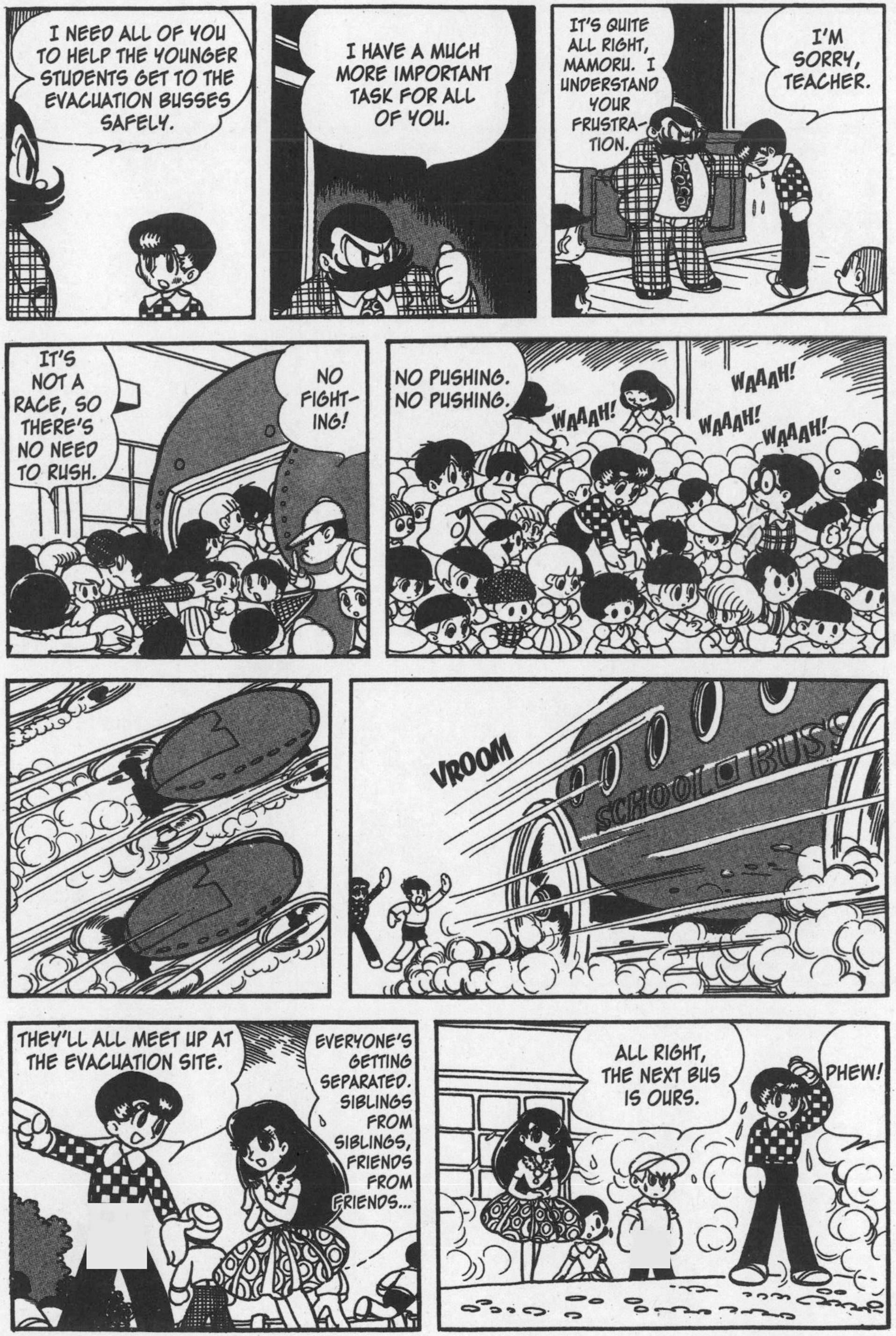
I'M SORRY, TEACHER.
IT'S QUITE ALL RIGHT, MAMORU. I UNDERSTAND YOUR FRUSTRATION.
I HAVE A MUCH MORE IMPORTANT TASK FOR ALL OF YOU.
I NEED ALL OF YOU TO HELP THE YOUNGER STUDENTS GET TO THE EVACUATION BUSSES SAFELY.
WAAAH!
WAAAH!
WAAAH!
WAAAH!
NO PUSHING. NO PUSHING.
NO FIGHTING!
IT'S NOT A RACE, SO THERE'S NO NEED TO RUSH.
SCHOOL BUS
VROOM
PHEW!
ALL RIGHT, THE NEXT BUS IS OURS.
EVERYONE'S GETTING SEPARATED. SIBLINGS FROM SIBLINGS, FRIENDS FROM FRIENDS...
THEY'LL ALL MEET UP AT THE EVACUATION SITE.

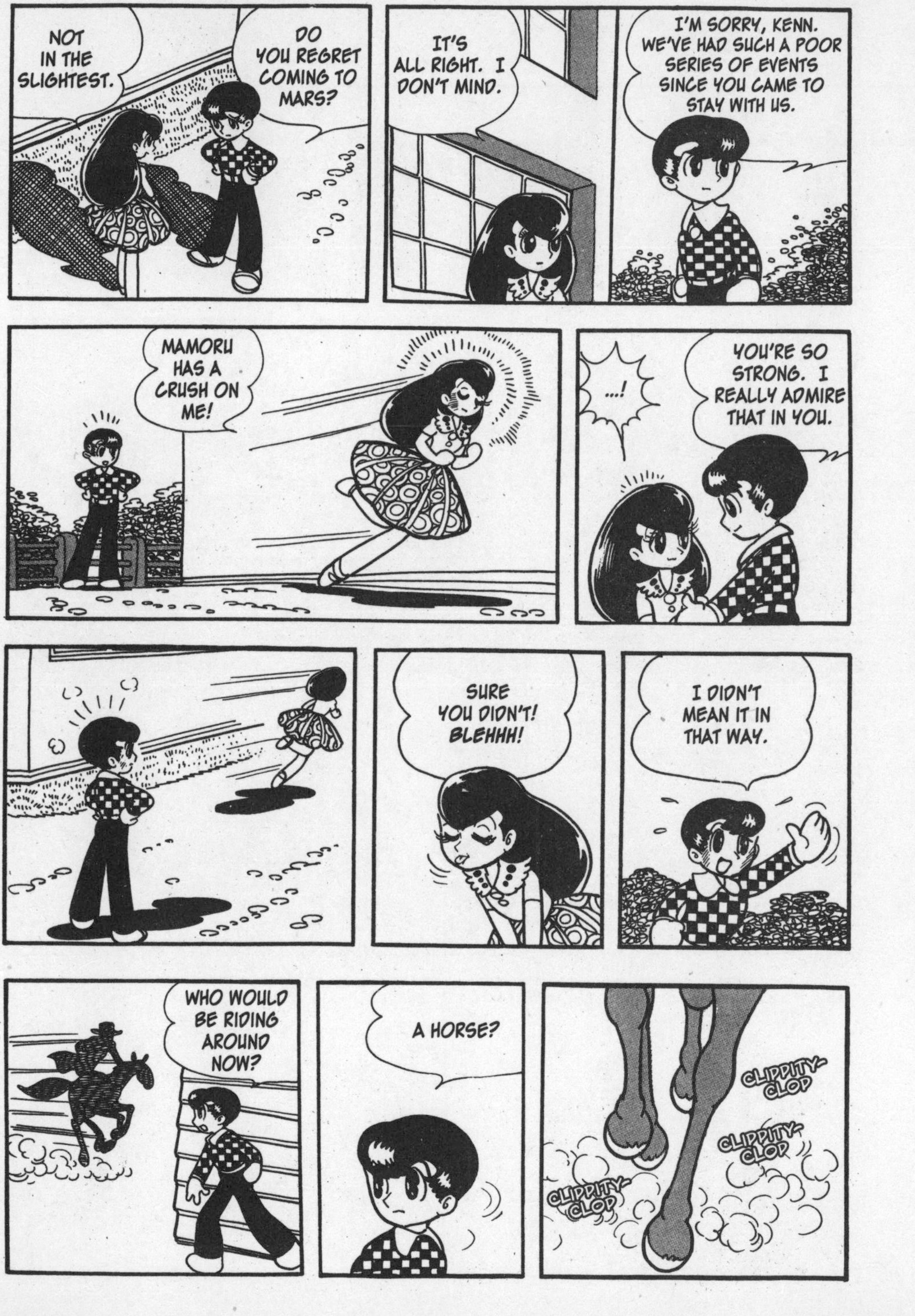
I'M SORRY, KENN. WE'VE HAD SUCH A POOR SERIES OF EVENTS SINCE YOU CAME TO STAY WITH US.
IT'S ALL RIGHT. I DON'T MIND.
DO YOU REGRET COMING TO MARS?
NOT IN THE SLIGHTEST.
YOU'RE SO STRONG. I REALLY ADMIRE THAT IN YOU.
...!
MAMORU HAS A CRUSH ON ME!
I DIDN'T MEAN IT IN THAT WAY.
SURE YOU DIDN'T! BLEHHH!
CLIPPITY-CLOP
CLIPPITY-CLOP
CLIPPITY-CLOP
A HORSE?
WHO WOULD BE RIDING AROUND NOW?

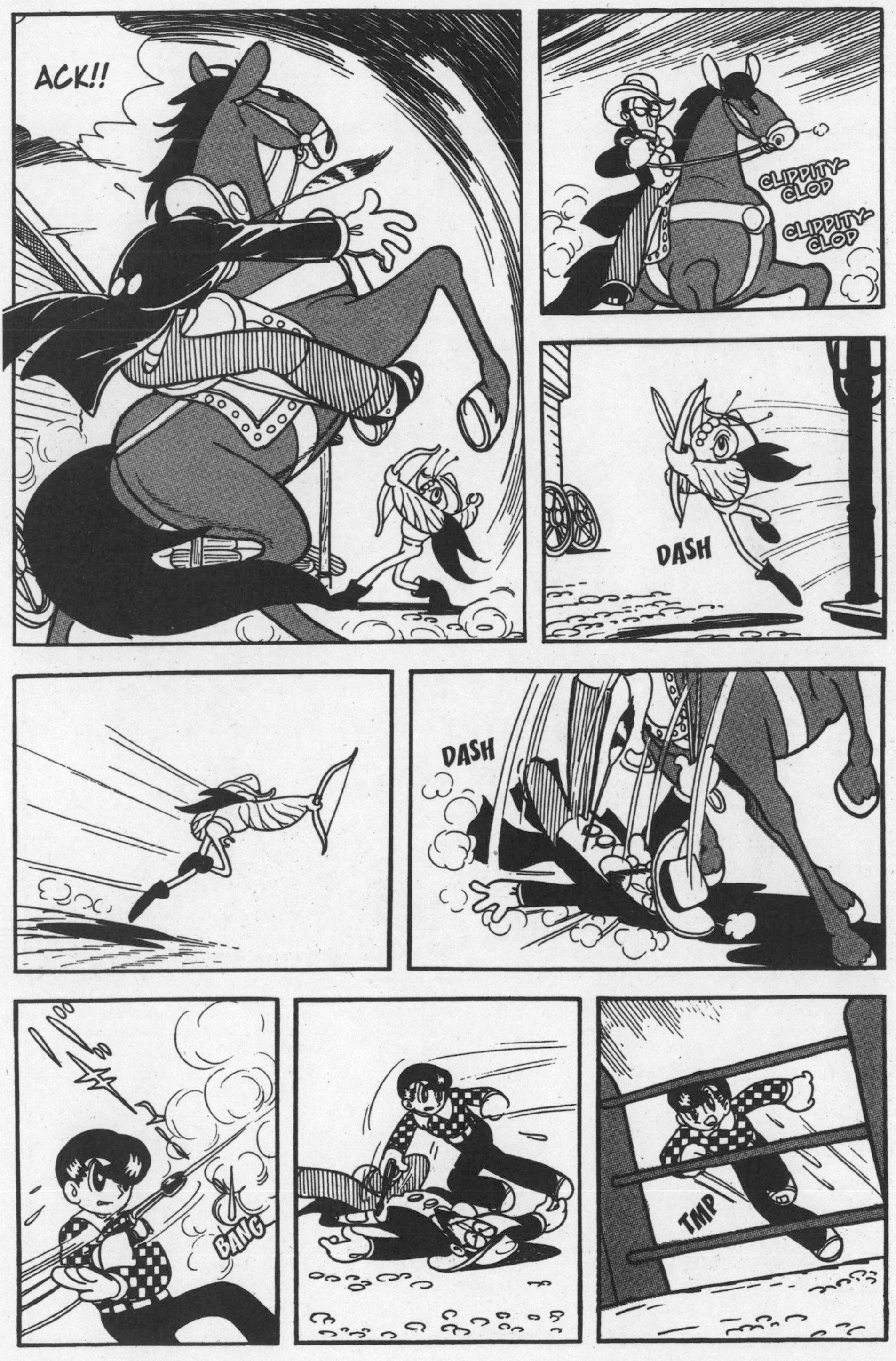
CLIPPITY-CLOP
CLIPPITY-CLOP
DASH
ACK!!
DASH
TMP
BANG

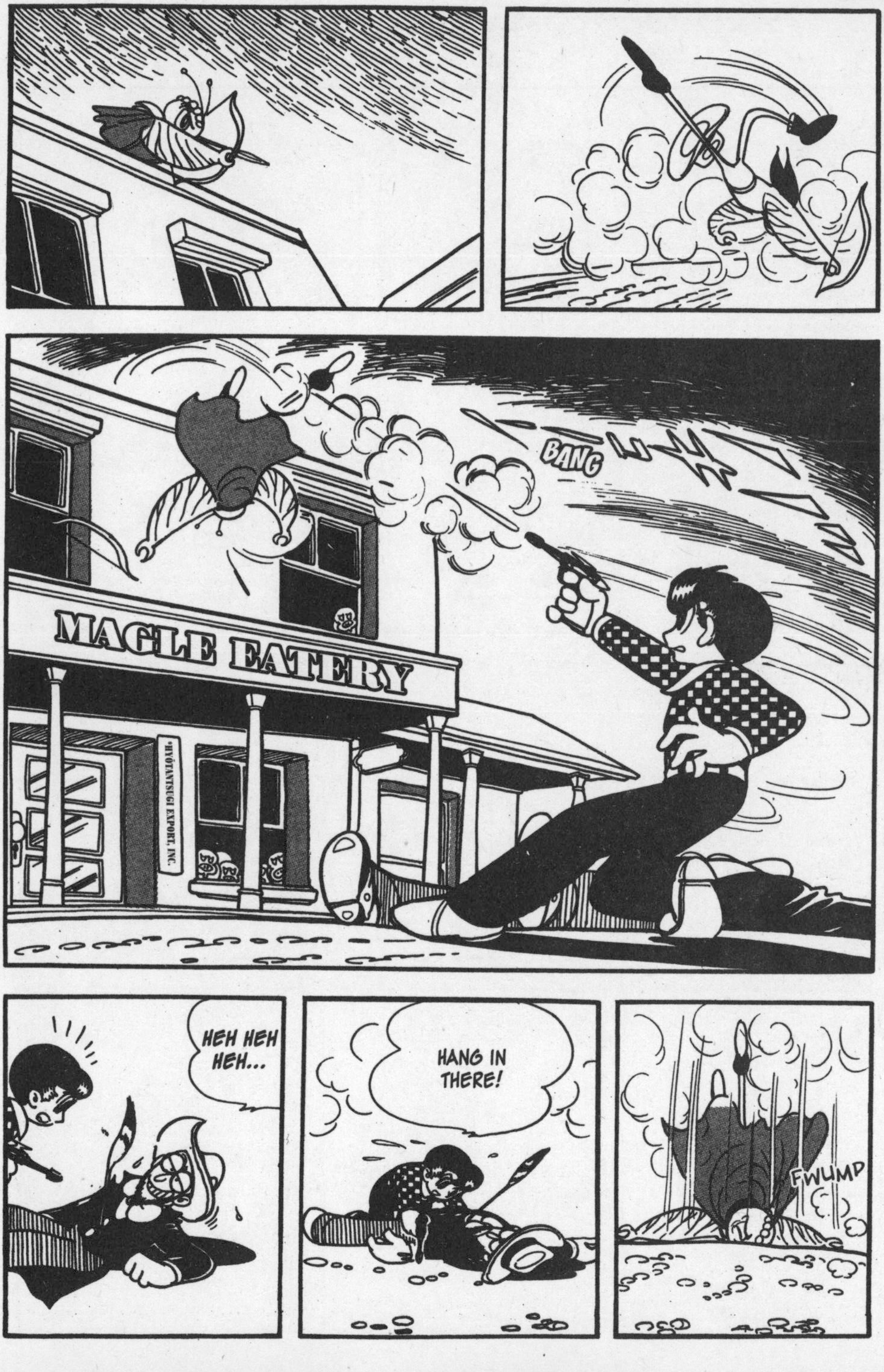
BANG
MAGLE EATERY
*HYŌTANTSUGI EXPORT, INC.
FWUMP
HANG IN THERE!
HEH HEH HEH...

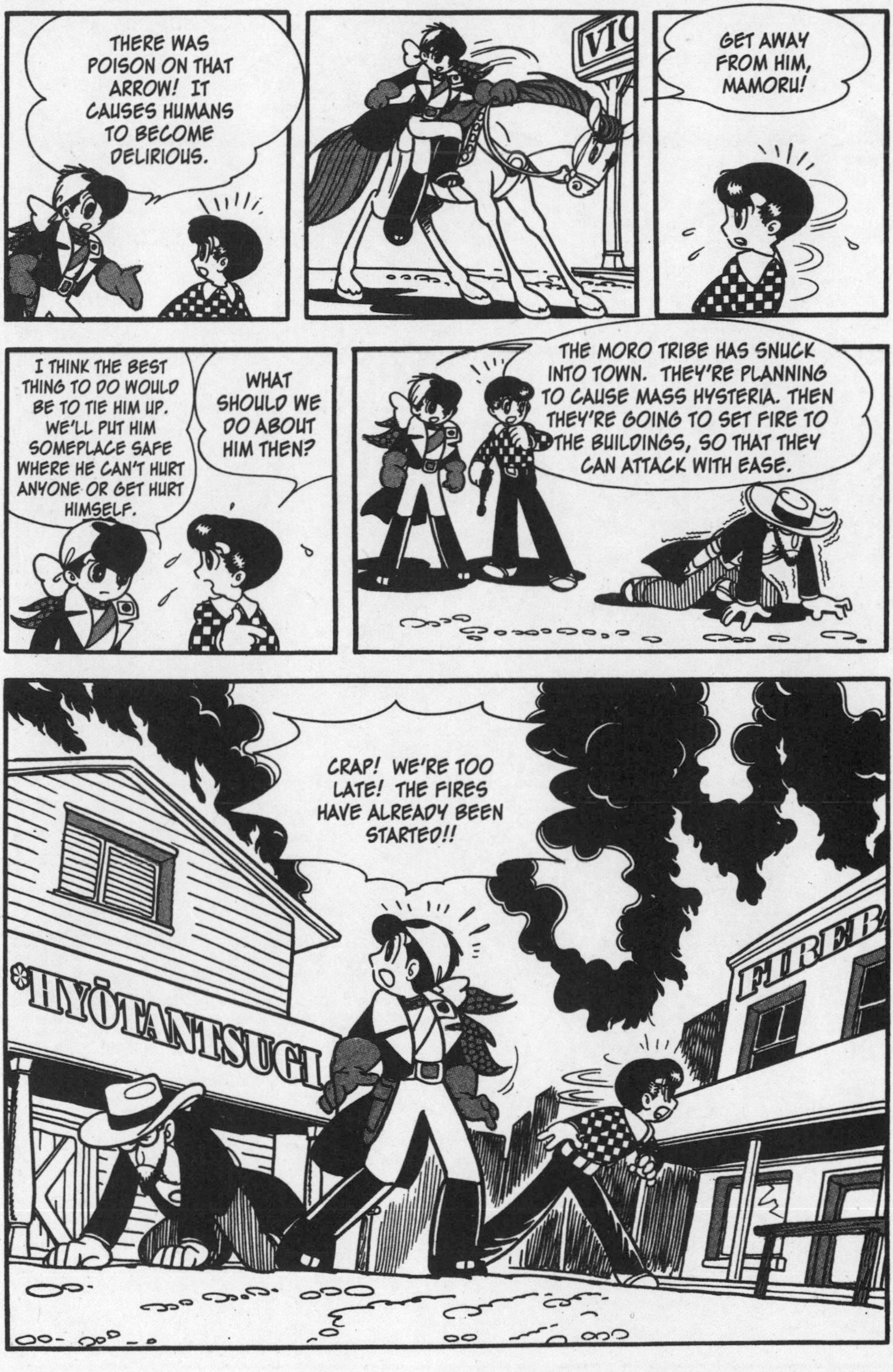
GET AWAY FROM HIM, MAMORU!
THERE WAS POISON ON THAT ARROW! IT CAUSES HUMANS TO BECOME DELIRIOUS.
THE MORO TRIBE HAS SNUCK INTO TOWN. THEY'RE PLANNING TO CAUSE MASS HYSTERIA. THEN THEY'RE GOING TO SET FIRE TO THE BUILDINGS, SO THAT THEY CAN ATTACK WITH EASE.
WHAT SHOULD WE DO ABOUT HIM THEN?
I THINK THE BEST THING TO DO WOULD BE TO TIE HIM UP. WE'LL PUT HIM SOMEPLACE SAFE WHERE HE CAN'T HURT ANYONE OR GET HURT HIMSELF.
CRAP! WE'RE TOO LATE! THE FIRES HAVE ALREADY BEEN STARTED!!
*HYŌTANTSUGI

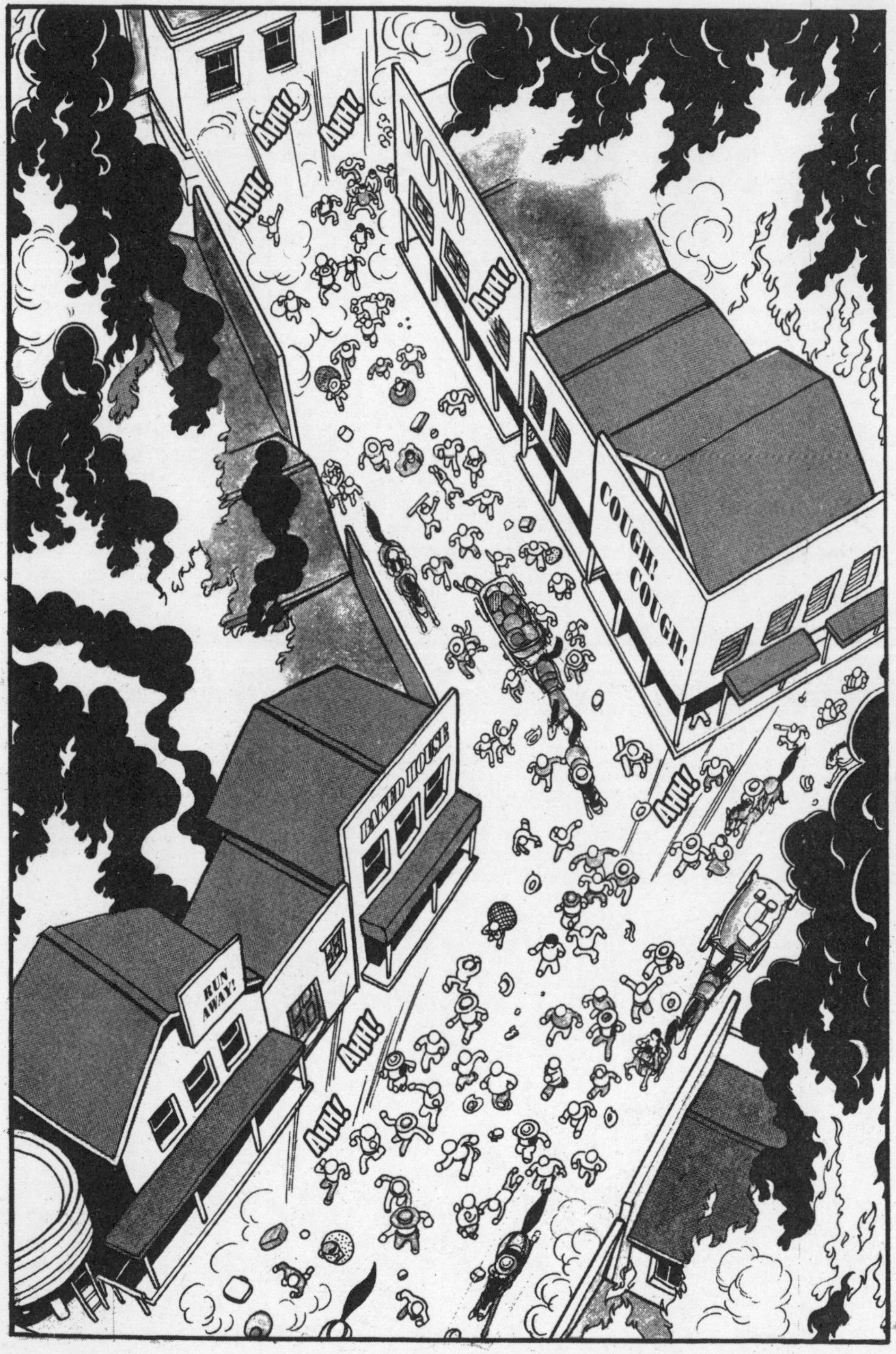
AHH!
AHH!
AHH!
AHH!
WOW!
AHH!
COUGH! COUGH!
BAKED HOUSE
AHH!
RUN AWAY!
AHH!
AHH!

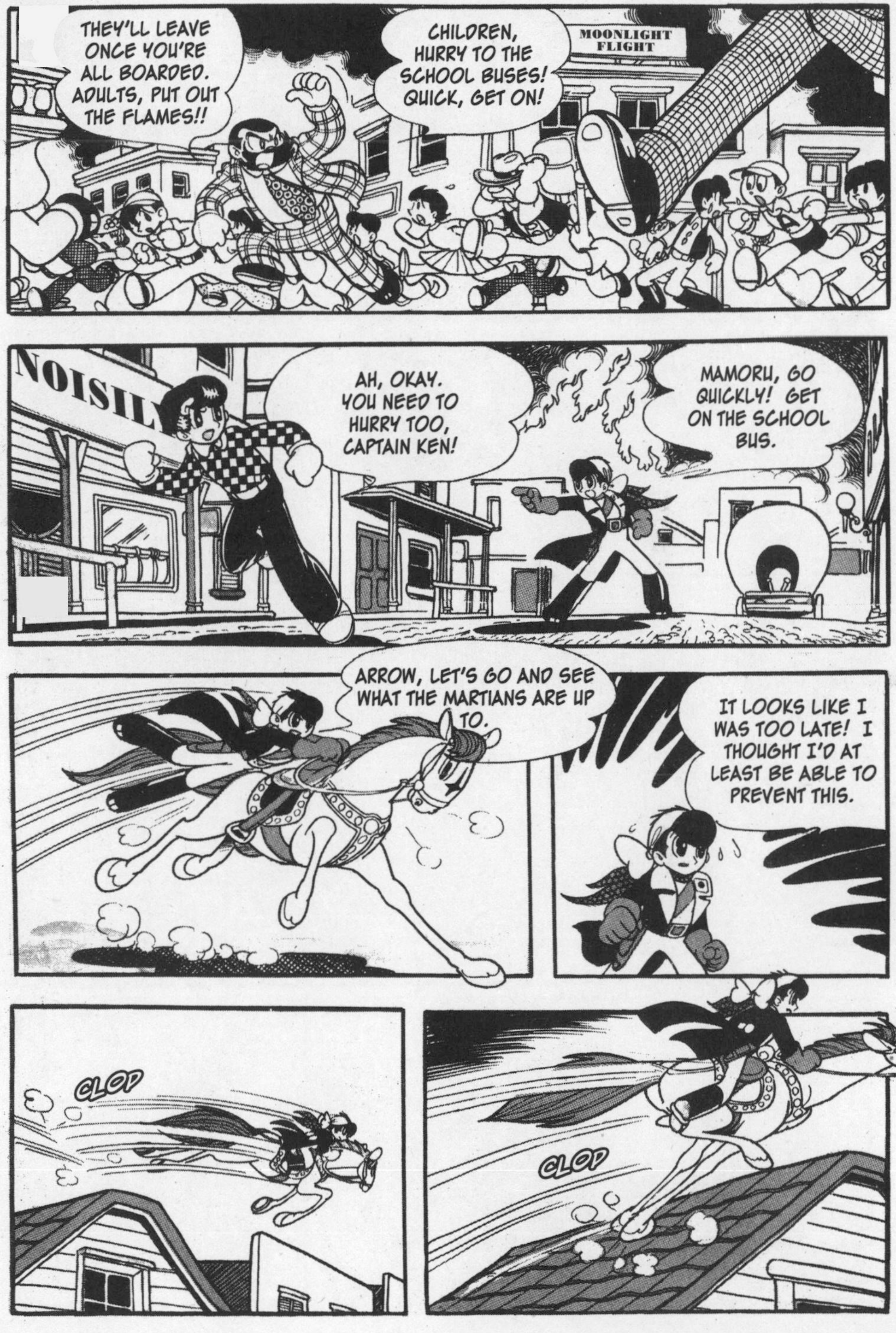
MOONLIGHT FLIGHT
CHILDREN, HURRY TO THE SCHOOL BUSES! QUICK, GET ON!
THEY'LL LEAVE ONCE YOU'RE ALL BOARDED. ADULTS, PUT OUT THE FLAMES!!
MAMORU, GO QUICKLY! GET ON THE SCHOOL BUS.
AH, OKAY. YOU NEED TO HURRY TOO, CAPTAIN KEN!
IT LOOKS LIKE I WAS TOO LATE! I THOUGHT I'D AT LEAST BE ABLE TO PREVENT THIS.
ARROW, LET'S GO AND SEE WHAT THE MARTIANS ARE UP TO.
CLOP
CLOP

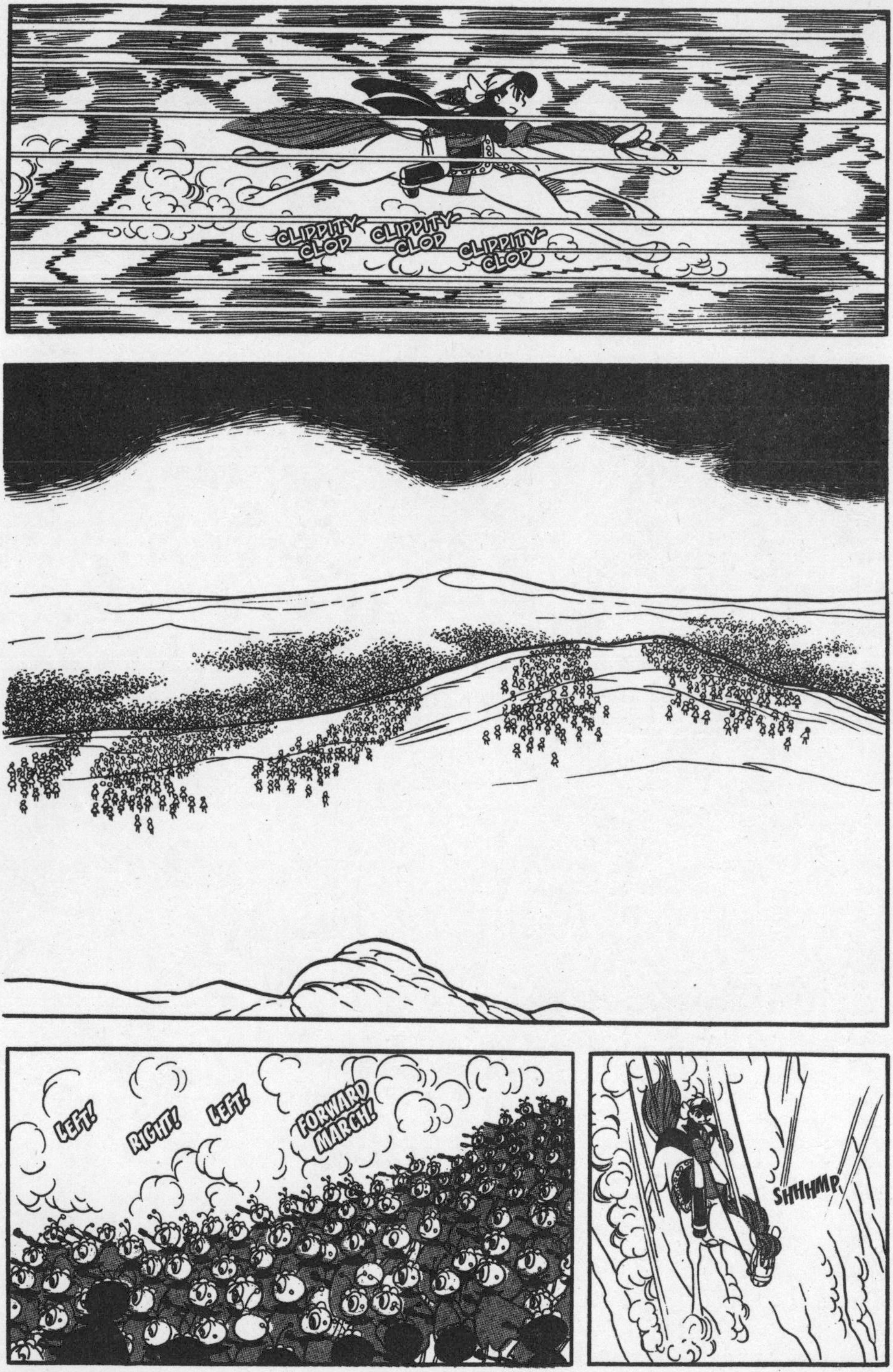
CLIPPITY-CLOP
CLIPPITY-CLOP
CLIPPITY-CLOP
SHHHMP
LEFT!
RIGHT!
LEFT!
FORWARD MARCH!

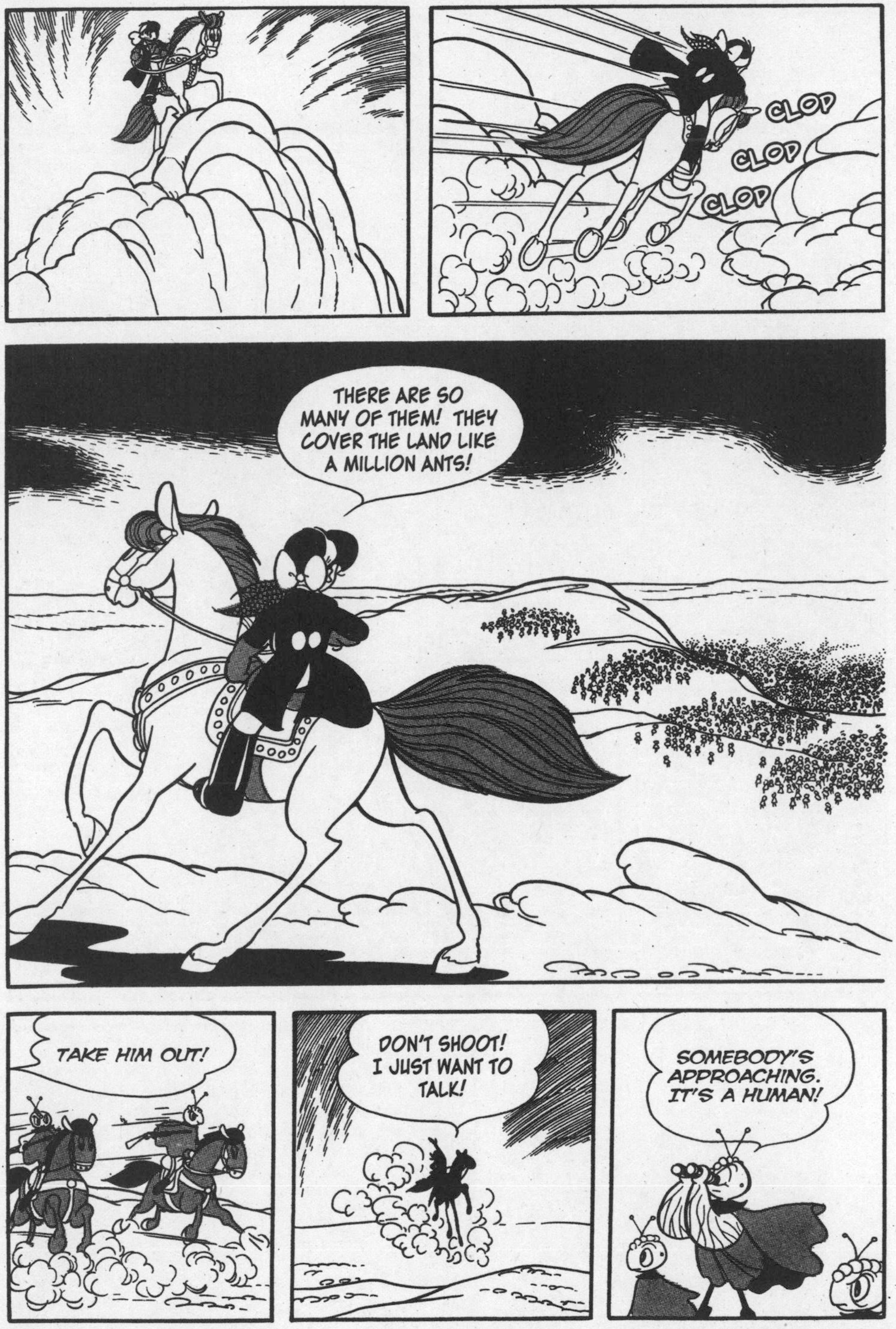
CLOP
CLOP
CLOP
THERE ARE SO MANY OF THEM! THEY COVER THE LAND LIKE A MILLION ANTS!
SOMEBODY'S APPROACHING. IT'S A HUMAN!
DON'T SHOOT! I JUST WANT TO TALK!
TAKE HIM OUT!

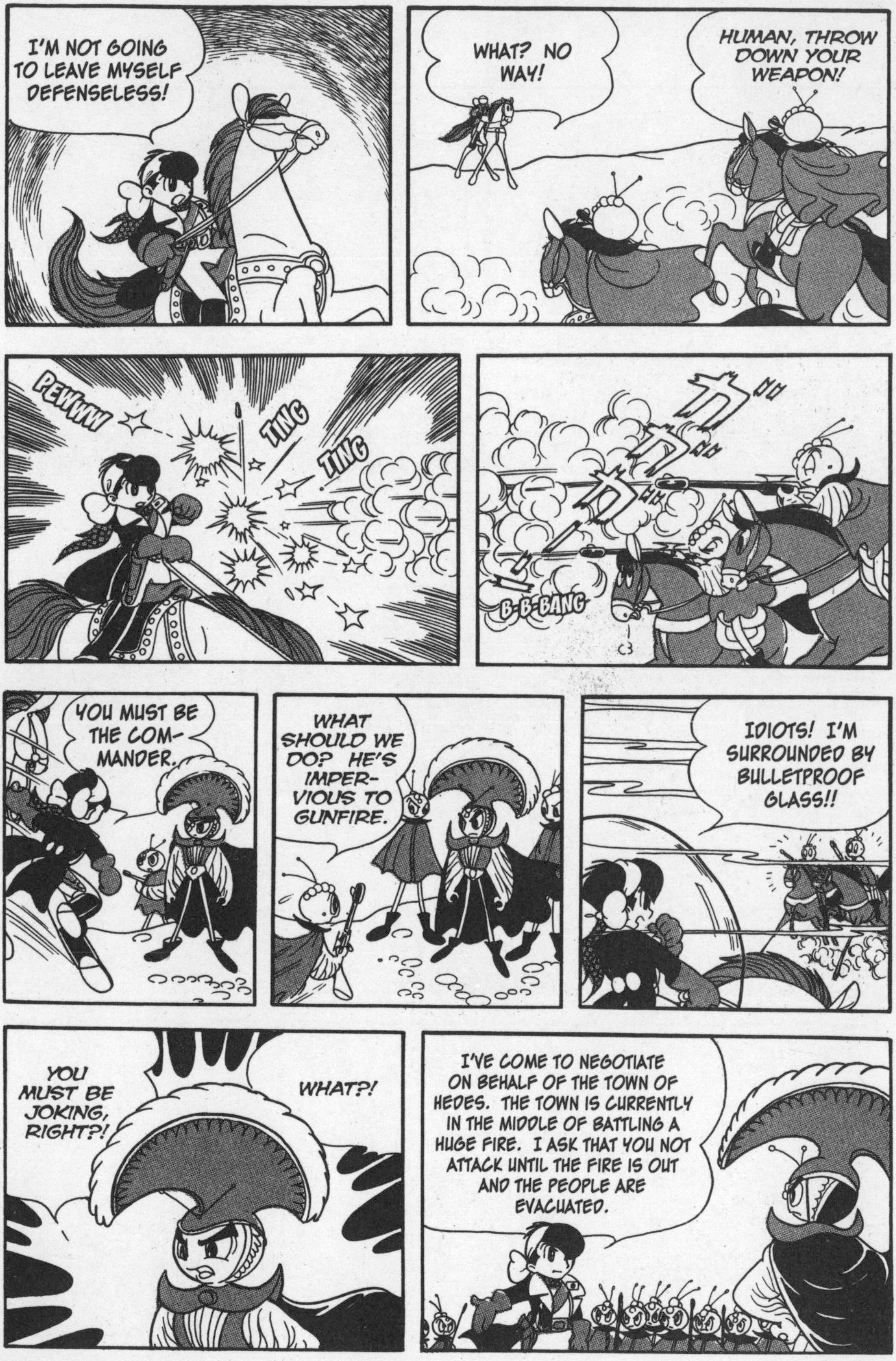
HUMAN, THROW DOWN YOUR WEAPON!
WHAT? NO WAY!
I'M NOT GOING TO LEAVE MYSELF DEFENSELESS!
B-B-BANG
PEWWW
TING
TING
IDIOTS! I'M SURROUNDED BY BULLETPROOF GLASS!!
WHAT SHOULD WE DO? HE'S IMPERVIOUS TO GUNFIRE.
YOU MUST BE THE COMMANDER.
I'VE COME TO NEGOTIATE ON BEHALF OF THE TOWN OF HEDES. THE TOWN IS CURRENTLY IN THE MIDDLE OF BATTLING A HUGE FIRE. I ASK THAT YOU NOT ATTACK UNTIL THE FIRE IS OUT AND THE PEOPLE ARE EVACUATED.
WHAT?!
YOU MUST BE JOKING, RIGHT?!

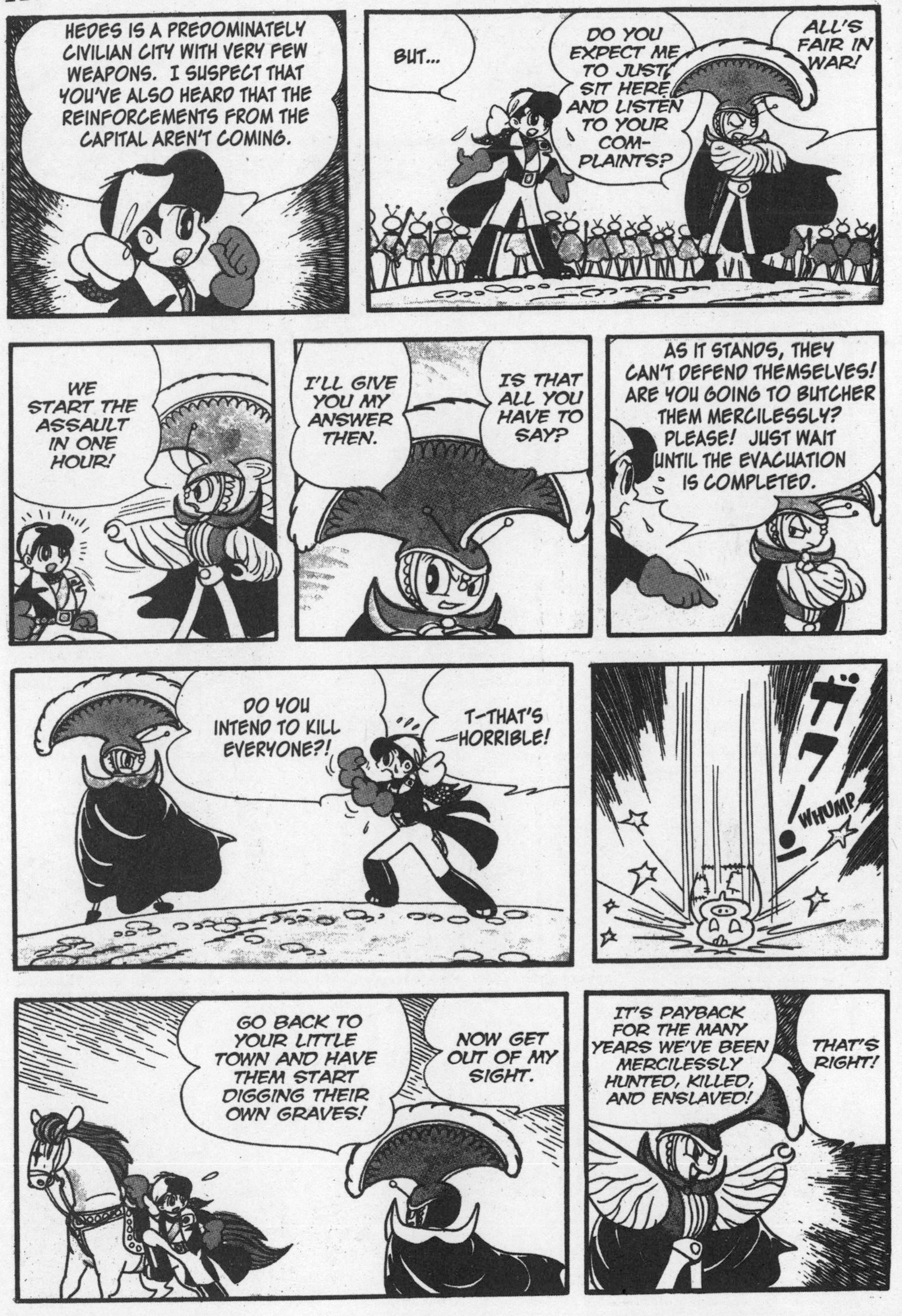
ALL'S FAIR IN WAR!
DO YOU EXPECT ME TO JUST SIT HERE AND LISTEN TO YOUR COMPLAINTS?
BUT...
HEDES IS A PREDOMINATELY CIVILIAN CITY WITH VERY FEW WEAPONS. I SUSPECT THAT YOU'VE ALSO HEARD THAT THE REINFORCEMENTS FROM THE CAPITAL AREN'T COMING.
AS IT STANDS, THEY CAN'T DEFEND THEMSELVES! ARE YOU GOING TO BUTCHER THEM MERCILESSLY? PLEASE! JUST WAIT UNTIL THE EVACUATION IS COMPLETED.
IS THAT ALL YOU HAVE TO SAY?
I'LL GIVE YOU MY ANSWER THEN.
WE START THE ASSAULT IN ONE HOUR!
ガク！
WHUMP
T-THAT'S HORRIBLE!
DO YOU INTEND TO KILL EVERYONE?!
THAT'S RIGHT!
IT'S PAYBACK FOR THE MANY YEARS WE'VE BEEN MERCILESSLY HUNTED, KILLED, AND ENSLAVED!
NOW GET OUT OF MY SIGHT.
GO BACK TO YOUR LITTLE TOWN AND HAVE THEM START DIGGING THEIR OWN GRAVES!

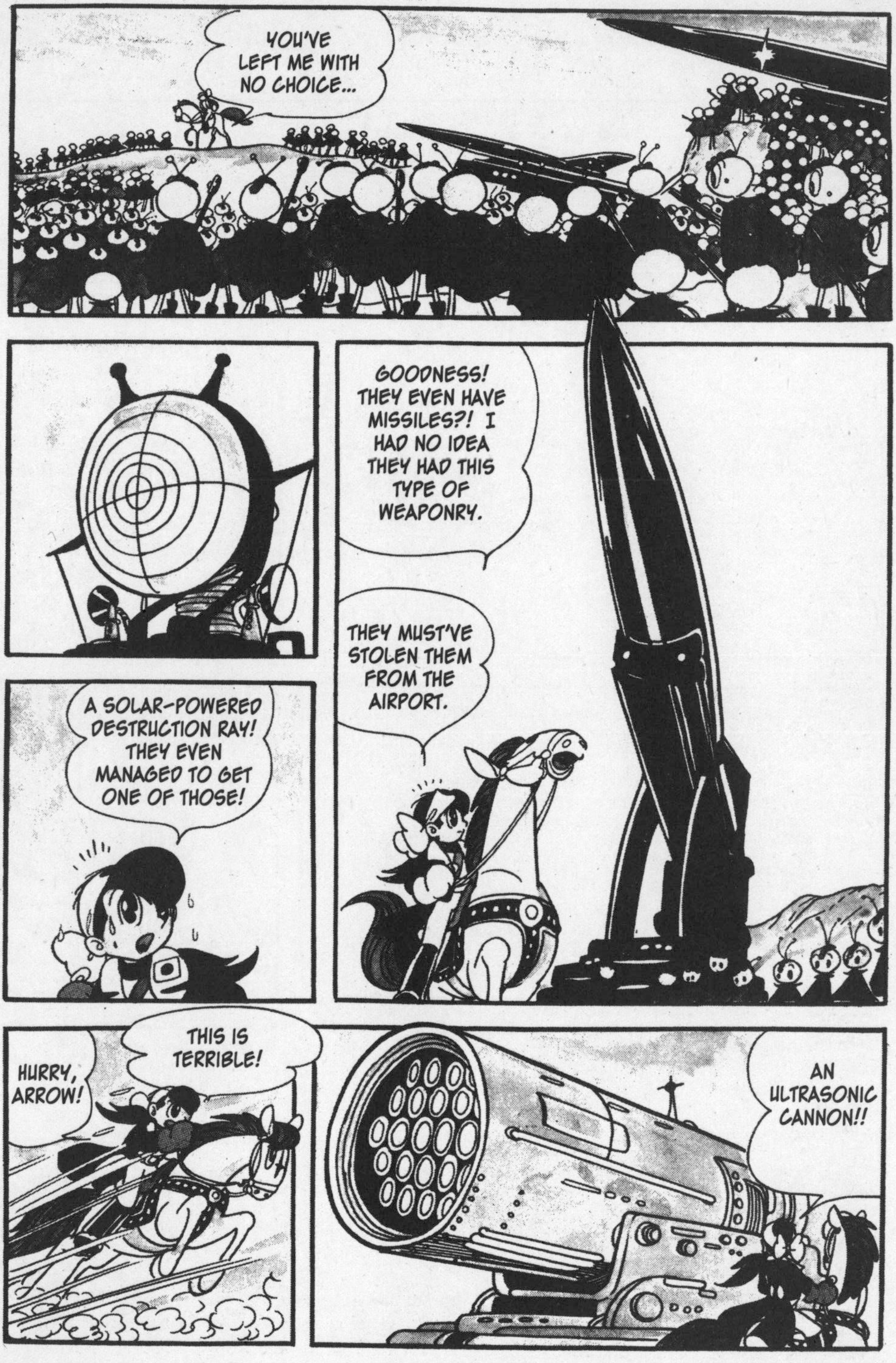
YOU'VE LEFT ME WITH NO CHOICE...
GOODNESS! THEY EVEN HAVE MISSILES?! I HAD NO IDEA THEY HAD THIS TYPE OF WEAPONRY.
THEY MUST'VE STOLEN THEM FROM THE AIRPORT.
A SOLAR-POWERED DESTRUCTION RAY! THEY EVEN MANAGED TO GET ONE OF THOSE!
AN ULTRASONIC CANNON!!
THIS IS TERRIBLE!
HURRY, ARROW!

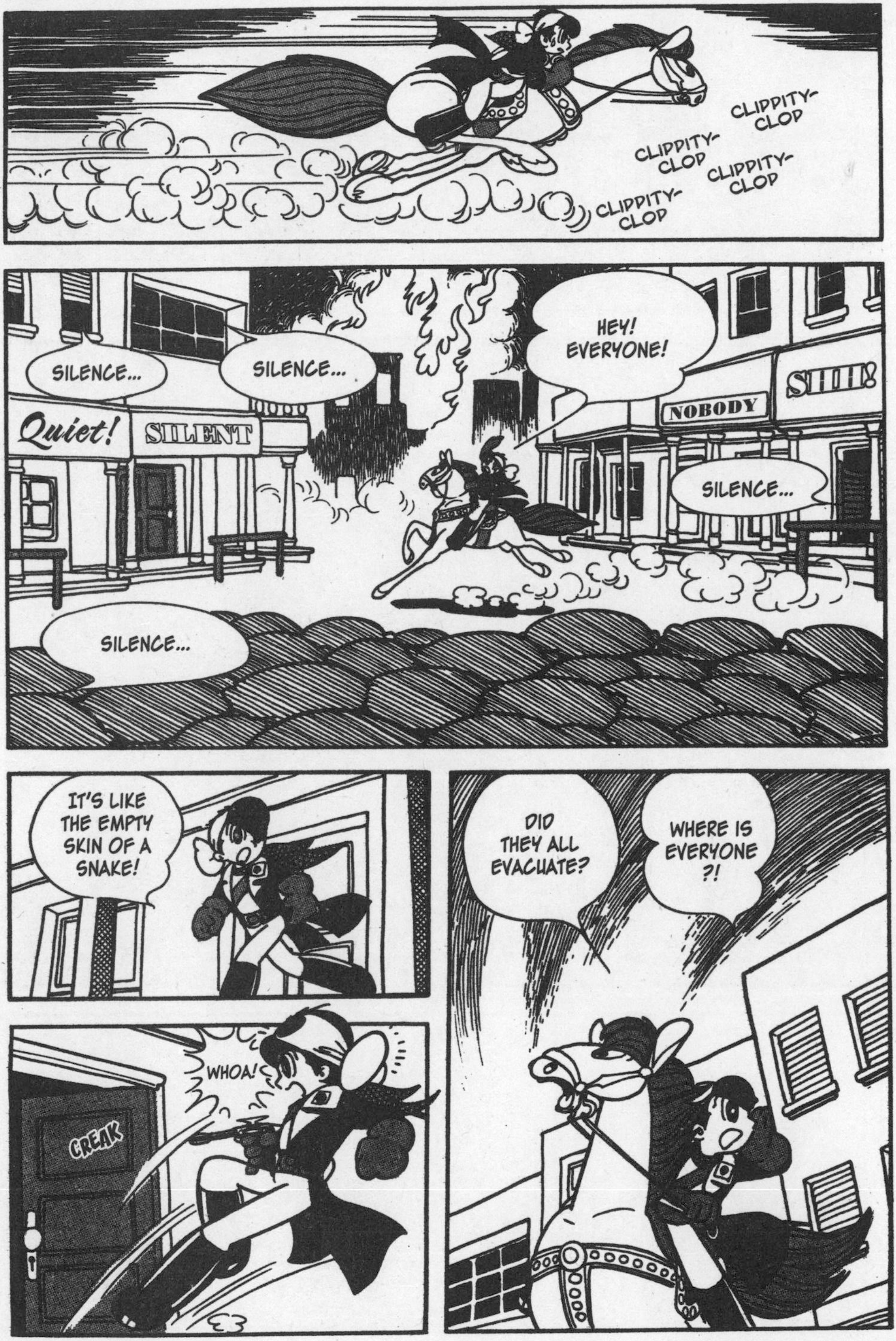
CLIPPITY-CLOP
CLIPPITY-CLOP
CLIPPITY-CLOP
CLIPPITY-CLOP
SHH!
HEY! EVERYONE!
NOBODY
SILENCE...
SILENCE...
SILENCE...
Quiet!
SILENT
SILENCE...
WHERE IS EVERYONE ?!
DID THEY ALL EVACUATE?
IT'S LIKE THE EMPTY SKIN OF A SNAKE!
WHOA!
CREAK

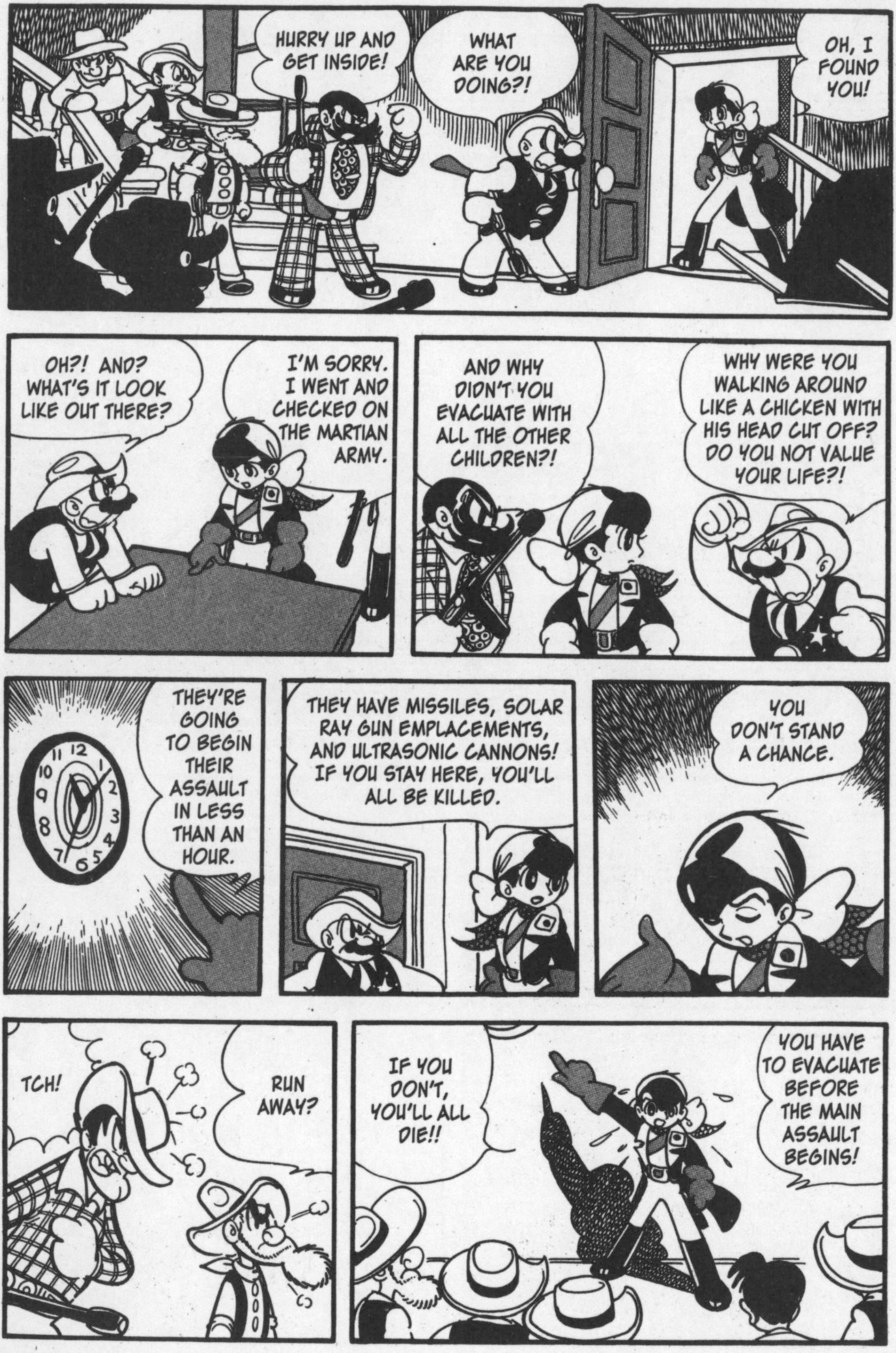
OH, I FOUND YOU!
WHAT ARE YOU DOING?!
HURRY UP AND GET INSIDE!
WHY WERE YOU WALKING AROUND LIKE A CHICKEN WITH HIS HEAD CUT OFF? DO YOU NOT VALUE YOUR LIFE?!
AND WHY DIDN'T YOU EVACUATE WITH ALL THE OTHER CHILDREN?!
I'M SORRY. I WENT AND CHECKED ON THE MARTIAN ARMY.
OH?! AND? WHAT'S IT LOOK LIKE OUT THERE?
YOU DON'T STAND A CHANCE.
THEY HAVE MISSILES, SOLAR RAY GUN EMPLACEMENTS, AND ULTRASONIC CANNONS! IF YOU STAY HERE, YOU'LL ALL BE KILLED.
THEY'RE GOING TO BEGIN THEIR ASSAULT IN LESS THAN AN HOUR.
YOU HAVE TO EVACUATE BEFORE THE MAIN ASSAULT BEGINS!
IF YOU DON'T, YOU'LL ALL DIE!!
RUN AWAY?
TCH!

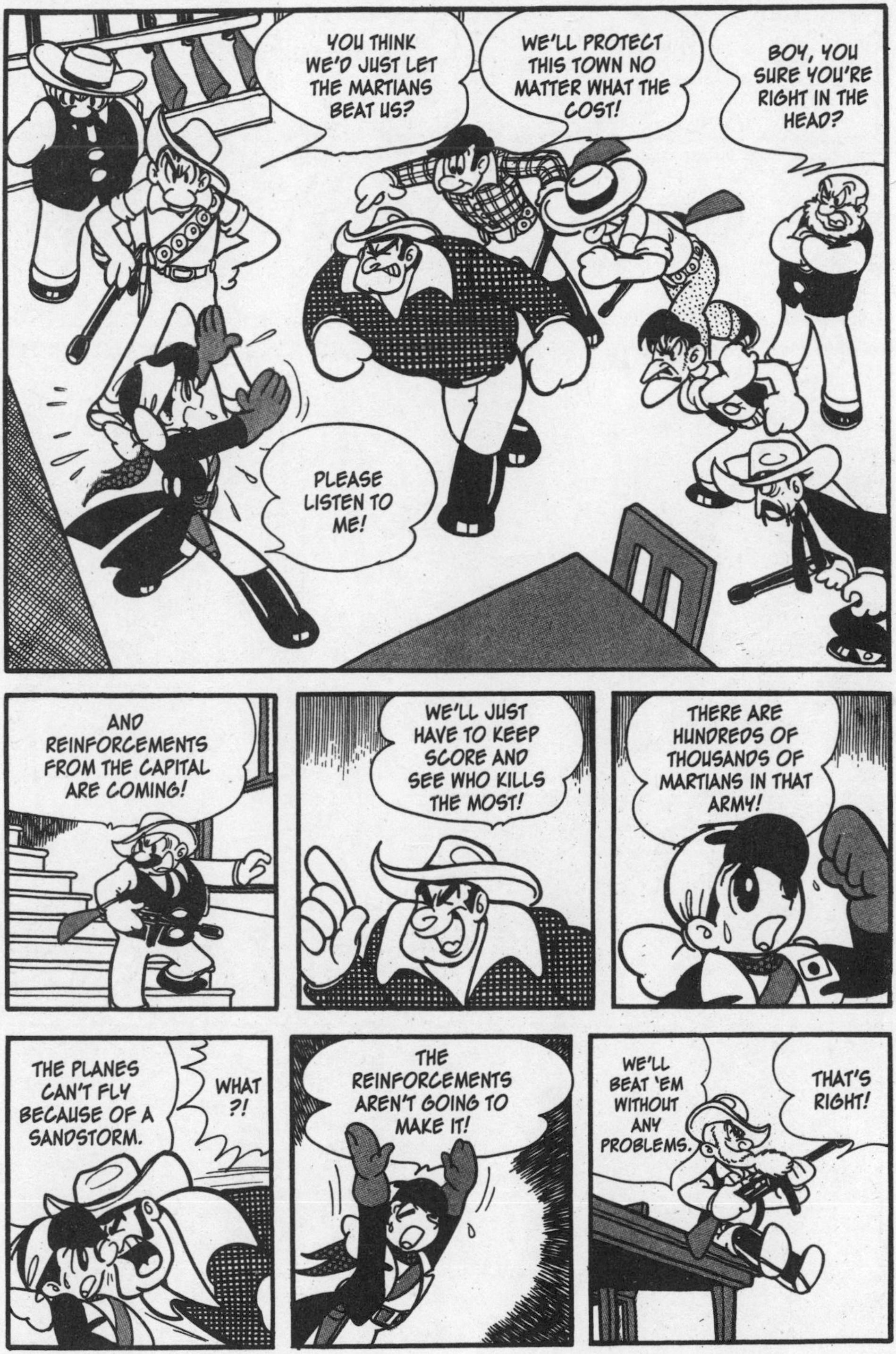
BOY, YOU SURE YOU'RE RIGHT IN THE HEAD?
WE'LL PROTECT THIS TOWN NO MATTER WHAT THE COST!
YOU THINK WE'D JUST LET THE MARTIANS BEAT US?
PLEASE LISTEN TO ME!
THERE ARE HUNDREDS OF THOUSANDS OF MARTIANS IN THAT ARMY!
WE'LL JUST HAVE TO KEEP SCORE AND SEE WHO KILLS THE MOST!
AND REINFORCEMENTS FROM THE CAPITAL ARE COMING!
WE'LL BEAT 'EM WITHOUT ANY PROBLEMS.
THAT'S RIGHT!
THE REINFORCEMENTS AREN'T GOING TO MAKE IT!
THE PLANES CAN'T FLY BECAUSE OF A SANDSTORM.
WHAT ?!

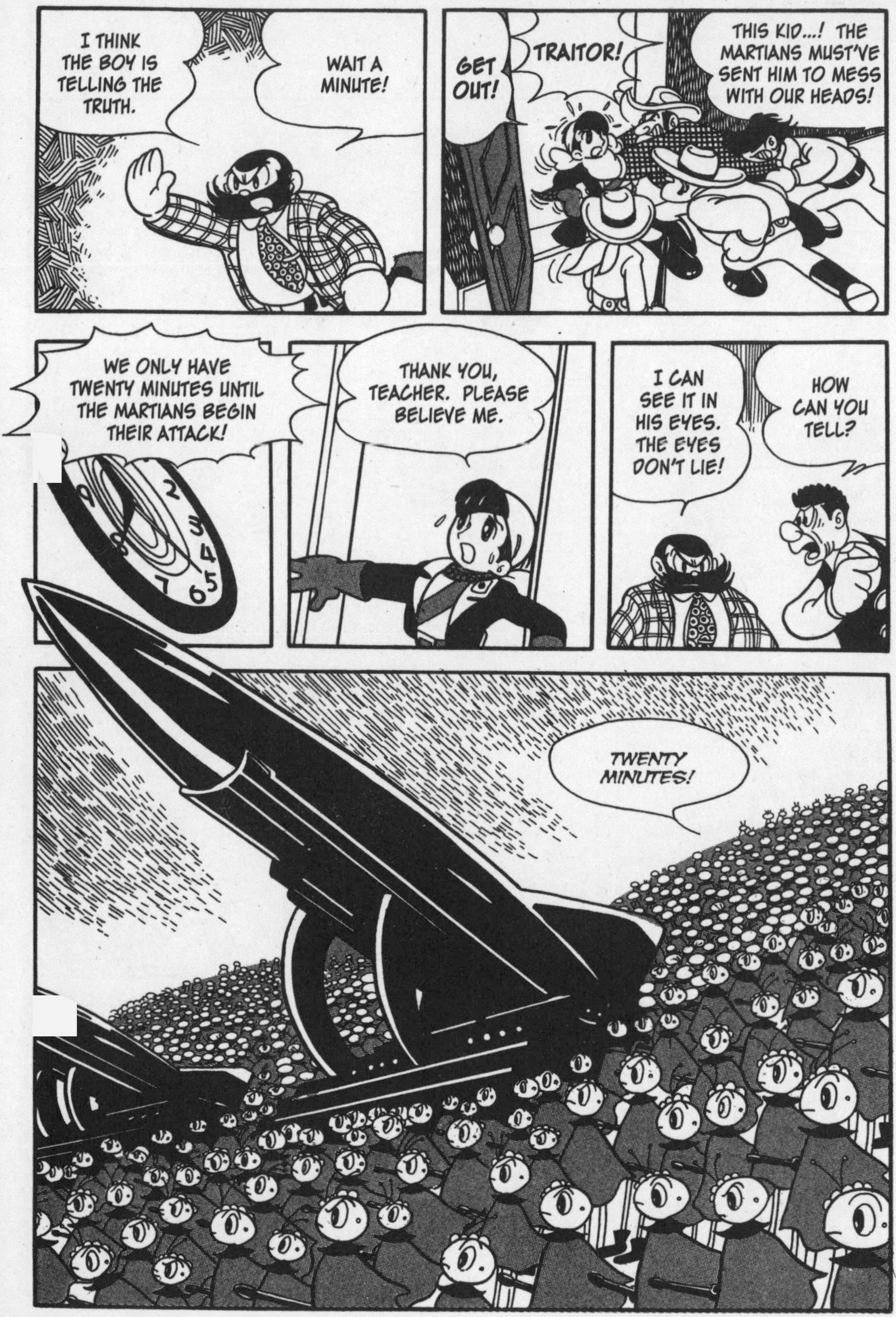
THIS KID...! THE MARTIANS MUST'VE SENT HIM TO MESS WITH OUR HEADS!
TRAITOR!
GET OUT!
WAIT A MINUTE!
I THINK THE BOY IS TELLING THE TRUTH.
HOW CAN YOU TELL?
I CAN SEE IT IN HIS EYES. THE EYES DON'T LIE!
THANK YOU, TEACHER. PLEASE BELIEVE ME.
WE ONLY HAVE TWENTY MINUTES UNTIL THE MARTIANS BEGIN THEIR ATTACK!
TWENTY MINUTES!

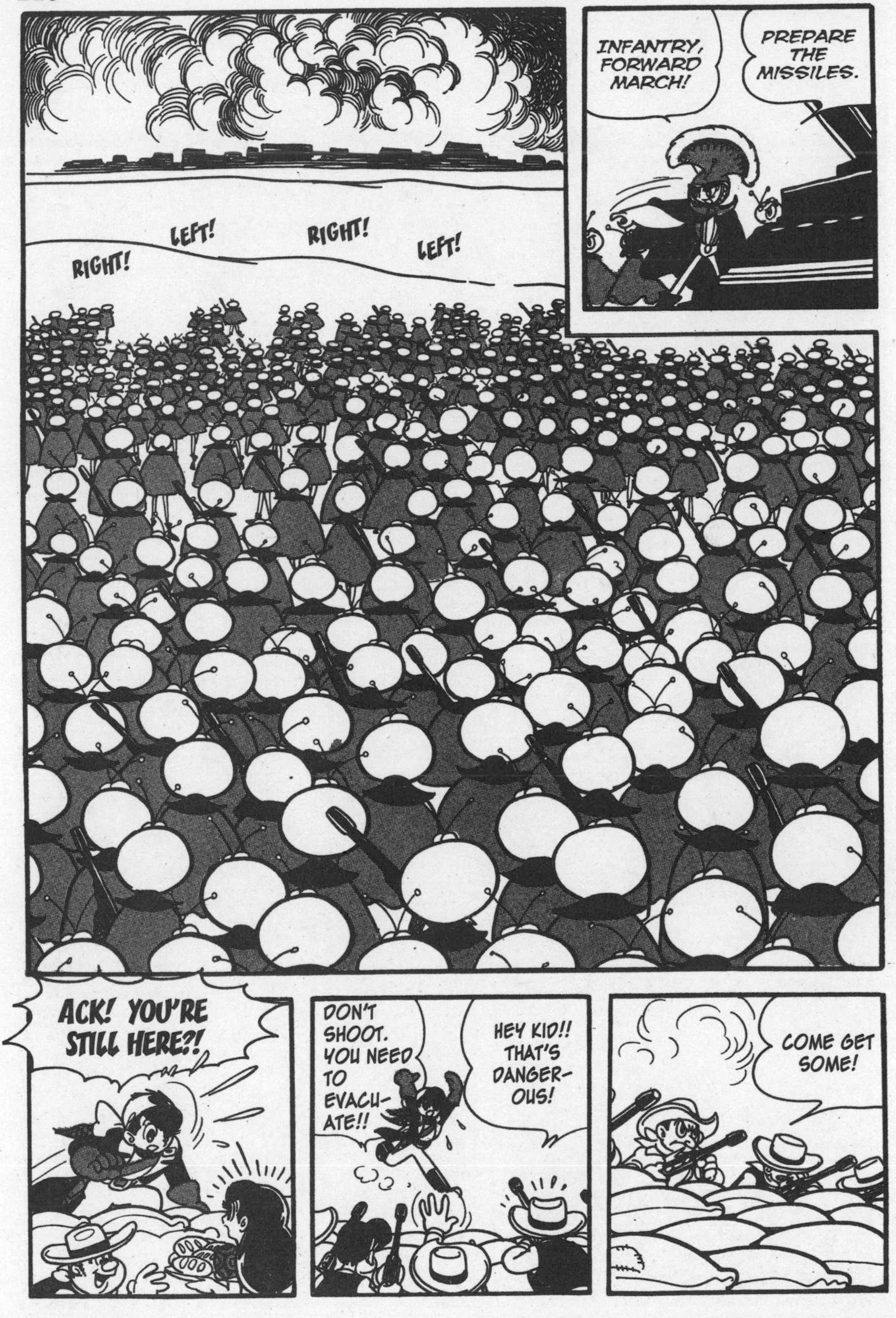
PREPARE THE MISSILES.
INFANTRY, FORWARD MARCH!
LEFT!
RIGHT!
LEFT!
RIGHT!
COME GET SOME!
HEY KID!! THAT'S DANGER-OUS!
DON'T SHOOT. YOU NEED TO EVACU-ATE!!
ACK! YOU'RE STILL HERE?!

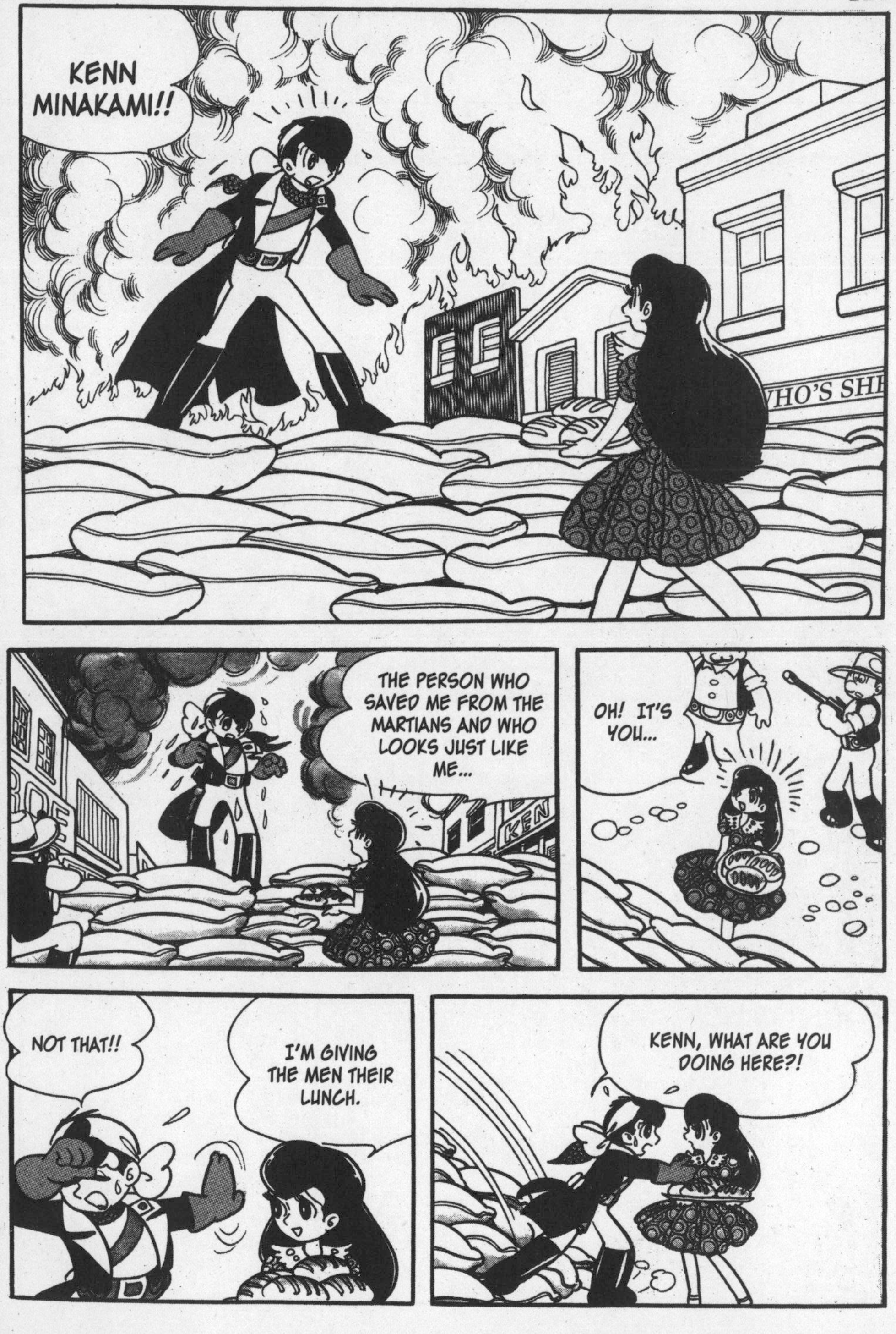
KENN MINAKAMI!!
OH! IT'S YOU...
THE PERSON WHO SAVED ME FROM THE MARTIANS AND WHO LOOKS JUST LIKE ME...
KEN
KENN, WHAT ARE YOU DOING HERE?!
I'M GIVING THE MEN THEIR LUNCH.
NOT THAT!!

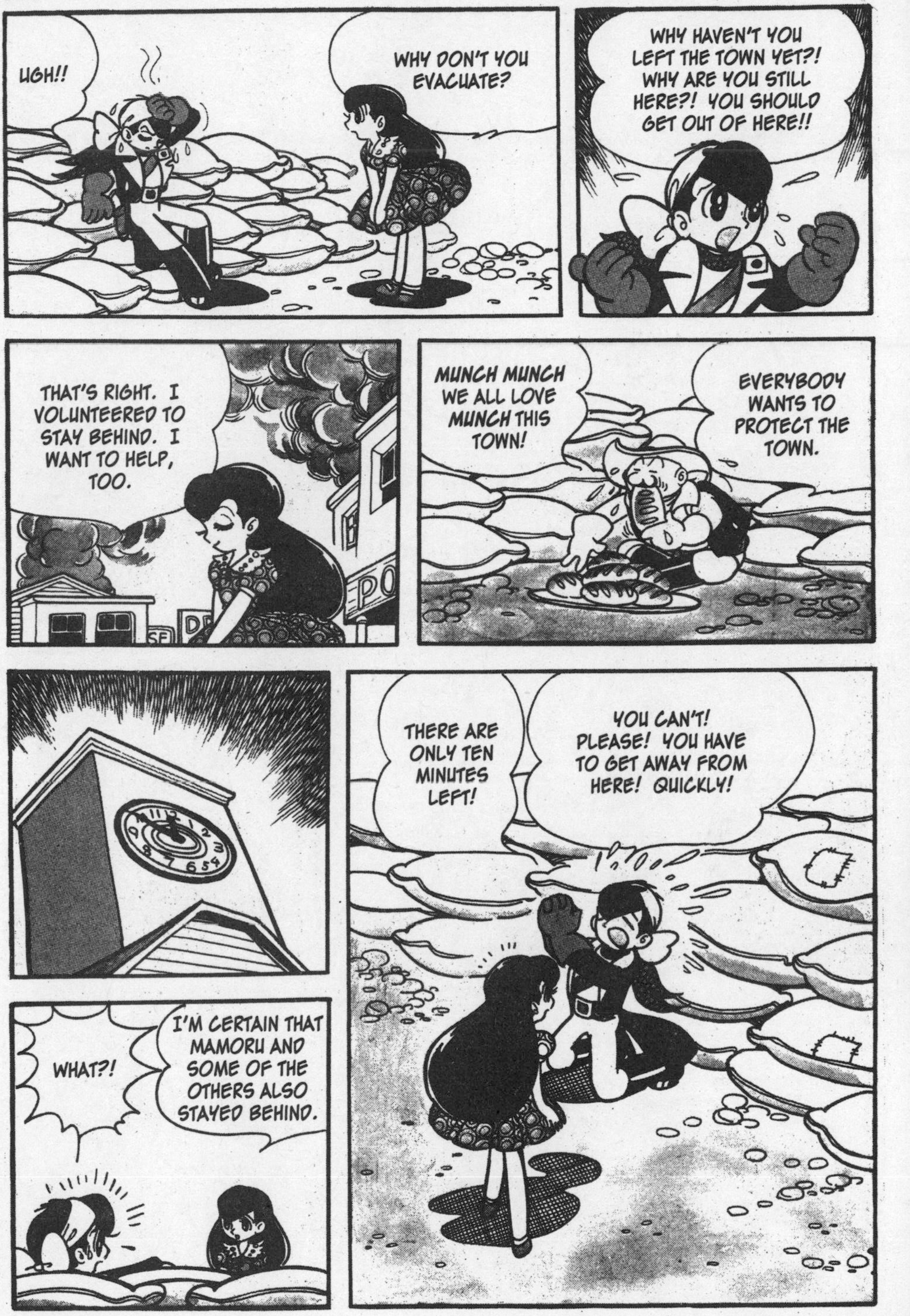
WHY HAVEN'T YOU LEFT THE TOWN YET?! WHY ARE YOU STILL HERE?! YOU SHOULD GET OUT OF HERE!!
WHY DON'T YOU EVACUATE?
UGH!!
EVERYBODY WANTS TO PROTECT THE TOWN.
MUNCH MUNCH WE ALL LOVE MUNCH THIS TOWN!
THAT'S RIGHT. I VOLUNTEERED TO STAY BEHIND. I WANT TO HELP, TOO.
YOU CAN'T! PLEASE! YOU HAVE TO GET AWAY FROM HERE! QUICKLY!
THERE ARE ONLY TEN MINUTES LEFT!
I'M CERTAIN THAT MAMORU AND SOME OF THE OTHERS ALSO STAYED BEHIND.
WHAT?!

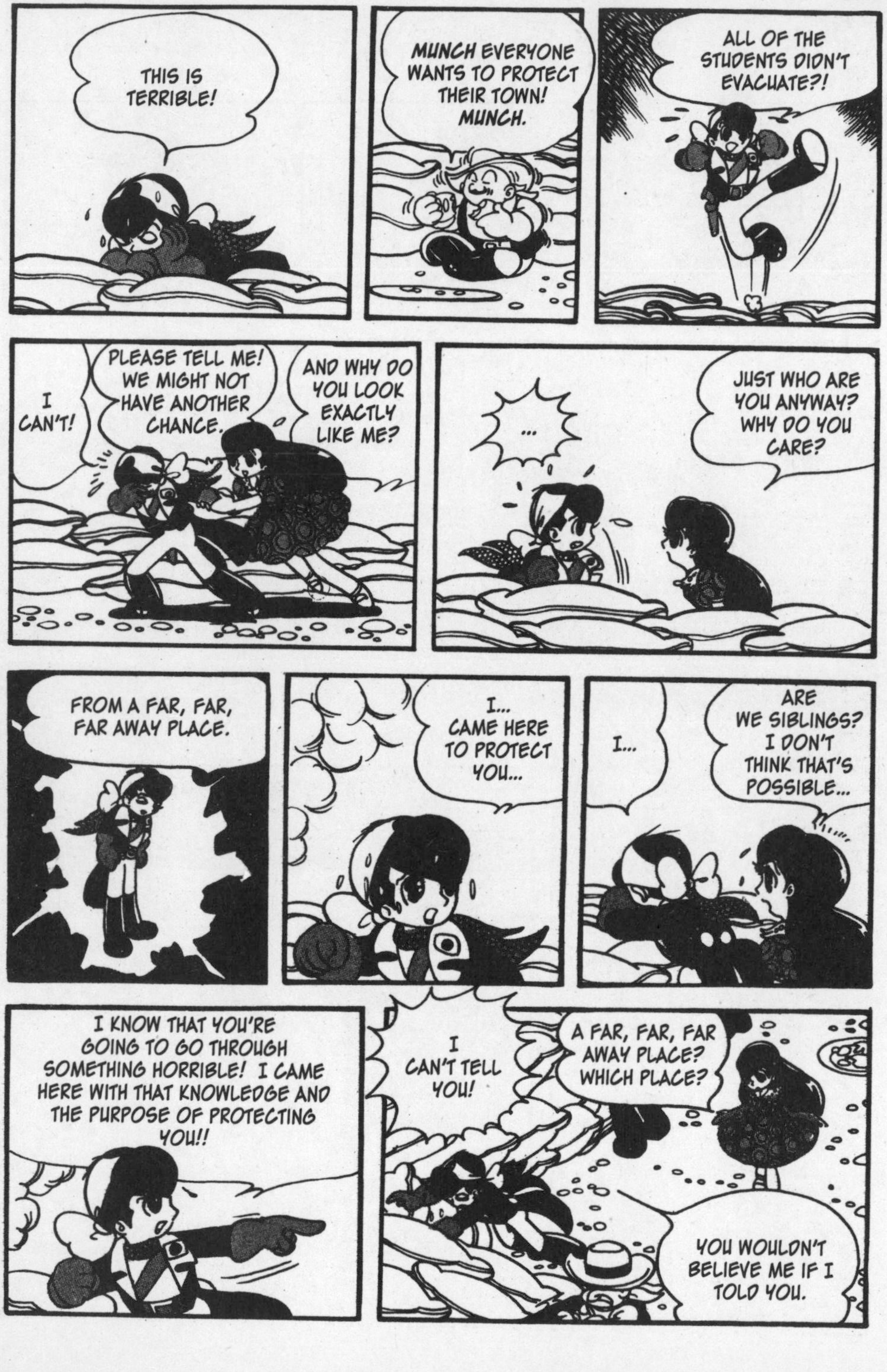
ALL OF THE STUDENTS DIDN'T EVACUATE?!
MUNCH EVERYONE WANTS TO PROTECT THEIR TOWN! MUNCH.
THIS IS TERRIBLE!
JUST WHO ARE YOU ANYWAY? WHY DO YOU CARE?
...
AND WHY DO YOU LOOK EXACTLY LIKE ME?
PLEASE TELL ME! WE MIGHT NOT HAVE ANOTHER CHANCE.
I CAN'T!
ARE WE SIBLINGS? I DON'T THINK THAT'S POSSIBLE...
I...
I... CAME HERE TO PROTECT YOU...
FROM A FAR, FAR, FAR AWAY PLACE.
A FAR, FAR, FAR AWAY PLACE? WHICH PLACE?
I CAN'T TELL YOU!
YOU WOULDN'T BELIEVE ME IF I TOLD YOU.
I KNOW THAT YOU'RE GOING TO GO THROUGH SOMETHING HORRIBLE! I CAME HERE WITH THAT KNOWLEDGE AND THE PURPOSE OF PROTECTING YOU!!

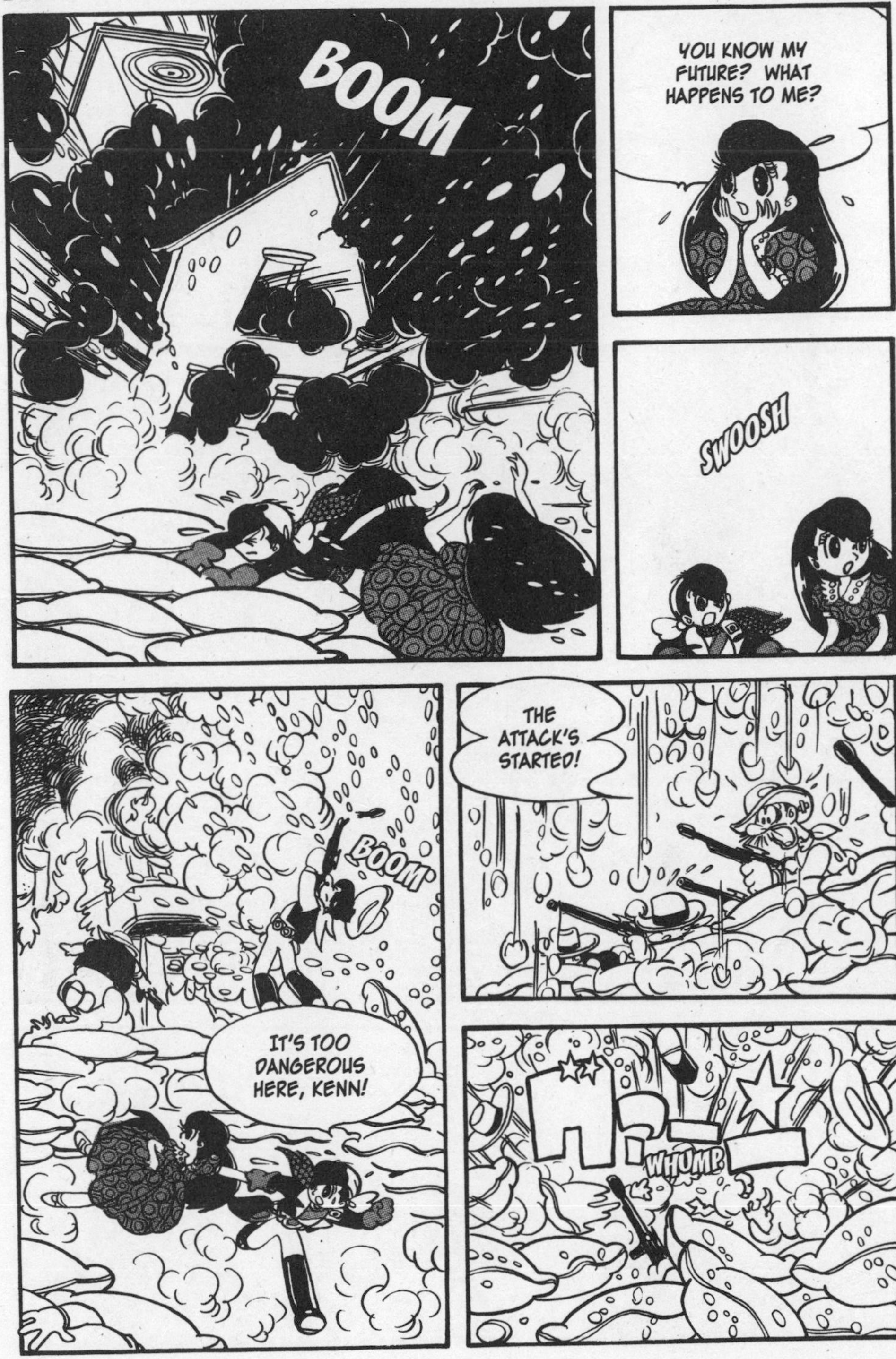
YOU KNOW MY FUTURE? WHAT HAPPENS TO ME?
SWOOSH
BOOM
THE ATTACK'S STARTED!
WHUMP
BOOM
IT'S TOO DANGEROUS HERE, KENN!

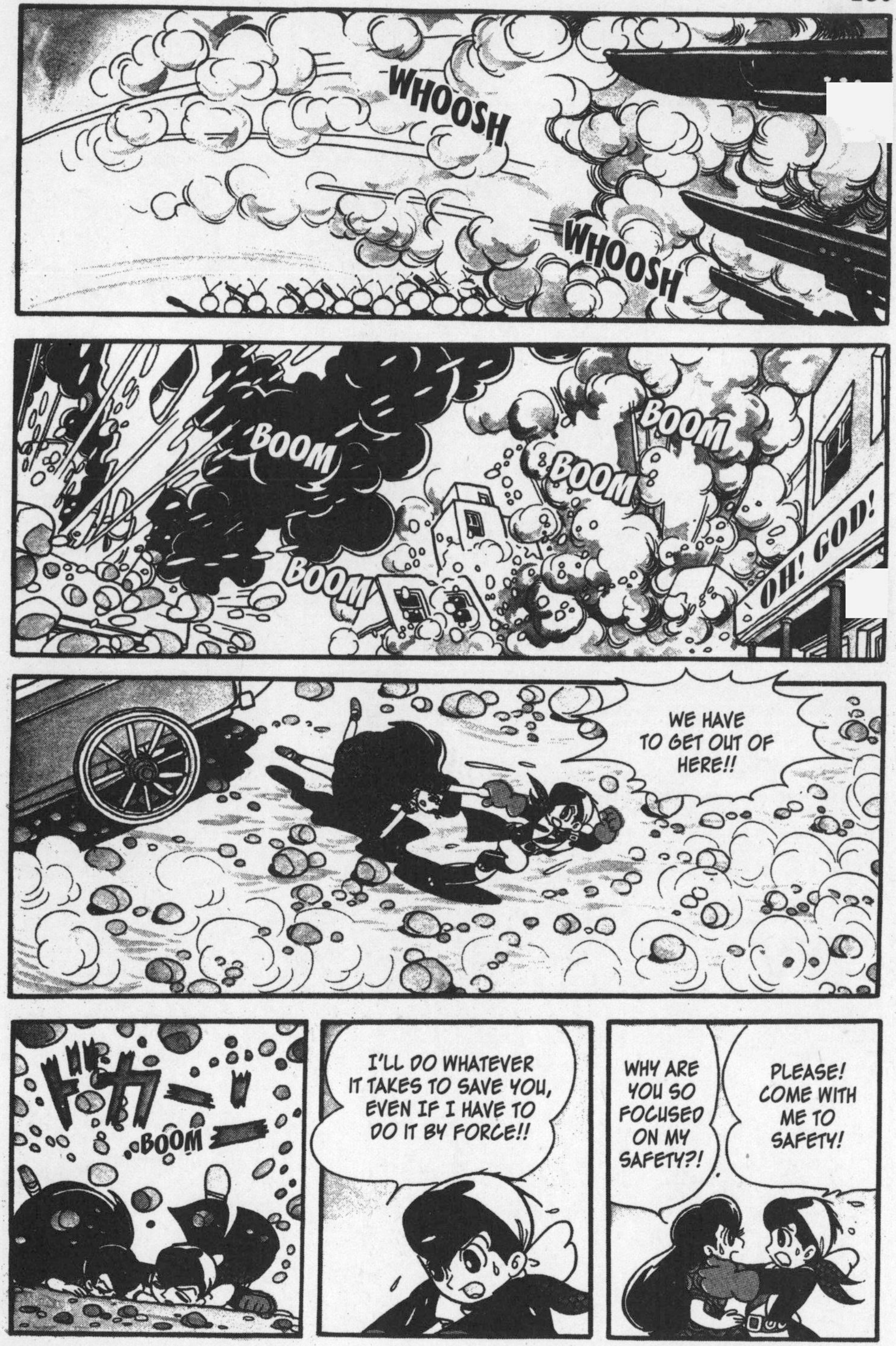
WHOOSH
WHOOSH
OH! GOD!
BOOM
BOOM
BOOM
BOOM
WE HAVE TO GET OUT OF HERE!!
PLEASE! COME WITH ME TO SAFETY!
WHY ARE YOU SO FOCUSED ON MY SAFETY?!
I'LL DO WHATEVER IT TAKES TO SAVE YOU, EVEN IF I HAVE TO DO IT BY FORCE!!
ドカー!
BOOM

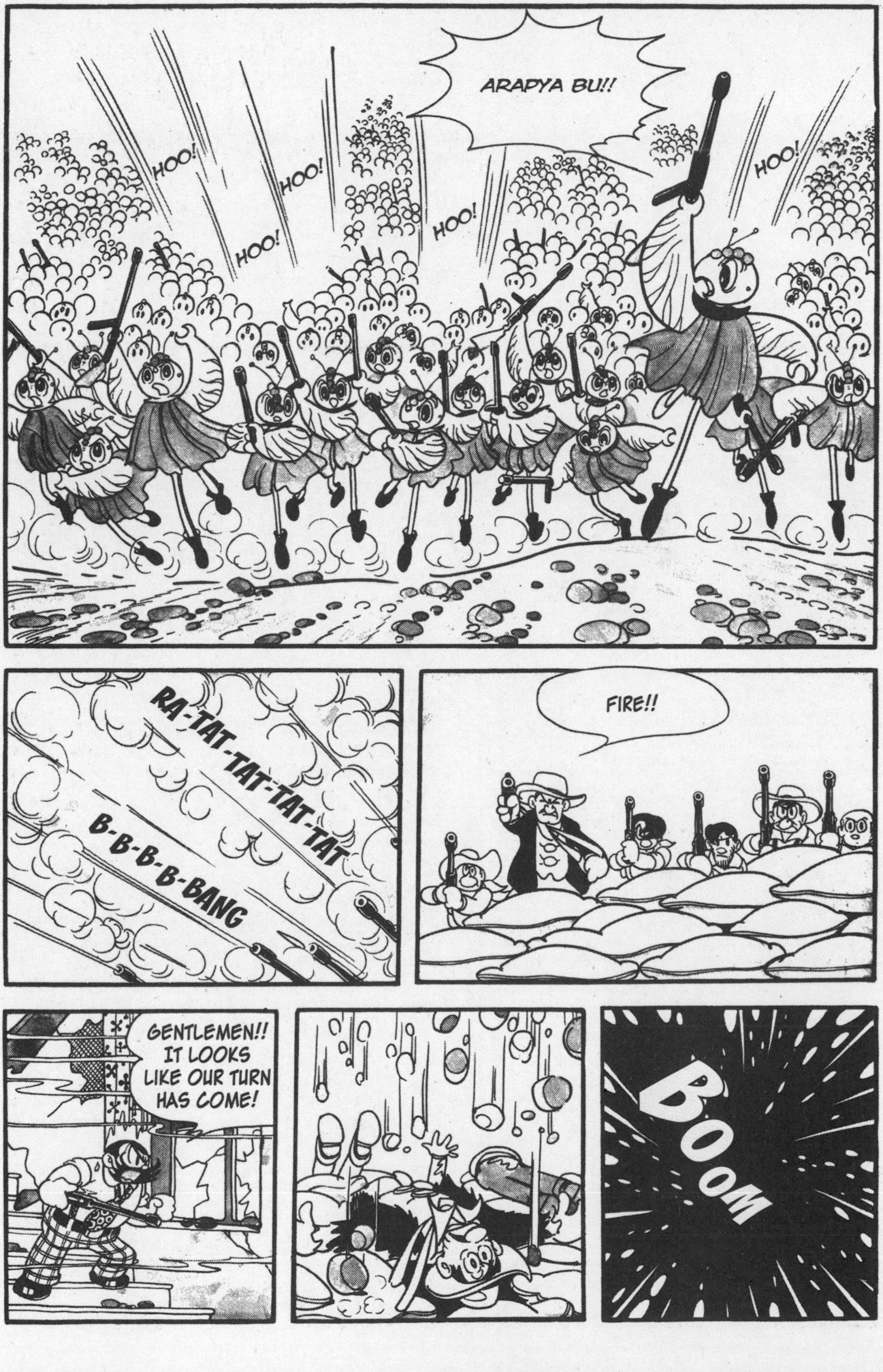
ARAPYA BU!!
HOO!
HOO!
HOO!
HOO!
HOO!
FIRE!!
RA-TAT-TAT-TAT-TAT
B-B-B-B-BANG
BOOM
GENTLEMEN!! IT LOOKS LIKE OUR TURN HAS COME!

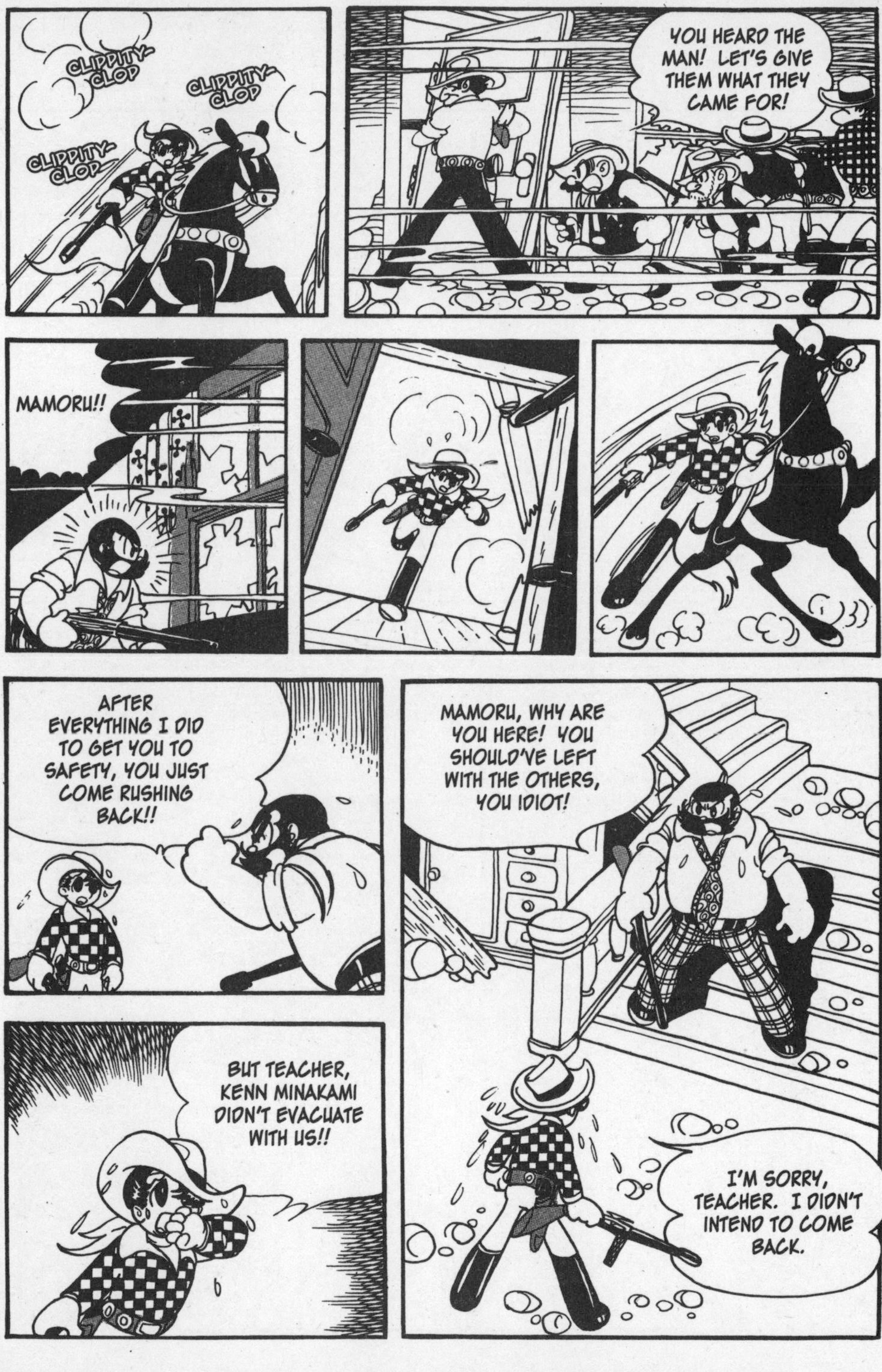
YOU HEARD THE MAN! LET'S GIVE THEM WHAT THEY CAME FOR!
CLIPPITY-CLOP
CLIPPITY-CLOP
CLIPPITY-CLOP
MAMORU!!
MAMORU, WHY ARE YOU HERE! YOU SHOULD'VE LEFT WITH THE OTHERS, YOU IDIOT!
I'M SORRY, TEACHER. I DIDN'T INTEND TO COME BACK.
AFTER EVERYTHING I DID TO GET YOU TO SAFETY, YOU JUST COME RUSHING BACK!!
BUT TEACHER, KENN MINAKAMI DIDN'T EVACUATE WITH US!!

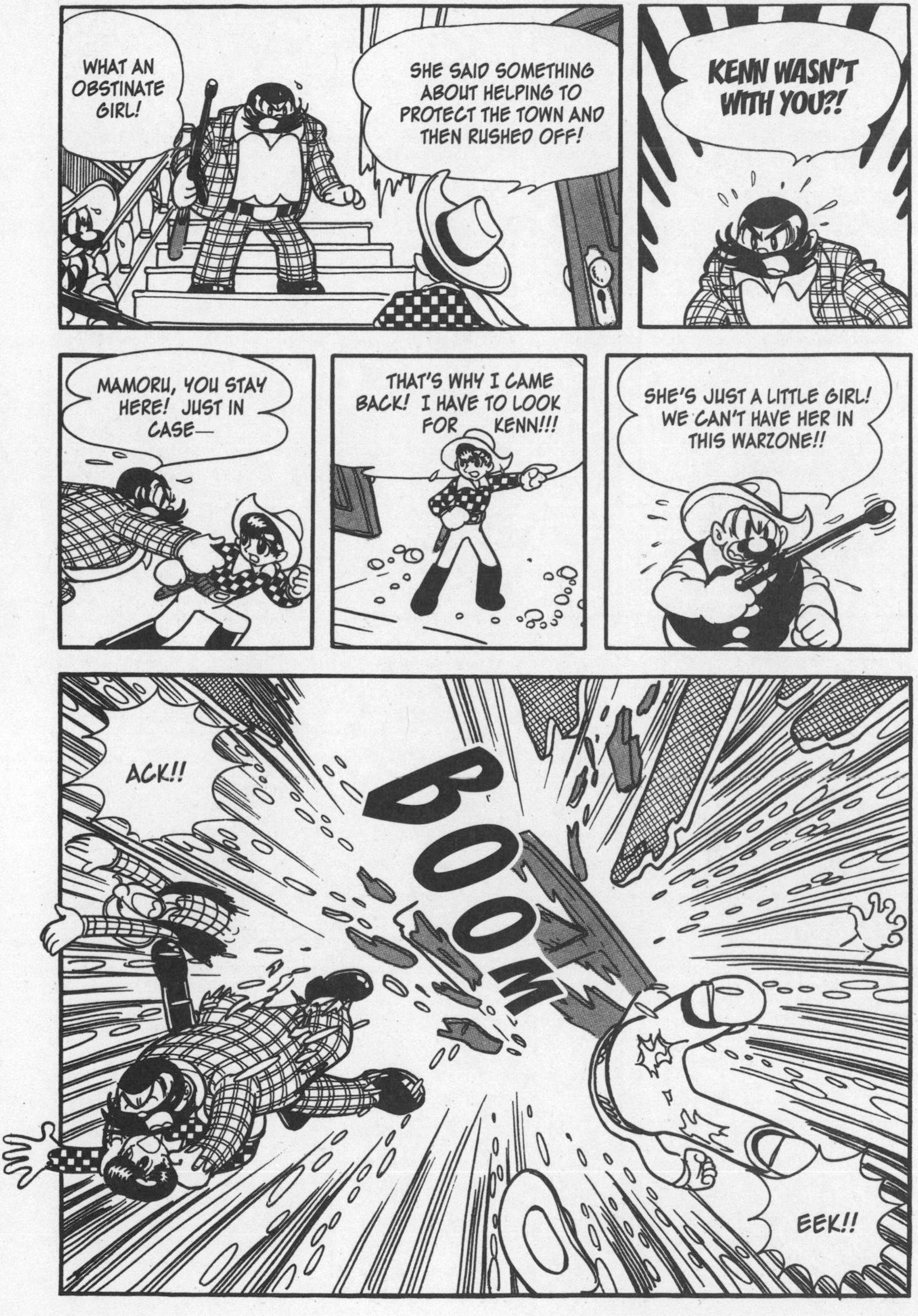
KENN WASN'T WITH YOU?!
SHE SAID SOMETHING ABOUT HELPING TO PROTECT THE TOWN AND THEN RUSHED OFF!
WHAT AN OBSTINATE GIRL!
SHE'S JUST A LITTLE GIRL! WE CAN'T HAVE HER IN THIS WARZONE!!
THAT'S WHY I CAME BACK! I HAVE TO LOOK FOR KENN!!!
MAMORU, YOU STAY HERE! JUST IN CASE—
BOOM
EEK!!
ACK!!

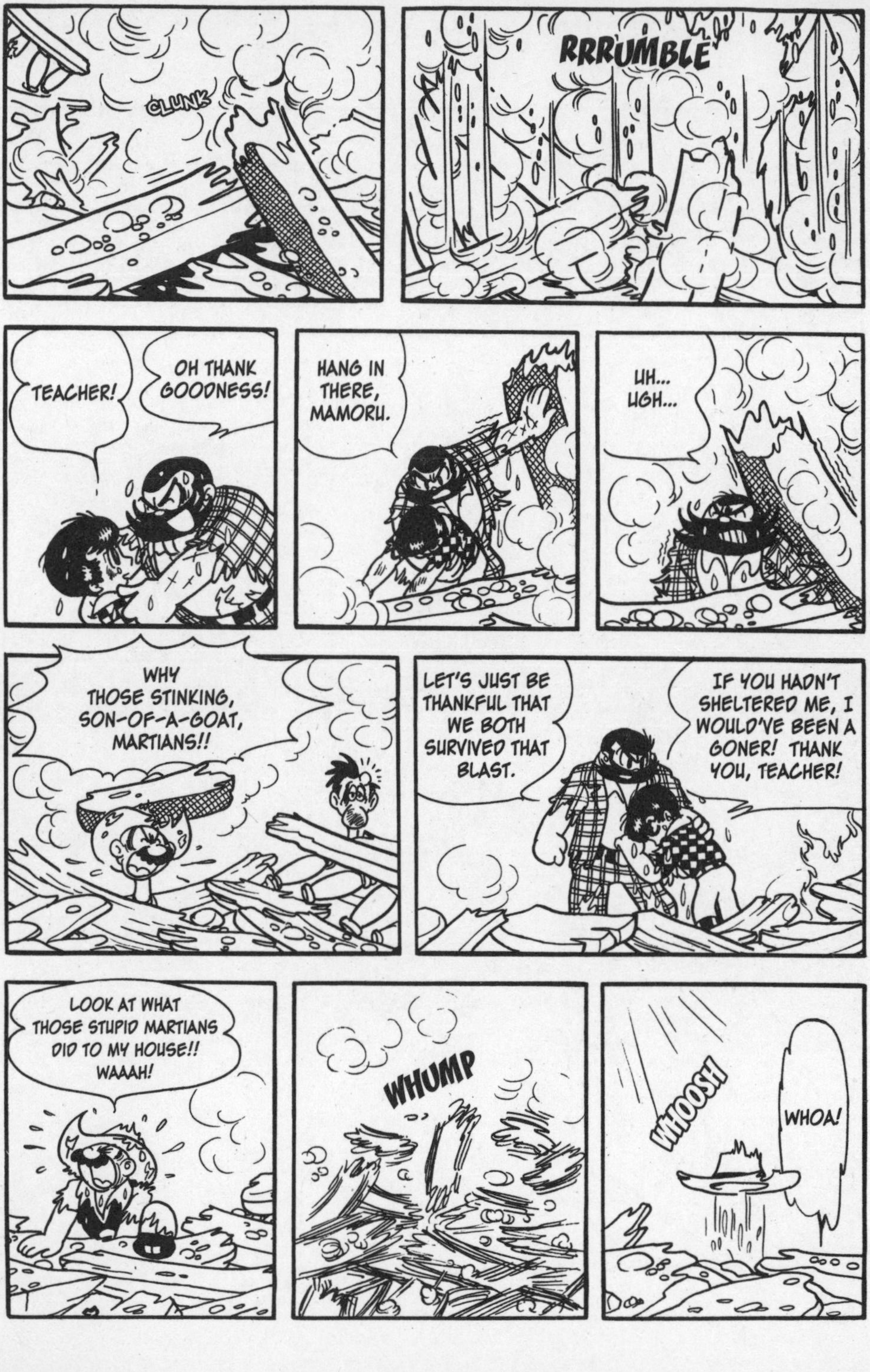
RRRUMBLE
CLUNK
UH... UGH...
HANG IN THERE, MAMORU.
OH THANK GOODNESS!
TEACHER!
IF YOU HADN'T SHELTERED ME, I WOULD'VE BEEN A GONER! THANK YOU, TEACHER!
LET'S JUST BE THANKFUL THAT WE BOTH SURVIVED THAT BLAST.
WHY THOSE STINKING, SON-OF-A-GOAT, MARTIANS!!
WHOA!
WHOOSH
WHUMP
LOOK AT WHAT THOSE STUPID MARTIANS DID TO MY HOUSE!! WAAAH!

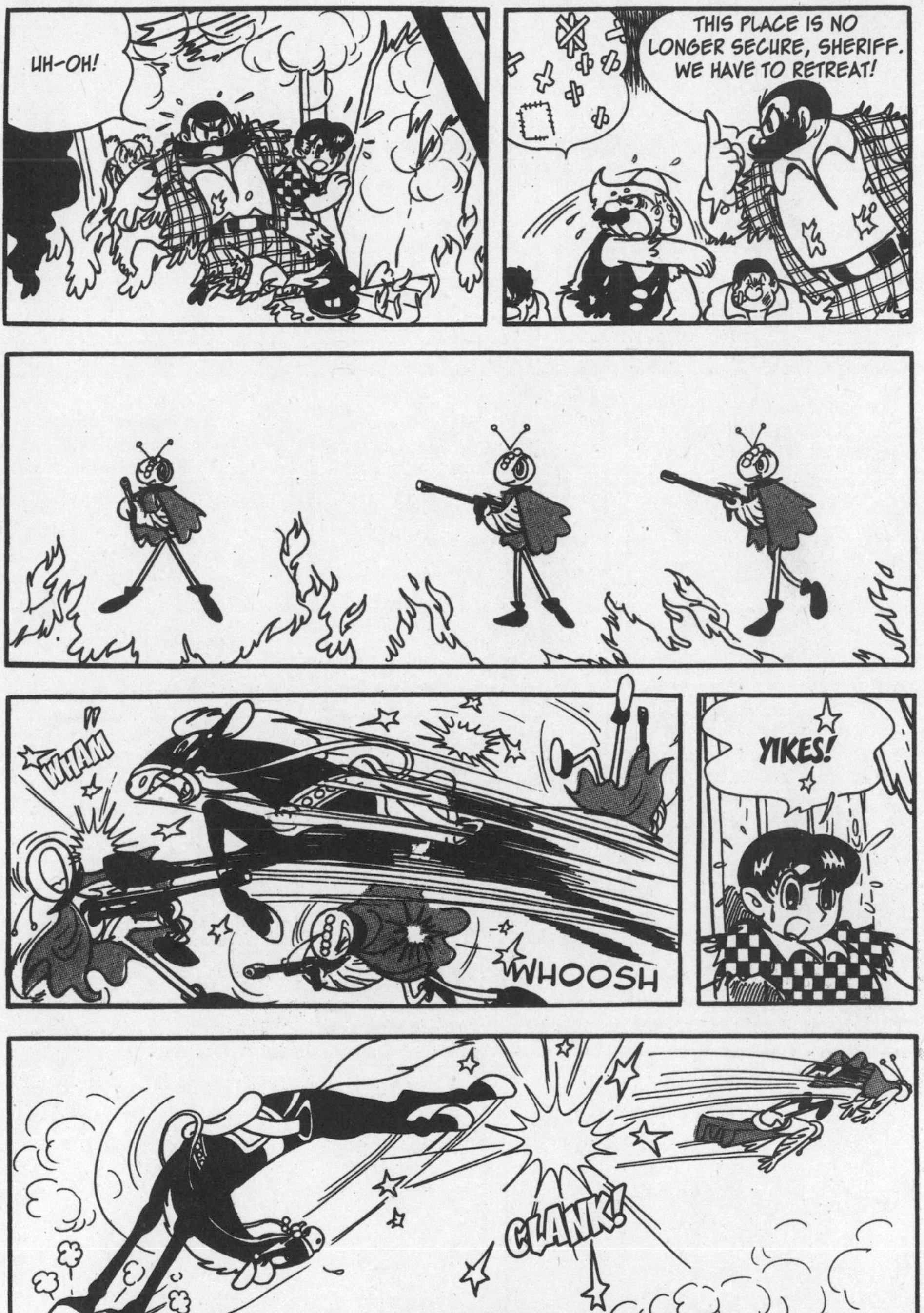
THIS PLACE IS NO LONGER SECURE, SHERIFF. WE HAVE TO RETREAT!
UH-OH!
YIKES!
WHAM
WHOOSH
CLANK!

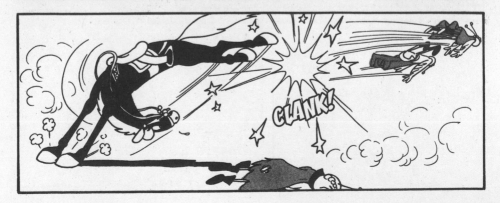

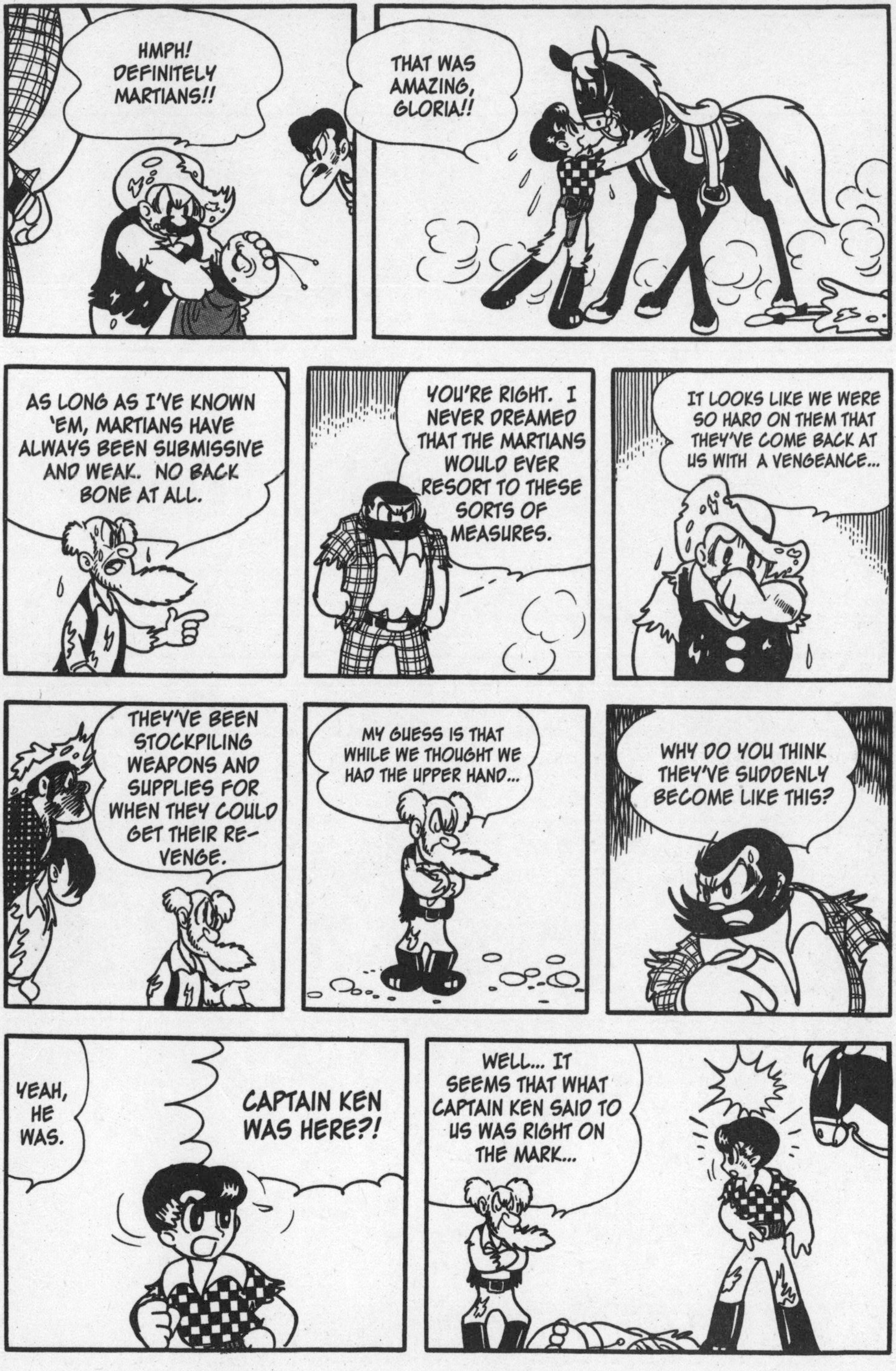
THAT WAS AMAZING, GLORIA!!
HMPH! DEFINITELY MARTIANS!!
IT LOOKS LIKE WE WERE SO HARD ON THEM THAT THEY'VE COME BACK AT US WITH A VENGEANCE...
YOU'RE RIGHT. I NEVER DREAMED THAT THE MARTIANS WOULD EVER RESORT TO THESE SORTS OF MEASURES.
AS LONG AS I'VE KNOWN 'EM, MARTIANS HAVE ALWAYS BEEN SUBMISSIVE AND WEAK. NO BACK BONE AT ALL.
WHY DO YOU THINK THEY'VE SUDDENLY BECOME LIKE THIS?
MY GUESS IS THAT WHILE WE THOUGHT WE HAD THE UPPER HAND...
THEY'VE BEEN STOCKPILING WEAPONS AND SUPPLIES FOR WHEN THEY COULD GET THEIR RE-VENGE.
WELL... IT SEEMS THAT WHAT CAPTAIN KEN SAID TO US WAS RIGHT ON THE MARK...
CAPTAIN KEN WAS HERE?!
YEAH, HE WAS.

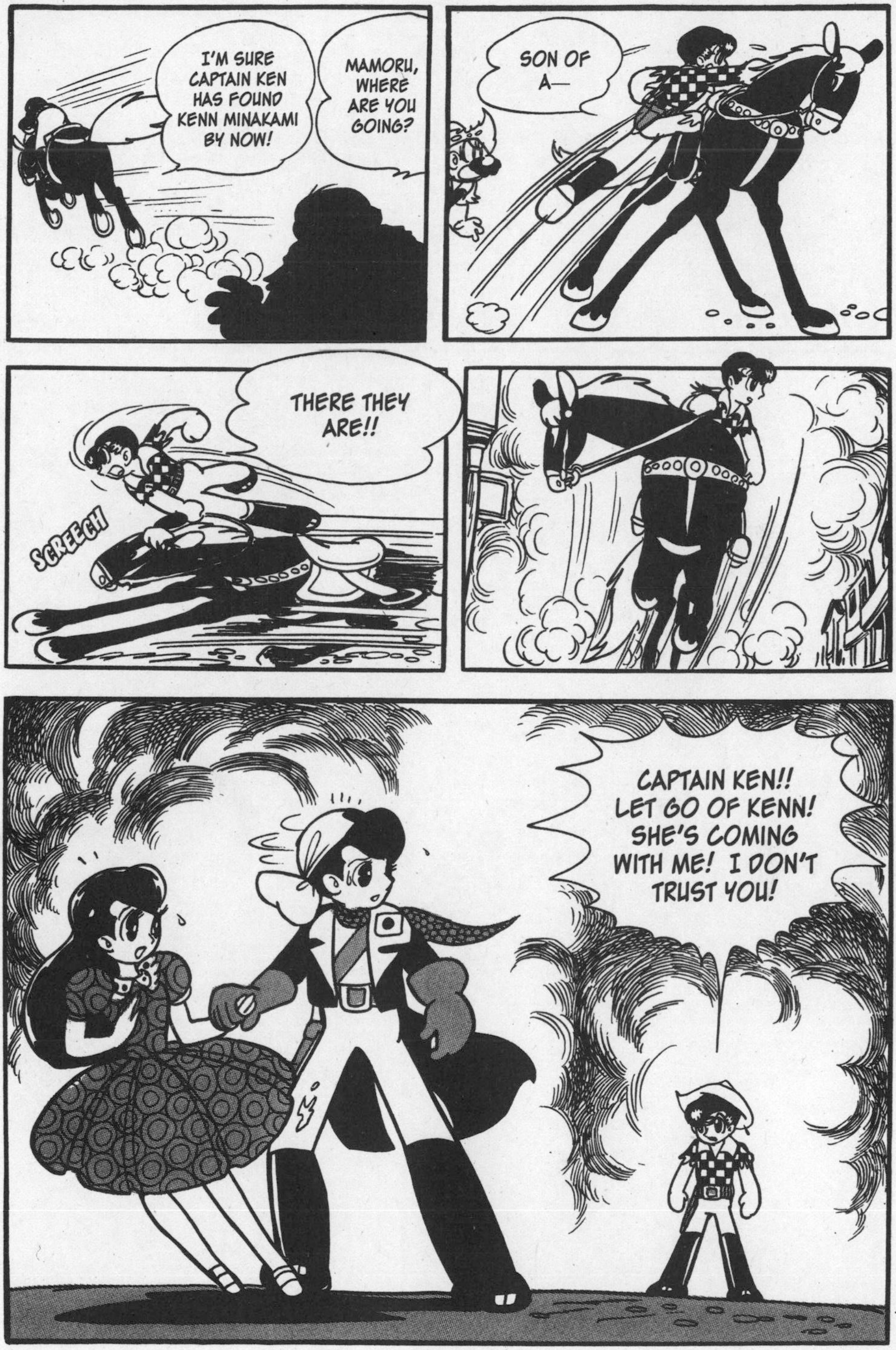
SON OF A—
MAMORU, WHERE ARE YOU GOING?
I'M SURE CAPTAIN KEN HAS FOUND KENN MINAKAMI BY NOW!
THERE THEY ARE!!
SCREECH
CAPTAIN KEN!! LET GO OF KENN! SHE'S COMING WITH ME! I DON'T TRUST YOU!

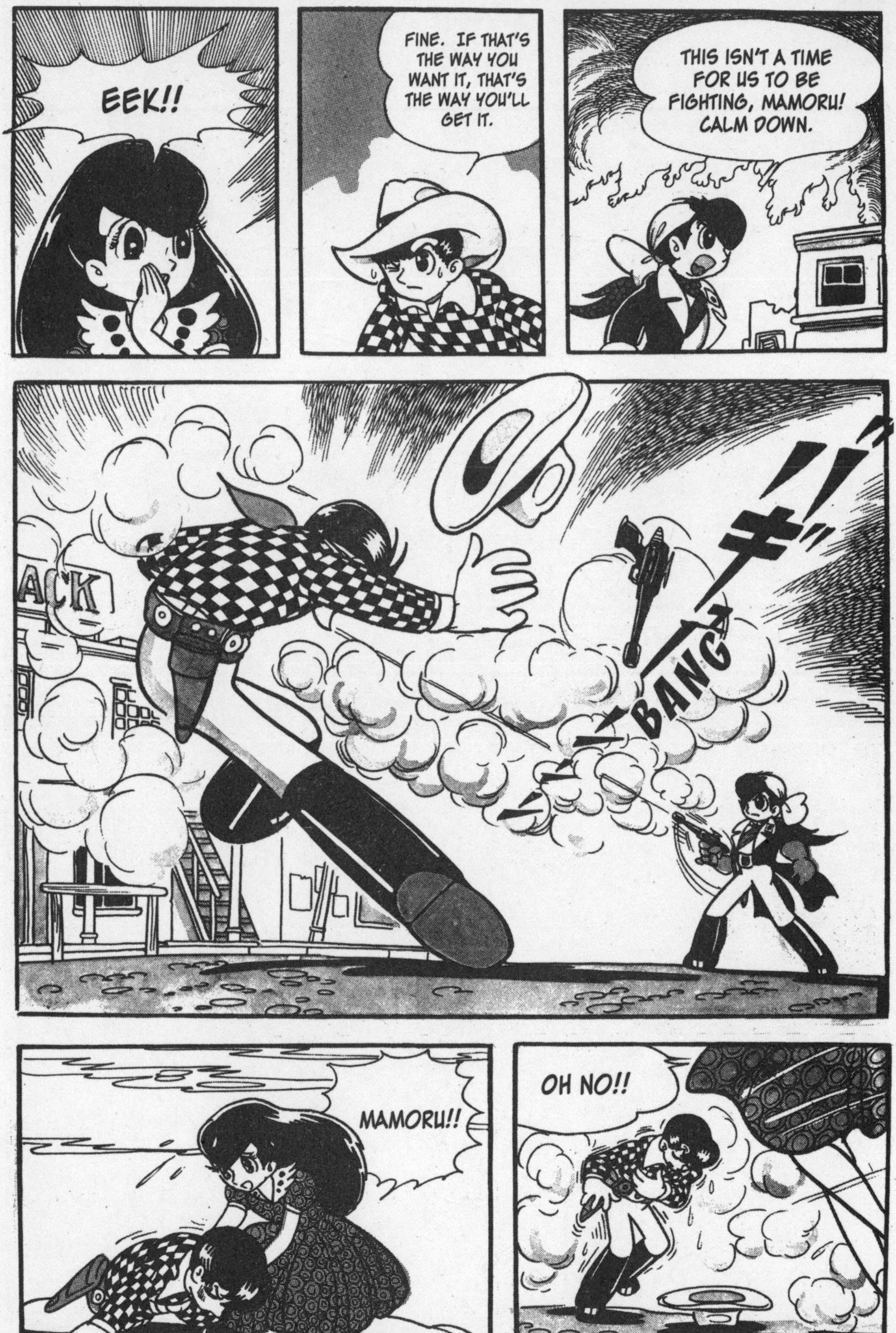
THIS ISN'T A TIME FOR US TO BE FIGHTING, MAMORU! CALM DOWN.
FINE. IF THAT'S THE WAY YOU WANT IT, THAT'S THE WAY YOU'LL GET IT.
EEK!!
BANG
OH NO!!
MAMORU!!

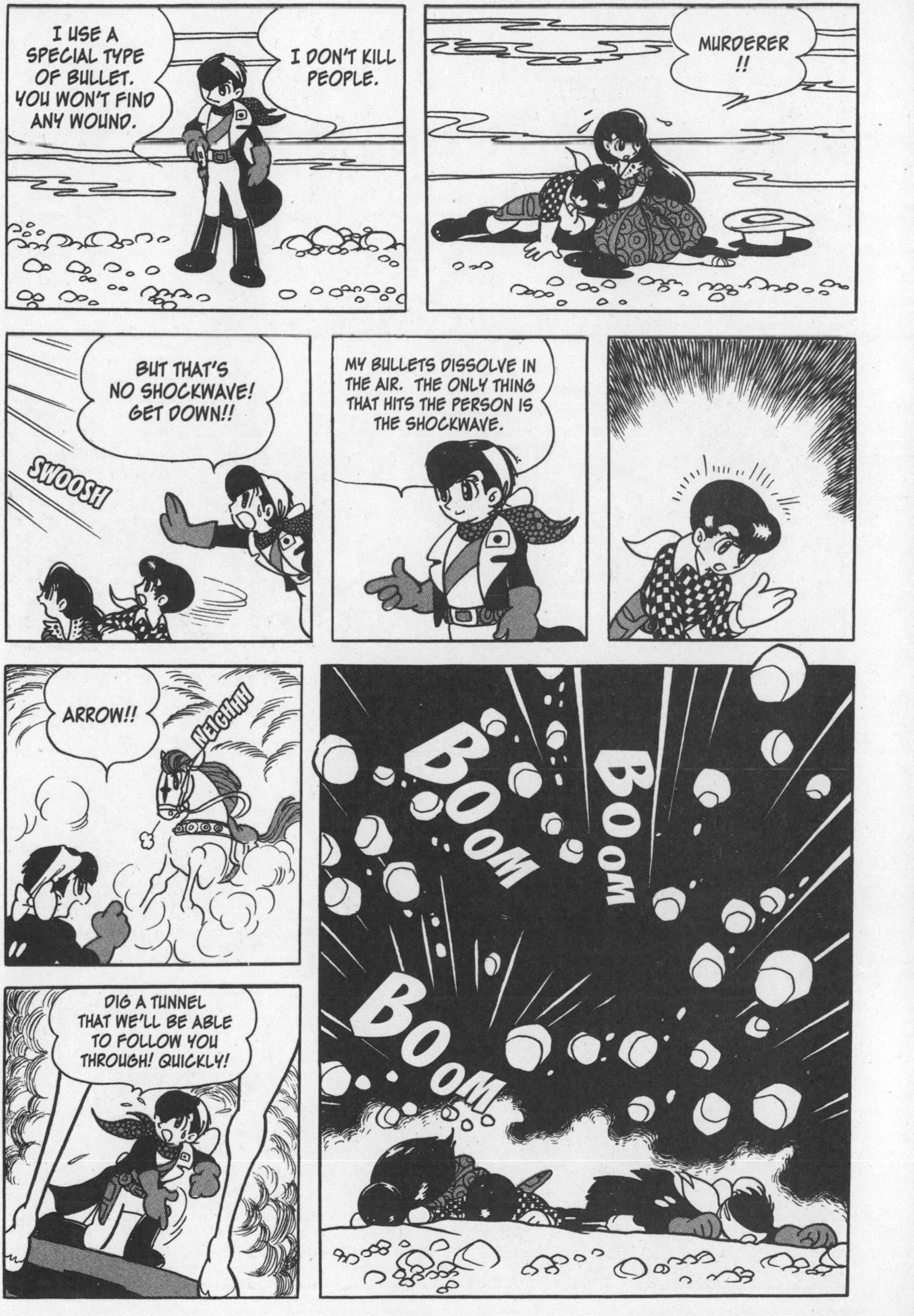
MURDERER !!
I DON'T KILL PEOPLE.
I USE A SPECIAL TYPE OF BULLET. YOU WON'T FIND ANY WOUND.
MY BULLETS DISSOLVE IN THE AIR. THE ONLY THING THAT HITS THE PERSON IS THE SHOCKWAVE.
BUT THAT'S NO SHOCKWAVE! GET DOWN!!
SWOOSH
BOOM
BOOM
BOOM
ARROW!!
NEIGHHH
DIG A TUNNEL THAT WE'LL BE ABLE TO FOLLOW YOU THROUGH! QUICKLY!

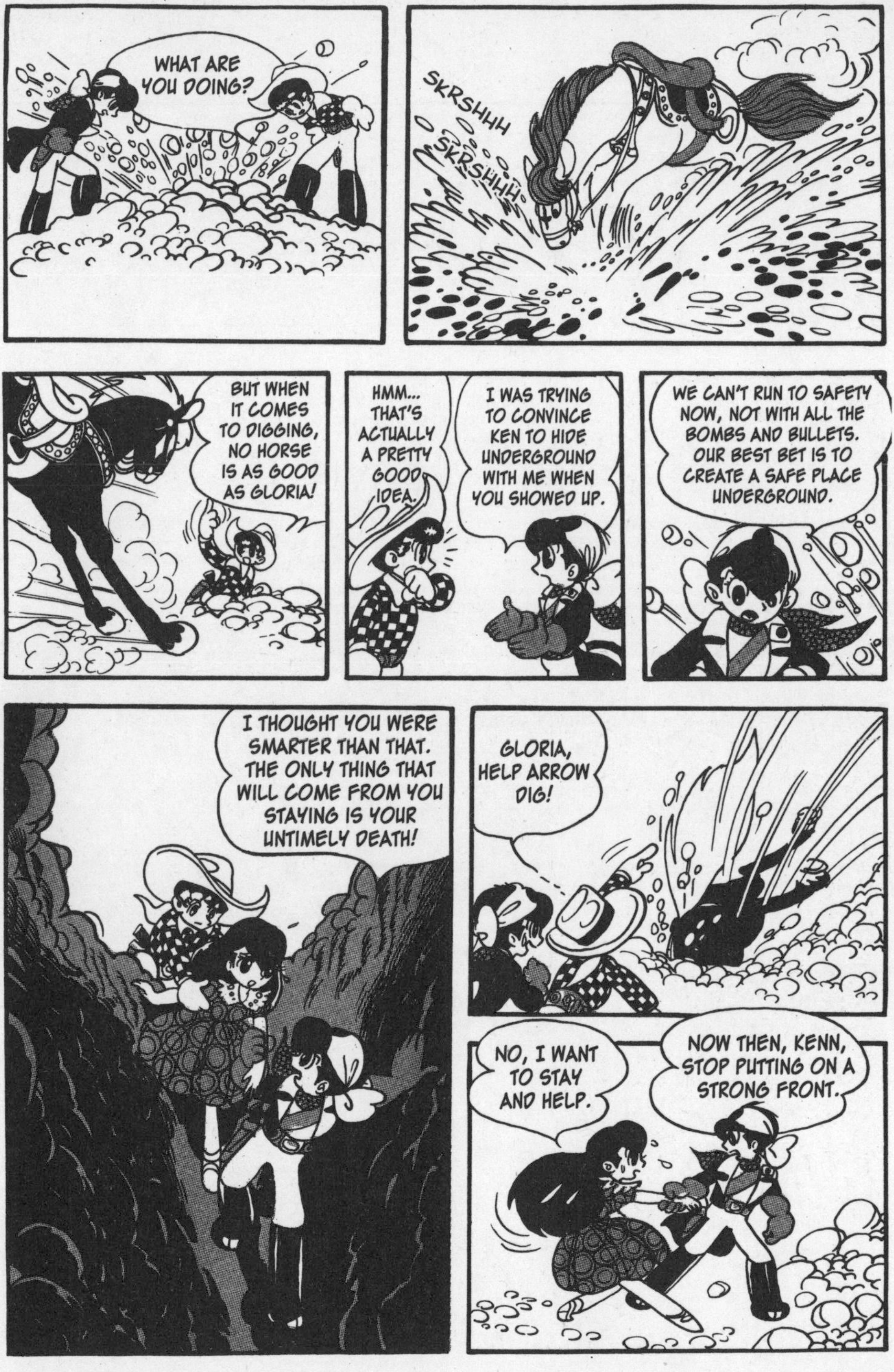
SKRSHHH
SKRSHHH
WHAT ARE YOU DOING?
WE CAN'T RUN TO SAFETY NOW, NOT WITH ALL THE BOMBS AND BULLETS. OUR BEST BET IS TO CREATE A SAFE PLACE UNDERGROUND.
I WAS TRYING TO CONVINCE KEN TO HIDE UNDERGROUND WITH ME WHEN YOU SHOWED UP.
HMM... THAT'S ACTUALLY A PRETTY GOOD IDEA.
BUT WHEN IT COMES TO DIGGING, NO HORSE IS AS GOOD AS GLORIA!
GLORIA, HELP ARROW DIG!
NOW THEN, KENN, STOP PUTTING ON A STRONG FRONT.
NO, I WANT TO STAY AND HELP.
I THOUGHT YOU WERE SMARTER THAN THAT. THE ONLY THING THAT WILL COME FROM YOU STAYING IS YOUR UNTIMELY DEATH!

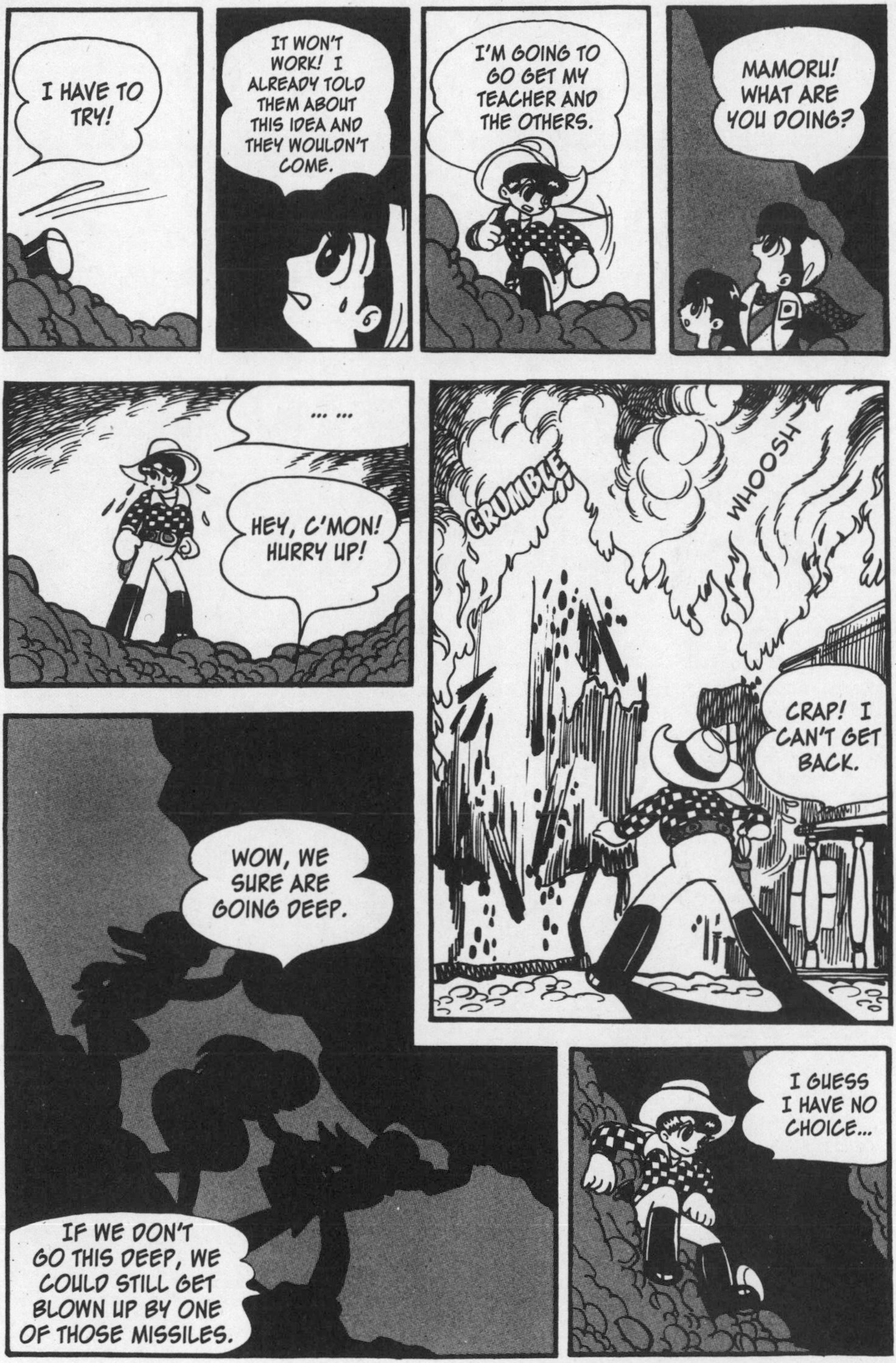
MAMORU! WHAT ARE YOU DOING?
I'M GOING TO GO GET MY TEACHER AND THE OTHERS.
IT WON'T WORK! I ALREADY TOLD THEM ABOUT THIS IDEA AND THEY WOULDN'T COME.
I HAVE TO TRY!
WHOOSH
CRUMBLE
CRAP! I CAN'T GET BACK.
... ...
HEY, C'MON! HURRY UP!
WOW, WE SURE ARE GOING DEEP.
IF WE DON'T GO THIS DEEP, WE COULD STILL GET BLOWN UP BY ONE OF THOSE MISSILES.
I GUESS I HAVE NO CHOICE...

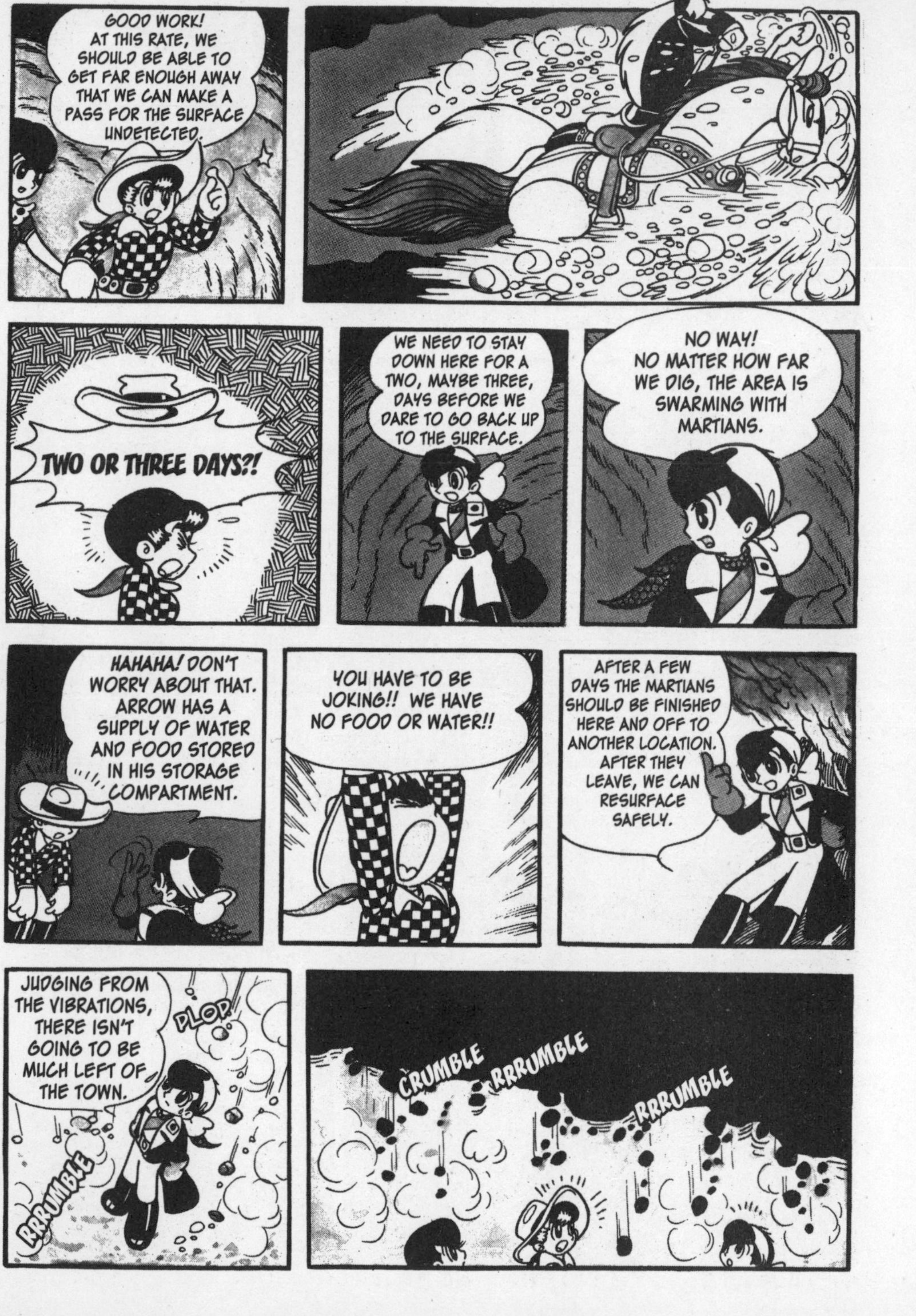
GOOD WORK! AT THIS RATE, WE SHOULD BE ABLE TO GET FAR ENOUGH AWAY THAT WE CAN MAKE A PASS FOR THE SURFACE UNDETECTED.
NO WAY! NO MATTER HOW FAR WE DIG, THE AREA IS SWARMING WITH MARTIANS.
WE NEED TO STAY DOWN HERE FOR A TWO, MAYBE THREE, DAYS BEFORE WE DARE TO GO BACK UP TO THE SURFACE.
TWO OR THREE DAYS?!
AFTER A FEW DAYS THE MARTIANS SHOULD BE FINISHED HERE AND OFF TO ANOTHER LOCATION. AFTER THEY LEAVE, WE CAN RESURFACE SAFELY.
YOU HAVE TO BE JOKING!! WE HAVE NO FOOD OR WATER!!
HAHAHA! DON'T WORRY ABOUT THAT. ARROW HAS A SUPPLY OF WATER AND FOOD STORED IN HIS STORAGE COMPARTMENT.
CRUMBLE
RRRUMBLE
RRRUMBLE
JUDGING FROM THE VIBRATIONS, THERE ISN'T GOING TO BE MUCH LEFT OF THE TOWN.
PLOP
RRRUMBLE

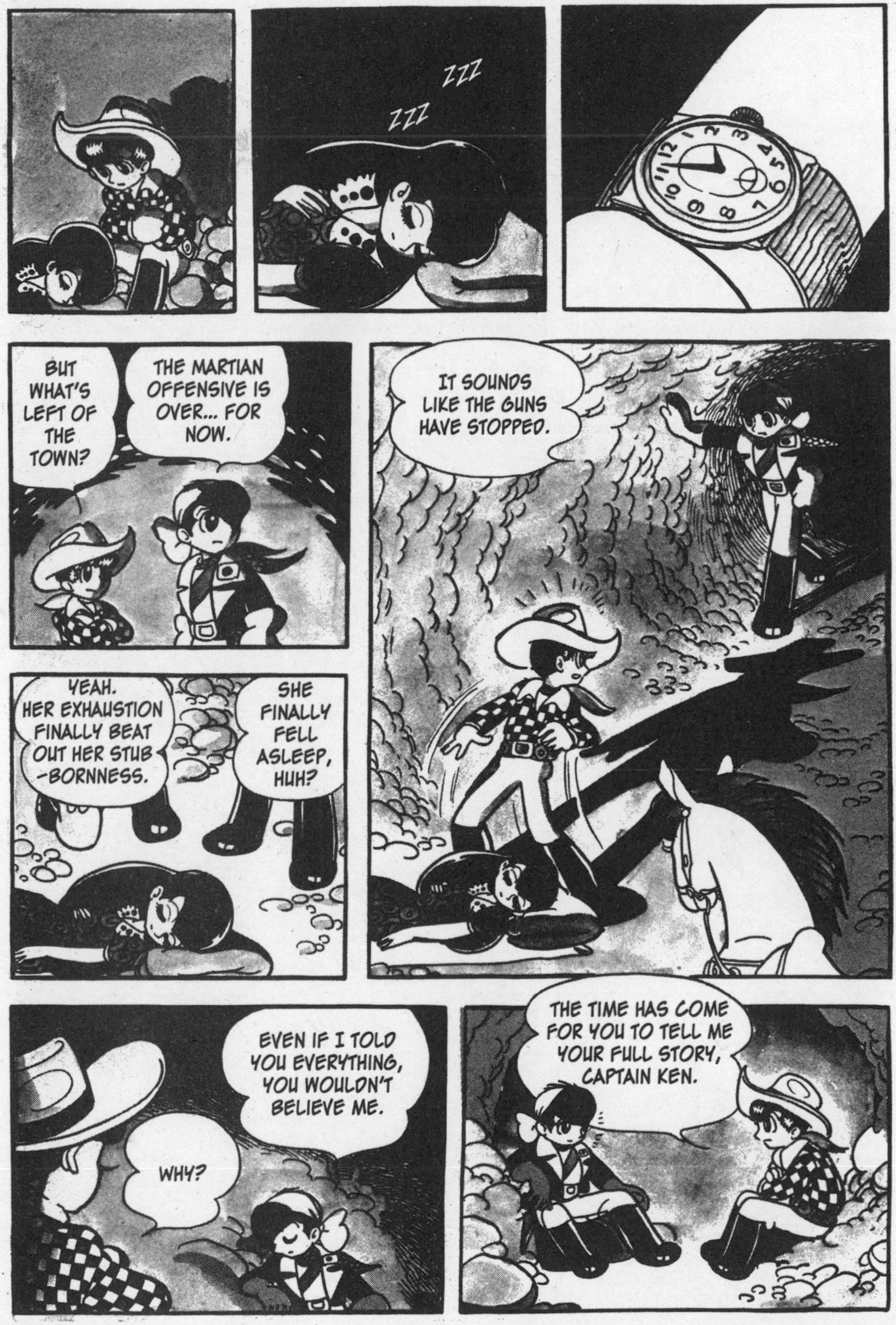
ZZZ
ZZZ
IT SOUNDS LIKE THE GUNS HAVE STOPPED.
THE MARTIAN OFFENSIVE IS OVER... FOR NOW.
BUT WHAT'S LEFT OF THE TOWN?
SHE FINALLY FELL ASLEEP, HUH?
YEAH. HER EXHAUSTION FINALLY BEAT OUT HER STUB-BORNNESS.
THE TIME HAS COME FOR YOU TO TELL ME YOUR FULL STORY, CAPTAIN KEN.
EVEN IF I TOLD YOU EVERYTHING, YOU WOULDN'T BELIEVE ME.
WHY?

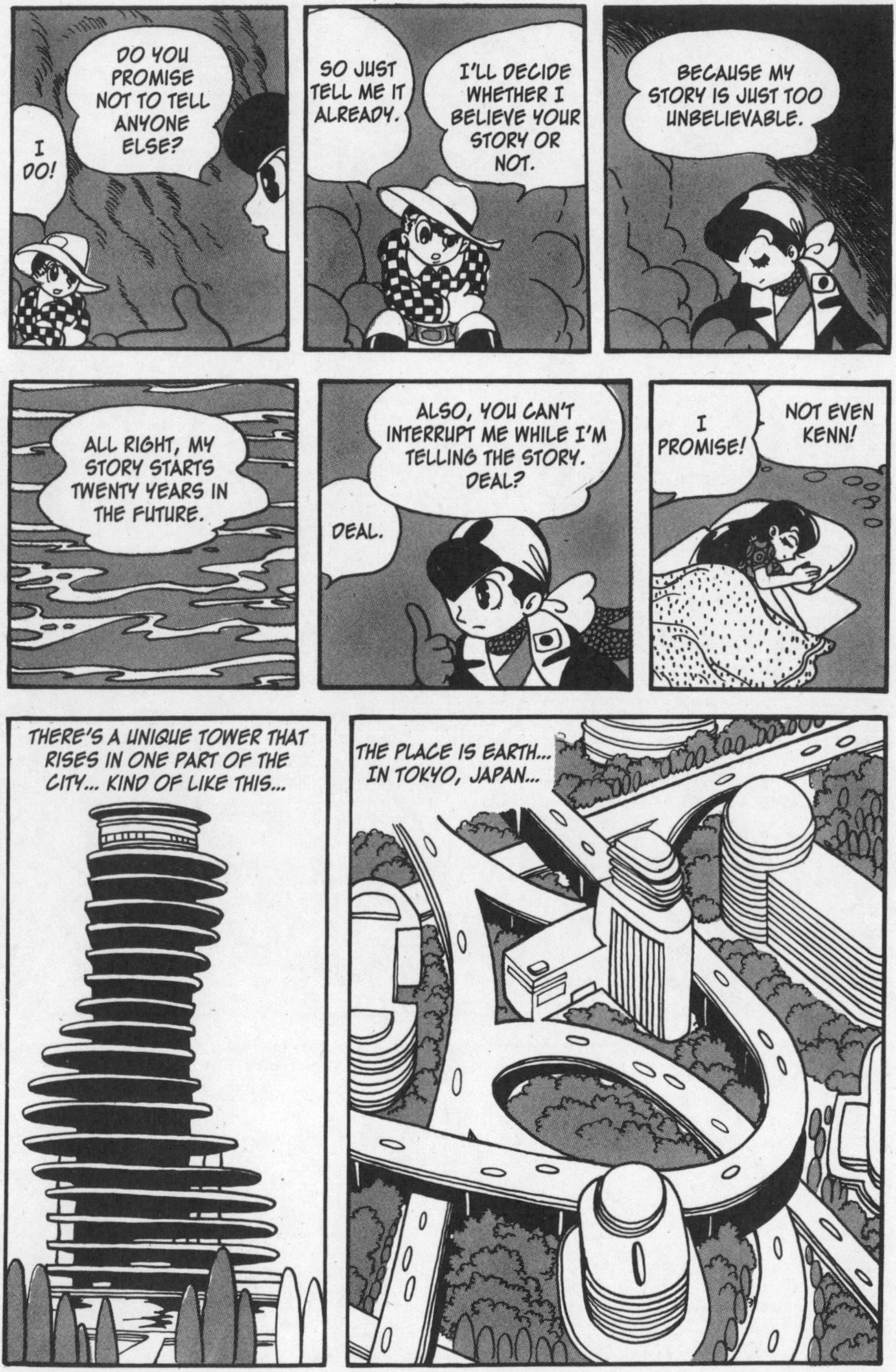
BECAUSE MY STORY IS JUST TOO UNBELIEVABLE.
I'LL DECIDE WHETHER I BELIEVE YOUR STORY OR NOT.
SO JUST TELL ME IT ALREADY.
DO YOU PROMISE NOT TO TELL ANYONE ELSE?
I DO!
NOT EVEN KENN!
I PROMISE!
ALSO, YOU CAN'T INTERRUPT ME WHILE I'M TELLING THE STORY. DEAL?
DEAL.
ALL RIGHT, MY STORY STARTS TWENTY YEARS IN THE FUTURE.
THE PLACE IS EARTH... IN TOKYO, JAPAN...
THERE'S A UNIQUE TOWER THAT RISES IN ONE PART OF THE CITY... KIND OF LIKE THIS...

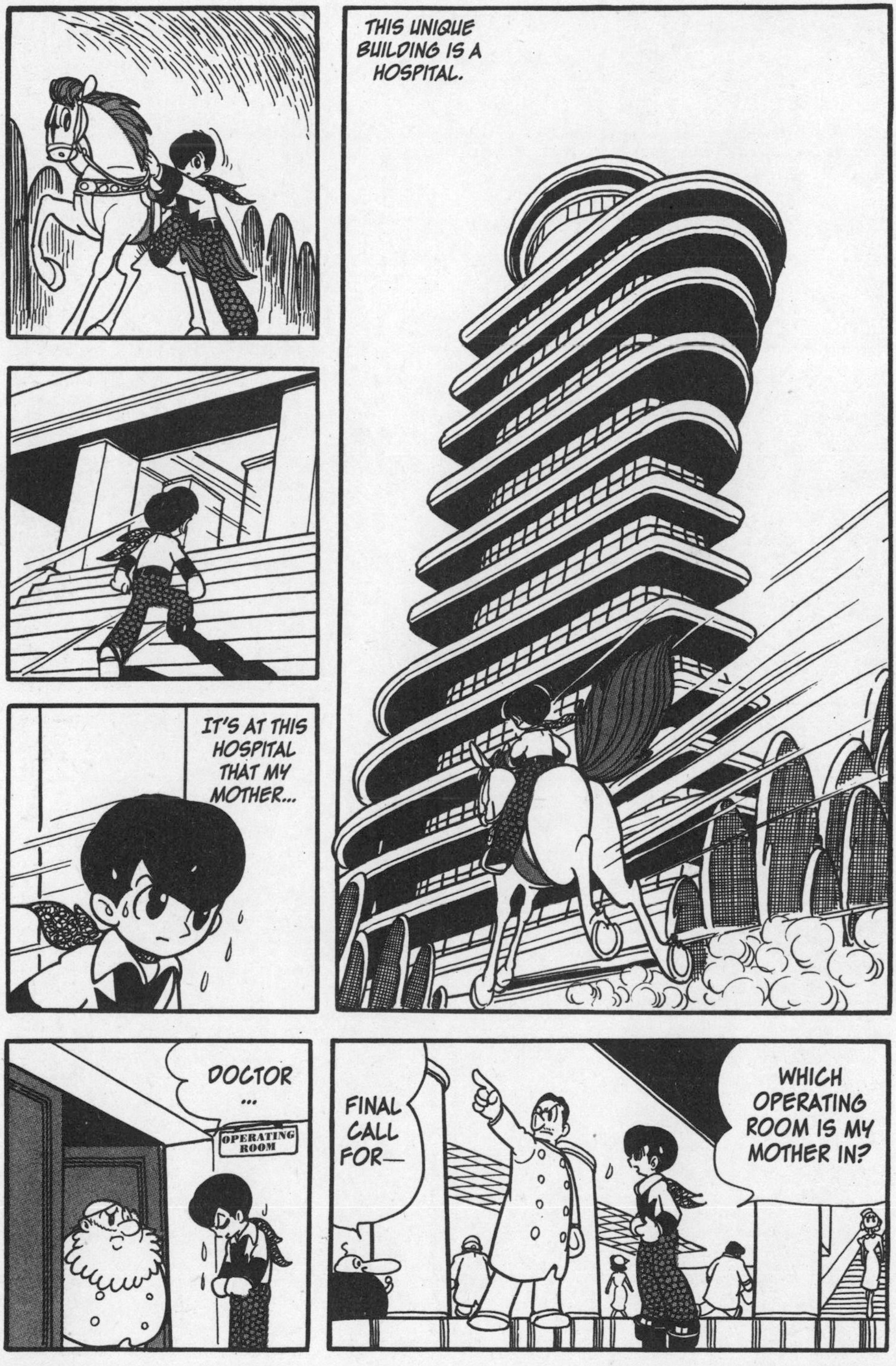
THIS UNIQUE BUILDING IS A HOSPITAL.
IT'S AT THIS HOSPITAL THAT MY MOTHER...
WHICH OPERATING ROOM IS MY MOTHER IN?
FINAL CALL FOR—
DOCTOR ...
OPERATING ROOM

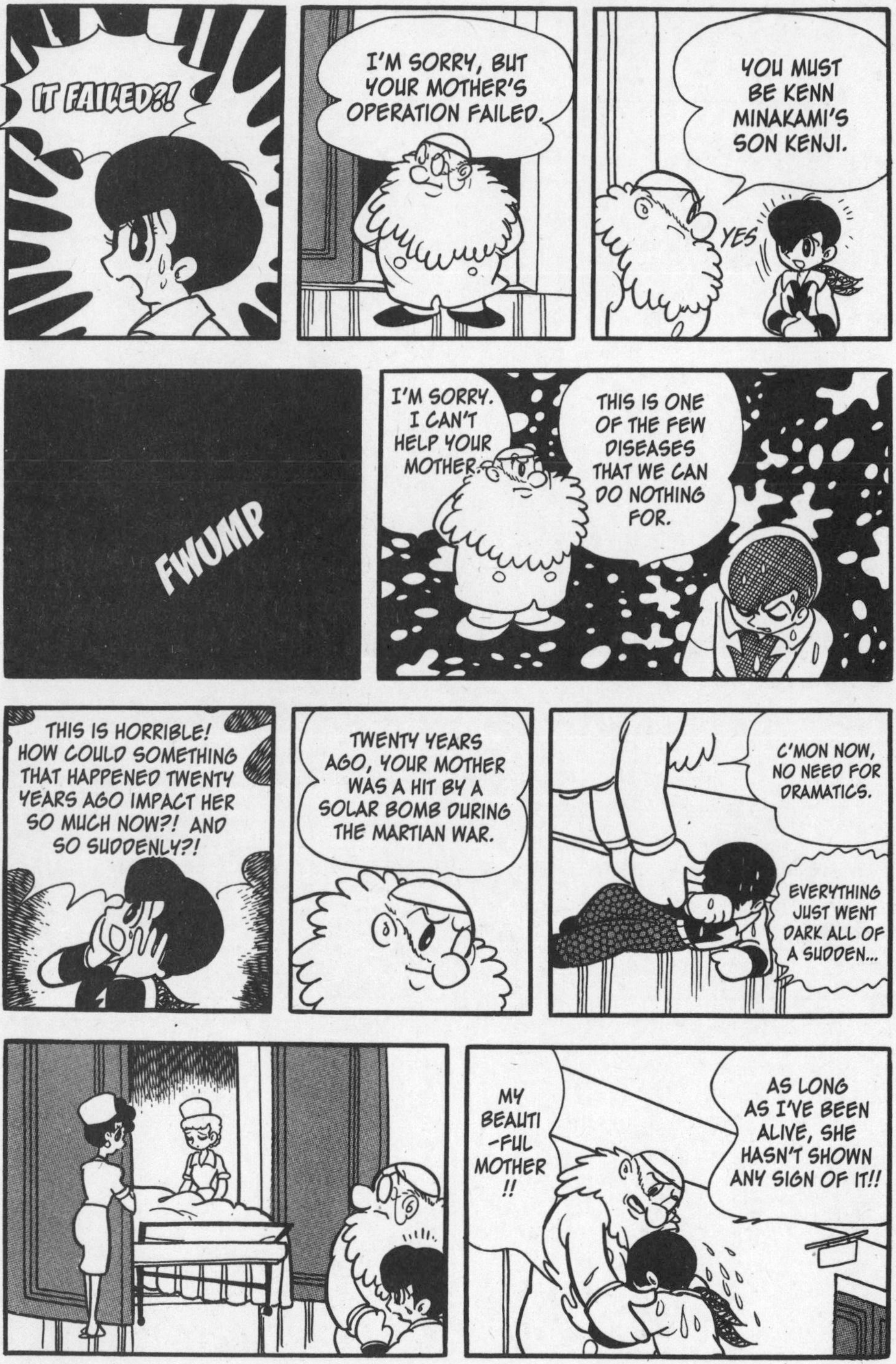
YOU MUST BE KENN MINAKAMI'S SON KENJI.
YES
I'M SORRY, BUT YOUR MOTHER'S OPERATION FAILED.
IT FAILED?!
THIS IS ONE OF THE FEW DISEASES THAT WE CAN DO NOTHING FOR.
I'M SORRY. I CAN'T HELP YOUR MOTHER.
FWUMP
C'MON NOW, NO NEED FOR DRAMATICS.
EVERYTHING JUST WENT DARK ALL OF A SUDDEN...
TWENTY YEARS AGO, YOUR MOTHER WAS A HIT BY A SOLAR BOMB DURING THE MARTIAN WAR.
THIS IS HORRIBLE! HOW COULD SOMETHING THAT HAPPENED TWENTY YEARS AGO IMPACT HER SO MUCH NOW?! AND SO SUDDENLY?!
AS LONG AS I'VE BEEN ALIVE, SHE HASN'T SHOWN ANY SIGN OF IT!!
MY BEAUTI-FUL MOTHER !!

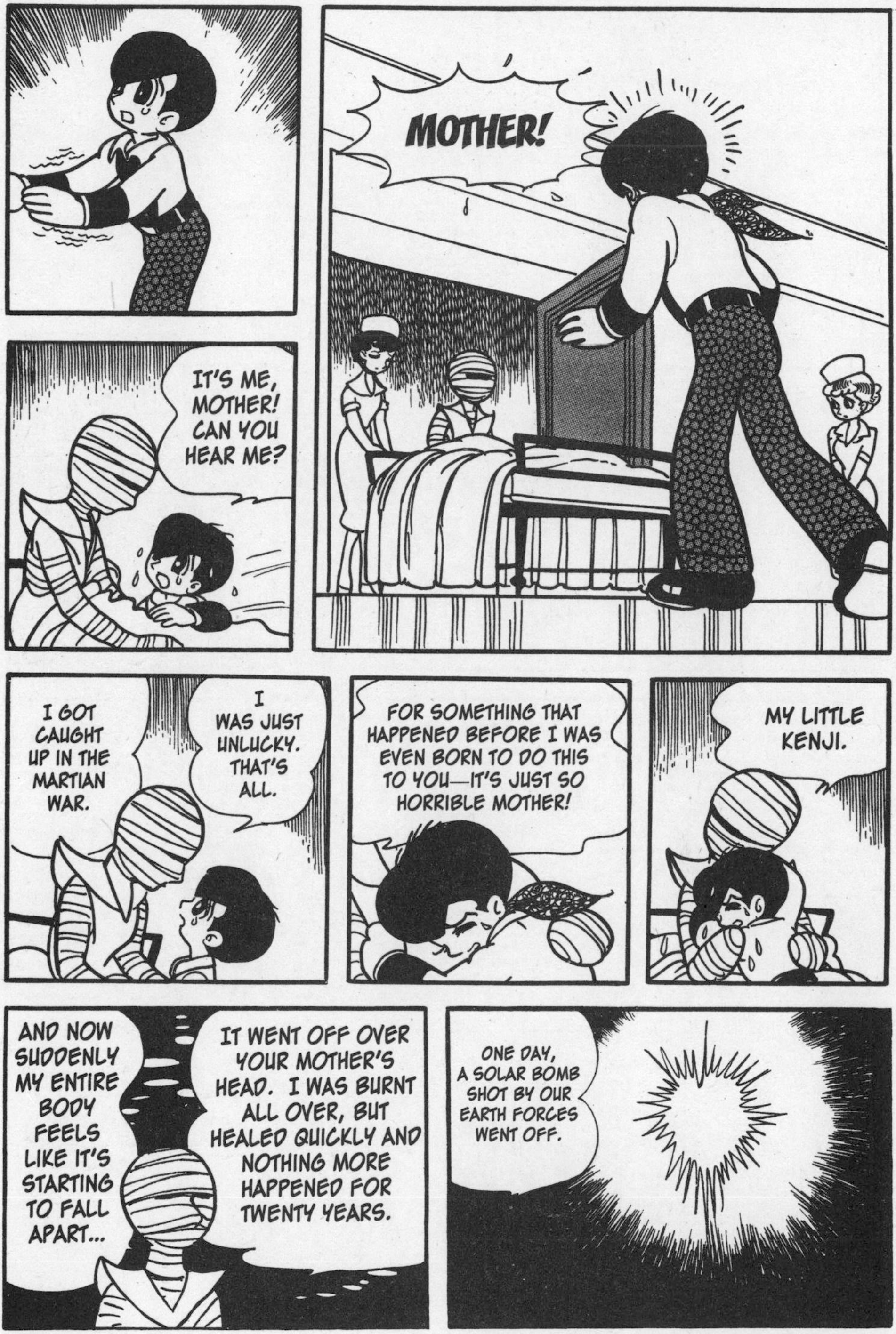
MOTHER!
IT'S ME, MOTHER! CAN YOU HEAR ME?
MY LITTLE KENJI.
FOR SOMETHING THAT HAPPENED BEFORE I WAS EVEN BORN TO DO THIS TO YOU—IT'S JUST SO HORRIBLE MOTHER!
I WAS JUST UNLUCKY. THAT'S ALL.
I GOT CAUGHT UP IN THE MARTIAN WAR.
ONE DAY, A SOLAR BOMB SHOT BY OUR EARTH FORCES WENT OFF.
IT WENT OFF OVER YOUR MOTHER'S HEAD. I WAS BURNT ALL OVER, BUT HEALED QUICKLY AND NOTHING MORE HAPPENED FOR TWENTY YEARS.
AND NOW SUDDENLY MY ENTIRE BODY FEELS LIKE IT'S STARTING TO FALL APART...

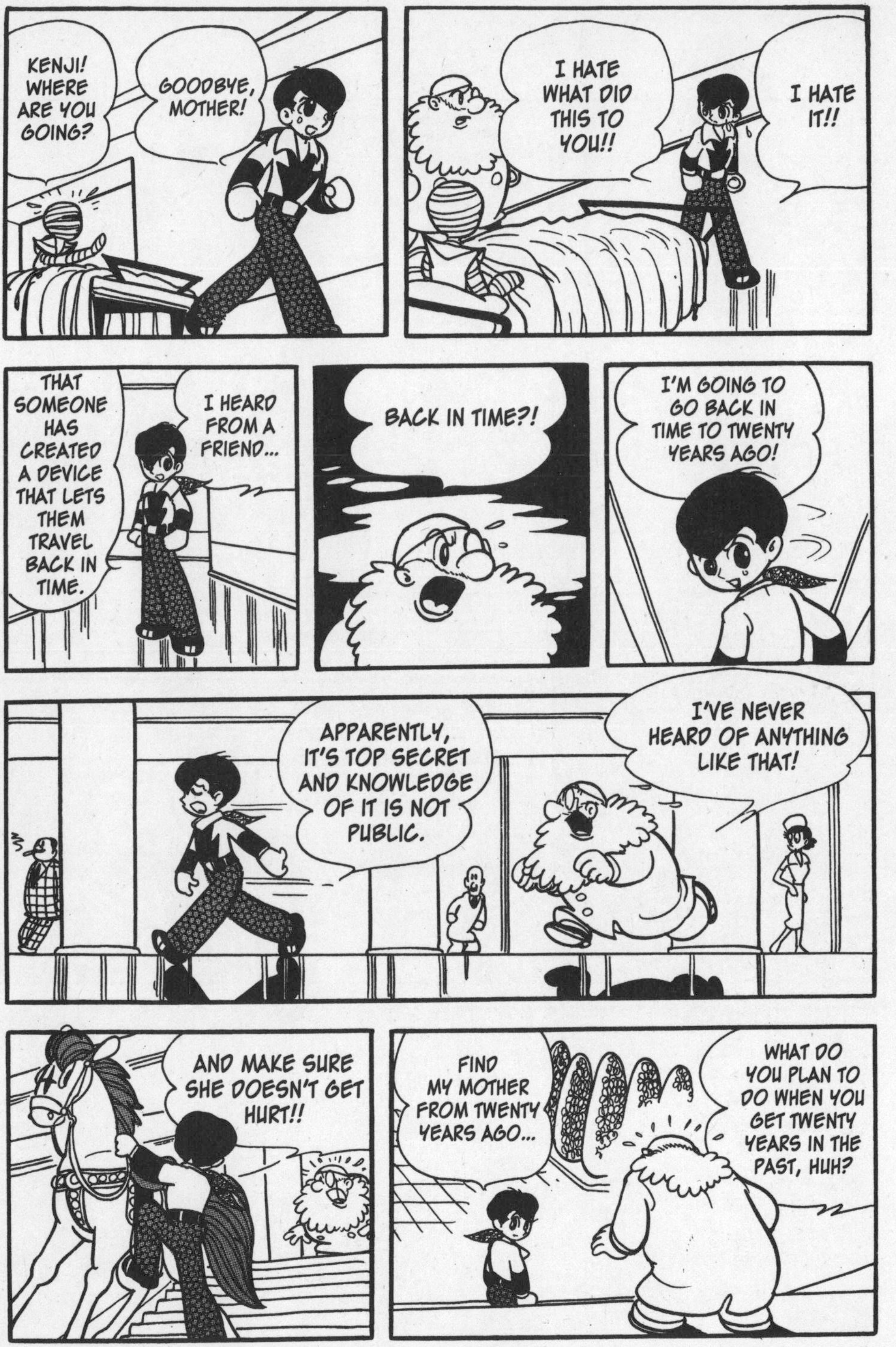
I HATE IT!!
I HATE WHAT DID THIS TO YOU!!
GOODBYE, MOTHER!
KENJI! WHERE ARE YOU GOING?
I'M GOING TO GO BACK IN TIME TO TWENTY YEARS AGO!
BACK IN TIME?!
I HEARD FROM A FRIEND...
THAT SOMEONE HAS CREATED A DEVICE THAT LETS THEM TRAVEL BACK IN TIME.
I'VE NEVER HEARD OF ANYTHING LIKE THAT!
APPARENTLY, IT'S TOP SECRET AND KNOWLEDGE OF IT IS NOT PUBLIC.
WHAT DO YOU PLAN TO DO WHEN YOU GET TWENTY YEARS IN THE PAST, HUH?
FIND MY MOTHER FROM TWENTY YEARS AGO...
AND MAKE SURE SHE DOESN'T GET HURT!!

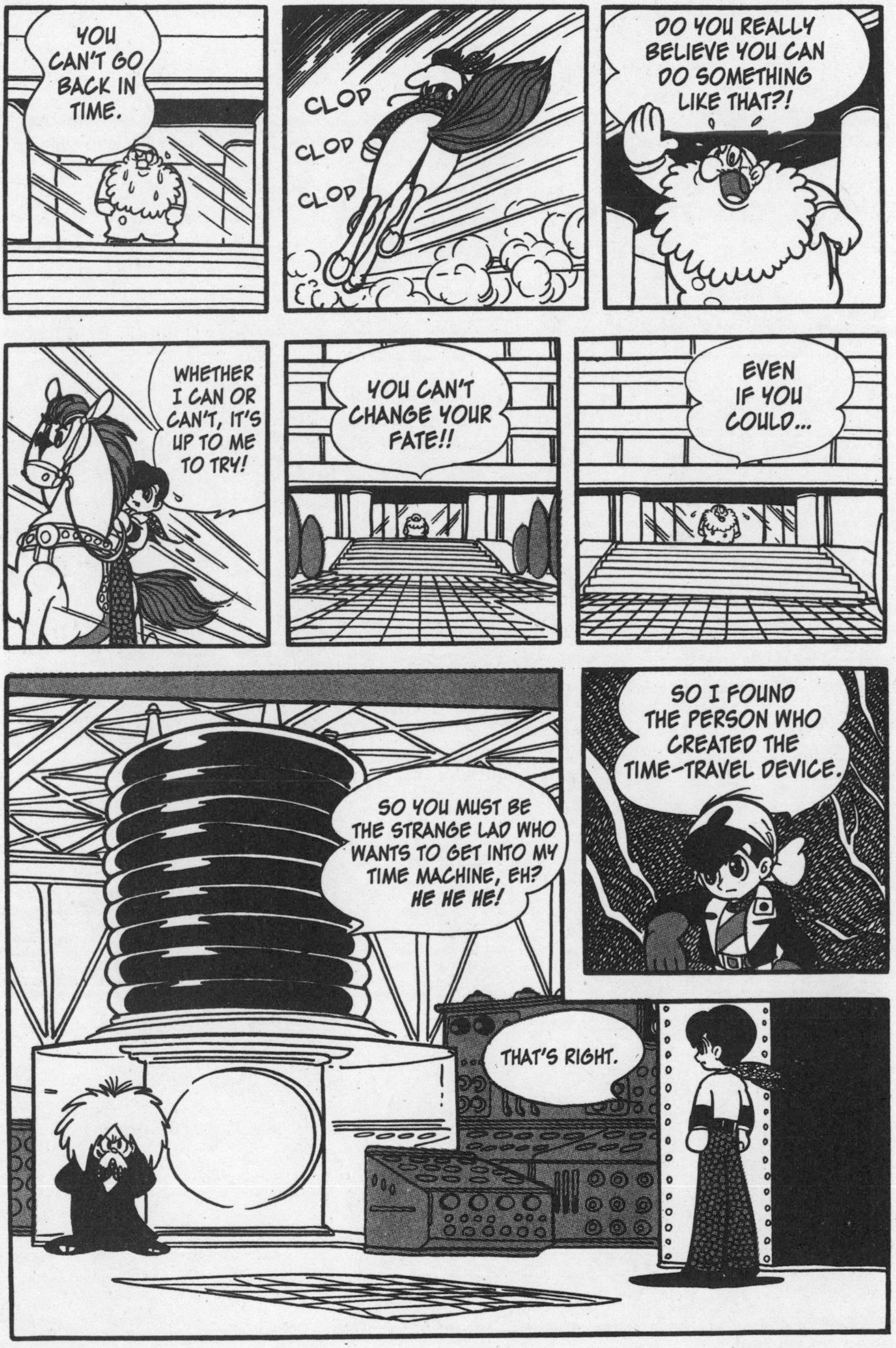
DO YOU REALLY BELIEVE YOU CAN DO SOMETHING LIKE THAT?!
CLOP
CLOP
CLOP
YOU CAN'T GO BACK IN TIME.
EVEN IF YOU COULD...
YOU CAN'T CHANGE YOUR FATE!!
WHETHER I CAN OR CAN'T, IT'S UP TO ME TO TRY!
SO I FOUND THE PERSON WHO CREATED THE TIME-TRAVEL DEVICE.
THAT'S RIGHT.
SO YOU MUST BE THE STRANGE LAD WHO WANTS TO GET INTO MY TIME MACHINE, EH? HE HE HE!

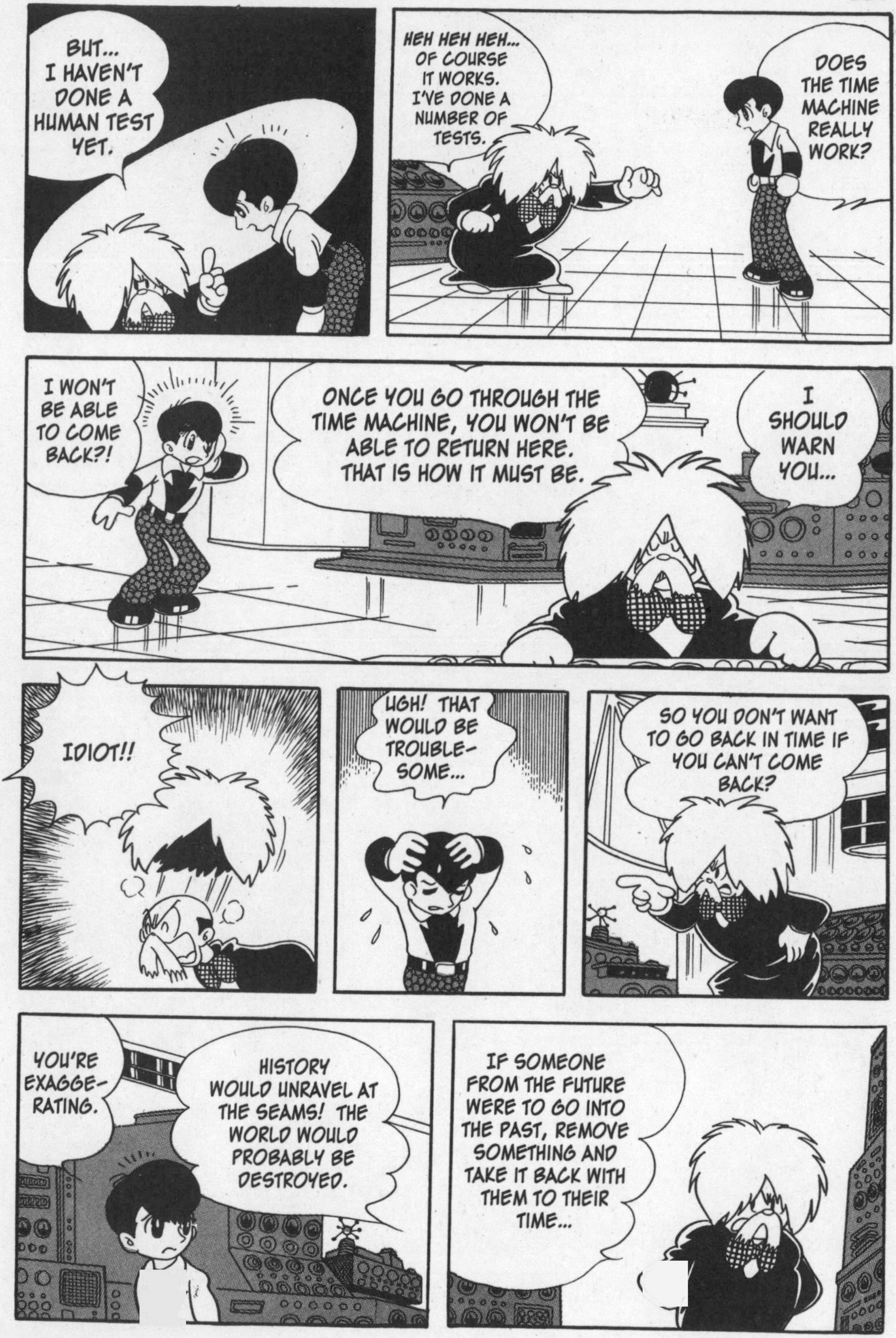
DOES THE TIME MACHINE REALLY WORK?
HEH HEH HEH... OF COURSE IT WORKS. I'VE DONE A NUMBER OF TESTS.
BUT... I HAVEN'T DONE A HUMAN TEST YET.
I SHOULD WARN YOU...
ONCE YOU GO THROUGH THE TIME MACHINE, YOU WON'T BE ABLE TO RETURN HERE. THAT IS HOW IT MUST BE.
I WON'T BE ABLE TO COME BACK?!
SO YOU DON'T WANT TO GO BACK IN TIME IF YOU CAN'T COME BACK?
UGH! THAT WOULD BE TROUBLE-SOME...
IDIOT!!
IF SOMEONE FROM THE FUTURE WERE TO GO INTO THE PAST, REMOVE SOMETHING AND TAKE IT BACK WITH THEM TO THEIR TIME...
HISTORY WOULD UNRAVEL AT THE SEAMS! THE WORLD WOULD PROBABLY BE DESTROYED.
YOU'RE EXAGGE-RATING.

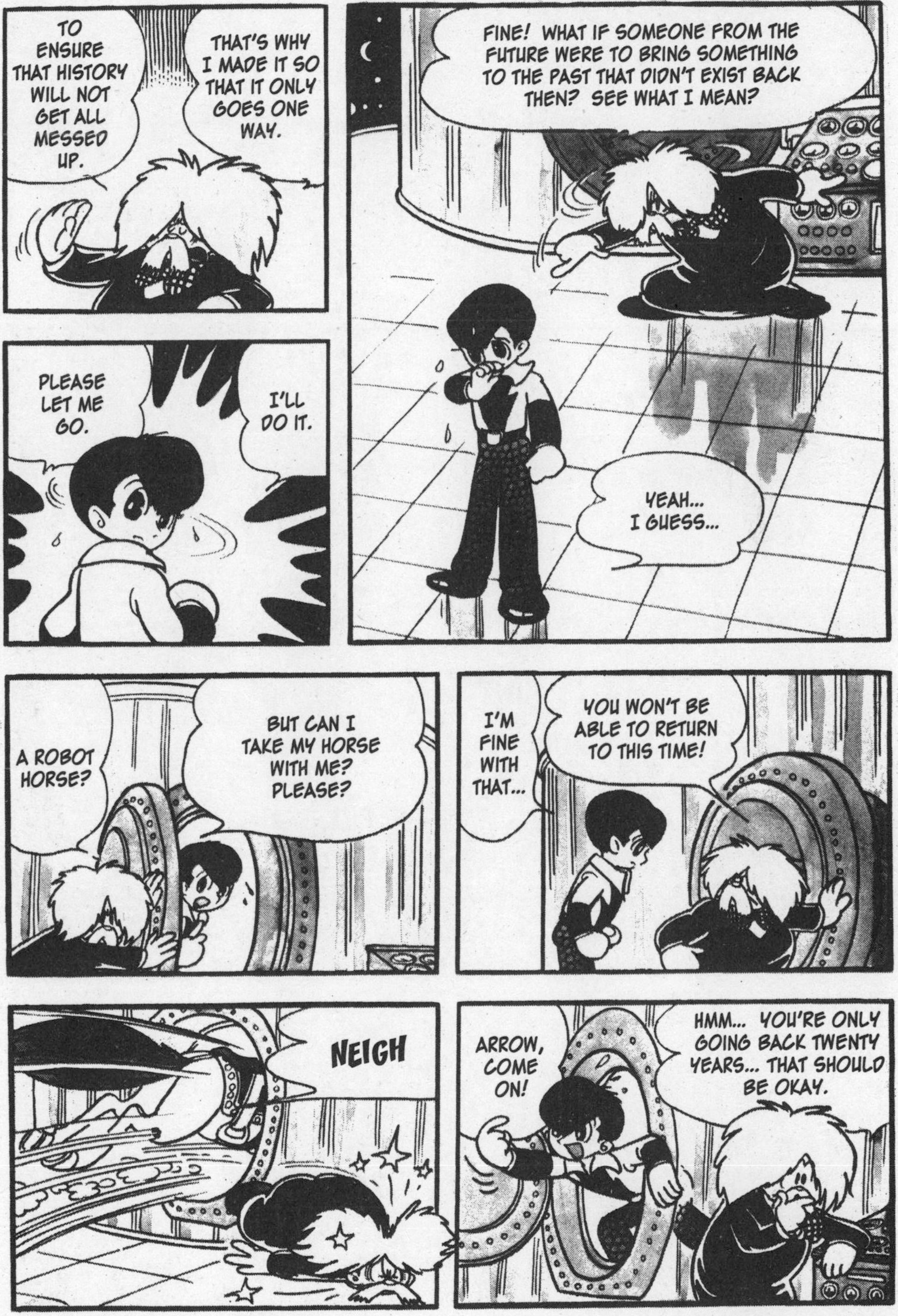
FINE! WHAT IF SOMEONE FROM THE FUTURE WERE TO BRING SOMETHING TO THE PAST THAT DIDN'T EXIST BACK THEN? SEE WHAT I MEAN?
YEAH... I GUESS...
THAT'S WHY I MADE IT SO THAT IT ONLY GOES ONE WAY.
TO ENSURE THAT HISTORY WILL NOT GET ALL MESSED UP.
I'LL DO IT.
PLEASE LET ME GO.
YOU WON'T BE ABLE TO RETURN TO THIS TIME!
I'M FINE WITH THAT...
BUT CAN I TAKE MY HORSE WITH ME? PLEASE?
A ROBOT HORSE?
HMM... YOU'RE ONLY GOING BACK TWENTY YEARS... THAT SHOULD BE OKAY.
ARROW, COME ON!
NEIGH

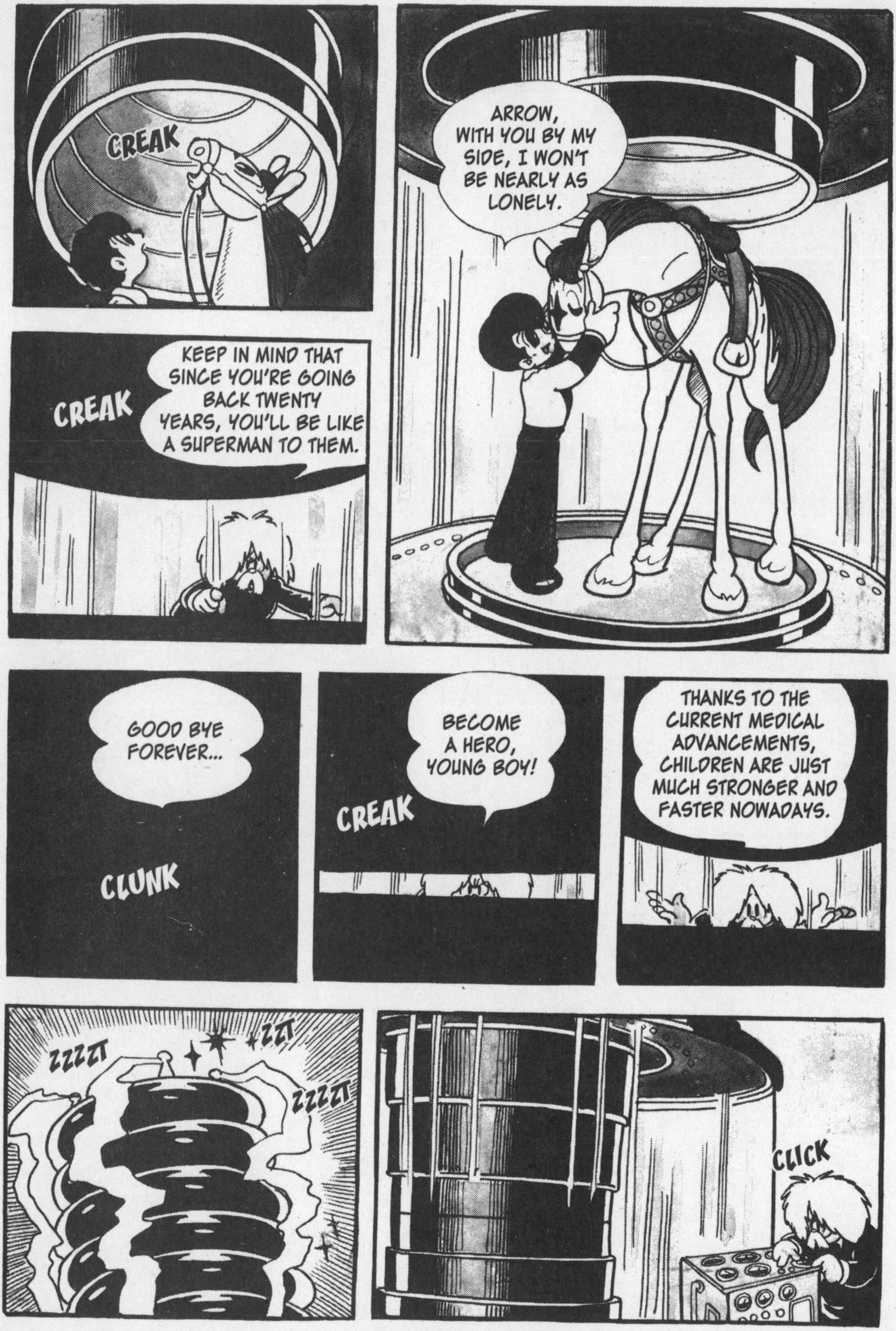
ARROW, WITH YOU BY MY SIDE, I WON'T BE NEARLY AS LONELY.
CREAK
KEEP IN MIND THAT SINCE YOU'RE GOING BACK TWENTY YEARS, YOU'LL BE LIKE A SUPERMAN TO THEM.
CREAK
THANKS TO THE CURRENT MEDICAL ADVANCEMENTS, CHILDREN ARE JUST MUCH STRONGER AND FASTER NOWADAYS.
BECOME A HERO, YOUNG BOY!
CREAK
GOOD BYE FOREVER...
CLUNK
CLICK
ZZZT
ZZZZT
ZZZZT

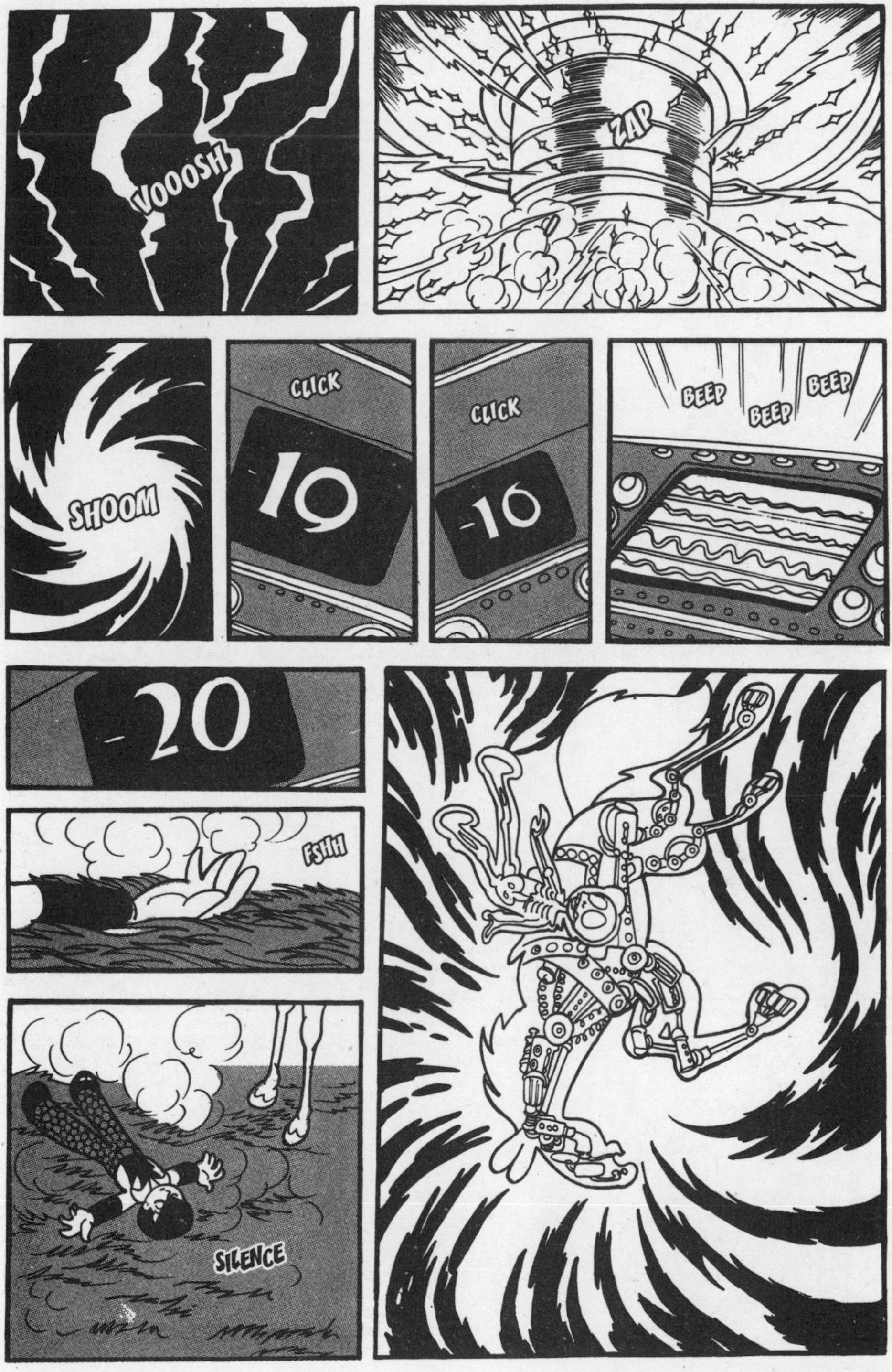
ZAP
VOOOSH
BEEP
BEEP
BEEP
CLICK
-16
CLICK
-19
SHOOM
-20
FSHH
SILENCE

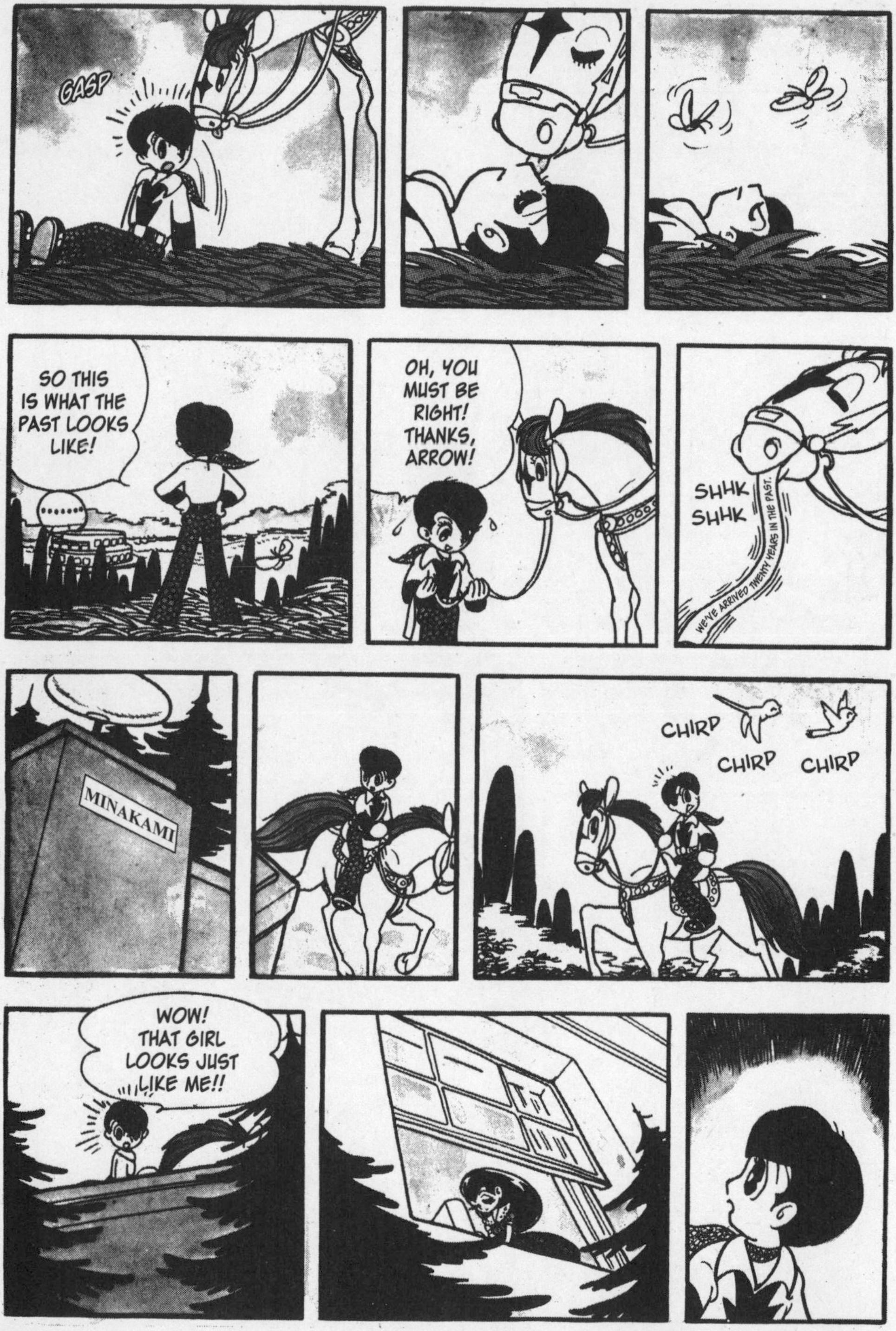
GASP
SHHK
SHHK
WE'VE ARRIVED TWENTY YEARS IN THE PAST.
OH, YOU MUST BE RIGHT! THANKS, ARROW!
SO THIS IS WHAT THE PAST LOOKS LIKE!
CHIRP
CHIRP
CHIRP
MINAKAMI
WOW! THAT GIRL LOOKS JUST LIKE ME!!

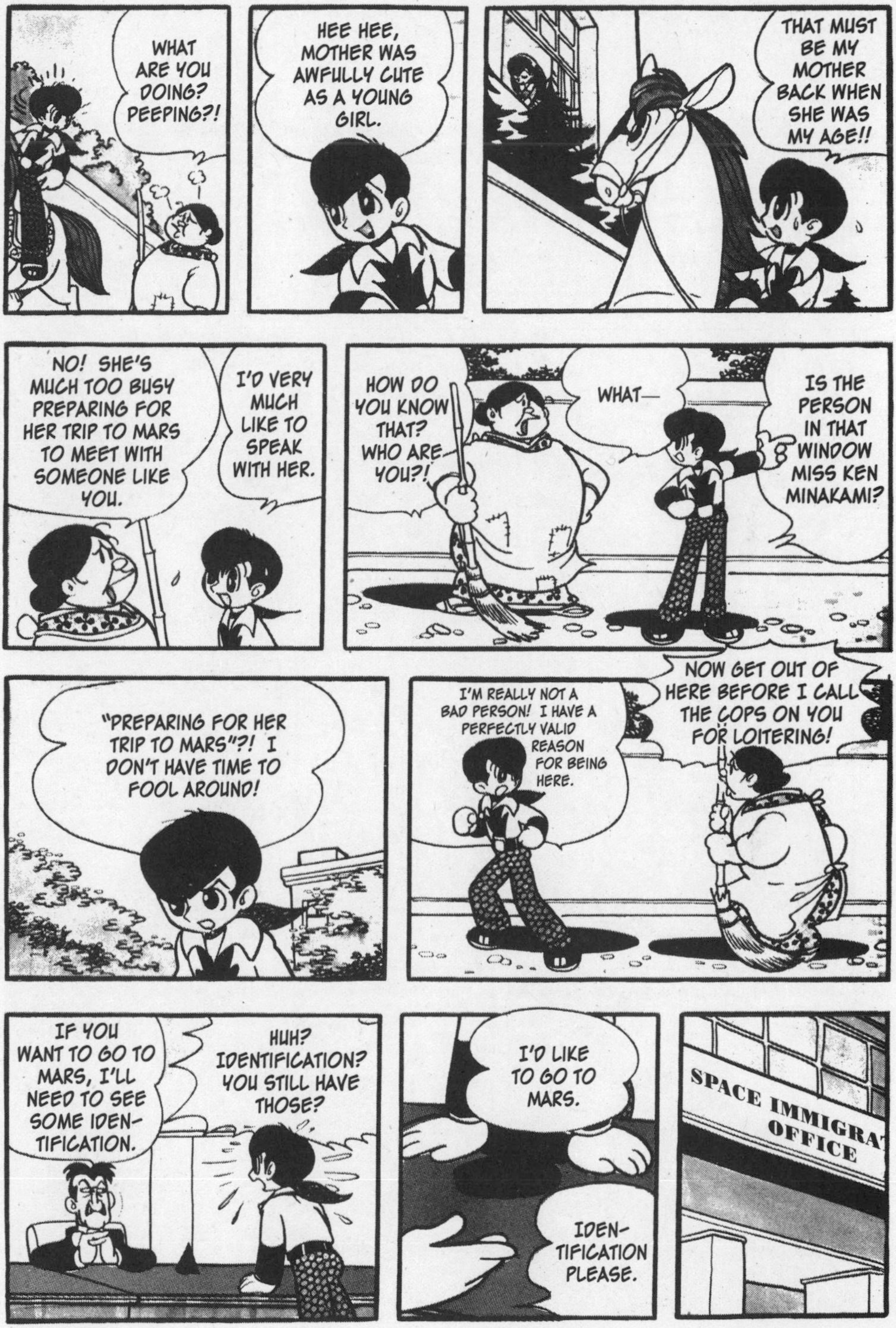
THAT MUST BE MY MOTHER BACK WHEN SHE WAS MY AGE!!
HEE HEE, MOTHER WAS AWFULLY CUTE AS A YOUNG GIRL.
WHAT ARE YOU DOING? PEEPING?!
IS THE PERSON IN THAT WINDOW MISS KEN MINAKAMI?
WHAT—
HOW DO YOU KNOW THAT? WHO ARE YOU?!
I'D VERY MUCH LIKE TO SPEAK WITH HER.
NO! SHE'S MUCH TOO BUSY PREPARING FOR HER TRIP TO MARS TO MEET WITH SOMEONE LIKE YOU.
NOW GET OUT OF HERE BEFORE I CALL THE COPS ON YOU FOR LOITERING!
I'M REALLY NOT A BAD PERSON! I HAVE A PERFECTLY VALID REASON FOR BEING HERE.
"PREPARING FOR HER TRIP TO MARS"?! I DON'T HAVE TIME TO FOOL AROUND!
SPACE IMMIGRAT
OFFICE
I'D LIKE TO GO TO MARS.
IDEN-TIFICATION PLEASE.
HUH? IDENTIFICATION? YOU STILL HAVE THOSE?
IF YOU WANT TO GO TO MARS, I'LL NEED TO SEE SOME IDEN-TIFICATION.

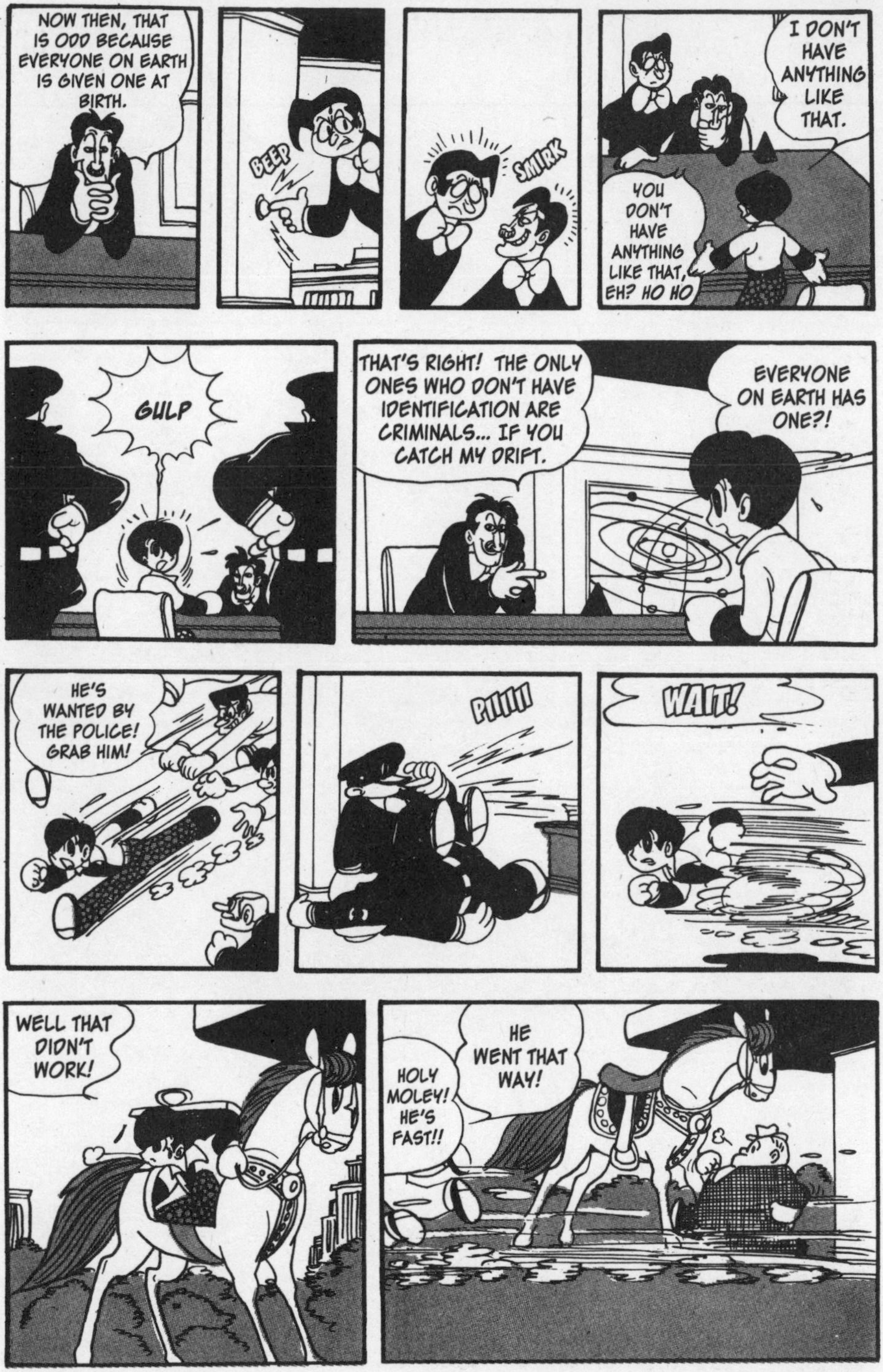
I DON'T HAVE ANYTHING LIKE THAT.
YOU DON'T HAVE ANYTHING LIKE THAT, EH? HO HO
SMIRK
BEEP
NOW THEN, THAT IS ODD BECAUSE EVERYONE ON EARTH IS GIVEN ONE AT BIRTH.
EVERYONE ON EARTH HAS ONE?!
THAT'S RIGHT! THE ONLY ONES WHO DON'T HAVE IDENTIFICATION ARE CRIMINALS... IF YOU CATCH MY DRIFT.
GULP
WAIT!
PIIIII
HE'S WANTED BY THE POLICE! GRAB HIM!
HE WENT THAT WAY!
HOLY MOLEY! HE'S FAST!!
WELL THAT DIDN'T WORK!

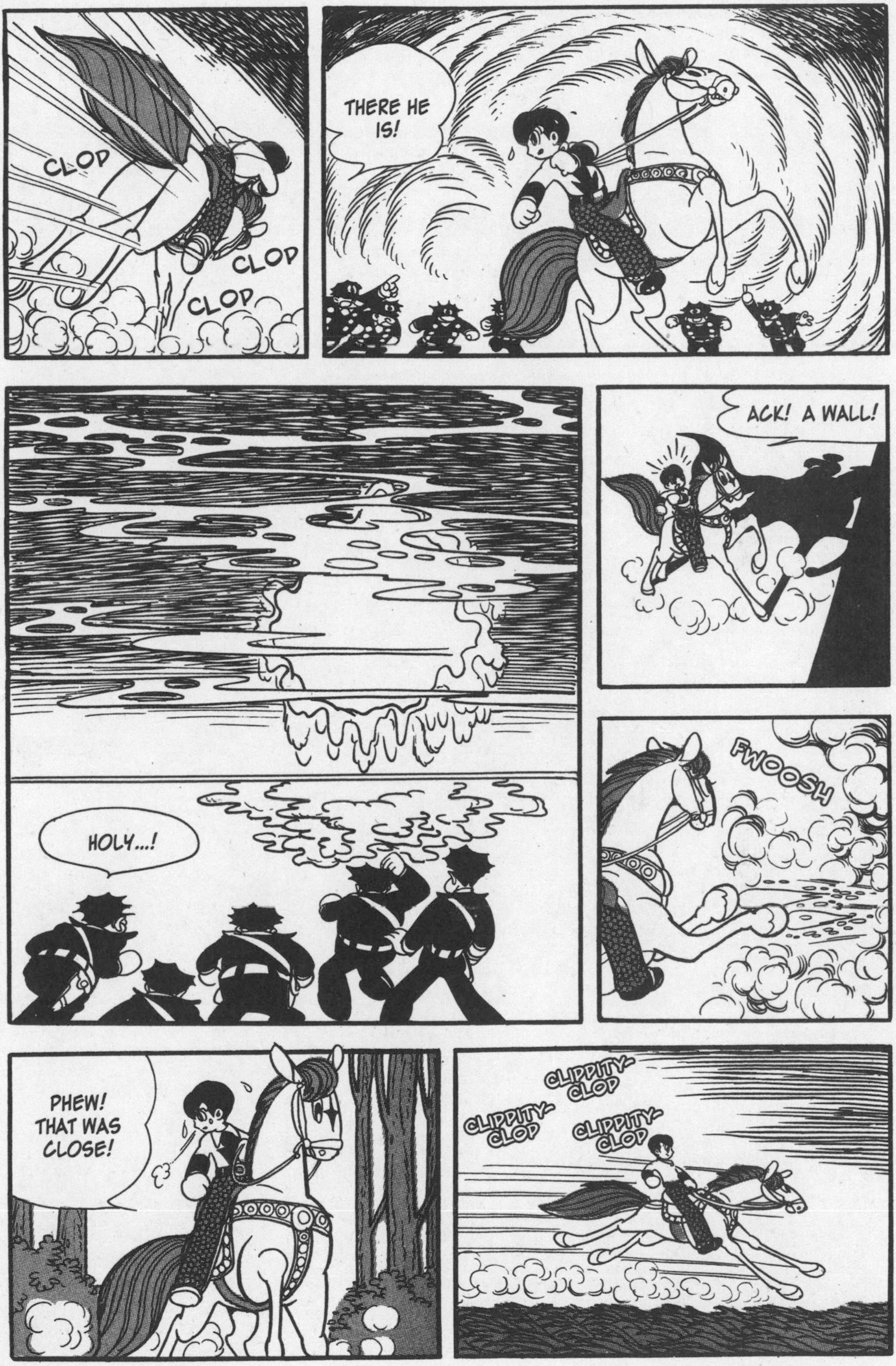
THERE HE IS!
CLOP
CLOP
CLOP
ACK! A WALL!
FWOOSH
HOLY...!
CLIPPITY-CLOP
CLIPPITY-CLOP
CLIPPITY-CLOP
PHEW! THAT WAS CLOSE!

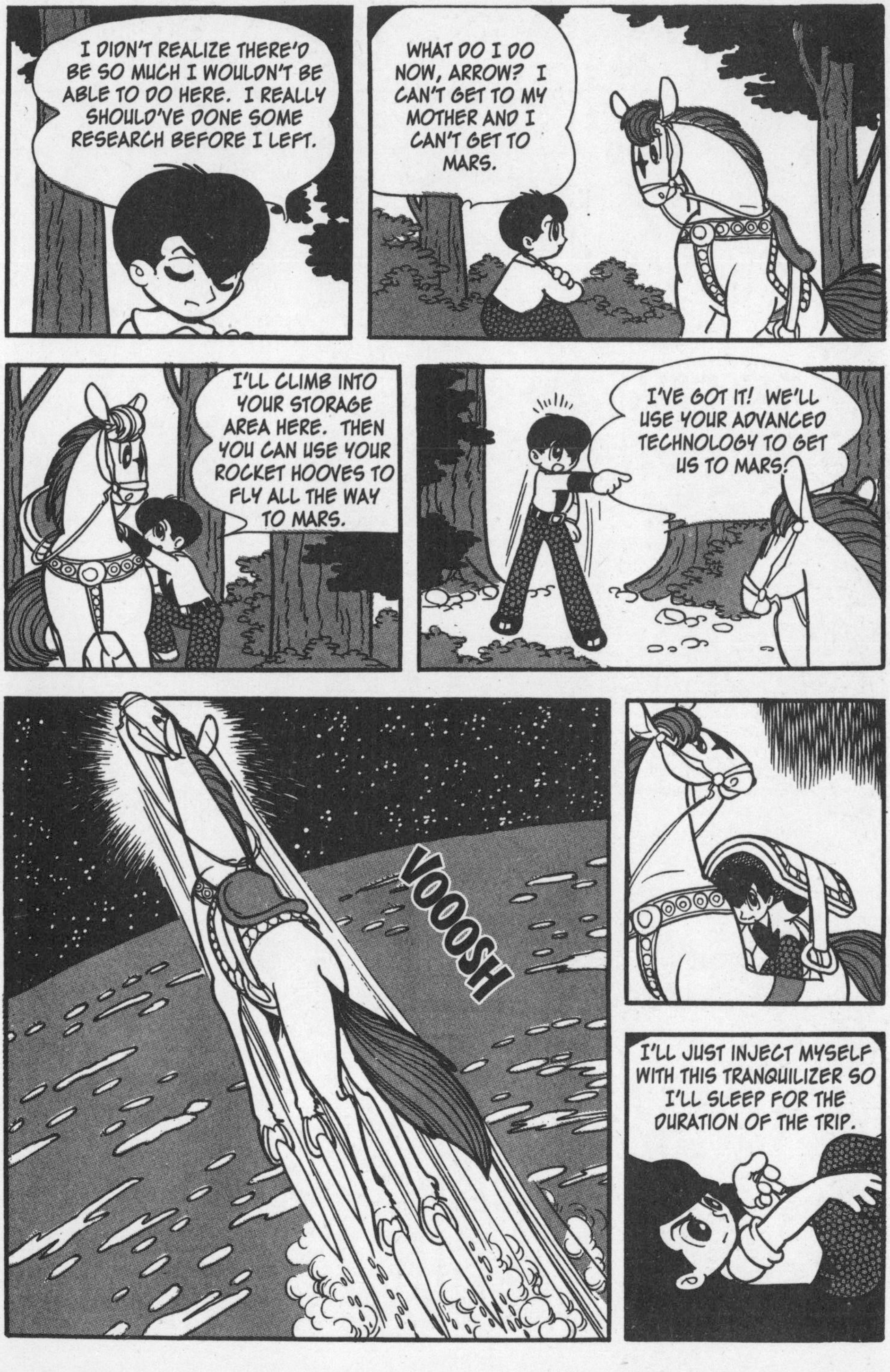
WHAT DO I DO NOW, ARROW? I CAN'T GET TO MY MOTHER AND I CAN'T GET TO MARS.
I DIDN'T REALIZE THERE'D BE SO MUCH I WOULDN'T BE ABLE TO DO HERE. I REALLY SHOULD'VE DONE SOME RESEARCH BEFORE I LEFT.
I'VE GOT IT! WE'LL USE YOUR ADVANCED TECHNOLOGY TO GET US TO MARS.
I'LL CLIMB INTO YOUR STORAGE AREA HERE. THEN YOU CAN USE YOUR ROCKET HOOVES TO FLY ALL THE WAY TO MARS.
I'LL JUST INJECT MYSELF WITH THIS TRANQUILIZER SO I'LL SLEEP FOR THE DURATION OF THE TRIP.
VOOOSH

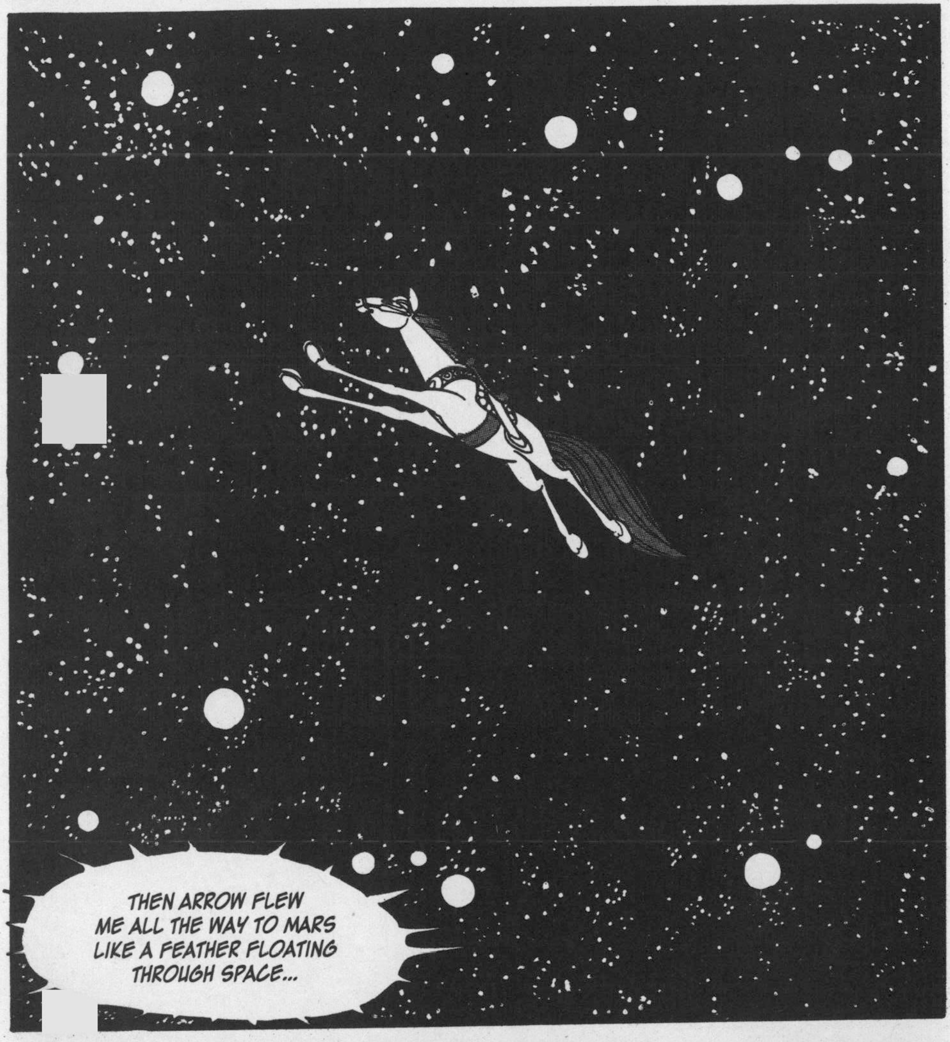
THEN ARROW FLEW
ME ALL THE WAY TO MARS
LIKE A FEATHER FLOATING
THROUGH SPACE...

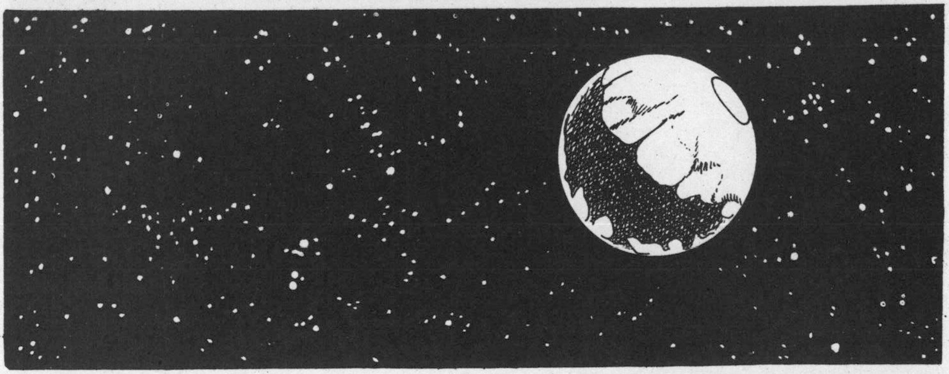

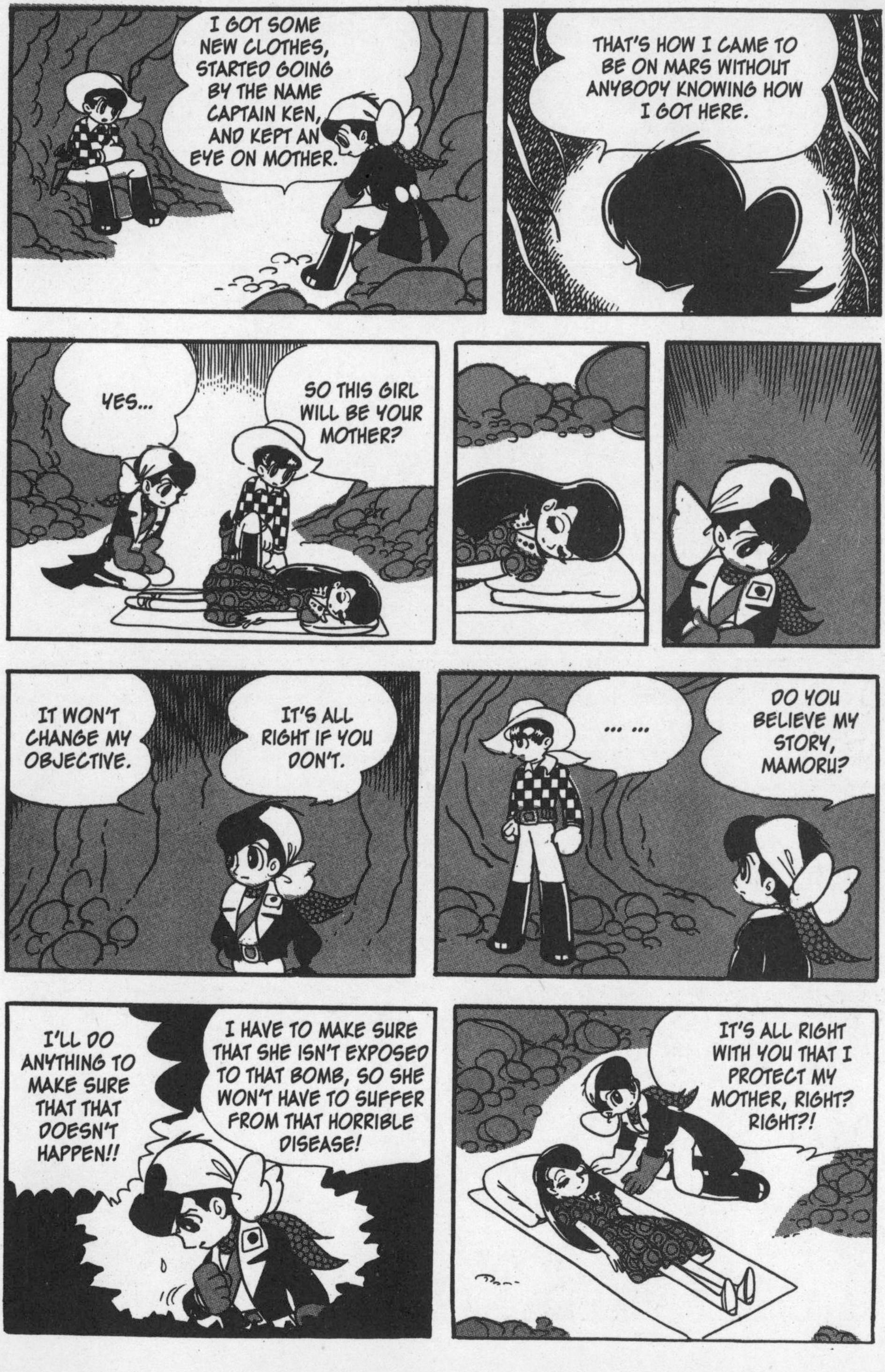
THAT'S HOW I CAME TO BE ON MARS WITHOUT ANYBODY KNOWING HOW I GOT HERE.
I GOT SOME NEW CLOTHES, STARTED GOING BY THE NAME CAPTAIN KEN, AND KEPT AN EYE ON MOTHER.
SO THIS GIRL WILL BE YOUR MOTHER?
YES...
DO YOU BELIEVE MY STORY, MAMORU?
... ...
IT'S ALL RIGHT IF YOU DON'T.
IT WON'T CHANGE MY OBJECTIVE.
IT'S ALL RIGHT WITH YOU THAT I PROTECT MY MOTHER, RIGHT? RIGHT?!
I HAVE TO MAKE SURE THAT SHE ISN'T EXPOSED TO THAT BOMB, SO SHE WON'T HAVE TO SUFFER FROM THAT HORRIBLE DISEASE!
I'LL DO ANYTHING TO MAKE SURE THAT THAT DOESN'T HAPPEN!!

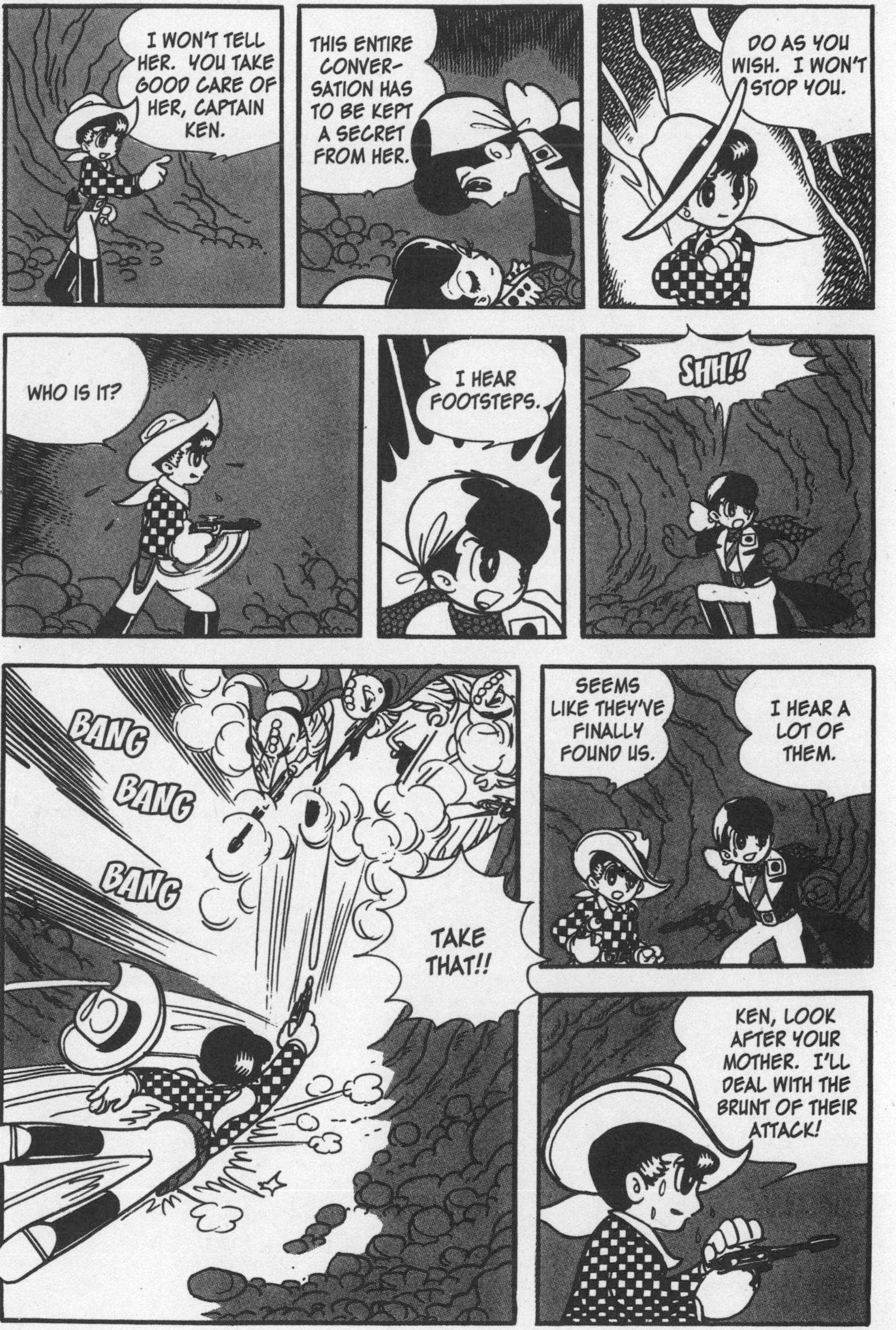
DO AS YOU WISH. I WON'T STOP YOU.
THIS ENTIRE CONVERSATION HAS TO BE KEPT A SECRET FROM HER.
I WON'T TELL HER. YOU TAKE GOOD CARE OF HER, CAPTAIN KEN.
SHH!!
I HEAR FOOTSTEPS.
WHO IS IT?
I HEAR A LOT OF THEM.
SEEMS LIKE THEY'VE FINALLY FOUND US.
KEN, LOOK AFTER YOUR MOTHER. I'LL DEAL WITH THE BRUNT OF THEIR ATTACK!
BANG
BANG
BANG
TAKE THAT!!

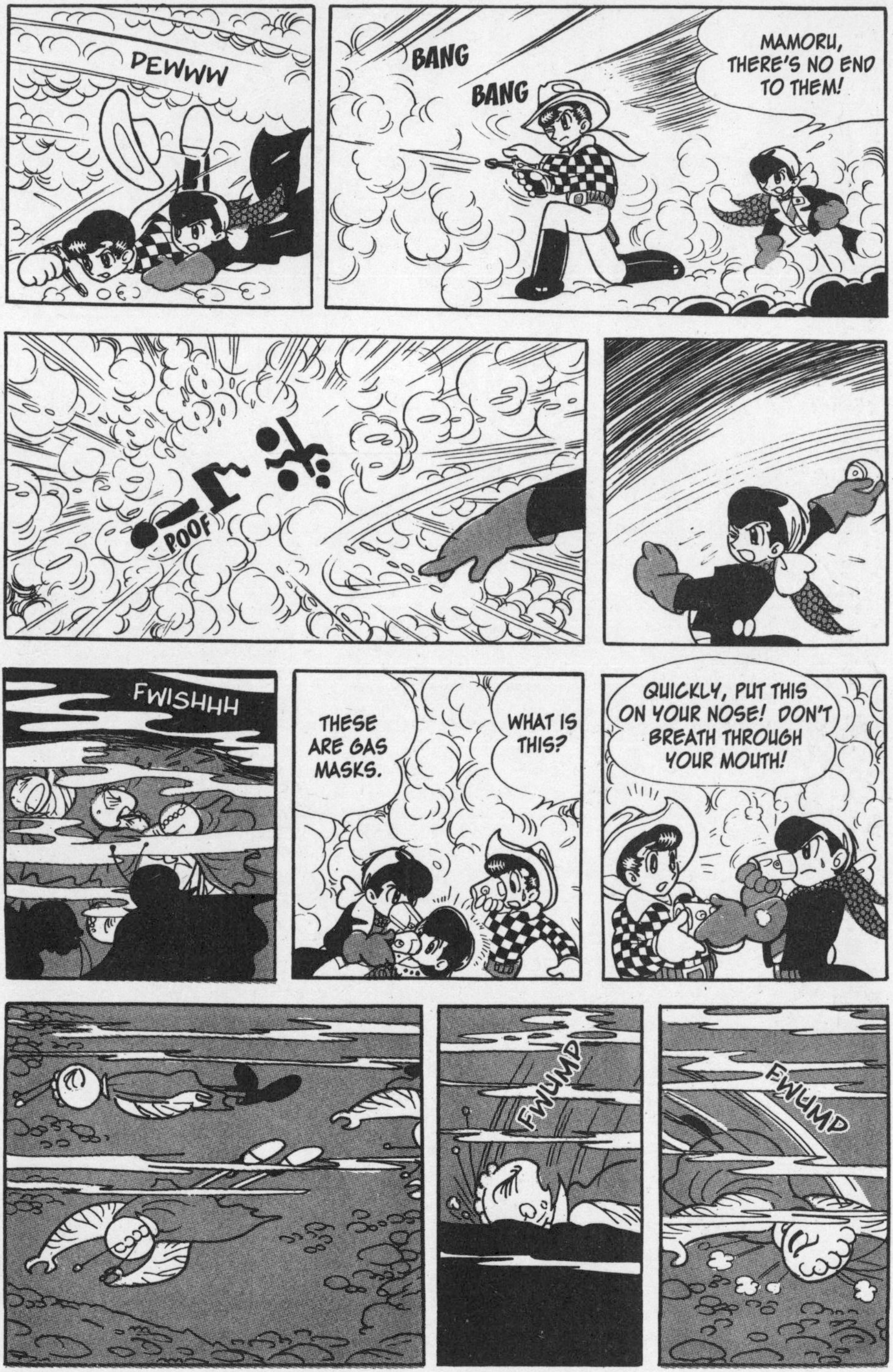
BANG
BANG
MAMORU, THERE'S NO END TO THEM!
PEWWW
POOF
QUICKLY, PUT THIS ON YOUR NOSE! DON'T BREATH THROUGH YOUR MOUTH!
WHAT IS THIS?
THESE ARE GAS MASKS.
FWISHHH
FWUMP
FWUMP

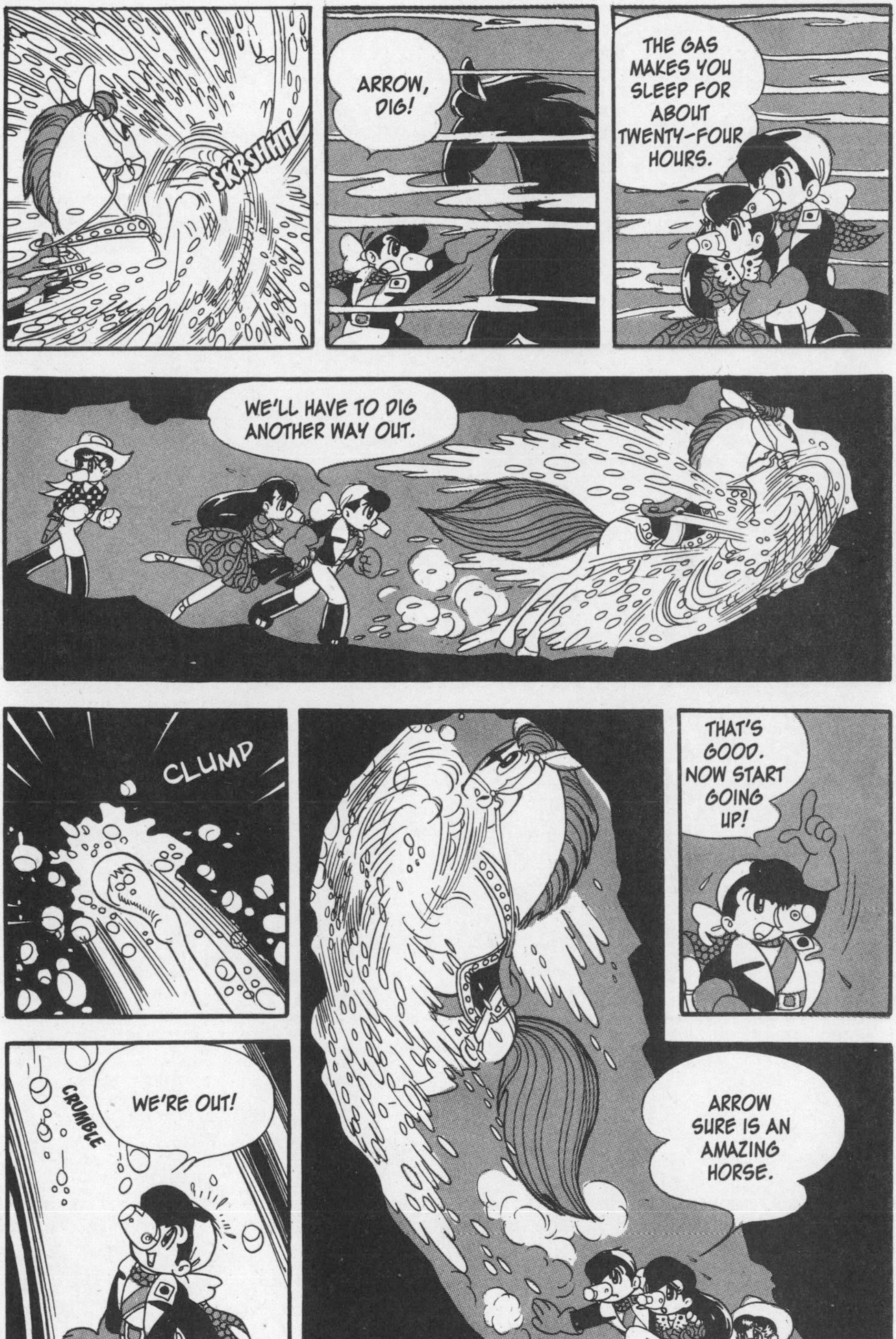
THE GAS MAKES YOU SLEEP FOR ABOUT TWENTY-FOUR HOURS.
ARROW, DIG!
SKRSHHH
WE'LL HAVE TO DIG ANOTHER WAY OUT.
THAT'S GOOD. NOW START GOING UP!
ARROW SURE IS AN AMAZING HORSE.
CLUMP
WE'RE OUT!
CRUMBLE

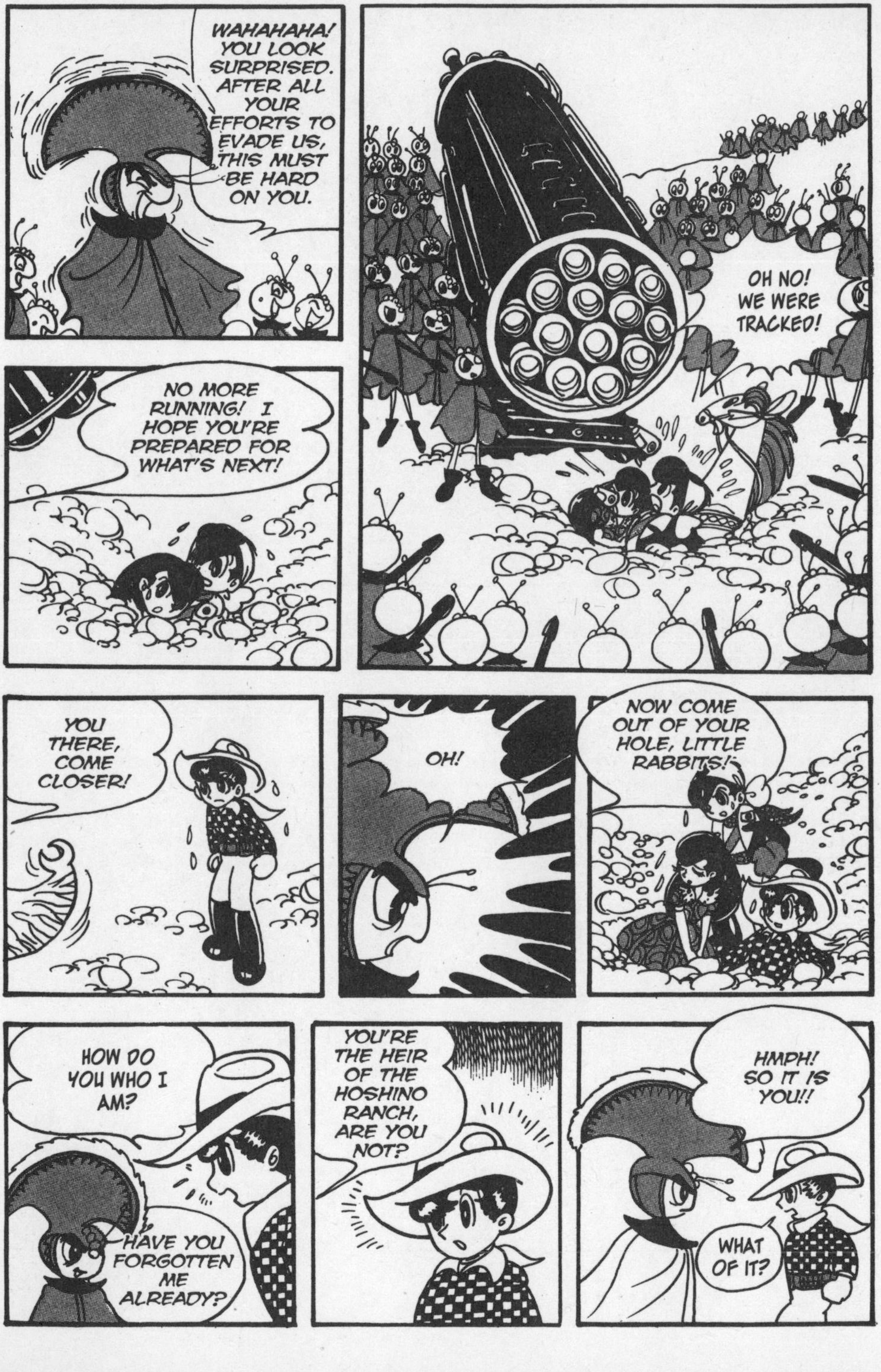
OH NO! WE WERE TRACKED!
WAHAHAHA! YOU LOOK SURPRISED. AFTER ALL YOUR EFFORTS TO EVADE US, THIS MUST BE HARD ON YOU.
NO MORE RUNNING! I HOPE YOU'RE PREPARED FOR WHAT'S NEXT!
NOW COME OUT OF YOUR HOLE, LITTLE RABBITS!
OH!
YOU THERE, COME CLOSER!
HMPH! SO IT IS YOU!!
WHAT OF IT?
YOU'RE THE HEIR OF THE HOSHINO RANCH, ARE YOU NOT?
HOW DO YOU WHO I AM?
HAVE YOU FORGOTTEN ME ALREADY?

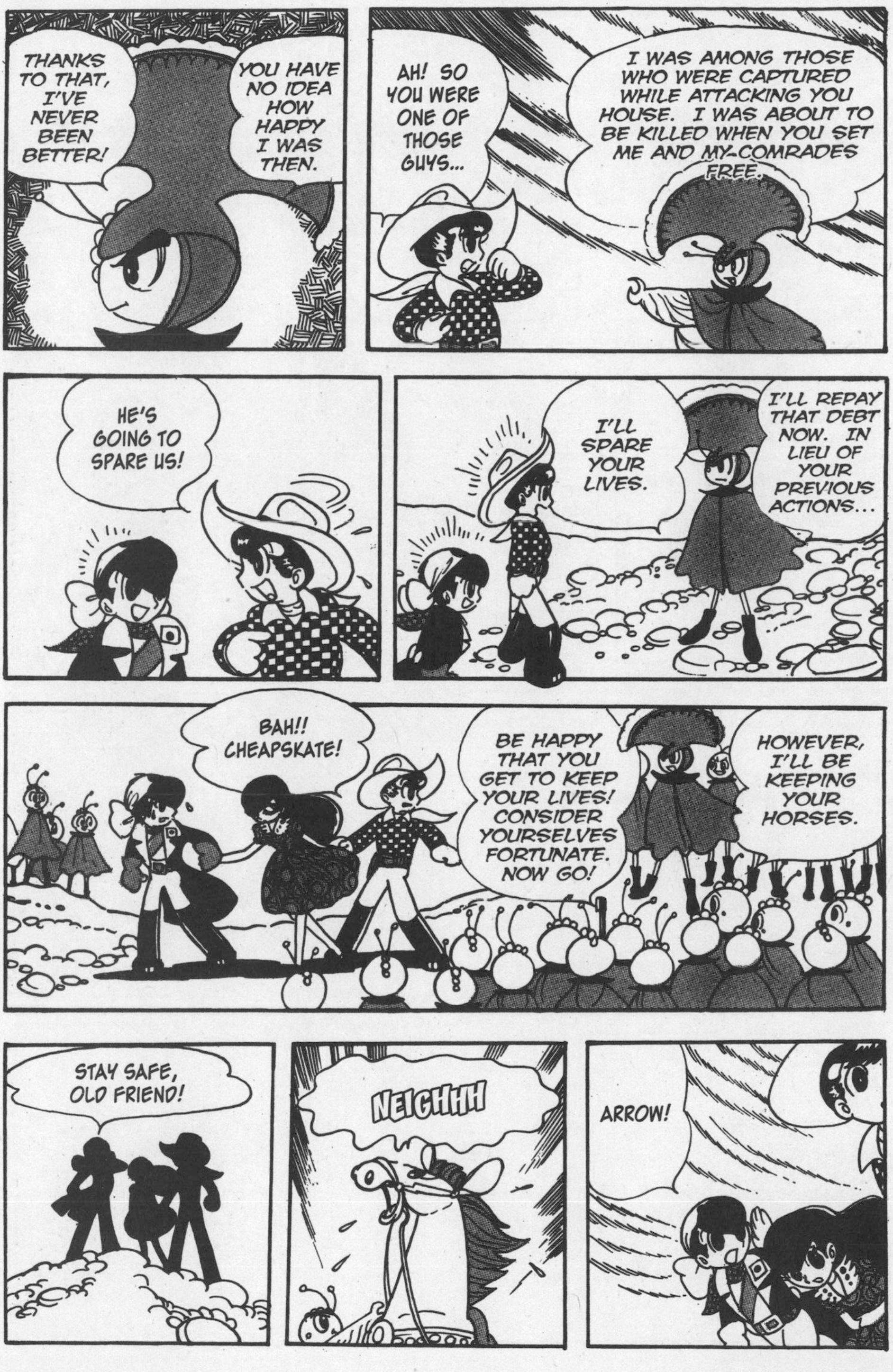
I WAS AMONG THOSE WHO WERE CAPTURED WHILE ATTACKING YOU HOUSE. I WAS ABOUT TO BE KILLED WHEN YOU SET ME AND MY COMRADES FREE.
AH! SO YOU WERE ONE OF THOSE GUYS...
YOU HAVE NO IDEA HOW HAPPY I WAS THEN.
THANKS TO THAT, I'VE NEVER BEEN BETTER!
I'LL REPAY THAT DEBT NOW. IN LIEU OF YOUR PREVIOUS ACTIONS...
I'LL SPARE YOUR LIVES.
HE'S GOING TO SPARE US!
HOWEVER, I'LL BE KEEPING YOUR HORSES.
BE HAPPY THAT YOU GET TO KEEP YOUR LIVES! CONSIDER YOURSELVES FORTUNATE. NOW GO!
BAH!! CHEAPSKATE!
ARROW!
NEIGHHH
STAY SAFE, OLD FRIEND!

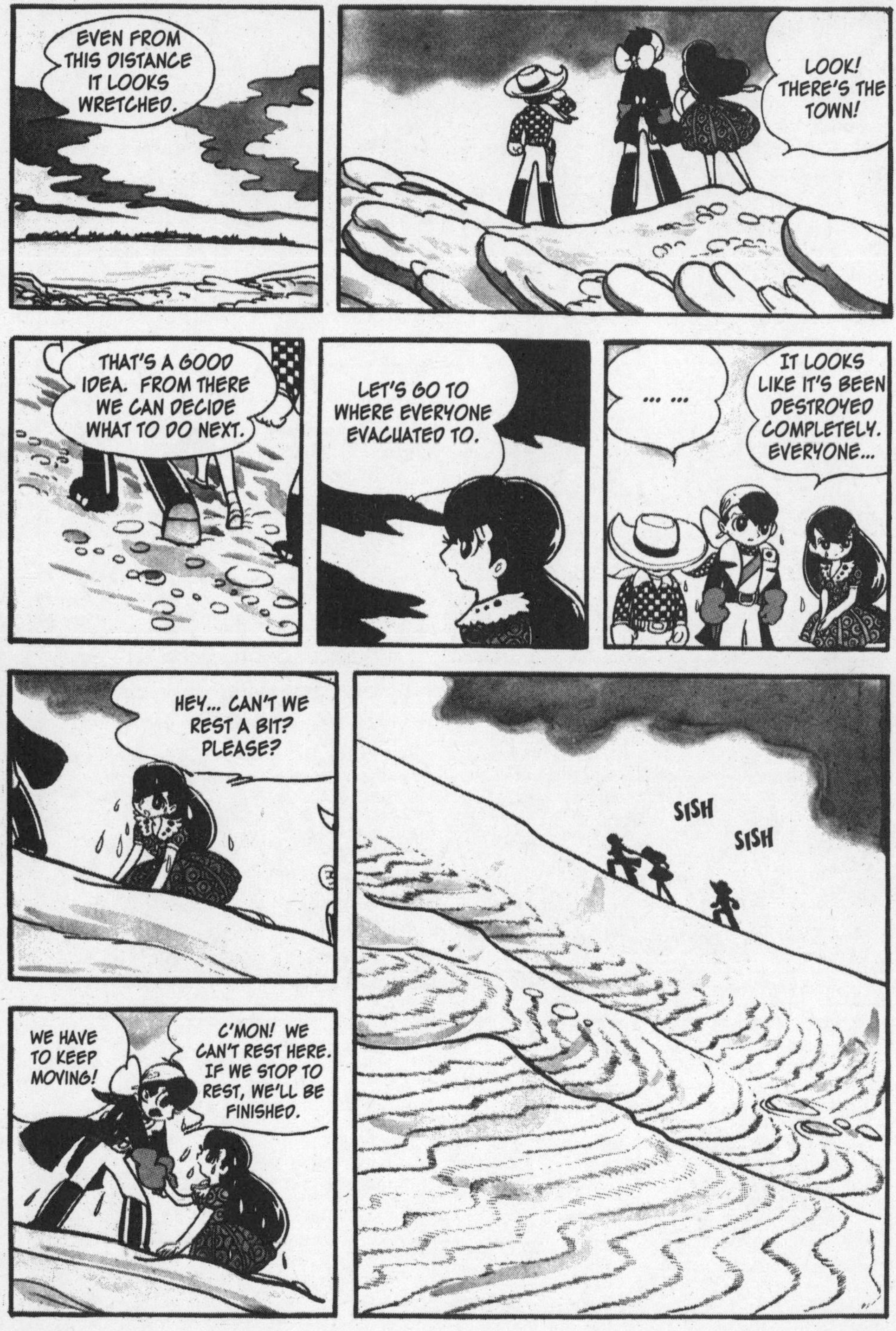
LOOK! THERE'S THE TOWN!
EVEN FROM THIS DISTANCE IT LOOKS WRETCHED.
IT LOOKS LIKE IT'S BEEN DESTROYED COMPLETELY. EVERYONE...
... ...
LET'S GO TO WHERE EVERYONE EVACUATED TO.
THAT'S A GOOD IDEA. FROM THERE WE CAN DECIDE WHAT TO DO NEXT.
SISH
SISH
HEY... CAN'T WE REST A BIT? PLEASE?
C'MON! WE CAN'T REST HERE. IF WE STOP TO REST, WE'LL BE FINISHED.
WE HAVE TO KEEP MOVING!

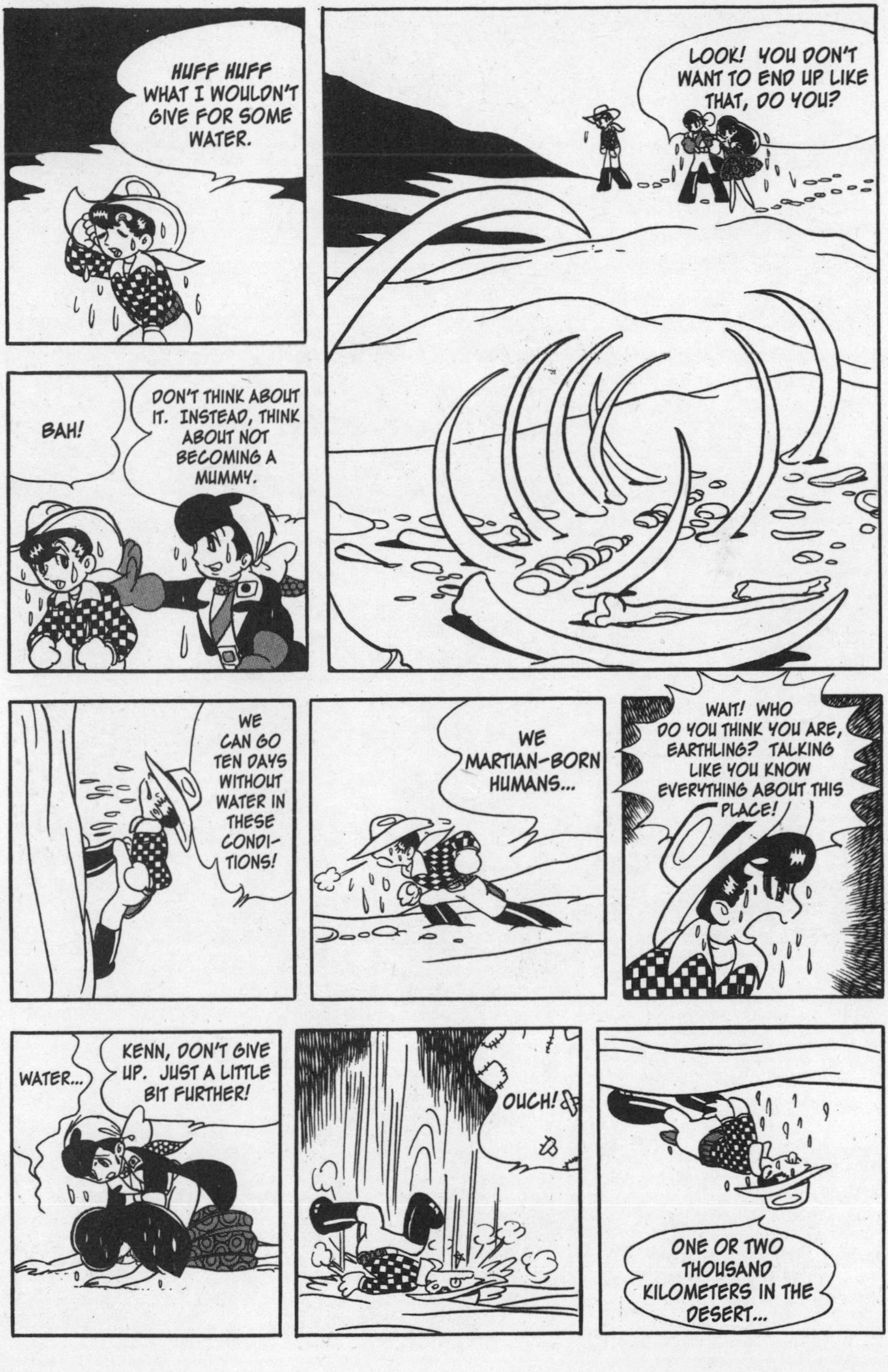
LOOK! YOU DON'T WANT TO END UP LIKE THAT, DO YOU?
HUFF HUFF WHAT I WOULDN'T GIVE FOR SOME WATER.
DON'T THINK ABOUT IT. INSTEAD, THINK ABOUT NOT BECOMING A MUMMY.
BAH!
WAIT! WHO DO YOU THINK YOU ARE, EARTHLING? TALKING LIKE YOU KNOW EVERYTHING ABOUT THIS PLACE!
WE MARTIAN-BORN HUMANS...
WE CAN GO TEN DAYS WITHOUT WATER IN THESE CONDI-TIONS!
ONE OR TWO THOUSAND KILOMETERS IN THE DESERT...
OUCH!
KENN, DON'T GIVE UP. JUST A LITTLE BIT FURTHER!
WATER...

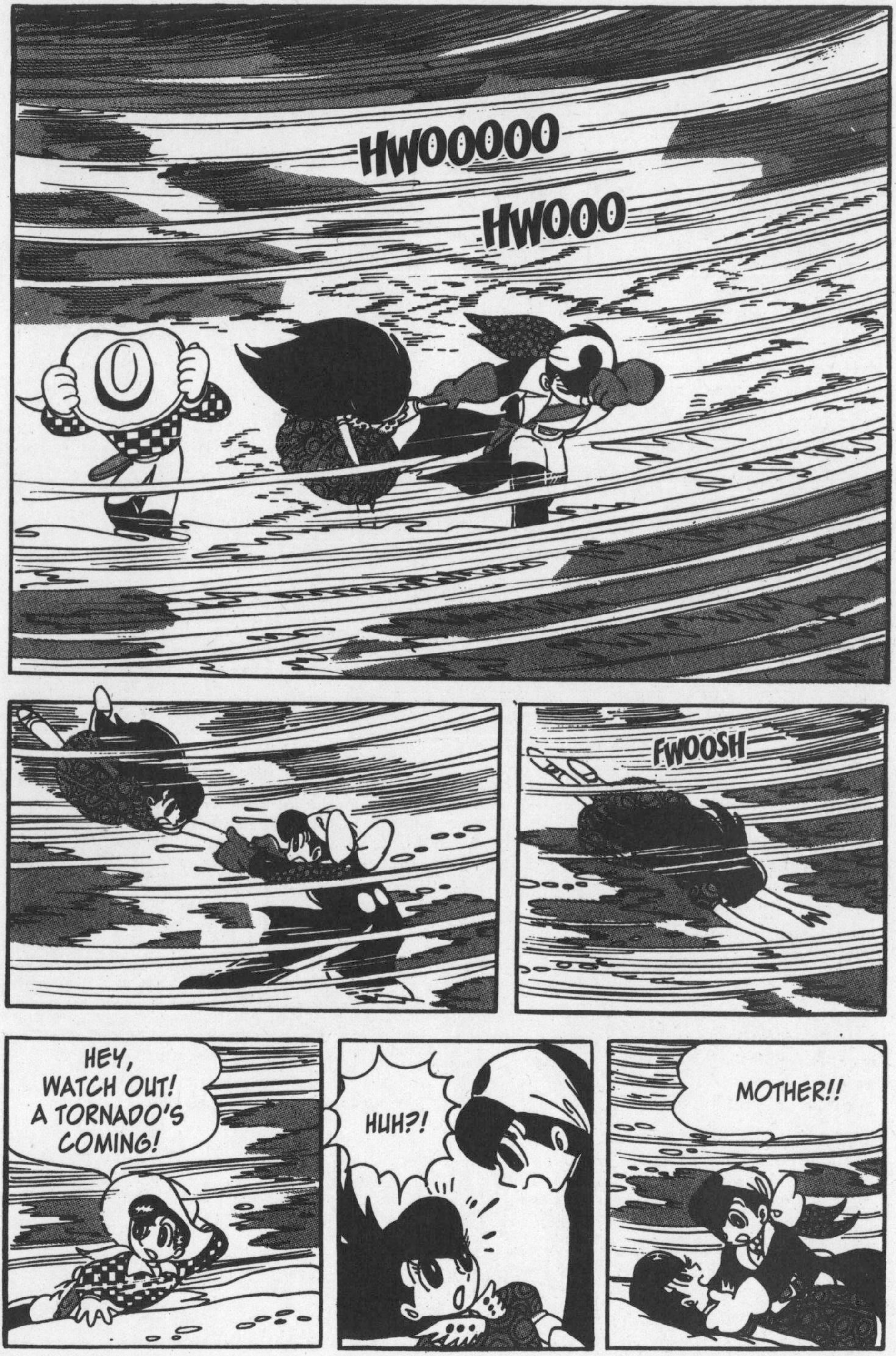
HWOOOOO
HWOOO
FWOOSH
MOTHER!!
HUH?!
HEY, WATCH OUT! A TORNADO'S COMING!

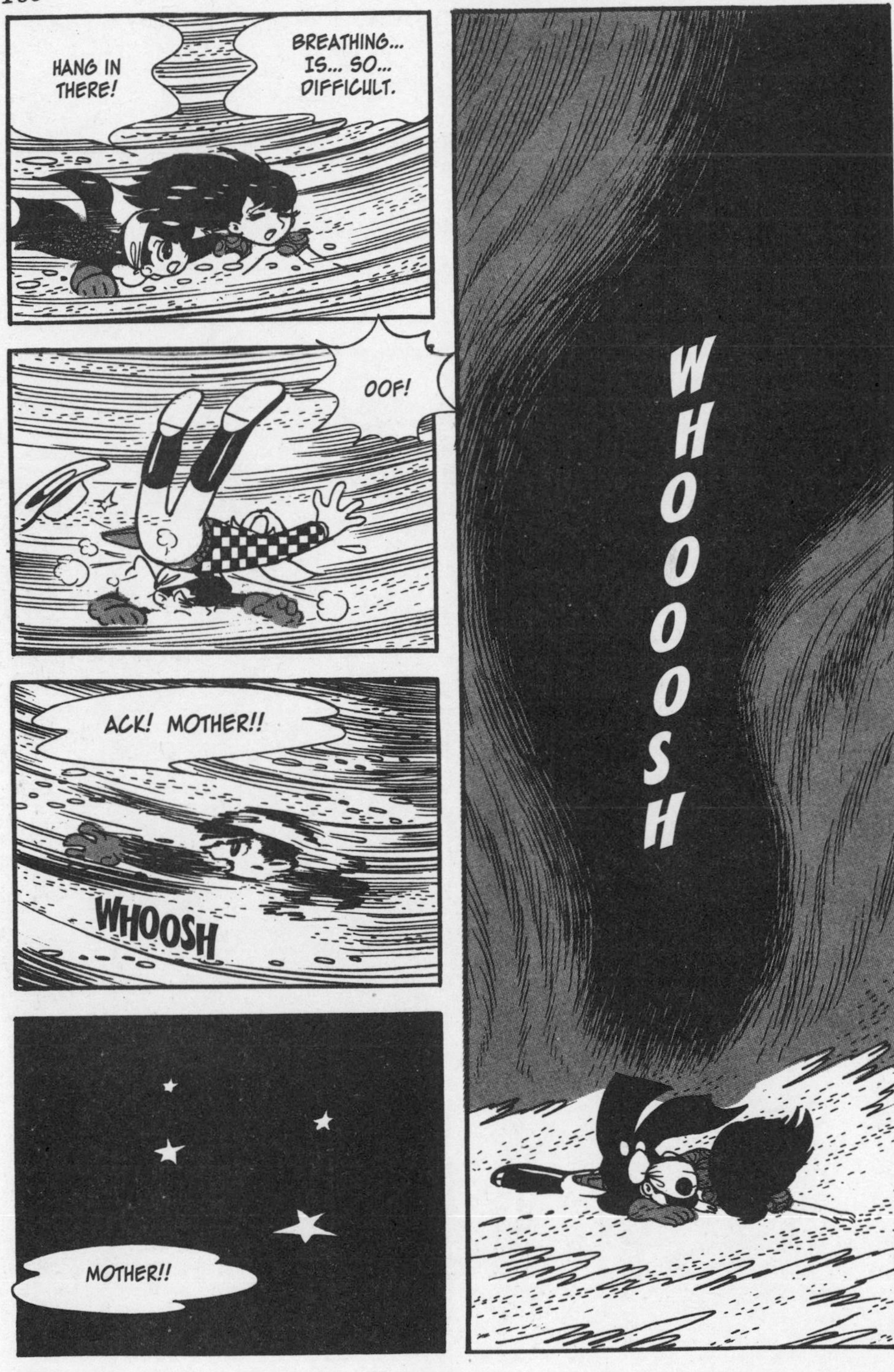
WHOOOOSH
HANG IN THERE!
BREATHING... IS... SO... DIFFICULT.
OOF!
ACK! MOTHER!!
WHOOSH
MOTHER!!

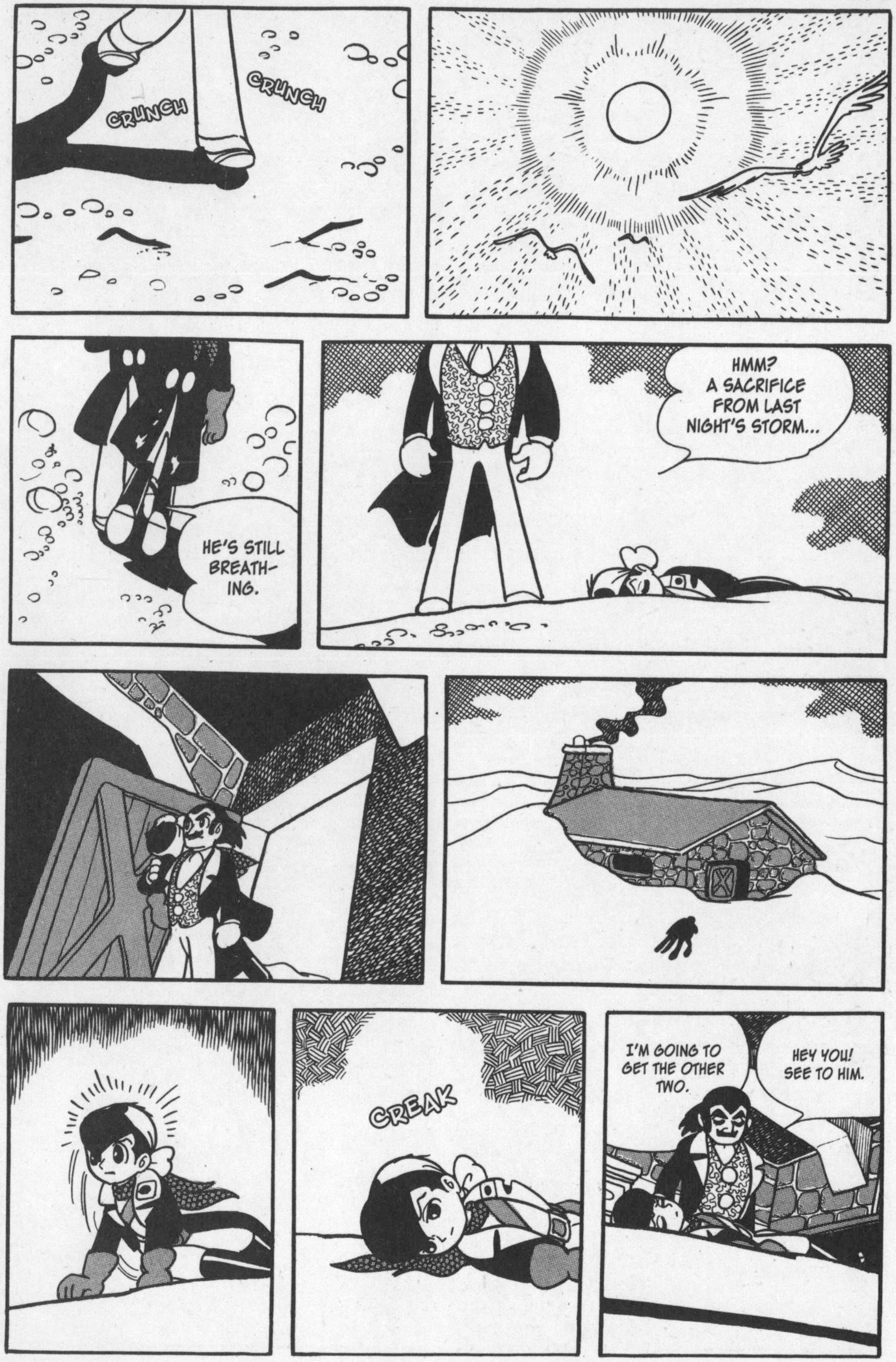
CRUNCH
CRUNCH
HMM? A SACRIFICE FROM LAST NIGHT'S STORM...
HE'S STILL BREATH-ING.
HEY YOU! SEE TO HIM.
I'M GOING TO GET THE OTHER TWO.
CREAK

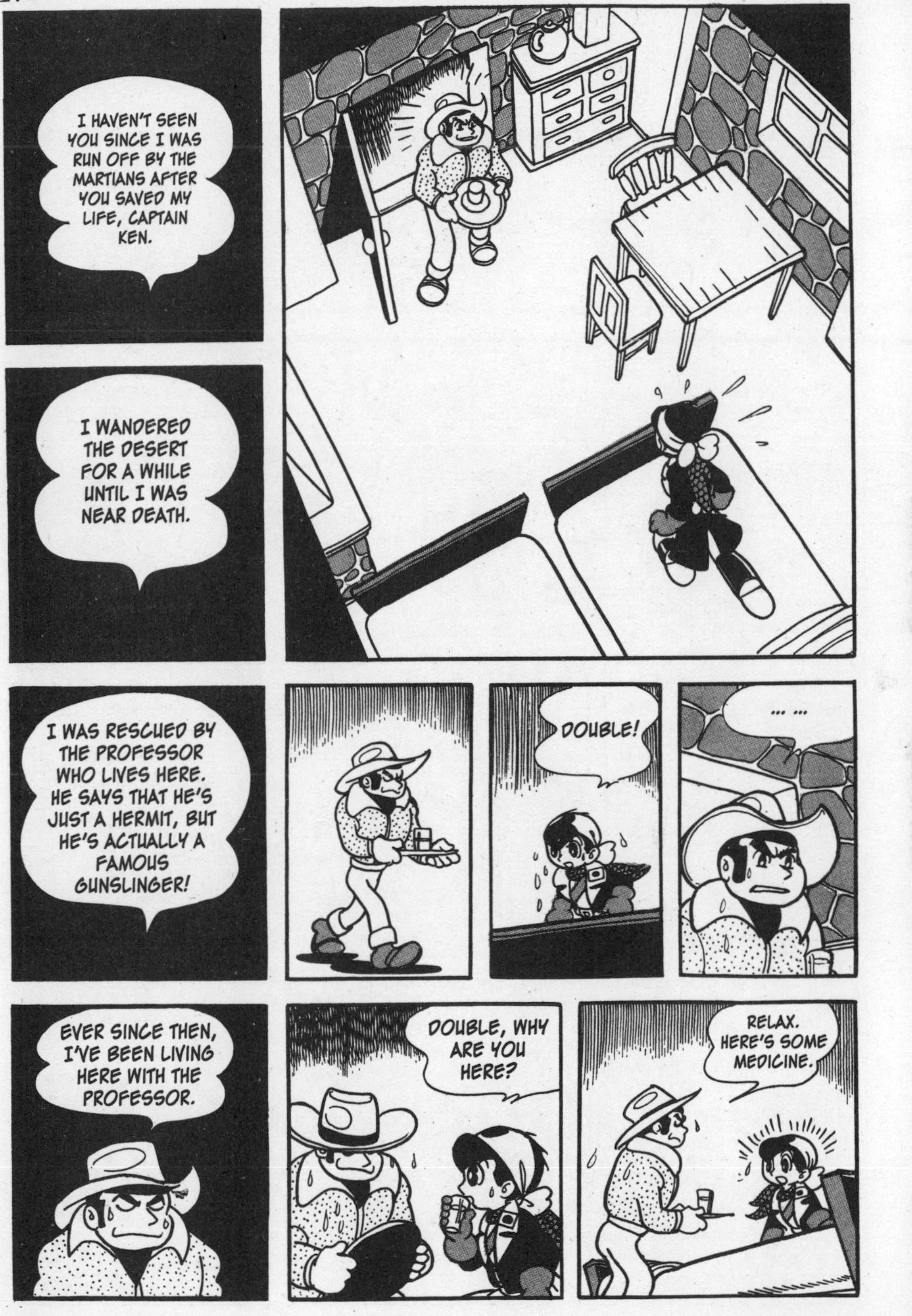
I HAVEN'T SEEN YOU SINCE I WAS RUN OFF BY THE MARTIANS AFTER YOU SAVED MY LIFE, CAPTAIN KEN.
I WANDERED THE DESERT FOR A WHILE UNTIL I WAS NEAR DEATH.
... ...
DOUBLE!
I WAS RESCUED BY THE PROFESSOR WHO LIVES HERE. HE SAYS THAT HE'S JUST A HERMIT, BUT HE'S ACTUALLY A FAMOUS GUNSLINGER!
RELAX. HERE'S SOME MEDICINE.
DOUBLE, WHY ARE YOU HERE?
EVER SINCE THEN, I'VE BEEN LIVING HERE WITH THE PROFESSOR.

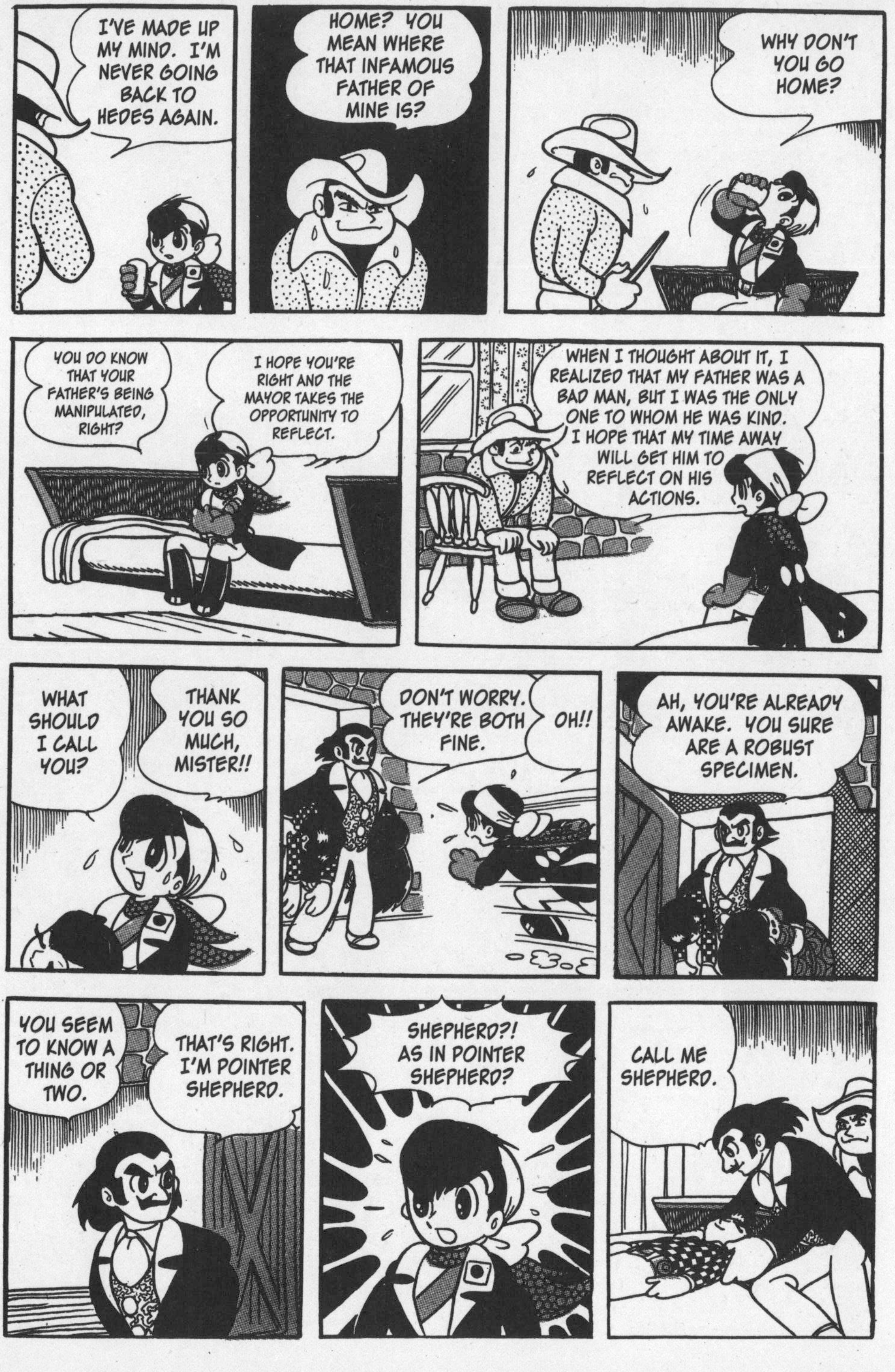
WHY DON'T YOU GO HOME?
HOME? YOU MEAN WHERE THAT INFAMOUS FATHER OF MINE IS?
I'VE MADE UP MY MIND. I'M NEVER GOING BACK TO HEDES AGAIN.
WHEN I THOUGHT ABOUT IT, I REALIZED THAT MY FATHER WAS A BAD MAN, BUT I WAS THE ONLY ONE TO WHOM HE WAS KIND. I HOPE THAT MY TIME AWAY WILL GET HIM TO REFLECT ON HIS ACTIONS.
I HOPE YOU'RE RIGHT AND THE MAYOR TAKES THE OPPORTUNITY TO REFLECT.
YOU DO KNOW THAT YOUR FATHER'S BEING MANIPULATED, RIGHT?
AH, YOU'RE ALREADY AWAKE. YOU SURE ARE A ROBUST SPECIMEN.
OH!!
DON'T WORRY. THEY'RE BOTH FINE.
THANK YOU SO MUCH, MISTER!!
WHAT SHOULD I CALL YOU?
CALL ME SHEPHERD.
SHEPHERD?! AS IN POINTER SHEPHERD?
THAT'S RIGHT. I'M POINTER SHEPHERD.
YOU SEEM TO KNOW A THING OR TWO.

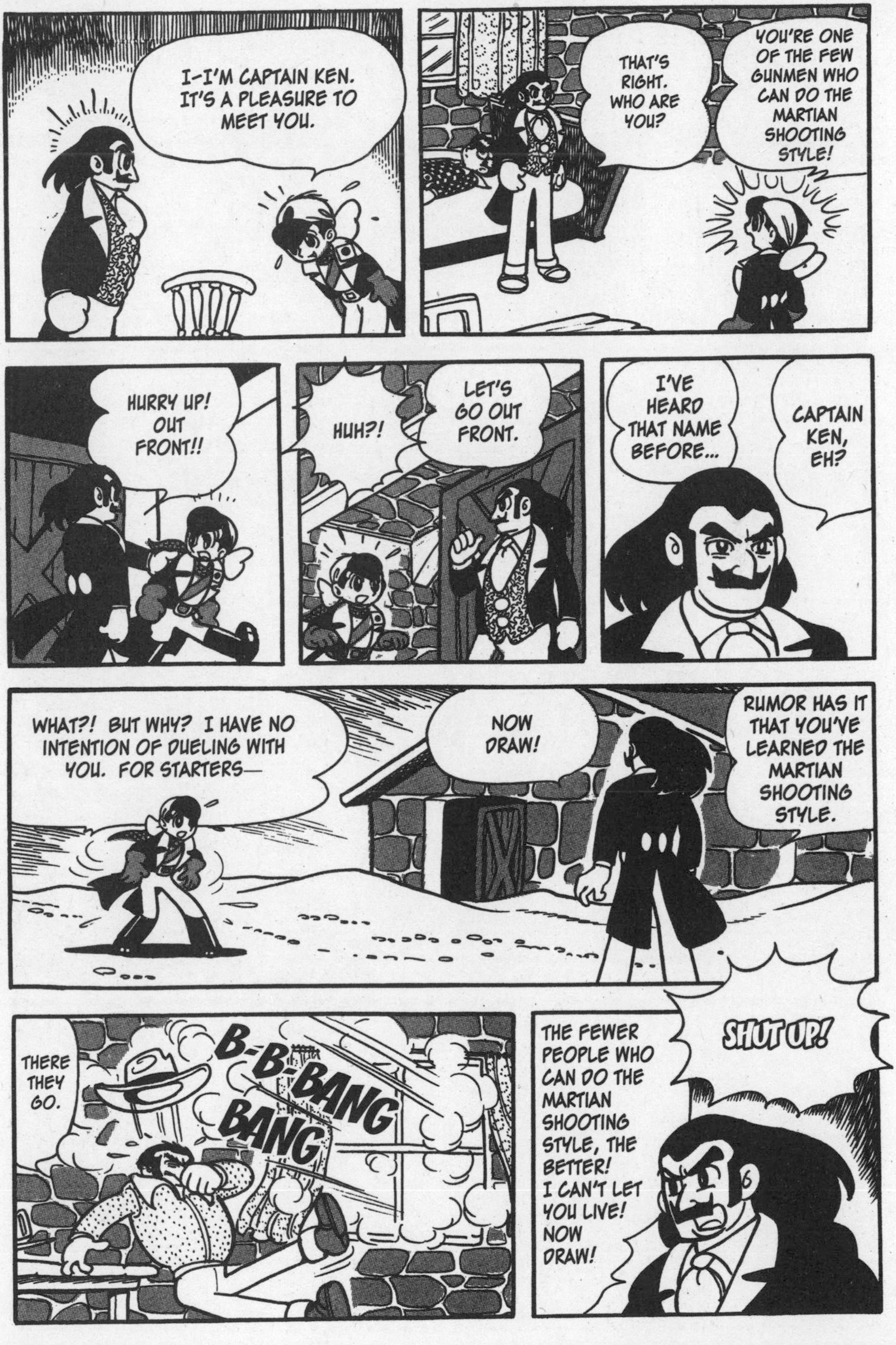
YOU'RE ONE OF THE FEW GUNMEN WHO CAN DO THE MARTIAN SHOOTING STYLE!
THAT'S RIGHT. WHO ARE YOU?
I-I'M CAPTAIN KEN. IT'S A PLEASURE TO MEET YOU.
CAPTAIN KEN, EH?
I'VE HEARD THAT NAME BEFORE...
LET'S GO OUT FRONT.
HUH?!
HURRY UP! OUT FRONT!!
RUMOR HAS IT THAT YOU'VE LEARNED THE MARTIAN SHOOTING STYLE.
NOW DRAW!
WHAT?! BUT WHY? I HAVE NO INTENTION OF DUELING WITH YOU. FOR STARTERS—
SHUT UP!
THE FEWER PEOPLE WHO CAN DO THE MARTIAN SHOOTING STYLE, THE BETTER! I CAN'T LET YOU LIVE! NOW DRAW!
B-B-BANG
BANG
THERE THEY GO.

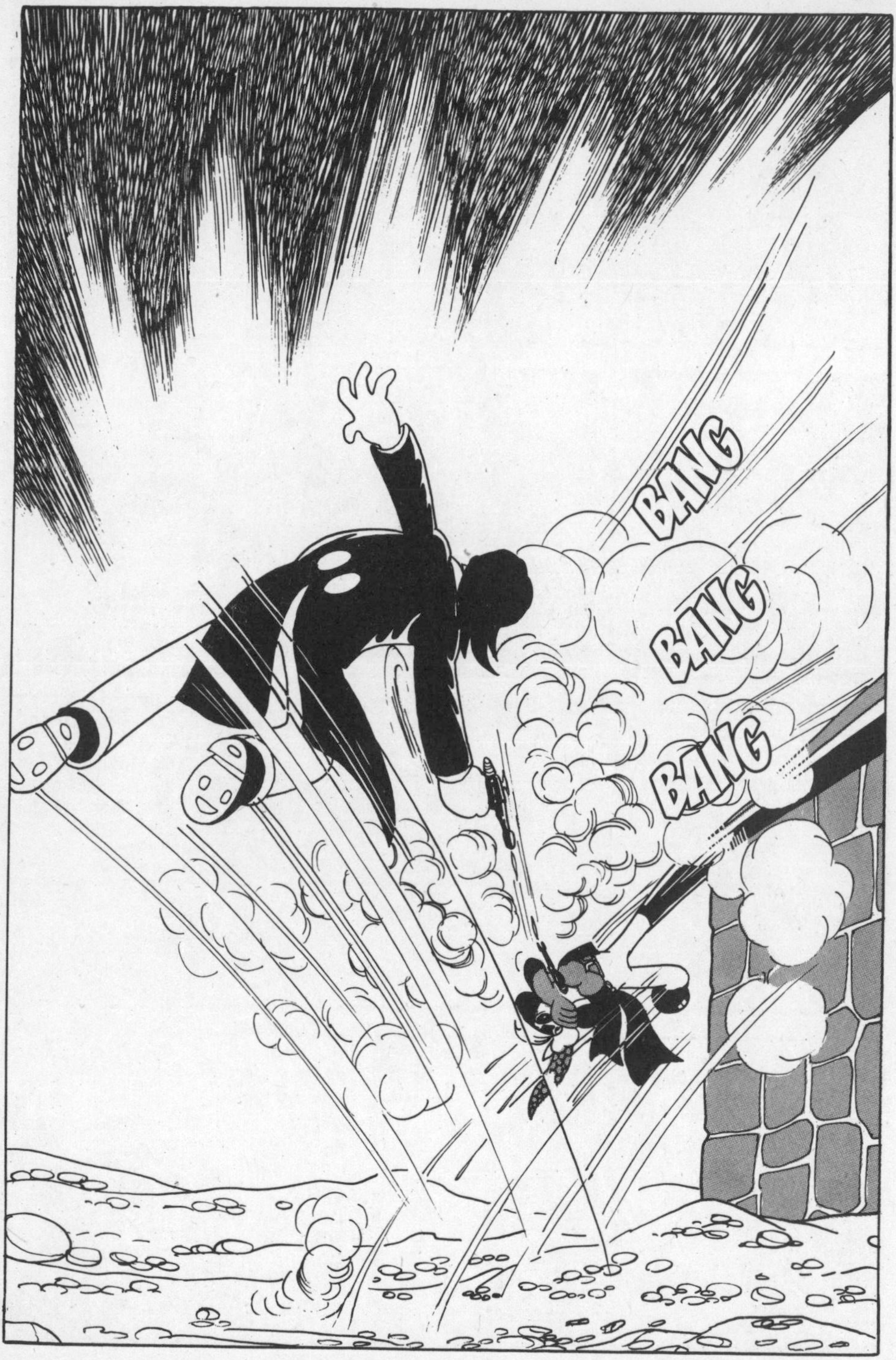
BANG
BANG
BANG

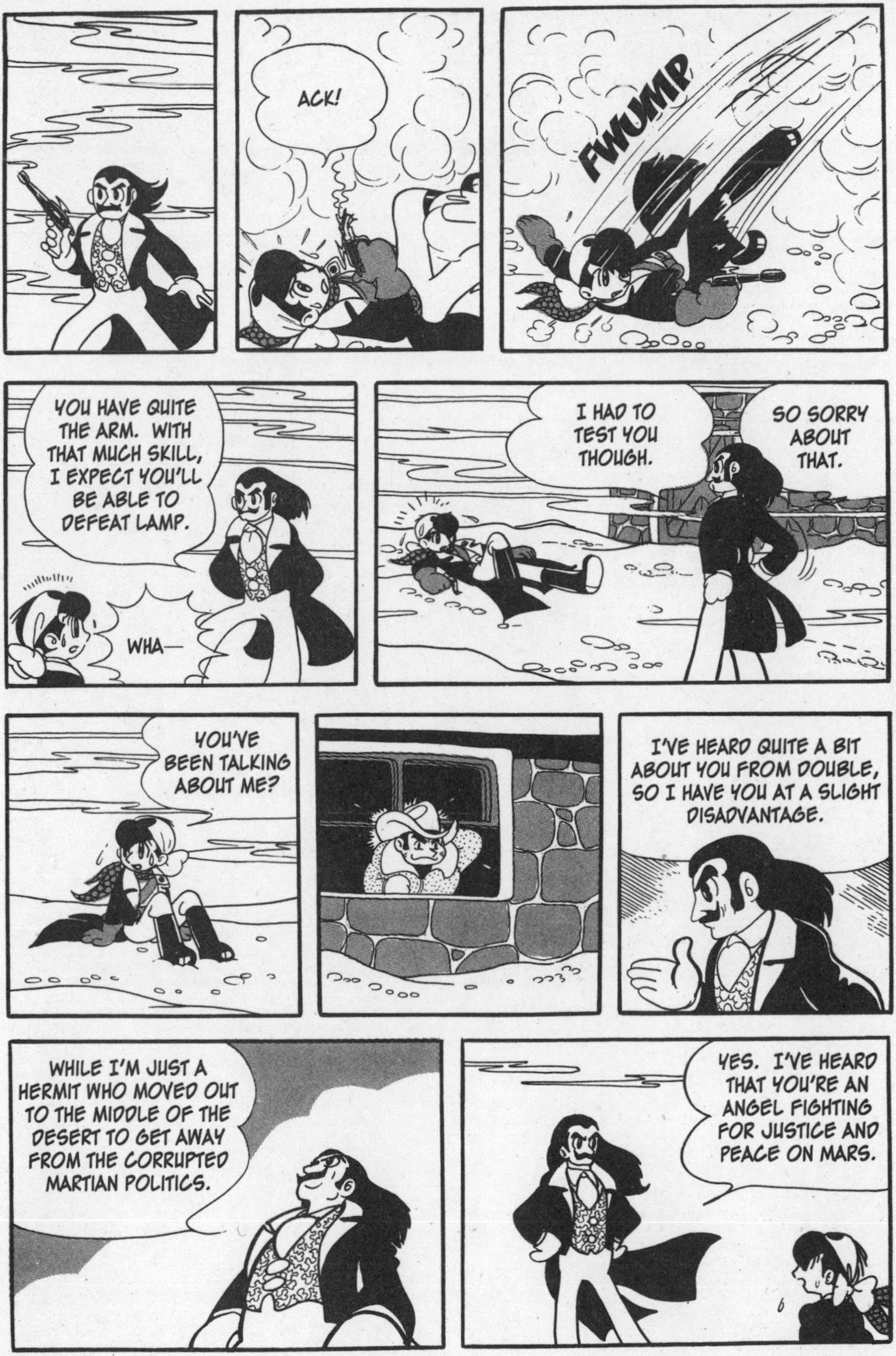
ACK!
FWUMP
YOU HAVE QUITE THE ARM. WITH THAT MUCH SKILL, I EXPECT YOU'LL BE ABLE TO DEFEAT LAMP.
WHA—
I HAD TO TEST YOU THOUGH.
SO SORRY ABOUT THAT.
YOU'VE BEEN TALKING ABOUT ME?
I'VE HEARD QUITE A BIT ABOUT YOU FROM DOUBLE, SO I HAVE YOU AT A SLIGHT DISADVANTAGE.
WHILE I'M JUST A HERMIT WHO MOVED OUT TO THE MIDDLE OF THE DESERT TO GET AWAY FROM THE CORRUPTED MARTIAN POLITICS.
YES. I'VE HEARD THAT YOU'RE AN ANGEL FIGHTING FOR JUSTICE AND PEACE ON MARS.

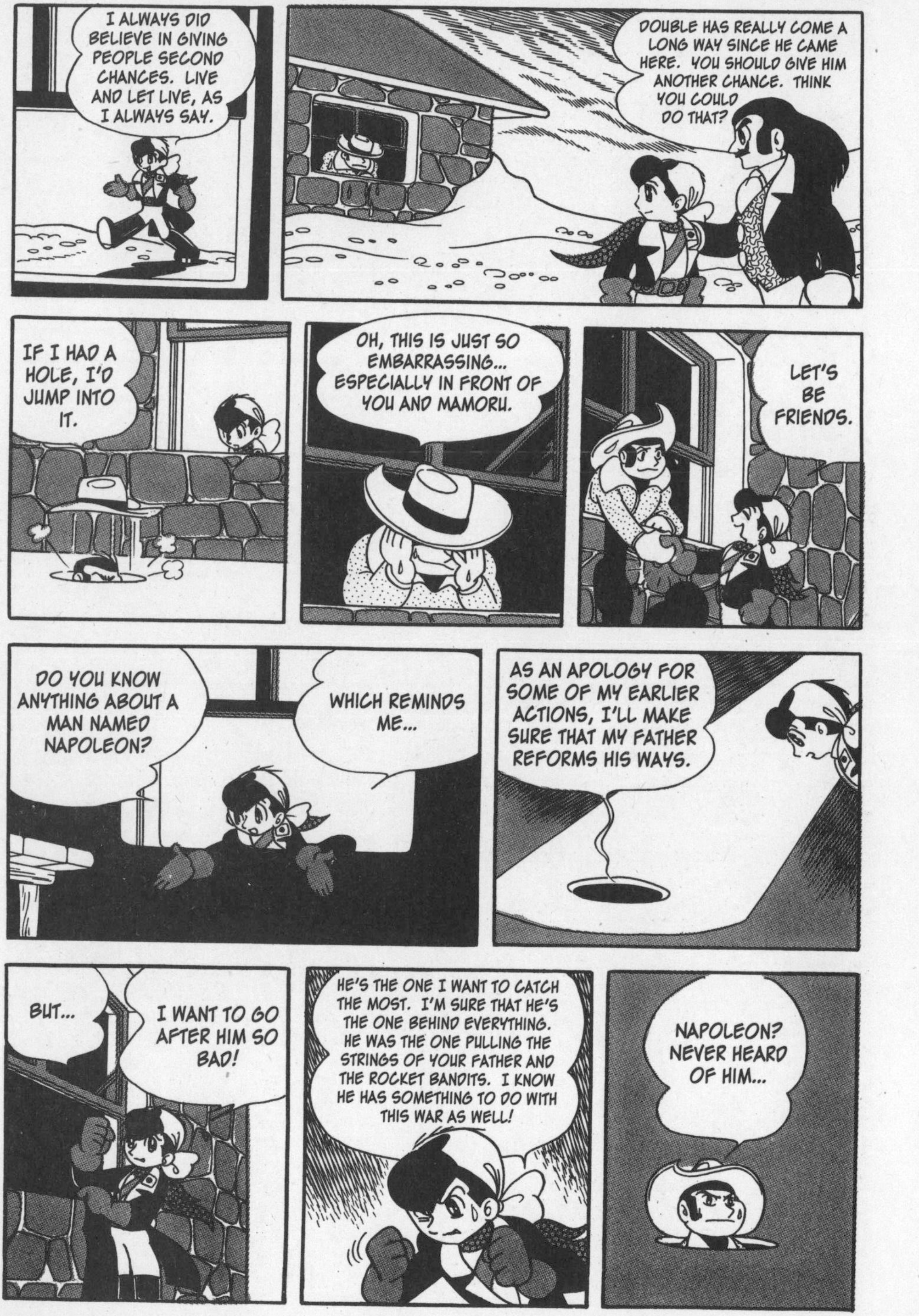
DOUBLE HAS REALLY COME A LONG WAY SINCE HE CAME HERE. YOU SHOULD GIVE HIM ANOTHER CHANCE. THINK YOU COULD DO THAT?
I ALWAYS DID BELIEVE IN GIVING PEOPLE SECOND CHANCES. LIVE AND LET LIVE, AS I ALWAYS SAY.
LET'S BE FRIENDS.
OH, THIS IS JUST SO EMBARRASSING... ESPECIALLY IN FRONT OF YOU AND MAMORU.
IF I HAD A HOLE, I'D JUMP INTO IT.
AS AN APOLOGY FOR SOME OF MY EARLIER ACTIONS, I'LL MAKE SURE THAT MY FATHER REFORMS HIS WAYS.
WHICH REMINDS ME...
DO YOU KNOW ANYTHING ABOUT A MAN NAMED NAPOLEON?
NAPOLEON? NEVER HEARD OF HIM...
HE'S THE ONE I WANT TO CATCH THE MOST. I'M SURE THAT HE'S THE ONE BEHIND EVERYTHING. HE WAS THE ONE PULLING THE STRINGS OF YOUR FATHER AND THE ROCKET BANDITS. I KNOW HE HAS SOMETHING TO DO WITH THIS WAR AS WELL!
BUT...
I WANT TO GO AFTER HIM SO BAD!

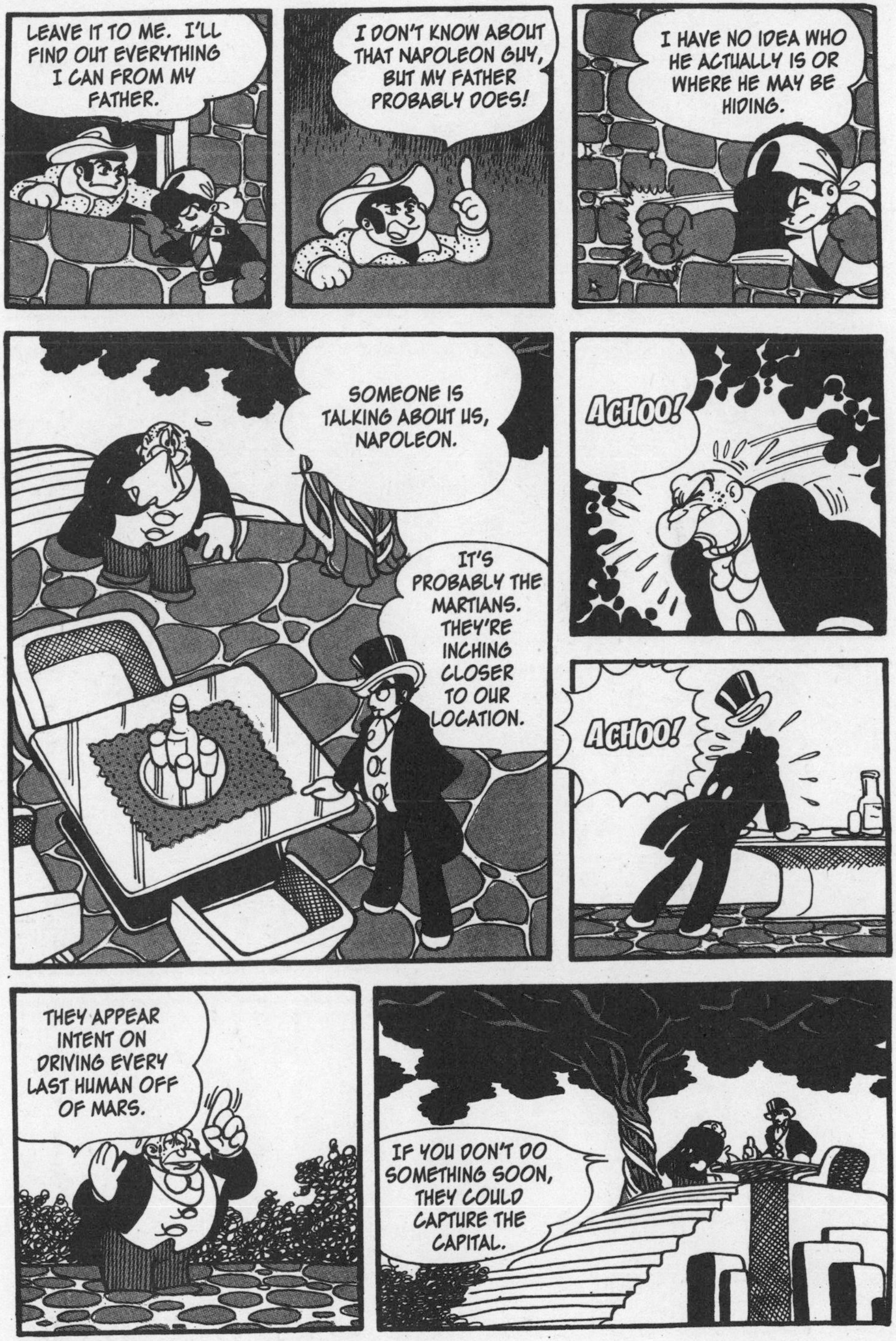
I HAVE NO IDEA WHO HE ACTUALLY IS OR WHERE HE MAY BE HIDING.
I DON'T KNOW ABOUT THAT NAPOLEON GUY, BUT MY FATHER PROBABLY DOES!
LEAVE IT TO ME. I'LL FIND OUT EVERYTHING I CAN FROM MY FATHER.
ACHOO!
ACHOO!
SOMEONE IS TALKING ABOUT US, NAPOLEON.
IT'S PROBABLY THE MARTIANS. THEY'RE INCHING CLOSER TO OUR LOCATION.
IF YOU DON'T DO SOMETHING SOON, THEY COULD CAPTURE THE CAPITAL.
THEY APPEAR INTENT ON DRIVING EVERY LAST HUMAN OFF OF MARS.

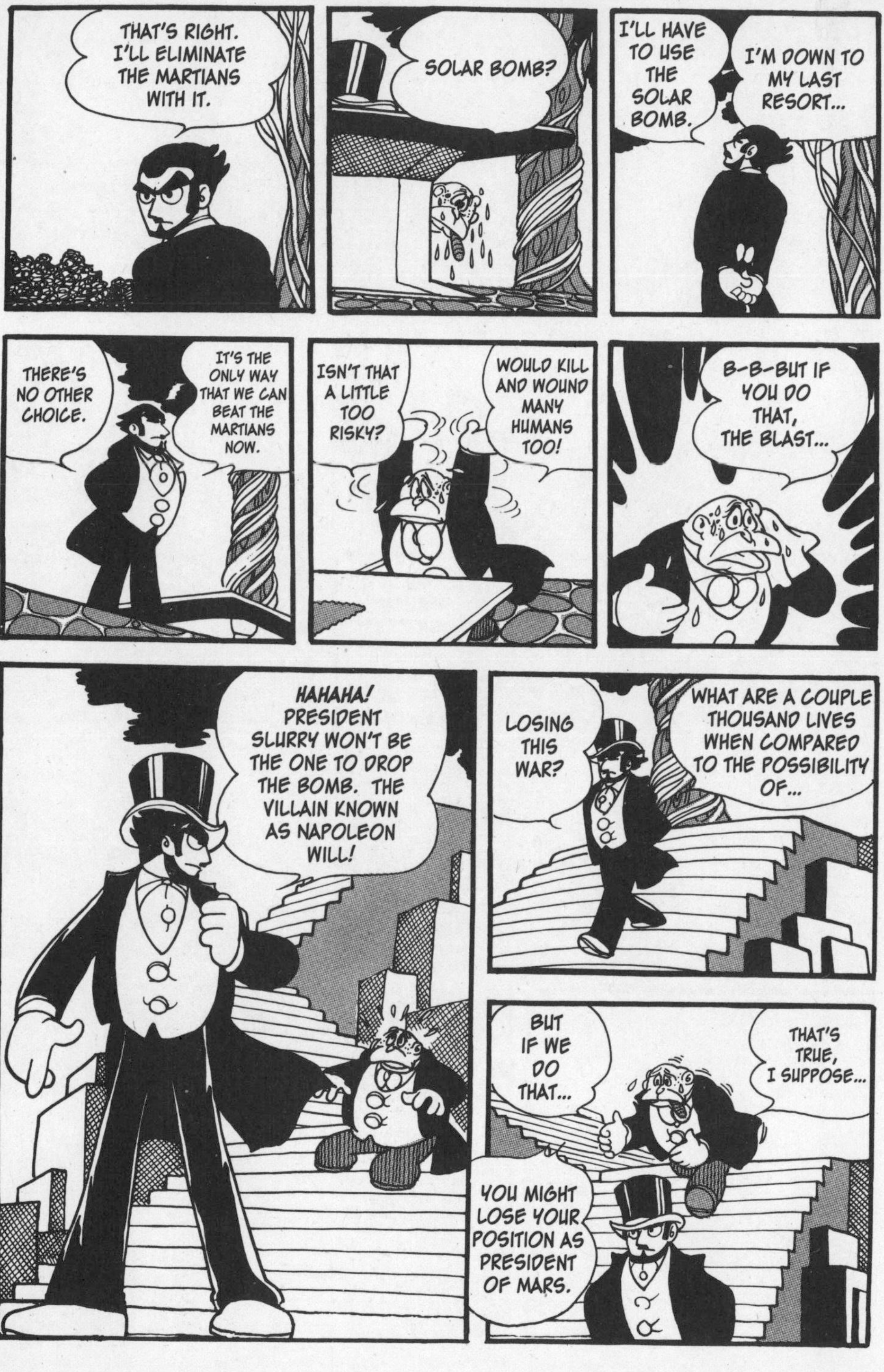
I'M DOWN TO MY LAST RESORT...
I'LL HAVE TO USE THE SOLAR BOMB.
SOLAR BOMB?
THAT'S RIGHT. I'LL ELIMINATE THE MARTIANS WITH IT.
B-B-BUT IF YOU DO THAT, THE BLAST...
WOULD KILL AND WOUND MANY HUMANS TOO!
ISN'T THAT A LITTLE TOO RISKY?
IT'S THE ONLY WAY THAT WE CAN BEAT THE MARTIANS NOW.
THERE'S NO OTHER CHOICE.
WHAT ARE A COUPLE THOUSAND LIVES WHEN COMPARED TO THE POSSIBILITY OF...
LOSING THIS WAR?
THAT'S TRUE, I SUPPOSE...
BUT IF WE DO THAT...
YOU MIGHT LOSE YOUR POSITION AS PRESIDENT OF MARS.
HAHAHA! PRESIDENT SLURRY WON'T BE THE ONE TO DROP THE BOMB. THE VILLAIN KNOWN AS NAPOLEON WILL!

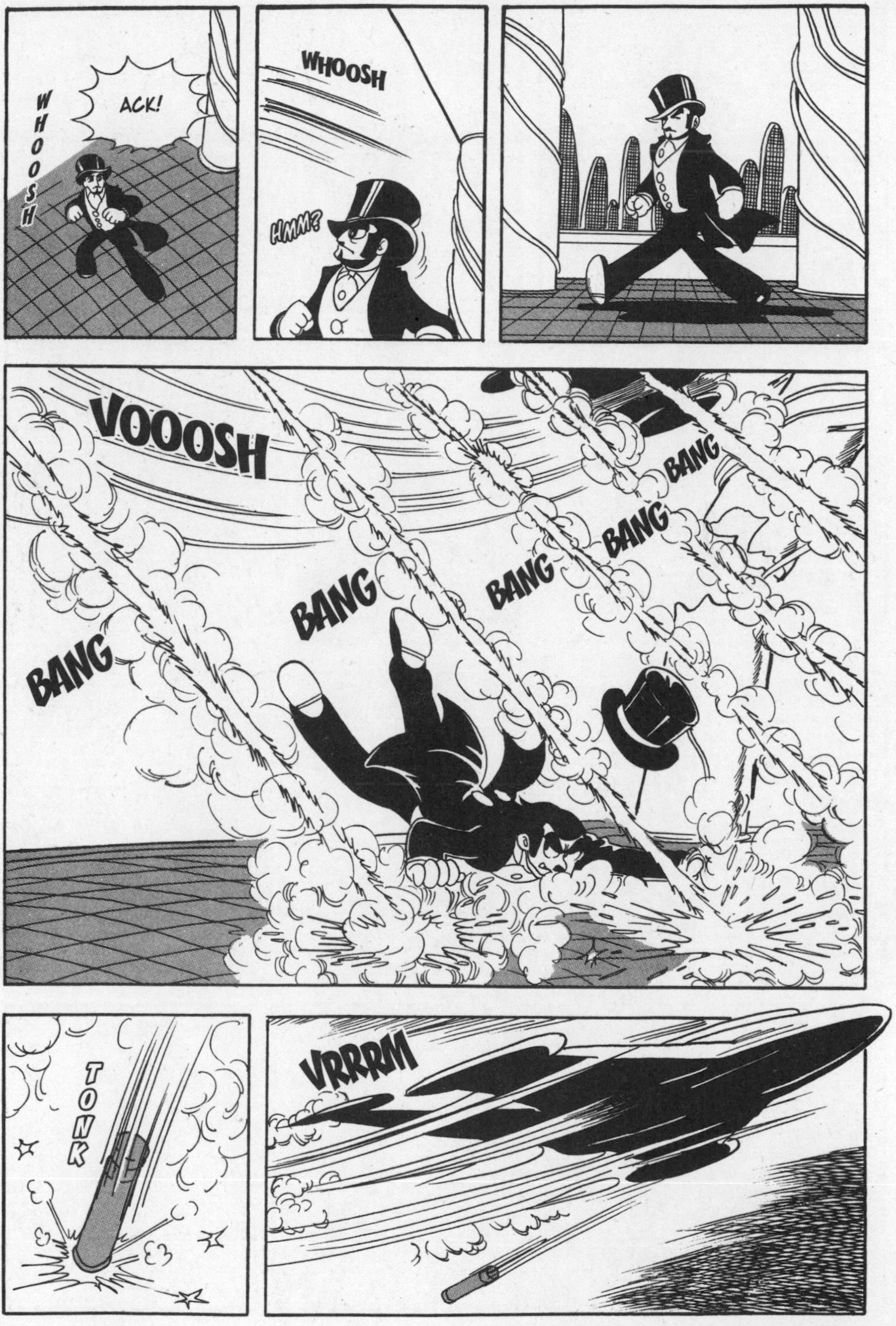
WHOOSH
HMM?
WHOOSH
ACK!
VOOOSH
BANG
BANG
BANG
BANG
BANG
VRRRM
TONK

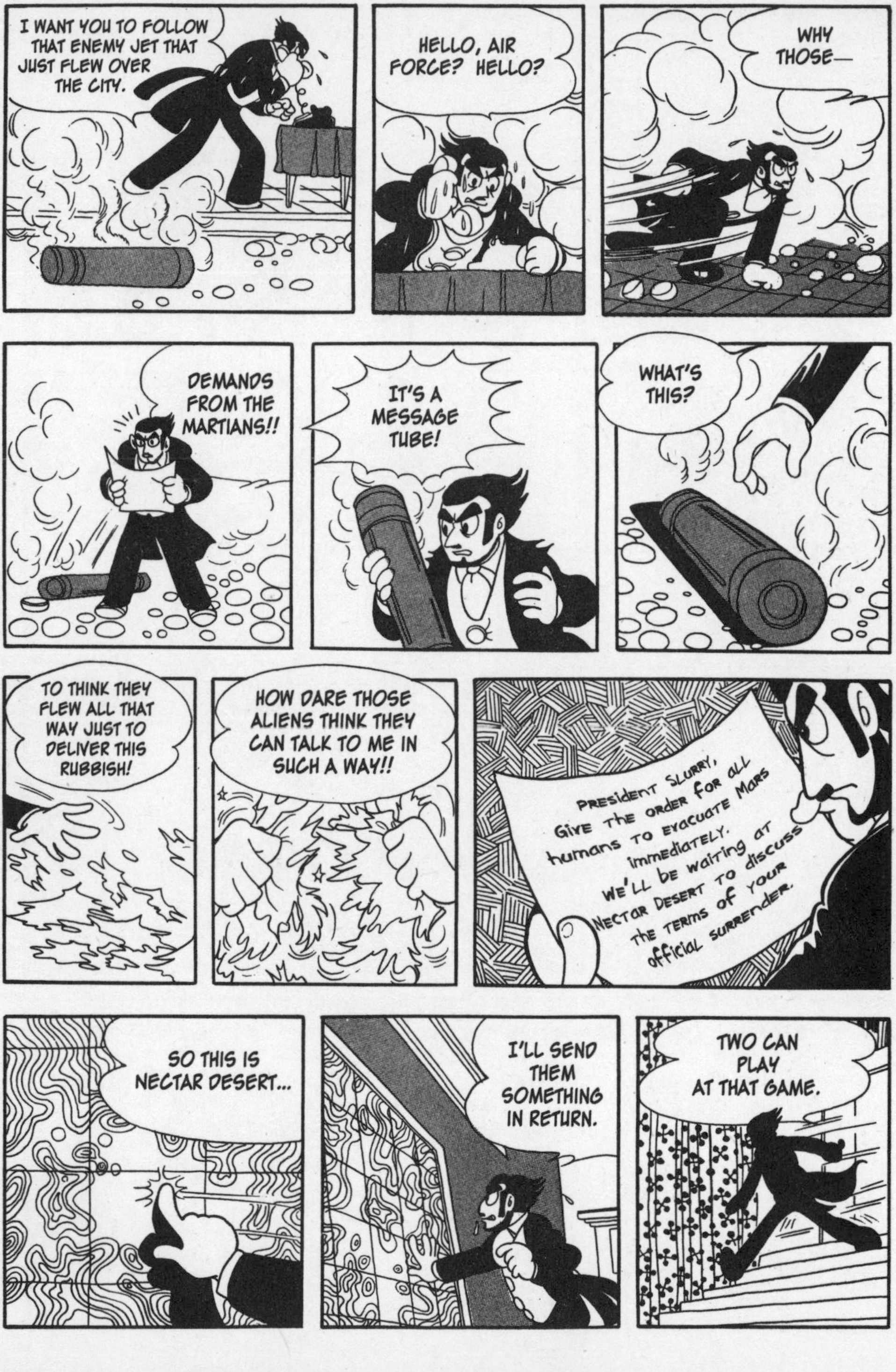
WHY THOSE—
HELLO, AIR FORCE? HELLO?
I WANT YOU TO FOLLOW THAT ENEMY JET THAT JUST FLEW OVER THE CITY.
WHAT'S THIS?
IT'S A MESSAGE TUBE!
DEMANDS FROM THE MARTIANS!!
PRESIDENT SLURRY, GIVE THE ORDER FOR ALL HUMANS TO EVACUATE MARS IMMEDIATELY. WE'LL BE WAITING AT NECTAR DESERT TO DISCUSS THE TERMS OF YOUR OFFICIAL SURRENDER.
HOW DARE THOSE ALIENS THINK THEY CAN TALK TO ME IN SUCH A WAY!!
TO THINK THEY FLEW ALL THAT WAY JUST TO DELIVER THIS RUBBISH!
TWO CAN PLAY AT THAT GAME.
I'LL SEND THEM SOMETHING IN RETURN.
SO THIS IS NECTAR DESERT...

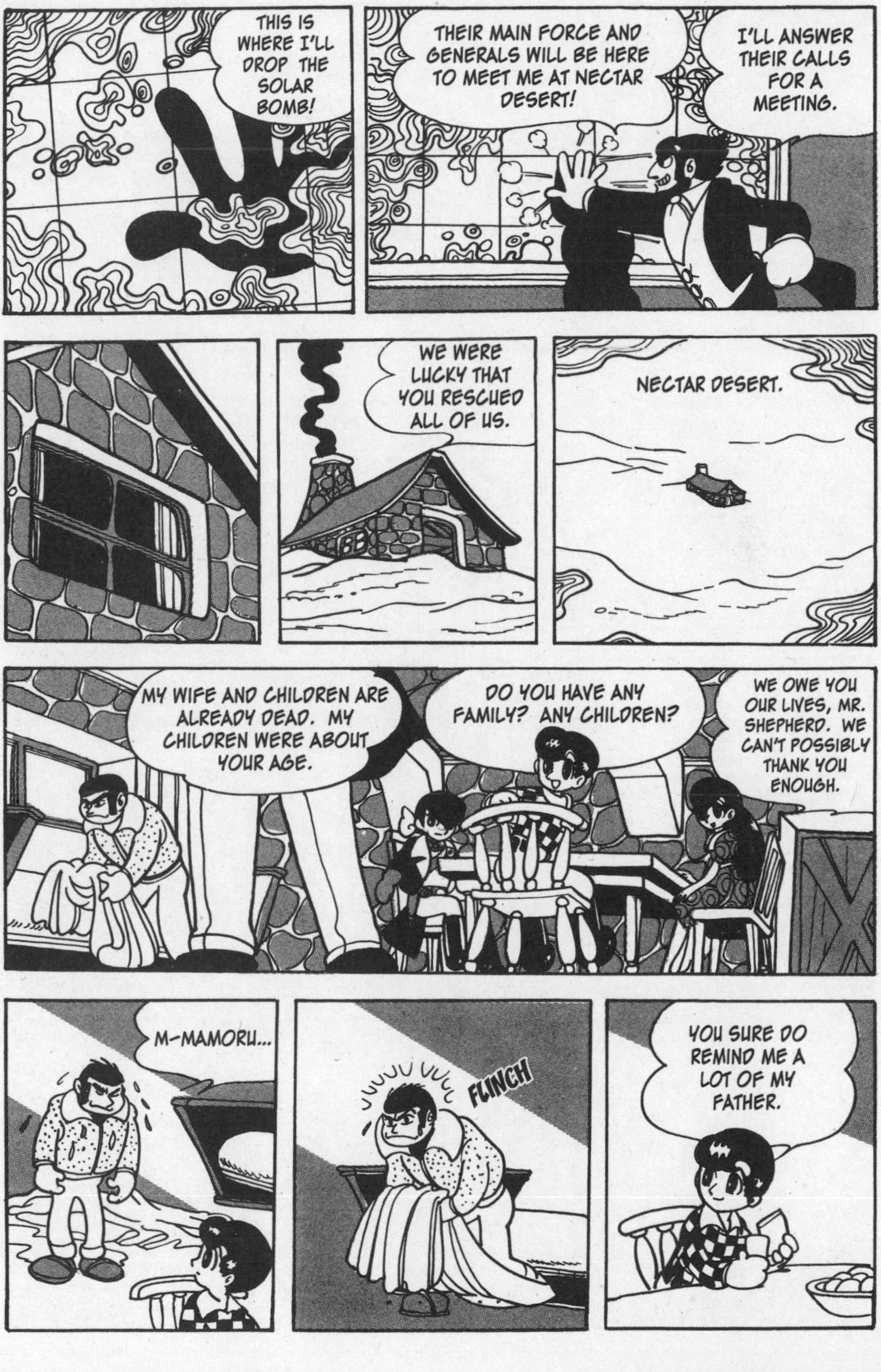
I'LL ANSWER THEIR CALLS FOR A MEETING.
THEIR MAIN FORCE AND GENERALS WILL BE HERE TO MEET ME AT NECTAR DESERT!
THIS IS WHERE I'LL DROP THE SOLAR BOMB!
NECTAR DESERT.
WE WERE LUCKY THAT YOU RESCUED ALL OF US.
WE OWE YOU OUR LIVES, MR. SHEPHERD. WE CAN'T POSSIBLY THANK YOU ENOUGH.
DO YOU HAVE ANY FAMILY? ANY CHILDREN?
MY WIFE AND CHILDREN ARE ALREADY DEAD. MY CHILDREN WERE ABOUT YOUR AGE.
YOU SURE DO REMIND ME A LOT OF MY FATHER.
FLINCH
M-MAMORU...

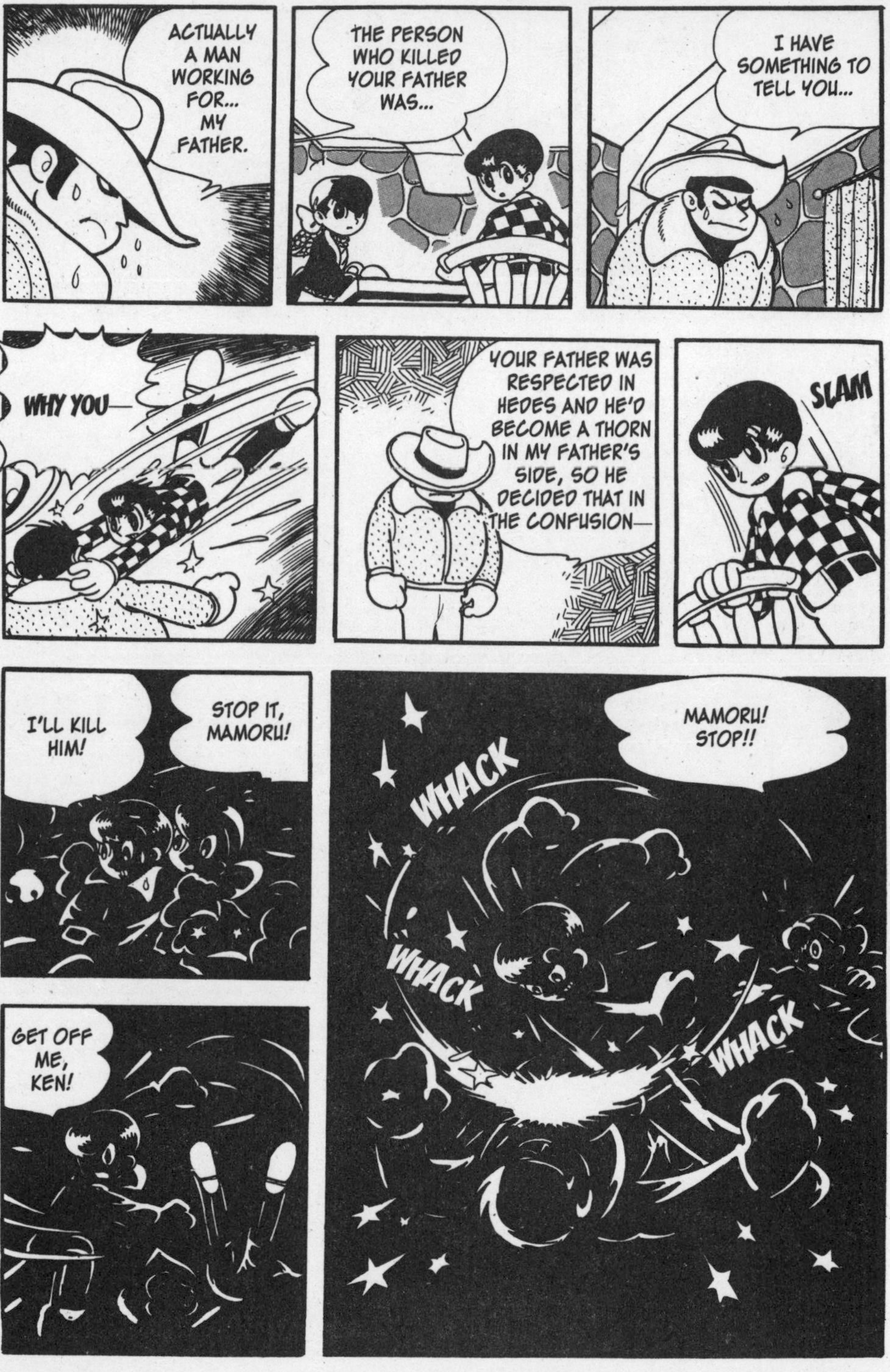
I HAVE SOMETHING TO TELL YOU...
THE PERSON WHO KILLED YOUR FATHER WAS...
ACTUALLY A MAN WORKING FOR... MY FATHER.
SLAM
YOUR FATHER WAS RESPECTED IN HEDES AND HE'D BECOME A THORN IN MY FATHER'S SIDE, SO HE DECIDED THAT IN THE CONFUSION—
WHY YOU—
MAMORU! STOP!!
WHACK
WHACK
WHACK
STOP IT, MAMORU!
I'LL KILL HIM!
GET OFF ME, KEN!

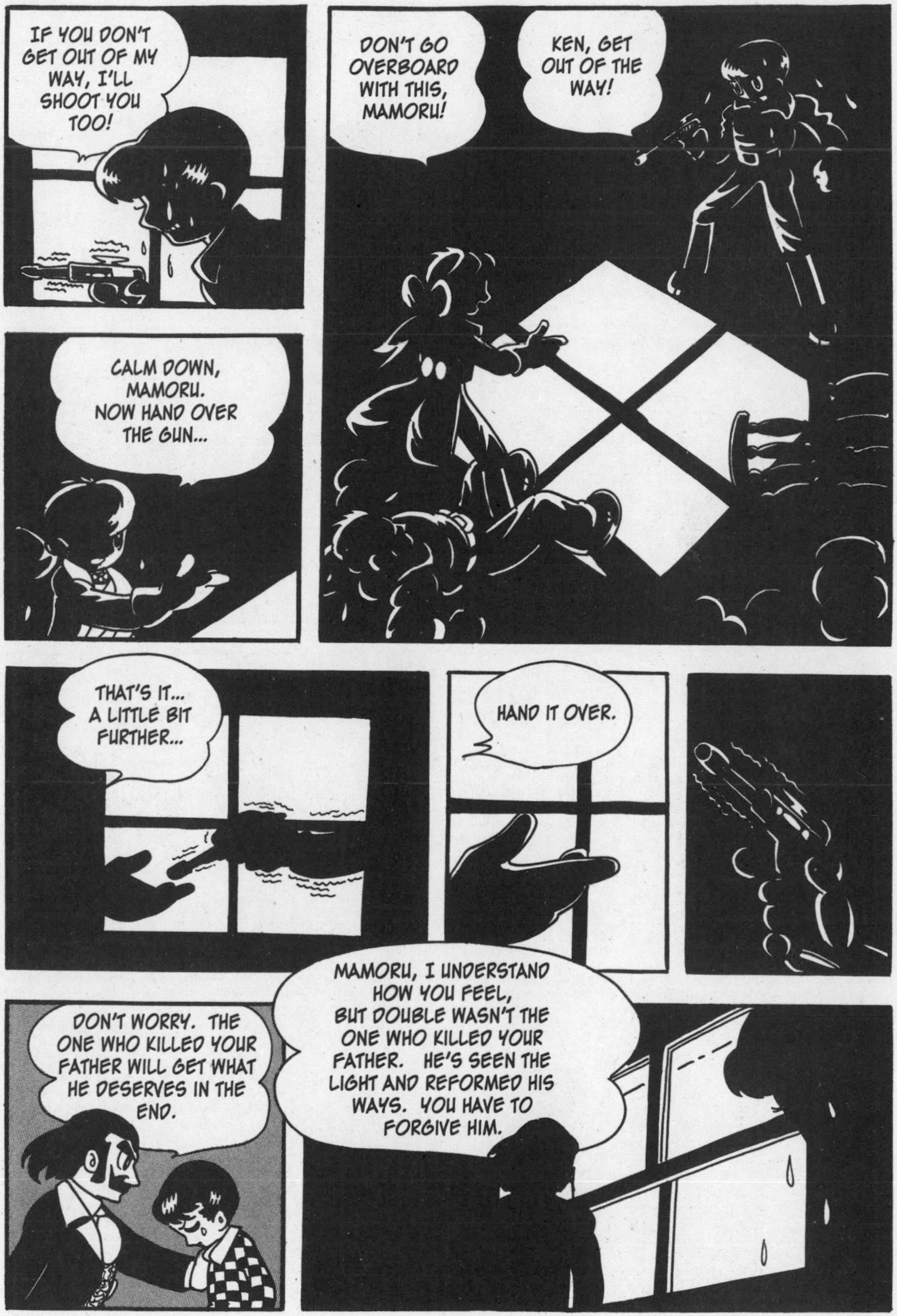
KEN, GET OUT OF THE WAY!
DON'T GO OVERBOARD WITH THIS, MAMORU!
IF YOU DON'T GET OUT OF MY WAY, I'LL SHOOT YOU TOO!
CALM DOWN, MAMORU. NOW HAND OVER THE GUN...
HAND IT OVER.
THAT'S IT... A LITTLE BIT FURTHER...
MAMORU, I UNDERSTAND HOW YOU FEEL, BUT DOUBLE WASN'T THE ONE WHO KILLED YOUR FATHER. HE'S SEEN THE LIGHT AND REFORMED HIS WAYS. YOU HAVE TO FORGIVE HIM.
DON'T WORRY. THE ONE WHO KILLED YOUR FATHER WILL GET WHAT HE DESERVES IN THE END.

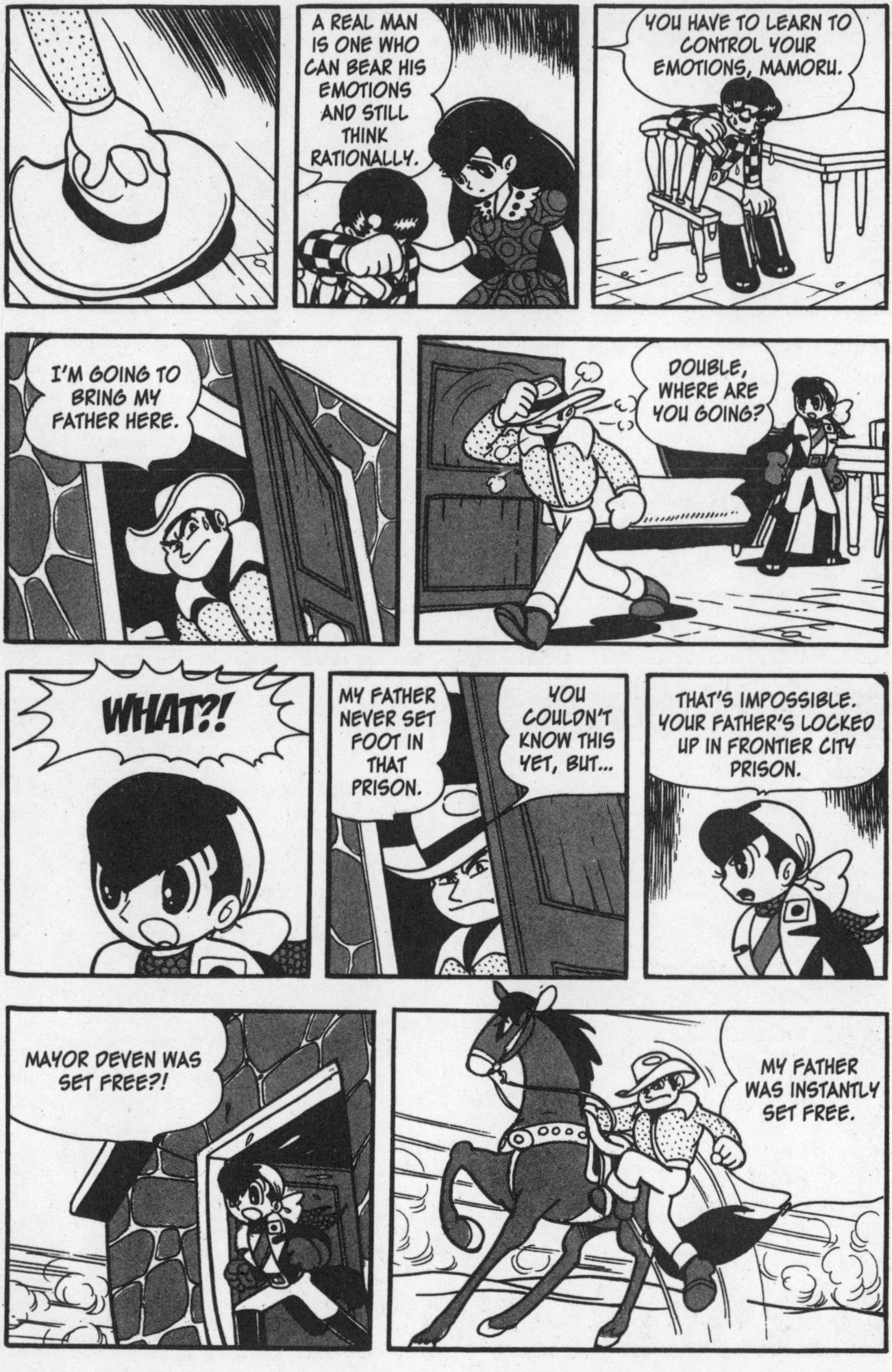
YOU HAVE TO LEARN TO CONTROL YOUR EMOTIONS, MAMORU.
A REAL MAN IS ONE WHO CAN BEAR HIS EMOTIONS AND STILL THINK RATIONALLY.
DOUBLE, WHERE ARE YOU GOING?
I'M GOING TO BRING MY FATHER HERE.
THAT'S IMPOSSIBLE. YOUR FATHER'S LOCKED UP IN FRONTIER CITY PRISON.
YOU COULDN'T KNOW THIS YET, BUT...
MY FATHER NEVER SET FOOT IN THAT PRISON.
WHAT?!
MY FATHER WAS INSTANTLY SET FREE.
MAYOR DEVEN WAS SET FREE?!

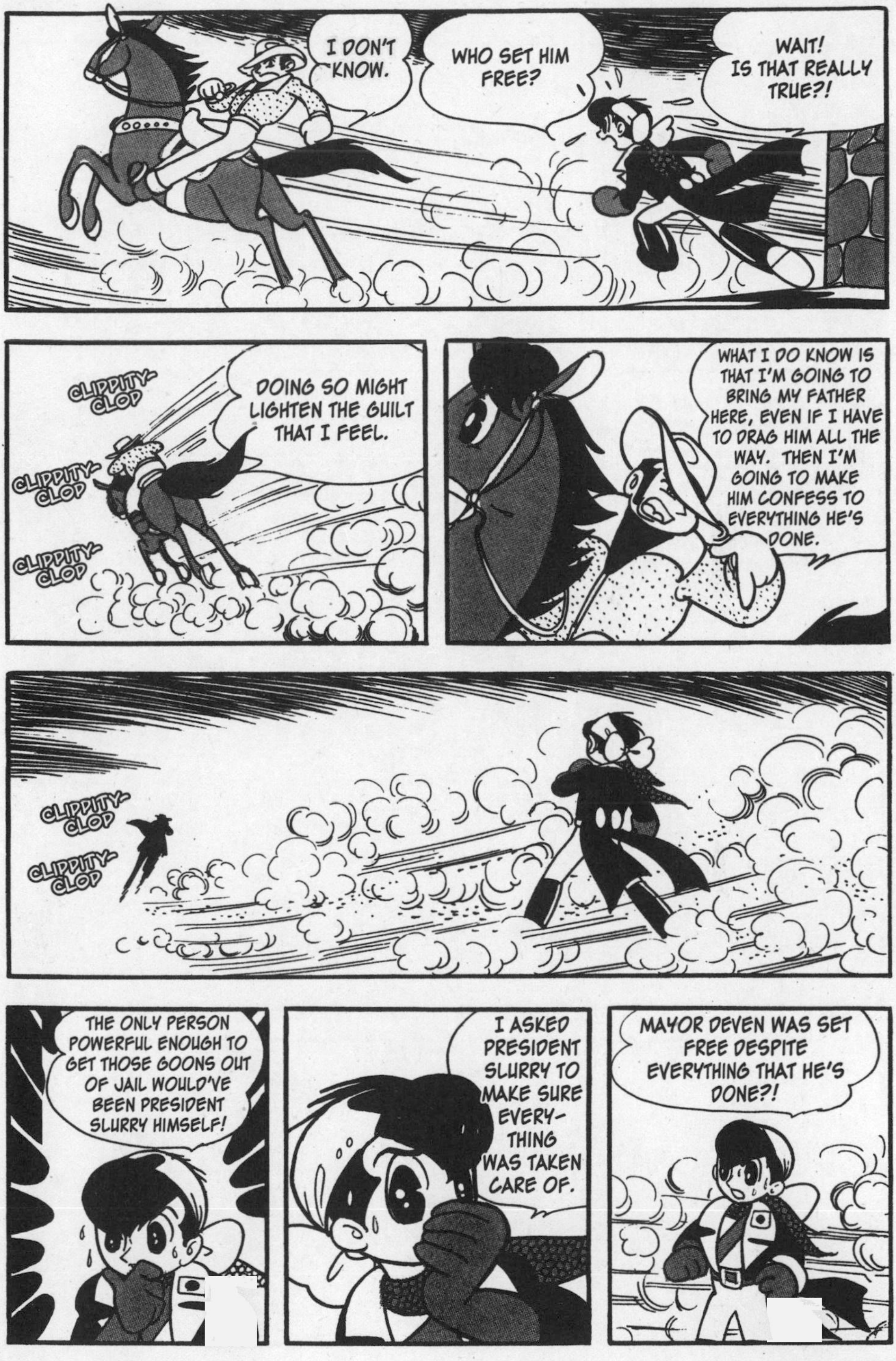
WAIT! IS THAT REALLY TRUE?!
WHO SET HIM FREE?
I DON'T KNOW.
WHAT I DO KNOW IS THAT I'M GOING TO BRING MY FATHER HERE, EVEN IF I HAVE TO DRAG HIM ALL THE WAY. THEN I'M GOING TO MAKE HIM CONFESS TO EVERYTHING HE'S DONE.
DOING SO MIGHT LIGHTEN THE GUILT THAT I FEEL.
CLIPPITY-CLOD
CLIPPITY-CLOD
CLIPPITY-CLOD
CLIPPITY-CLOD
CLIPPITY-CLOD
MAYOR DEVEN WAS SET FREE DESPITE EVERYTHING THAT HE'S DONE?!
I ASKED PRESIDENT SLURRY TO MAKE SURE EVERY-THING WAS TAKEN CARE OF.
THE ONLY PERSON POWERFUL ENOUGH TO GET THOSE GOONS OUT OF JAIL WOULD'VE BEEN PRESIDENT SLURRY HIMSELF!

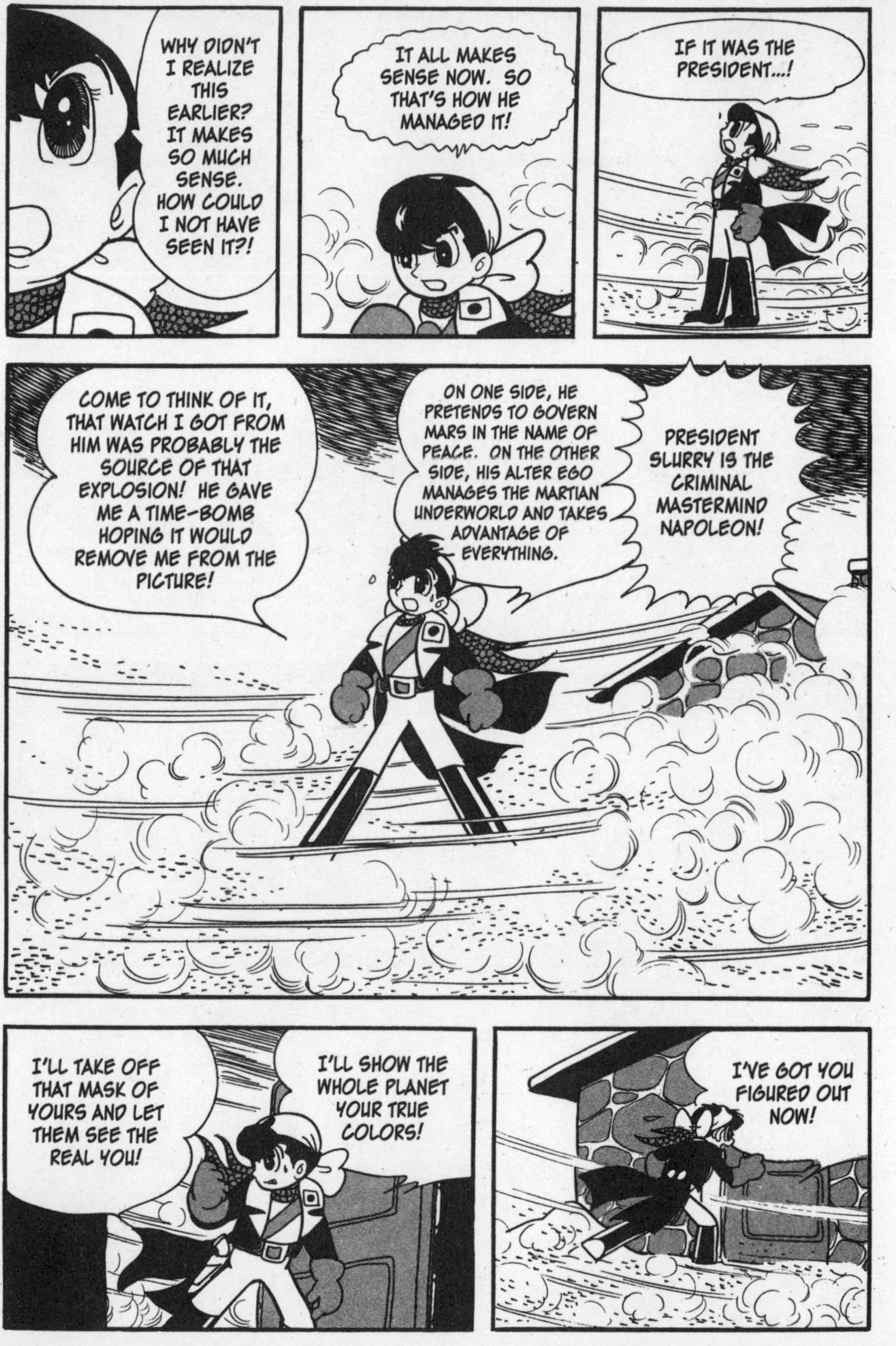
IF IT WAS THE PRESIDENT...!
IT ALL MAKES SENSE NOW. SO THAT'S HOW HE MANAGED IT!
WHY DIDN'T I REALIZE THIS EARLIER? IT MAKES SO MUCH SENSE. HOW COULD I NOT HAVE SEEN IT?!
PRESIDENT SLURRY IS THE CRIMINAL MASTERMIND NAPOLEON!
ON ONE SIDE, HE PRETENDS TO GOVERN MARS IN THE NAME OF PEACE. ON THE OTHER SIDE, HIS ALTER EGO MANAGES THE MARTIAN UNDERWORLD AND TAKES ADVANTAGE OF EVERYTHING.
COME TO THINK OF IT, THAT WATCH I GOT FROM HIM WAS PROBABLY THE SOURCE OF THAT EXPLOSION! HE GAVE ME A TIME-BOMB HOPING IT WOULD REMOVE ME FROM THE PICTURE!
I'VE GOT YOU FIGURED OUT NOW!
I'LL SHOW THE WHOLE PLANET YOUR TRUE COLORS!
I'LL TAKE OFF THAT MASK OF YOURS AND LET THEM SEE THE REAL YOU!

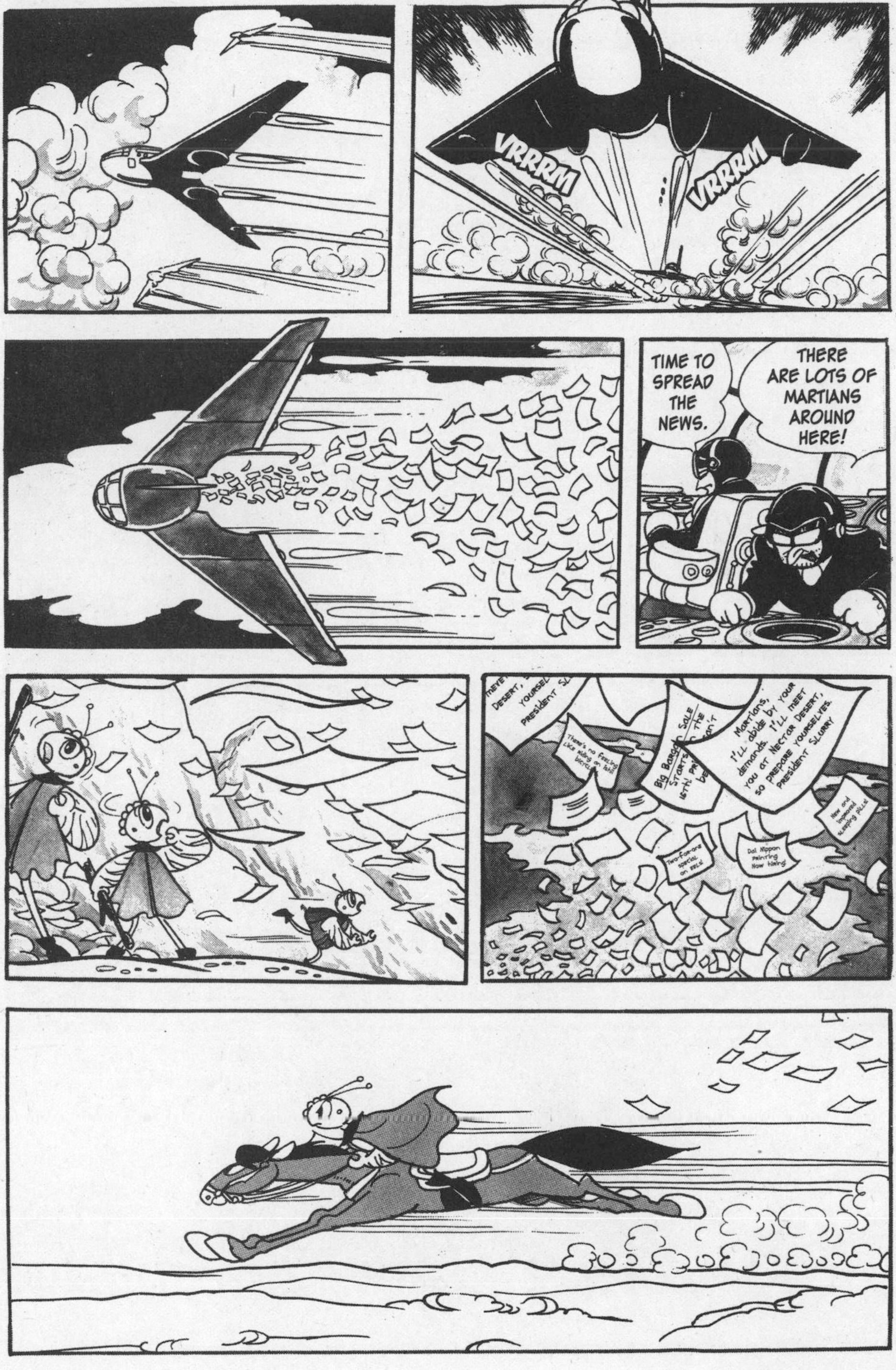
VRRRM
VRRRM
THERE ARE LOTS OF MARTIANS AROUND HERE!
TIME TO SPREAD THE NEWS.
Martians, I'll abide by your demands. I'll meet you at Nectar Desert, so prepare yourselves. President Slurry
New and improved sleeping pills!
Dai Nippon Printing Now hiring!
Two-for-one special on eels!

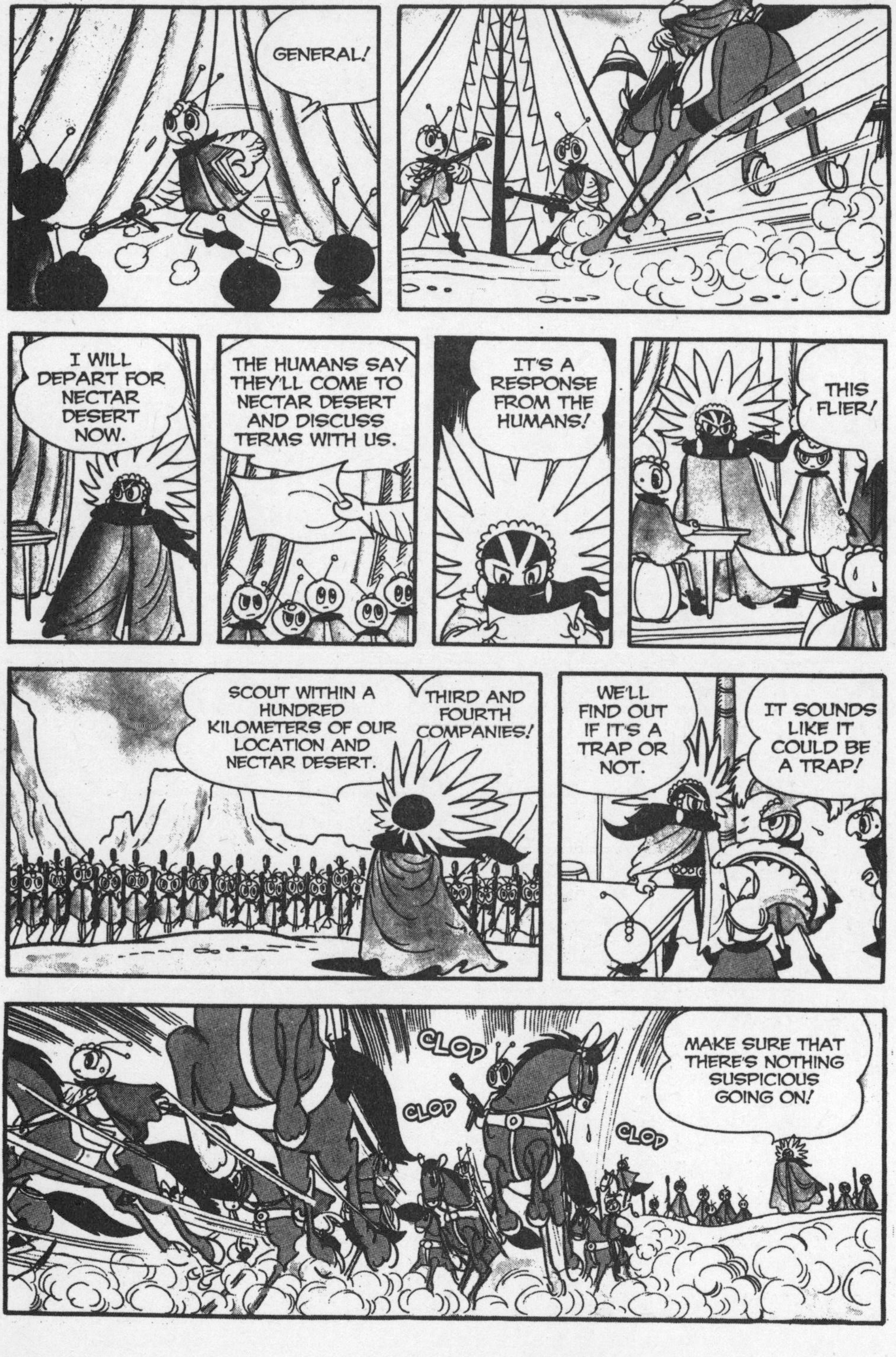
GENERAL!
THIS FLIER!
IT'S A RESPONSE FROM THE HUMANS!
THE HUMANS SAY THEY'LL COME TO NECTAR DESERT AND DISCUSS TERMS WITH US.
I WILL DEPART FOR NECTAR DESERT NOW.
IT SOUNDS LIKE IT COULD BE A TRAP!
WE'LL FIND OUT IF IT'S A TRAP OR NOT.
THIRD AND FOURTH COMPANIES!
SCOUT WITHIN A HUNDRED KILOMETERS OF OUR LOCATION AND NECTAR DESERT.
MAKE SURE THAT THERE'S NOTHING SUSPICIOUS GOING ON!
CLOP
CLOP
CLOP

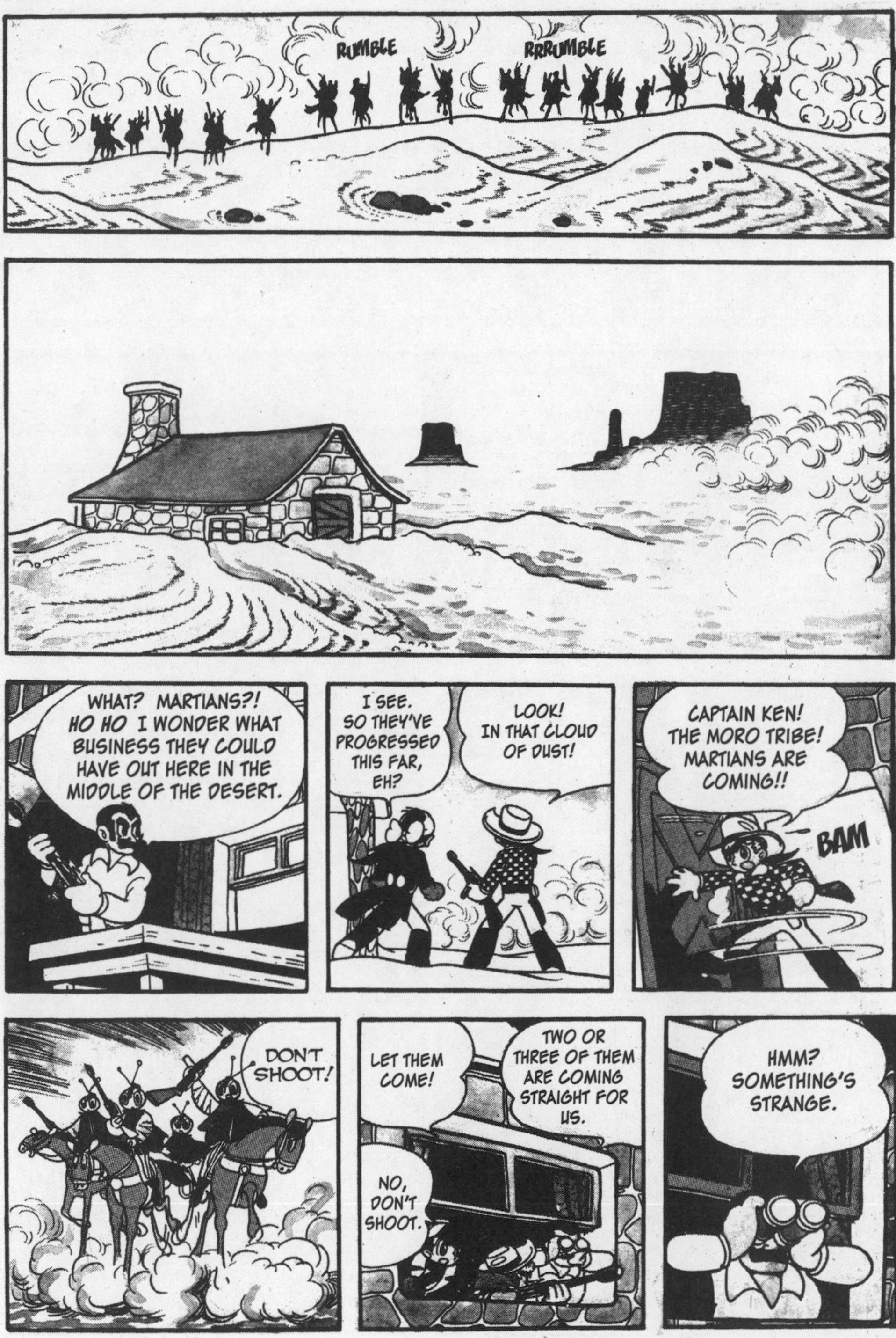
RRRUMBLE
RUMBLE
CAPTAIN KEN! THE MORO TRIBE! MARTIANS ARE COMING!!
BAM
LOOK! IN THAT CLOUD OF DUST!
I SEE. SO THEY'VE PROGRESSED THIS FAR, EH?
WHAT? MARTIANS?! HO HO I WONDER WHAT BUSINESS THEY COULD HAVE OUT HERE IN THE MIDDLE OF THE DESERT.
HMM? SOMETHING'S STRANGE.
TWO OR THREE OF THEM ARE COMING STRAIGHT FOR US.
LET THEM COME!
NO, DON'T SHOOT.
DON'T SHOOT!

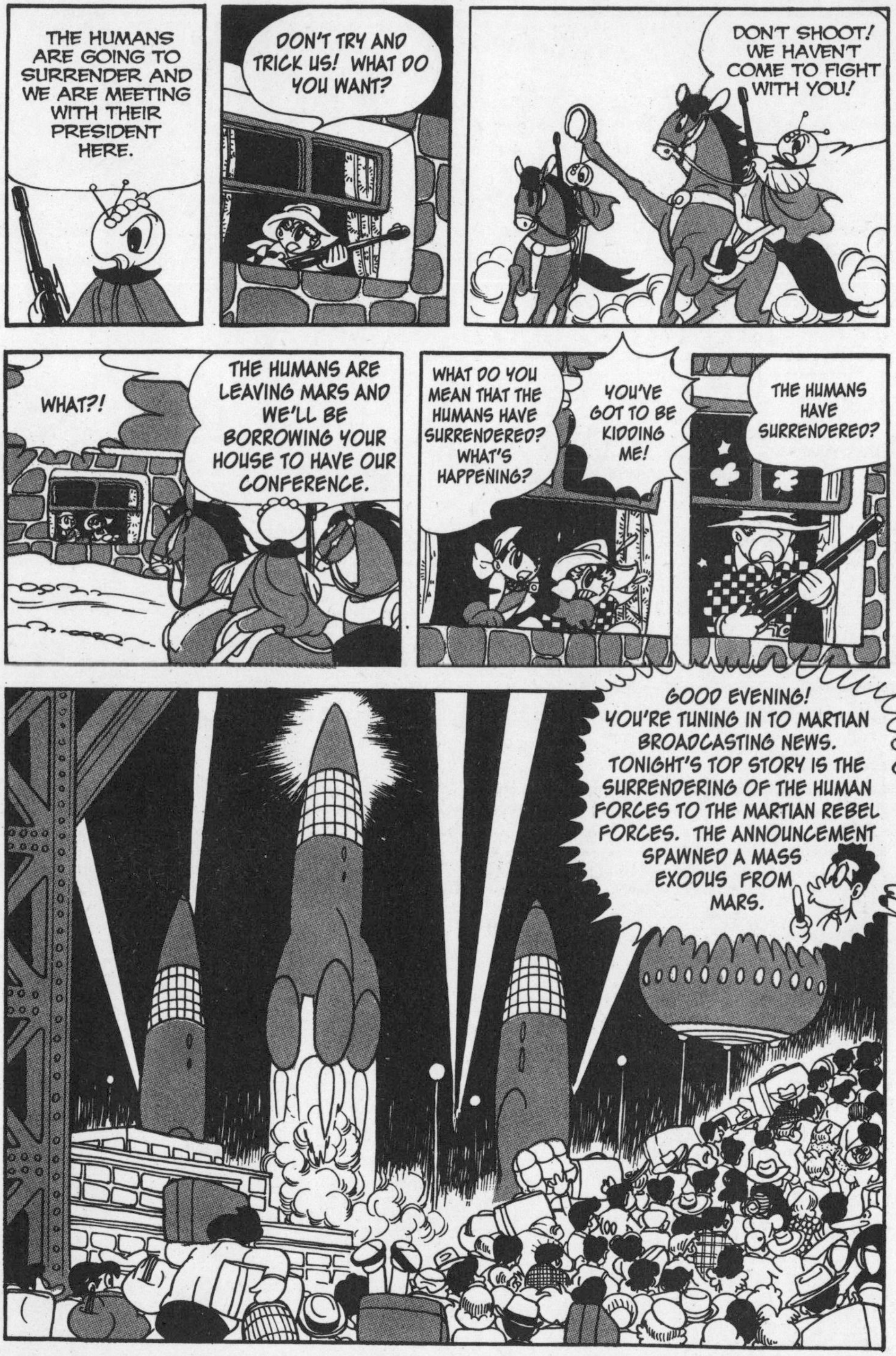
DON'T SHOOT! WE HAVEN'T COME TO FIGHT WITH YOU!
DON'T TRY AND TRICK US! WHAT DO YOU WANT?
THE HUMANS ARE GOING TO SURRENDER AND WE ARE MEETING WITH THEIR PRESIDENT HERE.
THE HUMANS HAVE SURRENDERED?
YOU'VE GOT TO BE KIDDING ME!
WHAT DO YOU MEAN THAT THE HUMANS HAVE SURRENDERED? WHAT'S HAPPENING?
THE HUMANS ARE LEAVING MARS AND WE'LL BE BORROWING YOUR HOUSE TO HAVE OUR CONFERENCE.
WHAT?!
GOOD EVENING! YOU'RE TUNING IN TO MARTIAN BROADCASTING NEWS. TONIGHT'S TOP STORY IS THE SURRENDERING OF THE HUMAN FORCES TO THE MARTIAN REBEL FORCES. THE ANNOUNCEMENT SPAWNED A MASS EXODUS FROM MARS.

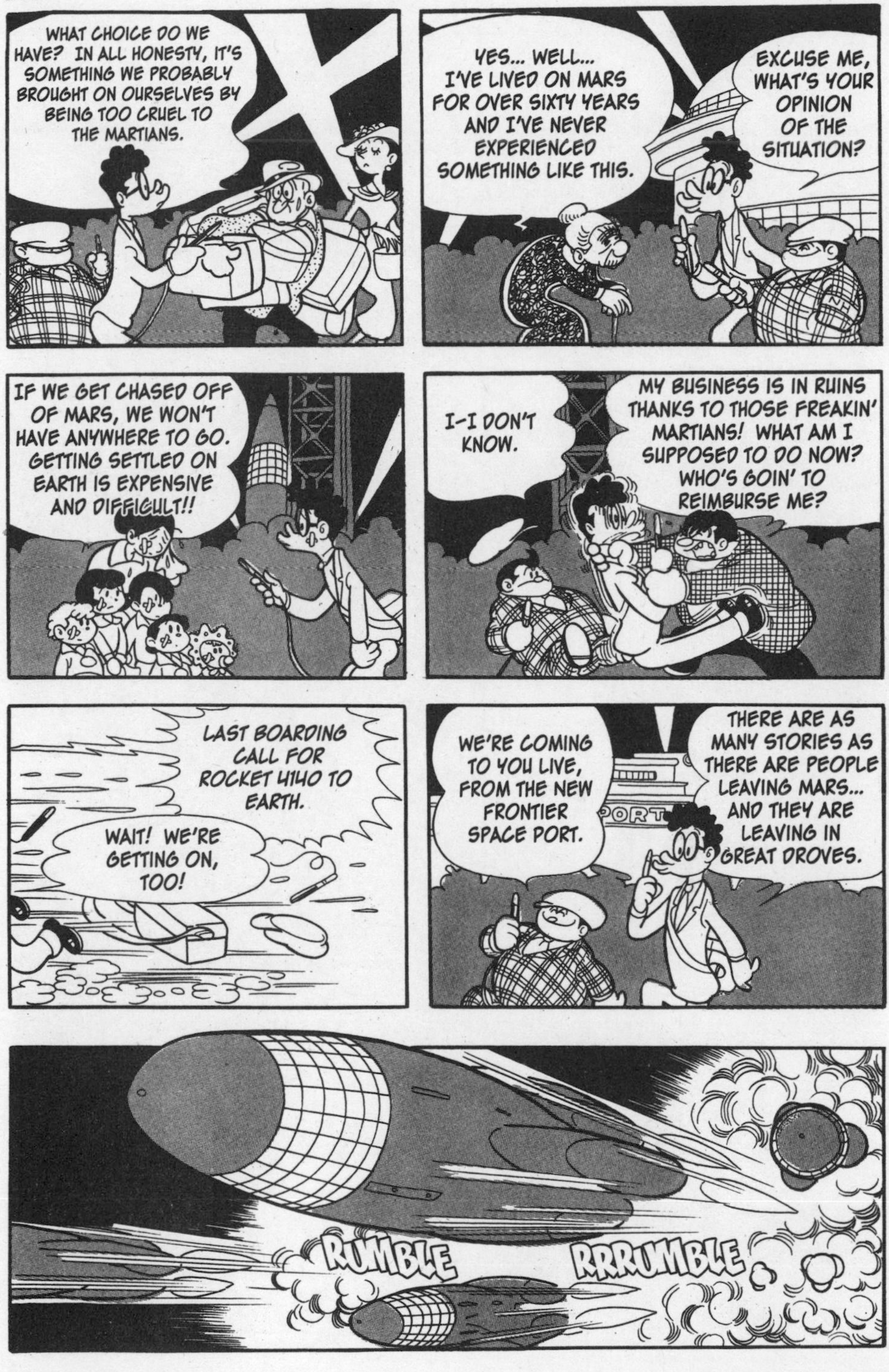
EXCUSE ME, WHAT'S YOUR OPINION OF THE SITUATION?
YES... WELL... I'VE LIVED ON MARS FOR OVER SIXTY YEARS AND I'VE NEVER EXPERIENCED SOMETHING LIKE THIS.
WHAT CHOICE DO WE HAVE? IN ALL HONESTY, IT'S SOMETHING WE PROBABLY BROUGHT ON OURSELVES BY BEING TOO CRUEL TO THE MARTIANS.
MY BUSINESS IS IN RUINS THANKS TO THOSE FREAKIN' MARTIANS! WHAT AM I SUPPOSED TO DO NOW? WHO'S GOIN' TO REIMBURSE ME?
I-I DON'T KNOW.
IF WE GET CHASED OFF OF MARS, WE WON'T HAVE ANYWHERE TO GO. GETTING SETTLED ON EARTH IS EXPENSIVE AND DIFFICULT!!
THERE ARE AS MANY STORIES AS THERE ARE PEOPLE LEAVING MARS... AND THEY ARE LEAVING IN GREAT DROVES.
PORT
WE'RE COMING TO YOU LIVE, FROM THE NEW FRONTIER SPACE PORT.
LAST BOARDING CALL FOR ROCKET 4140 TO EARTH.
WAIT! WE'RE GETTING ON, TOO!
RRRUMBLE
RUMBLE

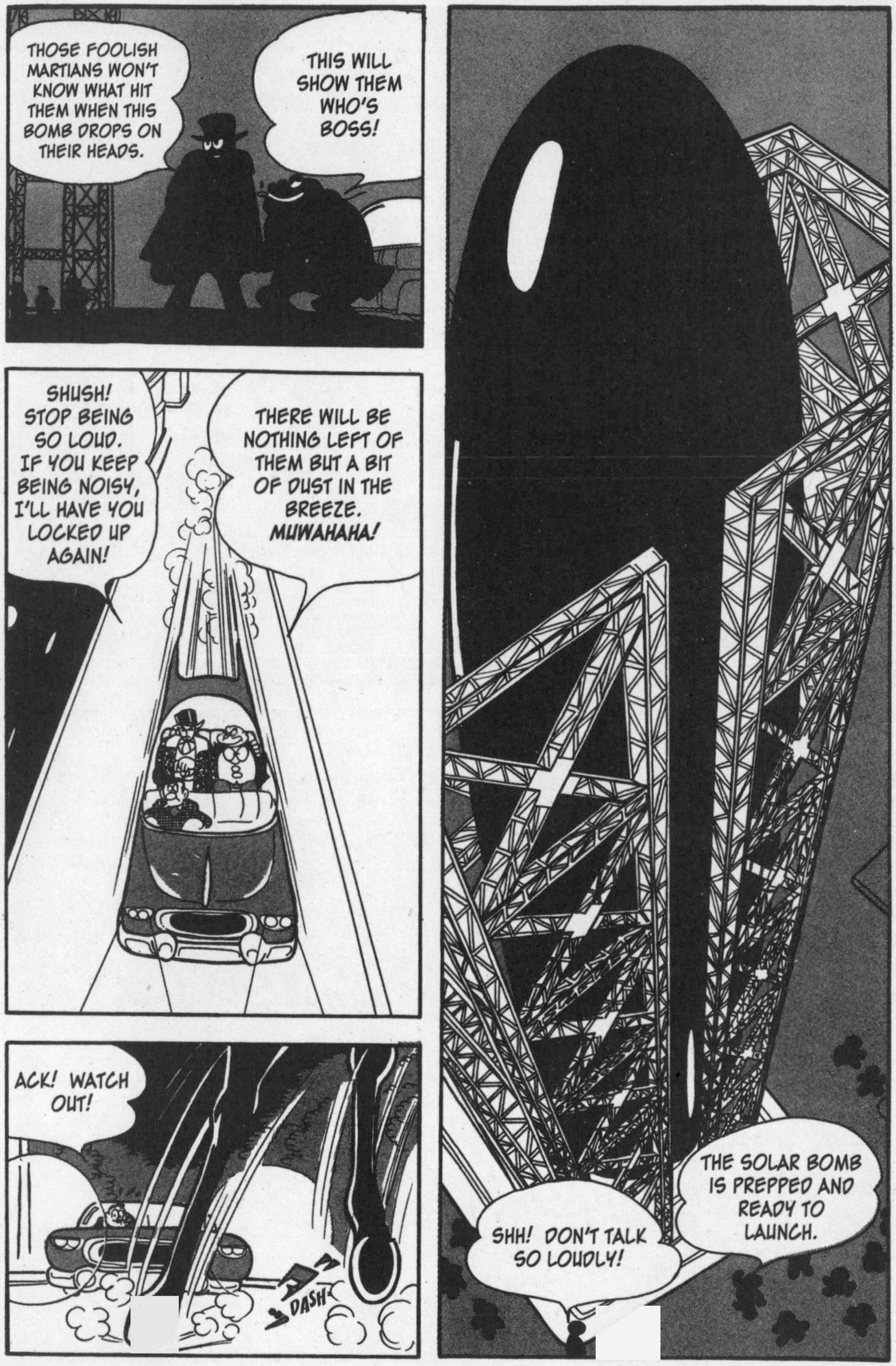
THE SOLAR BOMB IS PREPPED AND READY TO LAUNCH.
SHH! DON'T TALK SO LOUDLY!
THIS WILL SHOW THEM WHO'S BOSS!
THOSE FOOLISH MARTIANS WON'T KNOW WHAT HIT THEM WHEN THIS BOMB DROPS ON THEIR HEADS.
THERE WILL BE NOTHING LEFT OF THEM BUT A BIT OF DUST IN THE BREEZE. MUWAHAHA!
SHUSH! STOP BEING SO LOUD. IF YOU KEEP BEING NOISY, I'LL HAVE YOU LOCKED UP AGAIN!
ACK! WATCH OUT!
DASH

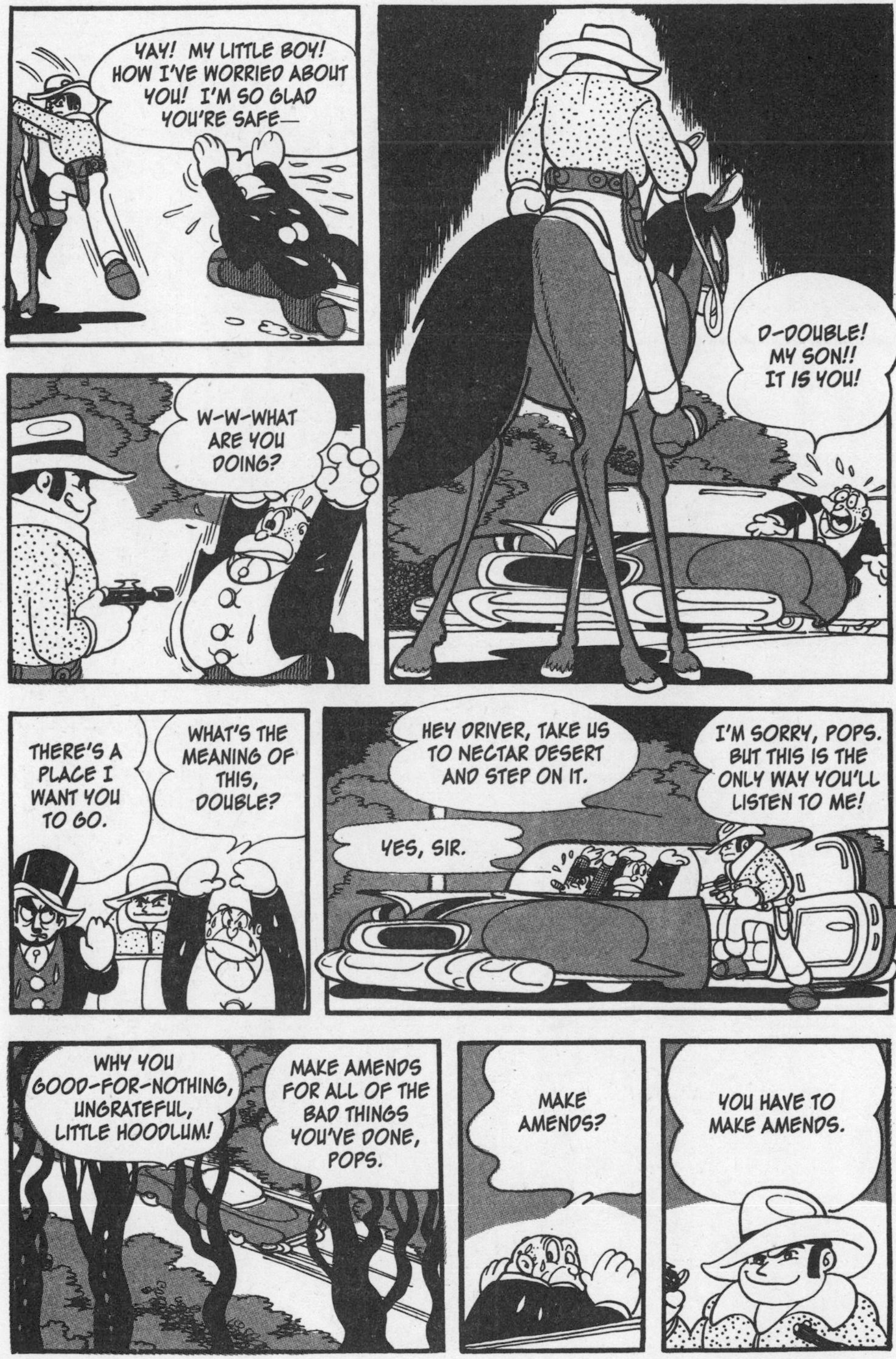
D-DOUBLE! MY SON!! IT IS YOU!
YAY! MY LITTLE BOY! HOW I'VE WORRIED ABOUT YOU! I'M SO GLAD YOU'RE SAFE—
W-W-WHAT ARE YOU DOING?
I'M SORRY, POPS. BUT THIS IS THE ONLY WAY YOU'LL LISTEN TO ME!
HEY DRIVER, TAKE US TO NECTAR DESERT AND STEP ON IT.
YES, SIR.
WHAT'S THE MEANING OF THIS, DOUBLE?
THERE'S A PLACE I WANT YOU TO GO.
YOU HAVE TO MAKE AMENDS.
MAKE AMENDS?
MAKE AMENDS FOR ALL OF THE BAD THINGS YOU'VE DONE, POPS.
WHY YOU GOOD-FOR-NOTHING, UNGRATEFUL, LITTLE HOODLUM!

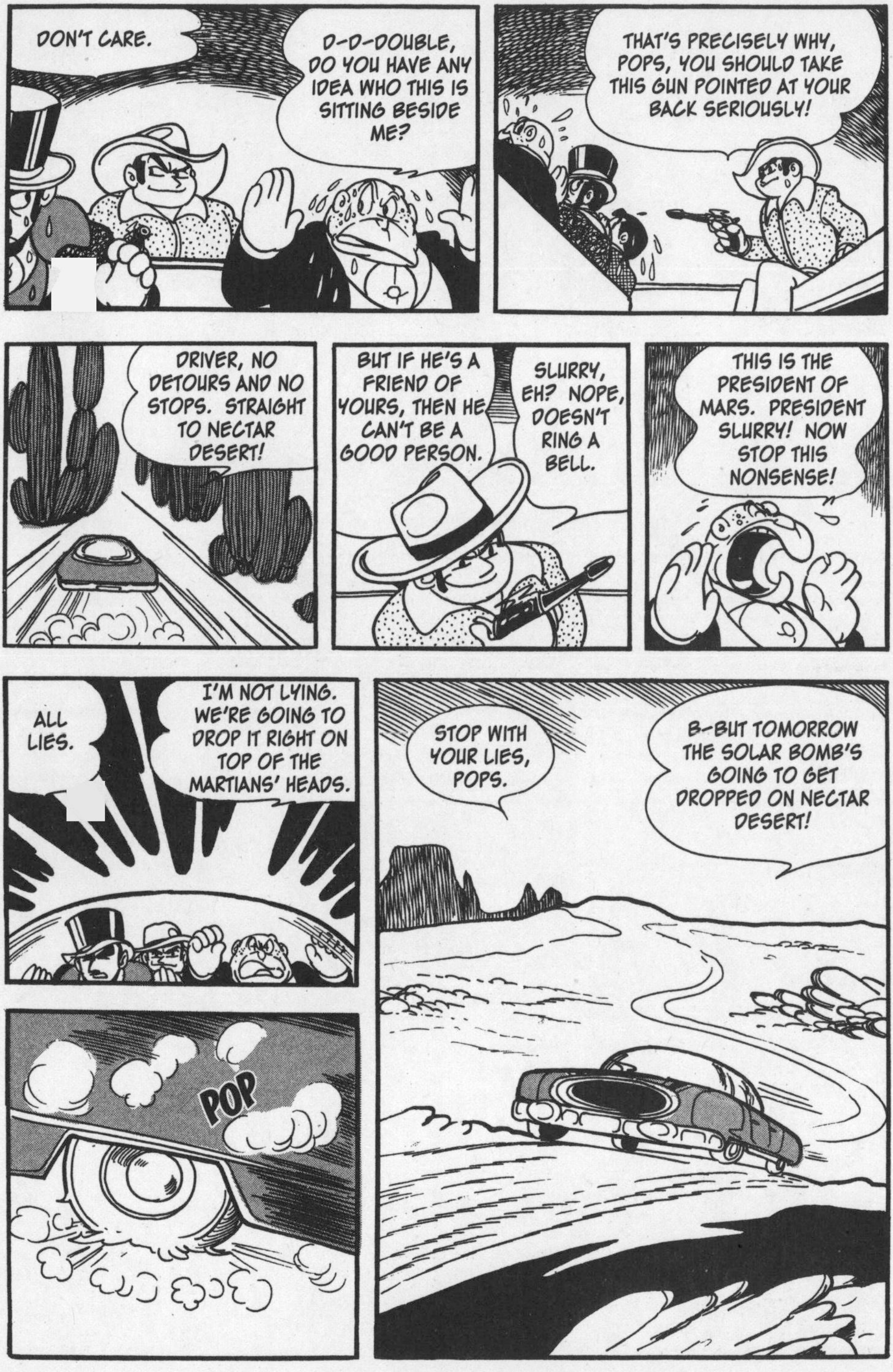
THAT'S PRECISELY WHY, POPS, YOU SHOULD TAKE THIS GUN POINTED AT YOUR BACK SERIOUSLY!
D-D-DOUBLE, DO YOU HAVE ANY IDEA WHO THIS IS SITTING BESIDE ME?
DON'T CARE.
THIS IS THE PRESIDENT OF MARS. PRESIDENT SLURRY! NOW STOP THIS NONSENSE!
SLURRY, EH? NOPE, DOESN'T RING A BELL.
BUT IF HE'S A FRIEND OF YOURS, THEN HE CAN'T BE A GOOD PERSON.
DRIVER, NO DETOURS AND NO STOPS. STRAIGHT TO NECTAR DESERT!
B-BUT TOMORROW THE SOLAR BOMB'S GOING TO GET DROPPED ON NECTAR DESERT!
STOP WITH YOUR LIES, POPS.
I'M NOT LYING. WE'RE GOING TO DROP IT RIGHT ON TOP OF THE MARTIANS' HEADS.
ALL LIES.
POP

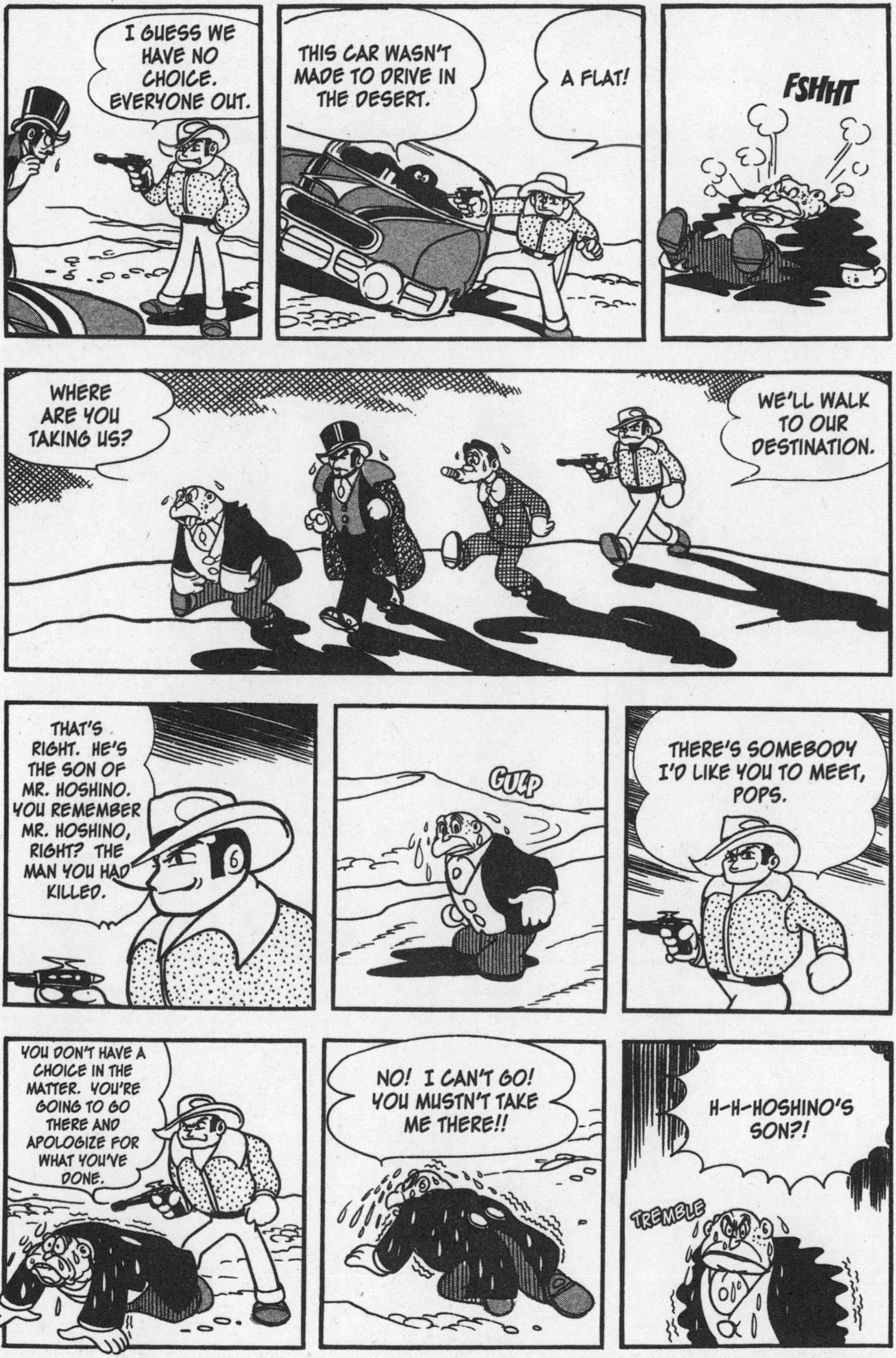
FSHHT
A FLAT!
THIS CAR WASN'T MADE TO DRIVE IN THE DESERT.
I GUESS WE HAVE NO CHOICE. EVERYONE OUT.
WE'LL WALK TO OUR DESTINATION.
WHERE ARE YOU TAKING US?
THERE'S SOMEBODY I'D LIKE YOU TO MEET, POPS.
GULP
THAT'S RIGHT. HE'S THE SON OF MR. HOSHINO. YOU REMEMBER MR. HOSHINO, RIGHT? THE MAN YOU HAD KILLED.
H-H-HOSHINO'S SON?!
TREMBLE
NO! I CAN'T GO! YOU MUSTN'T TAKE ME THERE!!
YOU DON'T HAVE A CHOICE IN THE MATTER. YOU'RE GOING TO GO THERE AND APOLOGIZE FOR WHAT YOU'VE DONE.

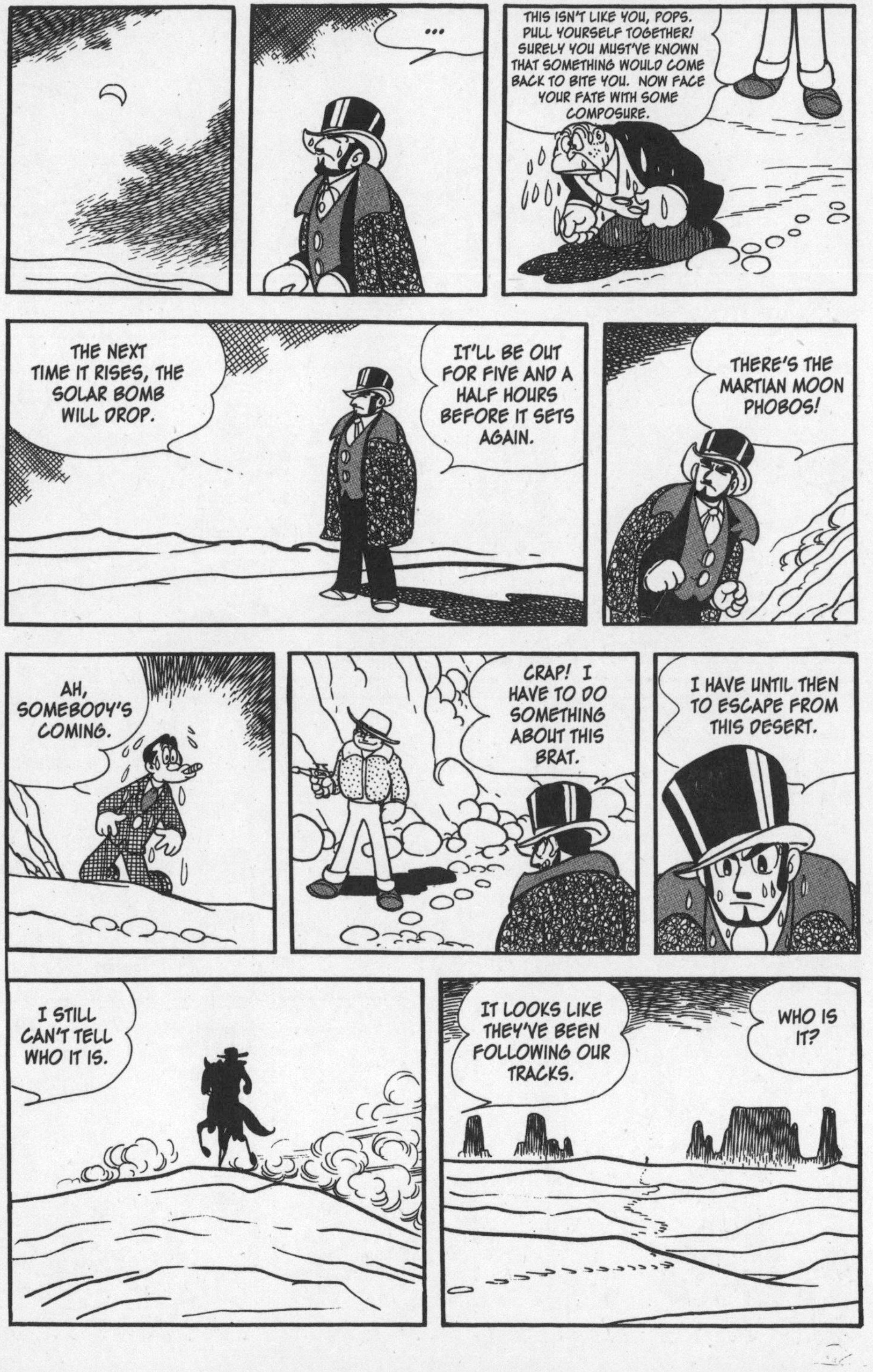
THIS ISN'T LIKE YOU, POPS. PULL YOURSELF TOGETHER! SURELY YOU MUST'VE KNOWN THAT SOMETHING WOULD COME BACK TO BITE YOU. NOW FACE YOUR FATE WITH SOME COMPOSURE.
...
THERE'S THE MARTIAN MOON PHOBOS!
IT'LL BE OUT FOR FIVE AND A HALF HOURS BEFORE IT SETS AGAIN.
THE NEXT TIME IT RISES, THE SOLAR BOMB WILL DROP.
I HAVE UNTIL THEN TO ESCAPE FROM THIS DESERT.
CRAP! I HAVE TO DO SOMETHING ABOUT THIS BRAT.
AH, SOMEBODY'S COMING.
WHO IS IT?
IT LOOKS LIKE THEY'VE BEEN FOLLOWING OUR TRACKS.
I STILL CAN'T TELL WHO IT IS.

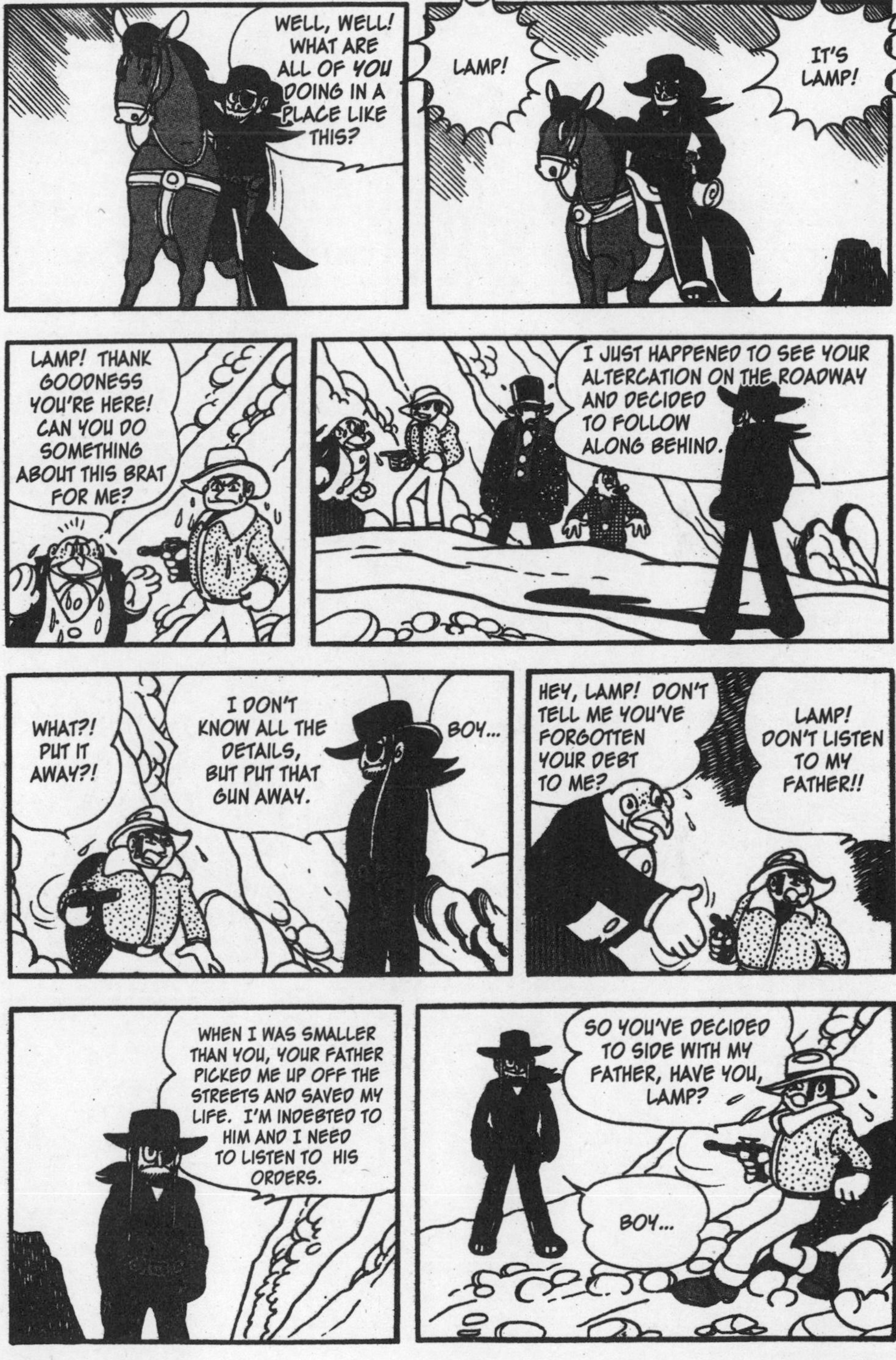
IT'S LAMP!
LAMP!
WELL, WELL! WHAT ARE ALL OF YOU DOING IN A PLACE LIKE THIS?
I JUST HAPPENED TO SEE YOUR ALTERCATION ON THE ROADWAY AND DECIDED TO FOLLOW ALONG BEHIND.
LAMP! THANK GOODNESS YOU'RE HERE! CAN YOU DO SOMETHING ABOUT THIS BRAT FOR ME?
LAMP! DON'T LISTEN TO MY FATHER!!
HEY, LAMP! DON'T TELL ME YOU'VE FORGOTTEN YOUR DEBT TO ME?
BOY...
I DON'T KNOW ALL THE DETAILS, BUT PUT THAT GUN AWAY.
WHAT?! PUT IT AWAY?!
SO YOU'VE DECIDED TO SIDE WITH MY FATHER, HAVE YOU, LAMP?
BOY...
WHEN I WAS SMALLER THAN YOU, YOUR FATHER PICKED ME UP OFF THE STREETS AND SAVED MY LIFE. I'M INDEBTED TO HIM AND I NEED TO LISTEN TO HIS ORDERS.

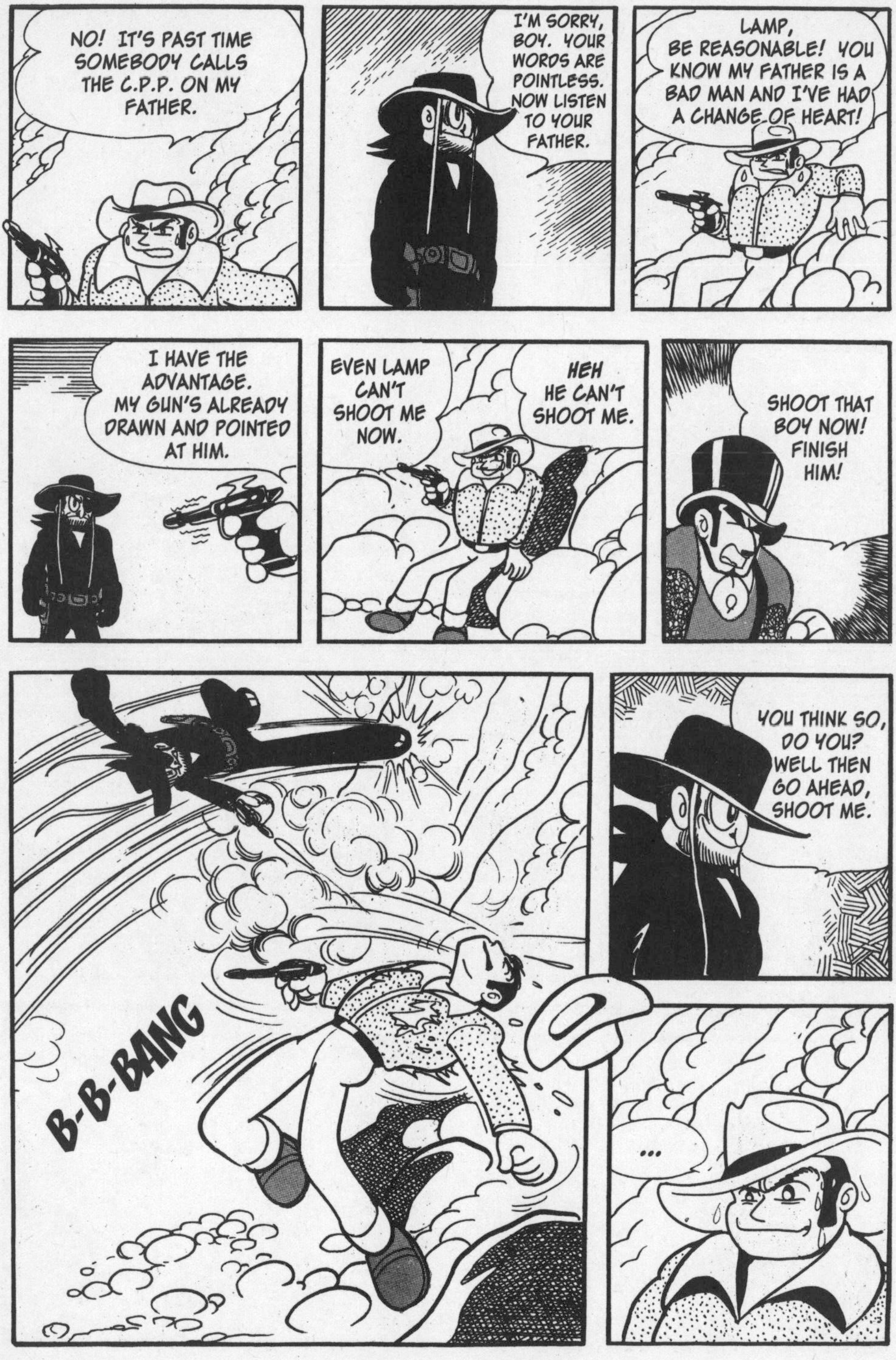
LAMP, BE REASONABLE! YOU KNOW MY FATHER IS A BAD MAN AND I'VE HAD A CHANGE OF HEART!
I'M SORRY, BOY. YOUR WORDS ARE POINTLESS. NOW LISTEN TO YOUR FATHER.
NO! IT'S PAST TIME SOMEBODY CALLS THE C.P.P. ON MY FATHER.
SHOOT THAT BOY NOW! FINISH HIM!
HEH HE CAN'T SHOOT ME.
EVEN LAMP CAN'T SHOOT ME NOW.
I HAVE THE ADVANTAGE. MY GUN'S ALREADY DRAWN AND POINTED AT HIM.
YOU THINK SO, DO YOU? WELL THEN GO AHEAD, SHOOT ME.
...
B-B-BANG

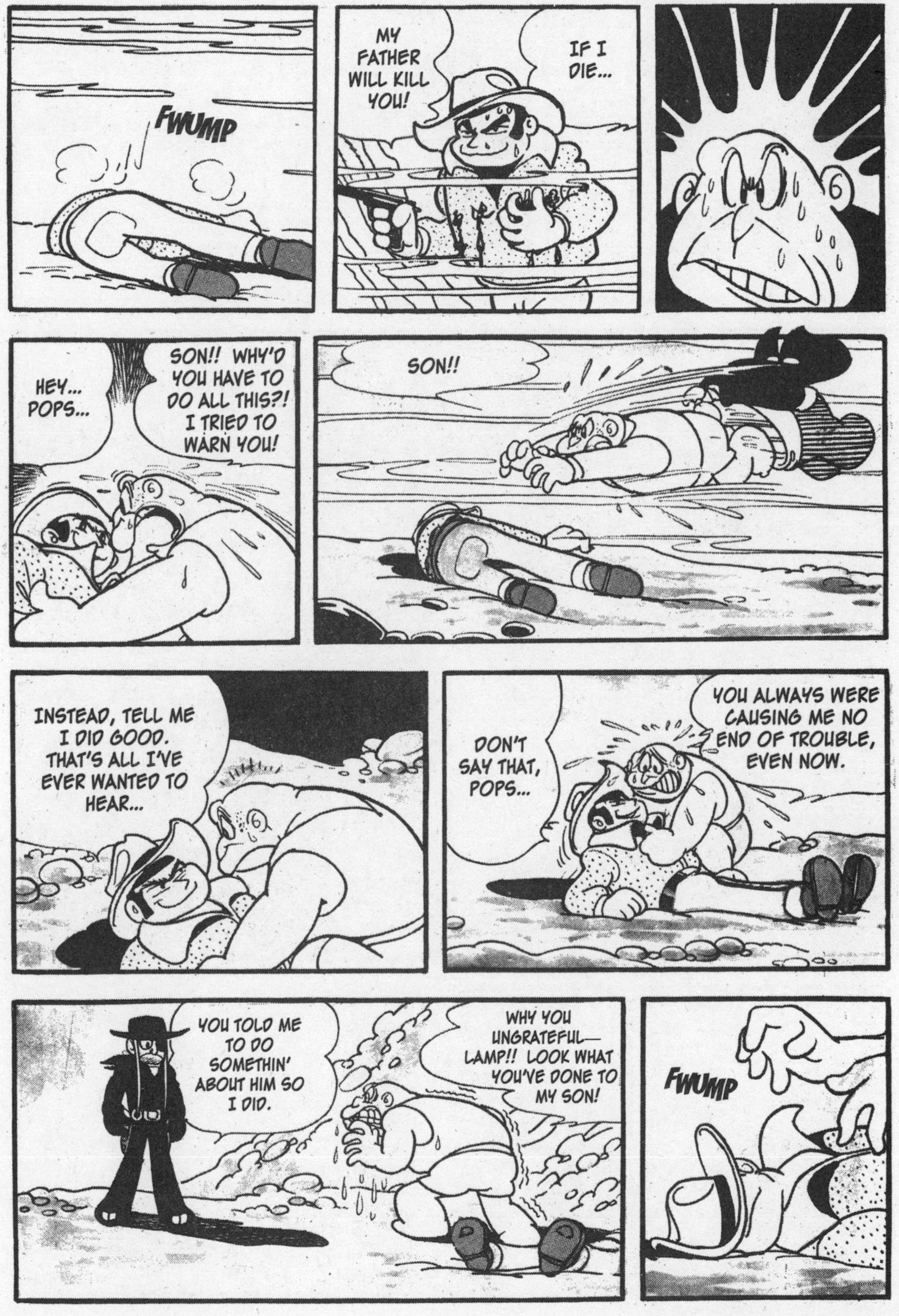
IF I DIE...
MY FATHER WILL KILL YOU!
FWUMP
SON!!
SON!! WHY'D YOU HAVE TO DO ALL THIS?! I TRIED TO WARN YOU!
HEY... POPS...
YOU ALWAYS WERE CAUSING ME NO END OF TROUBLE, EVEN NOW.
DON'T SAY THAT, POPS...
INSTEAD, TELL ME I DID GOOD. THAT'S ALL I'VE EVER WANTED TO HEAR...
FWUMP
WHY YOU UNGRATEFUL— LAMP!! LOOK WHAT YOU'VE DONE TO MY SON!
YOU TOLD ME TO DO SOMETHIN' ABOUT HIM SO I DID.

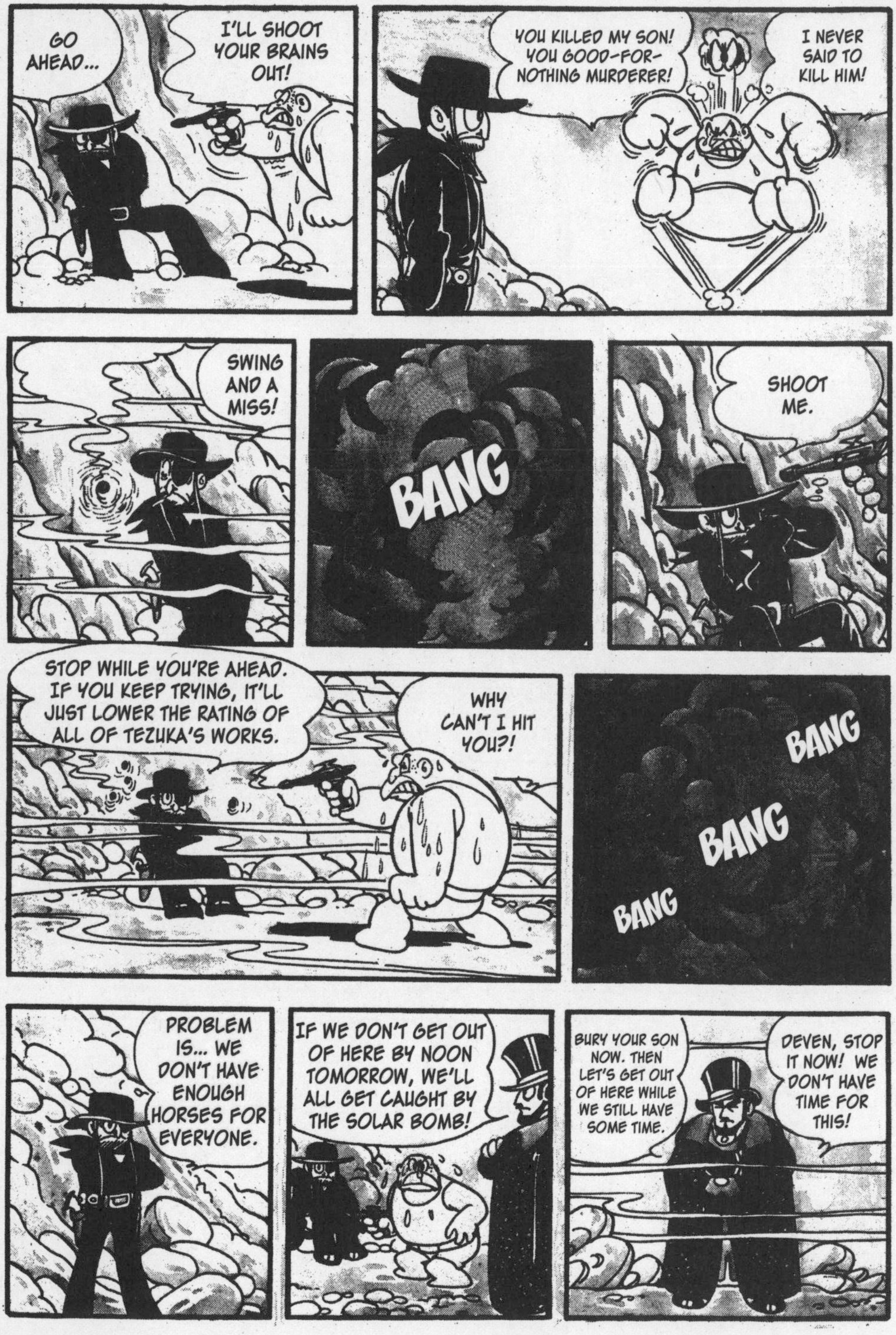
I NEVER SAID TO KILL HIM!
YOU KILLED MY SON! YOU GOOD-FOR-NOTHING MURDERER!
I'LL SHOOT YOUR BRAINS OUT!
GO AHEAD...
SHOOT ME.
BANG
SWING AND A MISS!
BANG
BANG
BANG
WHY CAN'T I HIT YOU?!
STOP WHILE YOU'RE AHEAD. IF YOU KEEP TRYING, IT'LL JUST LOWER THE RATING OF ALL OF TEZUKA'S WORKS.
DEVEN, STOP IT NOW! WE DON'T HAVE TIME FOR THIS!
BURY YOUR SON NOW. THEN LET'S GET OUT OF HERE WHILE WE STILL HAVE SOME TIME.
IF WE DON'T GET OUT OF HERE BY NOON TOMORROW, WE'LL ALL GET CAUGHT BY THE SOLAR BOMB!
PROBLEM IS... WE DON'T HAVE ENOUGH HORSES FOR EVERYONE.

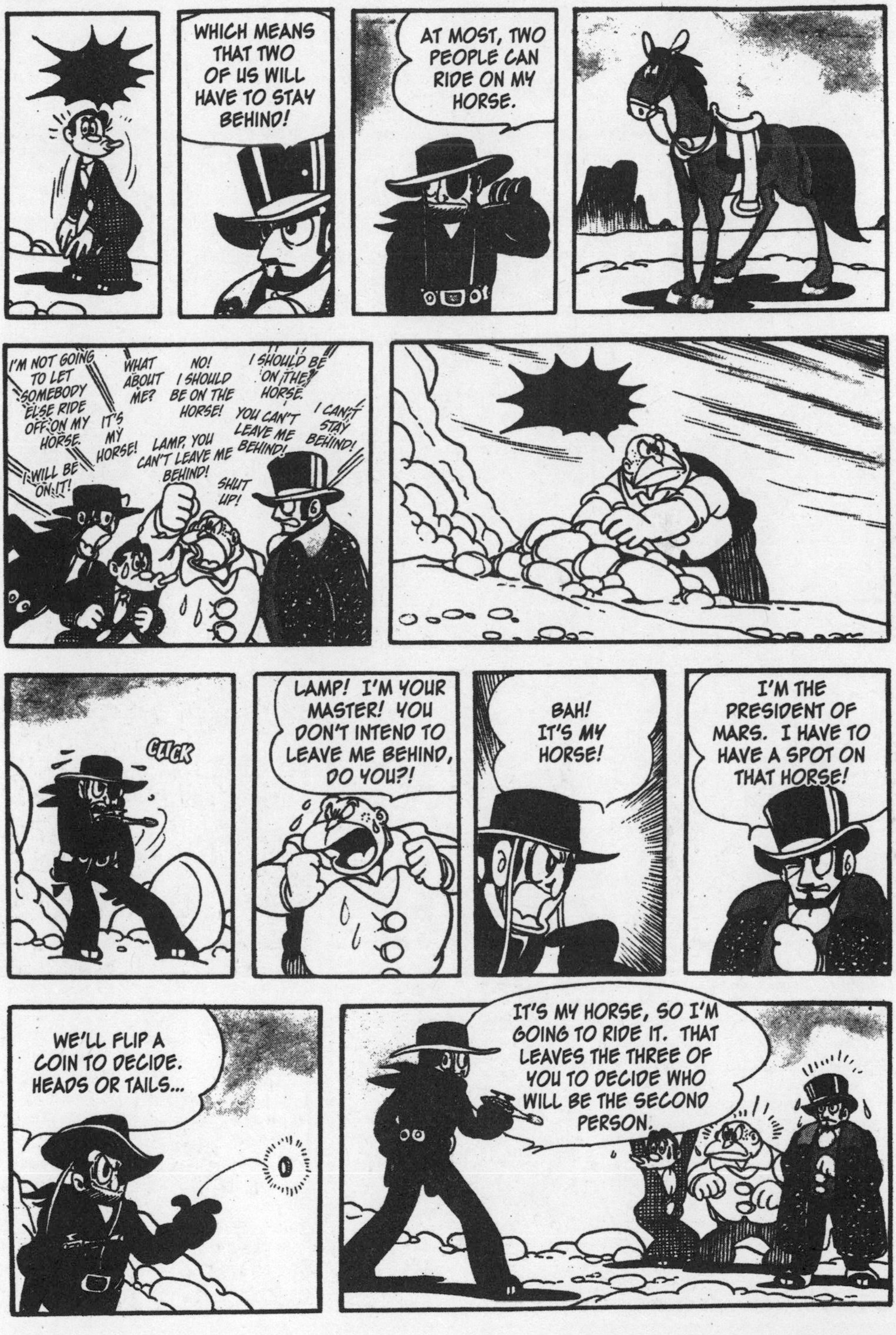
AT MOST, TWO PEOPLE CAN RIDE ON MY HORSE.
WHICH MEANS THAT TWO OF US WILL HAVE TO STAY BEHIND!
I SHOULD BE ON THE HORSE.
I CAN'T STAY BEHIND!
NO! I SHOULD BE ON THE HORSE!
YOU CAN'T LEAVE ME BEHIND!
WHAT ABOUT ME?
I'M NOT GOING TO LET SOMEBODY ELSE RIDE OFF ON MY HORSE.
IT'S MY HORSE!
LAMP, YOU CAN'T LEAVE ME BEHIND!
SHUT UP!
I WILL BE ON IT!
I'M THE PRESIDENT OF MARS. I HAVE TO HAVE A SPOT ON THAT HORSE!
BAH! IT'S MY HORSE!
LAMP! I'M YOUR MASTER! YOU DON'T INTEND TO LEAVE ME BEHIND, DO YOU?!
CLICK
IT'S MY HORSE, SO I'M GOING TO RIDE IT. THAT LEAVES THE THREE OF YOU TO DECIDE WHO WILL BE THE SECOND PERSON.
WE'LL FLIP A COIN TO DECIDE. HEADS OR TAILS...

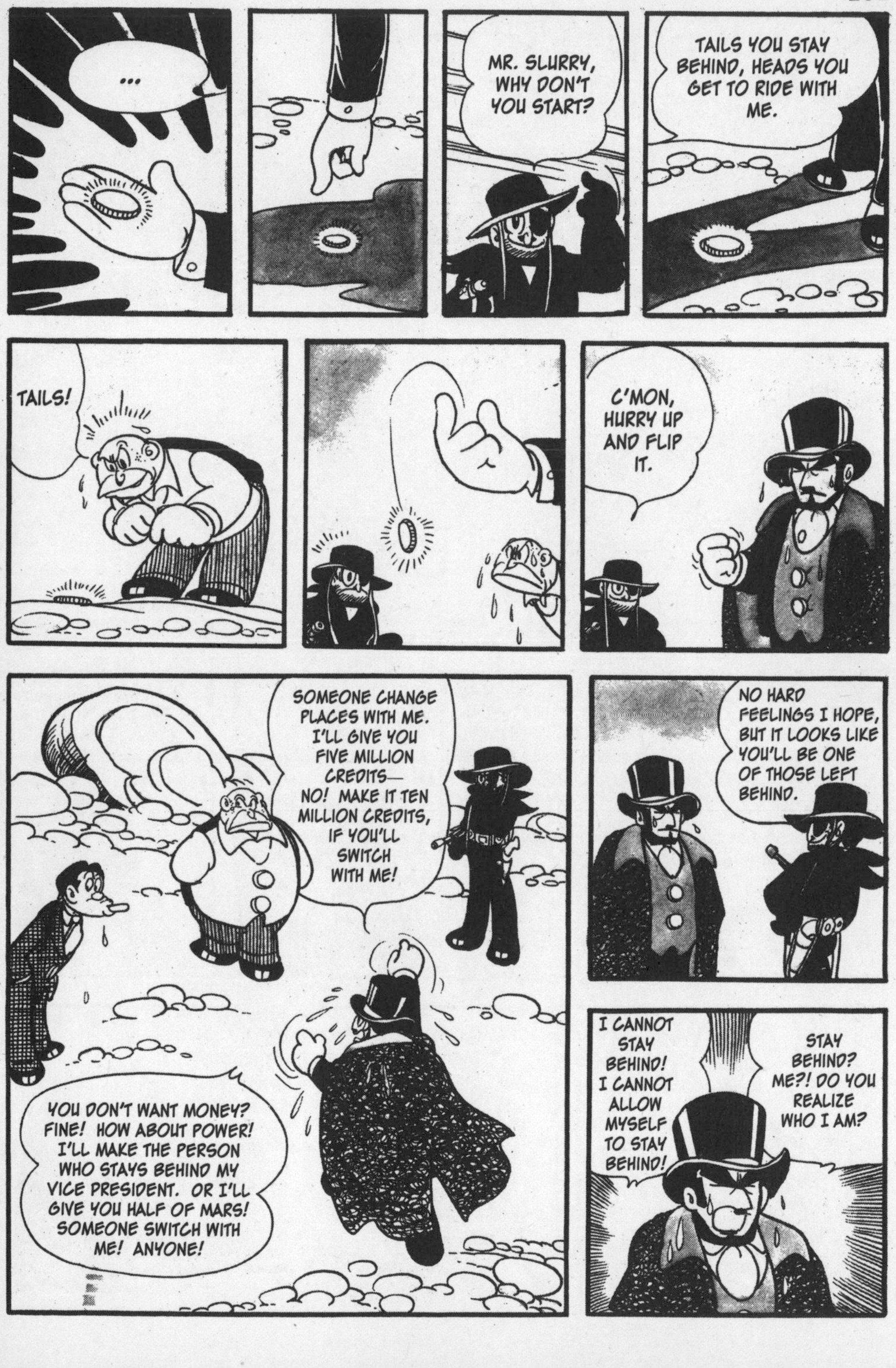
TAILS YOU STAY BEHIND, HEADS YOU GET TO RIDE WITH ME.
MR. SLURRY, WHY DON'T YOU START?
...
C'MON, HURRY UP AND FLIP IT.
TAILS!
NO HARD FEELINGS I HOPE, BUT IT LOOKS LIKE YOU'LL BE ONE OF THOSE LEFT BEHIND.
STAY BEHIND? ME?! DO YOU REALIZE WHO I AM?
I CANNOT STAY BEHIND! I CANNOT ALLOW MYSELF TO STAY BEHIND!
SOMEONE CHANGE PLACES WITH ME. I'LL GIVE YOU FIVE MILLION CREDITS— NO! MAKE IT TEN MILLION CREDITS, IF YOU'LL SWITCH WITH ME!
YOU DON'T WANT MONEY? FINE! HOW ABOUT POWER! I'LL MAKE THE PERSON WHO STAYS BEHIND MY VICE PRESIDENT. OR I'LL GIVE YOU HALF OF MARS! SOMEONE SWITCH WITH ME! ANYONE!

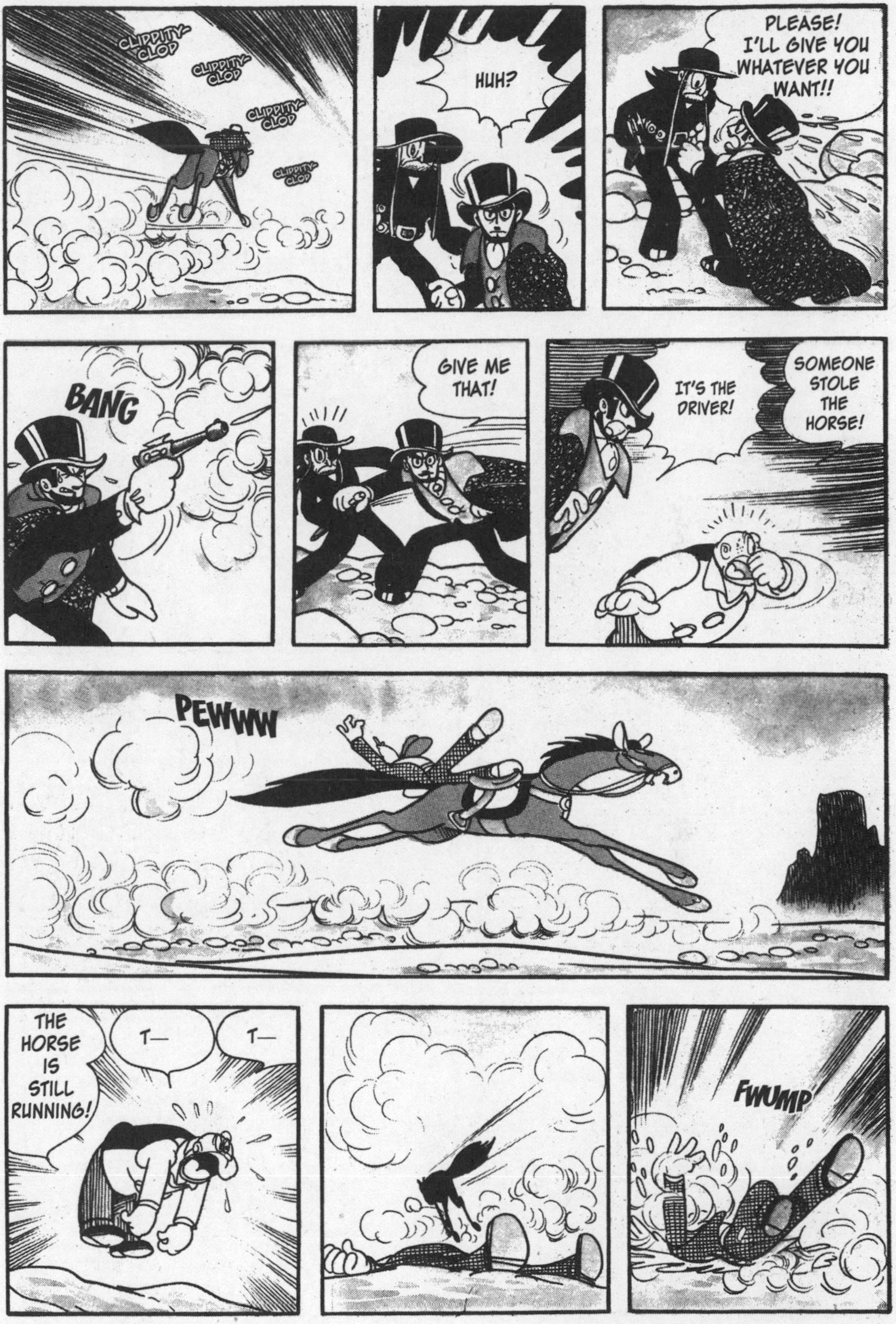
PLEASE! I'LL GIVE YOU WHATEVER YOU WANT!!
HUH?
CLIPPITY-CLOP
CLIPPITY-CLOP
CLIPPITY-CLOP
CLIPPITY-CLOP
SOMEONE STOLE THE HORSE!
IT'S THE DRIVER!
GIVE ME THAT!
BANG
PEWWW
FWUMP
T—
T—
THE HORSE IS STILL RUNNING!

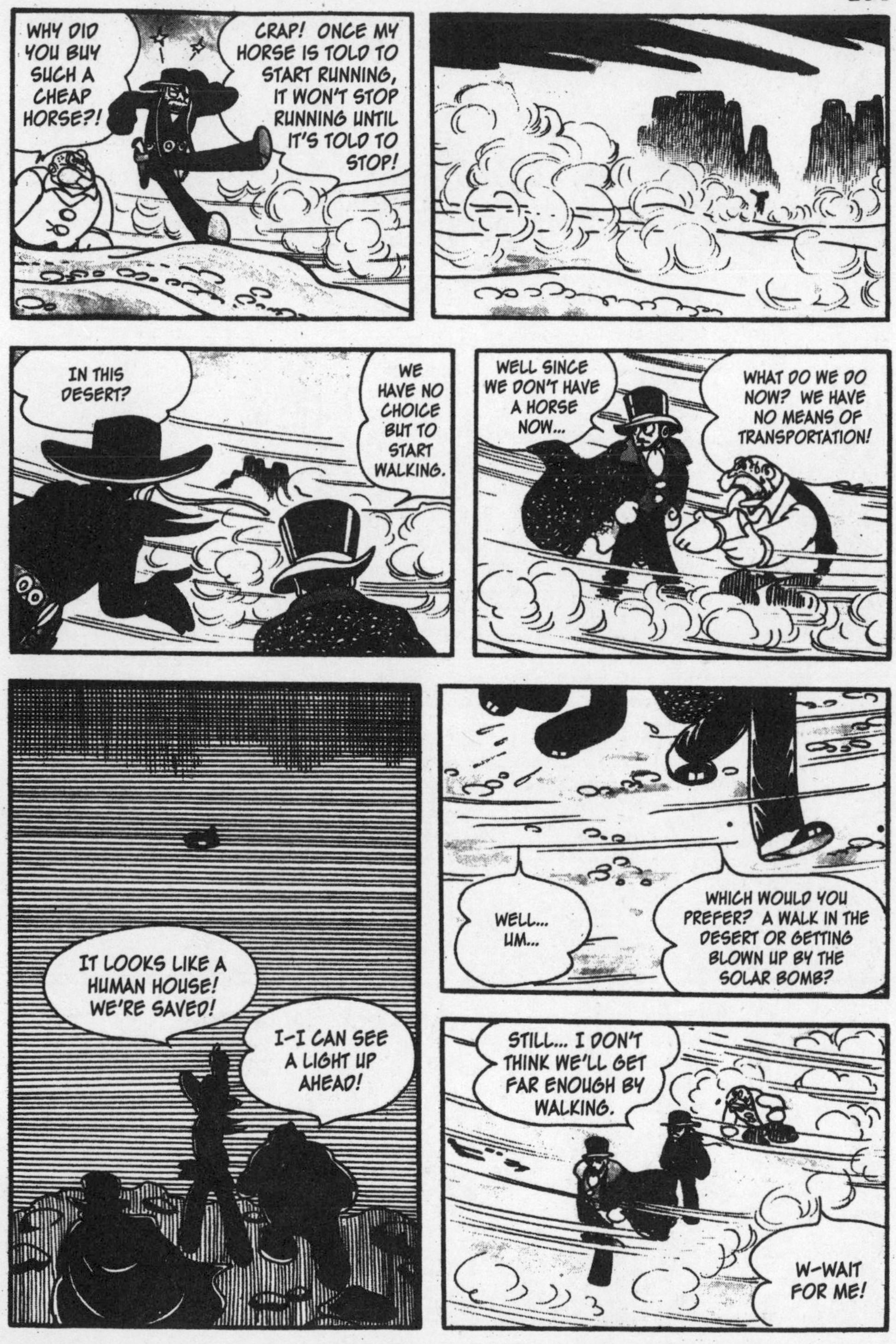
CRAP! ONCE MY HORSE IS TOLD TO START RUNNING, IT WON'T STOP RUNNING UNTIL IT'S TOLD TO STOP!
WHY DID YOU BUY SUCH A CHEAP HORSE?!
WHAT DO WE DO NOW? WE HAVE NO MEANS OF TRANSPORTATION!
WELL SINCE WE DON'T HAVE A HORSE NOW...
WE HAVE NO CHOICE BUT TO START WALKING.
IN THIS DESERT?
WHICH WOULD YOU PREFER? A WALK IN THE DESERT OR GETTING BLOWN UP BY THE SOLAR BOMB?
WELL... UM...
STILL... I DON'T THINK WE'LL GET FAR ENOUGH BY WALKING.
W-WAIT FOR ME!
I-I CAN SEE A LIGHT UP AHEAD!
IT LOOKS LIKE A HUMAN HOUSE! WE'RE SAVED!

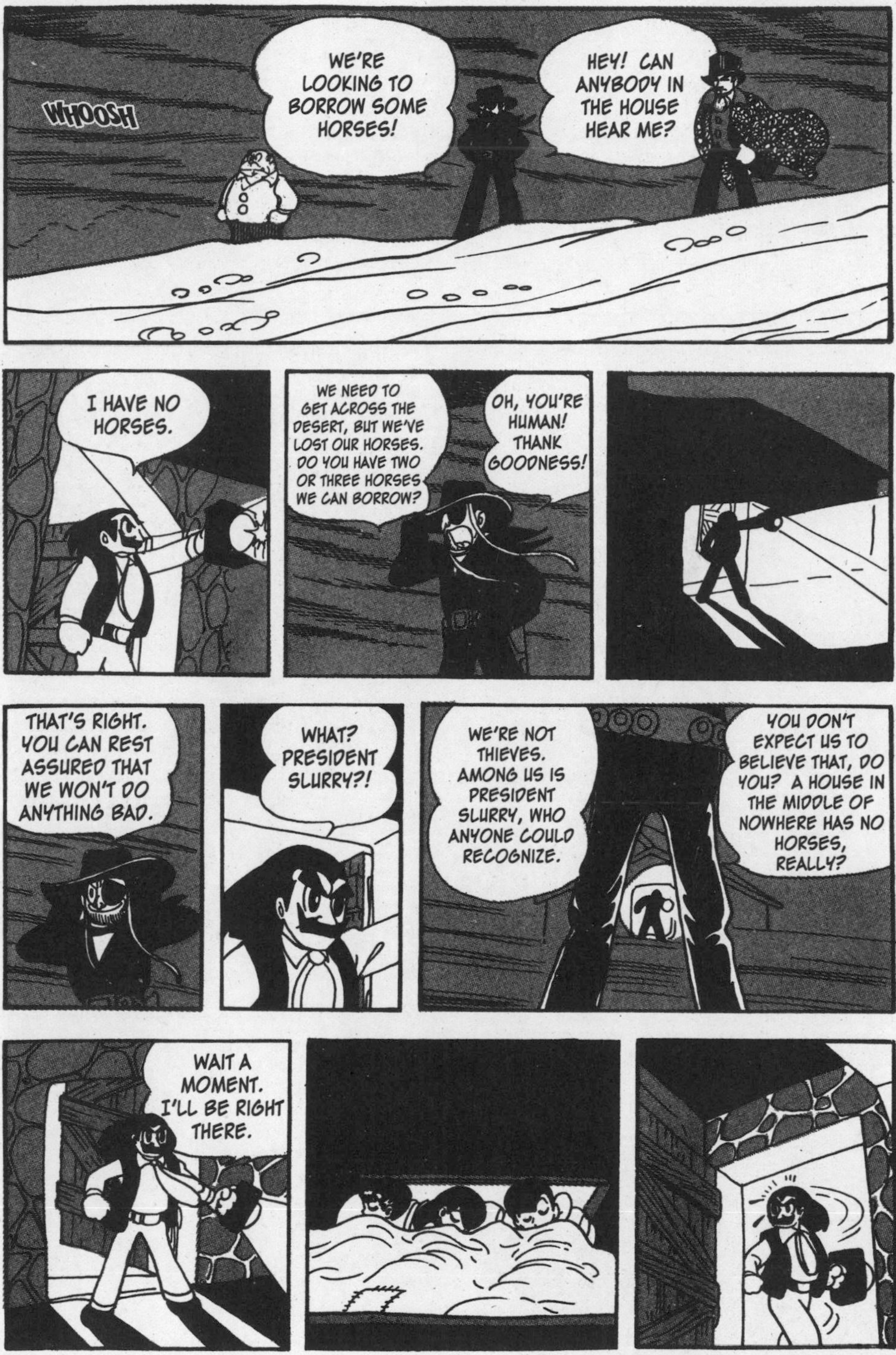
HEY! CAN ANYBODY IN THE HOUSE HEAR ME?
WE'RE LOOKING TO BORROW SOME HORSES!
WHOOSH
OH, YOU'RE HUMAN! THANK GOODNESS!
WE NEED TO GET ACROSS THE DESERT, BUT WE'VE LOST OUR HORSES. DO YOU HAVE TWO OR THREE HORSES WE CAN BORROW?
I HAVE NO HORSES.
YOU DON'T EXPECT US TO BELIEVE THAT, DO YOU? A HOUSE IN THE MIDDLE OF NOWHERE HAS NO HORSES, REALLY?
WE'RE NOT THIEVES. AMONG US IS PRESIDENT SLURRY, WHO ANYONE COULD RECOGNIZE.
WHAT? PRESIDENT SLURRY?!
THAT'S RIGHT. YOU CAN REST ASSURED THAT WE WON'T DO ANYTHING BAD.
WAIT A MOMENT. I'LL BE RIGHT THERE.

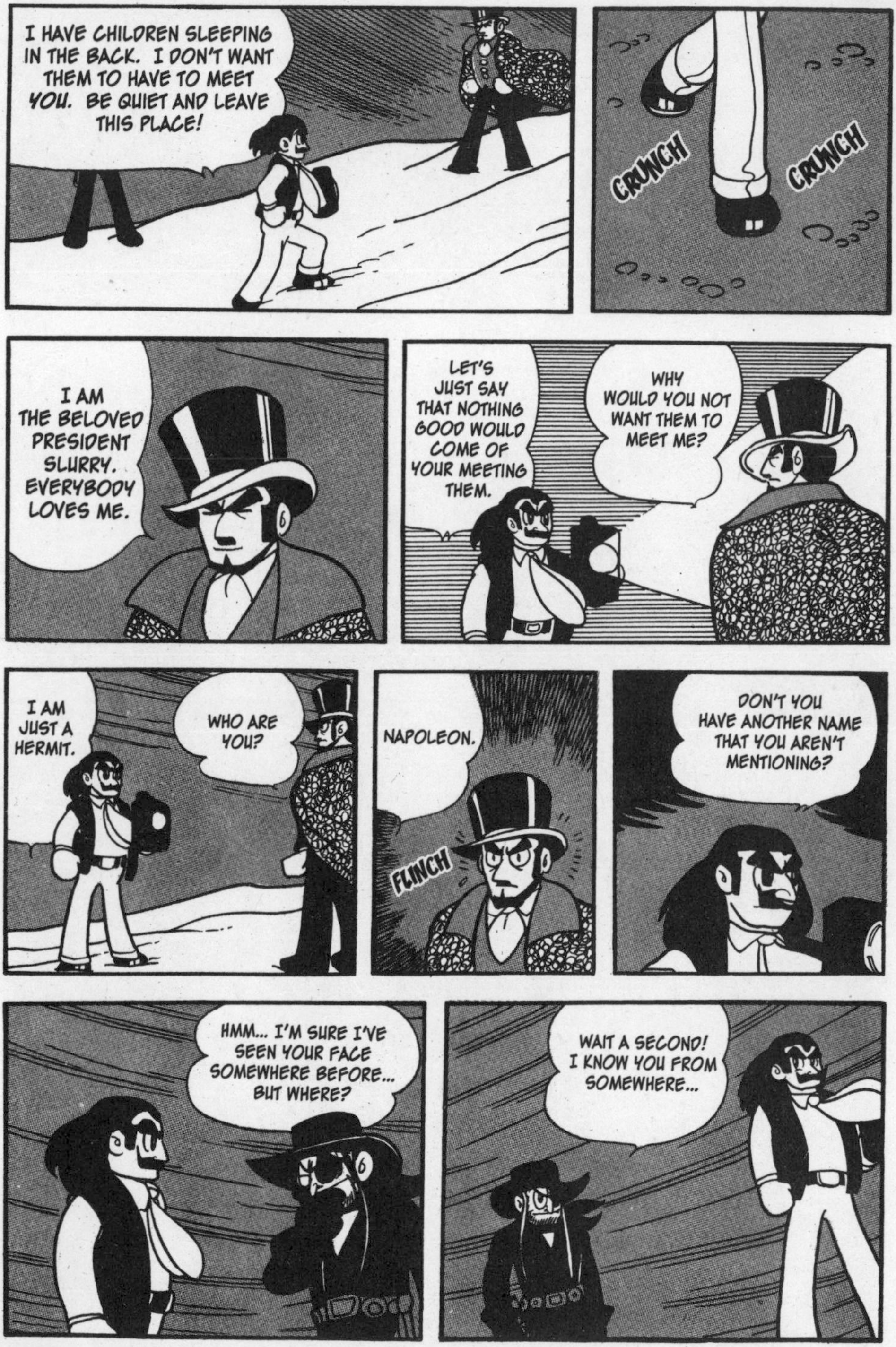
CRUNCH
CRUNCH
I HAVE CHILDREN SLEEPING IN THE BACK. I DON'T WANT THEM TO HAVE TO MEET YOU. BE QUIET AND LEAVE THIS PLACE!
WHY WOULD YOU NOT WANT THEM TO MEET ME?
LET'S JUST SAY THAT NOTHING GOOD WOULD COME OF YOUR MEETING THEM.
I AM THE BELOVED PRESIDENT SLURRY. EVERYBODY LOVES ME.
DON'T YOU HAVE ANOTHER NAME THAT YOU AREN'T MENTIONING?
NAPOLEON.
FLINCH
WHO ARE YOU?
I AM JUST A HERMIT.
WAIT A SECOND! I KNOW YOU FROM SOMEWHERE...
HMM... I'M SURE I'VE SEEN YOUR FACE SOMEWHERE BEFORE... BUT WHERE?

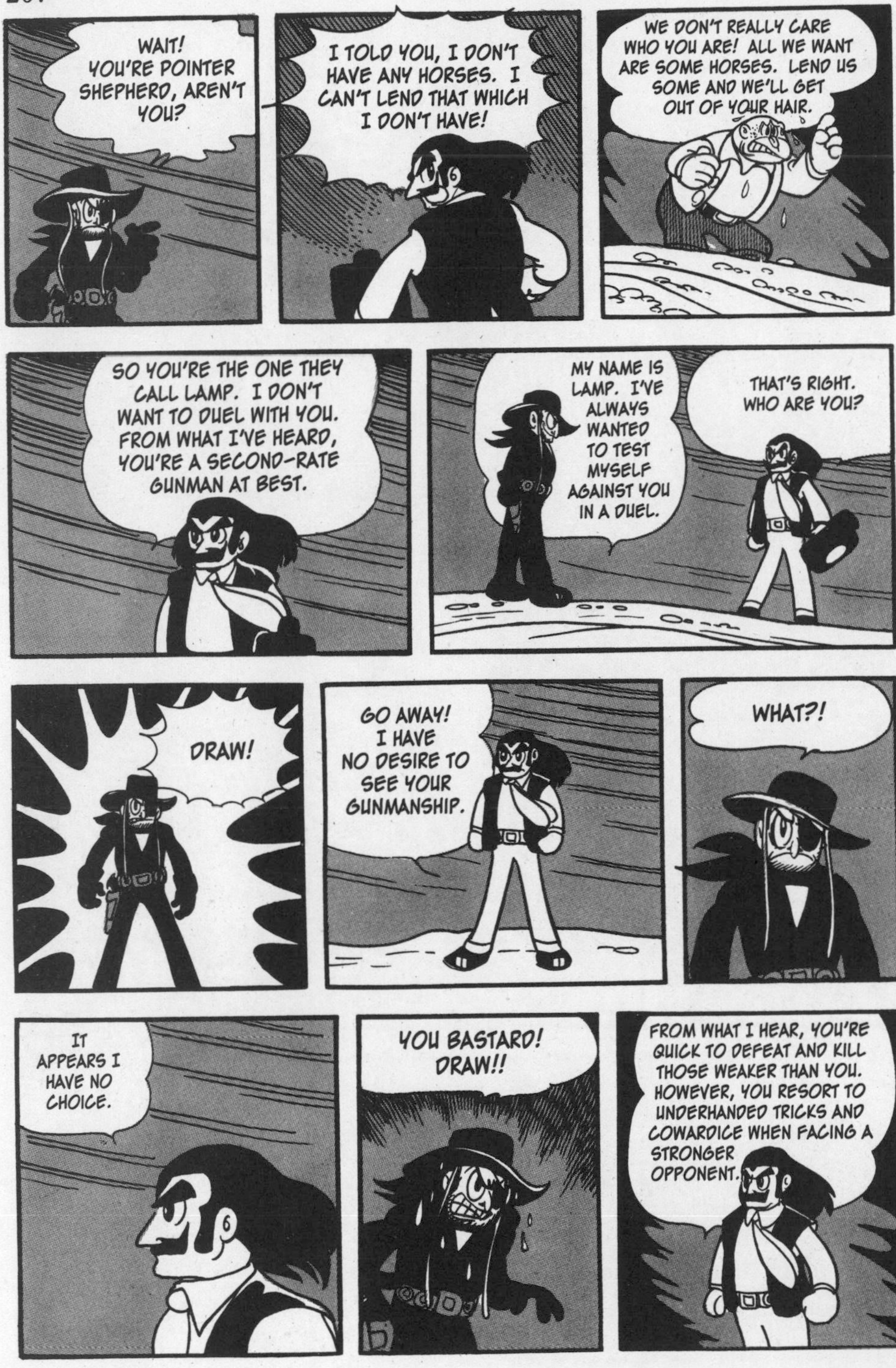
WE DON'T REALLY CARE WHO YOU ARE! ALL WE WANT ARE SOME HORSES. LEND US SOME AND WE'LL GET OUT OF YOUR HAIR.
I TOLD YOU, I DON'T HAVE ANY HORSES. I CAN'T LEND THAT WHICH I DON'T HAVE!
WAIT! YOU'RE POINTER SHEPHERD, AREN'T YOU?
THAT'S RIGHT. WHO ARE YOU?
MY NAME IS LAMP. I'VE ALWAYS WANTED TO TEST MYSELF AGAINST YOU IN A DUEL.
SO YOU'RE THE ONE THEY CALL LAMP. I DON'T WANT TO DUEL WITH YOU. FROM WHAT I'VE HEARD, YOU'RE A SECOND-RATE GUNMAN AT BEST.
WHAT?!
GO AWAY! I HAVE NO DESIRE TO SEE YOUR GUNMANSHIP.
DRAW!
FROM WHAT I HEAR, YOU'RE QUICK TO DEFEAT AND KILL THOSE WEAKER THAN YOU. HOWEVER, YOU RESORT TO UNDERHANDED TRICKS AND COWARDICE WHEN FACING A STRONGER OPPONENT.
YOU BASTARD! DRAW!!
IT APPEARS I HAVE NO CHOICE.

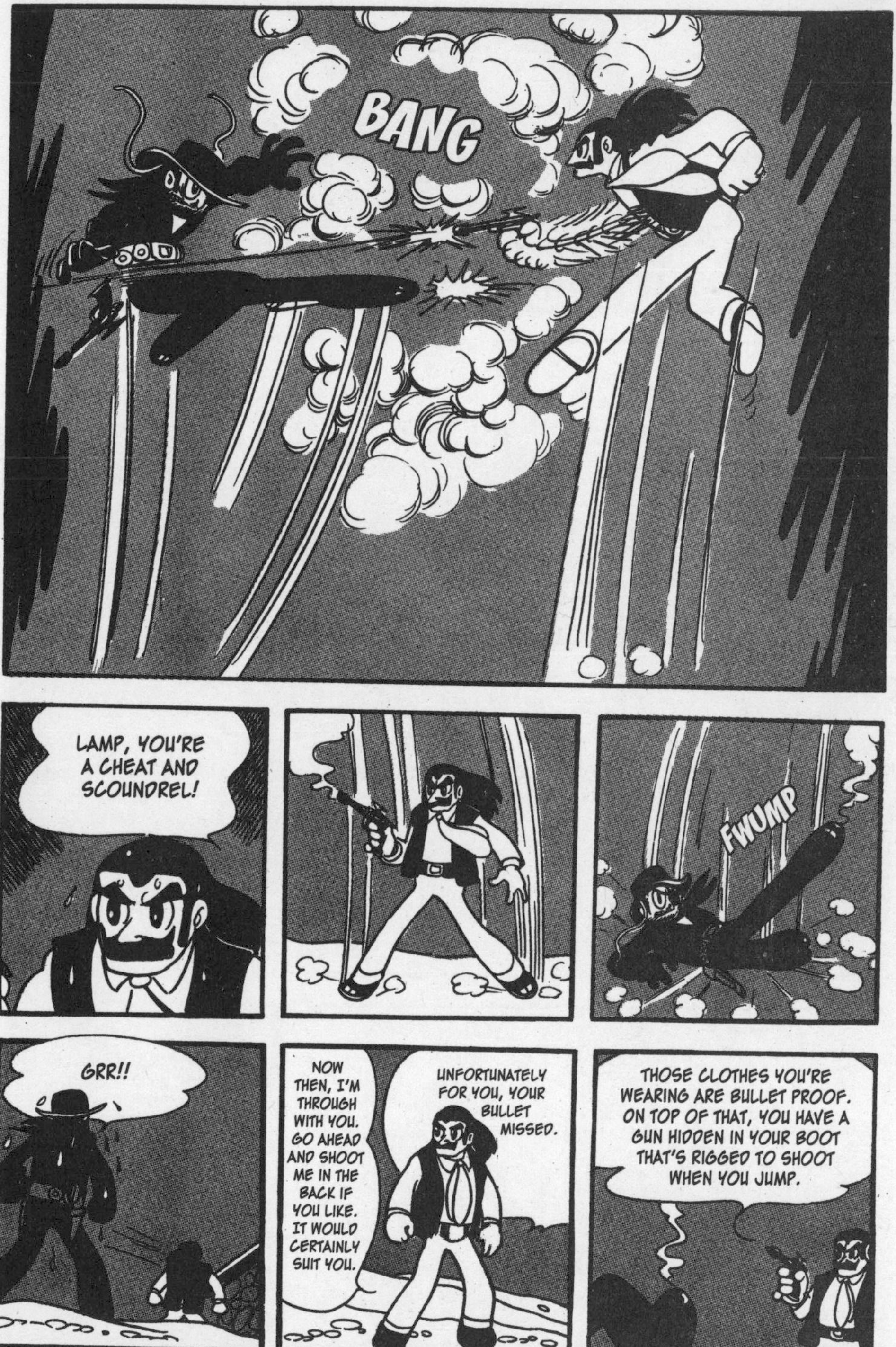
BANG
FWUMP
LAMP, YOU'RE A CHEAT AND SCOUNDREL!
THOSE CLOTHES YOU'RE WEARING ARE BULLET PROOF. ON TOP OF THAT, YOU HAVE A GUN HIDDEN IN YOUR BOOT THAT'S RIGGED TO SHOOT WHEN YOU JUMP.
UNFORTUNATELY FOR YOU, YOUR BULLET MISSED.
NOW THEN, I'M THROUGH WITH YOU. GO AHEAD AND SHOOT ME IN THE BACK IF YOU LIKE. IT WOULD CERTAINLY SUIT YOU.
GRR!!

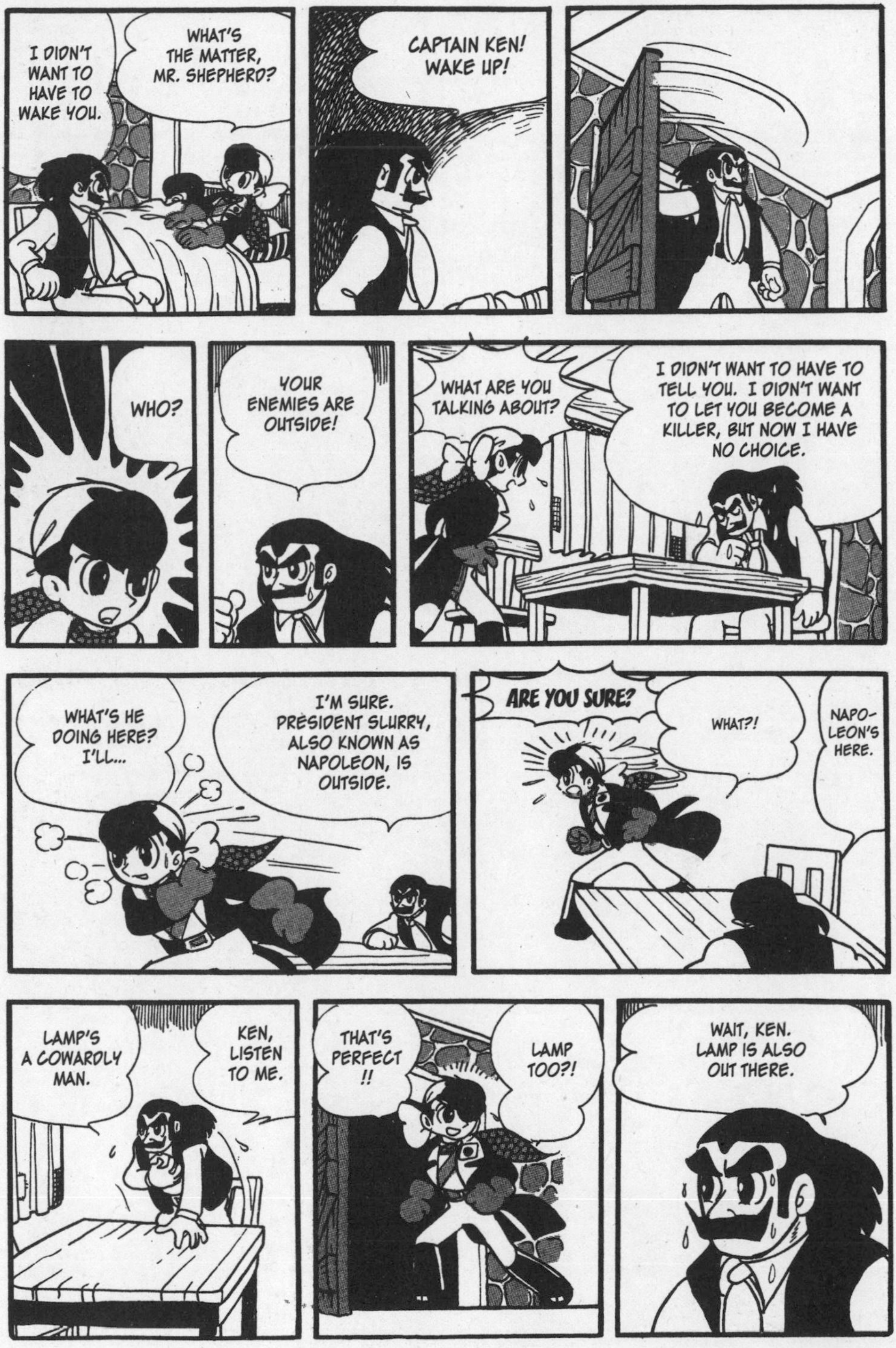
CAPTAIN KEN! WAKE UP!
WHAT'S THE MATTER, MR. SHEPHERD?
I DIDN'T WANT TO HAVE TO WAKE YOU.
I DIDN'T WANT TO HAVE TO TELL YOU. I DIDN'T WANT TO LET YOU BECOME A KILLER, BUT NOW I HAVE NO CHOICE.
WHAT ARE YOU TALKING ABOUT?
YOUR ENEMIES ARE OUTSIDE!
WHO?
NAPOLEON'S HERE.
WHAT?!
ARE YOU SURE?
I'M SURE. PRESIDENT SLURRY, ALSO KNOWN AS NAPOLEON, IS OUTSIDE.
WHAT'S HE DOING HERE? I'LL...
WAIT, KEN. LAMP IS ALSO OUT THERE.
LAMP TOO?!
THAT'S PERFECT !!
KEN, LISTEN TO ME.
LAMP'S A COWARDLY MAN.

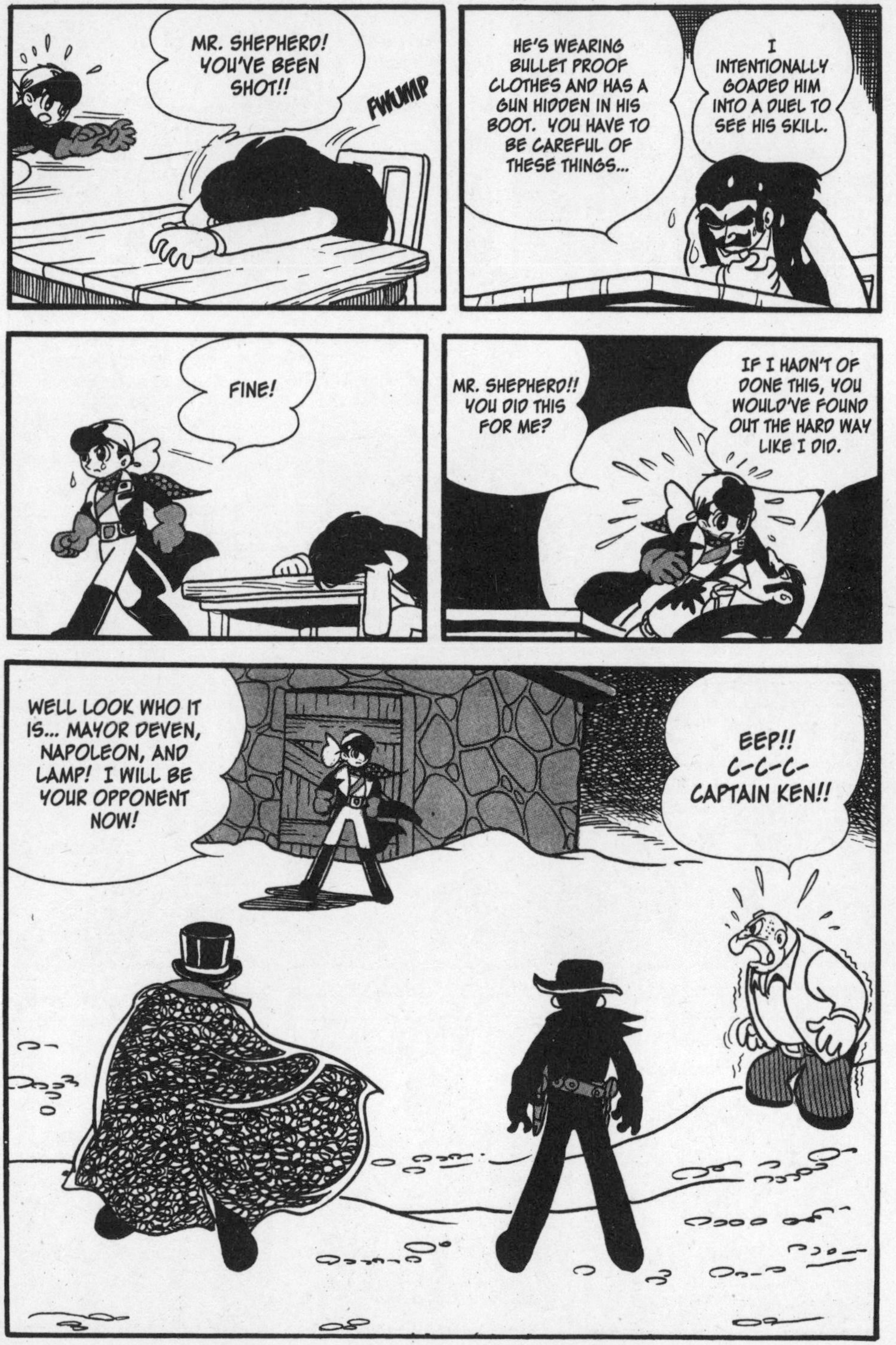
MR. SHEPHERD! YOU'VE BEEN SHOT!!
FWUMP
HE'S WEARING BULLET PROOF CLOTHES AND HAS A GUN HIDDEN IN HIS BOOT. YOU HAVE TO BE CAREFUL OF THESE THINGS...
I INTENTIONALLY GOADED HIM INTO A DUEL TO SEE HIS SKILL.
FINE!
MR. SHEPHERD!! YOU DID THIS FOR ME?
IF I HADN'T OF DONE THIS, YOU WOULD'VE FOUND OUT THE HARD WAY LIKE I DID.
WELL LOOK WHO IT IS... MAYOR DEVEN, NAPOLEON, AND LAMP! I WILL BE YOUR OPPONENT NOW!
EEP!! C-C-C- CAPTAIN KEN!!

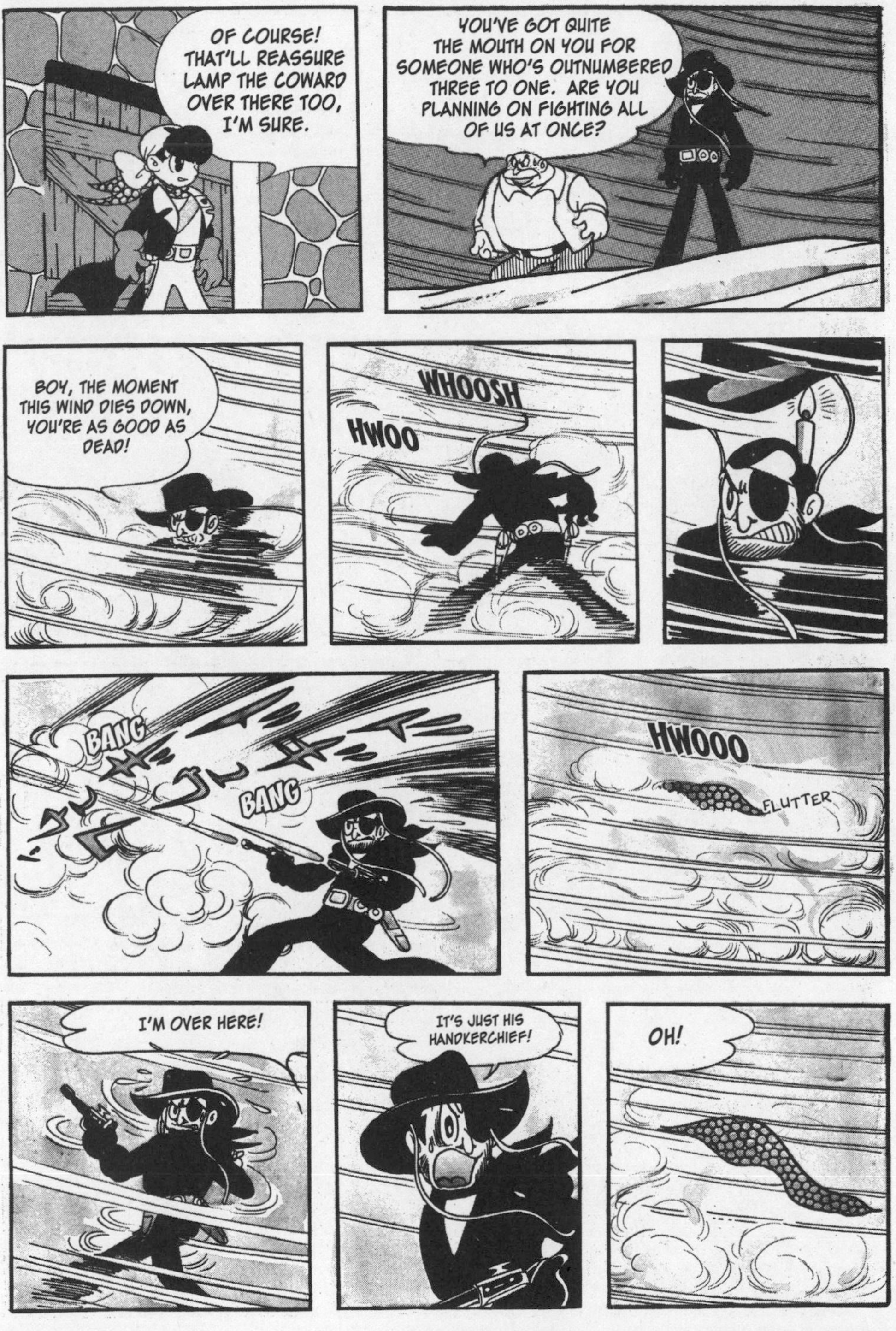
YOU'VE GOT QUITE THE MOUTH ON YOU FOR SOMEONE WHO'S OUTNUMBERED THREE TO ONE. ARE YOU PLANNING ON FIGHTING ALL OF US AT ONCE?
OF COURSE! THAT'LL REASSURE LAMP THE COWARD OVER THERE TOO, I'M SURE.
WHOOSH
HWOO
BOY, THE MOMENT THIS WIND DIES DOWN, YOU'RE AS GOOD AS DEAD!
HWOOO
FLUTTER
BANG
BANG
OH!
IT'S JUST HIS HANDKERCHIEF!
I'M OVER HERE!

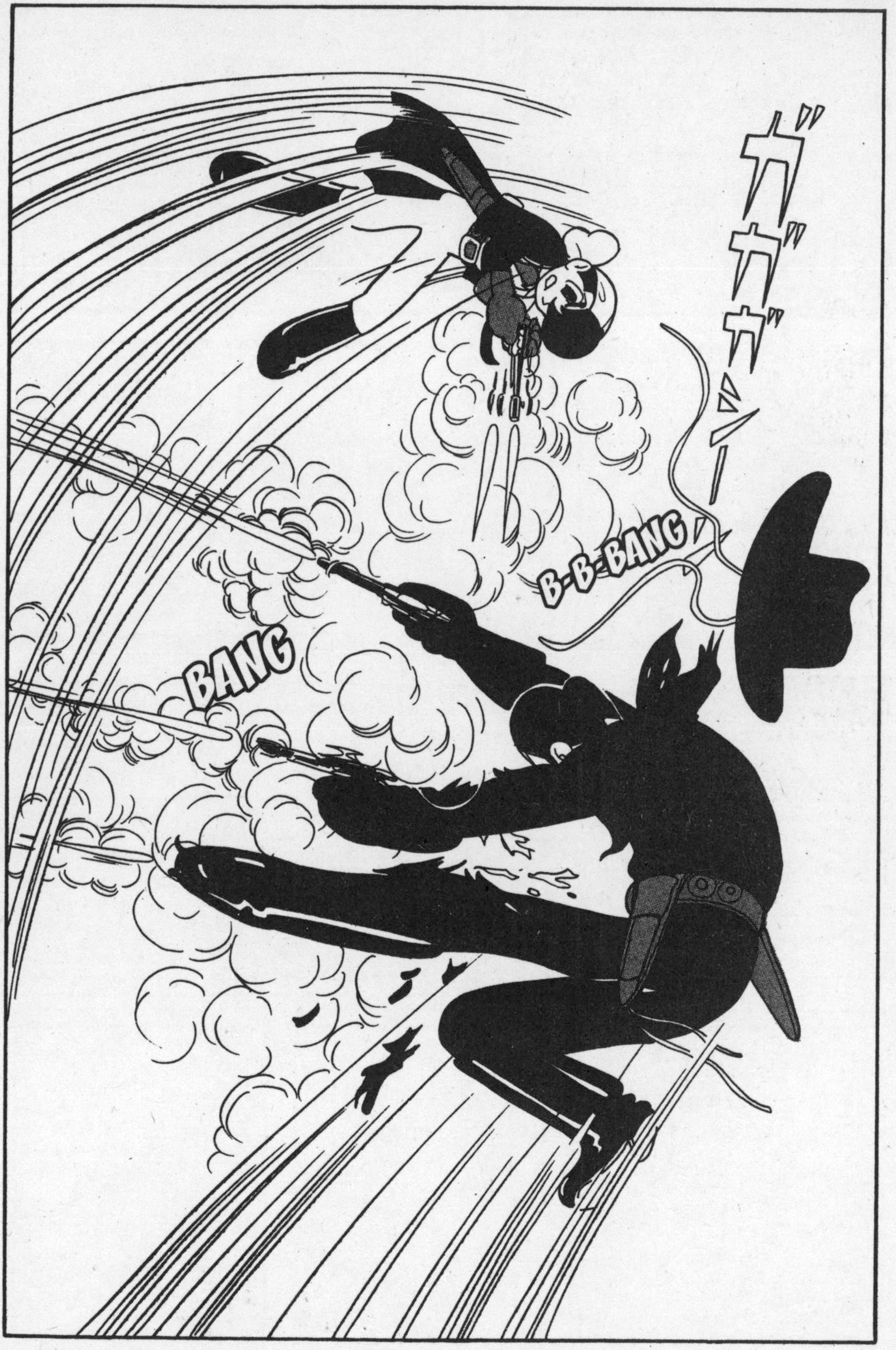
ガガガシーン
B-B-BANG
BANG

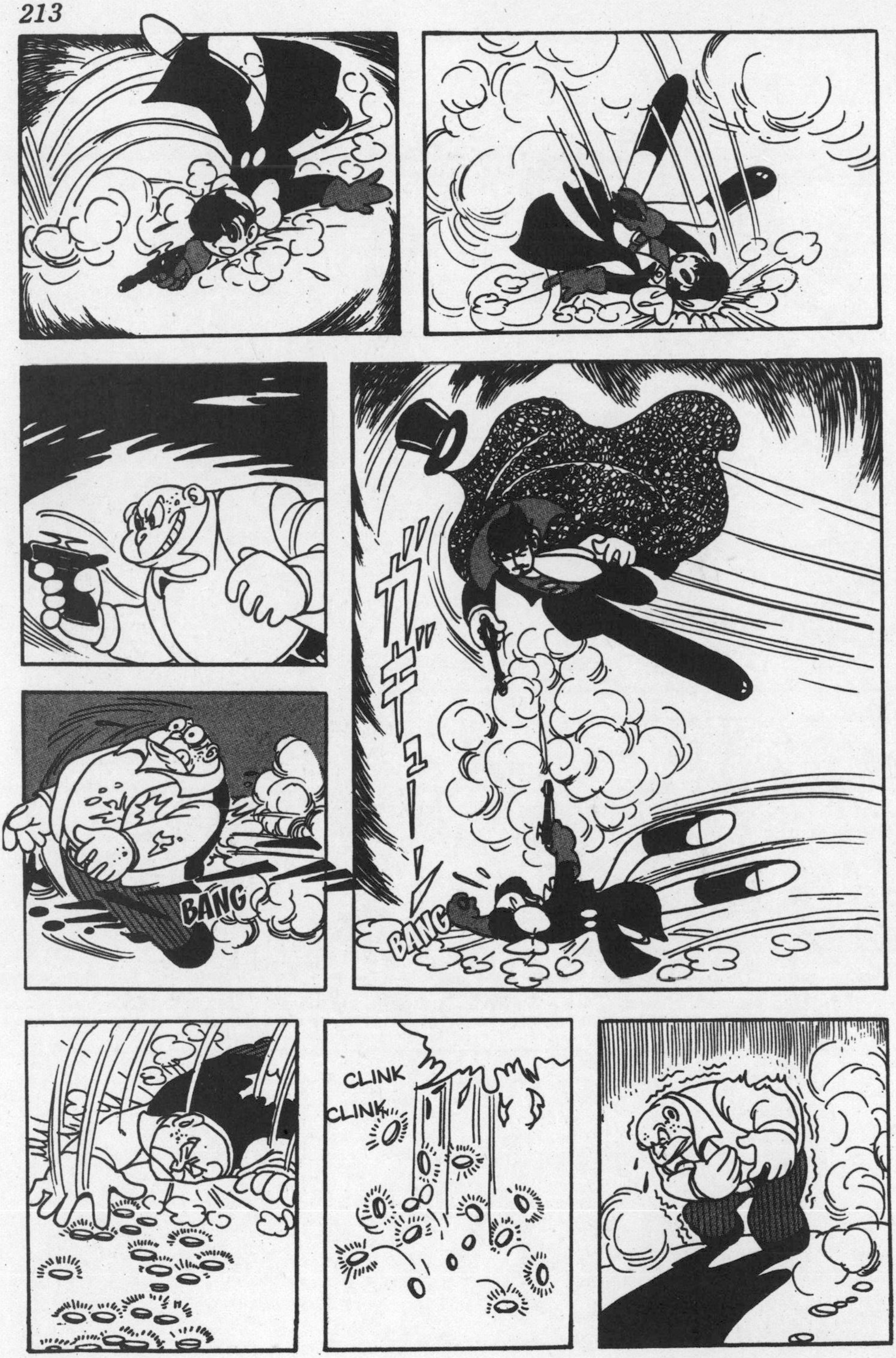
ガギューン
BANG
BANG
CLINK
CLINK

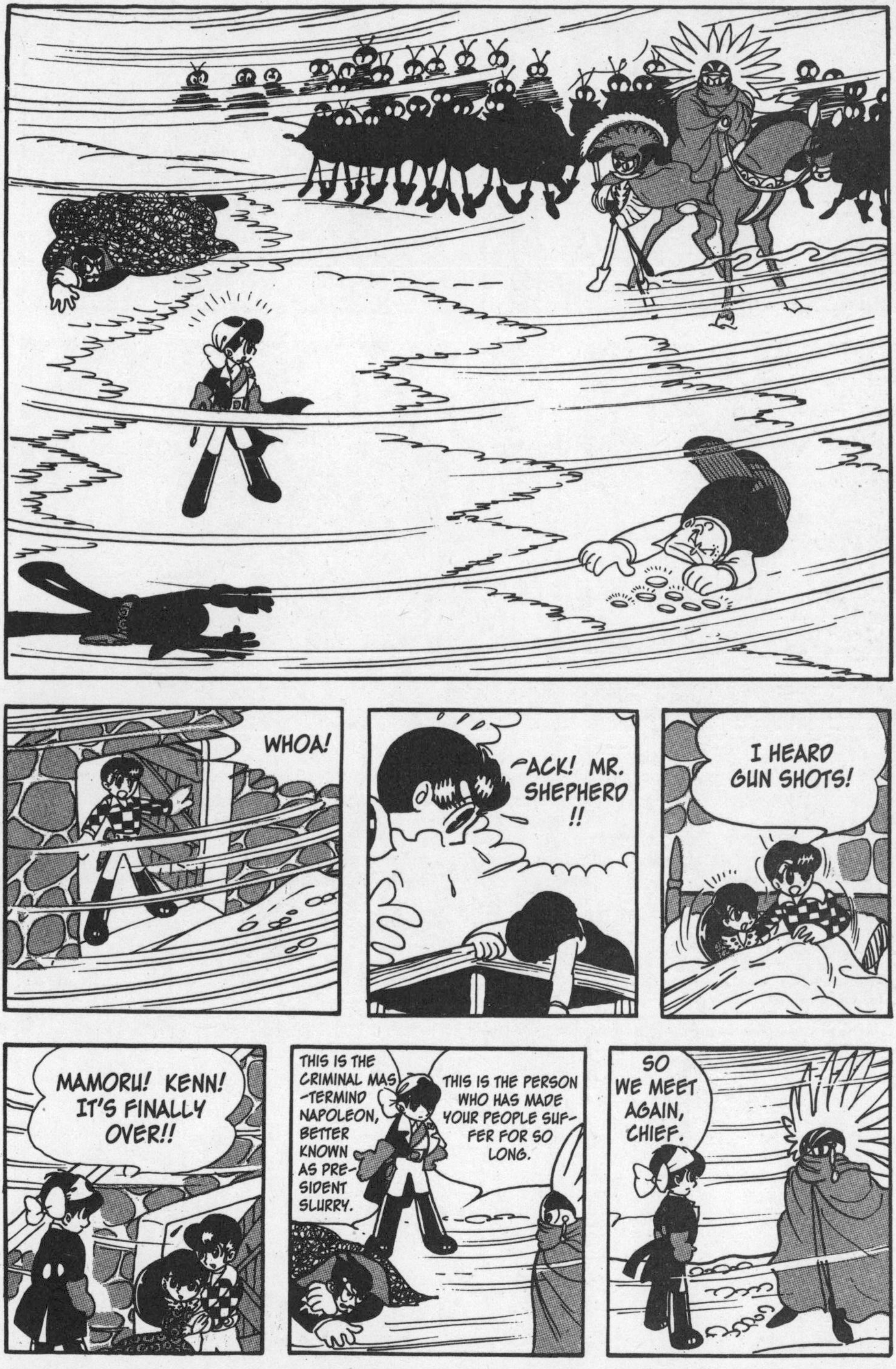
I HEARD GUN SHOTS!
ACK! MR. SHEPHERD !!
WHOA!
SO WE MEET AGAIN, CHIEF.
THIS IS THE PERSON WHO HAS MADE YOUR PEOPLE SUF-FER FOR SO LONG.
THIS IS THE CRIMINAL MAS-TERMIND NAPOLEON, BETTER KNOWN AS PRE-SIDENT SLURRY.
MAMORU! KENN! IT'S FINALLY OVER!!

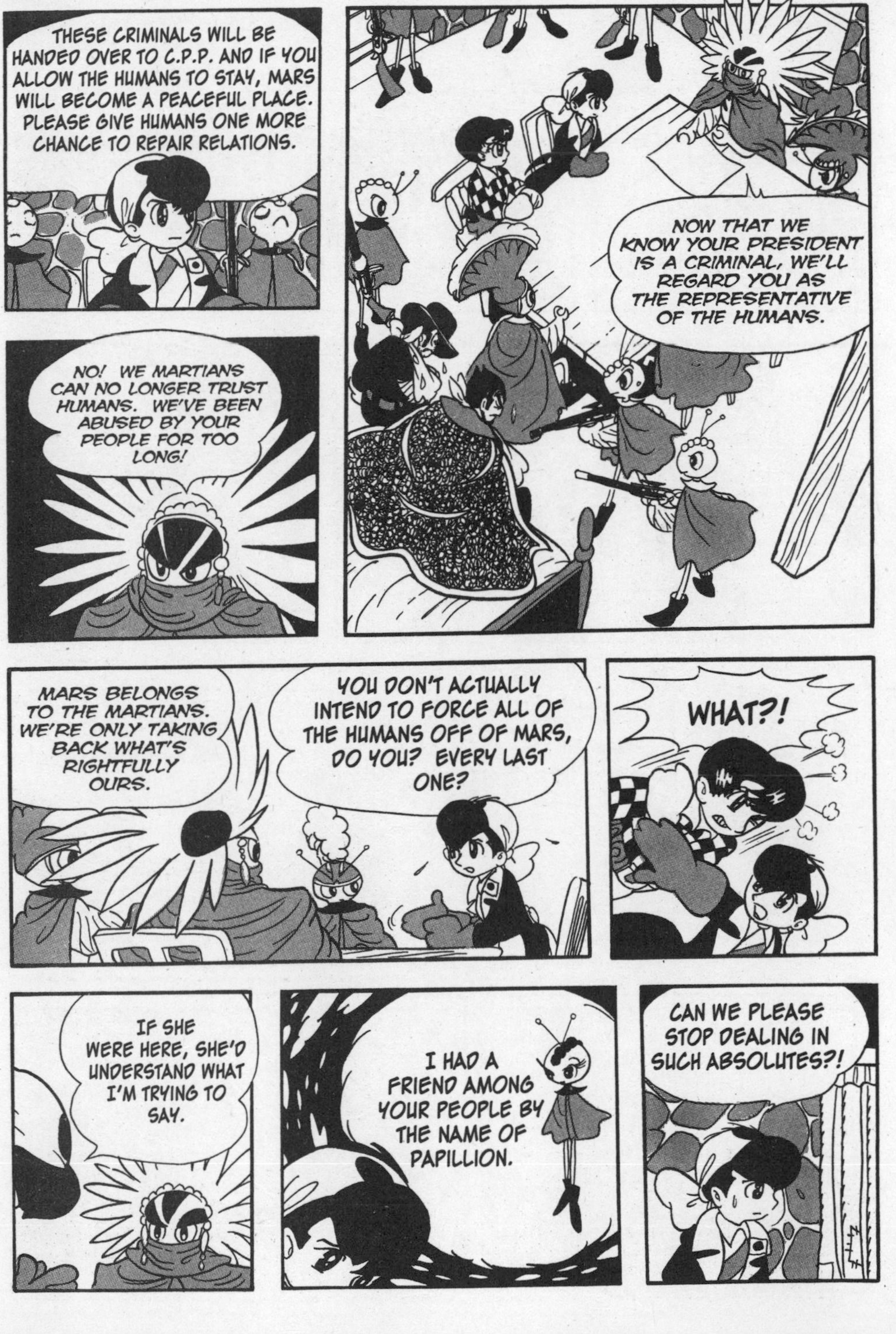
NOW THAT WE KNOW YOUR PRESIDENT IS A CRIMINAL, WE'LL REGARD YOU AS THE REPRESENTATIVE OF THE HUMANS.
THESE CRIMINALS WILL BE HANDED OVER TO C.P.P. AND IF YOU ALLOW THE HUMANS TO STAY, MARS WILL BECOME A PEACEFUL PLACE. PLEASE GIVE HUMANS ONE MORE CHANCE TO REPAIR RELATIONS.
NO! WE MARTIANS CAN NO LONGER TRUST HUMANS. WE'VE BEEN ABUSED BY YOUR PEOPLE FOR TOO LONG!
WHAT?!
YOU DON'T ACTUALLY INTEND TO FORCE ALL OF THE HUMANS OFF OF MARS, DO YOU? EVERY LAST ONE?
MARS BELONGS TO THE MARTIANS. WE'RE ONLY TAKING BACK WHAT'S RIGHTFULLY OURS.
CAN WE PLEASE STOP DEALING IN SUCH ABSOLUTES?!
I HAD A FRIEND AMONG YOUR PEOPLE BY THE NAME OF PAPILLION.
IF SHE WERE HERE, SHE'D UNDERSTAND WHAT I'M TRYING TO SAY.

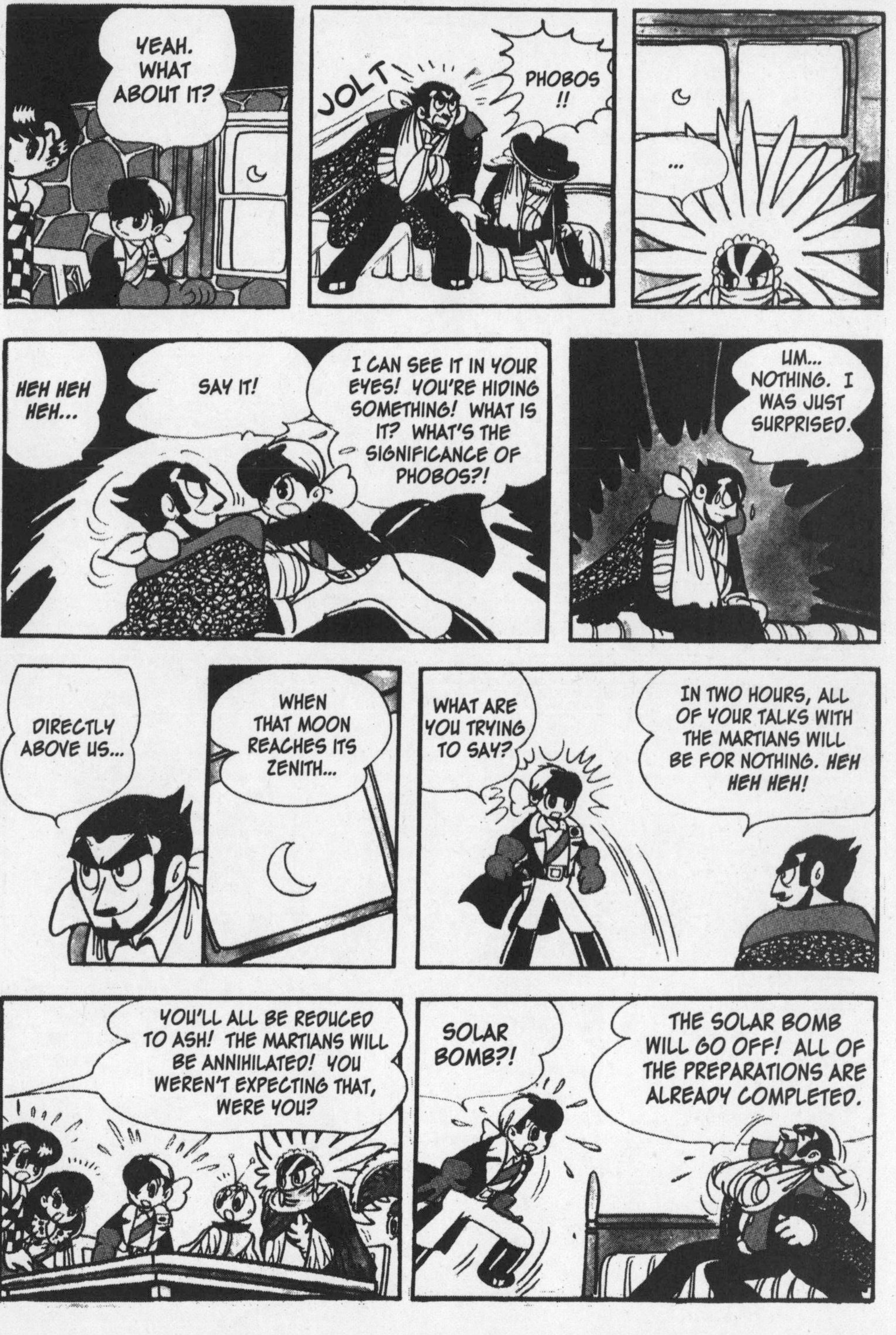
...
PHOBOS !!
JOLT
YEAH. WHAT ABOUT IT?
UM... NOTHING. I WAS JUST SURPRISED.
I CAN SEE IT IN YOUR EYES! YOU'RE HIDING SOMETHING! WHAT IS IT? WHAT'S THE SIGNIFICANCE OF PHOBOS?!
SAY IT!
HEH HEH HEH...
IN TWO HOURS, ALL OF YOUR TALKS WITH THE MARTIANS WILL BE FOR NOTHING. HEH HEH HEH!
WHAT ARE YOU TRYING TO SAY?
WHEN THAT MOON REACHES ITS ZENITH...
DIRECTLY ABOVE US...
THE SOLAR BOMB WILL GO OFF! ALL OF THE PREPARATIONS ARE ALREADY COMPLETED.
SOLAR BOMB?!
YOU'LL ALL BE REDUCED TO ASH! THE MARTIANS WILL BE ANNIHILATED! YOU WEREN'T EXPECTING THAT, WERE YOU?

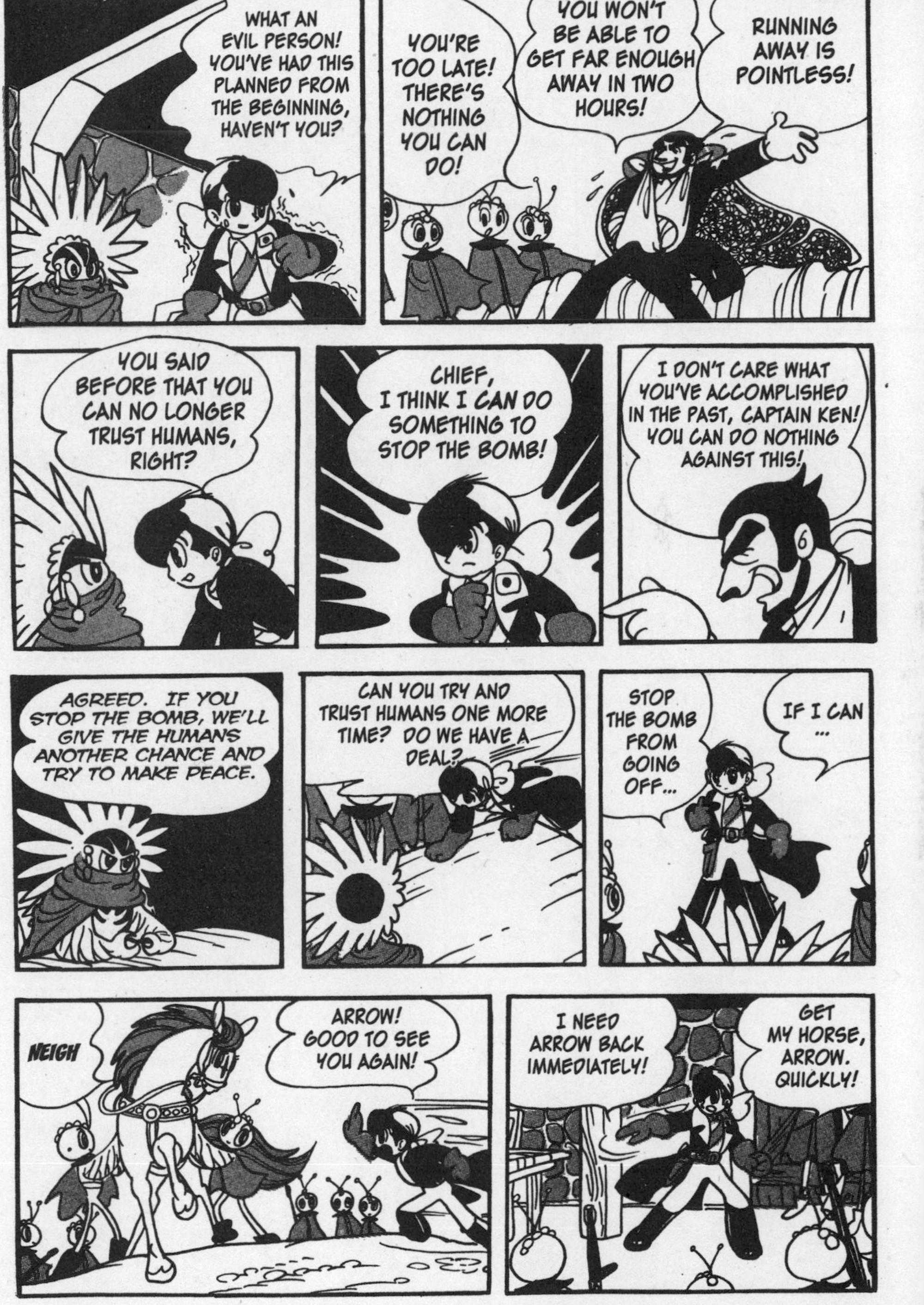
RUNNING AWAY IS POINTLESS!
YOU WON'T BE ABLE TO GET FAR ENOUGH AWAY IN TWO HOURS!
YOU'RE TOO LATE! THERE'S NOTHING YOU CAN DO!
WHAT AN EVIL PERSON! YOU'VE HAD THIS PLANNED FROM THE BEGINNING, HAVEN'T YOU?
I DON'T CARE WHAT YOU'VE ACCOMPLISHED IN THE PAST, CAPTAIN KEN! YOU CAN DO NOTHING AGAINST THIS!
CHIEF, I THINK I CAN DO SOMETHING TO STOP THE BOMB!
YOU SAID BEFORE THAT YOU CAN NO LONGER TRUST HUMANS, RIGHT?
IF I CAN ...
STOP THE BOMB FROM GOING OFF...
CAN YOU TRY AND TRUST HUMANS ONE MORE TIME? DO WE HAVE A DEAL?
AGREED. IF YOU STOP THE BOMB, WE'LL GIVE THE HUMANS ANOTHER CHANCE AND TRY TO MAKE PEACE.
GET MY HORSE, ARROW. QUICKLY!
I NEED ARROW BACK IMMEDIATELY!
ARROW! GOOD TO SEE YOU AGAIN!
NEIGH

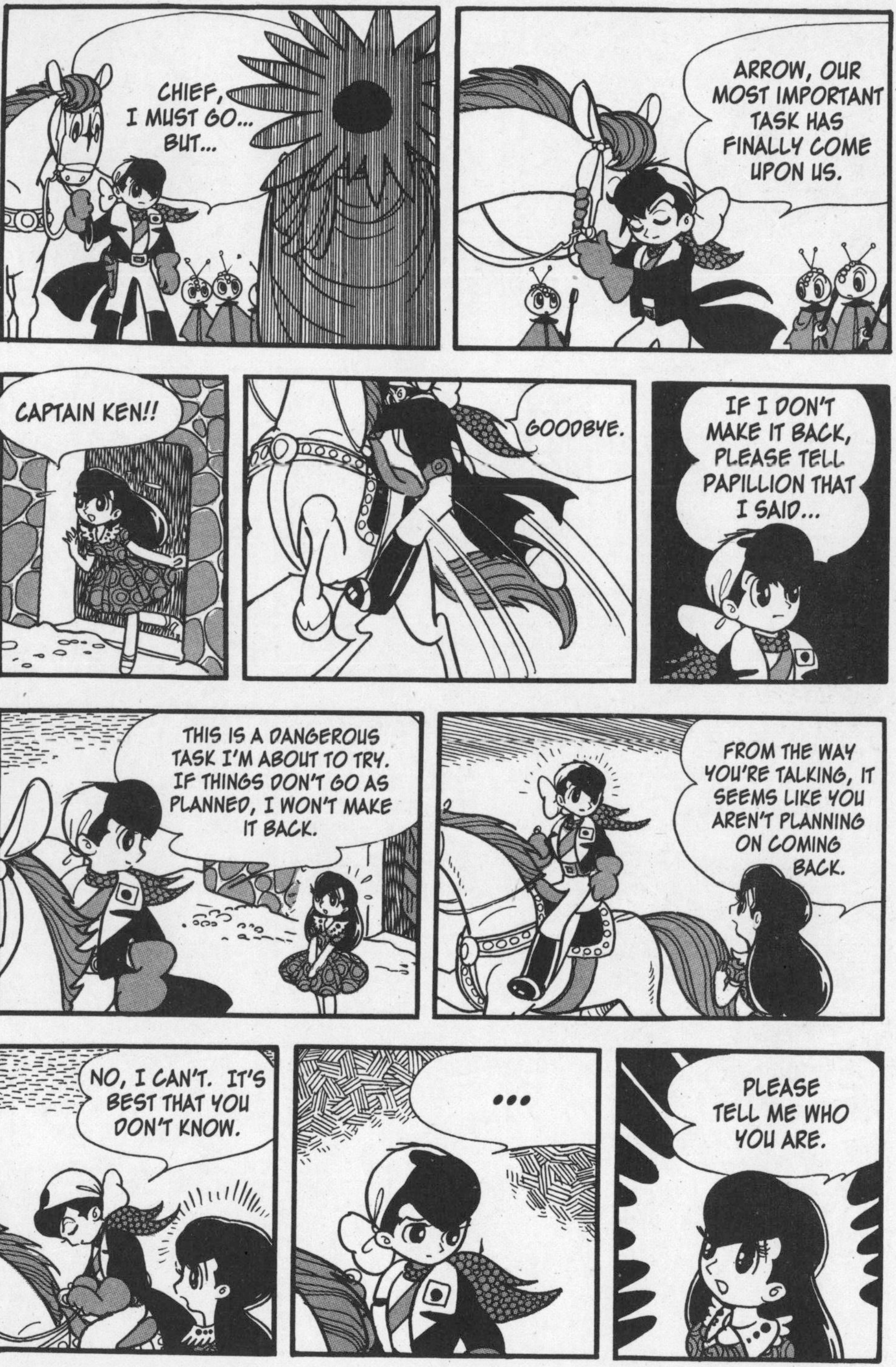
ARROW, OUR MOST IMPORTANT TASK HAS FINALLY COME UPON US.
CHIEF, I MUST GO... BUT...
IF I DON'T MAKE IT BACK, PLEASE TELL PAPILLION THAT I SAID...
GOODBYE.
CAPTAIN KEN!!
FROM THE WAY YOU'RE TALKING, IT SEEMS LIKE YOU AREN'T PLANNING ON COMING BACK.
THIS IS A DANGEROUS TASK I'M ABOUT TO TRY. IF THINGS DON'T GO AS PLANNED, I WON'T MAKE IT BACK.
PLEASE TELL ME WHO YOU ARE.
...
NO, I CAN'T. IT'S BEST THAT YOU DON'T KNOW.

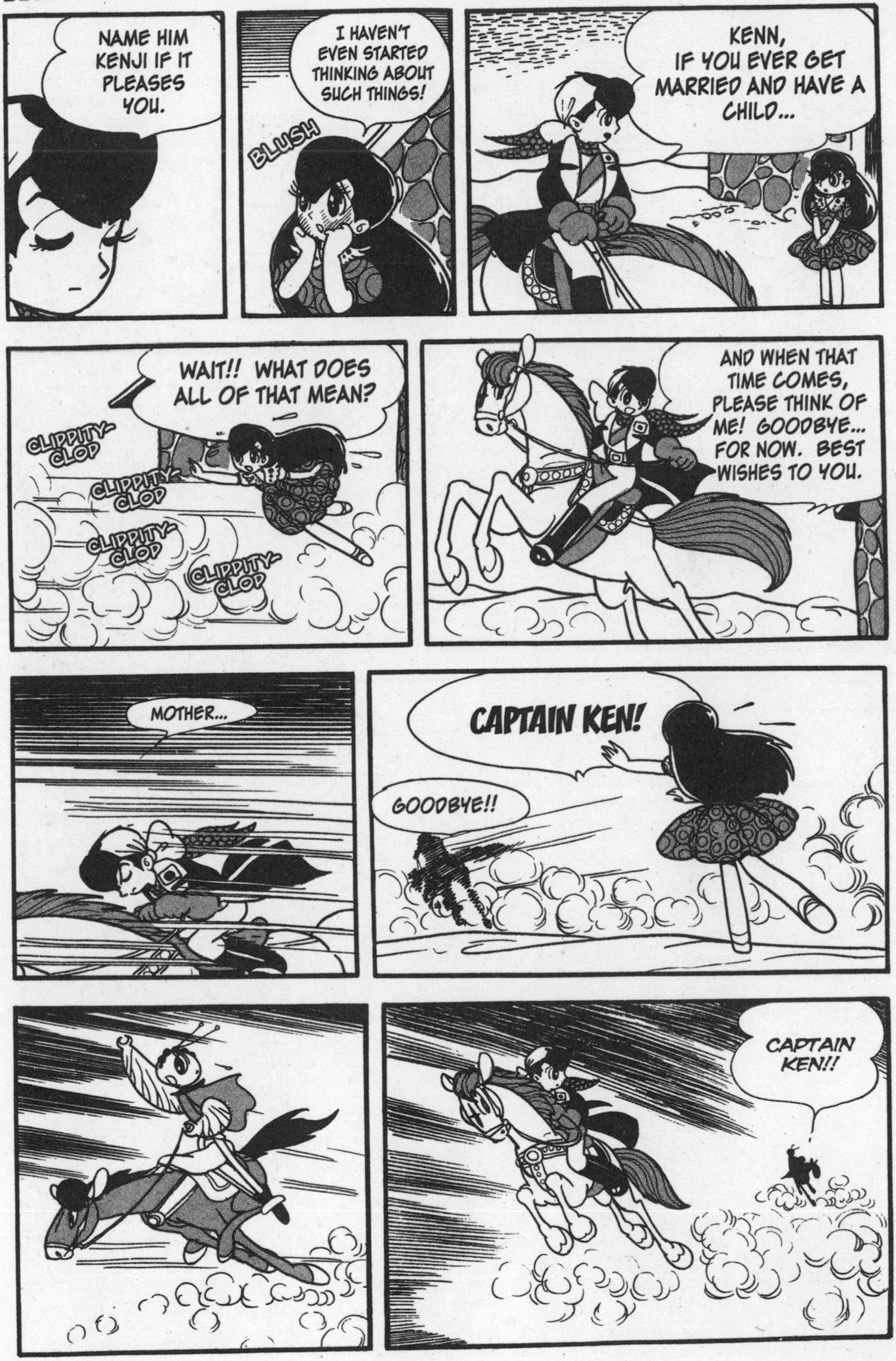
KENN, IF YOU EVER GET MARRIED AND HAVE A CHILD...
I HAVEN'T EVEN STARTED THINKING ABOUT SUCH THINGS!
BLUSH
NAME HIM KENJI IF IT PLEASES YOU.
AND WHEN THAT TIME COMES, PLEASE THINK OF ME! GOODBYE... FOR NOW. BEST WISHES TO YOU.
WAIT!! WHAT DOES ALL OF THAT MEAN?
CLIPPITY-CLOP
CLIPPITY-CLOP
CLIPPITY-CLOP
CLIPPITY-CLOP
CAPTAIN KEN!
GOODBYE!!
MOTHER...
CAPTAIN KEN!!

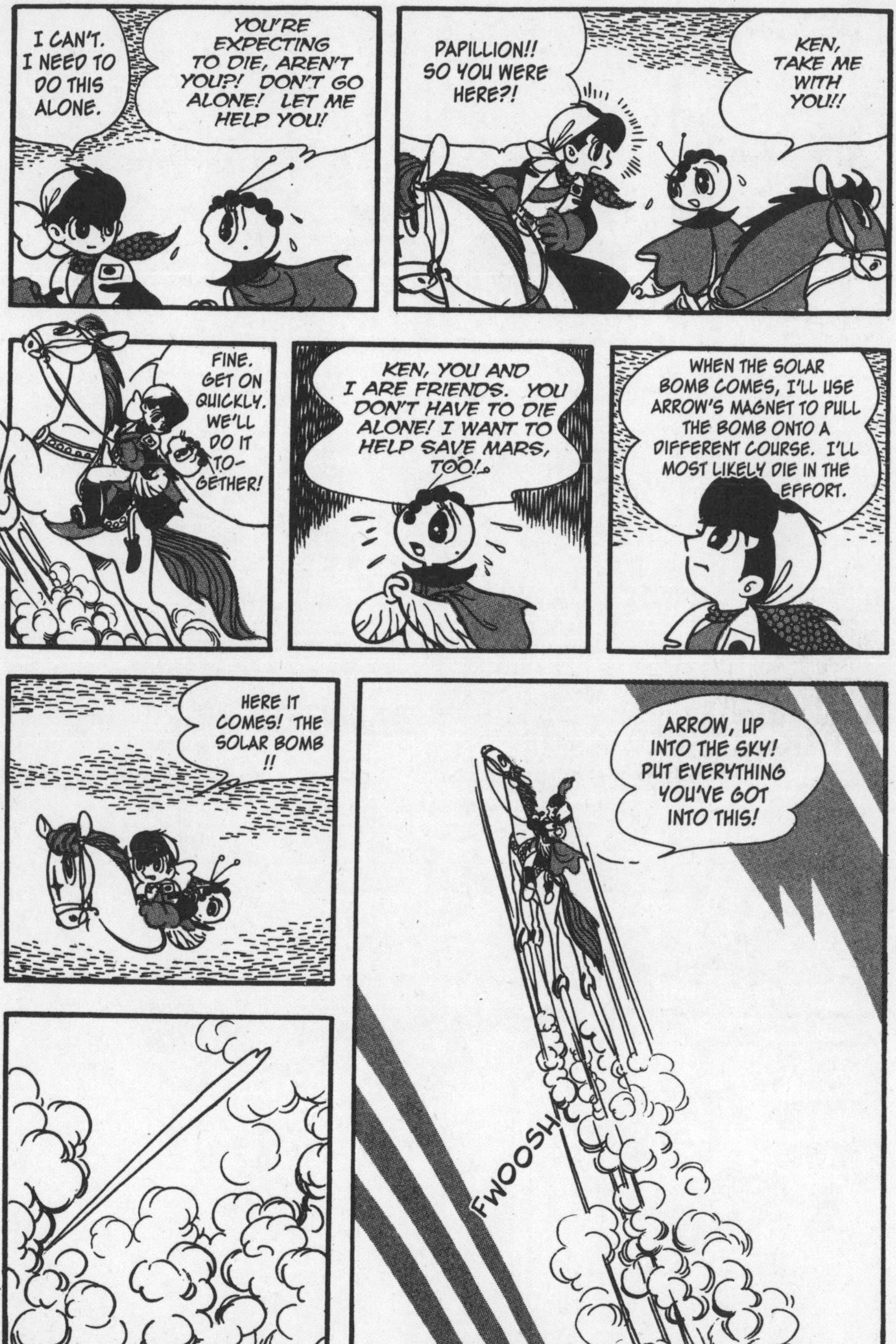
KEN, TAKE ME WITH YOU!!
PAPILLION!! SO YOU WERE HERE?!
YOU'RE EXPECTING TO DIE, AREN'T YOU?! DON'T GO ALONE! LET ME HELP YOU!
I CAN'T. I NEED TO DO THIS ALONE.
WHEN THE SOLAR BOMB COMES, I'LL USE ARROW'S MAGNET TO PULL THE BOMB ONTO A DIFFERENT COURSE. I'LL MOST LIKELY DIE IN THE EFFORT.
KEN, YOU AND I ARE FRIENDS. YOU DON'T HAVE TO DIE ALONE! I WANT TO HELP SAVE MARS, TOO!
FINE. GET ON QUICKLY. WE'LL DO IT TOGETHER!
ARROW, UP INTO THE SKY! PUT EVERYTHING YOU'VE GOT INTO THIS!
FWOOSH
HERE IT COMES! THE SOLAR BOMB !!

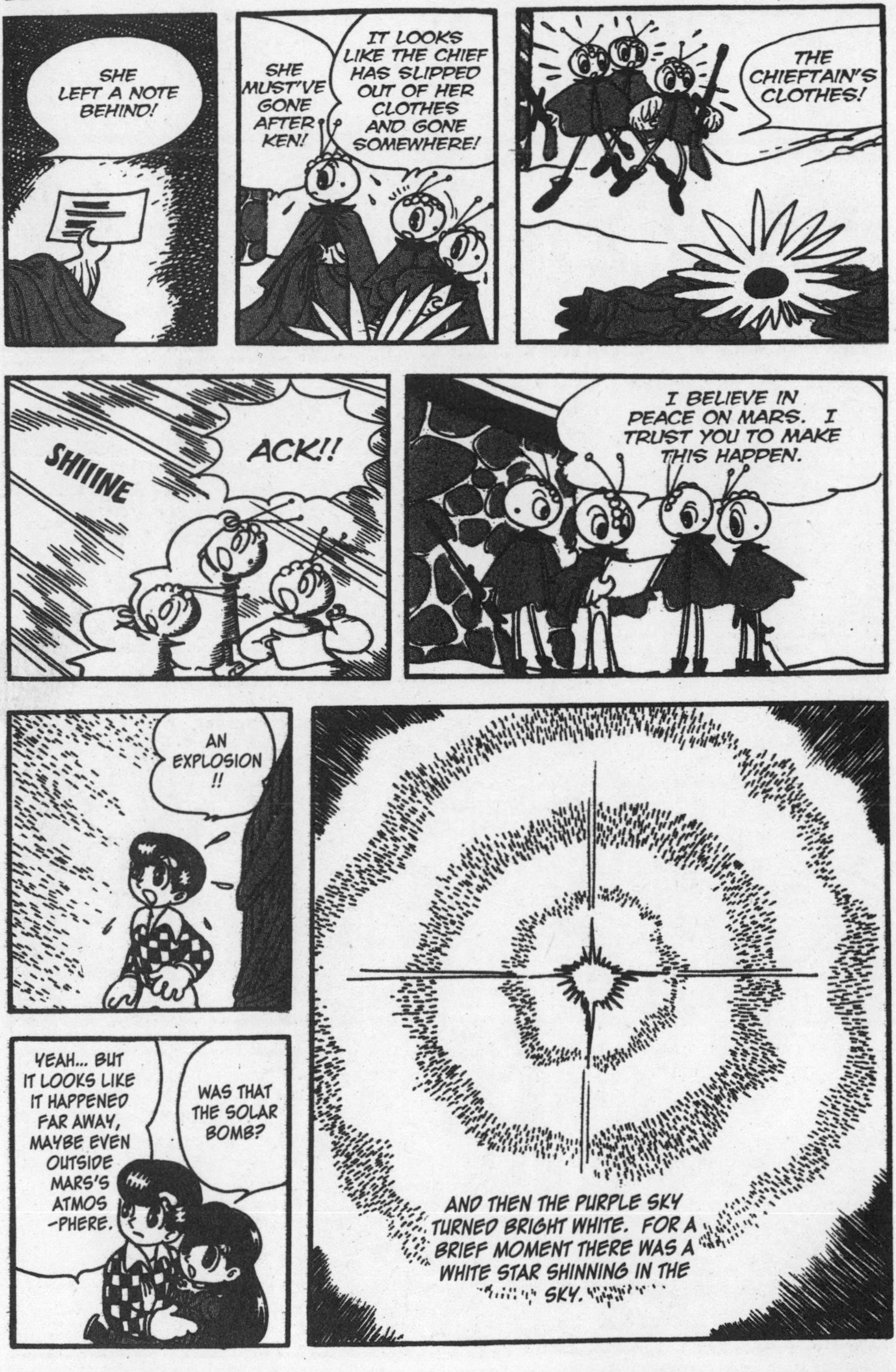
THE CHIEFTAIN'S CLOTHES!
IT LOOKS LIKE THE CHIEF HAS SLIPPED OUT OF HER CLOTHES AND GONE SOMEWHERE!
SHE MUST'VE GONE AFTER KEN!
SHE LEFT A NOTE BEHIND!
I BELIEVE IN PEACE ON MARS. I TRUST YOU TO MAKE THIS HAPPEN.
ACK!!
SHIIINE
AND THEN THE PURPLE SKY TURNED BRIGHT WHITE. FOR A BRIEF MOMENT THERE WAS A WHITE STAR SHINNING IN THE SKY.
AN EXPLOSION !!
WAS THAT THE SOLAR BOMB?
YEAH... BUT IT LOOKS LIKE IT HAPPENED FAR AWAY, MAYBE EVEN OUTSIDE MARS'S ATMOS -PHERE.

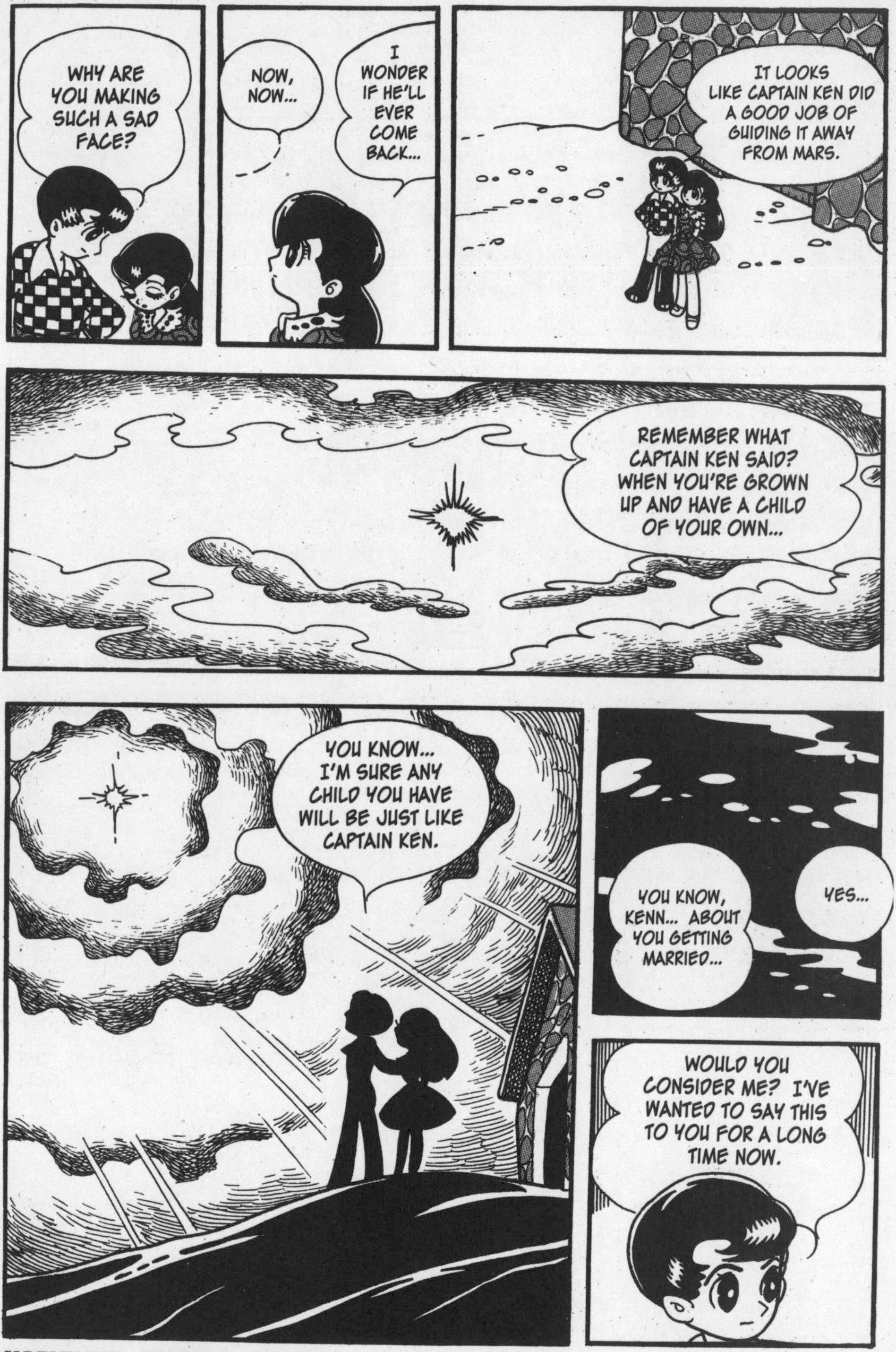
IT LOOKS LIKE CAPTAIN KEN DID A GOOD JOB OF GUIDING IT AWAY FROM MARS.
I WONDER IF HE'LL EVER COME BACK...
NOW, NOW...
WHY ARE YOU MAKING SUCH A SAD FACE?
REMEMBER WHAT CAPTAIN KEN SAID? WHEN YOU'RE GROWN UP AND HAVE A CHILD OF YOUR OWN...
YES...
YOU KNOW, KENN... ABOUT YOU GETTING MARRIED...
WOULD YOU CONSIDER ME? I'VE WANTED TO SAY THIS TO YOU FOR A LONG TIME NOW.
YOU KNOW... I'M SURE ANY CHILD YOU HAVE WILL BE JUST LIKE CAPTAIN KEN.

CAPTAIN KEN - VOLUME 2 - THE END

AFTERWORD

"CAPTAIN KEN" FOLLOWED "ZERO MAN" AS MY SERIALIZED SERIES IN THE WEEKLY SHONEN SUNDAY. MY READERS WERE A LITTLE BEWILDERED WITH THIS SCIENCE FICTION SET ON MARS, THUS IT WASN'T AS SUCCESSFUL AS THE PREVIOUSLY SERIALIZED "ZERO MAN."

WHILE "CAPTAIN KEN" WAS BEING SERIALIZED, I HAD A CONTEST AND ASKED THE READERS TO PREDICT WHO CAPTAIN KEN REALLY WAS. I RECEIVED MANY ANSWERS BACK, BUT OUT OF ALL OF THEM ONLY TWO WERE CORRECT. NO DOUBT THESE TWO PEOPLE WERE QUITE FAMILIAR WITH SCIENCE FICTION CONCEPTS. NINETY PERCENT OF RESPONDENTS THOUGHT THAT CAPTAIN KEN AND KENN MINAKAMI WERE THE SAME PERSON. OTHER COMMON RESPONSES WERE THAT THEY WERE BROTHER AND SISTER OR THAT CAPTAIN KEN WAS A ROBOT MADE TO LOOK LIKE KENN MINAKAMI. THE TWO WINNERS WERE SUPPOSED TO RECEIVE AN AUTOGRAPH FROM ME, BUT I NEVER ENDED UP SENDING THEM. I STILL FEEL GUILTY ABOUT IT TO THIS DAY.

ONE OF THOSE YOUTHS ENDED UP ACTUALLY WORKING AT TEZUKA PRODUCTIONS AND BECAME A VERY TALENTED ANIMATOR. EVERY TIME I SAW HIS FACE, I'D THINK BACK TO "CAPTAIN KEN" AND FEEL A LITTLE ASHAMED.

OSAMU TEZUKA

OSAMU TEZUKA MAGAZINE CLUB

DEAR READERS,

IN OSAMU TEZUKA'S WORKS THERE ARE MANY PORTRAYALS OF FOREIGNERS. RECENTLY, SOME OF THE WAYS IN WHICH FOREIGNERS WERE PRESENTED HAS BEEN CRITICIZED AS BEING RACIST. WE WOULD LIKE TO STATE THAT THE AUTHOR, IN CREATING THIS WORK, NEVER HAD ANY SUCH INTENTION. THE AUTHOR BELIEVES THAT ALL FORMS OF HATRED AND DISCRIMINATION ARE BAD, AND HOPES THAT YOU WILL FIND IN ALL HIS WORKS A LOVE FOR PEOPLE AS A WHOLE. WE THINK THAT RACISM IN ALL ITS FORMS ARE BAD, AND WOULD LIKE TO DISCOURAGE IT AS BEST WE CAN. AGAIN, ANY REPRESENTATIONS THAT MAY SEEM RACIST WERE NEVER INTENDED AS SUCH.

AS WE ENTER INTO THE TWENTY-FIRST CENTURY, WE WOULD LIKE TO PRESERVE THIS PIECE OF WORK IN ITS ORIGINAL FORM FOR A NUMBER OF REASONS. THE AUTHOR HAS ALREADY PASSED AWAY AND SO IT IS IMPOSSIBLE TO GET HIS FEEDBACK ON ANY PROPOSED CHANGES. THIS ENTIRE PIECE OF LITERATURE IS EMBEDDED WITH OSAMU TEZUKA'S FEELINGS AND MESSAGE, SO WE DO NOT WANT TO ALTER ANYTHING. THIS WORK HAS BECOME CONSIDERED A CULTURAL ARTIFACT AND WE WOULD LIKE TO KEEP IT IN ITS UNALTERED STATE SO THAT FUTURE GENERATIONS MAY LEARN SOMETHING FROM IT.

ONCE AGAIN, WE WOULD LIKE TO STATE THAT ALL OF US HERE AT TEZUKA PRODUCTIONS ARE AGAINST RACISM IN ALL ITS FORMS AND HOPE FOR THE END OF DISCRIMINATION.

WE HOPE THAT YOU THE READERS, THROUGH EXPOSURE TO OUR WORK, CAN BECOME MORE AWARE OF DISCRIMINATION AND ALL THE FORMS IT CAN TAKE, AND THAT THROUGH CONTINUED LEARNING AND AWARENESS WE CAN ALL LESSEN ITS IMPACT.

TEZUKA PRODUCTIONS

OSAMU TEZUKA

OSAMU TEZUKA WAS BORN ON MARCH 11, 1928 IN TOYONAKA, OSAKA, JAPAN. HE WAS RAISED IN TAKARAZUKA, YOKOHAMA. HE GRADUATED WITH A MEDICAL DEGREE FROM OSAKA UNIVERSITY AND WAS QUALIFIED TO BE A DOCTOR. INSTEAD HOWEVER, HE DEVOTED HIMSELF TO COMICS AND BECAME ONE OF JAPAN'S MOST FAMOUS AND BELOVED MANGA AND ANIME CREATORS. HIS FIRST WORK, "DIARY OF MA-CHAN" WAS PUBLISHED IN JANUARY OF 1946 WITHIN THE "SHOUKUKUMIN NEWSPAPER" WHICH IS NOW KNOWN AS THE "MAINICHI SHOUGAKUSEI NEWSPAPER." HIS MOST FAMOUS WORKS INCLUDE "ASTRO BOY," "PHOENIX," "JUNGLE EMPEROR," "BLACK JACK," "PRINCESS KNIGHT," "THE THREE-EYED ONE," "BUDDHA," AND "MESSAGE TO ADOLF." HE HAS MANY OTHER WORKS PUBLISHED AS WELL. HE DIED FEBRUARY 9, 1989 DUE TO STOMACH CANCER. IN FEBRUARY OF 1994 TAKARAZUKA CITY OPENED THE OSAMU TEZUKA MANGA MUSEUM.

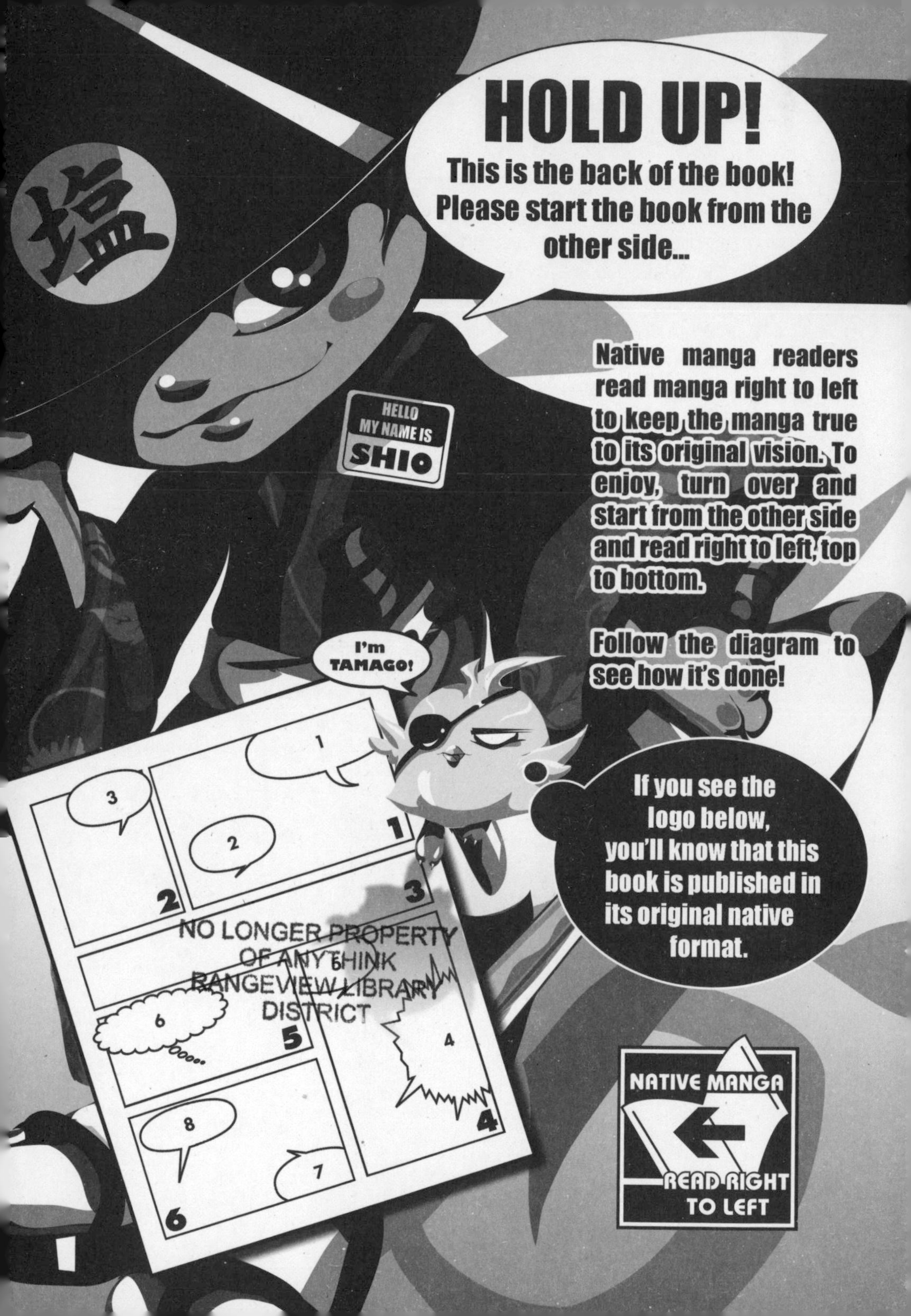
HOLD UP!
This is the back of the book! Please start the book from the other side...
塩
HELLO MY NAME IS SHIO
Native manga readers read manga right to left to keep the manga true to its original vision. To enjoy, turn over and start from the other side and read right to left, top to bottom.
Follow the diagram to see how it's done!
I'm TAMAGO!
If you see the logo below, you'll know that this book is published in its original native format.
NATIVE MANGA
READ RIGHT TO LEFT